Dispute Resolution Ethics

A Comprehensive Guide

Dispute Resolution Ethics

A Comprehensive Guide

Edited by Phyllis Bernard and Bryant Garth

Defending Liberty
Pursuing Justice

American Bar Association
Section of Dispute Resolution

Staff Editors:	Jack C. Hanna
	Gina Viola Brown
Managing Editor:	H. Kyo Suh
Assistant Editor:	Melody R. Daily
Research Assistants:	Tina Drake
	Khamisi Grace
	Kristin Guthrie
	Cailin Hammer
Cover Art:	Jeff Dionise

Published by the American Bar Association
Section of Dispute Resolution
740 15th St. NW, Washington, DC 20005
(202) 662-1680
Fax (202) 662-1683
dispute@abanet.org
www.abanet.org/dispute

The materials contained herein represent the opinions of the author(s) and should not be construed to be the action of either the American Bar Association or the Section of Dispute Resolution, unless adopted pursuant to the bylaws of the Association.

Nothing contained in this book is to be considered as the rendering of legal advice for specific cases, and readers are responsible for obtaining such advice from their own legal counsel. This book and any forms and agreements herein are intended for educational and informational purposes only.

ISBN: 1-57073-934-X

Discounts are available for members of the ABA Section of Dispute Resolution and for books ordered in bulk. Special consideration is given to state bars, CLE programs, and other bar-related organizations. For book orders, inquire at the American Bar Association Service Center, 750 North Lake Shore Drive, Chicago, Illinois 60611. (312) 988-5522. Or contact the Section of Dispute Resolution, (202) 662-1680.

For reprint inquiries, contact ABA Copyrights, (312) 988-6101.

Table of Contents

Introduction

By Phyllis Bernard and Bryant Garth

This volume signals the arrival of the field of "ethics in dispute resolution." The current focus on alternative dispute resolution (ADR) began in the late 1970s and moved gradually to a situation where the alternative processes – especially mediation but also arbitration – have become the normal. Recent studies suggest that virtually every state has some kind of mandatory referral of filed cases to mediation, and the many programs associated with the federal courts are to the same effect.[1] Arbitration has continued to play a major role, and the ethical issues have gained in importance with a strong movement by major corporations to place arbitration clauses in their standard form agreements with consumers and employees.

In the relative infancy of the ADR movement, a group representing the American Arbitration Association, the American Bar Association, and the Society of Professionals in Dispute Resolution (now the Association for Conflict Resolution) developed a set of *Model Standards of Conduct for Mediators* (*Joint Standards*) in the early 1990s. Since that time the number of court programs has multiplied, the number of provider organizations has both increased and been characterized by mergers and consolidations, and the Internet has become a central feature of our lives. One indicator of the growth in prominence in mediation is the recent promulgation of a Uniform Mediation Act by the National Conference of Commissioners on Uniform State Laws and by the American Bar Association Section of Dispute Resolution. For the first time in their 110 year history, the ABA and NCCUSL worked hand in hand drafting a Uniform Act.

The centrality of alternative dispute resolution to the legal profession was recently recognized by the American Bar Association's Commission on Evaluation of the Rules of Professional Conduct, which recommended changes last year to the *Model Rules of Professional Conduct*. The Rules provided explicit reference to the important role of lawyers in providing the services of mediator or other neutral. According to the Comment to the new Rule 2.4,

---

[1] *See* SARAH R. COLE ET AL., MEDIATION: LAW, POLICY & PRACTICE (2d ed. app. B 2001); *see also* John P. McCrory, *Mandated Mediation of Civil Cases in State Courts: A Litigant's Perspective on Program Model Choices*, 14 OHIO ST. J. ON DISP. RESOL. 813, 813-24 (1999).

Alternative dispute resolution has become a substantial part of the civil justice system. Aside from representing clients in dispute-resolution processes, lawyers often serve as third-party neutrals. A third-party neutral is a person, such as a mediator, arbitrator, conciliator or evaluator, who assists the parties, represented or unrepresented, in the resolution of a dispute or in the arrangement of a transaction. Whether a third-party neutral serves primarily as a facilitator, evaluator or decisionmaker depends on the particular process that is either selected by the parties or mandated by a court.[2]

Despite the urging of some of the leaders of the ADR community, in particular the CPR Institute for Dispute Resolution, the ABA Commission decided not to attempt to use the vehicle of the new rules to regulate lawyers practicing as ADR neutrals.[3] The Commission instead sought to make clear the situations where the lawyer serving as neutral has a role different from that of the traditional advocate. The proposed rules therefore do not provide specific guidance on the issues that are the subject of this volume. The field is still developing rapidly in case law and in a proliferation of state rules and regulations. If, as at least one of the chapters suggests, it is time to revise and update the *Model Standards of Conduct for Mediators*, we hope that the current volume will provide a basic reference.

In the meantime, in addition, the volume seeks to provide guidance to clients, litigants, lawyers, and third-party neutrals about issues of ethics and professional responsibility that arise in non-litigation processes, including negotiation, arbitration, and mediation, to offer solutions that are consistent with mandatory regulations or best practices, and to examine unresolved and currently debated issues. In order to highlight those issues, we have intentionally avoided imposing a single voice on the authors. The authors, as we shall suggest below, have some fundamental disagreements that, in our opinion, help define this field. The following paragraphs, which provide a general map of the volume, also highlight some of the variations in approach and tone in the different chapters.

After this introduction, the next seven chapters focus on mediation as the process currently favored as an alternative to litigation. Chapter I, by Lawrence Watson, begins by examining the question of how to move toward mediation and whether ethics or good practice require lawyers to advise their clients of the various possibilities for resolving a dispute. This is not a simple matter. While mediation can be an excellent solution for many situations, it is not appropriate for all circumstances. Some cases present a severe power imbalance which can

---

[2] MODEL RULES OF PROFESSIONAL CONDUCT, Rule 2.4 (2002).

[3] Margaret Colgate Love, ABA Ethics 2000 Commission, *Final Report - Summary of Recommendations* (June 9, 2001).

only be rebalanced through litigation. Or, a principle of law may be involved that requires a pronouncement by the court to elucidate a standard of conduct for society to follow. Mediation might be right for some issues in a case, while not for an entire case. Further, some critics, like Jay Folberg of the University of San Francisco, have expressed skepticism concerning the details for enforcing a requirement that lawyers must advise their clients about mediation. What form would that advice take? Would it become, over time, standardized -- and perhaps merely a hollow, *pro forma* "check off box" in filing a case?

Chapter II, by Douglas Yarn, takes on the question about how to select a mediator. Both of these chapters ground their discussions of ethics and professional responsibility in a commitment to the centrality of the mediation process. They suggest that the lawyer-participants in the mediation process should make success in mediation their first priority, and perhaps even that success should be defined according to criteria internal to mediation – party satisfaction and a solution that both parties feel is optimal.

The next chapter, authored by Lawrence Fox, a prominent litigator and former chair of the ABA's Litigation Section, takes a different approach. For Fox the main event is the litigation, and the quality of the outcome is to be measured first according to whether the client wins in either setting – be it the courtroom or the mediation room. This does not mean that Fox is opposed to ADR or to mediation in particular; but his focus and emphasis are on zealous representation in litigation. He starts with a client who is assumed to want to win the lawsuit on the client's desired terms. This means that any change in strategy – like negotiation or mediation – requires that the client be willing to settle for something less than what the client has demanded. Others, by comparison, suggest that the client should be assumed to want to resolve the dispute in a satisfactory manner, with adversarial litigation chosen only if all else fails. This is ostensibly the stance taken by the U.S. Department of Justice in civil cases since 1996, as directed in Executive Order No. 12988.[4] As the chapters make clear, both approaches can coexist within the current rules of professional responsibility as well as the proposed amendments offered by the recent ABA Ethics 2000 Commission. Kimberlee K. Kovach, in chapter IV, speaks to this issue on behalf of a more mediation-driven approach. Her chapter offers a contrast to the litigation-driven perspective, and articulates a view favored by some leaders of the ADR movement.

James Alfini, in chapter V, examines the state of regulation for mediators, analyzing the *Model Standards of Conduct for Mediators*, other sets of standards, and the case law that has arisen regarding the conduct of mediators. From his perspective, as suggested above, it may be time to reexamine the *Joint Standards*.

---

[4] Exec. Order No. 12988, 61 Fed. Reg. 4729 (February 5, 1996).

Phyllis Bernard, one of the editors, follows with a chapter on a subject that has increasingly arisen with respect to mediators. The question is whether, or when, mediation is the practice of law. The issues are more subtle and complicated than the question of whether non-lawyer mediation should trigger the potential criminal sanctions that proscribe "the unauthorized practice of law." They involve issues relating both to multidisciplinary practice (MDP) and to multijurisdictional (MJP) practice – both areas still characterized by intense debate in the organized legal profession. The final chapter specifically devoted to mediation, authored again by Kimberlee K. Kovach, asks about the enforcement of ethical rules. Her suggestion, which is consistent with this volume, is that the field has matured to the point where there should be more systematic attention to issues of enforcement.

The following chapters move to central issues that cut across or supplement the themes in the mediation chapters. The first of these chapters, chapter VIII, authored by Carrie Menkel-Meadow, discusses the controversial question of lawyers' ethics in negotiation. In addition to her examination of the specific rules and guidance concerning negotiation, Menkel-Meadow discusses at some length the fundamental questions of professional orientation implicit in the contrast between dispute resolution and adversarial litigation.

Sharon Press' contribution to this volume (chapter IX) explores the duties of provider organizations, which can apply to public entities, for-profit entities, and non-profit organizations. Provider organizations have become increasingly important in the market for dispute resolution with the emergence of a relatively few leading providers – led by JAMS on the for-profit side and the American Arbitration Association on the non-profit side. Both are quite active in mediation and in arbitration, and the dominance of these organizations leads to a number of particular ethical concerns – including especially issues of conflict of interest and potential issues respecting "repeat-players" in the market for dispute resolution. In addition to these private provider organizations, there are also questions as to what obligations bind the public entities that sponsor or administer a dispute resolution program, including questions of quality control.

The chapter by Richard Chernick and Kimberly Taylor (chapter X) addresses issues specific to arbitration. They examine the full context for arbitration, including again the complicated issues of conflict of interest, the differences between domestic and international arbitration, and the controversial questions that emerge when arbitration is more or less imposed on one of the parties. As with respect to the previous chapter, the positions that the major provider organizations have adopted – or are imposed on them -- are particularly important in helping to ensure that the arbitration processes will be fair.

Chapter XI, by Sharan Lee Levine, Philip Harter, Paula Aylward and Judith Kaleta, comes from the recognition that the ombuds institution, first developed in Scandinavia to help keep the government accountable to its citizens, is a key form of alternative dispute resolution that has spread to many different settings in the United States, both private sector and governmental. The discussion of questions of independence, impartiality, and confidentiality, makes clear that the ombuds raises precisely the same issues that surface in other major processes of dispute resolution.

The next chapter moves from an area with a long institutional history – the ombuds – to the Internet and the dispute resolution processes that are arising in virtual space. This chapter (chapter XII), by Sandra Sellers and Gina Viola Brown, focuses on ethical issues in Online Dispute Resolution (ODR). Once again, the new issues display considerable overlap with the ones addressed throughout this volume. Nevertheless, the Internet's ability to bridge great distances and to facilitate interactions among strangers put a special premium on full disclosure by the mediator and transparency in the process.

Finally, it is appropriate that John Feerick, the chair of the committee that produced the AAA-ABA-SPIDR *Model Standards of Conduct for Mediators*, provide a concluding comment. The field has developed and transformed since that first effort in the early 1990s, and Feerick has a unique vantage point from which to identify some of these changes and suggest future developments.

Chapter I

Initiating the Settlement Process – Ethical Considerations

By Lawrence M. Watson

Introduction – A Changing Civil Trial Culture

For years it has been true that only a small percentage of lawsuits filed in this country ever make it to the courtroom. Reconciliation of the dispute somewhere along the way to the courthouse occurs far more frequently than a final adjudication of the lawsuit, and the percentage of cases tried continues to decrease. In today's civil trial environment, where alternative dispute resolution processes are becoming more formalized and available to litigants, far more lawsuits will be settled than tried.

The reasons for this state of affairs are self-evident. Our existing judicial facilities and resources simply cannot handle the volume of litigation imposed upon them. There aren't enough courtrooms, and there aren't enough judges. Quite apart from physical constraints, the complexity of civil disputes – particularly those arising in the business community – often makes them inappropriate for resolution in a normal courtroom setting. The subject matter and laws governing these disputes are complicated and difficult for overworked judges and volunteer citizen jurors to fully appreciate or understand. Today's lawsuits tend to involve a greater number of parties with interrelated issues, a situation that adds to the time and difficulty of giving everyone a day in court. The costs associated with preparing and presenting these disputes for judicial resolution can be huge – often outweighing the value of the matters in dispute. Finally, the complexity of the issues, the number of interested parties, and the limitations on available judicial resources all combine to create lengthy delays that make it difficult to resolve problems in anything approaching a timely fashion.

The courts have been well aware of these conditions for a number of years. Although the degree of concern may vary from jurist to jurist and jurisdiction to jurisdiction, every trial court judge reflexively encourages, promotes and sometimes even mandates settlements.

As a result, most civil actions are (or should be) filed, prepared and prosecuted with every expectation of being settled before trial. In recent years, institutional alternative dispute resolution practices – most notably civil trial mediation programs -- have experienced exponential growth to keep up with this phenomenon. The trial community in America now embraces processes that resolve conflict in the conference room as well as the courtroom.

As the culture of trial practice has thus shifted, so have the role and responsibilities of the trial lawyer. Simply stated, in the civil trial profession, successful, competent, well-rounded representation of clients now requires proficiency and talent in alternative dispute resolution processes. A whole new set of practice skills is required of trial lawyers if they are to continue as major players in the civil dispute resolution business. With these new skills comes a need to reexamine the ethical standards controlling the relationship between trial lawyers and their litigation clients.

This chapter deals with the ethical responsibilities of trial lawyers to advise their clients of settlement opportunities, and to initiate the process.

The "Who Blinks First" Dilemma – Trial Lawyer to the Client and Trial Lawyer to the Opposition

Notwithstanding the reality that more cases will settle than not, most clients (and trial lawyers) still approach the litigation process with a substantially different goal in mind. Typically, when a dispute first arises, litigation clients experience an immediate and intense desire to have their day in court -- to publicly vindicate their position and resolve the conflict by winning the dispute in the eyes of the law and the public. The client's emotional reaction both to the conflict and to participation in a lawsuit clouds any objective evaluation of the best process for resolving the problem. A gap between the client's desires and reality appears almost immediately.

This gap between desire and reality is often inadvertently widened by the trial lawyer during the process of his or her engagement. Trial lawyers are retained as litigation warriors. They are sought after and hired for their skills in aggressively advancing the client's cause in the courtroom and securing a judicial victory. The pre-engagement interviews and discussions that come with the selection process for the trial attorney focus on past courtroom victories and a plan of attack for the subject litigation – the more aggressive the better. In this context, claims and defenses making up the dispute tend to expand during the process of retaining counsel to resolve the dispute. Conciliatory attitudes and discussions about settlement potentials are inconsistent with what the clients want to see or hear. As a general rule, trial lawyers are not hired to settle cases – they are hired to win cases. There is a perception that initiating settlement discussions with the client can impair the trial lawyer's image as the legal warrior.

Even after a client retains a trial lawyer, pays a few monthly bills, and begins to view the time and cost involved in a courtroom victory more realistically, problems with initiating settlement discussions remain. As in discussions between trial counsel and the client, initiating settlement discussions with the opposition is culturally regarded as a sign of weakness. The trial attorney is concerned that even mentioning settlement could send the wrong message to opposition. As a tactical matter, therefore, getting involved in starting settlement discussions may not be the best course for representing the client's interests.

Finally, lurking in the deep recesses of this dilemma is the fundamental fact that initiating settlement discussions and settling lawsuits may be in opposition to the short-term interests and natural inclinations of the trial lawyer. Litigation lawyers fare better economically if the lawsuit is prolonged or even carried through to an ultimate conclusion in the courtroom – or better yet, the appellate courts. Perhaps more significantly, a trial attorney's skills and reputation are best generated by actual courtroom experience and exposure. Future business is often won from the publicity accompanying completion of a trial in the courtroom. From a professional point of view, trial lawyers need to try lawsuits.

If we are to determine when and how settlement overtures are to be made, and who has the responsibility for initiating them, the client's subjective mindset concerning the dispute and the trial lawyer's natural instincts for the best way to resolve the dispute must be balanced against reality and what is really in the client's best interests.

For the most part, there are no clear mileposts for the trial lawyer in this situation. What guidance we can find will be implied in ethical standards, procedural rules and "best practices" arising from the trial profession. This chapter deals with those guidelines.

Advising the Client of ADR Options - Ethical Standards Requiring Trial Lawyers to Advise Litigation Clients of Settlement Options and Initiate Settlement Overtures

Is the trial lawyer ethically obliged to advise a client of settlement possibilities and options? Current ethical standards do not reveal a direct ruling on point, but there is much to suggest the answer might impliedly be "yes."[1]

No specific ethical rule in the American Bar Association's *Model Rules of Professional Conduct* (*Model Rules*)[2] requires a trial lawyer to advise a client

---

[1] For an excellent and far more detailed treatment of this issue, see, Marshall J. Breger, *Should an Attorney Be Required to Advise a Client of ADR Options*, 13 GEO. J. LEGAL ETHICS 427 (2000).

[2] For purposes of this chapter, references to ethical standards will be based on the American Bar Association *Model Rules of Professional Conduct (Model Rules)*. It should be noted that while

regarding settlement options or to suggest settlement overtures. There are a number of rules, however, that would strongly suggest ethical representation of a client in litigation would nonetheless require trial counsel to initiate those sorts of discussions reasonably early in the representation.

Model Rule 1.4(b), for example, requires a lawyer to offer legal explanations that are "reasonably necessary to permit the client to make informed decisions regarding the representation." *Model Rule 1.2(a)* requires a lawyer to "consult" with the client as to the "means" by which the client's objectives are to be achieved. *Model Rule 3.2* requires the trial lawyer to "make reasonable efforts to expedite litigation consistent with the interests of the client." Finally, *Model Rule 2.1* requires a trial lawyer to "exercise independent judgment and render candid advice" in representing a client, and the rule expands the definition of "candid advice" to include "moral, economic, social and political factors that may be relevant to the client's situation."

Some ethics commentators have emphatically suggested these four model rules establish (or should establish) a clear ethical duty for the trial attorney to counsel the litigation client on ADR options.[3] Other commentators have suggested that these model rules (along with the growing institutionalization of ADR processes in general) clearly impose a duty on trial attorneys to counsel litigation clients as to ADR alternatives as a best practice measure, and may raise implications of malpractice if they do not.[4] In jurisdictions with mandatory ADR processes in place,[5] a failure to counsel the litigation client as to what will certainly occur in the process of the lawsuit may indeed establish something more than a departure from best practice. Many of these states also impose

---

most states have substantially adopted the *Model Rules*, there might be variations or modifications in any given locale. The *Model Rules* referenced in this chapter are the revised *Model Rules*, based upon recommendations from the "Ethics 2000 Commission" and approved by the ABA House of Delegates in February 2002.

[3] Carrie Menkel-Meadow, *Ethics in ADR: The Many "Cs" of Professional Responsibility and Dispute Resolution*, 28 FORDHAM URB. L. J. 979, 981 (2001); Carrie Menkel-Meadow, *Ethics and Professionalism in Non-Adversarial Lawyering*, 27 FLA. ST. L. REV. 153; 167-168 (1999).

[4] See, Robert F. Cochran Jr., *Professional Rules and ADR: Control of Alternative Dispute Resolution Under the ABA Ethics 2000 Commission Proposal and Other Professional Responsibility Standards*, 28 FORD. URB. L. J. 895 (2001); Robert F. Cochran Jr., *Legal Representation and the Next Steps Toward Client Control: Attorney Malpractice for the Failure to Allow the Client to Control Negotiation and Pursue Alternatives to Litigation*, 48 WASH. & LEE L. REV. 819 (1990); Monica L. Warmbrod, Comment, *Could An Attorney Face Disciplinary Actions or Even Legal Malpractice Liability for Failure to Inform Clients of Alternative Dispute Resolution?*, 27 CUMB. L. REV. 791 (1996-1997).

[5] *See*, e.g. FLA. STAT. § 44.102(b) giving Florida trial courts the power to order the parties to mediate all or any part of a civil trial action. See also, Breger, *supra* note 1, Appendix II at 466 for a listing of states with mandatory ADR provisions.

ethical, procedural or statutory requirements for trial counsel to advise their litigation clients about all available ADR options.[6]

The ABA Section of Litigation recently formed a special task force to address the question of ethical standards for lawyers engaged in settlement negotiations. Recognizing that settlement negotiations are an "essential part of litigation," the Litigation Section Task Force On Ethical Guidelines for Settlement Negotiations (Task Force) has spent the last two years attempting to develop a practical, user-friendly guide for lawyers engaged in settlement programs. The Task Force has concluded there is a duty to "promptly advise" a client as to settlement options. Rule 3.1.1 of the Task Force Guidelines proposed in April 2002 states:

> *3.1.1. Prompt Discussion of Possibility of Settlement*
> A lawyer should consider and should discuss with the client, *promptly after retention in a dispute, and thereafter*, possible alternatives to conventional litigation, including settlement.[7]

If a trial lawyer is ethically obliged to raise settlement options with the client, the next question becomes, "What are a lawyer's ethical obligations with respect to initiating settlement discussions with, or responding to settlement discussions from, the opposition – independent of client consent?"

Initiating Settlement Discussions With the Opposition – Who Is in Charge?

Under *Model Rules 1.2 (a)* and *1.4(a)(2)* a lawyer is required to "abide" by a client's decisions concerning the "objectives" of representation, and "consult" with the client concerning the "means" of achieving those objectives. The duty to consult as to the means of meeting client objectives obviously contemplates more of a joint decision or undertaking between the client and the lawyer than suggested by the duty to strictly abide by a client's decisions regarding the objectives to be reached. Logically, settlement negotiations and settlement process decisions would be included in the list of potential means to achieve the objectives of legal representation and would fall more under the trial lawyer's professional tent. The settlement agreement itself, however, would seem to fall under the category of the objectives of the representation and clearly come under the client's control. It would thus stand to reason that the *Model Rules* would allow a lawyer more latitude in participating in the decision (and exercising independent professional judgment) to *initiate and conduct* a

---

[6] Breger, *supra* note 1, Appendix I at 462.

[7] ABA Section of Litigation, Task Force on Ethical Guidelines for Settlement Negotiations, *Ethical Guidelines for Settlement Negotiations*, Rule 3.1.1, April. 2002 Draft (Emphasis added).

settlement process, while still leaving the ultimate decision to *accept or reject* the settlement to the client.

Model Rule 1.2(a) specifically states, "A lawyer may take such action on behalf of the client as is impliedly authorized to carry out the representation. A lawyer shall abide by a client's decision whether to settle a matter."

In discussing the "consult with the client as to the means" requirement under *Model Rule 1.4(a)(2)*, the Comments add this note:

> In some situations – depending on both the importance of the action under consideration and the feasibility of consulting with the client – this duty will require consultation prior to taking action. In other circumstances . . . the *exigency of the situation may require the lawyer to act without prior consultation.* (Emphasis added).

If settlement discussions (not the acceptance or rejection of a specific settlement offer) are fairly considered the means to reaching objectives of representation, it would seem the *Model Rules* would at least allow a trial lawyer to react to a settlement offer by participating in the discussion (if not initiate a settlement overture when and if the opportunity presented itself) without the client's prior consent.

The Restatement (Third) of the Law Governing Lawyers tends to support this position. The Comments to Section 22 note, "[A] lawyer normally has authority to initiate or engage in settlement discussions, although not to conclude them."[8]

The Task Force on Ethical Guidelines, however, came down on the other side of the issue. The proposed *Guideline 3.1.2* titled "Client's Authority Over Initiation of Settlement Discussions*"* suggests this rule:

> The decision whether to pursue settlement discussions belongs to the client. A lawyer should not initiate settlement discussions without authorization from the client.

The Task Force's logic for this sentiment can be found in the Comments:

> Although the decision to initiate settlement discussions does not reflect a binding commitment of any kind, the initiation of such discussions can effect a significant alteration in the dynamic of a dispute. Clients therefore may want to discuss and approve in advance the initiation of settlement discussions. . . . [T]he better practice is to obtain the client's express consent prior to initiation

---

[8] RESTATEMENT (THIRD) OF THE LAW GOVERNING LAWYERS §22 cmt. (2000).

of settlement negotiations. The circumstances of a representation rarely present situations in which there is a need for the lawyer, acting in client's interests, to initiate such discussions without prior consultation with the client. Similarly, when opposing counsel first raises the possibility of settlement, better practice is to offer no immediate response (other than inquiries into what the counsel may have in mind) until the lawyer consults with the client, unless the client has already authorized such discussions or given pertinent directions.[9]

Once settlement discussions have been broached, however, it is clear a trial lawyer's ethical duties to the client require full and timely disclosure of all communications in that regard. *Model Rule 1.4(a)(1)* requires a lawyer to "promptly inform" the client of "any decision or circumstance" that would require the client's consent. *Model Rule 1.4(a)(4)* requires a lawyer to "promptly comply with reasonable requests for information." Under the Comments to *Model Rule 1.4*, specifically with respect to settlement negotiations, the authors provide, "A lawyer who receives from opposing counsel an offer of settlement in a civil controversy . . . must promptly inform the client of its substance" unless the client has otherwise made it clear that the proposal would not be acceptable.

The Section of Litigation Task Force on Ethical Guidelines in Settlement Negotiations would agree with that requirement. *Ethical Guideline 3.1.4* proposed by the Task Force succinctly states, "A lawyer must keep the client informed about settlement discussions and must promptly and fairly report settlement offers, except when the client has directed otherwise."

The Best Practice – Advising the Client of ADR Options

While there may be some doubt as to the existence of an ethical duty to unilaterally explore or develop settlement options for a client with the opposition, it seems clear that ethical standards would require an attorney to explain those options to the client at some point in time. Because *Model Rule 1.4(b)* imposes a duty to explain legal options in a manner "reasonably necessary to permit the client to make informed decisions regarding the relationship," it would seem early is better than late for this discussion.

Further, in those states having court-ordered ADR statutes where there is a relative certainty of going into settlement programs, common sense would dictate that explanation of these options would go hand in hand with an early and appropriate explanation of the overall litigation process. In those jurisdictions, the "Who blinks first?" and "litigation warrior" problems are eliminated since trial counsel can justify initiating settlement discussions with both the client and

---

[9] *Ethical Guidelines in Settlement Negotiations*, *Ethical Guideline 3.1.2* and Comments.

the opposition on the basis that the court will be ordering the process in any event.

In those jurisdictions where ADR is merely an option, trial attorneys can justify early discussion of settlement possibilities either as part of a litigation budget exercise with the client, or as case management planning with opposition counsel.

Clearly, best practices would require the attorney to engage in a forthright discussion with the litigation client very early in the process. What follows is a suggested two-step process for bringing the litigation client into the settlement arena without losing the hard-won image of a litigation warrior.

Step One: Preparing the Client for the Mediation Experience – Explaining the Mediation Process in Terms Consistent with the Client's Goals

As part of a discussion of the overall litigation process, the fact that the court may (or will) instigate settlement processes is hard to avoid. Some explanation of ADR processes likely to appear on the client's horizon must be part of the trial lawyer's performance agenda. Combining that explanation with a suggested strategy for achieving beneficial goals for the client – pointing out how the process can benefit the client's interests regardless of the outcome – will go a long way toward bringing the client into full support of those settlement programs. Because mediation is the most commonly encountered settlement process in today's courtroom environment, a suggested means of explaining and identifying goals in that process will follow.

The first step is to explain the process. Most sophisticated litigation clients today have some working knowledge of mediation. Risk managers, insurance adjusters and claims specialists have probably participated in several mediation sessions. First time litigants, however, have probably not been through a mediation. Their knowledge of the process will be anecdotal at best. More often than not, they will tend to confuse mediation with arbitration or some sort of administrative adjudication. These clients would benefit from an explanation of the process in advance. (In truth, many seasoned participants of mediation would also benefit from a review of the basics every now and then.)

It is critically important to have the clients understand that almost any settlement outcome of a mediation process contemplates a win-win, as opposed to a win-lose, result. Settlement is a process that seeks to reconcile disputes. Litigation is a process that seeks to adjudicate disputes. The outcome of reconciliation is an agreement with the other side. The outcome of adjudication is a judgment against the other side. There are big differences between securing a judgment and reaching an agreement. To secure a judgment, one party must prevail in the positional debates staged in the adjudication process – go win the lawsuit. To secure an agreement, both sides must find mutual accommodation for the interests and concerns driving each side in the dispute – frame an agreement.

The client should understand that an agreement reconciling a dispute is reached by developing terms that mutually satisfy the interests of the parties rather than confirm their concepts of right and wrong. Judgments, not agreements, define and validate concepts of right or wrong. Agreements mutually satisfy interests and concerns. Reaching settlement agreements, therefore, is a problem-solving exercise that deals with the challenge of finding a mutually acceptable way to satisfy often conflicting interests and concerns. Obtaining judgments, on the other hand, is a faultfinding exercise that involves efforts to convince a third party on issues of right and wrong.

The mediation of a civil lawsuit involves realistically analyzing the adjudicatory option available to the parties, then attempting to build a more mutually viable reconciliation alternative.

The attorney should inform the client, therefore, that the first part of mediation, the opening presentations, seeks only to define and explore the adjudicatory option – not to decide the case. At the end of the opening presentations, both parties should have a realistic and balanced view of their adjudication option. The second phase of the mediation (which may include a private caucus process) begins the problem-solving task of creating a reconciliation option that deals with both parties' interests in an acceptable manner. At that point, a choice is made between accepting a reconciliation option or continuing with litigation.

Clients should understand in advance that the mediation process does not dwell on who may be proven right or wrong in court. The probability of various adjudication outcomes is a factor, but not a controlling factor, in considering settlement options. To be successful at mediation, the client must understand the focus ultimately comes to creating the best possible reconciliation option through an agreement that will mutually satisfy the interests of all parties to the dispute. Creating the best settlement option will involve compromise – giving as well as getting.

The attorney should give the client a realistic definition of exactly what it means to be "successful" in mediation – what it means to prevail in the mediation process. To many participants, a successful mediation would be one that gets them settlement terms that they perceive would approximate a favorable court judgment. The attorney must immediately and forcefully readjust such thinking. Winning in the mediation process does not mean successfully convincing the other side to buy into a settlement agreement that would mirror a one-sided victory in court. Winning in mediation is not defined as making the other side lose. The ultimate objective of a civil trial mediation is to put the client in a position to make a meaningful choice between continuing litigation and accepting the best settlement option available. The goal of mediation is to develop and present the best settlement option available and thus create the opportunity to accept (or reject) a viable option to the lawsuit. The winner in mediation, therefore, is the party that persuades the other side to offer up its very last and best option to litigation before any decision to accept or reject is made. The loser in mediation is the party that causes the termination of the process without getting the other side to extend its best alternative available.

Success in mediation isn't getting everything the parties think they want or deserve. Success in mediation is getting the parties into a position of being able to make an intelligent choice between the best options available.

It is critical that trial counsel thus steer a mediation-bound client away from bottom-line-dollar thinking. To do that, counsel should avoid articulating preconceived absolutes of what must be taken or what will never be paid to settle the case. Becoming entrenched with positional anchors on settlement terms destroys the flexibility and creativity that are critical to any successful negotiator.

The attorney often needs to remind the client that there are things other than money that can settle lawsuits. One salient difference between resolving disputes through adjudication and resolving disputes through reconciliation is the range of settlement mechanisms available to the parties if they choose to reconcile. Judicial resolution of a dispute is generally restricted to money judgments reached through legal damage formulas that focus on remedying past offenses. Often the damages available fail to meet the parties' real needs in the resolution of the matter. Reconciliation offers far more choices for crafting a customized settlement of the conflict that can look forward to the future relationship as well as deal with past offenses. By thinking through and developing contingent plans to utilize these options and by doing feasibility research on settlement alternatives before the mediation starts, an attorney can dramatically increase the potential for a successful outcome. Structured annuities, future work, letters of apology, product discount programs, bartered services, use of equipment, joint undertakings to raise settlement dollars, introductions and bid invitations – the realm of possible settlement tools is limited only by the creativity of the mediator, the parties and counsel. That creativity should never be chained with fixed-dollar concepts.

A good method for getting clients off bottom-line thinking is to explore what constructive steps must be taken to resolve the damage done. Rather than focus a pre-mediation client on dollar amounts, the attorney should focus on how the dollars would be used to remedy the damage done. This approach encourages the client to define the interests that have been directly impacted by the dispute and look at the widest range of possibilities for accommodating those interests.

Before a mediation session, the attorney and client should discuss the structure, overall objectives, and various settlement scenarios available through reconciliation. Perhaps the best advance preparation for the client, however, is to get the client directly involved in actually preparing for the mediation itself. In truth, the negotiation forum presented through mediation belongs to the client. In the final analysis, the client must make the ultimate decision to accept or reject the settlement option reached. Counsel should give the client the opportunity to take an active role in the process.[10]

Step Two: Defining the Overall Goals of Mediation –
What Are We Trying to Achieve Through This Mediation?

The first step of any journey is to decide where we want to go. In mediations, the destination of choice is obviously a full settlement of the case. As noted, an attorney initially prepares for that destination by simply sitting down with the client and mutually agreeing on a range of acceptable outcomes to the mediation process without fixating on bottom-line-dollar absolutes. However, other equally important objectives that can be obtained through mediations do not include a full settlement of the dispute.

A Partial Settlement of Peripheral Issues

One reality of litigation is that all claims and all defenses arising out of the same facts and circumstances must be asserted in the same lawsuit. The judicial goal here – to avoid multiplicity of suits – is important to the judicial system and must be met. An unfortunate consequence of the rule, however, is that many lawsuits end up filled with peripheral arguments that really aren't determinative of the central issues between the parties. This tendency to expand, rather than narrow, the focus of the trial drives up the time and cost of an adjudicated resolution. Mediation can serve to eliminate those peripheral disputes by final or interim partial settlement agreements, stipulations to abate certain portions of the trial, or agreements to informally set certain issues aside pending the resolution of the main claims.

A Process to Move Toward Final Settlement

Many times, despite our best efforts to prepare for every contingency in advance, mediations become stalemated because of insufficient information or lack of agreement on what the facilitated negotiations reveal to be core or pivotal issues of fact or law. Rather than calling impasse and returning to the litigation path, attorneys can use the mediation process to facilitate an agreed "downstream" program that defines and schedules further steps aimed at breaking those logjams and continuing toward reconciliation.

---

[10] For a more comprehensive discussion of preparing the client for mediation, please see, THE FLORIDA BAR, ALTERNATIVE DISPUTE RESOLUTION IN FLORIDA, Vol. II, Section 2.6, pp. 2-6 (1995).

A Better Understanding of the Opposition's Case

An attorney should listen to everything said during a mediation. Despite the considerable discovery skills developed by practitioners within the trial bar, it is seldom that the opposition's full story – complete with intended themes, nuances and emphasis – is flushed out during discovery. More often than not, discovery will reluctantly yield only what we ask – not what we need to know. More importantly, mediation can provide the critical opportunity to see both sides of the story contrasted against each other. This unique opportunity to hear both sides of the issues presented side by side in their best light is never available through traditional discovery tools. Finally, with the consent of the party and with the right mediator, a neutral third party's reaction to the issues is also available through mediation.

Obviously, any preparation for mediation should be undertaken with a full understanding of all the goals available through the dispute resolution process.

Conclusion

Current ethical standards clearly signal a duty for the trial lawyer to advise the litigation client as to available ADR options. Many states have adopted procedural rules or policies making ADR such a significant part of their dispute resolution landscape that the requirements both to advise the client of ADR options and to perform appropriately during ADR processes have become issues of professional competence. By explaining to clients that ADR offers a commendable means of achieving valuable goals that advance clients' interests, trial lawyers can not only satisfy their duties to their clients, but also develop better ways of providing successful representation.

Chapter II

Ethical Duties and Best Practices When Engaging a Mediator

By Douglas Yarn

Introduction

After considering your advice and recommendations, your client has decided that mediation sounds like a good idea. Now what? In voluntary, private mediation, you must see if the other side will agree to mediate, and together you must choose and engage a mediator. Bearing in mind the fact that collaboration among the disputants or their attorneys is crucial to the initial stages of mediation, this chapter will address some of the ethical issues that arise when attorneys[1] are engaging a mediator. With the exception of the last section of this chapter, I am proceeding under the assumption that the mediation is private and contractual rather than court-ordered.

In a sense, mediation really begins when the parties agree to mediate, and those first interactions among the disputants, their attorneys, and the mediator will set the stage for the entire process that follows. These first encounters are likely to raise some of the same ethical issues for representatives, neutrals, and provider organizations covered in other chapters, so please refer to those chapters for additional discussion.

Competence – The Pervasive Ethics Theme

Where can one find ethical guidance on engaging a mediator? When the American Bar Association (ABA) promulgated the *Model Code of Professional*

---

[1] The term seems preferable to "advocate," which is so closely connected with adversary adjudication, and to "lawyer representative," which is ungainly. A lawyer with a client is an "attorney-at-law," a distinction often ignored in the United States. In addition, lawyers can be involved in ADR as counselors or advisors while not serving as a representative in the process.

Responsibility (*Model Code*)[2] and the *Model Rules of Professional Conduct* (*Model Rules*)[3], mediation was not even on the radar screen, much less the ethics of contacting and contracting a mediator. Outside of arbitration, the concept of engaging an impartial third party to resolve a dispute was completely antithetical to the prevailing practice of attorneys in an adversarial adjudicative system. In that system, attorneys do not contract with a judge,[4] nor do they have any meaningful control over who the judge might be. In contrast, one of the distinct advantages of mediation is choosing the third-party intervener. The rules that pertain to judges and to the attorneys who interact with them provide little guidance in a form of dispute resolution that presumes the disputants will "shop" for a third party, negotiate terms of engagement and compensation, and often conduct extensive ex parte communications. Because mediation is far more common than trial in many jurisdictions, it is time to consider the unique ethical problems that may arise in this context. However, there is a dearth of authoritative guidance. What little guidance exists is largely in the form of voluntary standards of practice for mediators, a topic covered in another chapter. Although knowledge of these standards is helpful to the attorney, it is the responsibility of the mediator, not the attorney, to adhere to them.

This leaves us with the general ethics theme that overshadows any discussion of professional responsibility in this and other stages of mediation--attorney competence. The *Model Rules of Professional Conduct* affirmatively require competence in representation:

> A Lawyer shall provide competent representation to a client. Competent representation requires the legal knowledge, skill, thoroughness and preparation reasonably necessary for the representation.[5]

To competently represent clients at this stage of mediation, attorneys must

---

[2] MODEL CODE OF PROFESSIONAL RESPONSIBILITY, in effect as of August 1982 ("MCPR").

[3] MODEL RULES OF PROFESSIONAL CONDUCT (1983) as amended in 2002. The American Bar Association's Commission on Evaluation of the Rules of Professional Conduct, nicknamed "Ethics 2000" (hereinafter also referred to as the "Commission"), reviewed the *Model Rules* and made recommendations for revision, some of which directly addressed the ethical problems of lawyers serving in ADR processes. On November 27, 2000, the Commission released its report. The Commission's recommendations were circulated among the public and approved by the ABA House of Delegates in February 2002.

[4] An exception is the statutory system of trial by reference, sometimes called "rent-a-judge" which has a long history in some states.

[5] MODEL RULES OF PROFESSIONAL CONDUCT Rule 1.1 (2002).

know what must be done and the best ways of doing it. You must know how to discuss mediation with the other side, the best way to draft an agreement to mediate, what to look for in and how to interact with a potential mediator or ADR provider organization, what to expect in fees and charges, and what ethical standards mediators should be following. As mediation has become more sophisticated, it is not enough simply to know the difference between mediation and arbitration. A competent attorney must know about different types and styles of mediation and must anticipate problems that might be caused by the choice of mediator or the selection process. In short, any chapter on the ethics of engaging a mediator cannot ignore competent practices.

As a consequence, this chapter risks repeating advice on how to pick a mediator found in the many "how to" treatises, books, and articles on mediation,[6] to which I refer you. Bear in mind that any such advice, if unqualified, is immediately suspect. The culture of mediation varies considerably across the country. In some jurisdictions, there is a long history of lawyers and courts using mediation and a large and varied market of qualified mediators available, while in others, mediation is still relatively new or rarely used with few mediators locally available. In some types of disputes or lawyering subspecialties, mediation has its own distinct character. Moreover, mediation is more an art than a science, with little agreement even among the most experienced mediators of what is the "right" or "wrong" way of doing things. Likewise, the choices attorneys make at this stage are rarely right or wrong, they simply have some foreseeable consequences, some of which have ethical implications beyond the issue of competence.

Attitude and Responsibility to the Process

The choices the attorney makes in initiating the mediation process will reveal, subtly or not so subtly, the attorney's attitude toward that process. Attorneys should consider whether they are responsible for the integrity of the mediation process and what attitude is consistent with that responsibility.

We recognize that lawyers are officers of the court and have certain overarching responsibilities toward the legal process; for example, lawyers should use the legal process for legitimate purposes only and not to harass others, they should show respect for the legal system, and they should work to improve the law and the administration of justice.[7] The lawyer who uses the legal process to

---

[6] One of the better sources on how to select a mediator is "A Consumer Guide to Selecting a Mediator," developed by the Alaska Judicial Council under a grant from the State Justice Institute. This guide can be found on several web sites, including www.state.oh.us/cdr/brochures/cgmediator.htm.

[7] *See* MODEL RULES OF PROFESSIONAL CONDUCT Preamble.

intimidate others, is openly disdainful and cynical when referring to the legal system, and ignores opportunities to improve the legal process is failing to meet his or her responsibility to preserve the integrity of the legal process. Indeed, as representatives of the legal system, any ethical breach by lawyers is potentially corrosive to its integrity.

Do we have analogous responsibilities to the mediation process? Certainly we do if mediation is considered part of the legal process and system, and there is a good argument that it is becoming so and that court-connected mediation already is. Even if, despite the increased use of mediation by lawyers and courts, one views the process as independent of the legal system, the professionalism or civility movement in the bar indicates that lawyers have analogous responsibilities toward mediation. This is illustrated by the following aspirations, from the State of Georgia Bar's professionalism regime:[8]

> As a lawyer, I will aspire:
>   * * *
>
> To preserve and improve the law, the legal system, and *other dispute resolution processes* as instruments for the common good.
>
> To make the law, the legal system, and *other dispute resolution processes* available to all.

Using professionalism ideals such as these as a guideline, lawyers have a duty to ADR processes – to preserve and improve them and to make them accessible. Behaviors and attitudes that undermine mediation are inconsistent with that duty. Just as the professionalism movement questions competitive behaviors associated with unrestrained zeal in advocacy and calls for more cooperative behaviors as a counterbalance, ADR proponents question the accepted standards of advocate behavior when attorneys participate in mediation.[9] They call for a new paradigm of lawyering for this process[10] in which Rambo litigation is incompatible with

---

[8.] *See* State Bar of Georgia Handbook, Aspirational Statement on Professionalism, p. H-124 (emphasis added). A discussion of how the ideals of professionalism affect settlement negotiations can be found in *Evanoff v. Evanoff*, 262 Ga. 303, 418 S. E. 2d 62 (1992).

[9] *See e.g.*, Jacqueline M. Nolan-Haley, *Lawyers, Clients, and Mediation*, 73 NOTRE DAME L. REV. 1369, 1371 (1998) (arguing that zealous advocacy as currently understood is incompatible with good representation in ADR). *But see contra* Craig McEwen et al., *Bring in the Lawyers: Challenging the Dominant Approaches to Ensuring Fairness in Divorce Mediation*, 79 MINN. L. REV. 1317 (1995).

[10] *See* Chief Judge Judith S. Kaye, *Lawyering for a New Age*, 67 FORDHAM L. REV. 1 (1998) (positing that societal changes and changes in the courts, particularly the introduction of court-

compromise and settlement and merely adds to the client's costs.[11] Effective adversary behavior for litigation may simply be counterproductive in mediation. Proponents of ADR have expressed their concern with adversarial behaviors by attorneys in mediation and have called for revisions to ethical standards in order to control such behaviors. The professionalism and ADR movements envision a behavioral model of the peacemaker-lawyer in contrast with the hyper-competitive, uncooperative behavior of the zealous advocate. The peacemaker engages in objective problem solving and wisely counsels clients to avoid exacerbating the conflict and to explore reconciliation. Such a lawyer is sensitive to the drawbacks of adversarial adjudication and seeks an outcome that is less destructive to human relationships while stressing civility, compromise, cooperation, and mutual respect.

Attitude implicates ethics, competence, and best practice in mediation. The peacemaker model is more compatible with the underlying ethos of mediation. If an attorney initiates mediation with the attitude that this is merely an opportunity to gain tactical advantages over an opponent, to browbeat the other side, and to treat the process like adjudication by trying to convince the mediator of the strength of one's legal case, then the attorney is undermining the mediation process in dereliction of the responsibility to preserve its integrity. This general theme overshadows the various more specific ethical issues that follow.

For the next several sections, I will follow a "Q & A" format, using commonly posed questions to explore the ethical issues in the initiating stages of mediation.

Getting the Process Underway

I feel I have a duty not to compromise my client's negotiating position by being the first to suggest mediation to the other side. How can I initiate the process without compromising my client?

In voluntary, private mediation, someone must initiate the mediation process. Typically, one of the disputants suggests it to the other; however, for many advocates, the strategic issue of how to approach an opponent about mediating is a delicate one. Initiating mediation, like initiating any settlement discussions, raises fears of perceptions of weakness, "who blinked first," and of compromising a client's

---

connected ADR and client-driven ADR, are creating pressures for a new type of problem-solving lawyering and reducing the demand for or relevance of the Rambo litigator).

[11] *See* Carrie Menkel-Meadow, *Pursuing Settlement in an Adversary Culture: A Tale of Innovation Co-opted or "The Law of ADR,"* 19 FLA. ST. U. L. REV. 1 (1991) (pointing out that the adversary system itself may be incompatible with some of the fundamental principles of ADR).

negotiating position. I think such fears are overstated and any related ethical concerns are moot. These fears reflect some kind of macho gamesmanship in a very primitive concept of negotiation. The vast majority of legal disputes settle prior to trial, as your client's likely will, but you have to come to the table to reach settlement. Although timing may be important in gauging the readiness of both sides to negotiate, waiting out the other side to see who blinks first is more likely to create delay, increase costs, foment distrust, and undermine the negotiation than gain your client any psychological leverage. Why not call the other lawyer and say "I feel so good about this case that I think your client should consider mediated settlement discussions." In some jurisdictions, you can point out that if the disputants do not mediate now, the court will direct them to do so down the road.

My client wants to talk directly to the other disputant about mediating their dispute, but the other side is represented. Is this a problem?

It sounds very promising to me. The client-to-client approach is particularly useful when the disputants are still on relatively civil speaking terms. Clearly, there are ethical limitations on you communicating directly with a represented disputant.[12] The situation seems more problematic though when the opposing attorney appears to be obstructionist and the attorney advises the client to go directly to the other disputant in order to bypass the other lawyer. Bear in mind that *Model Rule 4.2* prohibits attorneys from communicating directly with represented parties about the subject of representation. In addition, an attorney should not be able to accomplish indirectly through the client what is prohibited to be done directly; however, this limitation should not apply in the case of client-to-client discussions about the future of their own dispute.

I think the other disputant would be better off agreeing to participate in a mediation, and I think I can convince him to do so; however, he is not represented by an attorney.

In this situation, the offer to join together in mediation should not be couched as advice nor should you represent yourself as disinterested in the matter;[13] otherwise, there is no limitation on your suggesting and explaining the process. Alternatively, you might consider initiating the process through the mediator or through a neutral administering agency, or "ADR Provider Organization,"[14] which is experienced in

---

[12] *See* MODEL RULES OF PROFESSIONAL CONDUCT Rule 4.2.

[13] *See* MODEL RULES OF PROFESSIONAL CONDUCT Rule 4.3.

[14] *See* Chapter IX regarding the ethical issues for these organizations. There is a wide variety of

educating disputants about the process. Other than wanting to provide the service, such agencies are disinterested and relieve you from the possibility of being perceived by the pro se party as advising them on process. Bear in mind that it might be a constructive courtesy to give the other side notice, whether represented or not, that you are going to ask an agency to call them about the possibility of mediating.

Who should pay for the mediator? The other side is balking at the cost of a mediation but appears otherwise willing to participate. My client wants to offer to pay the mediator's fees to get the other side into the process.

In order to convince a reluctant party to participate in a mediation, the initiator may offer to pay some or all of the costs of the process. Typically, the disputants split the costs of a mediation as a show of good faith commitment and as a symbol of the mediator's equal commitment to all the parties. Disproportionate cost-sharing is common, particularly in personal injury mediation where the insurance carrier offers to pay the costs to entice the claimant's attorney to participate for the first time. Sometimes the parties agree that the initiating party will pay the costs unless the mediation results in a settlement, in which case the costs will be shared in some fashion. This is a functional arrangement, particularly if the costs are relatively nominal; however, the cost of the mediation itself could become an issue in the bargaining.

In more complex cases, involving many hours or several mediation sessions, the parties could agree for the initiating party to front the costs up to a point, after which the parties will split the remaining costs if they continue. The drawback to this arrangement is that the point of assessment is arbitrary and may deter the parties from continuing even though the potential for a mediated settlement exists.

There is nothing wrong with making the offer, but one must do it in such a way as to prevent any possible perceptions of bias. Best practice would dictate that the offer be discussed with the other side before mentioning it to the mediator. If the other side is comfortable with it, then let the mediator know who's paying. Alternatively, the parties could agree to pay the mediator through a third party or an administrating agency in such a way that the mediator does not know who is paying the fees. This might assuage any doubts that the non-paying party might have.

The other side has agreed to mediate, but they have forwarded a rather detailed draft agreement to mediate. Is this customary?

Maybe it is customary in your locality, but I have some qualms about

---

public and private, for profit and not for profit provider organizations with varying degrees of experience, service, and reputability.

proceeding this way. Over the last several years, I have been shown increasingly complex and lengthy written agreements to participate in mediation and have some ambivalence about them. On one hand, these complex written agreements seem like an unnecessary formalization and legalization of what could be viewed as a mere informal extension of private, voluntary negotiation. Attorneys may be more comfortable with a formal approach, but unnecessary legalization of the process can set a negative tone and increase disputant paranoia in an already tense situation. Much like the fabled Japanese negative reaction to the lengthy contracts proffered by American lawyers, a formal agreement signals that there is already a problem with the relationship. On the other hand, such an agreement can serve several useful purposes. By referring to a set of institutional mediation rules, which are largely descriptive, or by otherwise describing the process, the mediation agreement clarifies the parties' expectations and helps insure that they have an understanding of the nature and purpose of the process. In an atmosphere of distrust, a carefully crafted agreement to use mediation can set a positive tone, lower the level of anxiety, and empower clients.

Needless legal formality, however, is a threat to the very ethos of the mediation process, and I would tactfully avoid it. Assuming the agreement to use mediation is reached without the aid of and prior to engaging a mediator,[15] my preference would be to reach the agreement orally, usually by phone, and follow up with a brief confirmation letter containing the essential details discussed, which should be whether to proceed ad hoc or through an administering agency, and if proceeding ad hoc, the name of the mediator or the method of selecting a mediator; respective responsibilities for fees and expenses of the mediation; and, a realistic time frame within which to start mediating.

Whether your mediation agreement is a contractual clause for future disputes or a submission for an existing dispute, the content issues are much the same, but I would avoid specificity that unnecessarily restricts the inherently beneficial flexibility of the process. For example, I have seen agreements to use mediation for an existing dispute that specify the nature of the dispute. However, I generally disagree with this practice as needlessly limiting the scope of discussions and potentially encouraging positional frames. Also, agreements to use mediation might include a high degree of specificity about time, location, and steps in the mediation process, but as a mediator, I would rather see an agreement that is more general thereby giving me and the participants more flexibility to shape the process together. Very general statements that describe the process are useful, examples include the use of the term

---

[15] I assume for purposes of answering this question that a mediator or administering agency has not been involved in helping the parties agree to mediate. In such cases, ad hoc mediators and administering agencies might supply their own draft versions of mediation agreements that also incorporate provisions for engagement of their services.

"nonbinding" or the phrase "use of a neutral third party to facilitate settlement discussions." In some disputes, specificity about confidentiality and who will attend the mediation are useful.

The agreement can help set the tone and encourage collaboration and compromise. As part of this agreement, you should explicitly agree that the parties are committed to using their best good faith efforts in mediation to reach a settlement that satisfies their interests. This sets the stage for overcoming the inertia of the current impasse and of the fear of "bidding against oneself." Arguably, it reduces the possibility of innumerable small positional moves and encourages significant mutual concessions at the onset. The mere fact that the parties have agreed on a process to resolve their dispute should be acknowledged as a step toward resolution, and by formalizing their aspirations to resolve the matter through mediation, the parties may feel more committed to the process.

If the parties decide to use an administering agency, most agencies have procedural rules that the parties can incorporate by reference into their agreement. In addition to describing the process, method of mediator selection, allocation of fees, and confidentiality rules, such rules also incorporate many elements of a mediator engagement agreement discussed in more detail below. Although it is tempting to merely incorporate such rules, the attorneys should be sure that they and their clients understand the nature of these rules and that they can mutually modify these rules to better meet the parties' needs. Any such modifications should be clear in the mediation agreement.

Whether you do or do not draft an agreement to mediate, the disputants are likely to be asked to agree to something that has the same elements in it. Many mediators have parties sign an agreement to mediate either in advance of the first mediation session, often as part of the mediator's engagement agreement (see below), or immediately after the mediator's introductory remarks. This latter approach is influenced by the practice of many court-connected mediators who are required in some programs to have the parties sign an agreement to mediate after hearing the mediator's explanation of the process and the mediator's role. Ethically, most mediators subscribe to the concept of self-determination[16] as the fundamental principle of mediation. Self-determination would dictate that the parties make informed choices about the use of mediation.[17] The attorney should also have a

---

[16] American Arbitration Association, American Bar Association Section of Dispute Resolution, Society of Professionals in Dispute Resolution, MODEL STANDARDS OF CONDUCT FOR MEDIATORS (1994) (*Joint Standards*), Standard I. *See also* Society for Professionals in Dispute Resolution, ETHICAL STANDARDS OF PROFESSIONAL RESPONSIBILITY (1986), General Responsibilities (be sure the parties are informed of the process) and American Bar Association, STANDARDS OF PRACTICE FOR LAWYER MEDIATORS IN FAMILY DISPUTES, I (duty to define and describe the process of mediation).

[17] In the court-ordered context, the responsibility of the mediator may be higher as reflected in the

commitment to self-determination, not only to preserve the integrity of the process but also to promote client autonomy and act consistently with the ethical duty of fully informed client decision making and advisement on means by which to reach the client's objectives.[18] In this sense, the mediation agreement serves the ethical concerns of attorney and mediator alike.

Finding a Mediator

What is the best way to go about locating a mediator?

This is really more of a best practices question than an ethical question; however, there are subtle ethical undertones. The search for a mediator can involve considerable ex parte communications with mediator candidates. Unless the disputants and their attorneys have a clear understanding of the nature of this interaction, distrust and questions about impartiality can arise to undermine the process.

If the disputants or their attorneys know a mutually-acceptable mediator in whom they have confidence and who otherwise meets the needs of the dispute, then by all means approach that mediator directly as agreed. Word of mouth is probably the way most people find mediators. Otherwise, the easiest way is to use an ADR Provider Organization, particularly one with a reputation for having a large and varied list of experienced mediators. Some court-connected mediation programs will also have such a list available, often at no charge. The advantages are many. Larger ADR Provider Organizations are not promoting a small group of mediators, who are often owners, and are more concerned and experienced with helping disputants find the right mediator for the case. Such organizations are more objective sources of information about the mediators and usually have standards and requirements that members of their rosters must meet. A large and varied list provides the disputants with more choices and thus more confidence in the choice they make.[19]

One of the greatest advantages of using an administering agency is that it provides a neutral buffer between the participants and the mediator. During the period in which you are locating, choosing, and contracting with a mediator, you will

---

Georgia Commission on Dispute Resolution ETHICAL STANDARDS FOR MEDIATORS, Standard I, A, requiring a list of nine points to be fully explained by the mediator.

[18] *See* MODEL RULES OF PROFESSIONAL CONDUCT Rules 1.2(a) and 1.4.

[19] Consider what other services the private administrating agency offers in addition to simply providing a means of locating a mediator. For example, it might offer neutral conveniently-located meeting space or provide logistical support. Many mediators operate as sole practitioners and can provide similar services, so consider the alternative of jointly creating a list of individual mediators.

probably be engaged in numerous ex parte discussions with mediator candidates and your final choice of mediator. These discussions are not prohibited, in fact they are necessary and expected; however, there are two potential problems. The first problem involves the content of the communications. An attorney should refrain from discussing the substance of the actual dispute until the mediator asks for this information, usually after establishing an understanding among the participants about how such information will be presented.[20] This avoids biasing the mediator, who is ethically bound to maintain neutrality. The downside of biasing the mediator is that the other side may sense it from the mediator's comments either before or during the mediation conference, lose confidence in the mediator, and withdraw from the process, which they are free to do at any time. In the early stages of contracting with the mediator, the potential mediator who has heard one side of the story already may make references to the dispute that the other side could perceive as biased or just become suspicious about the ex parte discussion that took place. The second problem involves the impression that the mere occurrence of ex parte discussions with one side before contact with the other has undermined the mediator's impartiality. The disputants' attorneys should confer on the ground rules for ex parte contact in advance of any overtures to mediator candidates. The use of an administrative agency, however, goes a long way to reduce problems around ex parte discussions when locating and contracting a mediator.

I and other members of my firm have considerable confidence in a particular mediator that we use a lot. Should I suggest this mediator to the other side?

Another issue with the potential for undermining the integrity of the mediation process while locating a mediator is the repeat player problem. One of the parties or their attorney may have a mediator in mind, but if they have used the same mediator before, the potential for bias or a perception of bias increases. On the other hand, previous experience with a mediator is one of the best ways to determine who is a competent mediator. Good information for all the participants to know in such a case is the number of mediations and the extent to which this mediator's practice consists of cases involving one of the parties or attorneys.

One of the most disconcerting situations would involve some form of contractual relationship, an ongoing mediation services contract for example, between the mediator and a repeat player. This has the potential of undermining the integrity of mediation as well as confidence in the impartiality of the mediator for any

---

[20] In most classic mediations, presentations of the parties' perspectives on the issues in dispute are made immediately after the mediator makes an introductory statement during a meeting in which everyone is present. In other forms of mediation, however, the participants agree to share information about the dispute in advance of a joint session.

future mediation.[21] Although the repeat player may feel strongly that such a contract assures the availability of a competent mediator (perhaps at a locked in discounted fee), that long term contractual relationship is just as likely to make the mediator suspect in the eyes of the other disputants. In my view, the mediator is ethically required to disclose the relationship, and the other disputants are unlikely to go along with the appointment. Rather than contract for future disputes, it may be better practice to simply wait until the next dispute and then suggest to the other side that based on previous experience, which should be fully disclosed, this is a good mediator. A mutually-agreed appointment on an ad hoc basis is healthier than a unilateral contract and provides flexibility to appoint different mediators who may be more suited to the dispute.[22]

Picking a Mediator

I know there are different styles of mediation, and frankly, this dispute will not be settled if the mediator is a warm and fuzzy type. My fellow lawyer representing the other side agrees with me that we should engage a no-nonsense, aggressive lawyer-mediator, preferably an ex-judge, who tells it like it is. There are no ethical problems in that, are there?

---

[21] It also has the potential of impugning the integrity of the last mediation. Although there may have been no impropriety, it could appear that the subsequent offer for the longer term services contract was being held out as an inducement for the mediator to favor the repeat player in the previous mediation. In my view, this has the potential to undermine the integrity of the process in the eyes of the other participants in the former mediation, particularly if the contract offer comes close on the heels of the prior mediation.

[22] This should be distinguished from a mediation clause in a contract between the parties that designates a mediator or provider organization in case of future disputes. I have heard of mediation provider organizations seeking to contract with repeat players, particularly insurance companies and large employers. Although making one's services known to these entities is just part of the business of mediation, such mediation provider contracts are very problematic. Also problematic for the same reasons are mediation clauses in commercial and employment contracts that specify the mediator for any future disputes arising among the parties. Contracting with an administrative agency that has a stable of qualified mediators is less problematic, yet many such organizations are owned and managed by the very mediators that are on the list. An alternative is to this approach is use or name in contracts a provider organization that is independent of the individual mediators, such as the American Arbitration Association. Also, it is increasingly common for larger organizations to employ a corporate or internal ombudsman, who may serve as a mediator. Although it would seem that being an employee of one of the disputants would undermine the perception of impartiality, the ombuds exists in an institutional framework which supports the independence of the position. In addition, the non-corporate complainant should have the option of selecting a mutually-agreeable external mediator.

I applaud your collegial reference to the opposing attorney. It bodes well for a lawyer-to-lawyer negotiation if they have already reached an agreement on the process and treat each other with respect. However, in response to your question, the phrasing of which we might work on another time, I do believe that choosing a mediator for their style of mediating can implicate ethics.

As you indicate, different mediators may exhibit a preference for a particular mediation style or approach, and commentators have spilt considerable ink over this subject.[23] In a sense, "style" refers to the skills the mediator employs during the mediation. Different mediators may emphasize different mediation styles and hence different skills.[24] Although all mediators should have good listening skills, family mediators emphasize improving communication between the disputants and may not use caucuses, community mediators may use a transformative approach emphasizing party empowerment and a non-directive mediator role, labor and public policy mediators may focus on the logistics of group management, mediators of commercial disputes may facilitate creative problem solving, and mediators who handle insurance claims disputes may focus on reality testing and helping the parties make economically rational decisions. Recent research indicates that good mediators may be equally fluent in a range of styles.[25] Although I'm not sure where "warm and fuzzy" fits in the spectrum of styles, your description might be more closely associated with less directive, somewhat therapeutic mediation in which the mediator focuses on improving the parties' communication and relationship or on party recognition and empowerment.

If your client's objective is to use the mediation to negotiate settlement of a dispute, then you should consider the extent to which mediation style and negotiation

---

[23] *See* Leonard L. Riskin, *Understanding Mediators' Orientations, Strategies, and Techniques: A Grid for the Perplexed*, 1 HARV. NEGOT. L. REV. 7 (1996). Professor Riskin divides mediators into the following styles: facilitative-narrow, facilitative-broad, evaluative-narrow and evaluative-broad. *See also* Jeffrey W. Stempel, *Beyond Formalism and False Dichotomies: The Need for Institutionalizing a Flexible Concept of the Mediator's Role*, 24 FLA. ST. U. L. REV. 949, 953 n.7 (1997) (listing sources on this topic).

[24] Mediator competence can be judged based on the tasks a mediator must perform and the skills required to preform those tasks. Different categories of cases may require different tasks, therefore different skills. SPIDR's Commission on Qualifications developed a list of skills, 1st Report, 1989, for neutrals in general. Subsequently, the "Test Design Project" which developed a methodology for the selection, training, and evaluation of mediators published a list of common mediator tasks and associated skills, NATIONAL INSTITUTE FOR DISPUTE RESOLUTION, PERFORMANCE BASED ASSESSMENT: A METHODOLOGY FOR USE IN SELECTING, TRAINING, AND EVALUATING MEDIATORS (1995).

[25] *See* Dwight Golann, *Variations in Mediation: How - and Why - Legal Mediators Change Styles in the Course of a Case*, 2000 J. DISP. RESOL. 41.

style are related. Certain types of mediators promote different types of negotiation among the disputants. Typically, most mediators ascribe to interest-based negotiation and integrative bargaining; however, many evaluative, directive mediators as easily promote and encourage (or at least do not discourage) positional negotiation and distributive bargaining. The ethical concern that comes to mind is the extent to which positional negotiation may be detrimental to your client. If you seek out a mediator who is known to promote positional negotiation, you may be doing your client a disservice. Positional negotiation is accompanied by a higher risk of impasse and may fail to produce an optimal settlement that maximizes the client's benefits in relation to their interests. Interest-based bargaining that also seeks to provide mutual gains and maximal benefits to the other side as well may actually improve the benefits for your client. Evaluative mediators, more often associated with a positional negotiation, distributive bargaining approach, may actually inhibit creative, integrative solutions that could be of more benefit to your clients and better satisfy their interests.

In imagining a stereotype of the mediator you seem to be looking for, an additional, related ethical issue comes to mind around informed consent. An "aggressive" mediator favoring positional negotiation could press your client into a settlement that is ill-considered and not fully informed. There is an excellent argument that mediation has the potential to improve negotiation and negotiated solutions[26] with a higher quality of client consent achievable.[27] As an attorney, do you not owe a duty to your client to maximize the potential of the dispute resolution process? In addition, and as argued above, you may have a responsibility to preserve the integrity of the process through the choice of mediation style. Certain types of mediators may not maximize the potential of mediation. Indeed there is an argument that directive evaluative mediation may not be mediation at all.[28] If the parties are looking for case evaluation or non-binding arbitration, then it is better for the

---

[26] *See* John Lande, *How Will Lawyering and Mediation Practices Transform Each Other?*, 24 FLA. ST. U. L. REV. 839 (1997).

[27] Lande, *supra,* note 26, lists the following factors as present in a mediation that yields high quality consent: (1) explicit identification of the principals' goals and interests, (2) explicit identification of plausible options for satisfying these interests, (3) the principals' explicit selection of options for evaluation, (4) careful consideration of these options, (5) mediators' restraint in pressuring principals to accept particular substantive options, (6) limitation on use of time pressure, and (7) confirmation of principals' consent to selected options.

[28] Some critics would say that evaluative mediation is not "pure" mediation. See Kimberlee K. Kovach and Lela P. Love, *'Evaluative' Mediation is an Oxymoron*, 14 ALTERNATIVES TO HIGH COST LITIG. 31 (1996). Evaluative mediation also prompts many to question whether mediation should be considered the practice of law. *See* Carrie Menkel-Meadow, *Is Mediation the Practice of Law?* 14 ALTERNATIVES TO HIGH COST LITIG. 57 (1996); *But see* Bruce Meyerson, *Lawyers Who Mediate Are Not Practicing Law*, 14 ALTERNATIVES TO HIGH COST LITIG. 74 (1996).

integrity of the process to make the distinction and be clear about what kind of intervention you want from the neutral third party.

Your question raises another ethical issue that I can only describe as a possible conflict between attorney preferences and client preferences. Attorneys are more likely to pick mediators with styles with which they are more comfortable. You and the other disputant's attorney might like to have a mediator that promotes more traditional positional bargaining, which is familiar to most lawyers, but with what would your client be more comfortable? Indeed, if your style of negotiation and your concept of good mediating and representation in mediation are not compatible with maximizing that particular client's interests in that particular dispute, you should consider bringing in an attorney with more compatible skills.

Certainly, it is in everyone's interest to be cognizant of what kind of mediation your client will experience. Understanding mediator styles and being able to match the most effective style of mediation with the client's problem is fundamental to competence at this stage of the process. You may have rightly determined that this dispute and these disputants will not respond constructively to a warm and fuzzy mediator. If the disputants have no on-going relationship, or possibility of one, and are involved in a dispassionate legal disagreement (if there is such a thing) over a fixed resource over which they have mutually exclusive conflicting interests, they certainly may benefit from a mediator that is directive, evaluative, and good at reality testing. But be sure you're not merely reflecting your biases and consider, as one always should, involving your client in the decision of how best to use mediation.

I'm looking for a mediator who will be favorable to my client's position.

So is the other side. Mediators have a responsibility to be impartial. Impartiality can be described as freedom from bias or favoritism and a lack of any interest in the outcome of the dispute. Granted that a mediator has no power to bind the parties or impose a decision, to that extent bias is not a considerable problem. A disputant can always walk out or ask the mediator to withdraw if he feels the mediator's bias is harming the negotiations. But even the perception of bias can be harmful to the negotiations, so it is important to select a mediator whose impartiality is not questioned by either party. You may believe that your best friend or your law partner has the requisite qualities to mediate, but in the unlikely event that an informed opposing party agrees with your choice, it is likely to backfire at a critical decision-making point in the mediation and make the mediator's job even more difficult. Perhaps "equal partiality" is what you're looking for.

I want a credible mediator with enough substantive knowledge and experience to appreciate this case.

For some disputes, it may be helpful to have a mediator with expertise in the subject matter in dispute. Substantive expertise is particularly helpful in a specialized area such as construction, environment, securities, computer technology, divorce, class actions, child custody, probate, or insurance coverage. In addition to getting "up to speed" faster and at less expense to the parties, mediators with substantive expertise have more credibility with the disputants and often are better able to assist the parties in analyzing their positions and alternatives. Many mediators have learned about different substantive areas in order to mediate effectively in those areas. The Ethical Standards of Professional Responsibility of the Society of Professionals in Dispute Resolution (SPIDR, recently renamed the Association for Conflict Resolution) provide that a neutral should accept responsibility only in cases where the neutral has sufficient knowledge regarding the appropriate process and subject matter to be effective.[29]

I am somewhat skeptical of choosing mediators on the basis of substantive knowledge. A substantive expert may have an investment in a certain approach to the problem or be too ready to impose his knowledge on the participants. Although general knowledge of the subject matter in dispute may give the mediator credibility and enhance trust building, an essential element of mediation, technical expertise would typically be called upon only if the mediator is to play an assertive role. A Panel on Mediator Qualifications recommended that subject matter knowledge in mediator selection should "relate only to its value in facilitating the process, and not to the influence such knowledge might have on the outcome of the negotiations."[30] In addition, mediators with particular substantive expertise rarely have extensive mediation expertise, although this is changing with the increased use of mediation in particular areas. I have mediated successfully dozens of highly technical disputes about which I had no clue as to what was being discussed. I rely on the parties, their attorneys, and their experts, all of whom will have more knowledge about the problem than most mediators ever will. My preference is to look for mediation experience first and substantive knowledge second. Consider co-mediators, one with process experience and the other with substantive knowledge and experience.

Some mediators say that they are "certified" and have special training. Are these indicators of competence?

---

[29] It is probably advantageous to concentrate on finding a mediator with process knowledge, training, and experience over substantive knowledge. If you cannot find an experienced and impartial mediator with substantive knowledge, then consider letting the mediator bring in a neutral expert or co-mediating with a less experienced mediator who has the substantive expertise.

[30] Margaret Shaw, *Mediator Qualifications: Report of a Symposium on Critical Issues in Alternative Dispute Resolution*, 12 SETON HALL LEGIS. J. 125,132(1998).

The ethical standard for mediators is that they can refer to meeting particular state, national, or private organization qualifications if that entity has procedures for qualifying mediators and the mediator has been granted that status. I'm always suspicious of a mediator that holds himself out or promotes himself as "expert," "qualified," or "certified." Outside of court-connected mediation, there are no public licensing or educational requirements for mediators. Some ADR provider organizations have education and experience requirements. Certification usually consists of having a certificate from a mediation training program or being registered with a court-connected mediation program. Virtually anyone can hold himself out as a mediator, and mediation has become a cottage industry with little or no control over quality and competency. Should there be such controls? One school of thought supports the traditional model of disputants' freely choosing a trusted third party to help them resolve their disputes. The disputants are seeking someone familiar, perhaps authoritative, with a reputation for interpersonal skills, fairness, and mental acumen. Training in process is irrelevant -- let the marketplace decide. An opposing school of thought supports a model of trained, professional mediators. Practitioners would have to obtain certification and maintain skills through continuing education.

Although there is considerable discussion about setting standards of competency, there is little data to support the proposition that such standards actually improve the quality and success of the processes. Indeed, there is little consensus on what constitutes a successful process; however, if disputant satisfaction is the primary criterion, some of the best neutrals may have little or no formal training, while some of the worst may have the most training. Currently, the trend is to set standards of competency for court-connected neutrals while not regulating neutrals in private, voluntary processes. Since many "professional" neutrals rely primarily on court-connected processes for their income, active practitioners are usually competent under the prevailing court standards. Training programs for court-connected neutrals are often regulated. Outside the courts, most private practitioners in mediation adhere to competency standards created by professional societies, such as the Association for Conflict Resolution. Many private providers of dispute resolution services provide training for their panels of neutrals, and if the parties desire, they can ascertain a potential neutral's level of training from the information provided by the company.

Contracting to Reinforce Standards of Practice

Once you locate the appropriate mediator, you will enter into a mediator engagement agreement. If you have not yet drafted an agreement to mediate, you can use the mediator engagement agreement to serve as a consent to mediate and accomplish the same goals (see discussion above).

Applicable standards of practice

Judges, arbitrators, and mediators adhere to various ethical standards when deciding whether to serve in a particular matter. Other chapters discuss these duties for arbitrators and mediators in more detail. It is the responsibility of the neutral to adhere to their standards. When contracting with a mediator, however, the attorneys should know the ethical standards to which the mediator adheres, recognize those ethical restraints, and perhaps reinforce them.

Confidentiality

Attorneys must maintain client confidences.[31] This raises the issue of what attorneys may disclose to the mediator. In turn, mediators consider themselves bound to protect the confidentiality of information disclosed in confidence during the mediation.[32] In a matter in which confidentiality is important, the attorney should have a thorough understanding not only of the applicable law[33] protecting the confidentiality of the mediation but also the extent to which the mediator will protect confidentiality. What will the mediator do if subpoenaed by one of the disputants or a third party? The parties can make their own rules with respect to confidentiality, which should be respected by the mediator; however, mediators may determine that they are required by law or public policy to disclose matters that the parties expected to be confidential. What will the mediator do if he or she feels an ethical or moral obligation to breach confidentiality? Lawyer-mediators are bound to their ethical obligations as lawyers in addition to those as mediators, and sometimes these may conflict as in the case of revelations regarding the unethical behavior of a fellow lawyer. The attorneys should have an understanding of these thresholds when contracting with the mediator.

Impartiality

Mediators should strive to be impartial and evenhanded in the conduct of the mediation. Mediators who believe they are not or cannot remain impartial in a

---

[31] MODEL RULES OF PROFESSIONAL CONDUCT Rule 1.6. The client can authorize the attorney to reveal information.

[32] *Joint Standards*, V.

[33] Depending on the jurisdiction, these may include evidentiary exclusion rules, law enforcing contractual agreements to maintain confidentiality, and court rules or statutes providing special protection to mediations.

particular matter should not accept the engagement.[34] The concept has been discussed in more detail above.

Conflicts and Disclosures

Mediators should disclose all dealings and relationships which might create an impression of bias and should decline an engagement if a conflict of interest casts doubt on the integrity of the process.[35] If, after disclosure, all the parties still wish to engage the mediator, then the mediator can accept the case. In a similar spirit, the attorneys and their clients should disclose any dealings or relationships with the mediator that the mediator may have failed to disclose. Future relationships may also raise problems and should be carefully considered if not altogether avoided.[36]

Fees

In most private mediation, the mediator charges a fee, and if you are using an ADR provider, there is normally an additional administrative fee. The amount and method of calculating fees varies widely among mediators. Mediators typically charge per hour or per diem, particularly on matters that normally require no more than one or two days to resolve. In complex cases that may require several days of mediation, some mediators give bids, require deposits, or may work within budgets established by the parties.

The prevailing ethical standard is that mediators should not enter into fee arrangements that are contingent on the results or on the amount of settlement. This creates a potential conflict of interest for the mediator and perverse incentives. Referral fees among mediators are also frowned upon.

Mediators have an ethical obligation to fully inform the parties as to the fees and not to prolong proceedings which would cost the parties more money but not be productive to settlement. Be sure the fee arrangements are clear and in writing before engaging the mediator. Mediators have a responsibility not to charge unreasonable fees; however, notions of reasonableness can vary widely. Factors include the customary rates in the community, the service provided, the expertise of the mediator, the complexity of the matter, and the time involved. Mediators should return

---

[34] *Joint Standards*, II.

[35] *Joint Standards*, III.

[36] *See e.g., Poly Software Intern., Inc. v. Su*, 880 F. Supp. 1487 (D. Utah, 1995) (how serving as a mediator in one case and then serving as an attorney in a related case may raise special ethical issues). *See also Cho v. Superior Court*, 45 Cal. Rptr. 2d 863 (Cal.App.2.Dist.1995) (how ex parte and caucus discussions raise downstream ethics issues).

unearned portions of any prepaid fees.

Timing

The timing of an intervention by a mediator can be crucial in the resolution of a dispute. When choosing a mediator, attorneys should know when the mediator will be available and whether the mediator's availability is congruent with the ripeness of the dispute. Mediators should accept cases only when they are prepared to spend the time and attention necessary and when they can satisfy the parties' reasonable expectations concerning the timing of the process.[37]

Engaging a Mediator in Court-Connected Programs

It is difficult to comment on the ethics of engaging a mediator in court-connected mediation ("CCM") programs because of the diversity of such programs. In some CCM programs, the parties are free to choose whatever mediator they like and pay a negotiated fee directly. Such programs are more akin to private, contractual mediation and share the ethical issues discussed above. In contrast, there are CCM programs in which the disputants have little or no control over choice of mediator. Mediators are assigned as they rotate up a list, for example. Fees can be fixed by a court and even paid out of a pool rather than directly by the parties. Even the timing and length of a mediation session may be fixed by local CCM rules. The less control that the parties and their attorneys have over choice, the more the burden of choosing a competent mediator and shaping an appropriate process shifts over to the courts and program administration.

From the competence perspective, attorneys should have a thorough grasp of the local CCM program rules, which in addition to dictating the method of mediator selection usually provide direction on timing, attendance, confidentiality, and perhaps what constitutes good faith participation. From a process integrity point of view, disputant consent and control are central to the ethos of alternative dispute resolution processes. If at all possible, attorneys should attempt to bypass CCM programs that limit consent and control in favor of private, voluntary, contractual mediation.

---

[37] *Joint Standards*, VI, Comments.

Chapter III

Mediation Values and Lawyer Ethics: For the Ethical Lawyer the Latter Trumps the Former

By Lawrence Fox

To read the scripture of mediation, one might conclude that lawyers – particularly unreconstructed trial lawyers – have no place in mediation[1] and that, therefore, the question of the role of ethical lawyers in mediation is irrelevant because for successful mediation the first thing we need to do is get rid of all of the trial lawyers – ethical or otherwise. The thesis of this chapter however, is not only that trial lawyers can play an effective role in mediation, but that the ethics of the profession require that clients be represented by effective advocates – whether trial lawyers or not. Further, the only way clients can be ill-served in mediation is if their lawyers abandon the fundamental ethical precepts of the profession simply because they are engaged in something called mediation, rather than civil litigation or arbitration. To demonstrate the point, permit me to review those core principles and demonstrate how each of them in fact is consistent with the process of mediation and why their abandonment will ill serve the clients. Thereafter, I will address other ethical issues lawyers may confront in the mediation context, issues that are not unique to mediation but important to recognize nonetheless.

Lawyers' Duties Are to Their Clients, Not the Process

The mediation literature is filled with eloquent paeans to the mediation process. We are told that compared to trial work, this thing called mediation is

---

[1] What we mean by mediation is a topic not free from dispute. For purposes of this chapter – and probably this chapter only – I include all forms of negotiated settlement processes, either voluntary or mandated, in which the parties either select or have imposed upon them a neutral third party facilitator whose role it is to help the parties find a solution through devices as simple as face to face negotiations and as elaborate as a mini-trial in which the parties engage in litigation-lite and the mediator is authorized to render an "opinion" on the merits. *See* Lawrence J. Fox, *Mini-trials*, LITIG., Summer 1993.

refreshing, uplifting, satisfying, soothing, relationship building, anxiety eliminating, dignifying and otherwise the next best thing to heaven itself. While I take a back seat to no one in my admiration for the effort and talent required to pull off a successful mediation, and the benefits from doing so, all this playing of lute and lyre should not obscure the fact that mediation – at least for the parties – is not an end in itself. It might be perfectly all right for mediators to view a commitment to the process as their goal, but for the lawyers who represent clients in mediation, that must never be the case.

Some assert that the role of the lawyer in mediation is not to advocate for the client, but to assure the process is a fair one that results in a settlement satisfactory to all participants.[2] But the ethical lawyer cannot apply that standard to his or her conduct in mediation. Whatever outward appearance the lawyer representing a client in mediation may assume, the duty of the lawyer must be clear: to represent the client and only the client during the entire mediation process. If that goal requires the lawyer to feign or even exhibit genuine concern for the plight of the other side; if that goal requires the lawyer to concede some point or appear reasonable or act gracious; if that goal requires discussions about fair process and satisfactory result, that may be perfectly acceptable behavior – but only if its sole purpose is to advance the interests of the client. If the client will be served best by a process of mediation that is glacial in its pace and gives each party hours to vent or to assert their best arguments regarding the merits, that goal is what should guide the lawyer's conduct.

The day lawyers embark on any activity – trials, depositions, negotiations, mediation – where the goal is something other than the best interests of the client (running the meter; satisfying the lawyer's penchant for strutting her stuff; humiliating the opposition; getting high cooperation marks from a mediator) is the day we lose our right to call ourselves lawyers. We then might become judges or mediators or facilitators or convenors, but we will not be officers of the court dedicated to our clients before all others.

Zealous Advocacy and Mediation Are Compatible Concepts

---

[2] For example, Professor Steven Hobbs writes that the mediation lawyer should be "an instrument of peace" recommending a course of conduct that is "most beneficial to the individual client as well as other interested parties (e.g. grandparents and children) and society." Steven H. Hobbs, *Facilitative Ethics in Divorce Mediation: A Law and Process Approach*, 22 U. RICH. L. REV. 325, 338-39 (1988). For this and so many other of these sources I am deeply indebted to Professor Jean R. Sternlight, whose splendid article, *Lawyers' Representation of Clients in Mediation: Using Economics and Psychology to Structure Advocacy in a Nonadversarial Setting*, 14 OHIO ST. J. ON DISP. RESOL. 269 (1999), is a rich compendium of the literature on this topic.

Some mediation partisans are offended by the notion that trial lawyers might play a meaningful role in mediation. Because they are so wedded to the idea that everything that is wrong with litigation must be avoided in mediation, it is not far-fetched to say that some opponents of civil litigation sound as if they wish the litigators be cordoned off from the mediation temple lest this holy of holies be sullied by the shrill advocacy of these obstreperous trial lawyers, these zealous advocates.[3] The last thing we need, they argue, are crusading legal eagles destroying this far more enlightened way of settling disputes.[4]

This caricature of trial work serves the purpose of advancing mediation as a desirable alternative method of dispute resolution. But those lawyers who set out to participate in mediation should not allow this argument to confuse or compromise an important principle. In mediation, the zeal is the same; it is simply the means of demonstrating the zeal that may be different.

Indeed, zealous advocacy, even in litigation, is not synonymous with table-pounding, endless discovery or boisterous behavior. One can be a zealous advocate and never raise one's voice, never cause anyone's blood pressure to rise, never file a motion for sanctions. More importantly, zealous advocacy on behalf of one's client is every bit as required in mediation as it is in full bore civil litigation.

Does mediation advocacy appear more subtle? For sure. Should mediation advocacy employ more diplomatic language? Perhaps. But the lawyer entering into mediation still has the obligation to represent her client with zeal, even if the zeal is not reflected in a withering cross-examination or a stentorian closing argument. Mediation is not a process in which the ethical lawyer lets down her guard or pulls any punches; it is simply that the ever-vigilant lawyer may cloak her advocacy in garb which is more consistent with the tone of mediation.

The Same Rules Governing Allocation of Authority Between Lawyer and Client Apply in Mediation

Another mantra of mediation is that it is client-centered. Unlike litigation, which the proponents of mediation consider quite correctly a lawyer-

---

[3] "For mediation to succeed as a profession and to reach its highest objectives, advocacy has no place in any part of the process. For outside counsel to advocate a client's interests contradicts the very essence of mediation and can produce inequitable results." Mark C. Rutherford, *Lawyers and Divorce Mediation: Designing the Role of "Outside Counsel,"* MEDIATION Q., June 1986, at 17, 27.

[4] *See* THOMAS E. CARBONNEAU, ALTERNATIVE DISPUTE RESOLUTION: MELTING LANCES AND DISMOUNTING THE STEEDS 174 (1989).

dominated process, mediation is supposed to take the resolving of disputes away from the $400 an hour trial lawyers and "empower" (a favorite word in the mediation world) the clients to resolve their own differences.[5] Thus, it is asserted, lawyers should fade into the background and permit the clients to take control.

While it is great sport for those advocating mediation to suggest that in the litigation process unchaperoned lawyers run wild, driving fast cars and drinking in the back seat, the truth is far less interesting, mundane even, as lawyers conscientiously consult with their clients. But once having set the stereotype up as a basis for promoting mediation, some advocates for mediation feel compelled to perpetuate it as a basis for keeping the unreconstructed trial lawyers out of the new mediation process.

Rule 1.2 of the American Bar Association (ABA) *Model Rules of Professional Conduct* establishes the groundwork in our own ethical rules for allocation of responsibility between client and lawyer. That rule, in relevant part provides:

> *RULE 1.2 Scope of Representation and Allocation of Authority Between Client and Lawyer*
> (a) ... [A] lawyer shall abide by a client's decisions concerning the objectives of representation and, as required by Rule 1.4, shall consult with the client as to the means by which they are to be pursued. A lawyer shall abide by a client's decision whether to accept an offer of settlement of a matter.

The same rule applies whether the matter is a transactional one, is in mediation, or is in litigation. Moreover, despite all of the rhetoric surrounding the exalted role clients should play in the mediation process, that same rule should apply equally to mediation.

This does not mean that the client may not play a bigger role in the mediation process than might be played in the trial of a case. But that decision should not be made because of some desirable characteristic some proponents of mediation think every successful mediation "should" reflect. Rather, the decision should be made through consultation between lawyer and client, considering whether it is in the best interests of the client for the client to undertake any given task or role, whether the client is totally comfortable in doing so, and whether lawyer and client believe that the client's participation

---

[5] *See* ROBERT A. BARUCH BUSH & JOSEPH P. FOLGER, THE PROMISE OF MEDIATION: RESPONDING TO CONFLICT THROUGH EMPOWERMENT AND RECOGNITION 81-112 (1994).

will contribute either directly or psychologically to achieving a satisfactory result.

The reason clients consult lawyers, in part, is because they are uncomfortable dealing with confrontation, they are nervous, they do not enjoy public speaking, or they otherwise want someone – someone they believe is better at this than they are – standing in for them, representing them. For some clients, playing an active role in mediation is a terrifying thought. Whatever these clients think of the merits of mediation versus trial, they do not want a lead role or even a one-line walk-on part. Other clients, even if they wished for it, are not really capable of undertaking that responsibility, and should at least be so advised. A third group of clients may be fully capable and so inclined, but still should neither enter mediation unrepresented nor have their lawyer act as a potted palm.[6] And there clearly is at least a fourth category where all the vectors line up and the process and result will be better because of the active participation – even control – by the client.

So lawyers have to be very careful in the roles they assign to clients as part of the mediation process. Quite simply, many clients don't want to be "empowered." And they should not be unless (a) there is a good reason to do so; (b) the client has been consulted about and is comfortable with the decision; and (c) the lawyer thinks it is in the client's best interest, for example, to have the client give an opening speech, meet alone with the principal on the other side or with the mediator, or appear as a "witness" to tell the client's side of the story or simply explain the client's frustration with the controversy. There is, however, no independent value in granting the client a larger role beyond fulfilling the lawyer's mandate to make decisions in the best interests of the client.

It is also critical to remember that it is solely up to the client to decide the objectives of the representation. In that connection, in the mediation context, the lawyer must be mindful that the objectives to be achieved may come from a broad menu of possibilities. Clients may want complete vindication, an unlikely result from any settlement. Clients may want to continue a business relationship at all costs. Clients may want to save face. Finally the mediation literature teaches us that many clients will feel really well served by the process if they have achieved procedural justice. For them the fact that they were heard (either directly or through the lawyer), their views were considered by a third party and they were treated in a respectful and dignified manner, may be enough without achieving a financial result that the lawyer believes is a fair one.[7]

---

[6] The reference is to a comment by Brendan Sullivan while representing Oliver North. *See* ASSOCIATED PRESS, July 10, 1987.

[7] See Nancy A. Welsh, *Making Deals in Court-Connected Mediation: What's Justice Got to Do With It?*, 79 WASH. U. L.Q. 787, 820 (2001).

The Ethical Lawyer Will Not Abandon Positional Advocacy

One of the reasons some proponents of mediation want to keep the trial lawyers out of the cathedral of pacification is the idea that heretical litigators are too interested in positional advocacy ("my client's case is a winner"), and not interested enough in interest analysis ("what is my client's real goal in pursuing this matter and how can it be achieved?").[8] In their model, the mediation process would focus almost exclusively on the latter and not at all on the former. Positional advocacy, they assert, simply gets in the way of mediated solutions. Moreover, since litigators, they contend, are not very good at this skill which they are also not very interested in pursuing,[9] real benefit can be achieved by having the client represented by someone committed to interest analysis.

The ethical lawyer cannot permit her skills to be so circumscribed. It is the author's view that advocacy – raw, unmitigated, positional advocacy – is as important in a mediation as it is when the lawyer fills that box of twelve plus two. While mediation advocacy may not be as overt and transparent as advocacy in trial work, it is critical that it be undertaken as carefully and with as much preparation as any closing argument the seasoned trial lawyer has ever delivered. Indeed, in many ways this advocacy is more difficult and calls on more classic courtroom skills than a typical trial.

No matter what the interest analysis folks say, the two major ethical obligations in any mediation are to convince the other side of the merits of your position and to convince the mediator of the same thing. The lawyers who enter mediations without these two objectives firmly in view are disserving both their clients and the mediation process.

But some mediators say positional advocacy gets in the way. That can be true if the entire mediation is dedicated to arguing the merits. And true enough, at some point debate solely on positions can interfere with the ability to achieve the goal – a settlement that is in the best interests of the client. Still, each side wants the mediation to result in an inevitably unacknowledged yet, nonetheless, real recognition that its case is strong. If this does not occur, then

---

[8] Carrie Menkel-Meadow calls "mediation advocacy" "oxymoronic" and courses designed to teach lawyers to "win" at ADR as fundamentally inconsistent with the goals of mediation. Carrie Menkel-Meadow, *Ethics in ADR Representation: A Road Map of Critical Issues*, 4 DISP. RESOL. MAG. 3 (Winter 1997). Carrie Menkel-Meadow, *Ethics in Alternative Dispute Resolution: New Issues, No Answers from the Adversary Conception of Lawyers' Responsibilities*, 38 S. TEX. L. REV. 407, 408 (1997).

[9] Carrie Menkel-Meadow does believe that some lawyers might be educable. 38 S. TEX. L. REV. 407 at 427, 429.

the search for "flexibility" in the mediation process is doomed to failure. Similarly, the party to a mediation who does not strike a responsive chord in the mediator and provide the mediator with ammunition to soften up the other side has missed one of the great opportunities mediation provides. Even the mediator who announces she is purely a facilitator – and not an evaluator – will undertake some evaluation in her search for points on the merits that can be used in the mediation process to bring reality to bear upon otherwise hardened positions. And no one is better at bringing the advocacy skills to bear on the mediation process in this way than the seasoned trial lawyer. Having spent years trying to strike responsive chords in judges, law clerks, magistrates and jurors, trial lawyers are steeped in an understanding of how all of these decision-makers are affected by proof and how they make decisions, skills that easily transfer to the mediation environment.

All Advocacy – Not Just Mediation Advocacy – Requires Consideration of Both the Merits and Other Matters

I admire and recognize of the importance of advocacy on the merits, but that principle should not obscure the fact that in full bore litigation as well as mediation, lawyers who simply focus on advocating the merits of the client's case are disserving the clients and failing their ethical obligations. While it should go without saying, let me say it lest anyone misconstrues my view of the proper approach to these matters.

There are two aspects to this. First, the zealous advocate has an obligation to make sure that both lawyer and client do not get carried away with the sound of the lawyer's voice. By this I mean, no matter how facile the arguments, how elegant the distinguishing of adverse precedent, how compelling the factual analysis, the lawyer owes the client – a debt that may have to be paid many times if it is to "sink in" – an objective view of the likelihood of success. No case is risk free and most are quite risky. It is the lawyer's job to give that difficult assessment despite the inevitable consequence that in emphasizing the negative it can damage essential client confidence and take away from the aura of invincibility that surrounds the advocate's best efforts – an aura that otherwise may only disappear when the Court's opinion is issued or the jury returns its verdict. When *Model Rule 2.1* declares that it is our ethical duty that "a lawyer shall exercise independent professional judgment and render candid advice" it is referring to exactly what I have just described.

Second, the lawyer should remind the client that the "merits" of the controversy is only one matter the client should be considering in litigation and, particularly, in considering a mediated solution. Are there real possibilities that the relationship with the adverse party can be restored, preserved or, even, enhanced through some negotiated settlement? Will the result of a "victory" in court on the merits come at too great a cost, creating a pyrrhic victory for the client? Is the client psychologically prepared to endure the expense, delay and intrusiveness a litigated solution is likely to impose on the client? Will a victory in court be viewed by the client's customers and suppliers as vindication or oppressive conduct by a bully who should demonstrate more compassion?

These considerations – and others – are just as real and important for the lawyer to discuss with the client in litigation as in mediation. The lawyer who limits her advice only to the "merits" of the matter, ignores the ethical injunction in *Model Rule 2.1* that "in rendering advice, a lawyer may refer not only to law but to other considerations such as moral, economic, social and political factors, that may be relevant to the client's situation."

Confidentiality

Mediation is a conciliatory process. As a result there are two tendencies that potentially affect a lawyer's performance as a mediation advocate. First, there is a real desire to get along, to please the mediator, to encourage cooperation with the other side. Second, there is an inclination to lower one's guard. This process does not look like a discovery battle where one side asks for too much information through lengthy requests for documents, and the other side gives as little as possible (or even less). Nonetheless, the ethical lawyer must always remember that the lawyer's obligation of confidentiality remains in full force and effect; this duty is in no way trumped by any mediation-imposed obligation to disclose either voluntarily or upon request valuable information.[10] No information may be shared with the other side unless the client has impliedly or specifically authorized it. This goes for everything from attempts to use the mediation process as a means for merits discovery to matters relating to the clients' bottom line. If the client has not granted the lawyer permission, one way or the other, no matter how many points the lawyer might earn in good will by "sharing," *Model Rule 1.6* applies and must be complied with. And *Model Rule 1.6*, we must remember, comprehends all information – whether privileged or not – learned in the course of the representation.

Equally important, there is a tendency for lawyers to want to be "frank" with the mediator and even the other side about difficulties the lawyer might be having with the client. Unless the "trashing" of the client ("he's being so unrealistic," "he's a pain in the ...") is part of a deliberate strategy developed with the client, disparaging the client to either mediator or the other side is also a violation of *Model Rule 1.6*. It is, therefore, prohibited, no matter how good it

---

[10] *See* Sternlight, *supra* note 2, at 281 and n.37 (collecting sources for an alternative formulation).

might make the lawyer feel and no matter how much the lawyer believes it might be in the client's best interest to be frank.

While the attorney-client privilege is not a creature of the ethics rules, the lawyer's obligation to recognize that the privilege belongs to the client and that, absent explicit client consent, it must be protected at all costs, raises another important consideration in this context. Any sharing of information with the other side or the mediator could well be deemed a waiver of the privilege that may require the disclosure of what was said as well as any other privileged material on the same or related topics both in the underlying litigation and in any related matters that might arise in the future. Some of the subject matter waiver cases are quite expansive[11] and stand as a graphic reminder to any lawyer why the protection of the privilege is an important topic to consider while engaging in expansive conversations with the participants as one mediates.

Model Rule 4.2

Mediation may go on for many days. It may include face to face meetings and follow-up telephone conferences or *ex parte* discussions with a shuttling mediator. So long as everyone is together, *Model Rule 4.2* is unlikely to play a role. That rule provides:

> *RULE 4.2 Communication With Person Represented by Counsel*
> In representing a client, a lawyer shall not communicate about the subject of the representation with a person the lawyer knows to be represented by another lawyer in the matter unless the lawyer has the consent of the other lawyer or is authorized to do so by law or a court order.

When everyone is in the same place at the same time, all discussions will be fairly carefully orchestrated and the chance for such contacts (except to exchange pleasantries) are remote. As the process proceeds to less formal contacts or to contacts in-between formal mediation sessions, it is not unusual – as it is not unusual in many other forms of negotiation – for lawyers to be contacted by the client on the other side. Such conversations typically begin "I gotta get around my shyster lawyer" or "I respect you and know that you and I can settle this matter." Before the wave of flattery causes the lawyer to eagerly respond "you are so right," the lawyer must recognize that even though the other lawyer's client called you (you, of course, would never call the other party), that

---

[11] *See* RESTATEMENT (THIRD) OF THE LAW GOVERNING LAWYERS § 79, cmt. f and Reporter's Note f (collecting cases) (2000).

does not remove the other side's client from the protections of the rule.[12] Only with the permission of the lawyer on the other side are you permitted to talk to that client. And even if the client tells you he has fired his lawyer, the ethical lawyer will confirm that fact before initiating any discussions.

Model Rule 4.2 raises a second issue. The rule does not prohibit the parties to a matter, including a mediation matter, from contacting each other directly.[13] On the other hand, a lawyer may not do through the acts of another what the lawyer cannot do directly.[14] This has generally been held not to prohibit a lawyer from helping a client with a direct approach to the other side, to engage in what is commonly referred to as "scripting." However, that proposition is not free from doubt.[15] Therefore the well-advised lawyer participating in a mediation might have his client use the mediator as the intermediary to abrogate any argument that the lawyer was, in effect, violating *Model Rule 4.2* by assisting the client in this way. In any event, if the client plans to contact the other side directly, the lawyer should keep in mind the potential ethical dilemma raised by the "scripting" issue. The lawyer must decide the proper scope of counseling with her client on how to handle the contact.

Candor, Truthfulness and Puffing

One of the greatest ethical issues raised by the mediation process is the obligation of the lawyer to truthfulness. The analysis of this problem must address two different problems. The first is raised by the following conflict. In negotiations a lawyer is bound by the obligations of *Model Rule 4.1*, which provides:

RULE 4.1 Truthfulness in Statements to Others

---

[12] "The Rule applies even though the represented person initiates or consents to the representation." *Model Rule 4.2*, comment [5] (2002).

[13] *Model Rule 4.2*, Comment [2] provides that "Parties to a matter may communicate directly with each other."

[14] "A lawyer may not make a communication prohibited by this Rule through the acts of another." *Id.*

[15] See ABA Comm. On Ethics and Professional Responsibility, Formal Op. 92-362 (1992) stating that "The prohibition of this Rule against a lawyer's violating the Rules through the acts of another raises a number of questions about, *inter alia*, what a lawyer may or may not say to the lawyer's client...."

In the course of representing a client a lawyer shall not knowingly:

    (a) make a false statement of material fact to a third person; or

    (b) fail to disclose a material fact to a third person when disclosure is necessary to avoid assisting a criminal or fraudulent act by a client, unless disclosure is prohibited by rule 1.6.

as well as *Model Rule 8.4* which provides in applicable part:

RULE 8.4   Misconduct
It is professional misconduct for a lawyer to:

    (a) violate or attempt to violate the Rules of Professional Conduct, knowingly assist or induce another to do so, or do so through the acts of another;

    (b) commit a criminal act that reflects adversely on the lawyer's honesty, trustworthiness or fitness as a lawyer in other respects;

    (c) engage in conduct involving dishonesty, fraud, deceit or misrepresentation.....

In litigation, a lawyer is bound by the same rules insofar as the lawyer is dealing with third parties. To the extent the lawyer is dealing with a tribunal, then *Model Rule 3.3* must be observed as well. That rule, captioned Candor Toward the Tribunal, in relevant part provides:

(a) A lawyer shall not knowingly:

    (1) make a false statement of fact or law to a tribunal or fail to correct a false statement of material fact or law previously made to the tribunal by the lawyer;

    (2) fail to disclose to the tribunal legal authority in the controlling jurisdiction known to the lawyer to be directly adverse to the position of the client and not disclosed by opposing counsel; or

    (3) offer evidence that the lawyer knows to be false. If a lawyer, the lawyer's client, or a witness called by the lawyer, has offered material evidence and the lawyer comes to know of its falsity, the lawyer shall take reasonable remedial measures, including, if necessary, disclosure to the tribunal. A lawyer may refuse to offer evidence, other than the testimony of a

defendant in a criminal matter, that the lawyer reasonably believes is false.

(b) A lawyer who represents a client in an adjudicative proceeding and who knows that a person intends to engage, is engaging or has engaged in criminal or fraudulent conduct related to the proceeding shall take reasonable remedial measures, including, if necessary, disclosure to the tribunal.

(c) The duties stated in paragraphs (a) and (b) continue to the conclusion of the proceeding, and apply even if compliance requires disclosure of information otherwise protected by Rule 1.6.

With these two very different standards as the bookends of lawyer obligations, what of mediation? Is it a negotiation? Is the mediator the equivalent of a tribunal? In this author's view, the mediation process, even when it is court-annexed, is simply a high falutin' form of negotiation. Therefore, the lawyer's obligation in mediation is no higher than that imposed by *Model Rule 4.1*. But some have argued otherwise.[16] And we may see a day when the argument will be accepted that, as mediations take more and more the form of a mini-adjudication, particularly when the mediation is court annexed, the *Model Rule 3.3* standard should apply.

Even assuming the *Model Rule 4.1* standard applies, ethical issues still abound. First, there is the puffing issue. While lawyers must be truthful under *Model Rule 4.1*, a comment to the rule makes it clear that this obligation to truth telling does not extend to the bargaining process itself. The applicable comment observes,

> This Rule refers to statements of fact. Whether a particular statement should be regarded as one of fact can depend on the circumstances. Under generally accepted conventions in negotiation, certain types of statements ordinarily are not taken as statements of material fact. Estimates of price or value placed on the subject of a transaction and a party's intentions as to an acceptable settlement of a claim are ordinarily in this category, and so is the existence of an undisclosed principal except where

---

[16] The Ethics 2000 Commission of the American Bar Association was asked to include mediation in the definition of tribunal, but that request was rejected. Letter from ABA Section of Dispute Resolution and the CPR-Georgetown Commission on Ethics and Standards in ADR Joint Initiative to Professor Nancy Moore, Chief Reporter, ABA Commission on the Evaluation of the Rules of Professional Conduct, April 8, 1999 (on file with author) (Dispute Resolution Letter).

nondisclosure of the principal would constitute fraud. Lawyers should be mindful of their obligations under applicable law to avoid criminal and tortious misrepresentation.

While it is clear that this comment provides sanctuary for such obviously false statements as "my client won't take less than $5,000" or "your claim is worthless," drawing the line between comments like that and statements like "I have an expert who will blow your case out of the water," when no expert, in fact, has been hired, raise quite different concerns.

Second, lawyers must deal with the situation in which the lawyer learns after the fact that the lawyer has passed on information to the mediator on the other side that was inaccurate or has become inaccurate with the passage of time. Under *Model Rule 1.2* a lawyer may not knowingly assist a client crime or fraud, but here the lawyer knowingly did nothing but now knows the information is incorrect. Under these circumstances the lawyer should remonstrate with the client to make the appropriate correction. If the client refuses, the lawyer may be required to resign the representation.[17] In addition the lawyer may be required to give notice of the fact of withdrawal and to disaffirm any opinion, document or affirmation of the lawyer.[18]

Using the Mediation Process

While lawyers have an ethical obligation not to pursue a litigation tactic solely for the purpose of delay, contrary to the views of some,[19] I believe there is nothing wrong with recommending that your client pursue mediation and actually embarking on mediation for the principal purpose that the passage of time will benefit your client in some particular way. The applicable *Model Rule 4.4* provides:

In representing a client, a lawyer shall not use means that have no substantial purpose other than to embarrass, delay, or burden

---

[17] *Model Rule 1.16(a)* provides that the lawyer must withdraw if the continued representation will result in a violation by the lawyer of the rules of professional conduct or other law.

[18] *See Model Rule 1.2*, comment 10.

[19] *See* Rutherford, *supra* note 3, at 28; Kimberlee K. Kovach, *Good Faith in Mediation -- Requested, Recommended or Required*, 38 S. Tex. L. Rev. 575, 593 (1997) ("[L]awyers must not be able to use the process to gain adversarial advantage which intentionally disadvantages other parties." *Id.* at 581).

a third person, or use methods of obtaining evidence that violate the legal rights of such a person.

Thus, if the lawyer thinks there is any meaningful chance the mediation may result in bringing the parties closer to a settlement, then the lawyer certainly can recommend and pursue that course of action even though the argument that prompts the decision to mediate is that a much sought delay will likely result. Similarly, if there is an opportunity as a result of the mediation process to learn information about the other side's case – either the kind that would be discoverable or simply the sizing up of the lawyer and party on the other side or the demeanor and credibility of likely witnesses – in my view the lawyer has an obligation to take advantage of free information gathering if the opportunity presents itself. Moreover, that obligation could even extend to using mediation to create the opportunity, so long as the interdictions of *Model Rule 4.4* are not violated.

The mediation lawyer also has the ethical obligation to consider, under appropriate circumstances, playing her hand as close as possible to her vest. The following illustration demonstrates the point. There may be some key confidential information the lawyer knows would help the mediation process. But disclosure of this information would destroy the element of surprise at a trial. The lawyer exercising professional judgment concludes that disclosure now is less likely to benefit the client than preserving the confidence until later. I firmly believe that neither client nor lawyer has a duty to the mediation process which outweighs the obligation to act in the best interests of the client, even if that means the mediation is fated to fail.[20] Indeed, any time mediation is taking place against the backdrop of either pending or threatened litigation, it is absolutely critical that all mediation decisions - whether to meet face-to-face; whether to allow your client to speak; whether to allow your client to submit to questions – must be answered with a view to the total context. Mediation might succeed, but it often fails. The lawyer must address the risk that the client may engage in the process and emerge from mediation more vulnerable to an unfavorable result in the underlying dispute, and if that occurs the lawyer better have had a sound reason for having chosen that riskier course.

---

[20] In that sense the author rejects Professor Menkel-Meadow's view that the "zealous advocate who jealously guards (and does not share) information, who does not reveal adverse facts (and in some cases, adverse law) to the other side, who seeks to maximize gain for his client," may lack the creativity, the ability to "focus on the opposing sides' interests," and the ability to broaden rather than narrow issues that can be critical in mediation). Menkel-Meadow, 38 S. TEX. L. REV. 407 at 427.

Finally, the lawyer is free to encourage the client to pursue mediation, particularly mediation that may result in some "on the merits" advisory opinion from the mediator, if the lawyer's purpose is to provide the client or the other side with a reality check. Even though mediation may be informal and only result in a sketchy presentation on the merits (not nearly as persuasive and riveting as a "real trial"), there can be nothing more bracing for the parties to a mediation than to have a true neutral, respected by all, candidly tell that party that this case seems quite weak or is otherwise flawed. The identical message that a lawyer has been delivering to his client for months may suddenly be "heard" by the client when it comes out of the mouth of the mediator.

Does the Lawyer Have an Ethical Duty To Recommend Mediation?

A client comes to a lawyer with a dispute. "I want to sue X," the client proclaims. Can the lawyer follow that instruction consistent with the lawyer's professional responsibility obligations? Or must the lawyer mention, recommend or insist that the client pursue mediation before the "ultimate sanction," a full-blooded lawsuit, is launched.

The Ethics 2000 Commission of the American Bar Association was importuned, as part of its review of the *Model Rules of Professional Conduct*, to add to the *Model Rules* "an ethical obligation to inform clients that choices exist with respect to different forms of dispute resolution."[21] The proposal was rejected, not for lack of situations where it may be in the best interests of a client to pursue mediation. Rather, the Commission (dare I speak for the entire Commission) held the view that there are many matters, depending on the facts, about which lawyers must advise clients. The subject matter of lawyer advice literally would fill encyclopedias. To single out mediation in this way would be wrong for two reasons.

First, hundreds of required actions by lawyers never mentioned in the *Model Rules of Professional Conduct*, are subsumed under obligations to be competent and diligent, to communicate with the client, and to put the client's interests ahead of the lawyer's. Thus, including mediation would represent special pleading for alternative dispute resolution otherwise unwarranted in the rules.

Second, as benighted as mediation may be considered by some, there are clearly situations in which a lawyer can appropriately determine, without consultation with the client, that lawyer and client need not consider these alternatives. Think of a client that must establish a legal precedent, a client who

---

[21] *See* Dispute Resolution Letter, *supra* note 15.

considers settlement a sign of weakness, or a client who needs the benefit of a court order. The reader will immediately recognize that to make the recommendation of mediation an ethical requirement – the violation of which would be punishable by discipline – is not only unwarranted but sometimes contrary to the lawyer's actual ethical obligations.

Client, Not Lawyer, Gets to Decide About Settlement

A mediation process has been launched. It is going swimmingly. The mediator brings all of her talent, patience and good humor to bear. Shuttle diplomacy has worked. The other side is finally acting realistic. The mediator brings to lawyer and client the other side's final proposition. The lawyer is thrilled with the mediator's work, her own contribution to the process and is concerned that if client were to return to litigation, even after trial, such a wonderful result could not be achieved. But the client balks. "It's not enough!" the client exclaims. "It's the best that I can do," the mediator intones, letting her voice betray her disappointment. "It's a good result," the lawyer observes. "We'll never do better at trial; a court could never award us a long term contract this deal includes." Lengthy remonstration ensues yet the client remains adamant.

No matter how ill-served the lawyer feels at this moment, the lawyer must remember this decision is one for the client to make – not the mediator and not the lawyer. While the lawyer must offer her best advice to the client, the line between advice and overwhelming the client can be a very fine one which the lawyer, as a matter of professional responsibility, may not cross. Client autonomy may not mean giving the entire mediation process over to the clients; it does, however, mean that the decision to settle is the client's and it is the lawyer's obligation to act on that decision.[22]

Conclusion

Perhaps even through a bit of rhetorical excess, I hope I have demonstrated that a lawyer's primary responsibility is to protect the interests of her client. But I must concede, yes, even celebrate the fact that providing such protection is not necessarily inconsistent with participating in a process that aims for collaboration and integrative solutions. Indeed, I will further concede that there are many instances where this process may be more consistent with protecting a client's interests than the litigation process, where even successful

---

[22] See *Model Rule 1.2 (a).* ("A lawyer shall abide by a client's decision whether to accept an offer of settlement.")

outcomes carry some heavy costs. At times, however, a conflict may arise between the client's interests and the goals of the mediation process. When that occurs, let no lawyer be confused: the lawyer's responsibility is to her client, not to the process.

Chapter IV

Ethics for Whom?
The Recognition of Diversity in Lawyering Calls for
Plurality in Ethical Considerations and
Rules of Representational Work

By Kimberlee K. Kovach

The practice of law has experienced and will continue to undergo considerable transformation. Alternatives to the litigation or adversary system for problem solving and dispute resolution exist, and practice in these processes will continue to increase. Additional examples of the diverse aspects of law practice in the 21st century include the interdisciplinary nature of problem solving, which encompasses collaborative lawyering; multidisciplinary practice; the need for lawyers to work with other professionals and be educated in other disciplines; and the increase of technology that allows communication to occur in a wide range of innovative mediums. In these and other contexts, lawyers serve their clients in a variety of roles and, in doing so, take on numerous diverse tasks. No longer can one-size-fits-all ethical standards serve to guide the conduct of lawyers. Diverse legal practice arenas demand distinct rules and guidelines to establish the constraints of such work.

This chapter looks at the ethical considerations of those who represent individuals or entities in mediation and other less or non-adversarial processes. One underlying theme is that mediation is quite different in many ways from the adversary system – in its goals, objectives and procedures. Consequently, the conduct, behaviors and strategies that might serve clients well in an adversary system are often, at best, inappropriate in the non-adversarial setting. In some cases behaviors inconsistent with mediation have even proven to be quite detrimental to the process. Such adversarial approaches may obstruct and hinder the opportunities and activities fundamental to the mediation process.

Accordingly, new approaches to dispute resolution call for new and different ethical guidelines and rules.[1]

Perspectives in Emerging Alternatives to the Adversary System

While the adversarial court system has been the dominant method of dispute resolution in the United States for more than 200 years,[2] that time has also been one of complaints and dissatisfaction with the system. Although this chapter is not intended to be a dissertation on the crisis with the legal system, there is some merit in understanding that the use of mediation and other dispute resolution processes was, at least in part, advanced in response to the problems within the court system. As a consequence the initial use of the term *alternative* meant to signify and underscore that mediation is quite different and distinct from adversarial approaches, including trial and more traditional settlement negotiation.

Even though the mediation process offers participants many opportunities for creative problem solving, when introduced to the court system, mediation was viewed primarily as a method to increase and accelerate the settlement of lawsuits. Yet, even then, the bar was somewhat reluctant to utilize the process. As a result, in many jurisdictions, in an effort to encourage more use of mediation, courts began to mandate such use. Because mediation is not yet society's default paradigm, it must be introduced to potential consumers in order to achieve familiarity and acceptance. Compulsory usage is one way to introduce people to any new or innovative process. Judges and court administrators very quickly began to refer cases to mediation in order to expedite settlement. Currently, in many courts, in numerous state and federal jurisdictions throughout the United States, mediation was, and still is, suggested, urged, and ordered as a method to resolve or settle lawsuits. Objectives such as saving time and money, for the court system as well as the litigants, were cited as the primary motivators.

Other quite significant aspects of mediation were rarely mentioned, let alone stressed. These include aspects of mediation such as the use of creativity and the need for party participation in the process. Little was said about the fact that mediation differs so significantly from adversary practice. Mediation participants, lawyers and parties alike, were not educated about this very different process, and hence often carried with them to mediation the conduct and

---

[1] I have previously made this contention in greater detail. See Kimberlee K. Kovach, *New Wine Requires New Wineskins: Transforming Lawyer Ethics for Effective Representation in A Non-adversarial Approach to Problem Solving: Mediation* 28 FORDHAM U. L. J. 935 (2001).

[2] For a look at the history of the adversary system, see Stephan A. Lansman, A *Brief Survey of the Development of the Adversary System* 44 OHIO ST. L. J. 713 (1983).

behaviors with which they were familiar and comfortable. Unfortunately in many cases, mediation has begun to look more like "litigation-lite."[3]

Yet mediation is not a process that focuses on right and wrong or on winning and losing. Factual perspectives play a very small role in the mediation process. Although some discussion of the underlying suit or dispute is necessary for the parties to grasp other points of view, such is not the focus of mediation. Instead of attempting to prove or disprove that something occurred in the past (the primary activity of trial lawyers, in order to achieve a "legal result"), mediation is much more concerned with looking at the future and finding innovative and creative solutions to problems. Mediation does not declare a party a winner or loser. While some lawyers and judges view mediation as merely an event to precipitate the settlement of a legalized dispute, it offers much more. Parties are able to negotiate many resolutions that courts are unable to order or even create. These distinctions come with differences.

Different Processes Call for Different Behaviors

An example may help the reader better understand the distinctions that are necessary when practicing in the two different arenas. Football and basketball are two very popular sports activities in the United States. To do extremely well in either requires athletic skill and talent. But the games themselves are played quite differently. Strategies differ, and in some cases the talents and skills that are effective in one game would be detrimental in the other. For example, football requires that the players tackle one another, of course with guidelines in place. Physical contact is a major part of the game. On the other hand, one of the major tenets of basketball involves the finesse of playing without making contact with the players of the other team. When a coach prepares an athlete to play football, contact is emphasized; conversely, when a coach prepares an athlete for basketball, it is prohibited.

So too with the adversary and mediation processes. The lawyer is talented in representing people. And for quite some time the adversarial method was the primary avenue of such representations. Now competent representation involves much more than advocacy in a win-lose paradigm. To represent clients most effectively, lawyers must be familiar with the nuances of each procedure or process in which their clients participate. As in any system, if a process is to be effective, the conduct, performance and skills demonstrated by those who represent clients in the system must be consistent with the purposes and goals of that system. In terms of the mediation process, lawyer competency includes not only knowledge about more technical matters such as the referral process and

---

[3] Jack M. Sabatino, *ADR as "Litigation Lite": Procedural and Evidentiary Norms Embedded within Alternative Dispute Resolution*, 47 EMORY L.J. 1289 (1998).

agreement enforceability issues, but also the ethical and strategic parameters of such a practice.

Litigation and mediation embrace very different paradigms and theoretical underpinnings for dispute resolution and problem solving. The adversarial paradigm is concerned with finding truth, determining right and wrong, preserving individual rights and punishing wrongdoers. To effectuate these goals, lawyers offer proofs through evidence, and they engage in argument in a competitive setting.[4]

On the other hand, the fundamental goals and objectives of mediation are to determine the parties' needs and interests, to identify areas of mutual interest and to fashion innovative and mutually satisfactory solutions through the use of creative problem solving. The parties themselves participate directly in the process of resolving their dispute. Resolutions are achieved without the necessity of determining right or wrong.

Clearly mediation involves a radically distinct and contrasting paradigm, one that incorporates a mindset, vision, attitude and skill set quite distinct in many ways from that of the prevailing adversarial norm.[5] A different philosophical map[6] is needed when entering the mediation area. Although rules cannot effectively change philosophy and attitudes, they do serve to guide conduct. Like the skills of football and basketball, some of the skills of litigation and mediation are transferable, while others are not.

Ethical Considerations that Apply in Mediation

There are some rules of lawyer conduct and behavior that are imperative for competent practice regardless of the context of such practice. For example, good communication skills are essential to effective representation in any context. This includes communication between lawyer and client, between and among other parties, as well as with third parties, such as jurors, judges or mediators. A lawyer should be adequately prepared for each process he may participate in on behalf of a client, though manner of preparation will likely differ. Preparation is a vital part of competent lawyering in any situation.

Model Rule of Professional Conduct 1.2, which allocates decision-making between lawyer and client, appears to apply to all types of settings.

---

[4] *See* Paul T. Wangerin, *The Political and Economic Roots of the "Adversary System of Justice" and "Alternative Dispute Resolution,"* 9 OHIO ST. J. DISP RESOL. 203 (1994) for an in-depth discussion and comparison of the philosophical bases for these systems.

[5] Lela P. Love, *Introduction, Symposium, Teaching a New Paradigm; Must Knights Shed Their Swords and Armor to Enter Certain ADR Arenas?* 1 CARDOZO ONLINE J. CONFLICT RESOL. (1999) at http://cardozo.yu.edu/cojcr/new-site/issues/vol1/vol1.htm.

[6] Leonard L. Riskin, *Mediation and Lawyers*, 43 OHIO ST. L. J. 29 (1982).

Rules which prohibit lawyers from taking advantage of parties such as *Model Rule 4.2* and *Model Rule 4.3* would also have applicability in a mediation or problem solving setting. Rules concerning conflicts of interests likewise are generally applicable. And, of course, *Model Rule 8.4,* the general misconduct "catch-all," is plainly another imperative applicable to all contexts of the lawyer's work, including mediation.

Ethical Considerations that Do Not Apply in Mediation

Other current rules, however, can cause confusion in mediation. Truthfulness is one example. When examining the negotiation process, *Model Rule 4.1* provides a very nebulous truthfulness standard. And while more than 20 years ago there appeared, at least in early drafts, a provision calling for more honesty in negotiation, it was deleted and the current provision inserted. The current standard is used to support various methods of puffery and trickery in the context of negotiation. And while I do not support these "conventions in negotiation" because they allow representatives and those who negotiate to deceive the other side, that practice remains, at this point, the norm, and is still accepted in the direct negotiation of litigation cases.

What has made this standard particularly troublesome is that this conduct is now carrying over into the mediation context. If mediation is viewed as nothing more than facilitated negotiation, then what is acceptable conduct in the context of direct negotiation becomes, by extension, acceptable in facilitated negotiation. Such conduct is contrary to those qualities, attitudes, and conduct basic to the mediation paradigm. However, because much direct negotiation still takes place in the context of the adversary system, then perhaps the rule should remain as it is, but at least be qualified for mediation and other problem solving, non-adversarial processes. The current rule clearly should not be the standard in mediation, a process that is dependent upon the direct and truthful exchange of communication.

Other rules, such as those dealing with litigation, tribunals, and the like do not have relevance in the mediation or problem solving process. A final consideration looks at the end result of mediation. Mediation is a facilitated negotiation. Although the resolution often encompasses the settlement of a lawsuit, in most states, by statutes as well as common law, the end result of mediation is also the formation of a contract. Behavior during mediation could clearly impact enforcement of the contract. For where it is assumed, as has been done historically in litigation settlements, that "puffing or lying is part of negotiation" such conduct could serve as grounds to void the contract.

At least to some extent, this change to non-adversarial practices in the mediation process must be effectuated by changes in the codes of professional responsibility. While it is too late for real changes in the new model code produced by the American Bar Association's Commission on Ethics (also known as Ethics 2000), it is not too late to begin looking at the possibilities of establishing a separate or at least supplemental code for lawyers who represent clients in a non-adversarial forum for dispute resolution. These new standards could be created either by merely amending existing codes, or in the alternative, and perhaps more appropriately, by enacting a separate new code, operational when practicing in different fora. This suggestion is not made in isolation, as new ethical considerations and codes for lawyer conduct have been urged in a variety of different practice areas.[7] New and widely divergent processes and procedures call for different, tailored and process-specific ethics.

The Need for New and More Appropriate Ethical Considerations

The lawyer's practice is no longer a one-size-fits-all service. Consequently the rules and guidelines that establish parameters of conduct should be diverse and appropriate for the context of practice. There have been prior calls for ethical considerations for distinct types of practice. Now new rules and guidelines are necessary for lawyers who represent clients in mediation.

Rules guide lawyers' behavior. In fact, rules are the most likely way in which to change lawyer conduct. Because of their emphasis on rights and objectivity, lawyers are more willing to change their behavior to conform to a codified rule than to respond to a more intangible, subjective call for conduct.[8] Lawyers are familiar and comfortable with rules. For example, although continuing legal education (CLE) programs were offered in the past, it was not until the states required a specific number of CLE hours per year (in order to maintain licensure) that attendance escalated.[9]

Precisely what those distinct ethical considerations are or should be is too difficult and lengthy a discourse to include in this piece. However, it is worthwhile, and perhaps inevitable, that the types of ethical standards appropriate for lawyers representing clients in non-adversarial settings be considered. A few commentators have expressed views conveying the need for new and innovative guidelines for practice. One such recommendation is that the participants in

---

[7] Nancy B. Rapoport, *Our House, Our Rules: The Need for a Uniform Code of Bankruptcy Ethics*, 6 AM. BANKR. INST. L. REV. 45 (1998).

[8] *See* Susan Daicoff, *Asking Leopards to Change Their Spots: Should Lawyers Change? A Critique of Solutions to Problems with Professionalism by Reference to Empirically- Derived Attorney Personality Attributes*, 11 GEO. J. LEGAL ETHICS 547, 553 (1998).

[9] *E.g.,* Paul Michael Hassett, *Association and Annual Meeting Continuing Impressive Growth*, N.Y.L.J., Jan. 22, 2001, at 52 (attributing an increase in attendance of over 100% to the new requirement of mandatory continuing legal education).

mediation are, or should be, obligated to mediate in good faith.[10] While that concept may be problematic in some ways, it at least provides some guidance. Although this approach has been criticized for lack of specificity, good-faith proponents have begun to itemize the factors that would constitute such a requirement.[11] Another option may be the establishment of an ethic of care.

For others it might be a standard of altruism. A level of minimal, meaningful participation for mediation participants has also been suggested, along with focus on communication and client interaction.[12] Establishing such guidance, along with education, will enable lawyers to become ethical, competent and effective representatives in problem solving activities.

Law practice will continue to evolve. We need to develop specific ethical standards appropriate for those participating in a variety of situations so attorneys will have guidance in all aspects of law practice – the innovative as well as the traditional. The bar has an obligation to recognize, support and guide the great diversity in law practice – to ignore that obligation is a breach of ethics for the profession.

---

[10] Kovach, *supra* note 1, *See also* Maureen A. Weston, *Checks on Participant Conduct in Compulsory ADR; Reconciling the Tension in the Need for Good-Faith Participation, Autonomy and Confidentiality*, 76 IND. L.J. 591 (2001).

[11] Kimberlee K. Kovach, *Good Faith in Mediation: Requested, Recommended or Required: A New Ethic*, 38 S. TEXAS L. REV. 575 (1997).

[12] Kovach, *supra* note 1.

CHAPTER V

Mediator Ethics[1]

By James J. Alfini

Introduction

The subject of mediator ethics has received widespread attention. Interest in developing appropriate standards of conduct for mediators has been fueled by the increasing popularity of court-sponsored mediation programs during the final decade of the 20th century and into the 21st. Often borrowing language from standards of conduct for mediators that had been developed by professional organizations and ADR practitioners, state and federal courts in a number of jurisdictions have promulgated mediator ethics rules to prescribe and regulate the behavior of mediators to whom court cases are referred. In other jurisdictions, statewide standards have been published by state bar associations or ADR organizations.

The purpose of this chapter is to review and compare these various standards of conduct for mediators. Section B focuses on standards relating to the mediator's role, dealing with the subjects of impartiality, conflicts of interest, competence, and capacity to mediate. Section C focuses on the mediation process and covers party self-determination, confidentiality, process fairness, relations with the court or other referring body, and the drafting of agreements. Section D focuses on practice considerations, including the unauthorized practice of law, fees, advertising, multidisciplinary practice, and professional development.

Although model mediator standards of conduct have been developed by a number of professional organizations,[2] the commentary in this chapter will focus primarily on the two sets of standards that were developed by consortia of ADR

---

[1] The author expresses his gratitude to Sharon Press for reviewing an earlier version of this chapter.

[2] *See, e.g.*, American Bar Association Family Law Section, *Standards of Practice for Lawyer Mediators in Family Disputes*, 18 FAM. L. Q. 363 (1984); Colorado Council of Mediators, CODE OF PROFESSIONAL CONDUCT (1982).

organizations. The first, the *Model Standards of Conduct for Mediators* (*Joint Standards*), was developed and adopted by the American Arbitration Association, the American Bar Association Section of Dispute Resolution, and the Society of Professionals in Dispute Resolution in 1994.[3] The second, the *Model Standards of Practice for Family and Divorce Mediation* (*Model Family Standards*), was developed through a symposium convened in 2000 by the Association of Family and Conciliation Courts, the Family Law Section of the ABA, and the National Council of Dispute Resolution Organizations, including the ABA Section of Dispute Resolution.[4] The *Joint Standards* have been used as a model in many jurisdictions that have developed and adopted mediator standards of conduct and are often offered as a guide by state bar associations and other professional groups in states that have not yet adopted standards.

There are, however, important differences between these two sets of "national" standards. The *Joint Standards* are intended to offer ethical guidance to all mediators,[5] while the *Model Family Standards* are directed only to family mediators. Thus, the *Model Family Standards* contain significantly more detailed guidance in some areas because of problems such as domestic violence and child abuse that are unique to family mediation practice. Even then, the drafters of the *Model Family Standards* sought to make them as consistent as possible with other standards.[6] Indeed, it is clear that the drafters of the *Model Family Standards* borrowed liberally from the language of the *Joint Standards*.

In addition to the two sets of national standards, we will also consider standards adopted for statewide application in a number of jurisdictions. In some states (*e.g.,* Alabama, Florida, Georgia, Kansas, New Jersey, Oklahoma and Virginia), specific mediator standards of conduct have been adopted by the state's highest court and are mandatory for mediators in court-sponsored

---

[3] American Arbitration Association, American Bar Association Section of Dispute Resolution, Society of Professionals in Dispute Resolution, MODEL STANDARDS OF CONDUCT FOR MEDIATORS (1994).(*Joint Standards*). For a description of these standards and their development *see,* John D. Feerick, *Standards of Conduct for Mediators,* 79 JUDICATURE 314 (1996). The standards are reprinted at 5 WORLD ARB. AND MEDIATION REP. 223 (1994). The *Joint Standards* are also reprinted in Appendix A.

[4] *See* Symposium on Standards of Practice, *Model Standards of Practice for Family and Divorce Mediation,* 39 FAM. CT. REV. 121 (2001). The *Model Family Standards* were adopted by the House of Delegates of the American Bar Association at the ABA annual meeting in Chicago in August, 2001. The *Model Family Standards* are reprinted in Appendix B.

[5] Feerick, *supra* note 3.

[6] *See* Andrew Schepard, *Preface to the Draft Model Standards,* 38 FAM. & CONCILIATION COURTS REV. 106 (2000).

programs,[7] and in at least one state (California), a drafting effort is currently in progress.[8] In several states (Indiana, Maine, Minnesota, and Tennessee), the mediator standards are subsumed in standards of conduct for all neutrals involved in ADR processes.[9] In other states (Hawaii, Oregon, and Texas), the standards are advisory, and are generally viewed as aspirational guidelines.[10] In Iowa, the statewide standards cover only family mediators.[11]

The Mediator

Various ethics provisions call upon the mediator to adopt a role that is consistent with the unique character of mediation. Among these are standards that require the mediator to be and remain impartial, to identify and disclose potential conflicts of interest, and to insure that the parties have the capacity to

---

[7] *See, e.g.*, Alabama Supreme Court, ALABAMA CODE OF ETHICS FOR MEDIATORS (adopted effective March 1, 1996) (hereinafter *Alabama Standards*); Georgia Supreme Court, ETHICAL STANDARDS FOR MEDIATORS, Chapter 1A of Appendix C of ALTERNATIVE DISPUTE RESOLUTION RULES (effective September 28, 1995) (hereinafter *Georgia Standards*); Florida Supreme Court Standing Committee on Mediation and Arbitration Rules, FLORIDA RULES FOR CERTIFIED AND COURT-APPOINTED MEDIATORS (amended, 2000) (hereinafter *Florida Standards*); Kansas Supreme Court, KAN. SUP. CT. RULE 903, ETHICAL STANDARDS FOR MEDIATORS (2001); New Jersey Supreme Court, STANDARDS OF CONDUCT FOR MEDIATORS IN COURT-CONNECTED PROGRAMS (2000) (hereinafter *New Jersey Standards*); Oklahoma Supreme Court, 120. S. §1801 et seq. Appendix A. CODE OF PROFESSIONAL CONDUCT FOR MEDIATORS (adopted April 8, 1986); Judicial Council of Virginia, STANDARDS OF ETHICS AND PROFESSIONAL RESPONSIBILITY FOR CERTIFIED MEDIATORS (1997) (hereinafter *Virginia Standards*).

[8] Judicial Council of California, ETHICAL STANDARDS FOR MEDIATORS IN COURT-CONNECTED MEDIATION PROGRAMS FOR CIVIL CASES (preliminary draft) (hereinafter *California Draft Standards*).

[9] *See, e.g,.* Indiana Supreme Court Rules for Alternative Dispute Resolution, Rule 7, CONDUCT AND DISCIPLINE FOR PERSONS CONDUCTING ADR (adopted December 6, 1994) (hereinafter *Indiana Standards*); Maine Association of Dispute Resolution Professionals, STANDARDS OF PROFESSIONAL CONDUCT (1989) (hereinafter *Maine Standards*); Minnesota Supreme Court General Rules of Practice, Rule 114, ALTERNATIVE DISPUTE RESOLUTION, Appendix, CODE OF ETHICS (1997) (hereinafter *Minnesota Standards*); Tennessee Supreme Court, TENN. SUP. CT. RULE 31 APPENDIX A, STANDARDS OF PROFESSIONAL CONDUCT FOR RULE 31 NEUTRALS (2001). Note: The *Minnesota Standards* are based on the *Joint Standards* and have a separate provision for mediators, specifically dealing with party self-determination.

[10] *See, e.g.*, Hawaii State Judiciary, Program on Alternative Dispute Resolution, STANDARDS FOR PRIVATE AND PUBLIC MEDIATORS IN THE STATE OF HAWAII (1986) (hereinafter *Hawaii Standards*); Oregon Mediation Association, STANDARDS OF MEDIATION PRACTICE (2000) (hereinafter *Oregon Standards*); State Bar of Texas Alternative Dispute Resolution Section, ETHICAL GUIDELINES FOR MEDIATORS (1998) (hereinafter *Texas Standards*).

[11] Iowa Supreme Court, RULES GOVERNING STANDARDS OF PRACTICE FOR LAWYER MEDIATORS IN FAMILY DISPUTES (effective February 2, 1987) (hereinafter *Iowa Family Standards*).

accomplish the purposes of mediation. All of these responsibilities are threshold aspects of the mediator's role that are intended to set the stage for a successful mediation.

Impartiality

Impartiality is a hallmark of mediation and is accorded a prominent place in all mediator standards of conduct. Most of the state standards define impartiality in general terms similar to those offered in the *Hawaii Standards* (one of the earliest): "Impartiality means freedom from favoritism and bias in word, action and appearance."[12]

All standards impose a clear and unambiguous duty to be and remain impartial. Standard II of the *Joint Standards* states, "A Mediator Shall Conduct the Mediation in an Impartial Manner." The duty to be and remain impartial requires a mediator to adopt a role that is free of "partiality or prejudice based on the parties' personal characteristics, background or performance at the mediation."[13] Standard IV of the *Model Family Standards* has similar language. Both sets of standards also call upon the mediator to withdraw if "at any time the mediator is unable to conduct the process in an impartial manner"[14] or "the mediator believes the mediator's impartiality has been compromised . . . ."[15] The *Oregon Standards* are somewhat unique in couching the mediator's duty in terms of "impartial regard": "The mediator shall demonstrate and maintain a commitment to impartial regard by serving all participants at all times."[16]

Conflicts of Interest

The concept of mediator impartiality presumes that a mediator is free of conflicts of interest. Indeed, the *Model Family Standards* include conflicts of interest responsibilities in the impartiality standard and, borrowing the language from Standard III (Conflicts of Interest) of the *Joint Standards*, call upon the mediator to "disclose all actual and potential . . . conflicts of interest reasonably

---

[12] *Hawaii Standards*, III (1).

[13] *Joint Standards*, II, Comments.

[14] *Joint Standards*, II.

[15] *Model Family Standards*, IV (I).

[16] *Oregon Standards*, III.

known to the mediator."[17]   The *Joint Standards* define a conflict of interest as "a dealing or relationship that might create an impression of possible bias," while the *Model Family Standards* state that a conflict "means any relationship between the mediator, any participant or the subject matter of the dispute, that compromises or appears to compromise the mediator's impartiality."[18]

Both sets of standards permit the mediator to go forward with the mediation if, following disclosure of the conflict, all parties waive the conflict. *The Model Family Standards* require that the waiver be in writing and both sets of standards caution the mediator, regardless of the waiver, not to proceed if the conflict of interest "clearly impairs a mediator's impartiality"[19] or "casts serious doubt on the integrity of the process."[20]

Although both sets of standards view the duty to disclose conflicts as a continuing one, the *Model Family Standards* specifically require the mediator to make disclosure "prior to the start of a mediation and in time to allow the participants to select an alternate mediator."[21]   Both standards also caution the mediator to "avoid conflicts of interest in recommending the services of other professionals."[22]   While the *Model Family Standards* deal with post-mediation conflicts in general terms ("A family mediator shall not use information about participants obtained in a mediation for personal gain or advantage"[23]), the *Joint Standards* are more specific: "Without the consent of the parties, a mediator shall not subsequently establish a professional relationship with one of the parties in a related matter, or in an unrelated matter under circumstances which would raise legitimate questions about the integrity of the mediation process."[24]   Concern has been expressed over the open-ended nature of the *Joint Standards* language dealing with conflicts in unrelated matters on the grounds that this provision would unnecessarily discourage certain professionals (particularly lawyers in large firms) from becoming mediators or from taking cases out of fear that their firm might subsequently face conflicts challenges for vague or ambiguous

---

[17] *Model Family Standards*, IV.

[18] *Model Family Standards*, IV (D).

[19] *Id.*

[20] *Joint Standards*, III.

[21] *Model Family Standards*, IV (D).

[22] *Joint Standards*, III, Comments; *Model Family Standards*, IV (G).

[23] *Model Family Standards*, IV (H).

[24] *Joint Standards*, III.

reasons. Therefore, at least one jurisdiction that has used the *Joint Standards* as a model (Minnesota) has deleted this language.[25] The *New Jersey Standards* set a specific time period for dealing with conflicts in unrelated matters: "A mediator . . . shall not subsequently represent or provide professional services for any party to the mediation proceeding in any unrelated matter for a period of six months, unless all parties consent after full disclosure."[26]

Competence

An important ethical threshold consideration for a mediator is whether he or she is competent to accomplish the purposes of a particular mediation. Although both sets of national standards identify -- in general terms -- training, education and experience in mediation as potentially important components in establishing a mediator's qualifications,[27] the *Joint Standards* and the *Model Family Standards* adopt different approaches to dealing with the question of whether mediator competence includes substantive expertise. In general, the *Joint Standards* reject any notion that a mediator should possess expertise in the subject matter of the dispute,[28] while the *Model Family Standards* state that the mediator should have "knowledge of family law" and "knowledge of and training in the impact of family conflict on parents, children and other participants, including knowledge of child development, domestic abuse, and child abuse and neglect."[29] The *Joint Standards* thus anticipate that expectations concerning the mediator's competence should be considered beforehand by both the mediator and the parties: "Any person may be selected as a mediator, provided that the parties are satisfied with the mediator's qualifications."[30] Once these expectations are established, the mediator has a duty to satisfy these expectations: "A Mediator Shall Mediate Only When the Mediator Has the Necessary Qualifications to Satisfy the Reasonable Expectations of the Parties."[31] In institutional settings, however, the Joint Standards call upon the appointing

---

[25] *See Minnesota Standards*, Rule II.

[26] *New Jersey Standards*, III (B) (2).

[27] *See Joint Standards*, IV and *Model Family Standards*, II.

[28] *Joint Standards*, IV: "Any person may be selected as a mediator, provided that the parties are satisfied with the mediator's qualifications."

[29] *Model Family Standards*, II (A).

[30] *Joint Standards*, IV, Text.

[31] *Joint Standards*, IV.

agency to "make reasonable efforts to ensure that each mediator is qualified for the particular mediation."[32] Mediator qualifications in court-sponsored and other institutionalized programs are generally established by statute or court rule and are discussed in Chapters II and IX.

Because the *Joint Standards* place a burden on the parties for establishing their expectations concerning a mediator's qualifications, they call upon mediators to "have available for the parties information regarding their relevant training, education and experience."[33] The *Model Family Standards* are even more emphatic on this point: "Family mediators should provide information to the participants about the mediator's relevant training, education, and expertise."[34] Moreover, Standard XIII of *the Model Family Standards* explicitly requires a family mediator to "acquire and maintain professional competence in mediation."

Capacity to Mediate

Mediators cannot adequately fulfill their role in the mediation process if one or more parties to the mediation lack the capacity to mediate effectively. Disputants may suffer from any number of conditions or circumstances that would impair their ability to mediate. Among these circumstances are alcoholism, drug abuse, domestic abuse, and physical disability. The *Joint Standards* are silent as to a mediator's responsibility to identify, and act on, conditions or circumstances that would impair a party's capacity to mediate. The *Model Family Standards*, on the other hand, devote three standards (IX, X, and XI) to this problem.

Standard IX of the *Model Family Standards* states that a "family mediator shall recognize a family situation involving child abuse or neglect and take appropriate steps to shape the mediation process accordingly." Standard X has the same language except that it substitutes "domestic abuse" for "child abuse or neglect." Standard IX (B) would preclude the mediator from going forward with "a mediation in which the family situation has been assessed to involve child abuse or neglect," and Standard X (B) would prohibit "a mediation in which the family situation has been assessed to involve domestic abuse" unless the mediator has had "appropriate and adequate training." Standard X (C) requires a mediator to screen for domestic abuse prior to the mediation and to continue domestic abuse assessment throughout the mediation. If domestic abuse is present, Standard X (D) lists six measures a mediator should consider,

---

[32] *Joint Standards*, IV, Comments.

[33] *Joint Standards*, IV, Comments.

[34] *Model Family Standards,* II (B).

including "suspending or terminating the mediation sessions, with appropriate steps to protect the safety of the participants."[35] Termination, however, is listed last and the other measures would anticipate the mediation going forward by "establishing appropriate security arrangements,"[36] "holding separate sessions . . . even without the agreement of all participants,"[37] allowing a friend or other third party to attend the mediation,[38] encouraging attorney participation,[39] or making a community resource referral.[40] To the extent that these standards would thus permit certain cases involving domestic violence to go forward in mediation, these standards run counter to the advice of commentators who have argued, in absolute terms, that cases in which domestic abuse is present should never be mediated.[41]

Standard XI of the *Model Family Standards* requires the mediator to suspend or terminate a mediation if the mediator "believes that a participant is unable to effectively participate . . . ." Among the circumstances warranting suspension or termination listed in XI (A) are situations in which "the safety of a participant or well-being of a child is threatened"[42] or "a participant is unable to participate due to the influence of drugs, alcohol, or physical or mental condition."[43]

The Mediation Process

The manner in which a mediator conducts a mediation raises a number of ethical issues that implicate mediation's core principles and values. Among these are the commitment to the core concept of party self-determination, the

---

[35] *Model Family Standards,* X (D) (6). *Model Family Standards* IX (2) similarly calls upon the mediator to consider suspension or termination in light of child abuse and neglect allegations.

[36] *Model Family Standards,* X (D) (1).

[37] *Model Family Standards,* X (D) (2).

[38] *Model Family Standards,* X (D) (3).

[39] *Model Family Standards,* X (D) (4).

[40] *Model Family Standards,* X (D) (5).

[41] *See, e.g,.* Lisa G. Lerman, *Mediation of Wife Abuse Cases: The Adverse Impact of Informal Dispute Resolution on Women,* 7 HARV. WOMEN'S L. J. 57 (1984).

[42] *Model Family Standards,* XI (A) (1).

[43] *Model Family Standards,* XI (A) (3).

confidentiality of mediation communications, and the need to assure a fair or balanced process. Ethical issues are also raised by the mediator's conduct in connection with the drafting of mediation agreements, by the mediator's relations to the court or other case-referring agency, and by circumstances under which the mediation might be terminated.

Party Self-Determination

Party self-determination is the most fundamental principle of mediation.[44] Accordingly, the first standard of both sets of national standards requires the mediator to "recognize that mediation is based on the principle of self-determination . . . ."[45] Both standards stress the mediator's responsibility to facilitate "voluntary" and "informed" party decision-making. Toward that end, the standards explain the desirability of party consultation, when appropriate, with other professionals or with information sources during the mediation process. The *Model Family Standards* are more emphatic on this point, stating that the mediator "should inform the participants that they may seek information and advice from a variety of sources during the mediation process,"[46] while the *Joint Standards* simply make this a matter of "good practice."[47] Similarly, the *Model Family Standards* are more explicit in describing the "primary role" of the mediator in the mediation process, stating that it is "to assist the participants to gain a better understanding of their own needs and interests and the needs and interests of others and to facilitate agreement among the participants."[48] The *Joint Standards* simply explain in the comments to Standard I that the "primary role of the mediator is to facilitate a voluntary resolution of a dispute" and that to accomplish this goal the mediator "may provide information about the process, raise issues, and help the parties explore options."

To emphasize the goal of party self-determination, many standards explicitly caution the mediator to avoid coercion. The *Hawaii Standards* are among the more emphatic on this point: "At no time and in no way shall a mediator coerce any party into agreements or make substantive decisions for any

---

[44] For an expression of concern over the erosion of the principle of self-determination in mandatory, court-sponsored mediation programs, *see* Nancy A. Welsh, *The Thinning Vision of Self-Determination in Court-Connected Mediation: The Inevitable Price of Institutionalization?*, 6 HARV. NEGOT. L. REV. 1 (2001).

[45] *Joint Standards*, I; *Model Family Standards*, I.

[46] *Model Family Standards*, I (C).

[47] *Joint Standards*, I, Comment.

[48] *Model Family Standards*, I (B).

party."[49] Similarly, the Florida Standards state, "A mediator shall not coerce or improperly influence any party to make a decision or unwillingly participate in a mediation."[50] In connection with this concern, most standards offer guidance in practice terms. For example, the *Hawaii Standards* caution, "Mediators may make suggestions and may draft proposals for the parties' consideration, but all decisions are to be made voluntarily by the parties themselves."[51] The *North Carolina Standards* offer the following: "A mediator shall not exert undue pressure on a participant, whether to participate in mediation or to accept a settlement; nevertheless, a mediator may and shall encourage parties to consider both the benefits of participation and settlement and the costs of withdrawal and impasse."[52]

Confidentiality

Because confidentiality is very much a creature of state statutes and court rules, both sets of national standards use general terms to state a mediator's obligations with regard to the confidentiality of mediation communications. Standard V of *the Joint Standards* requires the mediator to "maintain the reasonable expectations of the parties with regard to confidentiality," and Standard VII of the *Model Family Standards* calls upon the mediator to "maintain the confidentiality of all information acquired in the mediation process, unless the mediator is permitted or required to reveal the information by law or agreement of the participants." Both sets of national standards state that the mediator should discuss the parties' expectations of confidentiality with them.[53] These standards also make it clear that the mediator's responsibilities concerning confidentiality are circumscribed by relevant law or public policy, and the *Model Family Standards* go a step further and require the mediator to "inform the participants of the limitations of confidentiality such as statutory, judicially or ethically mandated reporting."[54] Moreover, the *Model Family Standards* also include a *Tarasoff* exception: "As permitted by law, the mediator shall disclose a participant's threat of suicide or violence against any person to

---

[49] *Hawaii Standards*, VI (1).

[50] *Florida Standard,* 10.310.

[51] *Hawaii Standards*, VI (1).

[52] *North Carolina Standards*, 4 (B).

[53] *Joint Standards,* V, Comments; *Model Family Standards*, VII (A).

[54] *Model Family Standards*, VII (B).

the threatened person and the appropriate authorities if the mediator believes such threat is likely to be acted upon."[55] Because exceptions to confidentiality vary so much from jurisdiction to jurisdiction, the *Joint Standards* are silent as to a mediator's duties with regard to exceptions to confidentiality.

Process Imperatives and Issues

Standards of mediator conduct relating to mediation process imperatives are presented in relatively general terms in the *Joint Standards*, while the *Model Family Standards* are more prescriptive. Standard VI of the *Joint Standards* requires a mediator to "work to ensure a quality process . . . [that] requires a commitment by the mediator to diligence and procedural fairness." The *Model Family Standards*, on the other hand, do not contain analogous general statements relating to process fairness. They do, however, prescribe conduct that is intended to ensure party understanding of the process and procedural fairness. For example, Standard III (A) of the *Model Family Standards* lists nine components of what is generally referred to as the mediator's opening statement, intended to "provide the participants with an overview of the process and its purposes"; and Standard VI states, "A family mediator shall structure the mediation process so that the participants make decisions based on sufficient information and knowledge."

Most sets of state standards offer both general language and explicit guidance concerning process fairness. The *Florida Standards*, for example, require a "balanced process": "A mediator shall conduct mediation sessions in an even-handed, balanced manner . . . and encourage the participants to conduct themselves in a collaborative, non-coercive and non-adversarial manner."[56] These standards also then prescribe the elements of the "orientation session."[57] Although there are many variations among the state standards[58] as to the items the mediator should explain to the parties during the orientation session, the standards that offer explicit guidance include, at a minimum, the following: the role of the mediator, the mediation process, confidentiality, and party self-

---

[55] *Model Family Standards*, VII (C).

[56] Florida Standards 10.410. *See also North Carolina Standards* 5(d) (requires the mediator to "promote a balanced process").

[57] *Florida Standards,* 10.420.

[58] *See, e.g., Georgia Standards,* I (A) (requiring that the mediator's "explanation of the mediation process" include nine elements); North Carolina Standards 4 (A) (requiring that the discussion of "the rules and procedures of the mediation process" include six separate information items). Alabama Standards 3 (a) require the mediator to add to the five matters to be discussed during the orientation session two additional items if the parties are unrepresented.

determination. The *Oregon Standards* call upon the mediator to inform the parties of the mediator's "style": "To encourage self determination, the mediator should clarify the mediation process s/he proposes to use, including the particular style and structure . . . ."[59] Similarly, the *California Draft Standards* require the mediator to inform the parties at the outset that they "have a choice as to the nature of mediation process in which they will be involved, including whether or not the mediator will be called upon to offer evaluations, opinions, or recommendations about possible outcomes . . . ."[60]

A mediator's ability to work toward process fairness by ensuring that the disputants have sufficient information to make informed decisions is problematic. While the mediator may view certain information as essential to informed decision-making, if the mediator provides this information, he or she may be viewed as giving an advantage to a party, thereby running the risk of compromising his or her impartiality. Moreover, the parties may take the information as a form of advice, which would erode the goal of party self-determination.[61]

Both sets of standards therefore prescribe a *facilitative*, as opposed to an *evaluative* approach to mediation and attempt to draw a line between *information* and *advice*.[62] The comments to Standard VI of the *Joint Standards* include this statement: "The primary purpose of a mediator is to facilitate the parties' voluntary agreement . . . . A mediator should therefore refrain from providing professional advice." Similarly, Standard VI (A) of the *Model Family Standards* calls upon the mediator to "facilitate full and accurate disclosure and the acquisition and development of information during mediation so that the participants can make informed decisions." Furthermore, Standard VI (B) says that "a mediator may provide the participants with information that the mediator is qualified by training or experience to provide," but then clearly states that a "mediator shall not provide therapy or legal advice."

A number of the state standards are more permissive in connection with

---

[59] *Oregon Standards,* I, Comment 2.

[60] *California Draft Standards,* 4(a).

[61] *See, e.g.,* Robert A. Baruch Bush, *The Dilemmas of Mediation Practice: A Study of Ethical Dilemmas and Policy Implications,* 1994 J. DISP. RESOL. 1 (1994) (arguing generally against mediator intervention because it compromises mediator impartiality and undermines party self-determination).

[62] For contrary views arguing in favor of a more permissive approach to evaluative mediation *see* Robert B. Moberly, *Mediator Gag Rules: Is it Ethical for Mediators to Evaluate or Advise?* 38 S. TEX. L. REV. 669 (1997); James H. Stark, *The Ethics of Mediation Evaluation: Some Troublesome Questions and Tentative Proposals, from an Evaluative Lawyer Mediator,* 38 S. TEX. L. REV. 769 (1997).

the mediator's providing advice to the participants.[63] The *Alabama Standards* permit a mediator to "discuss possible outcomes of a case" and even to "offer a personal or professional opinion regarding the likelihood of any specific outcome," but only if the opinion is offered "in the presence of the attorney for the party to whom the opinion is given."[64] The difficulty in offering clear, ethical guidance in this area, however, is underscored by the double message sent by the *North Carolina Standards*: "[A] mediator may make suggestions for the parties' consideration. However, at no time shall a mediator make a decision for the parties, express an opinion about or advise for or against any proposal under consideration."[65] In taking a strong position against a mediator's offering professional advice, the *Georgia Standards* recognize that this prohibition presents a dilemma for lawyer mediators: "Lawyers, having been trained to protect others, agonize over the perception that missing information, poor representation, ignorance of a defense, etc. may place a party in danger."[66] However, the standards then offer the following analysis: "[F]ailure to honor the maxim that a mediator never offers professional advice can lead to an invasion of the parties' right to self-determination and a real or perceived breach of neutrality."[67] The *Florida Standards* attempt to balance these varying perspectives with the following provision: "Consistent with standards of impartiality and preserving party self-determination . . . a mediator may point out possible outcomes of the case and discuss the merits of a claim or defense."[68]

The *Oregon Standards* attempt to increase process fairness by requiring the mediator to encourage "good faith participation." These standards not only impose this requirement on the mediator, but also require the mediator to discontinue the mediation if "a participant's bad faith, dishonesty, or nondisclosure is so significant that the fairness and integrity of mediation cannot be maintained."[69] A related provision of the *Texas Standards* directs the mediator not to convene the mediation session unless "corporate parties are

---

[63] For a general analysis of state standards in connection with the propriety of "evaluative mediation", *see* Murray S. Levin, *The Propriety of Evaluative Mediation: Concerns About the Nature and Quality of an Evaluative Opinion*, 16 OHIO ST. J. ON DISP. RESOL. 267 (2001).

[64] *Alabama Standards*, III (7) (d).

[65] *North Carolina Standards*, 5 (B).

[66] *Georgia Standards*, I (E), Commentary.

[67] *Georgia Standards*, I (E), Recommendation.

[68] *Florida Standards*, 10.370 (c).

[69] *Oregon Standards*, VI.

represented by officers or agents who have represented to the mediator that they possess adequate authority to negotiate a settlement."[70]

Finally, the *Tennessee Standards* include a unique provision that attempts to impose process protections where there is more than one mediator. In a clause entitled "co-mediation," the *Tennessee Standards* provide that "each mediator has a responsibility to keep the others informed of developments essential to a cooperative effort."[71]

Nonparticipating Parties

Some standards require, or permit, a mediator to encourage the parties to consider the interests of nonparticipating parties when reaching an agreement. The *Hawaii Standards* call upon the mediator "to promote consideration of the interests of persons affected by actual or potential agreements and not present or represented at the bargaining table," and encourage the mediator to withdraw from the mediation if the mediator "believes the best interests of an absent party are not being served . . . ."[72] The *Alabama Standards* adopt a more discretionary approach: "A mediator may promote consideration of the interests of persons who may be affected by an agreement resulting from the mediation process and who are not represented in the mediation process."[73] The comments to a similar provision in the *Florida Standards* identify relevant third parties as "lienholders, governmental agencies, shareholders, and related commercial entities" and -- in family mediations – "children, grandparents or other related persons . . . ."[74] Because the interests of minor children are often a central concern in a divorce mediation, the *Model Family Standards* devote a standard to the specifics of a mediator's duty to "assist participants in determining how to promote the best interests of children."[75]

Mediated Agreements

The *Joint Standards* are largely silent and the *Model Family Standards*

---

[70] *Texas Standards*, 7.

[71] *Tennessee Standards*, 13 (a) (2).

[72] *Hawaii Standards*, VI (2).

[73] *Alabama Standards*, III (4) (e).

[74] *Florida Standards*, 10.320, Committee Notes.

[75] *Model Family Standards*, VIII.

offer only general guidance as to a mediator's duties in connection with the finalization of agreements. The *Model Family Standards* permit a mediator to "document the participants' resolution of their dispute" and direct the mediator to "inform the participants that any agreement should be reviewed by an independent attorney before it is signed."[76] A number of the state standards, on the other hand, specify a mediator's duties in connection with mediated agreements. The *Florida Standards*, for example, require the mediator to "cause the terms of any agreement reached to be memorialized appropriately and discuss with the parties and counsel the process for formalization and implementation of the agreement."[77] The comments to the Florida standard state that mediators must insure that Florida rules requiring that mediated agreements be in writing are complied with, but the mediators "are not required to write the agreement themselves."[78] The *Iowa Family Standards* include this requirement: "Any proposed agreement which is prepared in the mediation process should be reviewed separately by independent counsel before it is signed."[79] If the parties decide to proceed without counsel, the mediator is required to provide them with a written "WARNING" prescribed by the standard. The warning informs the parties of a number of legal rights they may be giving up as a result of their failure to have the agreement reviewed by counsel.

Termination of Mediation

The parties have an absolute right to terminate a mediation under both sets of national standards. Standard VI of the *Joint Standards* states, "The parties decide when and under what conditions they will reach an agreement or terminate a mediation." Standard I (D) of the *Model Family Standards* imposes an affirmative duty on the mediator to "inform the participants that they may withdraw from family mediation at any time and are not required to reach an agreement in mediation." On the related question of when a mediator should withdraw from a mediation, both sets of standards set forth specific circumstances that would require withdrawal. The comments to Standard VI of the *Joint Standards* require a mediator to "withdraw from a mediation when incapable of serving or when unable to remain impartial" and to "withdraw from

---

[76] *Model Family Standards,* VI (E).

[77] *Florida Standards,* 10.420 (c). *See also Hawaii Standards,* IX (1) ([A] mediator should discuss and reach a mutual understanding with the participants on how such agreements are to be finalized").

[78] *Florida Standards,* 10.420 (c), Committee Notes.

[79] *Iowa Family Standards,* 6 (C).

the mediation or postpone the session if the mediation is being used to further illegal conduct, or if a party is unable to participate due to drug, alcohol, or other physical or mental incapacity." Similarly, Standard XI of the *Model Family Standards* requires a mediator to "suspend or terminate the mediation process when the mediator reasonably believes that a participant is unable to effectively participate or for other compelling reason." Standard XI (A) lists seven circumstances "under which a mediator should consider suspending or terminating the mediation." In addition to those contained in the *Joint Standards*, the list includes situations in which "the safety of a participant or well-being of a child is threatened,"[80] "the participants are about to enter into an agreement that the mediator reasonably believes to be unconscionable,"[81] or "a participant is using the mediation process to gain an unfair advantage."[82]

Practice Considerations

Unauthorized Practice of Law

Although neither set of national standards addresses the question of the unauthorized practice of law (UPL) by a mediator, UPL concerns have been raised, particularly in connection with the practices of non-lawyer mediators, by a number of bar associations.[83] Because of these concerns, the subject of UPL and mediation has been dealt with extensively in at least two states. The Supreme Court of Virginia has promulgated *Guidelines on Mediation and the Unauthorized Practice of Law* and the North Carolina Bar has adopted *Guidelines for the Ethical Practice of Mediation and the Unauthorized Practice of Law*.[84] Both sets of guidelines are concerned with the giving of legal advice by mediators. Both stress that their mediator ethics rules preclude the giving of legal advice by a mediator, and they attempt to draw a line between offering legal *information* and giving legal *advice*. In addition, both are concerned with the drafting of mediated agreements, particularly by non-lawyer mediators or

---

[80] *Model Family Standards*, XI (A) (1).

[81] *Model Family Standards*, XI (A) (4).

[82] *Model Family Standards*, XI (A) (6).

[83] *See e. g.* Werle v. R.I. B. Ass'n, 755 F.2d 195 (1st Cir. 1985), (ruling that a bar association letter to a psychologist (non-lawyer) mediator asking the mediator to terminate the mediator's divorce mediation practice did not violate the U. S. Constitution).

[84] For an excellent analysis of both guidelines *see* David A. Hoffman and Natasha A. Affolder, *Mediation and UPL: Do Mediators have a Well-founded Fear of Prosecution?*, 6 DISP. RES. MAG. 20 (Winter 2000).

lawyers who are not admitted to the bar of the jurisdiction in which the mediation takes place. Both guidelines offer examples in an attempt to indicate what is permissible and what is impermissible. Although these guidelines may be seen as a good beginning in addressing troublesome issues, they underscore the difficulty of drawing lines or setting boundaries that are meaningful in all mediation practice settings.

Agreements to Mediate

Standard III (B) of the *Model Family Standards* states, "The participants should sign a written agreement to mediate their dispute and the terms and conditions thereof within a reasonable time after first consulting the family mediator." The *Joint Standards* have no analogous provision requiring or suggesting written mediation agreements. The various state ethical standards adopt different approaches as to what must be included in a required written agreement to mediate. For example, the *Virginia Standards* provide, "The parties and mediator must include in the agreement to mediate a general statement regarding the mediator's style and approach to mediation to which the parties have agreed."[85]

Compensation

Both sets of national standards require a mediator to "fully disclose and explain the basis of any compensation, fees and charges to the parties,"[86] and prohibit contingent fee arrangements[87] and fees for referring a matter to another person.[88] The *Joint Standards* set forth a reasonableness standard for computing fees: "If a mediator charges fees, the fees shall be reasonable, considering, among other things, the mediation service, the type and complexity of the matter, the expertise of the mediator, the time required, and the rates customary in the community."[89] The *Model Family Standards* require that a written description of the fee arrangement be included in the parties' written agreement to mediate.[90]

---

[85] *Virginia Standards*, D (1) (c).

[86] *Joint Standards*, VIII; *Model Family Standards, V.*

[87] *Joint Standards*, VIII, Comments; *Model Family Standards, V (C).*

[88] *Joint Standards*, VIII, Comments; *Model Family Standards, V (D).*

[89] *Joint Standards*, VIII.

[90] *Model Family Standards, V (B).*

Although the *Joint Standards* do not require the fee arrangement to be in writing, Standard VIII states that a written agreement is the "better practice." Both standards require the mediator to return unearned fees to the parties.[91]

While the state standards generally track the national standards with regard to fees, a few variations are worthy of note. The *Alabama Standards* permit the mediator to "specify in advance minimum charges for scheduling or conducting a mediation session . . . ."[92] The *Florida Standards* specify four matters that must be addressed in the mediator's written explanation of fees and costs: the basis for the fees, charges for postponed or canceled sessions, the amount of other charges, and the parties' pro rata shares of the fees.[93]

Some of the state standards call upon the mediator to provide mediation services at reduced rates to make mediation more accessible. The *Alabama Standards* state, "As a means of meeting the needs of those who are unable to pay, a mediator should provide mediation services pro bono or at a reduced rate of compensation whenever appropriate."[94] The Florida,[95] Georgia,[96] and Texas[97] standards have similar provisions.

Advertising and Solicitation

Ethical constraints on mediator advertising and solicitation are largely identical in both sets of national standards. Joint Standard VII and Model Family Standard XII require a mediator to be "truthful" in advertising and soliciting, and they instruct the mediator to "refrain from promises and guarantees of results." Both standards place the same restrictions on communicating the mediator's qualifications to the public: "[A] mediator may make reference to meeting state, national, or private organization qualifications only if the entity referred to has a procedure for qualifying mediators and the mediator has been duly granted the requisite status."[98] However, the national standards part company on a

---

[91] *Joint Standards*, VIII, Comments; *Model Family Standards,* V (E).

[92] *Alabama Standards*, III (8) (e).

[93] *Florida Standards,* 10.380 (c).

[94] *Alabama Standards*, III (8) (g).

[95] *Florida Standards,* 10.690 (a).

[96] *Georgia Standards*, V.

[97] *Texas Standards,* 3.

[98] *Joint Standards,* VII, Comment; *Model Family Standards,* XII (B).

mediator's ability to advertise, in quantitative terms, the mediator's "record of success." While Model Family Standard XII (A) prohibits mediators from advertising "statistical settlement data or settlement rates,"[99] the *Joint Standards* contain no such prohibition.

Most of the state standards track the *Joint Standards* with regard to advertising. However, some states explicitly bar solicitation. The *Texas Standards*, for example, include this provision: "Although a mediator may advertise the mediator's qualifications and availability to mediate, the mediator should not solicit a specific case or matter."[100] The *California Draft Standards* take a more limited approach to solicitation: "Mediators must not solicit business from a participant in a mediation proceeding while that proceeding is pending."[101] The *California Draft Standards* also prohibit mediators from advertising that they are "approved, endorsed, certified, or licensed by the court" unless specifically permitted to do so by the court.[102]

Relations with Courts and Other Referring Bodies

Because a number of the state standards of conduct are intended for mediators in court-sponsored programs, the standards impose ethical constraints in connection with the mediator's relationship or responsibilities to the courts. For example, the *Alabama Standards* instruct the mediator to "refrain from any activity that has the appearance of improperly influencing a court to secure placement on a roster of mediators or appointment to a case."[103] Additionally, the *Florida Standards* state that the mediator "shall be candid, accurate, and fully responsive to the court concerning the mediator's qualifications, availability and other administrative matters,"[104] and the *Hawaii Standards* make adherence to the ethical standards of a court or agency a "joint one between individual

---

[99] *Model Family Standards,* XII (A).

[100] *Texas Standards*, 2, Comment (d).

[101] *California Draft Standards,* 9.4.

[102] *California Draft Standards*, 9.2.

[103] *Alabama Standards*, III (2). *See also Florida Standards* 10.530 ("A mediator shall refrain from any activity that has the appearance of improperly influencing a court to secure appointment to a case."); *Texas Standards* 15 ("A mediator should avoid the appearance of impropriety in the mediator's relationship with a member of the judiciary or the court staff with regard to appointments or referrals to mediation.")

[104] *Florida Standards,* 10.510.

mediators and any organizations under whose auspices they are mediating."[105] The *California Draft Standards* impose upon mediators a "continuing obligation to truthfully represent their background to the court" and require the mediator to notify the court if the mediator has been disciplined by a "professional licensing authority" or if he or she has been "charged with a felony or convicted of any crime other than an infraction."[106]

Professional Development

While both Joint Standard IX and Model Family Standard XIII (A) call upon mediators to "improve their professional skills and abilities," the *Model Family Standards* are more prescriptive in connection with a mediator's professional development. The *Model Family Standards* state that mediators should participate in "relevant continuing education programs and should regularly engage in self-assessment,"[107] and they "should continuously strive to understand the impact of culture and diversity on the mediator's practice."[108] On the other hand, the *Joint Standards* are more specific concerning a mediator's overall obligation to improve the practice of mediation, informing mediators that they "have an obligation to use their knowledge to help educate the public about mediation; to make mediation accessible to those who would like to use it; to correct abuses . . . ."[109] The state standards are generally in accord.

Conclusion

The increased use of mediation in recent years has resulted in a proliferation of standards of conduct for mediators. The *Joint Standards*, as well as pre-existing state standards, have served as a model for the development during the past decade of numerous state standards and the drafting of the *Model Family Standards*. As we have seen, however, these efforts have yielded varying approaches to imposing ethical constraints on mediators.

These standards have also been subjected to criticism. Some have

---

[105] *Hawaii Standards*, XI (4).

[106] *California Draft Standards*, 7.2.

[107] *Model Family Standard*, XIII (A).

[108] *Model Family Standard*, XIII (C).

[109] *Joint Standards*, IX, Comments.

argued that the *Joint Standards* are too simplistic and vague.[110] Others have worried that the standards and commentary on the standards have failed to take account of diversity issues.[111] Still others have stated that the standards should be revised to reflect the variety of mediator styles that have emerged in practice.[112]

Perhaps the time has arrived to initiate a comprehensive revision of *the Joint Standards*. As we have noted, the *Joint Standards* are couched in general terms and fail to address certain areas (e.g. capacity to mediate) that have demonstrated their importance in practice.

---

[110] *See, e. g,.* Jamie Henikoff and Michael Moffitt, *Remodeling the Model Standards of Conduct for Mediators*, 2 HARV. NEGOTIATION L. REV. 87 (1997) (suggesting a framework for drafting model standards that provides greater information and guidance for mediator conduct).

[111] *See generally,* Isabelle R. Gunning, *Diversity Issues in Mediation: Controlling Negative Cultural Myths*, 1995 J. DISP. RESOL. 55 (1995).

[112] *See, e.g,,* Alison E. Gerencser, *Alternative Dispute Resolution Has Morphed into Mediation: Standards of Conduct Must Be Changed*, 50 FLA. L. REV. 843 (1998).

REFERENCES

Alabama Supreme Court, ALABAMA CODE OF ETHICS FOR MEDIATORS (adopted effective March 1, 1996).

American Arbitration Association, American Bar Association Section of Dispute Resolution, Society of Professionals in Dispute Resolution, STANDARDS OF CONDUCT FOR MEDIATORS (1994).

American Bar Association Family Law Section, *Standards of Practice for Lawyer Mediators in Family Disputes*, 18 FAM. L. Q. 363 (1984).

Brown, Jennifer Gerarda and Ian Ayres, *Economic Rationales for Mediation*, 80 VA. L. REV. 323 (1994).

Burns, Robert P., *Some Ethical Issues Surrounding Mediation*, 70 FORDHAM L. REV. 691 (2001).

Bush, Robert A. Baruch, *The Dilemmas of Mediation Practice: A Study of Ethical Dilemmas and Policy Implications*, 1994 J. DISP. RESOL. 1 (1994).

Judicial Council of California, ETHICAL STANDARDS FOR MEDIATORS IN COURT-CONNECTED MEDIATION PROGRAMS FOR CIVIL CASES (preliminary draft).

Colorado Council of Mediators, CODE OF PROFESSIONAL CONDUCT (1982).

Feerick, John D., *Standards of Conduct for Mediators*, 79 JUDICATURE 314 (1996).

Florida Supreme Court Standing Committee on Mediation and Arbitration Rules, FLORIDA RULES FOR CERTIFIED AND COURT-APPOINTED MEDIATORS (amended, 2000).

Georgia Supreme Court, ETHICAL STANDARDS FOR MEDIATORS, Chapter 1A of Appendix C of ALTERNATIVE DISPUTE RESOLUTION RULES (effective September 28, 1995).

Gerencser, Alison E., *Alternative Dispute Resolution Has Morphed into Mediation: Standards of Conduct Must Be Changed*, 50 FLA. L. REV. 843 (1998).

Gunning, Isabelle R., *Diversity Issues in Mediation: Controlling Negative Cultural Myths*, 1995 J. DISP. RESOL. 55 (1995).

Hawaii State Judiciary, Program on Alternative Dispute Resolution, STANDARDS FOR PRIVATE AND PUBLIC MEDIATORS IN THE STATE OF HAWAII (1986).

Henikoff, Jamie and Michael Moffitt, *Remodeling the Model Standards of Conduct for Mediators*, 2 HARV. NEGOT. L. REV. 87 (1997).

Furlan, Fiona *et al.*, *Ethical Guidelines for Attorney-Mediators: Are Attorneys Bound By Ethical Codes for Lawyers When Acting as Mediators?, 14* J. AM. ACAD. MATRIM. LAW 267 (1997).

Indiana Supreme Court Rules for Alternative Dispute Resolution, Rule 7, CONDUCT AND DISCIPLINE FOR PERSONS CONDUCTING ADR (adopted December 6, 1994).

Iowa Supreme Court, RULES GOVERNING STANDARDS OF PRACTICE FOR LAWYER MEDIATORS IN FAMILY DISPUTES (effective February 2, 1987).

Kansas Supreme Court, KAN. SUP. CT. RULE 903, ETHICAL STANDARDS FOR MEDIATORS (2001).

Laflin, Maureen E., *Preserving the Integrity of Mediation through the Adoption of Ethical Rules for Lawyer Mediators*, 14 NOTRE DAME J. L. ETHICS & PUB. POL'Y 479 (2000).

Lerman, Lisa G., *Mediation of Wife Abuse Cases: The Adverse Impact of Informal Dispute Resolution on Women*, 7 HARV. WOMEN'S L. J. 57 (1984).

Levin, Murray S., *The Propriety of Evaluative Mediation: Concerns About the Nature and Quality of an Evaluative Opinion*, 16 OHIO ST. J. ON DISP. RESOL. 267 (2001).

Maine Association of Dispute Resolution Professionals, STANDARDS OF PROFESSIONAL CONDUCT (1989)

MAINE CODE OF PROFESSIONAL RESPONSIBILITY, Rule 3.4 (h), Mediation.

Menkel-Meadow, Carrie, *Professional Responsibility for Third-Party Neutrals*, in DISPUTE RESOLUTION ALTERNATIVES (Practising Law Institute, 1994).

Menkel-Meadow, Carrie, *The Silences of the Restatement of the Law Governing Lawyers: Lawyering as Only Adversary Practice*, 10 GEO. J. LEGAL ETHICS 631 (1997).

Menkel-Meadow, Carrie, *Ethics in Alternative Dispute Resolution: New Issues, No Answers from the Adversary Conception of Lawyers' Responsibilities*, 38 S. TEX. L. REV. 407 (1997).

Menkel-Meadow, Carrie, *Ethics in ADR: The Many "Cs" of Professional Responsibility and Dispute Resolution*, 28 FORDHAM URB. L. J. 979 (2001).

Minnesota General Rules of Practice, Rule 114, ALTERNATIVE DISPUTE RESOLUTION, Appendix, CODE OF ETHICS (1997).

Moberly, Robert B., *Ethical Standards for Court-Appointed Mediators and Florida's Mandatory Mediation Experiment*, 21 FLA. ST. U. L. REV. 701 (1994).

Moberly, Robert B., *Mediator Gag Rules: Is it Ethical for Mediators to Evaluate or Advise?* 38 S. TEX. L. REV. 669 (1997).

Moffitt, Michael L., *Will this Case Settle? An Exploration of Mediators' Predictions*, 16 OHIO ST. J. ON DISP. RESOL. 39 (2000).

New Jersey Supreme Court, STANDARDS OF CONDUCT FOR MEDIATORS IN COURT-CONNECTED PROGRAMS (2000).

Nolan-Haley, Jacqueline M., *Informed Consent in Mediation: A Guiding Principle for Truly Educated Decisionmaking*, 74 NOTRE DAME L. REV. 775 (1999).

O'Brien, Regina A., *Amending the Model Rules to Include the Role of Lawyer as Mediator: The Latest in the Debate*, 12 GEO. J. LEGAL ETHICS 107 (1998).

Riskin, Leonard S., *Mediation and Lawyers*, 43 OHIO ST. L. J. 29 (1982).

Stark, James H., *The Ethics of Mediation Evaluation: Some Troublesome Question and Tentative Proposals, from an Evaluative Lawyer Mediator*, 38 S. TEX. L. REV. 769 (1997).

Symposium on Standards of Practice, *Model Standards of Practice for Family and Divorce Mediation*, 39 FAM. CT. REV. 121 (2001).

Tennessee Supreme Court, TENN. SUP. CT. RULE 31 APPENDIX A, STANDARDS OF PROFESSIONAL CONDUCT FOR RULE 31 NEUTRALS (2001).

State Bar of Texas Alternative Dispute Resolution Section, ETHICAL GUIDELINES FOR MEDIATORS (1998).

Judicial Council of Virginia, STANDARDS OF ETHICS AND PROFESSIONAL RESPONSIBILITY FOR CERTIFIED MEDIATORS (1997).

Webne-Behrman, Harry M., *The Emergence of Ethical Codes and Standards of Practice in Mediation: The Current State of Affairs*, 1998 WIS. L. REV. 1289.

Welsh, Nancy A., *The Thinning Vision of Self-Determination in Court-Connected Mediation: The Inevitable Price of Institutionalization?*, 6 HARV. NEGOT. L. REV. 1 (2001).

Chapter VI

Dispute Resolution and the Unauthorized Practice of Law

By Phyllis E. Bernard

Introduction

Is mediation the practice of law? Is arbitration? These simple questions have difficult answers. Moreover, the questions and answers form one of the most contentious areas in appropriate dispute resolution (ADR) today. Answers may depend upon local law, custom, history and perhaps even a touch of politics between the professions. Regardless, the debate illustrates a growing tension between the theory of ADR and its emerging practice.

There currently are few, if any, bright lines that everywhere demarcate attorney practice in ADR from non-attorney practice. Some participants in the debate would even question whether such boundary lines ought to exist. After all, the principle of self-determination would suggest that parties have an overarching right to give informed consent for a non-attorney mediator to offer comprehensive advice in reaching a settlement, or assistance in drafting an agreement. Nevertheless, as ADR practice grows increasingly widespread and generates ever more revenue for practitioners, the voice of the parties and the principle of self-determination seem to be muted.

Instead, the legal profession has undertaken to define the boundary lines. Although these lines remain blurry, they form around three groups of activities, as described below.

The Non-lawyer as Mediator

Appropriate dispute resolution theoretically encourages public access to a wide range of providers, including non-lawyers. One of the great benefits ADR brings to the contemporary legal system is the flexibility to explore non-legal issues that often drive individual and institutional conflict. At its best ADR offers opportunities for parties to customize out-of-court settlement processes in ways the courtroom cannot. Critical to this flexibility may be the ability to engage the different perspectives offered by psychologists, engineers, social workers, and lay people from a cross-section of society who serve as trained mediators or arbitrators. Yet, in practice this approach raises a question: *When a non-lawyer serves as a mediator, has she engaged in the unauthorized practice of law (UPL)?*

The Out-of-State Attorney as Arbitrator or Mediator

ADR has gained ever-expanding acceptance in the business community because of its simplicity and efficiency relative to courtroom litigation. These advantages can present a particular benefit for businesses operating in a domestic market that spans the nation. Further, the increasingly global nature of commercial transactions compels American businesses and their legal counsel to become comfortable with international expectations that parties will utilize arbitration and, to a somewhat lesser degree, mediation rather than litigation. This practice raises another question: *When an attorney arbitrates or mediates a case in a state or country where he is not a member of the bar, has this attorney engaged in the unauthorized practice of law?*

The Non-lawyer Assisting in Arbitration

Ostensibly, ADR provides conflict resolution services that do not necessarily require the presence of attorneys. Ideally, most mediations and arbitrations operate in a "user-friendly" manner that can readily accommodate the use of non-attorney representatives, such as a labor union staff specialist who assists a worker in a grievance. This situation raises a third question: *When a non-lawyer represents a party in arbitration, has she engaged in the unauthorized practice of law?*

This chapter surveys how the bar has handled these issues, highlighting the activities of the American Bar Association (ABA) and a few leading states. We shall focus on the first and dominant question, which has spurred vigorous debate and action, rather than on the rare occurrences comprising the latter two issues.

The Unauthorized Practice of Law Defined

The ABA Model Code of Professional Responsibility and the Model Rules of Professional Conduct

The American Bar Association Model Code of Professional Responsibility at *DR 3-101*[1] and the ABA Model Rules of Professional Conduct at *Rule 5.5*[2] both

---

[1] ABA MODEL CODE OF PROFESSIONAL RESPONSIBILITY, *DR 3-101* (1980):

Aiding Unauthorized Practice of Law
(A) A lawyer shall not aid a non-lawyer in the unauthorized practice of law.
(B) A lawyer shall not practice law in a jurisdiction where to do so would be in violation of

prohibit lawyers from engaging in the unauthorized practice of law. Both provisions derive from the rationale that it takes professional expertise to analyze the law and proffer fitting advice about a course of action. The requirements of the law may vary from jurisdiction to jurisdiction, making membership in the bar of the particular affected state not insignificant. Limiting authorized practice to members of the bar subjects practitioners to the bar's monitoring for ethical conduct and competence. Thus, the proscription exists to assure quality representation and to protect the public interest.

---

the regulations of the profession in that jurisdiction.

The Ethical Considerations elaborate as follows:

EC 3-1: The prohibition against the practice of law by a layman is grounded in the need of the public for integrity and competence of those who undertake to render legal services. Because of the fiduciary and personal character of the lawyer-client relationship and the inherently complex nature of our legal system, the public can better be assured of the requisite responsibility and competence if the practice of law is confined to those who are subject to the requirements and regulations imposed upon members of the legal profession.

EC 3-2: The sensitive variations in the considerations that bear on legal determinations often make it difficult even for a lawyer to exercise appropriate professional judgment, and it is therefore essential that the personal nature of the relationship of client and lawyer be preserved. Competent professional judgment is the product of a trained familiarity with law and legal processes, a disciplined, analytical approach to legal problems, and a firm ethical commitment.

EC 3-3: A non-lawyer who undertakes to handle legal matters is not governed as to integrity or legal competence by the same rules that govern the conduct of a lawyer. A lawyer is not only subject to that regulation but also is committed to high standards of ethical conduct. The public interest is best served in legal matters by a regulated profession committed to such standards. The Disciplinary Rules protect the public in that they prohibit a lawyer from seeking employment by improper overtures, from acting in cases of divided loyalties, and from submitting to the control of others in the exercise of his judgment. Moreover, a person who entrusts legal matters to a lawyer is protected by the attorney-client privilege and by the duty of the lawyer to hold inviolate the confidences and secrets of his client.

[2] ABA MODEL RULES OF PROFESSIONAL CONDUCT, *Rule 5.5*: UNAUTHORIZED PRACTICE OF LAW:

A lawyer shall not:
(a) practice in a jurisdiction where doing so violates the regulation of the legal profession in that jurisdiction; or
(b) assist a person who is not a member of the bar in the performance of activity that constitutes the unauthorized practice of law.

The Comment elaborates:

The definition of the practice of law is established by law and varies from one jurisdiction to another. Whatever the definition, limiting the practice of law to members of the bar protects the public against rendition of legal services by unqualified persons....

Neither the *Model Code*[3] nor the *Model Rules*[4] bar attorneys from delegating non-legal tasks or aspects of a case to non-attorneys, so long as the attorney remains in control of the case and exercises independent professional judgment. Recognizing that financial controls can often exert a major influence on decision-making – either directly or indirectly – the *Model Code*[5] and *Model Rules*[6] expressly forbid monetary arrangements that suggest non-lawyer control over the lawyer's professional responsibilities. That is to say, non-lawyers cannot practice law vicariously through

---

[3] *See EC 3-6*:

> A lawyer often delegates tasks to clerks, secretaries, and other lay persons. Such delegation is proper if the lawyer maintains a direct relationship with his client, supervises the delegated work, and has complete professional responsibility for the work product. This delegation enables a lawyer to render legal service more economically and efficiently.

[4] The *Model Rules* disaggregate the concept of non-lawyer assistance and addressed aspects of this relationship in more than one place:

Model Rule 5.3: RESPONSIBILITIES REGARDING NONLAWYER ASSISTANTS
With respect to a nonlawyer employed or retained by or associated with a lawyer:
(a) a partner and a lawyer who individually or together with other lawyers possesses comparable managerial authority in a law firm shall make reasonable efforts to ensure that they firm has in effect measures giving reasonable assurance that the person's conduct is compatible with the professional obligations of the lawyer;
(b) a lawyer having direct supervisory authority over the nonlawyer shall make reasonable efforts to ensure that the person's conduct is compatible with the professional obligations of the lawyer; and
(c) a lawyer shall be responsible for conduct of such a person that would be a violation of the rules of professional conduct if engaged in by a lawyer ....

Model Rule 5.4 PROFESSIONAL INDEPENDENCE OF A LAWYER
... (b) A lawyer shall not form a partnership with a nonlawyer if any of the activities of the partnership consist of the practice of law.
... (d) A lawyer shall not practice with or in the form of a professional corporation or association authorized to practice law for a profit, if: ...
(2) a nonlawyer is a corporate director or officer thereof or occupies the position of similar responsibility in any form of association other than a corporation; or
(3) a nonlawyer has the right to direct or control the professional judgment of a lawyer.

[5] *DR 3-102* Dividing Legal Fees with a Non-lawyer
(A) A lawyer or law firm shall not share legal fees with a non-lawyer ....
    DR 3-103 Forming a Partnership with a Non-lawyer
(B) A lawyer shall not form a partnership with a non-lawyer if any of the activities of the partnership consist of the practice of law.

[6] *See* ABA MODEL RULES OF PROFESSIONAL CONDUCT, *Rule 5.4* excerpted above in note 4. *Model Rule 5.7* discusses ancillary businesses, such as ADR practices, which will be covered in the next section of this chapter.

the attorney.

Still this prohibition begs the question: What is the practice of law? What factors describe the work that quintessentially belongs to the attorney, as compared to the work that belongs to the lay person or other trained professional? The line that separates authorized from unauthorized practice is dim at best.

In *EC 3-5* the *Model Code* explains the purpose behind the vagueness:

> It is neither necessary nor desirable to attempt the formulation of a single, specific definition of what constitutes the practice of law. Functionally, the practice of law relates to the rendition of services for others that call for the professional judgment of a lawyer. The essence of the professional judgment of the lawyer is his educated ability to relate the general body and philosophy of law to a specific legal problem of a client....

Because the work of a lawyer must extend to a wide variety of endeavors, only an equally elastic definition will fit.

EC 3-5 recognizes that some transactions of modern life entail aspects of the law but do not require the professional judgment of an attorney. In those situations, the *Model Code* permits the involvement of non-lawyers, "such as court clerks, police officers, abstractors, and many governmental employees."

The *Model Rules* do not contain a direct corollary to *EC 3-5*. However, within Rule 5.7, Responsibilities Regarding Law-Related Services, one can find indicia of unauthorized practice. In defining "law-related services" the penumbra is bordered by whether the service would be "prohibited as unauthorized practice of law when provided by a nonlawyer [sic]."[7] Comment 8 explains that the "economic and other interests of clients" may be met through services that involve some aspects of law; nevertheless, these legal aspects will play a secondary role. Examples include "providing title insurance, financial planning, accounting, trust services, real estate counseling, legislative lobbying, economic analysis, social work, psychological counseling, tax return preparation, and patent, medical or environmental consulting."[8]

Proposed Changes and ABA Policy Resolution

The new *Model Rule 2.4* explains the role of the Lawyer Serving as Third-

---

[7] ABA MODEL RULES OF PROFESSIONAL CONDUCT, *Rule 5.7(b)*.

[8] We shall return to a fuller discussion of ancillary business later in the sections on one-stop services and the ethics rules.

Party Neutral. Comment 1 defines this function as "a mediator, arbitrator, conciliator or evaluator, who assists the parties, represented or unrepresented, in the resolution of a dispute or in the arrangement of a transaction." The *Model Rules* clearly contemplate that both lawyers and non-lawyers may serve as third-party neutrals. But the lawyer-neutral confronts "unique problems as a result of differences between the role of a third-party neutral and a lawyer's service as a client representative."[9] The Comment highlights the need for the lawyer-neutral to disclose to the parties that the attorney-client evidentiary privilege would not apply.

The ABA Section of Dispute Resolution has reviewed this issue in depth. In its Resolution on Mediation and the Unauthorized Practice of Law the Section articulated the clearest statement yet on the issue:

> Mediation is not the practice of law. Mediation is a process in which an impartial individual assists the parties in reaching a voluntary settlement. Such assistance does not constitute the practice of law. The parties to the mediation are not represented by the mediator.[10]

The Resolution goes two steps further, explicitly answering implied, continuing questions about the nature of advice by a third-party neutral and the role of the third-party neutral in drafting settlement agreements. Namely, if a mediator discusses with parties matters that involve their legal rights and obligations, these discussions "do not create an attorney-client relationship, and do not constitute legal advice, *whether or not the mediator is an attorney.*"[11]

Once the parties have reached a settlement, they often ask the mediator to assist in memorializing that agreement. If the mediator does so, can that be considered the practice of law? The Resolution outlines some extremely helpful guidelines:

> (1) If the preparation incorporates "the terms of settlement specified by the parties," it is not the practice of law. But,
> (2) If the agreement "goes beyond the terms specified by the

---

[9] ABA MODEL RULES OF PROFESSIONAL CONDUCT, *Rule 2.4*: LAWYER AS THIRD PARTY NEUTRAL, Comment 3.

[10] American Bar Association Section of Dispute Resolution, *Resolution on Mediation and the Unauthorized Practice of Law*, adopted by the Section Council on February 2, 2002. The views expressed in the Resolution have not yet been approved by the ABA House of Delegates and accordingly should not be construed as representing the policy of the American Bar Association.

[11] *Id.* (emphasis added).

parties," it may constitute the practice of law.[12]

Notwithstanding this fundamental paradigm, typically parties and mediators alike know that "the devil is in the details," as the saying goes. The language of the written agreement memorializing the settlement can be as important to the success of the mediation as the oral negotiations that preceded. How active can a mediator be in attending to the details before she crosses the line into the practice of law?

The Resolution concludes that the involvement of party representatives is determinative. Thus, a mediator may draft an agreement that goes beyond the terms specified by the parties if

> (a) all parties are represented by counsel; and
> (b) the mediator discloses that any proposal that he or she makes with respect to the terms of settlement is informational as opposed to the practice of law, and that the parties should not view or rely upon such proposals as advice of counsel, but merely consider them in consultation with their own attorneys.[13]

The policy enunciated in this UPL Resolution attempts to complete the steps initiated in the new *Model Rule 2.4*. Meaningful, detailed guidance will be carved out on a case-by-case basis through factual situations presented to bar ethics and disciplinary committees and courts. Some states may attempt a legislative or rule-making approach. For example, the North Carolina legislature has amended its statute governing attorneys to expressly define the practice of law as excluding "the writing of memoranda of understanding or other mediation summaries by mediators at community mediation centers" in the court-annexed system.[14] The Supreme Court of Virginia Department of Dispute Resolution Services published guidelines that permit non-lawyer mediators to provide legal information to the parties, but not legal advice. What is the distinction? The UPL Resolution provides this summary:

> The Guidelines define legal advice as applying the law to the facts of the case in such a way as to (a) predict the outcome of the case or an issue in the case, or (b) recommend a course of action based on the mediator's analysis.[15]

---

[12] *Id.*

[13] *Id.*

[14] N.C. Gen. Stat. § 84-2.1 (1999).

[15] *Resolution on Mediation and the Unauthorized Practice of Law, supra* note 10.

The guidelines adopted by North Carolina and Virginia were based upon extremely specific statutory definitions of their respective jurisdictions. The ABA Dispute Resolution Section suggests that such guidelines may create more confusion than they solve. The difference between information and advice hinges upon how the mediator presents the information/advice. As the Resolution notes, such an approach would require the mediator "in the midst of a discussion of relevant legal issues, [to determine] which particular phrasings would constitute legal advice and which would not." The illustration offered makes the mediator's dilemma quite tangible:

[D]uring mediation of a medical malpractice case, if a mediator comments that "the video of the newborn (deceased shortly after birth) has considerable emotional impact and makes the newborn more real," is this legal advice or prediction or simply stating the obvious? In context, the mediator is implicitly or explicitly suggesting that it may affect a jury's damage award, and thus settlement value. ... Is the mediator absolved if s/he phrases the point as a "probing question"? [16]

Some observers may find it ironic that the nation's chief professional association for lawyers would be a leading advocate for non-lawyers in ADR. Yet, the stated position of the Dispute Resolution Section derives from its longstanding cooperation between the professions. This cooperation is both a cause and effect of the relatively large proportion of non-attorney Section members, compared to other ABA sections.[17] Section policy encourages programs to include individuals from all professions as neutrals: "The Section believes that eligibility criteria for dispute resolution programs should permit all individuals who have appropriate training and qualification to serve as neutrals, regardless of whether they are attorneys."[18] The Section has published practice tips, organized CLE presentations, implemented a law school competition and established a major Section Committee on appropriate representation in mediation by attorneys. Having attorneys present offsets concerns about improper influence by a non-attorney neutral.

The Evolving Concept of the Practice of Law

Discussions about mediation and the unauthorized practice of law typically configure around two questions: (1) What is mediation? and (2) What is the practice of law? Discussants use this dualistic approach to define the legally permissible role

---

[16] *Id.*

[17] American Bar Association, *Section Lawyer Membership Report*, Fiscal Year 2000-2001, As of August 31, 2001, Chart A: Total Section Membership All Categories. Approximately 15% of the Dispute Resolution Section's members are associates (non-attorneys). This compares to highs of 12% for Law Practice Management and 11% for International Law & Practice; ranging to lows of 3% for Business Law and 1.5% for Labor & Employment Law.

[18] *ABA DR Section Votes for Inclusion*, JUST RESOLUTIONS NEWSLETTER, May 1999, at 12.

of mediators: *i.e.*, if XYZ activities define law practice, then a non-lawyer mediator may not engage in XYZ activities without risking penalties. This framing of the issues can quickly degenerate into debates that the public may perceive as a mere "power play" or "turf battle" between lawyers and non-lawyers.

Bryant Garth has cautioned against such dualism both because it undermines the credibility of the profession, and because it operates from a fundamentally wrong premise. The debate assumes the practice of mediation and the practice of law are "fixed categories." But they are not.

> Indeed, not only have the practices that have been characterized by those terms changed greatly over time, but they also remain subjects of intense debates. Indeed, empirical research shows that what was called "arbitration" a few decades ago looked much like what is sometimes called "mediation" today.[19]

Unfortunately, to date, relatively little attention has focused on the constantly changing nature of law practice or on the consumer's perspective.

The Lawyers' Perspective

That which we today consider legal work might typically have been the work of other professionals or lay persons in earlier decades (and still is in some regions of the country). History offers intriguing examples of activities that have shifted between (virtual) monopolies.[20] Looking at the current debate about UPL and ADR, we can readily see parallels. We are in a period of transition as the definition of lawyering seeks to keep pace with societal change.

---

[19] Bryant Garth, *Is Mediation the Practice of Law: The Wrong Question*, 33 NIDR FORUM 34 (June 1997) at 34.

[20] For a review of the history and politics of the struggle between attorneys and other professionals who offer services that border on the practice of law, *see* Mary C. Daly, *Choosing Wise Men Wisely: The Risks and Rewards of Purchasing Legal Services from Lawyers in a Multidisciplinary Practice*, 13 GEO. J. LEGAL ETHICS 217, 248-252 (2000). In his comprehensive study, A History of American Law (New York: 1973, 1985), Lawrence M. Friedman chronicles the changing definition of what constitutes the practice of law. He neatly highlights the 19th century's increasingly more complicated economy:

> Automation and technological change posed dangers to lawyers, just as they posed dangers to other occupations. Social invention constantly threatened to displace them. It was adapt or die. For example, lawyers in the first half of the century had a good thing going in title searches and related work. After the Civil War, title companies and trust companies proved to be efficient competitors. By 1900, well-organized, efficient companies nibbled away at other staples of the practice, too: debt collection and estate work, for example.

Id. at 634.

Generations ago former ABA President Chesterfield Smith was quoted as saying, "The practice of law is anything my client will pay me to do."[21] It is unlikely that legislatures, courts, the Federal Trade Commission or the Department of Justice's Antitrust Division would countenance such a statement today – if used to define the law profession's monopoly. Nevertheless, Smith's bald assertion serves as a marker for the most expansive definition of the practice of law.

Clearly a perspective this wide would embrace the role of the mediator or arbitrator, since disputants regularly share the cost of the third-party neutral's fee. But who would the client be in such a setting? Smith's construct presupposes a relationship of loyalty, advocacy and confidentiality that does not exist in a neutral conflict-resolution session. The mediator or arbitrator has no "client" in the classic sense of the term, as contemplated under bar regulatory systems.[22] Prof. Stephen Gillers[23] has suggested a New Mexico case to mark the most conservative end of the spectrum. In *Norvell v. Credit Bureau*, the New Mexico Supreme Court neatly set out six indicia to recognize the practice of law when the matter involves court proceedings:

---

[21] Alan Morrison, *Defining the Unauthorized Practice of Law: Some New Ways of Looking at an Old Question*, 4 NOVA L. J. 363, 365 (1980).

[22] The recommendation of the Ethics 2000 Commission have served a timely role. New *Model Rule 2.4*: LAWYER SERVING AS THIRD-PARTY NEUTRAL reads:

> (a) A lawyer serves as a third-party neutral when the lawyer assists two or more persons who are not clients of the lawyer to reach a resolution of a dispute or other matter that has arisen between them. Service as a third-party neutral may include service as an arbitrator, a mediator or in such other capacity as will enable the lawyer to assist the parties to resolve the matter.
> (b) A lawyer serving as a third-party neutral shall inform unrepresented parties that the lawyer is not representing them. When the lawyer knows or reasonably should know that a party does not understand the lawyer's role in the matter, the lawyer shall explain the difference between the lawyer's role as a third-party neutral and a lawyer's role as one who represents a client.

Comment 2 notes:

> The role of a third-party neutral is not unique to lawyers…. In performing this role, the lawyer may be subject to court rules or other law that apply either to third-party neutrals generally or to lawyers serving as third-party neutrals. Lawyer-neutrals may also be subject to various codes of ethics, such as the Code of Ethics for Arbitration in Commercial Disputes … or the Model Standards of Conduct for Mediators….

Comment 3 points to some of the differences between the lawyer's role as third-party neutral and a lawyer's role as a client representative, including "the inapplicability of the attorney-client evidentiary privilege."

[23] STEPHEN GILLERS, REGULATION OF LAWYERS: PROBLEMS OF LAW AND ETHICS, 5th ed., Aspen Law & Business (New York, 1998).

(1) representation of parties before judicial or administrative bodies;

(2) preparation of pleadings and other papers incident to actions and special proceedings;

(3) management of such actions and proceedings, and non-court related activities such as giving legal advice and counsel;

(4) rendering a service that requires the use of legal knowledge or skill;

(5) preparing instruments and contracts by which legal rights are secured.[24]

Some of the mediator activities most likely to be challenged fit probably five of the six factors laid out above. A New Jersey attorney-mediator offered a helpful overview of overlapping activities. His description could apply in almost any jurisdiction: mediators – both attorney mediators and non-attorney mediators – will "prepare and execute legal documents, prepare drafts of the parties' agreements, prepare a Memorandum of Understanding (a proposed settlement agreement)." Both attorney and non-attorney mediators will "participate in discovery, review legal documents, tax forms, tax statements, financial statements, accountings, and evaluations or appraisals prepared by other professionals." Depending upon the needs of the parties and the custom of the locality, some mediators will "prepare settlement agreements." In the process of performing this list of functions, non-attorney practitioners often will "offer legal advice." And, not infrequently, parties are not represented by counsel, but instead rely upon the advice proffered by the mediator.[25]

The *Model Rules* and *Model Code* might be said to adopt the middle position, as articulated in *R.J. Edwards, Inc. v. Hert* (a pre-Rules case), where the Oklahoma Supreme Court defined the practice of law as "the rendition of services requiring the knowledge and application of legal principles and techniques to serve the interests of another with his consent."[26] This intermediate position – which tracks the language of the *Model Code EC 3-5* – proceeds from the assumption that only an attorney can assess whether a situation actually requires an attorney's services. The intermediate view also presumes only regulation through the bar can assure quality.

---

[24] State ex rel. Norvell v. Credit Bureau of Albuquerque, Inc., 514 P.2d 40, 45 (N.M. 1973).

[25] Ron Kubiak, *Is ADR Practice by Non-Attorneys Authorized?*, N. J. LAW J. (January 30, 1995) at 37.

[26] R. J. Edwards, Inc. v. Hert, 504 P.2d 407, 416 (Okla. 1972).

The Consumers' Perspective

Few courts have adopted the approach suggested by a number of thoughtful scholars that we undertake a market analysis of UPL.[27] What are the costs and the benefits to the client? To what extent should the legislatures, courts and bar intervene to impose their own, perhaps expensive, determination of which matters require attorneys and which do not?[28] The expressed concern is that lay persons may seek to economize by using the services of people who are not attorneys; however, matters may be more complex than a non-attorney can recognize, ultimately leading to great harm. While this argument has a long tradition,[29] it has not withstood empirical examination.[30]

---

[27] Prof. Bryant Garth addressed this issue back in the 1980s. He asked the bar to confront candidly the economic basis for many UPL restrictions; to look beyond the veil of concern about the quality of services provided to the public. Garth brought to the reader's attention a 1938 observation by Prof. Karl Llewellyn inquiring in a symposium "'Who is worrying about unauthorized practice, and why? Is it the public, complaining of quacks? Is it the profession concerned about the public welfare? Or who and why?' As Llewellyn and other commentators have recognized, the lack of paying work in the Depression to a large extent explained the bar's sensitivity to the problem of unauthorized practice, or competition by nonlawyers. Neither public demand nor concern about public welfare adequately justified the sudden emphasis on eliminating the unauthorized practice of law. It was primarily the profession's issue – not that of the general public." Bryant G. Garth, *Rethinking the Legal Profession's Approach to Collective Self-Improvement: Competence and the Consumer Perspective*, 1983 WIS. L. REV. 639, 650 (1983). More recently this approach has been taken up by a new generation of scholars, *e.g.*, Benjamin Hoorn Barton, *Why Do We Regulate Lawyers?: An Economic Analysis of the Justification for Entry and Conduct Regulation*, 33 ARIZ. ST. L. J. 429 (Summer 2001); John S. Dzienkowski & Robert J. Peroni, *Multidisciplinary Practice and the American Legal Profession: A Market Approach to Regulating the Delivery of Legal Services in the Twenty-First Century*, 69 FORDHAM L. REV. 83 (October 2000).

[28] Garth recommends an approach that incorporates important consumer values: "A consumer perspective on the issue of the quality of the lawyer product would have to preserve the pro-access, pro-client autonomy direction of recent professional reforms while providing the means for clients: (1) to make intelligent choices regarding legal services investment; (2) to evaluate the results of professional services; and (3) to obtain redress if lawyers have provided less than was promised. We also must ask more generally how the quality of professional services can be improved consistently with values of accessibility and autonomy." One major way to achieve this would be to apply the doctrine of informed consent, "to ensure that the client has the ultimate power of choice and can obtain enough information about the various options to make the choice intelligently. The lawyer would have a duty to make the client aware of competing options." Garth, *supra* note 15, at 671-672.

[29] *See EC 3-4*: A layman who seeks legal services often is not in a position to judge whether he will receive proper professional attention. The entrustment of a legal matter may well involve the confidences, the reputation, the property, the freedom, or even the life of the client. Proper protection of members of the public demands that no person be permitted to act in the confidential and demanding capacity of a lawyer unless he is subject to the regulations of the legal profession.

[30] In Professor Rhode's empirical study she found the public's rate of satisfaction with non-lawyer representation exceeded the public's satisfaction with services rendered by attorneys. Deborah L.

Alongside the bar's interests, courts will also consider the interests of the public and others. The Washington State Supreme Court framed the inquiry in this way: "Whether non-lawyers should be allowed in the public interest to engage in activities that may constitute the practice of law." Particularly in non-criminal proceedings, the court may examine whether the interests of the bar outweigh the right of a party "to proceed without counsel."[31] Some 37 states have determined that the public interest in protecting against the downside risks of UPL are so significant that criminal penalties may be imposed.[32]

By contrast, other courts have recognized the need to protect the right of a person to appear *pro se*. Part and parcel of this right to self-representation is the need to have adequate information about the law. Can non-lawyers provide legal information? Can they provide guidance in filling out legal forms? This area has become a battleground (especially in family law and immigration law matters[33]), with attorneys on one side and paralegals, legal secretaries and other non-lawyers on the other. Arguably, the work of some mediators in drafting settlement agreements comes within the ambit of this line of litigation.

Various legal venues exist that seek to be less adversarial than standard

---

Rhode, *The Delivery of Legal Services by Non-Lawyers*, 4 GEO. J. LEGAL ETHICS, 209 (1990); *also Professionalism in Perspective: Alternative Approaches to Non-Lawyer Practice*, 1 J. INST. STUD. LEGAL ETHICS 97 (1996). Joyce Palomar, *The War Between Attorneys and Lay Conveyancers - Empirical Evidence Says "Cease Fire!"*, 31 CONN. L. REV. 423 (1999).

[31] Cuttum v. Heritage House Realtors, Inc., 694 P.2d 630, 633-635 (Wash. 1985). *Cuttum* concerned whether real estate brokers and title insurance companies could do the work oftentimes reserved to lawyers in residential house closings. *See also* In re Opinion No. 26, 654 A.2d 1344 (N.J. 1995), which described the great variation in custom that informs the expectations of the public and various professions. "Historically residential house closings in the southern and northern halves of New Jersey have proceeded differently. In the south it is routine not to use a lawyer. In the north, it is routine to use one." We have yet to develop as firmly entrenched a custom of ADR. However, this example highlights the necessity for flexibility, even within the same state.

[32] This figure comes from Prof. Rhode's statutory review, found in *The Delivery of Legal Services by Non-Lawyers, supra* note 18.

[33] In uncontested divorces: Florida Bar v. Brumbaugh, 355 So. 2d. 1186 (Fla. 1978); State Bar v. Cramer, 249 N.W. 2d 1 (Mich. 1976). Third-party or public insurance adjusters, not acting as an agent or employee of the insurance company: Professional Adjusters, Inc. v. Tandon, 433 N.E. 2d 779 (Ind. 1982); Utah State Bar v. Summerhayes & Hayden, 905 P.2d 867 (Utah 1995). Another version of this same struggle between the bar and non-lawyer efforts to provide legal information enabling lay persons to act *pro se* is found in the burgeoning area of legal software. In Texas the Unauthorized Practice of Law Committee attempted to enjoin the distribution of the software known as "Family Lawyer"; the Texas legislature enacted a statute specifically designed to permit the distribution of such software, so long as it was labeled to indicate the information provided did not substitute for the advice of a lawyer. Unauthorized Practice of Law Committee v. Parsons Technology, Inc., 179 F.3d 956 (5th Cir. 1999).

courtroom litigation. In administrative agency adjudications, for example, many jurisdictions favor an informal style, especially when the dollar amounts at issue are so small that it is generally not cost-effective to hire an attorney. Some courts have held that in these circumstances non-attorney representation ought to remain a viable option.[34] Other scholars have suggested that the legal profession should revamp its own approach to advocacy, to develop necessary proficiency in the less adversarial style that is increasingly needed, irrespective of the dollar amount in controversy.[35]

Distilling a Profile of UPL in ADR

Despite the efforts of some bar associations to articulate a set of guidelines for UPL in ADR, a workable picture of unauthorized practices must emerge not by fiat but from facts of cases as they arise. This section offers an overview of leading cases and bar opinions, organized around major themes identified as ethical problems.

Is ADR Ancillary to a Law Practice, or at its Center?
The Answer Depends Upon Where and When One Asks the Question

If an activity does not constitute the practice of law, then non-lawyers may engage in it without running afoul of the state bar. If the bar deems an activity "non-legal," then attorneys and non-attorneys may engage in it together so long as they maintain a firewall between the law firm and ancillary functions. The saga of UPL and ADR in New Jersey presents an unusual twist to this question. In 1991 the New Jersey Advisory Committee on Professional Ethics issued Opinion No. 657 in which it pronounced the practice of mediation by attorney dispute resolution professionals to be a non-legal service. Therefore, two attorneys could own and operate a mediation service so long as the service was entirely separate. Thus, the location had to be physically distinct from the law practice. No finances could be commingled. There could be no joint advertising or marketing; no demonstration of a shared relationship.

Most states reviewing the question have reached this same conclusion. Indiana's state bar, for example, found that:

the nature of a mediation practice differs substantially from the

---

[34] *See* Florida Bar v. Moses, 380 So. 2d 412, 418 (Fla. 1980) (unfair labor practice hearing); Denver Bar Association v. Public Utilities Commission, 391 P.2d 467, 469-471 (Colo. 1964); Hunt v. Maricopa County Employees Merit System Commission, 619 P.2d 1036 (Ariz. 1980); Henize v. Giles, 490 N.E. 2d 585 (Ohio 1986).

[35] *See* Carrie Menkel-Meadow, *Ethics and Professionalism in Non-Adversarial Lawyering*, 27 FLA. ST. U. L. REV. 153 (1999).

nature of the practice of law. Unlike the attorney who "should act with commitment and dedication to the interests of the client and with zeal in advocacy on the client's behalf," [cites omitted] ... the mediator is required to advise the parties that he does not represent either or both of them.[36]

The ethics committee concluded that because mediation was not the practice of law, an attorney-mediator could use a trade name and could solicit business for the mediation service. However, the attorney must maintain a strict separation between the two activities, in terms of publicity, advertising and solicitation. This position conforms to those taken by the bars of New York,[37] Tennessee,[38] the District of Columbia,[39] Kentucky,[40] Washington state,[41] and Maine.[42]

By 1994, the New Jersey bar had occasion to review its position and made a unique shift. Several professional ADR practitioners -- retired and former judges, attorney and non-attorney neutrals -- advertised their services in an ADR directory. A

---

[36] Indiana State Bar Association, Legal Ethics Committee, Opinion NO. 5 of 1992, National Reporter on Legal Ethics and Professional Responsibility, LEXIS Library: Ethics, File: INETH.

[37] New York State Bar Ass'n, Committee on Professional Ethics, Opinion No. 678 (1/10/96) - which barred an attorney from participating in a divorce-mediation-referral service that was neither operated, sponsored nor approved by the bar association.

[38] Tennessee Supreme Court, Disciplinary Board, Formal Ethics Opinion 83-F-39 (1/25/83) - which proscribed even a non-practicing attorney's practicing mediation with a non-lawyer.

[39] The notes to D.C. Court of Appeals Rule 49 - Unauthorized Practice of Law state:

> The Rule is not intended to cover the provision of mediation or alternative dispute resolution ... services. This intent is expressed in the first sentence of the definition of the "practice of law" which requires the presence of two essential factors: The provision of legal advice or services and a client relationship of trust or reliance. ADR services are not given in circumstances where there is a client relationship of trust or reliance; and it is common practice for providers of ADR services explicitly to advise participants that they are not providing the services of legal counsel.

[40] Kentucky Bar Ass'n Ethics Opinion No. 377 (1995) - holding that "Mediation is not the practice of law," as cited in the ABA Draft Resolution on Mediation and the Unauthorized Practice of Law (July 27, 2001) n. 1.

[41] Washington State Bar Ass'n, Committee to Define the Practice of Law, Final Report (July 1999, adopted by the Washington State Bar Ass'n Board of Governors September 1999, as cited in the *Resolution on Mediation and the Unauthorized Practice of Law*, *supra* note 10.

[42] Maine Bar Rule 3.4(h)(4) - "The role of the mediator does not create a lawyer-client relationship with any of the parties and does not constitute representation of them." As cited in the *Resolution on Mediation and the Unauthorized Practice of Law*, *supra* note 10.

complaint was filed charging that five attorneys who were arbitrators and/or mediators were engaged in activities that should in fact be considered the practice of law, in contravention of Opinion 657. The New Jersey Supreme Court Committee on Advertising and the Advisory Committee on Professional Ethics (known as the Joint Committee) determined in Joint Opinion 676/18 (April 4, 1994) that ADR had moved from being a mere ancillary activity to being "part and parcel of the practice of law." Moreover, the Joint Committee found that ADR "constitutes a tool of equal rank with litigation to achieve, in the proper case, prompt and cost-effective dispute resolution." The Joint Committee noted that this finding concurs with the approach taken by professional liability insurers, which cover attorneys in their activities as arbitrators, mediators and third-party neutrals.

Thus, an attorney engaged in ADR activities – mediation or arbitration requiring training and experience in the role – would be considered as engaging in the practice of law. New Jersey does not treat mediation as a separate profession. This leads to a paradoxical result. Rather than making it more difficult for attorney-neutrals to work closely with non-attorneys engaged in an ADR practice, the Joint Committee's opinion makes it easier. Because ADR is not an ancillary service, non-lawyer neutrals may render "ADR services in the same location as and jointly marketed or advertised with an attorney's legal practice."[43] While the result surely facilitates the marketing of full-spectrum ADR services, it is anomalous. The New Jersey bar has built its opinion primarily on the services rendered, with remarkably little consideration of a critical gap: there is no client relationship between the mediator and the parties.

One-Stop Service and the Ethics Rules

Within the American Bar Association the debate over multidisciplinary practice (MDP) has typically centered on how closely a law firm is allowed to work with accountants and business or financial advisors. The most frequently cited examples of MDP included strategic alliances to provide comprehensive services in complex commercial "often international" cases.[44] Nevertheless, the desire to offer attorney and non-attorney mediation services has also implicated this controversial topic.

The attorney's codified provisions outlining professional responsibilities did not originally envision one-stop, comprehensive service for clients. By the 1980s,

---

[43] New Jersey Supreme Court, Joint Opinion 676 - Advisory Committee on Professional Ethics, Opinion 18 - Committee on Attorney Advertising Alternative Dispute Resolution. National Reporter on Legal Ethics and Professional Responsibility, LEXIS Library: Ethics, File: NJETH.

[44] *See The Challenges Facing the Legal Profession in the 21st Century*, Appendix to American Bar Association Commission on Multidisciplinary Practice Report to the House of Delegates (May 2000).

however, mental health professionals and attorneys had begun to recognize the value of offering a range of services to families in need. This collaboration has encountered resistance in some states. Few situations, though, have reached the level of reported case law. We shall examine the handful of representative cases.

Rhode Island – Attorney's Role on the Team Weak and Undefined

In Rhode Island, Dr. Michael Werle, a psychologist, established the Werle Consultants Family Mediation Center, which marketed itself as "a place where cooperative resolution of marital problems could be undertaken."[45] The Center would provide mediation and arbitration services for resolving financial and child custody issues.

A closer look at the Center's staffing revealed the core problem: Dr. Werle was the only "mediation consultant" named in the Center's brochure. The Center proclaimed itself as having an "advisory attorney" who would "provide legal and tax advice" and "draft formal settlement agreements."[46] However, the legal counsel role remained unnamed and unfilled.

The billing arrangements also presented ethical problems. A couple using the Center's services would pay a deposit sufficient to cover 10 hours of mediation time and three hours of the "advisory attorney's" time. The deposit would be paid directly to the Center, and the Center would then disburse payments to the attorney. What type of engagement this deposit purchased remained murky. Ostensibly the attorney represented the couple jointly, or perhaps the mediation itself? Nevertheless, the failure to adequately define and delineate the attorney's role suggested to the Rhode Island Bar that Werle did not properly separate the legal and psychological aspects of the counseling services. Nor, in fact, could he.

Although the Rhode Island Attorney General had not filed a UPL case in approximately 10 years, he brought one against Dr. Werle. Dr. Werle was charged with the following violations: "[t]endering of legal advice; legal representation of an individual in a civil dispute; drafting of legal documents; the collection of what were in effect legal fees; the advertising of legal services; and the advertising of assistance in divorce proceedings."[47]

New York – Attorney's Role Limited to "Scribe" or Consultant

In a similar case, an attorney and a psychologist requested an advisory opinion from the Suffolk County (New York) Bar Ethics Committee to obtain

---

[45] Werle v. Rhode Island Bar Association, 755 F.2d 195 (1st Cir. 1985).

[46] Id.

[47] Suffolk Bar Ethics Opinion 95-2, published in N.Y.L.J. (March 6, 1996).

advance approval for their proposed professional venture. Like Werle, the attorney and psychologist sought to provide a fully integrated divorce-mediation service. They would confer with the divorcing couple to develop a voluntary agreement to resolve all issues. The attorney would review with the parties the available options for settling all issues, which would of necessity include explaining the controlling law. When the parties reached agreement, the attorney would prepare a separation agreement suitable for filing in court. The psychologist characterized the attorney's role as being a mere "scribe" or "consultant."[48] The couple would pay a fee to the organization, which, in turn, would pay the attorney.

This fully integrated approach created an insurmountable ethical quandary. The ethics committee found that "it is no more possible to segregate the portion of fees paid for legal services as distinguished from psychological, financial, and other services, than it is to segregate the nature of the specific services and the provider or providers thereof in the case presented. The consequence of such an arrangement is the division of legal fees with a non-lawyer." The characterization of the lawyer's role as that of a mere scribe confirmed to the Suffolk County Bar that the attorney had surrendered his independent professional judgment, subordinating his work to that of a non-attorney, the psychologist.

Minnesota - The Attorney's Role in Ethical Conflict of Loyalty

The case of Dean A. Nyquist[49] presents a strong cautionary tale for the attorney who seeks to offer non-adversarial representation in an adversarial world. A petition was filed for disciplinary action against this attorney for the comprehensive services offered by his Family Conflict Resolution Center. The Center offered legal services, along with mediation and counseling, in cases of divorce, child custody, and post-decree modifications to child custody orders. Nyquist's Center contrasted with other disciplinary situations where the one-stop services failed to provide a sufficient role for the attorney. Instead, the problem was that in an attempt to de-escalate conflict, the attorney attempted to serve both spouses/parents. This attempt, unfortunately, led to charges that the attorney had an irreconcilable conflict of interests, was unable to fulfill duties of loyalty to both sides, and was unable to fully preserve and act upon confidential communications by each.

Does *Nyquist* stand for the proposition that a non-adversarial approach is unworkable? Certainly not. Rather, *Nyquist* instructs us that cases of high emotional conflict and complex legalities may require separate legal counsel at some stages. Can such counsel be provided through the same firm? Possibly not, although

---

[48] *Id.*

[49] Petition for Disciplinary Action Against Dean A. Nyquist (In Re Nyquist) 493 N.W. 2d 538 (Minn. 1992).

rigorously enforced screening procedures – or the use of attorneys from offices in two different locations – could be sufficient so long as clients are fully informed in advance and their consent is obtained in writing.[50]

Overextending the Mediator's Role?

A recent Arizona case probably comes closest to describing the scenario many lawyers and bar UPL committees dread. Which aspect of the situation was most daunting? A hybrid firm – lawyers? mediators? consultants? – held itself out as providing services most lay people would likely consider to be those ordinarily provided by a lawyer. However, the firm had not designated or authorized a lawyer to actually perform such services. They were provided by the non-attorney members.

The mediation firm, calling itself Levin Grant & Associates, brought an attorney, Kenn Hanson, into its business. The verb phrase used here "brought into" is purposefully vague. Shortly after Hanson joined, the name of the firm changed to Levin Grant Hanson & Associates. The changes to letterhead, business cards and oral representations would suggest that Hanson had joined the mediation firm as a partner. Notwithstanding these external changes, Hanson was not a principal of the firm, but only an employee. None of Levin Grant's principals was a lawyer.

Levin Grant offered the public another version of an integrated ADR service. Levin Grant obtained names of litigants from court records and mailed them letters soliciting their business. Levin Grant offered clients a full range of ADR services, which included providing legal advice, consulting with regard to preparation of answers in the discovery process, and contacting parties for settlement discussions and negotiated resolutions.[51] Levin, a non-attorney, provided most of these services,

---

[50] A Seventh Circuit case concerning retaliatory discharge offers an excellent summary and update on successful institutional mechanisms to protect the confidentiality of the attorney-client relationship when *Model Rule 1.7* (client-client conflict), *Model Rule 1.8* (attorney-client conflict) or *Model Rule 1.9* (conflict with former client) are implicated. Some of those pertinent to our discussion include: (a) informing the entire law office of the conflict – including any necessary recusals; (b) banning all communications with attorneys who have been recused or screened off from the case; (c) limiting access to files, computer records, etc. through keys, secret codes and passwords. Courts will also consider: "the size of the law firm, the structural divisions, the 'screened' attorney's position in the firm, the likelihood of contact between the 'screened' attorney and one representing another party, and the fact that a law firm's and lawyer's most valuable asset is 'their reputations for honesty and integrity, along with competence.'" Further, the court expects the attorneys in the firm under question to have affirmed under oath that these screening devices were in place and in force. Cromley v. Board of Education, 17. F.3d 1059, 1065 (7th Cir. 1994).

[51] A typical solicitation letter was reprinted as an attachment to In the Matter of Kenn M. Hanson, Ariz. S. Ct. No. SB-00-0102-D, 2001 Ariz. LEXIS 7 (January 5, 2001):

Mr. Joseph Knapp
1256 West Atlantic
Gilbert, Arizona 85233

not Hanson. Hanson worked with Levin Grant only about six months. Hanson quickly recognized the major UPL problems embedded in the solicitation letter and brought them to Levin's attention, with suggested changes. Levin refused to consider the redrafted solicitation letter. Hanson consequently resigned.

It is difficult to find a more egregious situation reported in the courts or in the press. Yet *Hanson* may be a case that sets out helpful guidance for those who wish to offer comprehensive ADR services. At a minimum, the traditionally legal tasks of advising parties about (1) how the law would apply to the facts of their specific case and (2) drafting and responding to discovery requests must be handled

---

Re: Case No. DR 98-15540

Dear Joseph:

We are writing to you because we noticed you are a participant in divorce litigation. Levin Grant Hanson and Associates is a mediation firm not a law firm and we assist men who cannot afford an attorney to represent themselves.

After meeting with you, if I or my associate attorney Kenn Hanson determine that mediation is not immediately possible, we will cause to be prepared an Answer to your wife's Petition for Dissolution. If you feel it would be helpful to have the court establish a visitation schedule so you can exercise visitation with your children on a consistent basis, we will cause to be prepared a Petition for Pendente Lite Relief and a Petition for an Order to Show Cause re: Custody, Visitation and Child Support.

All issues of dissolution in Maricopa County are subject to Maricopa County Superior Court Guidelines and Community Property Law. After listening to those issues about which you are concerned we should be able to give you a good indication of the possibility of your case being successfully mediated. We'd like you to be aware however, that if you choose not to consider retaining an attorney or a private mediation firm like ours, the court provides a free mediation service which will attempt to resolve custody issues only. That service is provided to most parties to domestic relations actions who cannot agree on custody or visitation provisions only, as they relate to their children. Notwithstanding the foregoing, we'd be happy to answer your questions if you'd like to call us.

If your wife is represented by an attorney, the issues may still be successfully mediated. As a matter of fact, often it is helpful if her attorney is involved in the mediation process.

We have provided our service for nearly 1,000 couples in the last five years. We have helped to prevent their children from being embroiled in ongoing conflict. We have helped to limit the high cost of the dissolution process. We will be happy to permit you to speak with any former or current client so you will be more certain of how we can help you.
...
Sincerely,

Michael Levin
Levin Grant Hanson and Associates

by an attorney. Other activities, such as bringing the parties to the negotiation table or helping them resolve the problem, can be done by non-attorneys so long as their role remains to facilitate communication, not to define legal obligations.

Conclusion

The battleground and battle lines for UPL in ADR may remain hazy for the immediate future. The details that distinguish appropriate from inappropriate conduct will continue to evolve as the practice of mediation itself changes. Confidentiality protections severely limit the amount of information that can be offered about a mediator's conduct in a session. Limited provable facts will result in limited case law. Nevertheless, the ADR field already experiences substantial anxiety about the issue.

Will that anxiety be allayed through statutory definition? Unlikely, for the complexity of this issue exceeds the grasp of statutory language. Thus far, the Resolution of the ABA Dispute Resolution Section comes closest to offering meaningful guidance – at least when attorneys are involved. Some bar associations have undertaken a review and amendment of their rules to address the issue. Some cases have suggested answers, although we have yet to see detailed, consistent indicia. In coming years the "turf wars" may be fought not over UPL statutes or rules, but over the definition of mediation embodied in legislative standards for mediator certification.[52] And, of course, despite any efforts to legislate an answer, the true testing ground will be the individual, case-by-case instances of how particular words or behaviors by mediators are perceived by the parties – especially when appearing *pro se*.

---

[52] *See, e.g.*, legislation introduced February 2001 in the Illinois General Assembly which provides that mediation is not the practice of law. "When mediation is performed by a non-attorney certified mediator, it is not considered the unauthorized practice of law provided the mediator does not give legal advice." As reported by Thomas F. Gibbons, *Certification, Ethics Standards Proposed*, CHICAGO DAILY LAW BULLETIN, March 19, 2001, at 6.

Chapter 7

Enforcement of Ethics in Mediation

By Kimberlee K. Kovach

Ethical conduct in mediation practice involves a number of important factors. As set out in this book, diverse issues surround the drafting, enactment and implementation of codes of ethics for mediators as well as for others who participate in the mediation process. One aspect not yet focused on, but critical to the process, is the enforcement of codes or standards of ethics.

While codes of ethics that are aspirational – that is, those lacking any real enforcement mechanisms – can be valuable in improving the profession of mediation, it is only with strict enforcement mechanisms that parties can be assured of consistently high standards for the mediation process. Professions that are self-regulating, such as law, have in place internal enforcement procedures for addressing violations of ethical provisions. As the mediation profession moves toward regulation, the time is ripe for considering appropriate procedures to enforce ethical rules. This chapter examines critical considerations involved in the enforcement of ethical codes for mediators.

Overview of Issues to Address in Enforcement of Ethics

The enactment of any ethical code raises difficult questions. Additional thorny issues surround enforcement mechanisms. While some mediators may argue that the mere existence of ethical standards, in and of itself, is sufficient for professional regulation, and that individual mediators should, and will, voluntarily abide by them, that approach does not guarantee ethical conduct. If one of the primary objectives of enacting ethical standards is to protect the general public, then an ability to assure compliance is necessary. An enforcement procedure would dictate that mediators are responsible for more than voluntary compliance with guidelines. To make compliance with ethical standards compulsory, we must establish consequences for violations. The majority of the current codes of ethics have been created as guidelines for mediator conduct, and consequently no real sanctions exist for violations. Thus, even mediators who knowingly violate ethical guidelines usually continue to practice without consequence.

One troublesome issue that has rarely been addressed in the creation of ethical guidelines for mediation is the determination of *who is to enforce them*. In most instances no enforcement entity exists. In a few situations mediators may be prohibited from retaining membership in the organization that enacted the standards. But these mediators may, and do, continue to mediate. Mechanisms of enforcement are critical. And an essential component of enforcement is the establishment of an enforcement agency.

Another major consideration involves just *how* these ethical rules or guidelines are to be enforced. In other words, what methods will be used to monitor individual mediators to assure that they do not violate the rules -- or if they do, that appropriate action is taken? One critical component of the process is establishing a procedure that allows the consumer (that is, the user of the process -- a party, lawyer or other representative for a party) to lodge a complaint.

An additional issue that must be considered is the impact of enforcement on other aspects of mediation such as confidentiality. Using an investigative process, for example, almost necessitates an exception for confidentiality. Alternatively, perhaps it is appropriate that the complaint process begin with a less adversarial approach. Although several approaches to complaint investigation have been utilized with mediators, very little has been documented.

Another aspect of the enforcement process involves the determination of appropriate sanctions or consequences. Should it be determined that a mediator has not complied with an ethical rule, then a particular consequence might be appropriate. Currently, however, specific penalties or consequences appropriate for various ethical violations rarely exist. Potential sanctions range from a remedial or educational consequence to a rather severe suspension-from-practice option. If penalties or consequences are established, then it is also imperative that they be known in advance. Mediators must be informed about both the procedure for, and consequences of, ethical breaches. Therefore an educational component of the enforcement process is also essential.

Thus, in the view of many, the most important consideration of ethics enforcement involves the introduction of ethical codes to new mediators. Perhaps an even more difficult dilemma may be how to educate experienced mediators. In many jurisdictions and programs, there is only a minimal, one-time training requirement for mediators. Programs to train and educate mediators are far from standardized. Consistency with regard to course content is lacking, and it is often difficult to ascertain whether trainings actually include ethical components. Although some mediator membership organizations have implemented ethical guidelines for their members, it is difficult to determine whether the mediators are familiar with them. Because no standard testing of mediators currently exists, it is possible that many mediators may not even be aware that ethical guidelines or standards exist. In many cases, novice mediators are provided with copies of the ethical codes during training and are educated with regard to the content. Yet very little has been done to assure that they are really familiar with or understand the ethics rules. Therefore, a mandatory educational component is appropriate and necessary to create and implement policies and procedures for enforcing mediator ethics.

Another related aspect of ethics concerns the mediation participants. This aspect of mediation in ethics is considered in this book, and while an in-depth discussion of all possible consequences is a complex endeavor, such an issue is worth some consideration and is addressed at the end of this chapter.

Potential Oversight or Enforcement Organizations

One of the most basic or preliminary considerations in the enforcement of ethical standards or codes is the identification of *who* will be responsible for enforcement. This issue is at the core of why most codes lack enforcement. No entity with jurisdiction over mediators exists. Currently only a few regulatory schemes provide a clear entity that is responsible for monitoring mediator conduct. One example is in the state of Florida where several years ago the Florida Supreme Court assumed the role of establishing a certification procedure for mediators, which was accomplished through court rules. These rules also include *Standards of Professional Conduct for Mediators,* as well as a process for discipline. Appointed panels make decisions about conduct and may impose a variety of sanctions that are enumerated in the rules.

One concern with the Florida model, however, is that it does not apply to all mediators. The court can exercise jurisdiction over only those who mediate cases filed and pending in Florida courts. Mediators in private practice who mediate non-litigation cases are not subject to the standards or the enforcement process. It would seem that all professional mediators should be treated evenly by the oversight organization.

In most jurisdictions, however, no organization has assumed a regulatory role. Although many codes of ethics and standards for mediator conduct exist, the mechanisms for enforcement are lacking. Until specific processes and procedures are identified and put in place, it is quite difficult, if not actually impossible, to monitor mediator conduct. Therefore, designating the oversight organization is a critical first step in the enforcement process.

A variety of options exist. For example, in some professions oversight is accomplished by a state agency or quasi-governmental group. In these situations legislation establishes a requirement that a specific entity license the professionals. A component of licensing is oversight, including ethical enforcement.

In other instances, professional associations establish ethics panels or committees to serve in the oversight, investigatory and enforcement roles. Often the chair of the committee is given the initial investigatory responsibility while the entire panel is convened to make final determinations. Another model, used, for example, by the American Institute of Architects, is the creation of a National Ethics Council that is given the responsibility for enforcement policies and procedures.

In terms of the mediation profession, any of these options would likely be workable. National as well as state associations and organizations are in place although no requirement of membership exists. In those instances, should a procedure for enforcement be created, it would be a voluntary one. Establishing a mandatory scheme for the enforcement of mediator ethics necessitates that other options be considered and eventually implemented. One example is a state licensing board. Once an organization assumes an enforcement role, various methods for its work must be considered.

Methods of Enforcement of Mediator Ethics

Enacting a specific and detailed code of ethics for mediators is a good foundation upon which to foster trust and build confidence in the mediation process. The consumers of mediation services, however, must also be assured that the mediators are being held to such standards on a regular and continuing basis. Those who must comply with codes of ethics must be aware not only of the actual contents and provisions of the ethical code, but also the consequences of failing to comply with the code. If violations occur, procedures should be in place to investigate a report or grievance, as well as determine consequences. This section discusses some of the primary options available to entities and organizations that are, or in the future may be, in the position of investigating charges of ethical violations against mediators.

Several methods exist by which a violation of an ethical code might be brought to the attention of an enforcement official or entity. The first is through the reporting of a grievance by a consumer of mediation services. This consumer could be a party at the mediation or a party's lawyer or other representative. The enforcement entity should be sure that mediation participants know how to make a complaint, and once a complaint is lodged, what procedures are in place to address it.

In mediations conducted or administered by a large provider organization, the organization may have an obligation to monitor the panel members. Should ethics rules be enacted for the providers (as urged by some), enforcement might be their responsibility. In that situation, the reporting would begin within the organization. The same might also be true of not-for-profit mediation centers.

An enforcement entity could also learn of violations from other mediators or staff members. Many professions include in their ethical standards a requirement that each professional must report ethical violations of colleagues. While such provisions have not yet made their way into the codes of ethics for mediators, it would not be surprising to see such an addition. An ethical rule that obligates mediators to report the unethical conduct of other mediators is not an unforeseen possibility.

Some types of ethics violations occur during the mediation session. Another concern, however, involves the violations that occur before or after the mediation session. In these instances also, the participants should be aware of the procedures available to voice a complaint or concern.

Once a complaint is lodged, the next step is to investigate the matter or address it in some other way. Historically, the initial means of addressing an ethics violation or complaint made against lawyers, accountants and other professionals has been an investigatory procedure. At first, a screening process may make an initial determination as to whether the complaint has merit. If it does not, summary dismissal may result. If the grievance is found to be credible (by some entity or person), then the complaint proceeds through an evidentiary hearing where findings of fact are made. From those, consequences are then derived.

Interestingly, however, in mediation practice some of the programs and centers in the United States have decided to employ a more facilitative approach before progressing to a full hearing. Various alternative procedures exist through which an organization could address complaints lodged against mediators for ethics violations.

Adjudicatory approaches consist of methods such as fact-finding, arbitration, or administrative hearing. In these instances, it is important that both the mediator and the consumer understand what kind of hearing may take place. Rules with regard to the presentation of evidence should be specified. These procedures are somewhat formal in nature, although not as formal as court proceedings, and result in official outcomes.

Another option is to begin with a less formal investigation to determine whether there is "probable cause" to proceed to the next step.

Where an adjudicatory process is used, parties should know in advance who will be making the decisions. As is the case in a number of other professions, it is essential that those who make the decisions are knowledgeable and have experience in the field.

In situations where there may have been a misunderstanding between the mediator and the participants, it would be possible to utilize a less formal method for ascertaining what the consequences may be. A mediation-like process may be appropriate. If mediation is used, however, a number of additional considerations arise. One concerns confidentiality. Another is whether mediation should be mandatory on the part of the mediator. Another important matter involves who may serve as mediators for this process and whether additional training may be necessary. Who may attend, including the other party, should be addressed, along with the role of any lawyer representatives. Yet another issue is that of possible ramifications for the complaint process if no agreement is achieved in mediation.

Potential Consequences of Violations of Mediator Ethics

In any disciplinary process, the enforcement entity must determine the consequences of violations. That is, what happens to the mediator should a finding be made that a violation of an applicable ethical code has occurred?

A number of possibilities exist. Options may include a series of sanctions, progressive in severity, with the ultimate sanction being suspension from the program or even from the practice of mediation. There is also the possibility that, for some violations, immediate suspension would be appropriate. Alternatives include, but are not limited to, requiring the mediator to do the following: attend a remedial education program; shadow another experienced mediator; co-mediate only; observe a specific number of mediations conducted by other mediators, or pay fees, should any damages be established. In addition, the mediator could be suspended from the list for a specific period of time and even suspended permanently.

Another approach might be to establish a rule that no mediator can register to be on approved lists until after he or she has demonstrated compliance with the ethical and educational requirements of the organization. In some instances, if a broad licensure or certification scheme were in place, then to maintain one's license would necessitate compliance with ethical rules and standards.

Most of the potential consequences have both advantages and drawbacks. To require the mediator to attend remedial training programs or spend time with a more experienced mediator in a mentoring relationship would improve the profession and maintain the individual's ability to mediate. Suppose, for example, that a more or less novice mediator becomes biased and takes sides, and the session results in no agreement. If a party complains and the enforcer finds that the mediator violated the ethics of neutrality, it might be helpful to require the mediator to engage in more training with a focus on neutrality issues. Such training might include adopting a mentor, shadowing an experienced mediator, or engaging in co-mediation for a period of time. One difficulty, however, is identifying sufficient mediators who would work with others.

In those instances where noncompliance with ethics is more severe, stringent consequences may be appropriate. For example, violation of confidentiality may be not only an ethics violation but also something akin to malpractice.

While more mediative and remedial (more collaborative) approaches are in sync with the mediation approach to problem solving, there also exists the downside that if mediators -- as professionals -- are not "punished," then the mantra that lawyers have heard (protecting their own) may reverberate throughout mediation practice.

A final consideration concerns the dissemination of information about alleged or actual ethical violations by mediators. For example, where the enforcement entity finds a violation, should that information be kept confidential by the oversight organization, or alternatively is a public reprimand of sorts a desired consequence?

Enforcement Considerations for Mediation Participants

Discussion of ethics in mediation also has focused on the possibility of enacting ethical requirements for all who participate in mediation: the parties as well as their representatives, including lawyers for the parties. While the nature and content of those ethical rules differ vastly, no mechanism for real enforcement exists. One option for enforcement involves the courts that refer cases to mediation. In some instances, referring courts are very involved in overseeing or superintending the mediation process.

If, as some urge, lawyers specifically must abide by the purely adversarial win-lose paradigm of ethical guidelines -- even in a context where that paradigm is at best inappropriate and at worst disruptive and damaging -- then enforcement would seem to remain attached to the original lawyer regulating groups, state or local bar associations. Still outstanding, however, is the question of how information about one lawyer's conduct in mediation can be disclosed to anyone, whether judge of case, bar association or other independent entity.

With regard to other representatives, such as CPAs, therapists, financial advisors, or real estate representatives, the matter can be even more complex. Most professions have some sort of ethical requirements, although great variation and diversity exist. The interplay of these professions' ethics with requirements for mediation presents complex issues.

Conclusion

While discussions of mediator ethics have not focused on enforcement mechanisms, procedures and consequences, as the profession becomes more regulated, these considerations are necessary. A number of different options and alternatives exist for the reporting, investigation, and mediation of complaints made against mediators for ethical violations. Alternatives also exist for the implementation of consequences of violations. If in fact the ethical codes and standards are to have real meaning for the consumers, some enforcement process is essential.

Chapter VIII

Ethics, Morality and Professional Responsibility in Negotiation

By Carrie Menkel-Meadow

Introduction: The Issues and Layers of Ethics

Negotiation necessarily involves interaction with other human beings. By definition we negotiate when we "seek to do together what we cannot do alone,"[1] by "conferring with another so as to arrive at the settlement of some matter or to transfer to another by delivery or endorsement in return for equivalent value."[2] In legal negotiation more than a few human beings are usually involved, since lawyers are representing clients who seek to resolve a dispute in a litigation matter or who seek to plan a transaction, create a new entity or structure a contract, treaty, agreement or deal. How we should behave toward and with those people in legal negotiations remains a troubling and unresolved question in legal ethics.

This chapter addresses issues of ethics in negotiation at several different levels, reflecting the often wide disparity between what is "good" or "moral" behavior as we claim it aspirationally and what we actually do in negotiation (what I here call "instrumental" negotiation ethics and what others have called "market"[3] or "pragmatic"[4] ethics). In between these levels of aspiration and actual behavior are the rules or laws that seek, quite unsuccessfully in my view, to regulate ethics in

---

[1] Carrie Menkel-Meadow, *Toward Another View of Legal Negotiation: The Structure of Problem Solving*, 31 UCLA L. REV. 754 (1984).

[2] MERRIAM-WEBSTER DICTIONARY, "Negotiate" (1974).

[3] Eleanor Holmes Norton, *Bargaining and the Ethic of Process*, 64 N.Y.U. L. REV. 493 (1989).

[4] G. RICHARD SHELL, BARGAINING FOR ADVANTAGE: NEGOTIATION STRATEGIES FOR REASONABLE PEOPLE (1999).

negotiation, in the hope that some regulation will provide at least de minimus standards of fairness and fair dealing when lawyers negotiate legal arrangements on behalf of their clients. In addition to what might be considered behavioral or "micro" ethics concerns – how should a given lawyer-negotiator make choices about what to do in a given negotiation – there are larger, "macro" ethical issues implicated in negotiation. When is a negotiated outcome just or fair? What should our judicial and dispute resolution systems allow as systematic approaches to the resolution of conflicts or facilitation of transactions? Do accumulations of behaviors create expectations about how the "system" operates and what it provides, what one philosopher has called an "ethical climate"?[5] Have we created a trusted and "fair" system or one in which manipulation, power or deception prevail, producing cynicism and lack of compliance? Should we base our negotiation ethics rules and practices on the current empirical reality[6] of expectations of "generally accepted conventions"[7] ("background norms")[8] or should we aspire to make current practices more fair or just?

Many scholars and practitioners view candor, deception or lying as the key ethical issue in negotiation – what exactly do we have to tell the other side about ourselves and our actual goals, desires and interests in a negotiation? How much can we withhold about what we truly value or what we know (because we fear someone on the other side of a negotiation will take strategic advantage of us)? But, in reality there are many more issues implicated in negotiating to resolve disputes or create commercial, personal or international relationships, than "mere" considerations of "truth-telling" in strategic interactions.

This chapter will focus on the deception or "misrepresentation" issues, but it will also focus on issues of substantive fairness of outcomes negotiated for, our treatment of the human beings we are negotiating with, the relationship of one-shot negotiations to longer-term negotiations and relationships and the place of negotiation ethics in the increasingly complex legal worlds of litigation, compliance with governmental regulations and transactional work. In addition to these general ethical issues of fairness in information sharing and in substantive agreements reached in negotiation, there are ethical issues implicated in the duty of lawyers to

---

[5] SIMON BLACKBURN, BEING GOOD: AN INTRODUCTION TO ETHICS 3 (2001).

[6] "We suppose that the world is exhausted by what *is* the case." *Id.* at 29.

[7] *See* MODEL RULES OF PROFESSIONAL CONDUCT (2002), *Rule 4.1*, Comment 2, discussed more fully infra.

[8] Donald C. Langevoort, *Half-Truths: Protecting Mistaken Inferences By Investors and Others*, 52 STAN. L. REV. 87 (1999).

inform, counsel and consult with clients about settlement offers and proposals made and considered in negotiations, and the respective roles of lawyers and clients in representational negotiations. Ethics and professional responsibility in negotiation should also encourage us to consider the others affected by any negotiated outcome, what some call the "externalities" of negotiated agreements (such as children in a divorce negotiation or future generations in environmental negotiations). Finally, there is the question of whether honest, fair and efficient completion or satisfaction of negotiated agreements is also a part of negotiation ethics. Thus, broadly considered, ethical concerns in negotiation go well beyond the explicit rules of our profession, beyond the customs, cultures and habits of actual negotiators and even beyond those formally sitting at any negotiation table.

Most modern treatments of negotiation ethics take the current world as given;[9] that is, negotiation is a strategic process in which we assume a certain amount of dissembling, "puffery"[10] and even deception. In the words of one commentator, the very purpose of the negotiator is to "mislead his opponent. Like the poker player, a negotiator hopes that his opponent will overestimate the value of his hand. . . . To conceal one's true position, to mislead an opponent about one's true settling point, is

---

[9] What we actually know about lawyer negotiation in the real world is quite thin and contradictory. In the earliest study of actual lawyer negotiation practices Stephen D. Pepe (now a Magistrate Judge and formerly a negotiation teacher and researcher at the University of Michigan) found evidence of fairly widespread acceptance of deceptive practices; *see Standards of Legal Negotiations: Interim Report for ABA Commission on Evaluation of Professional Standards and ABA House of Delegates* (1983). Just a little bit later, Professor Gerald Williams surveyed lawyers in several locations about what they considered effective or ineffective among the other lawyers they negotiated with. Williams found that there were in fact greater numbers of "cooperative" and truth-telling lawyers among those rated "effective." GERALD R. WILLIAMS, LEGAL NEGOTIATION AND SETTLEMENT (1983). These attempts to study real-world legal negotiations remain largely unreplicated 20 years later. Most other studies of negotiation behavior have been conducted in social psychology laboratory settings (or in attitudinal research) and tell us next to nothing about what really is happening in legal negotiations today. For summaries of empirical research on negotiation behavior, *see e.g.* JEFFREY Z. RUBIN & BERT BROWN, THE SOCIAL PSYCHOLOGY OF BARGAINING AND NEGOTIATION (1975); DEAN G. PRUITT, NEGOTIATION BEHAVIOR (1981); MAX H. BAZERMAN & MARGARET A. NEALE, NEGOTIATING RATIONALLY (1992); LEIGH L. THOMPSON, THE MIND AND HEART OF THE NEGOTIATOR (2d ed. 2000). For an interesting computer simulation of theorized approaches to "repeat-play interactions" of the "prisoner's dilemma" game, *see* ROBERT AXELROD, THE EVOLUTION OF COOPERATION (1984) (suggesting that even in assumed competitive situations some forms of "forgiving cooperative" behavior may be more effective over the long run).

[10] "Puffing" or exaggerations of value or other statements have actually been formally recognized in the Comments to lawyers' professional ethics rules, *see* MODEL RULES OF PROFESSIONAL CONDUCT *Rule 4.1,* Comment 2, and in securities disclosure standards, *see also* Langevoort, *supra* note 8, at 121.

the essence of negotiation."[11] Like others who have gone before me,[12] I want to suggest here that we need not take the world as we find it (though I am an empiricist-realist), but should, instead, consider what would make for good and moral, as well as "optimal" behavior in negotiations. Whether rule changes, market forces or additional ethical discourse is likely to be effective in changing the strategic present to the more trustworthy future, it is, in my view, useful to interrogate our assumptions that the way things are is the way they have to be. If changing dispute resolution practices and procedures, such as mediation, now encourage us to approach legal problems with a different mindset of "problem-solving," rather than purely adversarial self-interest, then negotiation ethics will emerge either as the middle ground between problem-solving mediation and adversarial trial ethics or as the model for ethics in all dispute settlement[13].

While the rules of professional ethics and the law of fraud and misrepresentation are the principal regulatory sources for considering what is proper or unlawful conduct in negotiation behavior, actual conduct is in fact quite context-dependent, and thus attempts to craft universal rules of behavior are indeed quite difficult in this area. One important ethical and policy concern then is to determine the extent to which our ideas of ethical behavior in negotiation must be relative and conditional, based on the context in which the negotiation occurs. Is it possible or desirable to craft a set of universal behavioral exhortations in this area?

Perhaps a greater negotiation ethics problem lies in the enforcement of whatever standards we do set for ourselves. If professional disciplinary bodies (which enforce professional ethics codes) and courts (which enforce the law of fraud) are our sole sources of regulatory enforcement, with their cumbersome rules of evidence,

---

[11] James J. White, *Machiavelli and the Bar: Ethical Limitations on Lying in Negotiation*, 1980 AM. B. FOUND. RES. J. 926, 927.

[12] *See* Alvin B. Rubin, *A Causerie on Lawyers' Ethics in Negotiation*, 35 LA. L. REV. 577 (1975). Gary Tobias Lowenthal, *The Bar's Failure to Require Truthful Bargaining By Lawyers*, 2 GEO. J. LEGAL ETHICS, 411 (1988); Roger Fisher, *A Code of Negotiation Practices for Lawyers*, 1 NEGOTIATION. J. 2 (1985); Walter W. Steele, Jr., *Deceptive Negotiating and High Toned Morality*, 39 VAND. L. REV. 1387 (1986); Gerald B. Wetlaufer, *The Ethics of Lying in Negotiations*, 76 IOWA L. REV. 1219 (1990); Reed Elizabeth Loder, *Moral Truthseeking and the Virtuous Negotiator*, 8 GEO. J. LEGAL ETHICS 45 (1994).

[13] The question of whether mediation, which is facilitated negotiation, and "unassisted" negotiation can have different ethics rules and practices is quite complex; *see* Bruce E. Meyerson, *Telling the Truth in Mediation: Mediator Owed a Duty of Candor*, 4 DISP. RES. MAG. 17 (Winter, 1997) (suggesting that the same duty of candor is due to a judge in a tribunal (MODEL RULES OF PROFESSIONAL CONDUCT, *Rule 3.3*), to a mediator and to opposing counsel negotiating a settlement agreement directly with the other side (MODEL RULES OF PROFESSIONAL CONDUCT, *Rules 4.1, 1.2(d)* and *8.4(c)*).

procedure and proof, how can we effectively monitor, scrutinize and sanction departures from ethics rules and laws? As at least one influential commentator suggested when the ABA last tried to regulate negotiations substantively, since negotiations are almost always conducted in private (and usually with only the principal negotiators themselves present), how can we ever know what was said and whether there has been an "ethical" violation?[14]

Because formal sanctioning of unethical behavior in negotiation is so rare, we must, in fact, turn to other methods of norm development and enforcement. In this chapter I suggest three. The first, most commonly suggested by most commentators, is that of market or reputational norm setting. To the extent that lawyer negotiators are often repeat players, if not with each other, then in the same profession or same speciality or sub-set of the profession, a person's value, at an instrumental level, as a negotiator, will often depend on what others think of the reliability and truthfulness of what he or she does in a negotiation. Note that even this version of instrumental reputational ethics is not confined to simple truth-telling in a negotiation. Reliability in the follow-through of what is promised in a negotiation and the ability to reasonably and efficiently draft an agreement and deliver on its promises, are all part of the negotiator's reputation. As the chapters in this book on the ethical duties of the attorney representatives in mediation and arbitration and the duties of mediators and other third-party neutrals make clear, what lawyers say to each other -- and now to third-party neutrals like mediators and arbitrators, as well as to judges and opponents or other parties who are present in larger negotiation settings -- is now witnessed and remembered by growing numbers of participants in these processes. Add to these new processes the possibilities of enhanced communication between and among lawyers, clients and third-party neutrals through Internet communication, and a lawyer's reputation as a negotiator is likely to spread further and wider than ever before. If a lawyer wishes to promise a client effectiveness as a negotiator, he or she must tend carefully to his or her reputation as a trustworthy negotiator who follows through on the implementation, as well as the negotiation, of agreements, settlements and transactions.[15]

---

[14] White, *supra* note 11, at 926-938. (White argued against substantive regulation of negotiation and more intrusive regulation of candor, as proposed by the Kutak Commission in its 1983 proposals for *Model Rules 4.2* and *4.3*, because, in his view, the private nature of negotiation would result in virtually no transparency of negotiation behavior making enforcement of such rules unlikely to impossible, and the inability to enforce these rules might damage the legitimacy of the rest of the Model Code of Professional Conduct for lawyers.)

[15] *See* Ronald J. Gilson & Robert H. Mnookin, *Disputing Through Agents: Cooperation and Conflict Between Lawyers in Litigation*, 94 COLUM. L. REV. 509 (1994) (suggesting that a reputation for being a collaborative, cooperative, and value-creating negotiator will enhance the value of a particular lawyer and law firm with such reputations).

Beyond the instrumental value of being known as a fair, effective and trustworthy negotiator for client acquisition and satisfaction, as well as trust from opposing lawyers and other parties, the negotiator must also maintain an internal standard of negotiation ethics and morality. While other commentators shy away from such "personal" morality as being too "idealistic"[16] in the rough and tumble of modern day negotiations, most human beings "know" when they have taken unfair advantage of someone else, whether by deception, manipulation, use of superior economic or informational power, brute strength or general unfairness. For some, this standard of morality is one of "intentionality"[17] – internally a person "knows," even if outsiders may not be able to discern enough evidence of intent, whether he or she intended to deceive or take advantage of the other side. This internal standard (which I have called the "Can you look at yourself in the mirror?" test) is probably the single most important determinant of what we actually do in negotiations.[18] In legal negotiation this "internal" standard is more complicated and the subject of its own negotiation because lawyers and clients as agents and principals must negotiate what the "internal" standard of their functional and professional relationship is to be, and a professional ethic of "advocacy" allows lawyers and clients to create a "community of two"[19] against the other side. Whatever rules, standards or laws we adopt in this area, in my view, it is ultimately this level – how we each judge our own behavior – that controls most negotiation ethics.

---

[16] Richard Shell eloquently describes three possible ethical modes for negotiators, "idealists," "game-players" and "pragmatists" in Chapter 11 of BARGAINING FOR ADVANTAGE, *supra* note 4. He suggests that idealists will have a hard time in this less-than-idealistic world and might be taken advantage of by the game-players and pragmatists. He does suggest, however, one useful internal standard, and that is individual consistency. A negotiator who does not know his/her own ethical limits is more likely to be taken advantage of than one who finds some knowable "self" in negotiating limits of behavior.

[17] SISSELA BOK, LYING: MORAL CHOICE IN PUBLIC AND PRIVATE LIFE 8 (Pantheon Books, 1st ed. 1978).

[18] Others have called this the "would you tell a family member or loved one what you have done, or be pleased if what you had done was reported in the newspaper" test; *see e.g.* David Lax & James Sebenius, *Three Ethical Issues in Negotiation*, 2 NEGOTIATION. J. 363, 366 (1986). Lax and Sebenius also ask the question of whether you would advise others to use the tactic or would design a system with a particular tactic to be used by everyone (the organizational development version of Kant's Categorical Imperative!). Peter Drucker has also suggested the "mirror" test in the business context, "when you look at yourself in the mirror the next morning, will you like the person you see?", *Id.* at 366. The philosopher Seneca perhaps captures the "inner judge" best by suggesting that "I am content if you only act, in whatever you do, as you would act if anyone else at all were looking on." Bok, *supra* note 17, at 99.

[19] William H. Simon, *Homo Psychologicus: Notes on a New Legal Formalism*, 32 STAN. L. REV. 487 (1980).

Finally, all negotiators act within a context. There are facts, bargaining endowments and situations that people find themselves in. Much discussion of negotiation ethics assumes bilateral parity between negotiators or their principals. In my view, negotiation ethics must consider the underlying structure in which the negotiation occurs – to what extent are negotiators justified in taking advantage of some bargaining inequality (the standard professional-role "defense" of the lawyer as zealous advocate) and to what extent must negotiators be accountable for failing to take into account distributional justice concerns as they divide whatever pie they have "baked," whether expanded or not? This element of structural distribution in negotiation can be considered both at the substantive level and at the process level, as sometimes negotiators do not even know what the rules or customs are that they are expected to be playing by,[20] whatever their substantive endowments might be.

What we as ethicists and professionals can do is to encourage raising the standards of what is good and moral behavior by discussing the issues at all levels and considering the contexts and impacts of our behaviors in different negotiation environments, what I and others have called a "moral dialogue"[21] with our clients and ourselves. Then there is always the issue of whether we take the world as we find it and adapt to its customs and practices or whether we seek to change it.

A Brief Philosophical and Historical Review

The issues implicated in how we should treat people with whom we have professional relationships are as old as humankind itself. From the multi-religious convergence on a "golden rule"[22] to treat other people as we would want to be treated by them, which creates an almost universal rule of aspirational "reciprocity," to the extreme variability of market ethics in acceptable bargaining tactics,[23] customs and cultures have developed understandings, norms and questions about how we should

---

[20] Bok, *supra* note 17, at 138. This applies particularly in situations of unequal bargaining power, such as in employer-employee negotiations, some merger or acquisition negotiations and in one-shot vs. repeat-player litigation. *See* Carrie Menkel-Meadow, *Do the "Haves" Come Out Ahead in Alternative Judicial Systems?: Repeat Players in ADR*, 15 Ohio St. J. Disp. Res. 19 (1999).

[21] *See* Menkel-Meadow, *supra* note 1, at 813-817.

[22] For different religion's formulations of the "golden rule," *see* Bok, *supra* note 17, at 98. For application of a "golden rule" of candor in lawyer-client relations, *see* Carrie Menkel-Meadow, *Lying to Clients for Economic Gain or Paternalistic Judgment: A Proposal for a Golden Rule of Candor*, 138 U. Penn. L. Rev. 761 (1990).

[23] *See e.g.* Steven Lubet, *Notes on the Bedouin Horse Trade or "Why Won't the Market Clear, Daddy,"* 74 Tex. L. Rev. 1039 (1996).

treat others while conducting business with them. Virtually all treatments of professional ethics acknowledge role-based exceptions to the commandment that we should "not bear false witness against [our] neighbor."[24] Lawyers are expected to be loyal and zealous advocates for their clients, justifying some exaggerations, some puffing and even some deception in protective roles; doctors deceive or lie to protect their clients' health or confidentiality; journalists, police officers and social scientists use deception to learn the "truth" and protect their sources; and public officials lie to protect national security, as well as to get elected by large, diverse and contentious constituencies.[25] Even highly regulated corporations successfully argue for some degree of protective secrecy to shield the "property" interests of proprietary research and development.[26]

When we consider ethics standards for lawyer-negotiators, we generally assume the point of view of the lawyer protecting the client – we want to be able to deceive, puff or "get the best possible deal" for our client, as a "zealous advocate,"[27] often without considering that the other side will want to justify doing exactly the same things.[28] So rule drafters or justification proponents often start from a partisan perspective.

Might we look at different sources of rules or ethics if we stood slightly outside of our role as advocates and thought about legal negotiations as having

---

[24] "Thou shall not bear false witness against thy neighbor" is often read narrowly to refer to the prohibition of perjury in a courtroom, but some read it more broadly to prohibit lying more generally.

[25] *See* Bok, *supra* note 17; ARTHUR ISAK APPLBAUM, ETHICS FOR ADVERSARIES: THE MORALITY OF ROLES IN PUBLIC AND PROFESSIONAL LIFE (1999).

[26] Langevoort, *supra* note 8.

[27] The notion of the "zealous advocate" is found in the former ABA MODEL CODE OF PROFESSIONAL RESPONSIBILITY, *Canon 7*. In the current formulation of the ABA ethics rules, the MODEL RULES OF PROFESSIONAL CONDUCT, "zeal" has been dropped from the black-letter rules to the comments of *Model Rule 1.3*, now requiring "only" "reasonable diligence" in client representation. The comment to 1.3 provides that "[a] lawyer must act with commitment and dedication to the interests of the client and with zeal in advocacy upon the client's behalf. A lawyer is not bound, however, to press for every advantage that might be realized for a client." Whether the dropping of "zeal" from the black-letter to the comment has made any difference in any lawyer's behavior or conception of his role remains to be seen and studied. Most lawyers continue to routinely describe themselves as having a duty to be a "zealous advocate" in both litigation and transactional settings.

[28] For a moving account of how "adversarialism" and "patriotism" blind us to seeing that the other side wants the same thing as we do – victory – *see* MARK TWAIN, THE WAR PRAYER (1923), *reprinted in* ELIZABETH DVORKIN ET AL., BECOMING A LAWYER: A HUMANISTIC PERSPECTIVE ON LEGAL EDUCATION AND PROFESSIONALISM at 202 (1981).

something to do with justice (the outcome) – or at least fairness (the process) – and the effects on parties outside the negotiation? (I will return below to the relationship of the substantive law and legal entitlements as a measure of fairness in negotiation outcomes.) It is useful to ask from whose perspective we should take the measure of negotiation ethics. The partisan advocate? The tough deal-maker? The righteous justice seeker? The person on the other side of the negotiation table? The clients affected by any agreement reached? Those, other than clients, affected by a negotiated agreement? Philosopher and public ethicist Sissela Bok made an eloquent statement some years ago about looking at the limits of acceptable lying from the perspective of the person to whom less-than-truths are often told (the client, the child, the patient, the citizen), even when there is some institutionalized role or paternalistic justification (such as well-being of the other) offered. When, in the late 1970s, Bok documented the public's loss of faith in a number of American professionals, different professions responded differently.

Following the crisis of credibility the legal profession suffered after Watergate, the ABA's Kutak Commission suggested in 1980 that an enhanced duty of care, candor and conscionability might be appropriate in legal negotiations. Proposed *Model Rule 4.2* would have required lawyers to be "fair" in their dealings with third parties in negotiation, including full disclosure where necessary to "correct a manifest misapprehension of fact or law resulting from a previous representation made by the lawyer or known by the lawyer to have been made by the client."[29] And Proposed *Model Rule 4.3* would have required lawyers not to permit an "unconscionable" agreement to be agreed to.[30] These proposals were based on the notion that it was precisely because in a private negotiation session (unlike a court) there would be no third-party neutral (such as a judge) to monitor the truth-telling and general advocacy of the lawyers[31] that a duty of candor and fairness should be enacted by ethics rule to require honest behaviors when negotiators deal directly, but privately, with each other.

These proposals were defeated by an active professional debate that sought to preserve the caveat emptor culture of both the litigator and transactional dealmaker. A zealous advocate protects his or her own client and does not do the work of protecting the other side. As one commentator has put it, the adopted version of

---

[29] ABA Commission on Evaluation of Professional Standards, MODEL RULES OF PROFESSIONAL CONDUCT, DISCUSSION DRAFT 40 (1980), *Rule 4.2 (*discussing fairness to other participants); *see* discussion of subsequent history of this rule in Geoffrey C. Hazard, Jr., *The Lawyer's Obligation to be Trustworthy When Dealing With Opposing Parties*, 33 S.C. L. REV. 181 (1981).

[30] *See* MURRAY L. SCHWARTZ, LAWYERS AND THE LEGAL PROFESSION 204 (2d ed. 1985).

[31] Murray L. Schwartz, *The Accountability and Professionalism of Lawyers*, 66 CAL. L. REV. 391 (1978).

Model Rule 4.1, prohibiting only "material" misrepresentations of fact or law, "unambiguously embraced 'New York hardball' as the official standard of practice."[32] Or, to put it another way, "the language of the market can be used as justification for *our* high prices"[33] or *our* hard-bargaining tactics.

For many ethicists, the question of whether a rule or precept requires too much of those regulated often forces such rules of "realism" to conform to actual practices. Thus, in 1983 those who defeated the more demanding rules of candor and fair dealing in negotiation suggested that ethics rules would not be effective in changing the ingrained practices of lawyer-advocates and would cause serious damage to the legitimacy of the remainder of the ethics rules.[34] Philosophers have noted the tendency, especially by lawyers, to create loopholes, exceptions and excluding definitions when the general rule or law is too "harsh," strict or impossible to live by.[35]

Thus, while philosophers and ethicists might begin with general -- and in some cases categorical -- rules such as "thou shalt not lie or dissemble" or "bear false witness,"[36] professional ethicists have tended to begin the inquiry within the narrower focus of professional-role morality[37] and the justifications that are offered for

---

[32] Gary Lowenthal, *The Bar's Failure to Require Truthful Bargaining by Lawyers,* 2 GEO. J. LEGAL ETHICS 411, 445 (1988). *See also* James J. Alfini, *Settlement Ethics and Lawyering in ADR Proceedings: A Proposal to Revise 4.1,* 19 N. ILL. U. L. REV. 255 (1999).

[33] Blackburn, *supra* note 5, at 7.

[34] *See* White, *supra* note 11 and critiques of White's position in CHARLES WOLFRAM, MODERN LEGAL ETHICS 726 (1986); Loder, *supra* note 12.

[35] "Whenever a law or rule is so strict that most people cannot live by it, efforts to find loopholes will usually ensue; the rules about lying are no exception." Bok, *supra* note 17, at 15. *See also* Heidi Li Feldman, *Codes and Virtues: Can Good Lawyers be Good Ethical Deliberators?,* 69 S. CAL. L. REV. 885 (1996) and the "bad man" in OLIVER WENDELL HOLMES, THE PATH OF THE LAW (1897).

[36] Ethicists, theologians and philosophers who have urged categorical rules against lying include St. Augustine, Thomas Aquinas and Immanuel Kant. Recognition that elimination of all falsehoods was impossible began with Blaise Pascal, Cardinal Newman and Erasmus. Grotius, a lawyer-philosopher, probably began the role-differentiated argument for justifying some lies. He argued that some people had no "right" to be told the truth – other liars, lawbreakers or wrong-doers. *See* Bok, *supra* note 17, at 34-49. Thus begins the utilitarian defense of lying or deceptions as being justified by consequences, weighing of costs and benefits and/or necessity of role.

[37] For key sources on the uses of "role morality" *see, e.g.* LON L. FULLER, THE MORALITY OF LAW 193 (Rev. Ed. 1969); DOROTHY MARY EMMET, RULES, ROLES AND RELATIONS (1966); Richard Wasserstrom, *Roles and Morality* in THE GOOD LAWYER: LAWYERS' ROLES AND LAWYERS' ETHICS (David Luban, ed. 1983); Stephen Pepper, *The Lawyer's Amoral Ethical Role: A Defense, A Problem and Some Possibilities,* 1986 AM. B. FOUND. Res. J. 613; Schwartz, *supra* note 31.

departures from more general personal morality.

In some sense it is odd that a profession that is, at least in principle, dedicated to the discovery of truth (at least in theory in adversarial trial settings) is equally committed to the notion that advocacy for a client allows a lawyer to tell less than the whole truth when negotiating outside of the courtroom setting. As more fully discussed below, the ABA's *Model Rules of Professional Conduct*, while prohibiting "false statements of material fact or law to third persons" (*Model Rule 4.1*), require slightly more candor when the lawyer is before a tribunal. For example, *Model Rule 3.3(a)(3)* requires a lawyer to disclose to a tribunal controlling legal authority, even if directly adverse to the lawyer's client, even where the opposing counsel is not aware of that authority. Thus, negotiation responsibilities are demarcated from the lawyer's trial obligations, and "private" negotiations are considered different from what goes on in the public settings of courts.[38]

The absence of a positive duty to be truthful or candid or to tell an opposing lawyer about a case or fact helpful to that lawyer's matter is based on the principle that each client is entitled only to one zealous representative – his or her own lawyer. The adversary system allows a client a zealous advocate, but no more. The other side has no duty to do the work of its opposite number in either a litigation matter (adversary ethics) or a transaction (market ethics, subject to the exceptions of substantive law discussed below, such as general fraud law and specific disclosure rules). All of this special "role morality" of the advocate is premised on a long-standing American belief (still unsubstantiated by empirical verification) that the adversary system is the best way to get at the "truth" or "justice," and the adversary system itself is best conducted when two advocates zealously present their own "best case" without regard for the case of "the other guy." Just how much of the practices of zealous, aggressive and inner-directed, (rather than other-directed) behavior should be justified on this single thread remains a hotly debated topic in legal ethics generally and dispute resolution ethics more specifically.[39]

---

[38] Whether you are cynical or not, the differences between duties of candor to the tribunal and duties to opposing counsel or other parties in a private negotiation appear to rest on the need to protect the judiciary from deciding a case on the basis of inaccurate law. Note there is no corresponding duty to tell a tribunal about an adverse witness or fact known to be adverse to the lawyer's case. Bad facts can make factually inaccurate decisions, but the harm is obviously considered less "harmful" in consequences to the larger public than a bad "law" decision. By this logic what transpires in a private negotiation is nobody's problem but the people engaged in the private negotiation. There is no duty to affirmatively tell an opposing lawyer of a case that would help his client if that lawyer has not discovered it.

[39] See e.g. David Luban, *The Adversary System Excuse* in Luban, *supra* note 37; Carrie Menkel-Meadow, *The Limits of Adversarial Ethics* in ETHICS IN PRACTICE (Deborah L. Rhode, ed. 2000); Carrie Menkel-Meadow, *The Trouble with the Adversary System in a Post-Modern, Multi-Cultural World*, 38 WM. & MARY L. REV. 5 (1996); DEBORAH L. RHODE, IN THE INTERESTS OF JUSTICE: REFORMING THE LEGAL PROFESSION, chs. 3 & 4 (2001).

Another philosophical defense of withholding information in negotiations is based, in part, on a "work product" or property-entitlement morality. Negotiators who do their own due diligence and investigation with respect to a transaction or litigation matter should not have to share their own superior information, based on their work and "moral desert" (called "deserved bargaining advantages"), with the other less-informed side.[40] In the opinion of some who have defended this claim, both in litigation and contractual or transactional contexts, a duty to disclose all that a negotiator learns about a case or deal to the other side would distort the incentives for lawyers and other negotiators to undertake their own investigations and fact gathering, and eventually sub-optimal amounts of information would be available in all negotiations.[41]

Thus, one important disciplinary dilemma for any consideration of ethical issues in negotiation is the domain from which we should we consider negotiation "ethics" (pure ethics or moral philosophy, economics, positive law and what is enforceable, or sociological or phenomenological accounts of what negotiation ethics as practiced actually are). Related to this dilemma has to be a concern about whether negotiation ethics rules should be designed with particular negotiators or negotiations in mind or whether rules and standards can be developed for more general social utility purposes. For example, should the ethics rules for corporate disclosures be different from used car sales or class action settlements,[42] and should the rules be dependent on whether the lawyer-negotiator is acting in a litigation or "advocate's" matter[43] or acting as a "non-advocate" in a transactional negotiation?[44]

---

[40] *See e.g. Alan Strudler, Moral Complexity in the Law of Non-Disclosure*, 45 U.C.L.A. L. REV. 337 (1997); Alan Strudler, *On the Ethics of Deception in Negotiation*, 5 BUS. ETHICS Q. 805 (1995). The standard case here is Laidlaw v. Organ, 15 U.S. (2 Wheat.) 178 (1817) in which the Supreme Court remanded to the trial court the question of whether a seller of tobacco had asked questions of a purchaser with superior knowledge (that the port of New Orleans was now open due to the end of the War of 1812 and the tobacco would fetch higher prices), suggesting that if he had not, the purchaser had no independent duty to reveal what he had learned.

[41] *See* Anthony Kronman, *Mistake, Disclosure, Information and the Law of Contracts*, 7 J. LEGAL STUDIES 1 (1978) for this economics based argument about disclosure and information incentives.

[42] Carrie Menkel-Meadow, *Ethics and the Settlement of Mass Torts: When the Rules Meet the Road*, 80 CORNELL L. REV. 1159 (1995).

[43] This distinction between the lawyer's duty to disclose or not depending on the forum was a hotly contested issue in the famous Kaye Scholer case where the law firm, supported in a opinion letter by noted legal ethicist Geoffrey Hazard, argued that since it was engaged in "advocacy" rather than a mere administrative regulatory reporting situation, it was entitled to withhold certain information and make argumentative claims, *see* Donald Langevoort, *What Was Kaye Scholer Thinking?* 23 LAW & SOC. INQUIRY 297 (1998); William Simon, *The Kaye Scholer Affair: The Lawyer's Duty of Candor and the Bar's Temptations of Evasion and Apology*, 23 LAW & SOC. INQUIRY 243 (1998). *Cf.* Geoffrey Hazard, *supra* note 29 (arguing for lawyer's duty to disclose and rectify client frauds

The Ethical "Rules": Model Rules of Professional Conduct

Most discussions of negotiation ethics begin with *Model Rule of Professional Conduct 4.1(a)* and *(b)* which provides that a lawyer shall *not*, in the course of representing a client,

> *make a false statement of material fact or law to a third person; or*
> *fail to disclose a material fact to a third person when disclosure is*
> *necessary to avoid assisting a criminal or fraudulent act by a client,*
> *unless disclosure is prohibited by Model Rule 1.6*
> [client confidentiality rule].

What the black-letter rule appears to require (a fair amount of candor) is in fact greatly modified by the Comments. For example, Comment 2 states that this rule applies only to "statements of fact," and "whether a particular statement should be regarded as one of fact can depend on the circumstances." "Opinions" (of value, of interpretations of facts or of case law) are not considered "facts" under this rubric. Most significantly, the Comment goes on to exempt from the operation of the rule three particular kinds of statements made in negotiation. According to the Comment, there are "generally accepted conventions in negotiation" (a nod to the sociological phenomenology of negotiation) in which no one really expects the "truth" because these statements are not "material" statements of fact. These are (1) estimates of price or value placed on the subject of the transaction, (2) a party's intentions as to an acceptable settlement of a claim and (3) the existence of an undisclosed principal, except where non-disclosure of the principal would otherwise (by other law) constitute fraud.

Thus, the exception in the Comment defines away, as not material, several key notions of how negotiations are conducted, including inflated offers and demands (otherwise known as "puffing" and "exaggeration"), failure to disclose "bottom lines" or "reservation prices," and non-disclosure of a principal (say Donald Trump or Harvard University) where knowledge of who the principal is might raise a price or demand, on the assumption that the principal has deep pockets. In addition, as

---

in certain circumstances).

[44] *See* Schwartz, *supra* note 31 for this distinction between the lawyer as "advocate" in the courtroom and "non-advocate" in negotiations. This distinction probably does not work as well as Schwartz originally intended the functional differentiation. Even in transactional negotiations lawyers are clearly "advocates" for their clients, and they certainly are so in negotiations conducted "in the shadow of litigation." *See* Robert Mnookin & Lewis Kornhauser, *Bargaining in the Shadow of the Law: The Case of Divorce*, 88 Yale L. J. 950 (1979).

discussed more fully below, Comment 1 suggests that while a negotiating lawyer "is required to be truthful when dealing with others on a client's behalf," a lawyer does not have an *affirmative duty* to inform an opposing party of relevant facts (subject to some further qualifications that failure to act or to correct may sometimes constitute a misrepresentation and that substantive law may, in fact, sometimes require affirmative disclosure -- see Comment 3).

A simple reading of these provisions demonstrates how indeterminate and unhelpful the formal rules of professional responsibility are. First, the claim that there are "generally accepted conventions" is an empirical one, without substantiation in the text of the Comments. Who, in fact, generally "accepts" these conventions? All lawyers? Lawyers who subscribe to the conventional, adversarial and distributive models of negotiation? Many lawyers would probably "accept" even more classes of "untruthful" or less-than-full-disclosure statements in negotiations. Consider, for example, the "tough negotiators" described by Herb Cohen and James Freund.[45]

In an important test of these "generally accepted conventions," Larry Lempert asked 15 legal and ethics experts how – under these rules -- they would resolve several important disclosure dilemmas, including lying about authorized limits given by the client, lying about the extent of a personal injury as a plaintiff's lawyer during a litigation negotiation, exaggerating an emotional distress claim in a torts negotiation, and failing to correct the other side's misimpression about the extent of injuries.[46] Not surprisingly, there was relatively little consensus among the experts about how far a lawyer-negotiator could go in lying about, deceiving or misrepresenting these issues, all of which could be argued to be within the three "generally accepted conventions" excluded from the general non-misrepresentation rule.

Recently, I have added to this list the following negotiator's ethical dilemmas in a variety of lawyer-negotiator ethics CLE programs. Consider what you would do in the following situations, in addition to those four listed above.

> 1. Just before the closing of a sale of a closely held business, a major client of the business terminates a long-term commercial relationship, thereby lessening the value of the firm being purchased and you represent the seller. Do you disclose this information to the buyer?

---

[45] HERBERT COHEN, YOU CAN NEGOTIATE ANYTHING (1980); JAMES FREUND, SMART NEGOTIATING: HOW TO MAKE GOOD DEALS IN THE REAL WORLD (1992).

[46] Larry Lempert, *In Settlement Talks, Does Telling the Truth Have Its Limits?*, 2 INSIDE LITIGATION 1 (1988) *reprinted in* LEGAL ETHICS 421-427 (Deborah L. Rhode & David Luban, eds., 2d ed. 1992).

2. On the morning of a scheduled negotiation about a litigation matter, you receive notice that your request for a summary judgment has been denied. The lawyer for the other side is coming to your office and clearly has no notice of the judge's ruling. Do you disclose it before negotiating or seek to "close the deal" quickly with an offer before the other side finds out about the summary judgment decision?

3. You receive, by mistake, a fax addressed to all of the counsel on the other side of a multi-party litigation. It contains important and damaging-to-the-other-side information that would enhance your bargaining position. What do you do?

4. A defense lawyer in a government-agency-employment matter demands a secrecy-and-confidentiality clause in a cash settlement of the claim. Can you agree, without disclosing what you know but the defense lawyer does not seem to know -- that there is an applicable Public Records Act that will make the settlement accessible, through a properly filed request by anyone with standing under the statute?

5. In a large money-demand case the defendants come to the table with a check written to your client and say they have no other available funds and this is a one-time-only offer. You and your client can accept this check or they will walk away. What do you do?

6. In seeking to see if your client's liability on a lease can be mitigated by having the new tenants move in early, you ask the landlord's lawyer for permission to contact the new tenants and he replies he has already asked the new tenants if they wanted to move in early and they said no. You independently find the new tenants, and they say they were never contacted by the landlord and would be happy to move in early. What do you do with the knowledge that the landlord's lawyer lied to you?[47]

7. In a hotly contested contractual negotiation the other side

---

[47] All of these "hypotheticals" are real and are based on inquiries I have had from practicing lawyer-negotiators about what they should do, under the currently existing ethics rules for lawyer-negotiators.

demanded the inclusion of a particular clause that your client did not want to agree to but finally did when it was made a "deal-breaker." The final draft of the contract, prepared by the other side, arrives at your office without the disputed clause, which you know the other side really wants included in the final deal. What do you do?[48]

8. Can a plaintiff's lawyer "threaten" a class action when she knows the plaintiff does not want to bear the risks, costs and stress of being a named class member? Can a lawyer "threaten" she will bring a lawsuit in a pre-filing negotiation, when she knows the client does not want to be part of a lawsuit?[49]

Remarkably, time after time, use of these hypotheticals reveals exactly the opposite of what Comment 2 to *Model Rule 4.1* so baldly states. In my experience, there are virtually no "generally accepted conventions" with respect to what should be done in these situations. Different negotiators bring to the table different assumptions of what they are trying to do, and with those assumptions come different ethical orientations.

Thus, for those who are "tough negotiators" or who see legal negotiation as an individual maximization game, whether in the litigation or transactional context, most of the deceptions above can be justified by reference either to "expectations" about how the legal-negotiation game is played, or to the lawyer's obligation to be a zealous advocate and not to "do the work" of the other side. For those lawyers who are concerned about making a good agreement "stick" – the instrumentalists – some disclosure is considered desirable (for example, in the scenarios above that describe the omission of a contract provision or the failure to correct misimpressions) because of a concern that some failures to disclose might lead to a post-hoc attack on the agreement (fraud, negligent misrepresentation, unilateral mistake).

Still others regard negotiations as opportunities for problems to be solved and so are more likely to thoughtfully consider the later impact of doing some of the

---

[48] This situation is drawn from an inquiry made to the American Bar Association Standing Committee on Ethics and Professional Responsibility, *see* ABA Standing Committee on Ethics and Professional Responsibility, Informal Op. 86-1518 (1986), *Notice to Opposing Counsel of Inadvertent Omission of Contract Provision, Feb. 9, 1986* and was recently used by me, Professor Eleanor Myers and Janet Perry, Esq. in a CLE Program, *Lies, Damn Lies and Misimpressions; Ethical Challenges in Negotiation and Mediation,* at the National Association of College and University Attorneys, 41st Annual Meeting, June 20, 2001.

[49] *See* Thomas F. Guernsey, *Truthfulness in Negotiation*, 17 U. RICH. L. REV. 99, 105-107 (1982); ABA Standing Committee On Ethics and Professional Responsibility, Informal Op. 1283 (1973) (opining that it is unethical for a lawyer to threaten a class action when he knows the plaintiff is unwilling to bear the costs of such an action).

things suggested above. These lawyers ask questions such as these: What would be gained or lost by revealing to the landlord's lawyer that you know he is lying? How can you honestly return the helpful fax and honestly disclose what you now know, but perhaps shouldn't use? When should clients be consulted about these ethical choices, as *Model Rule 1.2* suggests they should be, at least about some matters? And those who value their reputations and/or see negotiations as a method for achieving some modicum of justice outside of courtrooms or in deals would disclose (as some ethics opinions and fraud cases say they must) the omitted contract clause and the diminished value of the purchased company (is it a material matter?).

Thus, there are no "generally accepted conventions" in negotiation practice, especially as more and more lawyers and law students are trained in the newer canon of *Getting to Yes*,[50] collaborative, integrative and problem-solving negotiation models. Who decides what "generally accepted conventions" are? The drafters of the ethics rules, without empirical verification? And, more importantly, why should "generally accepted conventions" prevail in an ethics code? Are we looking at "generally accepted conventions" in other areas of the Rules? (See discussion of *Model Rule 3.3 (a) (3)* above.) The answer is usually "no" – we require lawyers appearing before tribunals to reveal adverse authority without regard to what "accepted conventions" of advocacy might suggest, e.g. that each side should do its own research and it is up to the judge or her clerk to find the cases.

After some discussion, the Ethics 2000 Commission of the ABA, tasked with amending the *Model Rules of Professional Conduct*, suggested virtually no "material" changes to *Model Rule 4.1*. Even though many commentators requested clarification of the candor obligations under *Model Rule 4.1*, the Ethics 2000 Commission declined to change any language in the black-letter rule. Some changes to the Comments make explicit that substantive fraud and "other applicable law" may, in fact "trump" the general language of *Model Rule 4.1*. Comment 2, for example, has been modified by the addition of the word "ordinarily" to the statement that estimates of price are not subject to the misrepresentation-of-fact requirement. This modification references the fact that in some contexts, under some other laws, some misstatements about the "generally accepted conventions" of price, value, and so forth could constitute actionable misrepresentation, and "lawyers should be mindful of their obligations under applicable law to avoid criminal and tortious misrepresentation."

In addition, changes to Comment 1 recognize that "partially true but misleading" statements, as well as failures to act, may also constitute a misrepresentation under some state or other laws[51] if they are "the equivalent of

---

[50] Roger Fisher & William Ury, Getting to Yes: Negotiating Agreement Without Giving In (2d. ed. 1991).

[51] *See* Donald C. Langevoort, *supra* note 8.

affirmative false statements."[52] Most significantly, Comment 3, which deals with the prohibition in *Model Rule 4.1 (b)* against the lawyer's assistance in a client's criminal or fraudulent acts, has been modified to reflect a growing consensus that lawyers have an increasing duty to reveal client crimes and frauds when necessary to prevent physical and some economic harm, and to either withdraw from representation or rectify certain crimes and frauds, especially when required to rectify a fraud committed upon a tribunal.[53] These proposed changes to the *Model Rules* have been adopted by the ABA House of Delegates, but do not become "law" with disciplinary consequences unless adopted by the appropriate body in each state, either court, legislature or disciplinary agency.

Model Rule 4.1, however, is not the only rule that might be seen to govern negotiation ethics.[54] *Model Rule 1.2*, defining the scope of legal representation, has implications for negotiation behavior in several respects. First, *Model Rule 1.2* provides for allocation of decision-making responsibility between lawyers and clients in any representation. Clients are to make decisions about the "objectives of

---

[52] ABA MODEL RULES OF PROFESSIONAL RESPONSIBILITY, *Model Rule 4.1*, Comment 1.

[53] See ABA MODEL RULES OF PROFESSIONAL RESPONSIBILITY, *Model Rule 3.3* (clarifying what is a fraud against a tribunal, removing "materiality" requirement, and when frauds must be rectified, even in circumstances requiring divulging of confidential information, ordinarily protected by *Model Rule 1.6*. Amended *Model Rule 1.0(m)* defines "tribunal" to include binding arbitration. Even this change continues the differentiation between negotiation candor (governed by *Model Rule 4.1*) and candor before a court or other "tribunal" (governed by *Model Rule 3.3*) so the *Model Rules*, by definition, recognize different duties of candor in different loci of the lawyer's work. This distinction is formally acknowledged in the Comments to *Model Rule 2.4*, which recognizes the role of lawyers as third-party neutrals without specifying much about their ethical duties. Complicated issues about the applicability and relation of these sections will remain, however. Is a mediation, for example, conducted in a court-annexed program, more like a "tribunal" because of its location (and not its function, since it does not "adjudicate" anything) or more like an unassisted negotiation? Does this change if the mediator "evaluates" on the basis of legal arguments and cases the lawyers present in the mediation? We still have to question what the rationale is for not requiring the same duty of candor with "third parties" (*Model Rule 4.1*) that is required before a tribunal (however inartfully defined in *Model Rule 1.0(m)*). For a more detailed treatment of these issues see CPR-Georgetown Commission on Ethics and Standards in ADR, *Proposed Model Rule of Professional Conduct for the Lawyer as Third Party Neutral* (1999); Carrie Menkel-Meadow, *Ethics and Professionalism in Non-Adversarial Lawyering*, 27 FLA. ST. U. L. REV. 153 (1999) and Carrie Menkel-Meadow, *The Silences of the Restatement of the Law Governing Lawyers: Lawyering as Only Adversary Practice*, 10 GEO. J. LEGAL ETHICS 631 (1997).

[54] The recent passage by the American Law Institute of the RESTATEMENT (THIRD) OF THE LAW GOVERNING LAWYERS (2000) suggests that there will be other sources for state rules about appropriate negotiation behavior and disclosure requirements; see e.g. Sections 66 (Disclosure of information to Prevent Death or Bodily Harm), 67 (Using or Disclosing Information to Prevent, Rectify or Mitigate Substantial Financial Loss, and 98 (Statements to a Non-Client).

representation," and lawyers, in consultation with clients, may make decisions about the "means" of representation. Some states now require, and others recommend, that this consultation about "means" should include counseling about and consideration of the forms of dispute resolution that should be considered in any representation, including negotiation, mediation, arbitration or other forms of "appropriate dispute resolution."[55] Some might think that such consideration of "means" should extend to the different models of negotiation or different strategies now possible within the growing sophistication about different approaches to negotiation.[56]

Second, and most importantly, *Model Rule 1.2* requires the lawyer to "abide by a client's decision whether to settle a matter" and thus requires the lawyer to transmit settlement offers to the client, especially in conjunction with the requirements of *Model Rule 1.4(a)(3)* that a lawyer "shall keep the client reasonably informed about the status of the matter" and *Model Rule 1.4(b)* that a lawyer "shall explain a matter to the extent reasonably necessary to permit the client to make informed decisions regarding the representation."[57] *Model Rule 1.2(d)* also admonishes lawyers not to counsel a client to engage in and not to assist the client in conduct the lawyer knows is fraudulent or criminal, and thus, once again, the Rule implicates the substantive law of fraud and crimes. Lawyers may not assist clients in such activities, and thus, what constitutes a misrepresentation in a negotiation is dependent on tort and criminal law, outside the rules of professional responsibility. The lawyer may, then, be more restricted in 1.2 (d) by what other laws prohibit clients from doing than by what the lawyer might be restricted from in 4.1.

Beyond these more specific requirements, *Model Rules 8.3* and *8.4* can be and have been invoked with respect to the lawyer's duty to be honest and fair in

---

[55] For a summary and review of state variations of this requirement and different state forms of *Model Rule 1.2*, see Marshall J. Breger, *Should An Attorney Be Required to Advise A Client of ADR Options?*, 13 GEO. J. LEGAL ETHICS 427 (2000).

[56] *See e.g.* ROBERT H. MNOOKIN ET AL., BEYOND WINNING: NEGOTIATING TO CREATE VALUE IN DEALS AND DISPUTES (2000).

[57] MODEL RULES OF PROFESSIONAL CONDUCT, *Rule 1.4*, Comment 2: "A lawyer who receives from opposing counsel an offer of settlement in a civil controversy . . . must promptly inform the client of its substance unless the client has previously indicated that the proposal will be acceptable or unacceptable or has authorized the lawyer to accept or to reject the offer." The clear violation of this language (and its applicable predecessor in Massachusetts, the Code of Professional Responsibility, EC 7-8 and EC 9-2) in the movie The Verdict, 1982 (Attorney Frank Galvin fails to transmit a large settlement offer to his clients, the family of a comatose victim of medical malpractice and thus, gets to go to trial, win the case and redeem himself from his alcoholism) demonstrates how little clients may understand of their "rights" to participate in the negotiation process. *See* Carrie Menkel-Meadow, *Can They Do That? Legal Ethics in Popular Culture: Of Character and Acts*, 48 UCLA L. REV.1305 (2001).

negotiation. *Model Rule 8.4* states that "it is professional misconduct for a lawyer to (c) engage in conduct involving dishonesty, fraud, deceit or misrepresentation," once again incorporating by reference not only substantive standards of legal fraud and misrepresentation, but also suggesting that certain forms of dishonesty or breach of trust or "serious interference with the administration of justice"[58] (especially when a "pattern of repeated offenses" exists) may subject a lawyer to discipline for his deceptive or other fraudulent actions in negotiations. *Model Rule 8.3* requires a lawyer who "knows that another lawyer has committed a violation of the *Rules of Professional Conduct* that raises a substantial question as to that lawyer's honesty, trustworthiness or fitness as a lawyer" to report such misconduct to the appropriate professional authority. Thus, lawyers who repeatedly deceive or play some versions of negotiation "hardball" or "hide and seek" may be subject to discipline for their professional misconduct, though such misconduct is rarely reported.

Several other ethics rules, seldom invoked, also have possible applicability to the conduct of negotiations. *Model Rule 4.4* prohibits lawyers from using means that have "no substantial purpose other than to embarrass, delay or burden a third person," and thus requires lawyers to exercise some degree of "care" toward third parties (such as opposing parties in a negotiation, whether in litigation[59] or transactional settings).

Finally, *Model Rule 5.6* prohibits any agreement "in which a restriction on the lawyer's right to practice is part of the settlement of a client controversy." This section is intended to prevent a common practice of defense counsel settling favorably with one plaintiff under the condition that the plaintiff's lawyer be barred from representing similarly situated plaintiffs, or alternatively, be prevented from using evidence or other information acquired in one representation in another, as a condition of the settlement.[60] Despite this rule, many civil settlements, including those in class-action and mass-torts settings, have utilized such conditions. Despite this ethics rule, a variety of case rulings now place substantial restraints on what some lawyers can negotiate for in settlements of civil matters, such as statutory attorneys fees.[61]

---

[58] MODEL RULES OF PROFESSIONAL CONDUCT, *Rule 8.4*, Comment 2.

[59] In at least one famous case, a noted and aggressive litigator has been barred from further pro hac vice appearances in litigation in Delaware due to his repeated harassment and arrogance in conducting depositions in litigation.

[60] *See* ABA Standing Committee On Ethics and Professional Responsibility, Formal Op. 00-417, Settlement Terms Limiting a Lawyer's Use of Information (opining that a lawyer may not, without violating *Model Rule 5.6 (b)*, agree to a settlement in which the lawyer is prevented from using information gained during that representation in later representations against the same party).

[61] *See e.g.* Evans v. Jeff D., 475 U.S. 717 (1986) (permitting one party to require the waiver of

Regardless of, or perhaps because of, the general inefficacy of the lawyers' general rules of professional conduct to affect negotiation ethics, various groups have suggested more specialized rules or guidelines. Recently, the ABA Section of Litigation has proposed a set of Ethical Guidelines for Civil Settlement Negotiations (for lawyers who "represent private parties in non-mediated settlement negotiations in civil cases"[62]), making suggestions about such matters as relations with clients, disputes with clients, fees, disclosures to third parties and other clients, but most specifically, authorizing a variety of conditions on settlement, including secrecy and confidentiality of agreements and information or evidence disclosed in the context of settlement negotiations[63] and the return of documents or evidence discovered during litigation or settlement talks. These provisions, drafted with a litigator's (and mostly "defense") view toward settlement-agreement issues, are unlikely to have the force of law in any jurisdiction.

Negotiation Ethics and the Law: Fraud, Misrepresentation, Good Faith and Required Disclosures

Because enforcement of lawyer ethics codes, usually, but not exclusively, through administrative disciplinary bodies, is so rare, due in large measure to the difficulties of reporting and proving essentially private "he-said/she-said" conversations, most actual regulation of lawyer "ethics" in negotiation is through more formal law – the law of contract, the law of fraud and, in some particular substantive areas, laws requiring disclosures of certain kinds. Most actual regulation of what lawyers may say and do in a negotiation occurs in post-hoc challenges to agreements already made that one party seeks to void. The problem with this approach, as many commentators have noted,[64] is that it converts the question from

---

statutory attorneys fees as a condition of settlement); Buckhannon Board & Care Home Inc. v. West Virginia Dept of Health and Human Resources, 532 U.S. 598 (2001) (disallowing statutory attorneys fees when party "voluntarily" changes its behavior pursuant to filed lawsuit, where there is no judicially entered consent decree or other order from the "voluntary" settlement).

[62] ABA Section of Litigation, Task Force on Ethical Guidelines for Settlement Negotiations, *Ethical Guidelines for Settlement Negotiations*, May 2002 Draft, *Preface*.

[63] The "secrecy" of negotiated agreements is one of the major "macro" ethics issues in this field. Many commentators suggest that making settlement agreements, especially in important cases with public significance, is itself "unethical" in the larger jurisprudential sense; *see e.g.* David Luban, *Settlements and the Erosion of the Public Realm*, 83 GEO. L. J. 2619 (1995). Thus, whether the rule "permits" or "prohibits" lawyers from agreeing to privatize or make secret or confidential their settlement agreements raises both "macro" jurisprudential ethical issues as well as more "micro" behavioral issues in negotiation.

[64] See Blackburn, *supra* note 7.

"Is it ethical to dissemble in negotiations?" to "Is it legal?"[65] The issue recapitulates the age-old jurisprudential question of the relationship of ethics and morality to positive law.[66]

A few significant cases have set the outer boundaries of what lawyers can and cannot do in civil-litigation negotiations. In *Virzi v. Grand Trunk Warehouse & Cold Storage*[67] a federal court found that a lawyer has an obligation to disclose the death of his client in a claim for personal injuries before settling the claim (under doctrines, see below, that require the correction of "material" misimpressions of the other side).[68] In probably the most famous case in the negotiation canon, *Spaulding v. Zimmerman*,[69] the court overturned a negotiated settlement of a personal injury claim on behalf of a minor when it learned that the defendant's lawyers had failed to reveal a life-threatening injury discovered in a defense-ordered medical examination.

Oddly enough, the courts in *Virzi* and *Spaulding* expressed very different assumptions about the negotiation process. The *Spaulding* court overturned the settlement only because the plaintiff was a minor and the settlement therefore needed court confirmation. Consequently, the failure to disclose the additional injury was really a fraud upon the court, not a misrepresentation made in the context of ordinary litigation negotiation. The court suggested that if the plaintiff had not been a minor, his only recourse would have been a malpractice action against his lawyer or doctor.

In contrast, the *Virzi* court expressed distaste for the conception of litigation negotiation as a place where one "deals with his adversary as he would deal in the

---

[65] For a good review of this issue, see G. Richard Shell, *When Is It Legal to Lie in Negotiations?*, Sloan Management Review 93 (Spring 1991).

[66] *See, e.g.* H.L.A. Hart, Law, Liberty and Morality (1963); Lon L. Fuller, The Morality of Law.

[67] Virzi v. Grand Trunk Warehouse & Cold Storage, 571 F. Supp. 507 (E.D. Mich. 1983).

[68] But note that several subsequent formal ethics rulings have taken different positions on this issue. ABA Standing Committee On Ethics and Professional Responsibility, Formal Op 94-387 (Sept. 26, 1994) suggests that a lawyer can settle a claim the lawyer knows is barred by the statute of limitations, without revealing that fact(?) or (law?) [see differences in *Model Rules 4.1* and *3.3* on this dividing line in negotiations and before tribunals discussed supra] to the other side because of the lawyer's duty to fully represent his client. But in ABA Standing Committee On Ethics and Professional Responsibility, Formal Op. 94-397 (Sept. 18, 1995) the Standing Committee endorsed *Virzi* because when a client dies, the claim is transferred to a new party and thus the lawyer's role is changed and must be disclosed to opposing counsel. *See* discussion of the differences in disclosure requirements in these cases because of court involvement vs. private negotiations in Geoffrey C. Hazard, Jr., et al., The Law and Ethics of Lawyering 5-13 (3d ed. 1999).

[69] Spaulding v. Zimmerman, 116 N.W. 2d 704 (Minn. 1962).

marketplace."[70] Despite these two cases, many other courts have diverged widely on the kinds of failures to disclose during litigation settlement discussions that can be used to subsequently attack settlement agreements,[71] and so case law in this area provides little further guidance on the vagueness of our profession's ethical rules.

Ironically for a profession whose ethical code is based on assumptions of the lawyer as advocate and litigator,[72] the applicable legal standards for transactional negotiation may be slightly more enlightening, as they are based on the law of contract, fraud and tort. The best modern treatment of the relationship of the law of fraud to commercial negotiations (with some applicability to other forms of negotiation, including litigation) is G. Richard Shell's review in his recent book, *Bargaining for Advantage: Negotiation Strategies for Reasonable People* (1999). Shell reminds all negotiators that, at the very least, they must obey the law – negotiated agreements should not run afoul of fraud or other laws that can cause agreements to be overturned. Thus, legality provides at least a floor for what can be done, even if ethics (and morality) aspire to higher levels of stairs and escalators.

While the standard elements of fraud – knowledge, misrepresentation of a material fact on which the listener reasonably relies and from which the victim suffers damages – should be well known to most lawyers, what is less well known is how these elements have changed in recent years, as state legislatures, courts and other regulatory bodies (including the National Commissioners on Uniform State Laws and the American Law Institute) broaden the meaning and scope of many of these elements. Thus, as the most significant example, fraud no longer is constituted only by an "affirmative" misstatement or misrepresentation. As the ethics rules discussed above and modern fraud law (both statutory and common law) now recognize, silence, incorporation of another's misapprehension, failure to correct bad information and failure to disclose certain required matters, may all now constitute fraud (or actionable intentional or negligent misrepresentation in certain

---

[70] Virzi, 571 F. Supp. At 512.

[71] *See* cases collected in NATHAN CRYSTAL, PROFESSIONAL RESPONSIBILITY: PROBLEMS OF PRACTICE AND THE PROFESSION 348-359 (1996) and DEBORAH RHODE, PROFESSIONAL RESPONSIBILITY: ETHICS BY THE PERVASIVE METHOD (2d ed. 1998).

[72] When the Kutak Commission originally proposed *Model Rules 4.2* and *4.3* requiring greater obligations of fairness and candor in negotiations, it was attempting to enact Judge Rubin's 1975 proposals, *see* Rubin, *supra* note 12, with particular attention to the lawyer's role as "the instrument of the transaction [who] should be the guardian of integrity [and whose duty should include disclosing those facts] of which the opposing party was obviously ignorant and which might affect the integrity of the transaction." Hazard, *supra* note 29, at 192. These proposals were defeated by bar groups fearful of increased civil liability, which they feared they would be subject to by enhanced ethical standards.

circumstances).

In specific areas such as real estate transactions, automobile sales and securities law, "half-truths" and failure to disclose certain information will constitute grounds for revoking contracts and agreements or for awarding damages and, in some cases, penalties. In addition to particular subject matter disclosures, certain relationships may also give rise to increased disclosure obligations (such as where there is a fiduciary relationship between negotiators). Fraudulent behavior can give rise to remedies that include revocation or rescission of negotiated agreements, civil damages and penalties and – in cases of criminal fraud – fines and even imprisonment.[73]

With all the attention that truth-telling has received in recent political scandals ("it all depends on what the meaning of *is* is"), law reformers have focused on the various definitions and meanings of "materiality." Former President Clinton's lawyers claimed that certain of his consensual and non-governmental-employee sexual relationships were not "material" or "relevant" to the disclosure and discovery obligations in the Paula Jones sexual harassment case.[74] These arguments about the extent of "materiality" for disclosure, discovery, fraud and perjury issues have their analogues in all negotiation ethics. Recall that both *Model Rule 4.1* and *3.3* had "material" modifiers in their requirements for candor to third parties and tribunals. Many commentators have argued for the elimination of "materiality" modifiers in these and other legal requirements precisely because there is no easy way to determine what is "material" in particular negotiation settings. Is the existence of another offer "material" to the price a negotiator might pay for some property or for a company?[75] Some have argued that this information is "ancillary to the deal," not

---

[73] Rex R. Pershbacher, *Regulating Lawyers' Negotiations*, 27 ARIZ. L. REV. 75 (1985); Charles Craver, *Negotiation Ethics: How To Be Deceptive Without Being Dishonest/How to Be Assertive Without Being Offensive*, 38 S. TEX. L. REV. 713 (1997).

[74] *See, e.g.* BOB WOODWARD, SHADOW: FIVE PRESIDENTS AND THE LEGACY OF WATERGATE (1999) (revealing strategy of President's counsel, Bob Bennett).

[75] In one CLE program I participated in, a well-known and successful lawyer claimed it was not improper to "fabricate" the existence of another offer to increase the pressure on a negotiator to make a higher offer. His justification was that "other offers are ancillary" to the intrinsic value of the item being bargained for and it is the buyer's duty to fully investigate and know what he is willing to pay, regardless of what others might pay. As a frequent real estate purchaser myself, I find this ludicrous. The value of real estate in the highly inflated markets in which I have purchased property is totally dependent on what other people offer (especially in multi-offer settings, common in both California and Washington DC). Thus, in my view, "other offers" are not ancillary to the deal, but material measures of the market price, and a "false" offer, in my view, is an actionable falsehood. See Shell's treatment of "bid-rigging" in the highly inflated New York real estate market, where one bidder on property uses "shills" to make several low-ball offers as a way of inducing a seller to revalue and drop her price, Shell, *supra* note 4 at 224-225. *See also* Kabatchnik v. Hanover-Elm Building Corp., 103 N.E. 2d 692 (Mass. 1952) (tenant successfully sued for fraud

part of the "value" of the item bargained for and besides, the value of a bargained-for item is itself a matter of opinion, not fact.

Although, in general, American law does not require affirmative disclosure of all "relevant" facts or information in a negotiation, and does not even require a general duty of "good faith" in commercial negotiations, duties both to negotiating "opponents" and to other "third parties" have, in fact, been increasing, and the lawyer who negotiates without a firm grasp of the changing standards does so at his or her peril.[76] "Good-faith bargaining" in labor law, for example, has not required much actual movement in the negotiation process, but the law does require that certain topics must be addressed and that certain practices ("bribes," promises) cannot be engaged in during the negotiation process.[77] Similarly, although courts are reluctant to look inside the substantive negotiations of either civil or criminal matters, there has been increasing scrutiny of lawyers' good-faith participation in court-annexed negotiations, through pre-trial conferences, mediation, early neutral evaluation and other court-mandated processes designed to encourage parties to engage in a negotiation process to settle cases. Lawyers have been sanctioned for failing to participate, and for participating in bad faith (i.e. listening to other parties' disclosures but not disclosing information, or failing to send the client with settlement authority to appropriate meetings).[78] Some commentators have urged the adoption of ethical, procedural or substantive rules to require honest, good-faith participation in negotiation and mediation processes.[79]

---

where landlord extracted high rent increase by claiming he had another tenant who would pay more, and tenant later learned it was a bluff).

[76] For example, some courts have begun to increase the circle of liability, including malpractice claims, to protect more or less "innocent" third parties who rely on what lawyers say to each other, in a variety of different contexts; *see Symposium, The Lawyer's Duty and Liability to Third Party*, 37 S. TEX. L. REV. 957-1315 (1996).

[77] *See, e.g.,* National Labor Relations Act, Sections 8(a) 5, 8(b)3 and 8(d) and the corresponding case law, which define "bad faith" both in terms of highly subjective and contextualized findings of fact and per se indicia of bad faith, without authorizing the National Labor Relations Board or courts to impose particular substantive standards. Per se violations include failure to provide financial information for wage bargaining, failure to "meet and confer," and unilateral changes in the employment relation (wages, hours or terms of employment). Certain subjects of bargaining are denominated "mandatory" subjects of bargaining in any labor negotiation. These include wages, hours and other "terms and conditions of employment." See General Electric Co. 150 NLRB Dec. 192 (1964), aff'd, NLRB v. General Electric, 418 F. 2d 736 (2d Cir. 1969); See also, DOUGLAS RAY ET AL., UNDERSTANDING LABOR LAW 198-217 (1999).

[78] *See, e.g.,* G. Heileman Brewing Co. v. Joseph Oat Corp., 871 F. 2d. 648 (7th Cir. 1989).

[79] *See, e.g.,* Edward Sherman, *Court-Mandated Alternative Dispute Resolution: What Form of Participation Should be Required?* 46 SMU L. REV. 2079 (1993); Kimberlee K. Kovach, *Good*

Issues of good faith and fraud come together when legal negotiators parse the meanings of making a "misrepresentation," especially when advising each other about appropriate strategies. Guides to negotiation often advise negotiators to "deflect" questions or "answer different questions" or "change the subject" as a way of avoiding giving an incomplete or untruthful answer to a specific request for information. Increasingly these tactics can give rise to post-hoc fraud or misrepresentation claims, especially if there is evidence that a negotiator deliberately refused to answer, "recklessly" gave incomplete or incorrect responses or allowed some incorrect fact or information to stand (such as the declining financial condition of a company or the condition of physical property, especially when one negotiator is in a superior position to know "the truth"). Recall that the Federal Rules of Civil Procedure now require litigators to correct information provided in discovery, such as depositions or interrogatories, when the lawyer has reason to know the facts have changed.[80]

Both case law and ethics opinions now make it clear that negotiators cannot take advantage of incorrect assumptions or mistakes of the other side when they know such mistakes are being made. In what has become standard fare for both contracts classes and negotiation courses, the case of *Stare v. Tate*[81] demonstrates what can happen when one side knowingly takes advantage of another. After a hotly contested divorce negotiation, especially focused on the value of some stock, the wife's lawyer made an arithmetic error in the final agreement, undervaluing the stock to be divided. The husband's lawyer knew about the error but didn't say anything. Later when the husband gleefully told his ex-wife how he had gotten the better of her in the negotiation, the court was so offended it reformed the divorce agreement (rather than rescinding or remanding it or suggesting a possible legal malpractice action against the wife's lawyer).

Other obvious cases of "bad faith" have been actionable too. Parties or lawyers who use the negotiation process unfairly (such as to get access to trade

---

Faith in Mediation – Requested, Recommended or Required? A New Ethic, 38 S. Tex. L. Rev. 575 (1997).

[80] Fed. R. Civ. P. 26(e). A party is required to supplement and amend disclosures and responses to discovery when the party learns that "in some material respect the information disclosed is incomplete or incorrect." (This version of the rule retains a "materiality" requirement). (Effective December 1, 2000.)

[81] Stare v. Tate, 98 Cal. Rptr. 264 (Cal. App. 1971). *See also* Comm. On Prof'l Ethics, Assn of Bar of City of NY, Op. No. 477 (1939) (the lawyer should reveal arithmetic errors made by the other side, even if they cause disadvantage to the lawyer's own client and even if the client doesn't want to reveal).

secrets,[82] or to tie up a competitor with negotiations while proceeding to do other business) may have to pay partial damages for lost opportunities or lost value, even if a whole agreement is not overturned.

Thus, while not often discovered, acts of bad faith in negotiation can be corrected by overturning agreements or by awarding damages in cases of completed contracts and negotiations. *Stare v. Tate* was an easy case because of the husband's need to get his "last licks" in. More often, such fraud will be harder to prove, dependent on often-conflicting testimony about what was said, and in these cases such questions often go to a jury for factual determination. Nevertheless, lay juries have often proven to have lower tolerance for hardball negotiation tactics than judges or lawyer disciplinary bodies who may be inured to "conventional" lawyer negotiation tactics.

Specific statutes, administrative regulations and even common law rulings now require particular kinds of disclosures that are more demanding than more general fraud law. California was the first state to require a list of specific disclosures with respect to sales of residential real estate. Now common in many other jurisdictions, such disclosures include matters such as conditions of parts of housing (for example, the roof), easements, and the existence of toxic substances (for example, lead paint, asbestos and radon). Federal law has long required a higher standard of candor in the issuance and sale of corporate securities.[83] Certain relationships are now defined as requiring greater disclosure in contract or other negotiations through the creation of either fiduciary or "repeat player" relationships (such as with insurers, franchisors, banks, and so forth). When it is obvious that one party has superior or exclusive information about a material fact, some courts will require disclosure.[84]

There are attempts to provide general rules of candor, either affirmatively or negatively, by definitions of actionable fraud or misrepresentation, such as in the Restatements of Torts (Sect. 551 (2)-Concealment and Non-Disclosure) and Contracts (Sect. 161-Misrepresentation). Increasingly, however, what is required of

---

[82] *See* Smith v. Snap-On Tools Corp. 833 F. 2d. 578 (5th Cir. 1988).

[83] *See* Securities Act Rule 10(b)-5, 17 C.F.R. § 240.10b-5 (2002).

[84] In the hotly debated case of Zimpel v. Trawick, 679 F. Supp. 1502 (W.D.Ark. 1988) a buyer with knowledge of likely oil on the property took advantage of a poor and ailing older woman to purchase her property at less than "market" value (if she had known the true value of her land). The court ruled that the buyer's failure to disclose what he knew amounted to fraud. The case has resulted in a great deal of commentary, not only because it challenges conventional ideas about what negotiators should disclose in arms-length bargaining situations, but because here it was the buyer, not the seller, who had superior information.

negotiators (in both transactional and litigation settings) may be governed by the context or subject matter of the negotiation, the parties to the negotiation, the jurisdiction in which the negotiation takes place (because states define fraud and mandatory disclosure law differently) and any number of other specialized rules or relationships that may make general rules of law and behavior less and less reliable for the well-prepared negotiator. Knowledge of specific and specialized duties and responsibilities in negotiation in different contexts is becoming more essential for a negotiator to be effective and successful (in the sense of crafting a negotiated agreement with staying power). At the same time, as others have suggested, having your own clear moral compass or negotiation "integrity"[85] may, in the end, provide guidance in those all-important moments where there is no clear rule of behavior and what is called for is judgment.

Fairness in Negotiation – Personal, Professional and Systemic

As this review of the governing ethical rules and legal principles makes clear, there are very few clear guideposts for what is considered ethical behavior in negotiation. We have competing conceptions of what the purpose of negotiation is – to accrete the most "gain" for a particular client, to solve a legal problem or to achieve a "just" result for all those affected by a dispute or transaction. We have competing theories about how those goals might be achieved – economic-efficiency theories, property-entitlement approaches, moral-desert justifications, empirically based phenomenological accounts of how the world is and how it can't be changed, limited professional-role exceptions to more general moral conceptions, and a sociological account of the enormous variability of contexts in which all negotiations, including legal ones, are conducted. These competing views have prevented us from developing any meta-theory of negotiation ethics.

Each of these theories or accounts of how negotiation is conducted resists another narrative about how negotiation could be. All theories and ethical prescriptions invoke stances with respect to whom the negotiation serves (the client in the professional-role story or the unequal bargaining "victim" in the justice-and-equity story) and who should be responsible for negotiated outcomes (the lawyer as loyal representative in the professional-role story or all of us as human beings in the larger-justice narrative). Like all attempts at human theorizing, negotiation ethics arguments are filled with assumptions about the quality of and malleability of human nature. The adversarialists or professional-role theorists tend to see negotiation as inherently distributional, competitive and economically wealth-maximizing. Those

---

[85] *See* Shell, *supra* note 4, at 17-18, for a discussion of "personal integrity" as one of the key elements of effective negotiation, suggesting that integrity in negotiation means "consistency" – a thoughtful set of principles and personal values that can be explained and defended to other people.

who see negotiation as an opportunity for mutual gains, for learning and for human coordination to solve human problems, see trust,[86] non-strategic communication and sharing (not division) of resources as animating principles. Is one world view more correct than the other or do they co-exist? And if they do co-exist, how do we choose our actions in negotiations?

More importantly, our assumptions and starting points can become self-fulfilling prophecies. As Sissela Bok noted when she began her study of lying and "moral choice in public and private life," the expectation of the telling of "little white lies" accumulates and in turn lowers our expectations of each other and the system as a whole. So, when we come to "expect" that "generally accepted conventions" of negotiation allow us to puff, dissemble, and exaggerate our preferences and needs, our "expectations" soon are experienced as requirements. It becomes dangerous to tell the truth or say what you or your client "really" wants, because you will be taken advantage of.

Perhaps this is why mediation and alternative approaches to negotiation have developed at this point in American legal history. Some of us have recognized that exaggerations and failure to disclose accurate information do not produce "efficient information searches" but instead produce "economic waste"[87] (both in transaction costs and in the sub-optimal arrangements arrived at in strategically deceptive processes). Others have noted that in addition to efficiency and economic concerns to the parties, there may be "externalities" – effects on others affected by, but not parties to, a particular negotiation. Thus, we now go to mediators and other third-party neutrals, in part, to be sure that important information is shared with someone who can help us determine if a better negotiated outcome is possible than the one we could accomplish on our own.[88] The decision to choose to work with a mediator is something of a recognition that our unassisted negotiation behaviors are faulty and we need some help. So much strategic behavior, perhaps, has lessened our trust in our fellow professionals, even those playing by the same rules or "generally accepted conventions."

Suppose then, as a thought experiment, we imagine ethical standards of

---

[86] For a powerful argument that we do not study and theorize adequately about the human trust that is essential for legal and other relationships to flourish, *see* Carol M. Rose, *Trust in the Mirror of Betrayal*, 75 B.U. L. REV. 531 (1995). As lawyers why are we more "programmed" to study what goes wrong (litigated cases) than to examine what goes smoothly (the millions of successfully completed contracts, legal relationships etc.)?

[87] *See* HOWARD RAIFFA, LECTURES ON NEGOTIATION ANALYSIS (1996) (describing the economic efficiencies of FOTE (Fair Open Truthful Exchange) in negotiations and the inefficiencies of POTE (partial exchange) and worse with lying and deception.

[88] *See* Howard Raiffa, *Post-Settlement Settlements*, 1 NEGOTIATION J. 9-12 (1985).

negotiation that approach what we hope are the standards parties and lawyers use with mediators[89] – probably greater candor than is presented to opposing lawyers in unassisted negotiations. We know that mediators seek to discover the real needs and interests of parties to look for complementary, as well as conflicting, preferences in relation to the other side. Mediators also seek to make agreements that are feasible, realistic, enforceable and sustainable. The mediator, like a lawyer in negotiation, is judged, in part, by whether agreements made will last. Furthermore, some mediators explicitly consider the impact of any agreement on others affected by the agreement and see it as their duty to consider possible unfairness to parties not present in a particular negotiation.[90] Because negotiators seek to have mediators help them achieve good solutions, they probably approach the mediator with an expectation of "trust." Imagine if negotiators approached each other with that same expectation.

Consider the objections consistently made to proposals that lawyers approach each other in negotiation with an obligation to affirmatively tell the truth. (1) The obligation would be unfair to the lawyer of greater technical skill[91] or his client. Heaven forbid that outcomes in negotiation turn on the "merits" rather than the lawyer's exercise of technical skill. (2) The requirement would reduce incentives to investigate information.[92] If a negotiator could trust the disclosures of the other side, information costs might actually decrease because each negotiator would have to investigate only that about which the other side wouldn't have superior knowledge. (3) It would be impossible to monitor whether someone was telling the truth (and what is "truth" in negotiation anyway?). Perhaps. It would be difficult, but who knows? We have never tried it. We do, however, allow legal actions for fraud and misrepresentations in all other forms of contracting (not to mention medical malpractice, corporate securities and a variety of other specific contexts). Should

---

[89] The issue of how much candor an attorney owes to a mediator is itself a difficult, and as yet unregulated, question. While we hope and some assume greater candor with mediators, especially in caucus settings, many mediators are also experiencing the same dissembling or "gaming" of the mediation process as occurs in strategic negotiations. *See* Chap. V (Alfini) of this volume on ethics in mediation; *see also* Carrie Menkel-Meadow, Pursuing Settlement in an Adversary Culture: A Tale of Innovation Co-Opted or "The Law of ADR," 19 FLA. ST. L. REV. 1 (1991) (fearing and predicting that adversarial processes will "co-opt" ADR, rather than having ADR ideology transform litigation practices, especially when ADR is moved into the formal court system).

[90] This is a more controversial aspect of mediation ethics but it offers an interesting analogue for negotiators to consider whether they have any responsibility to parties other than their own clients in negotiating agreements. For an eloquent statement of the mediator's accountability to parties outside of a mediation, in the environmental context, see Lawrence Susskind, Environmental Mediation and the Accountability Problem, 6 VT. L. REV. 1 (1981).

[91] Hazard, *supra* note 29.

[92] Kronman, *supra* note 41, Strudler, *supra* note 40.

lawyers be less subject to monitoring than others who negotiate (real estate agents, stockbrokers)? What is wrong with this picture?

Some years ago a savvy real estate broker[93] suggested to me that regardless of what ethical and disciplinary authorities do, eventually all middle persons would likely have to become more "honest" as increased information available on the Internet (about pricing, availability of products, land and services – not to mention laws and other people's form contracts) would make it more and more possible for "clients" to represent themselves in increasing numbers of transactions. Even if clients will never feel comfortable representing themselves in some kinds of legal negotiation, they are likely to be able to discover an increasing amount of information on their own. "Armed" with more knowledge and information, both clients and lawyers will be able to plant what I have called "trust land-mines" in all negotiations. I teach all negotiators to follow the advice often given to cross-examiners at trial – ask the other side questions "you already know the answer to." (As a mediator, I do this all the time, to both parties.) This technique enables you to learn how much you can trust the other side (so you can frame your "tit for tat" cooperation or defect strategy)[94] and at the same time requires the other side to wonder how much you already know[95] (this should instill a little honesty).

Consider how much more efficient and just, as well as fair, negotiations might be if the presumptive expectations about information and the purposes of negotiation were reversed. Clients would say what they really wanted and be required to produce what information they had to support their claims.[96] As Howard Raiffa and other negotiation analysts have explained, we already do this in negotiations with people we already trust (spouses, friends, children, some other relatives, business partners, colleagues and some adversaries – "intimate adversaries" who know everything about each other), with those who are required to reveal information (fiduciaries, doctors and accountants), with people who interact with us frequently

---

[93] *See* Carrie Menkel-Meadow, *The Art and Science of Problem Solving Negotiation*, TRIAL, 48 (June 1999) nn. 17.

[94] *See* Axelrod, *supra* note 9.

[95] As modern rules of civil discovery require more and more disclosure of information in formal litigation, the question of disclosure in negotiation is more often a question of timing than whether to disclose at all. (Of course, achieving a negotiated agreement is one way to avoid having to reveal some information that would come out later if there is a trial, so strategic considerations of information disclosure will continue to play a role in the interaction of litigation and negotiation in dispute negotiations.)

[96] This is currently the standard for "automatic disclosures" under FED. R. CIV. P. 26.

("repeat players"), and with those who have learned to negotiate differently.[97]

Much social-psychological research demonstrates that "fairness" principles explain a lot of negotiation behavior, even with strangers.[98] Thus, we must consider how, in fact, our expectations of ethics in negotiation are different in variable settings and wonder why our ethics "rules" enact the most minimal of obligations. Consider that we do specifically demand more candor, honesty and fairness in some settings and transactions than in others (civil discovery rules, corporate securities, statements signed under penalty of perjury). Might rules of ethics in negotiation (including both obligations of fairness in disclosure and justness of treatment and outcome) more formally recognize these different settings? Consider the following spectrum of negotiation settings in descending order of trust and possible disclosure and fairness obligations.[99]

1. Fiduciaries
2. Continuing relations[100] (on-going contractors, employees, family members)
3. Legally created relations of good-faith or truth-telling (e.g. banks and other lenders or credit agencies in Truth-in-Lending; residential-real-estate sellers; stockbrokers and so forth)
4. Special relationships of parties to each other
-- professionals-clients (lawyers, accountants, doctors, others)
-- regulable grossly unequal relations[101] (considering relative

---

[97] *See* Raiffa, *supra* note 87 at 7. Anne M. Burr, *Ethics in Negotiation: Does Getting to Yes Require Candor*, 56 DISP. RES. J. 8 (July, 2001).

[98] *See* reports of distributions in the "Ultimatum" game popular in negotiation laboratory settings, where parties evenly distribute dollars even where one could claim more; *see* MAX H. BAZERMAN, JUDGMENT IN MANAGERIAL DECISION MAKING (4th ed. 1998), ch. 5 for a discussion of how fairness concerns permeate negotiation choices and evaluation of decision.

[99] Others have suggested more variable tests for disclosure requirements in different settings, *see, e.g.*, Langevoort, *supra* note 8, at 100-125, for differentiation of disclosure requirements in the corporate securities context dependent on whether representations are made in face-to-face settings or in market settings and to which audiences – sophisticated market analysts, employees and managers, competitors or consumers and the general public.

[100] Of course, this category raises the question of how to act when we seek to terminate an on-going relationship, either in the commercial or in the personal sphere. Note that some courts have been imposing heightened requirements for truthfulness and good faith on employers in negotiations with potential, as well as actual, employees in some contexts; *see* Berger v. Security Pac. Info. Sys. Inc. 795 P.2d 1380 (Colo. Ct. App. 1990). *See also* Deborah A. DeMott, *Do You Have the Right to Remain Silent? Duties of Disclosure in Business Transactions*, 19 DEL. J. CORP. L. 65 (1994).

[101] From a jurisprudential perspective, many have argued that issues of equity and equality should

sophistication of parties, repeat players v. one-shotters,[102] "incompetent" negotiators)
5. Relative access to necessary information to conduct negotiation
6. Open market transactions (permitting some of the marketing and "optimistic" statements that accompany sales efforts, with fraud and other general contract rules as background norms)
7.Class-action-litigation negotiation (recognizing greater responsibilities for fairness and disclosures when large numbers of people are affected)[103]
8. Individual contested lawsuits

Note that our current ethical rules of disclosure and fairness take the last category as the model for all others (as the lawyers' ethics code takes as its model for most rules the lawyer as advocate) when it is likely that the other categories of negotiation relationships constitute the greater number of actual negotiations. So why don't we have ethics rules, standards or at least guidelines that are more responsive to the actual complexities of what we do?

Part of the answer to this question lies in our inability to confront the really big question about the objectives of negotiation. One scholar after another[104] and a few practitioners[105] have lamented our inability to come to grips with the fairness of what we do in negotiation. While the adversary system or market justifications of limited truth-telling and client wealth-maximization seem to be enacted in our current rules, other models are possible (e.g. fairness and justice in negotiation, "equity" or "do no harm"). As suggested above, concerns about both process disclosure and

---

trump values of economic wealth-maximization in suggesting proper rules of disclosure of legally relevant material; *see, e.g.,* KIM SCHEPPELE, LEGAL SECRETS: EQUALITY AND EFFICIENCY IN THE COMMON LAW (1988); Loder, *supra* note 12.

[102] *See* Marc Galanter, *Why The Haves Come Out Ahead: Speculations on the Limits of Legal Change*, 9 L. & SOC'Y REV. 95 (1974).

[103] *See* Menkel-Meadow, *supra* note 42.

[104] For a thoughtful catalogue of all of the elements of fairness in negotiation, *see* Cecilia Albin, *The Role of Fairness in Negotiation*, 9 NEGOTIATION J. 223 (1993), outlining issues of structural, process, procedural and outcome fairness.

[105] For a thoughtful review of ethics issues in negotiation from a practitioner's perspective, *see* Michael H. Rubin, *The Ethics of Negotiation: Are There Any?* 56 LA. L. REV. 447 (1995) (arguing for a single standard of lawyer honesty in both litigation and non-litigation negotiations and tracing the history of negotiation ethics and disclosure rules including the differences between the civil law and common law systems).

substantive fairness could be made to turn on contexts and different "locations" of negotiation, dependent on the relationships of the parties (such as repeat or long-term relationships, obvious bargaining superiority as in commercial-consumer relations[106] or special relationships governed by special duties). The claims of greater efficiency and/or just deserts of our more conventional withholding patterns are simply not empirically demonstrated. We could just as easily assert these and other claims for evaluating the effectiveness of negotiation behaviors and negotiated outcomes.

Alternatively, we could ask more searching questions of all negotiations:

1. Is the structure of the negotiation fair? (Are all relevant parties included? Are the physical space and time appropriate for the negotiation? Are there significant structural imbalances between the parties -- economics, information, quality of experts/representatives?)

2. Are the rules of process clear to all? (Are issues for the agenda transparent to all? Do all the parties understand the "rules of the game" being played? Has one party controlled the development of the rules or the agenda in an unfair way?)

3. Do the parties understand their respective purposes and goals? (Does it matter if the parties do not share distributive or integrative-problem-solving orientations to the negotiation? Is one party trying to create a long-term relationship while the other is not?)

4. Do the parties have a "fair" shot at achieving a mutually satisfactory solution, or is one party "unfairly" positioned to take advantage of the other side?

5. Do the parties share expected criteria for assessing outcomes? (One on-going debate in assessing the justice of outcomes in negotiation and other forms of dispute resolution involves the extent to which negotiated solutions must track legal entitlements.[107] In my own

---

[106] This factor has led many to suggest reforms in American arbitration law to reflect the different bargaining power of consumers and large commercial enterprises in compulsory arbitration clauses found in contracts; *see, e.g.,* Richard E. Speidel, Consumer Arbitration of Statutory Claims: Has Pre-Dispute (Mandatory) Arbitration Outlived Its Welcome?, 40 ARIZ. L. REV. 1069 (1998).

[107] *See, e.g.,* Jacqueline M. Nolan-Haley, *Court Mediation and the Search for Justice through Law,* 74 WASH. U. L.Q. 47 (1996); Robert Condlin, *"Cases On Both Sides": Patterns of Argument in Legal Dispute-Negotiation,* 44 MARYLAND L. REV. 65 (1985); *Cf.* Carrie Menkel-Meadow, *Whose Dispute Is It Anyway? A Philosophical and Democratic Defense of Settlement (In Some Cases),* 83 GEO. L. J. 2663 (1995).

suggested formulation, I would posit a rule that a lawyer should not agree to a negotiated outcome that he or she knows will cause substantial injustice to the other party or to a third party. In other words, a lawyer should do no unnecessary harm,[108] but I do not think all negotiated agreements have to track the law to be "just." Parties to a negotiation often seek to accomplish an outcome that is fair for them individually, while a statute or case was designed to deal with either the "average" or typical situation or the different facts of other parties.)

6. To what extent should the justice of negotiated outcomes be measured by principles outside of the parties' own criteria – equity, equality, need, social welfare, precedential value, likelihood of enforcement and effects on others.

7. Should we assess the justice or fairness of a negotiated outcome after we see what it actually accomplishes, after the agreement is reached? (Does this implicate another contested issue of macro negotiation ethics – should all negotiated agreements be available for public scrutiny and not be permitted to be made secret or confidential?)[109]

These broader ethical concerns might be difficult to craft into formal disciplinary rules (though I have tried – see Appendix F),[110] but to ask these questions is to consciously reflect on the questions of what negotiations are supposed to accomplish and what the lawyer's role is in doing this work on behalf of others.

Stuart Hampshire, the social philosopher, has recently suggested that since we will never agree "on the [substantive] good," we can at least agree on the process by which a civilized society decides how it will act to decide the good, by "hearing the other side (audi alteram partem)." This approach is process as justice.[111] Perhaps

---

[108] *See* Carrie Menkel-Meadow, (Proposed*) The Ten Commandments of Appropriate Dispute Resolution: An Aspirational Code*, in *Ethics and Professionalism in Non-Adversarial Lawyering*, 27 FLA. ST. L. REV. 153, 167 (1999).

[109] *See, e.g.,* Carrie Menkel-Meadow, *Public Access to Private Settlements: Conflicting Legal Policies*, 11 (6) ALTERNATIVES TO HIGH COST OF LITIG. 85 (June 1993); Frances Komoroske, *Should You Keep Settlements Secret?* TRIAL MAG. 55 (June 1999); David Luban, *Settlements and The Erosion of the Public Realm*, 83 GEO. L. J. 2619 (1995).

[110] *See Proposed Ten Commandments of Appropriate Dispute Resolution, supra* note 108.

[111] Hampshire calls it "Justice as Conflict," STUART HAMPSHIRE, JUSTICE AS CONFLICT (1999).

some will think that individuals or pairs of negotiators do not have the same obligations as the larger society to have "fair" processes in their negotiations of "private" matters, but I am not one of those. Single pairs of negotiations combine to form the "ethical climate" or "culture" of the whole. To the extent that we are all morally responsible for the "system" of negotiation that we create by our individual professional behaviors, might we not do better by at least asking these questions of ourselves? Shouldn't we aim for "generally accepted conventions" that seek to do the best for all parties,[112] rather than for only a few. Perhaps then we could, in the words of one modern ethicist, "live so that we can look other people, even outsiders [as well as ourselves] in the eye."[113]

---

[112] Yes, I am substituting utilitarian ethics (and an ethic of care); *see, e.g.,* Carrie Menkel-Meadow, *What's Gender Got to Do With It? The Morality and Politics of an Ethic of Care*, 22 N.Y.U. REV. L. & SOC. CHANGE 265 (1996) for a more limited professional-role ethics.

[113] Blackburn, *supra* note 5, at 128.

Chapter IX

Ethics for Provider Organizations

By Sharon Press

Introduction

While the ethical requirements for individual mediators and arbitrators have a long history,[1] it is only recently that the field has begun to look at the ethical requirements that should apply to provider organizations as distinct from the ethical requirements of the neutrals themselves. One of the first challenges in discussing "provider organization" ethics is to define what the phrase encompasses. A second challenge relates to the range of services that provider organizations may offer and the possibility that there may be different ethical obligations and expectations across these different ADR processes.

Definition of Phrase "Provider Organization" and Scope of Chapter

For purposes of this chapter, a "provider organization" is defined as an entity (or individual) that supplies or furnishes a dispute resolution neutral upon request.[2] This definition is meant to include both private (e.g., law firms with mediation divisions or dispute resolution firms) and public (e.g., courts or agencies) providers of neutrals. To the extent that there are or should be different standards applied, they will be pointed out.[3] For ease of discussion, this chapter will primarily focus on

---

[1] *See* Chapter V for a complete discussion of ethical standards for neutrals.

[2] The CPR-Georgetown Commission on Ethics and Standards of Practice in ADR (CPR-Georgetown Commission) defined an ADR provider organization as "any entity or individual which holds itself out as managing or administering dispute resolution or conflict management services."

[3] The CPR-Georgetown Commission issued a single set of standards stating: "A single set of standards was preferred because the Principles address core duties of responsible practice that

mediation and arbitration providers, which by analogy should cover the gamut of services. This chapter will not cover ethical issues relating to the decision by public entities to refer cases to alternative processes.[4]

Brief History of the Development of Provider Organization Standards

While as early as 1988 attention was focused on issues related to provider organizations, the early focus was on the policy implications of referrals from public entities rather that on the ethical issues confronted by provider organizations. Some of examples of this work include the Law and Public Policy Committee that was created by Lamont Stallworth, then President of the Society of Professionals in Dispute Resolution (SPIDR, one of the predecessor organizations to the Association for Conflict Resolution). The Committee was charged with examining and reporting on key legal and public policy issues relating to alternative dispute resolution. The Committee members came from a variety of backgrounds and worked in a range of dispute resolution sectors, including family, labor and employment, civil rights, community, environmental, commercial and criminal. The first report, entitled *Mandated Participation and Settlement Coercion: Dispute Resolution as it Relates to the Courts,* was published in 1991.

In 1993 the second report, entitled *Public Encouragement of Private Dispute Resolution: Implications, Issues and Recommendations, Report #2 of the*

---

apply to most organizations in most settings. The single set of Principles may also help alert the many kinds of entities providing ADR services of their essential, common responsibilities."

[4] For a more complete discussion of some these issues, see *Public Encouragement of Private Dispute Resolution: Implications, Issues and Recommendations, Society of Professionals in Dispute Resolution, Report #2 of the SPIDR Law and Public Policy Committee* [hereinafter *SPIDR Law and Public Policy Committee Report #2*]. This report grappled with the issues relating to the ethical and moral dilemmas faced when public entities rely on private dispute resolution. Specifically, the report stated the problem in the following way:

> [The] changed relationship between the public and private sectors in dispute resolution raise a number of public policy concerns. A hallmark of our system of democratic government has been that private individuals, including disadvantaged or less powerful segments of our society, have access to the political and legal processes, and that governmental decision-making is open to public scrutiny. We need to ensure that these values are not eroded by the government's increasing reliance on private dispute resolution. We also need to ensure that all disputants have equal access to justice, that the public justice system is not interfering with the "marketplace" checks on quality by steering disputants to particular providers, and that private providers are held sufficiently accountable to the public when dispute resolution responsibility has been delegated to them. Finally, inadequacies in our public justice system should be addressed directly, and not bypassed by increased referrals to the private sector forums. *Id.* at 2-3.

Law and Public Policy Committee of SPIDR, was published. The subject matter was expanded to include both court and agency referrals. The focus of these reports was on the policy implications of the decision by the public entities to make a referral to a provider organization, not on the ethical issues faced by the provider organizations.

In 1991 the Center for Dispute Settlement and the Institute of Judicial Administration joined together to create *National Standards for Court-Connected Mediation Programs.* Funded by the State Justice Institute, the standards were developed with the involvement of an 18-member Advisory Board. The Board included judges, state and local court administrators, mediators and mediation program administrators, attorneys, academics, evaluators, and officers of professional court and mediation organizations. While related specifically to court-connected mediation programs,[5] the report addressed a variety of issues including access to mediation and the various court responsibilities, qualifications and selection of the mediators, the role of lawyers in mediation, funding of programs and compensation of mediators. Given the broad definition of "court-connected," some of the standards are relevant to the ethical issues for provider organizations and some relate more specifically to individual neutrals.

In 1995, in response "to the growing need on the part of policy makers, government organizations and others to specify qualifications that ensure skillful, honorable and effective dispute resolution,"[6] SPIDR published a follow-up to its widely acclaimed *First Commission on Qualifications Report.* The second report started with the recognition that dispute resolution takes place in a broad range of contexts, and therefore the need to set standards must be balanced against "defining a single set of standards which could potentially limit and stifle the very skills, creativity and strengths that make this diverse field so valuable and rewarding."[7] Given this report's focus, its relevance to provider organization ethics relates mainly to the provider organization's responsibility for the qualifications and competence of its neutrals.

Shortly after the publication of the *Second Commission on Qualifications Report,* SPIDR, in cooperation with the National Center for State Courts and supported by a grant from the State Justice Institute, convened a group of judges, court managers, dispute resolution program administrators, practitioners, and

---

[5] *National Standards for Court-Connected Mediation Programs* [hereinafter referred to as *National Standards*]. The *National Standards* defined court-connected as "any program or service, including a service provided by an individual, to which a court refers cases on a voluntary or mandatory basis, including any program or service operated by the court."

[6] *SPIDR Law and Public Policy Committee Report #2.*

[7] *Id.* at 1.

researchers to recommend guidelines to assist courts in developing meaningful, achievable, and fair standards for qualifying, selecting, training, and evaluating dispute resolution practitioners. The guidelines were developed to apply to court-connected dispute resolution services both when a court actually maintains a roster and when the court refers the case to an individual or service funded or operated by the court or any other organization or individual.[8] This report recognized that a court, as a provider organization, is responsible for ensuring competence and quality in dispute resolution, for establishing and maintaining competency standards, for establishing and maintaining training standards, and for assuring program quality.

In 1998, in recognition of the increased use of ADR within agencies, SPIDR's ADR in the Workplace Initiative developed and published a set of guidelines.[9] As with the earlier work done by SPIDR (which focused on the courts), many of the recommended guidelines focus on mediation program design. On the other hand, because some agencies not only design and allow for the use of mediation but also serve as the "provider" of these services, the report does provide some guidance on the ethics of provider organizations.

The first comprehensive attempt to develop a set of ethical guidelines for provider organizations came in 1996 via the CPR-Georgetown Commission on Ethics and Standards of Practice in ADR. In June 2000, the draft principles[10] were circulated for public comments. CPR issued the final principles in May 2002. The remainder of this chapter will focus on the specific ethical duties related to provider organizations, as developed by these various reports.

Ethical Issues

Duty to Ensure Fair and Impartial Process

There is general agreement that individual mediators and arbitrators have an ethical obligation to provide a fair and impartial forum for dispute resolution.[11] The ethical issue for a provider organization is one step removed; in other words, the duty

---

[8] *Qualifying Dispute Resolution Practitioners: Guidelines for Court-Connected Programs*, 1996, at ii.

[9] *Guidelines for Voluntary Mediation Programs Instituted by Agencies Charged with Enforcing Workplace Rights*, published in 1998 by the Society of Professionals in Dispute Resolution, ADR in the Workplace Initiative (hereinafter referred to as *Guidelines for Voluntary Mediation*).

[10] *CPR-Georgetown Principles for ADR Provider Organizations*, May 2002 (hereinafter referred to as *CPR-Georgetown Principles*).

[11] *See* Chapter V. Substantive fairness in mediation is an issue that still generates a fair amount of debate.

for the provider organization is to "ensure that ADR processes provided under its auspices are fundamentally fair and conducted in an impartial manner."[12] While no one disagrees with this obligation, how one demonstrates and fulfills this duty has resulted in an intense debate. The surrogate for fulfilling this obligation has become careful scrutiny of conflicts of interest. Specifically, ethical concerns have been raised in the context of repeat users and/or contractual arrangements.

Repeat Players

Inherent in the development of organizational private providers is their need to generate work to sustain the organization. And equally as inevitable is the desire to create relationships with sources of work, which creates the ethical issue of the "repeat player." In a free market society we applaud the positive aspects of allowing the market to determine who will thrive and who will not. The very foundation of the free market is that those who do a good job will be rewarded with repeat business. For a provider organization the tension is between the desire to create "good will" in order to be sought out for repeat business, and the need to maintain both the appearance and the reality of impartiality. Particular concern is raised when a party moves from casual repeat user of services to one with a formalized contractual arrangement.

In a sharp critique of the current ethical state of affairs of provider organizations, Cliff Palefsky posits that mandatory arbitration provisions fundamentally changed the protections of fairness and neutrality by removing the fair market mechanism.[13] He argues that providers of arbitration services need only satisfy the large corporation to obtain repeat business. In contrast, when arbitration is voluntary, there is no need for administrative or judicial oversight because the parties define and control the process, and thus can protect themselves.

Solicitation of arbitration cases by provider organizations becomes even more problematic when one considers that individual arbitrators are prohibited from soliciting cases for themselves.[14] Currently, provider organizations have marketing staff that solicits cases. Palefsky believes that the appropriate standard should be that "if arbitrators cannot directly solicit cases, their paid agents certainly cannot do it for them."[15] The counterargument is that the provider organization actually serves as a

---

[12] *CPR-Georgetown Principles*, Principle III.

[13] Cliff Palefsky, *Only a Start*, 7 DISP. RES. MAG. 18 (Spring 2001). Mr. Palefsky cites specific examples of practices by the American Arbitration Association, JAMS and the National Association of Securities Dealers.

[14] *Code of Ethics for Arbitrators in Commercial Disputes* (1977), Canon 1-B.

[15] Palefsky, *supra* note 13, at 21.

buffer between the neutral and the litigant, and therefore, different rules should apply.[16]

While the ethical standards pertaining to individual mediators (who do not make decisions) do not generally prohibit advertising[17] or "soliciting" cases, the potential for a conflict of interest exists, and the issue for provider organizations remains. Mediation provider organizations still need to be concerned about contracts with institutions for bulk future services, the use of an ADR contract provision in consumer contracts, and of course, any financial or other interest the provider organization may have in the outcome of the individual case.

Disclosure

The *CPR-Georgetown Principle* on this general topic addresses the issue from a disclosure standpoint:

> Principle V. Disclosure of Organizational Conflicts of Interest
> a. The ADR Provider Organization should disclose the existence of any interests or relationships which are reasonably likely to affect the impartiality or independence of the Organization or which might reasonably create the appearance that the Organization is biased against a party or favorable to another, including (i) any financial or other interest by the Organization in the outcome; (ii) any significant financial, business, organizational, professional or other relationship that the Organization has with any of the parties or their counsel, including a contractual stream of referrals, a *de facto* stream of referrals or a funding relationship between a party and the organization; or (iii) any other significant source of bias or prejudice concerning the Organization which is reasonably likely to affect the impartiality or might reasonably create the appearance of partiality or bias.
>
> b. The ADR Provider Organization shall decline to provide its

---

[16] Michael D. Young, *The Right Balance,* 7 DISP. RES. MAG. 18 at 23 (Spring 2001). Mr. Young specifically cites fee arrangements as a useful way provider organizations can shield neutrals. At JAMS, he states, "the neutral is generally only aware of the amount she is receiving as compensation for her services, not of the allocation of responsibility between or among the parties or if there have been any problem in collecting the fees."

[17] *See, e.g.,* Florida Rules for Certified and Court-Appointed Mediators, Rule 10.610, which states that "a mediator shall not engage in marketing practices which contain false or misleading information. A mediator shall ensure that any advertisements of the mediator's qualifications, services to be rendered, or the mediation process are accurate and honest."

services unless all parties choose to retain the Organization, following the required disclosures, except in circumstances where contract or applicable law requires otherwise.

While this is the standard that specifically addresses disclosure, the concept is also found in Principle II entitled "Information Regarding Services and Operations." Provision b requires the ADR Provider Organization to provide "clear, accurate and understandable information about... the relevant economic, legal, professional or other relationships between the ADR Provider Organization and its affiliated neutrals."

While some argue that the standards do not go far enough to protect consumers against these practices, others may view the requirement as "unduly burdensome, irrelevant and/or intrusive."[18]

Stake in the Outcome

Another approach to the ethical requirement to provide a fair and impartial process is to identify specific actions that would be inappropriate. For example, provider organizations that have investigative or enforcement functions, along with neutral service provision, should provide a separation of these functions.[19] Some would extend this obligation to not intervening in any subsequent dispute between the parties since the duty of neutrality is owed to both.[20]

Additional Responsibilities of Public Justice System

The SPIDR Law and Public Policy Committee posited that the public justice system may have some enhanced responsibilities for ensuring a fair and impartial ADR process based on the presumptive attributes of the public justice system that promote "deeply held societal values."[21] These values include equal access, established rules that promote equal treatment and dignity, qualified neutrals,[22] and a

---

[18] Margaret L. Shaw & Elizabeth Plapinger, *Ethical Guidelines*, 7 DISP. RES. MAG. 14 at 15 (Spring 2001).

[19] *See, e.g., Guidelines for Voluntary Mediation Programs Instituted by Agencies Charged With Enforcing Workplace Rights*, at 2, "Agency personnel should not act as mediators on cases on which they have investigatory or enforcement responsibilities."

[20] The American Arbitration Association (AAA) filed an amicus curiae brief in Circuit City Stores v. Adams, 121 S.Ct. 1302 (2001) even though they were the designated provider in the underlying case. *See* Palefsky, *supra* note 13, at 22. Palefsky cites this action along with AAA's defense of the action as a flaw in the CPR proposal that will rely on self-regulation for enforcement.

[21] *SPIDR Law and Public Policy Committee Report #2* at 3.

[22] *Id.* at 3. *See also, Qualifying Dispute Resolution Practitioners: Guidelines for Court-Connected*

diverse pool of neutrals.[23] In fact, "courts ultimately are responsible for the quality of justice rendered in disputes brought before them. This responsibility extends beyond the traditional adjudicatory function of courts to non-traditional dispute resolution processes that occur under the administration, supervision, or encouragement of the court."[24]

Procedures and Guidelines

Another way for a provider organization to ensure fairness in an ADR process is by establishing specific procedural rules and guidelines. For example, allowing disputants the right to be accompanied by an advisor "will likely increase the opportunity for them to make informed, voluntary, uncoerced decisions in the mediation process."[25]   If disputants are not represented, procedures can be developed to allow disputants to leave at any time, or to provide disputants with an opportunity to confer with an attorney or advisor before an agreement is finalized. A provider organization would also have the obligation to ensure that disputants using its services understood the procedures and their rights.

Specific guidelines relating to confidentiality become particularly important for court and agency provider organizations where there is a close relationship between the ADR process and other organization functions. In such situations, if the ADR process does not result in a full, final agreement, the court or agency typically will be required to resolve the dispute in another forum. This scenario underscores the importance of the provider organization protecting confidentiality. Examples of confidentiality policies include "prohibit[ing] agency staff from asking mediators to reveal confidential mediation communications (including offers made during mediation)…comment[ing] on the merits of the case, mak[ing] recommendations about the case, or… subpoenaing mediators or disputants to testify about confidential mediation communications. These policies should also prohibit disputants from compelling mediators to testify concerning confidential mediation communications, absent appropriate waivers."[26]

Duty to Ensure Quality and Competence of Neutrals

Programs, 1996, at page 2 (hereinafter referred to as *Guidelines for Court-Connected Programs*).

[23] *See SPIDR Law and Public Policy Report #2*, Recommendation #4.

[24] *Guidelines for Court-Connected Programs* at 5.

[25] *Guidelines for Voluntary Mediation*, at 3, 7.

[26] *Guidelines for Voluntary Mediation*, at 5.

The quality and competency of neutrals are topics that have received a lot of attention and ink over the years.[27] There is general agreement that the duty to ensure quality and competence of neutrals exists.[28] The problem tends to be in how to define "competence" and "quality." In fact, the importance of quality and competence is so clear that one set of standards states, "It is better to have no mediation program at all than to allow unqualified mediators to participate in the program. If mediators are not qualified, they are unlikely to be able to ensure that the mediation process is fair and disputants' rights to make an informed, uncoerced, and voluntary decision are safeguarded ... ."[29]

Over the years, several ways to analyze this topic have emerged:

– Process expertise v. substantive expertise[30]
– Absolute duty v. "rule of reason"[31]

In describing the responsibilities for courts as provider organizations, the document *Qualifying Dispute Resolution Programs* contains several references to quality and competence. In general, the work posits that different categories of cases may require different types and levels of skills. However, in all cases "courts are responsible for assuring the quality of the dispute resolution process when they make referrals to a process, practitioner, or provider; provide specific information on a practitioner or provider, or maintain a list of practitioners or providers."[32] Further the standards state that courts "should (1) adopt or create standards for ensuring the competency of practitioners and providers and (2) implement a plan for maintaining

---

[27] *See, e.g., Qualifying Neutrals: The Basic Principles, Report of the SPIDR Commission on Qualifications*, 1989 (hereinafter *Commission on Qualifications I*); *Ensuring Competence and Quality in Dispute Resolution Practice*, Commission on Qualifications, 1995 (hereinafter *Commission on Qualifications II*); *Qualifying Dispute Resolution Practitioners: Guidelines for Court-Connected Programs*, 1996; *Interim Guidelines for Selecting Mediators*, NIDR 1993; *Performance-Based Assessment: A Methodology, for use in selecting, training and evaluating mediators*, NIDR 1995.

[28] *Commission on Qualifications II*, at 21."Program competence should be measured, in part, by the manner, fairness and consistency by which it ensures the competence of practitioners working under its auspices."

[29] *Guidelines for Voluntary Mediation*, at 6.

[30] *See Commission on Qualifications I* and *Commission on Qualifications II*.

[31] *CPR-Georgetown Principles.*

[32] *Guidelines for Court-Connected Programs*, Recommendation 1.1.

these standards."[33] In addition, courts "should ensure that practitioners of particular dispute resolution processes have mastery of the specific set of skills and knowledge needed to conduct the process."[34]

The *CPR-Georgetown Principles* contain a similar provision, albeit a more qualified approach. Specifically, Principle I states, "The ADR Provider Organization should take all reasonable steps to maximize the quality and competence of its services, *absent a clear and prominent disclaimer to the contrary*" [emphasis added].

Methods for Assessing Competence

Once one accepts the provider organization's responsibility for ensuring some level of competence and quality, one must then determine *how* the organization ensures this. Some of the common methods used by provider organizations include requiring minimum levels of training or mentorship/apprenticeship (pre-provision of neutral services activity), assessing settlement rates (post-provision of neutral services activity) or merely providing information so that the market can determine the level of competence desired. In addition to competency and quality issues, provider organizations should also pay attention to the demographics of the neutral pool, particularly for public provider organizations.[35]

Training

Some guidelines handle the issue of specifying the content areas in which program neutrals must be knowledgeable as a means of providing competence. The *Guidelines for Voluntary Mediation Programs Instituted by Agencies Charged with Enforcing Workplace Rights* include this provision: "An agency should ensure that program mediators are knowledgeable concerning: 1) the mediation process and professional ethics; 2) employment discrimination law; 3) outcomes in typical discrimination cases; and 4) diversity issues. In addition, the agency should ensure that qualifications of mediators are reviewed on an ongoing basis."[36] Other standards contain more generic provisions that call for the provider organization to determine

---

[33] *Guidelines for Court-Connected Programs*, Recommendation 2.1.

[34] *Guidelines for Court-Connected Programs*, Recommendation 2.3.

[35] "Courts should ensure that qualification requirements do not systematically exclude dispute resolution practitioners from any racial, ethnic, or cultural groups." *Guidelines for Court-Connected Programs*, Recommendation 2.2. See also "Programs should honor principles of diversity in selecting practitioners," *Commission on Qualifications II*, at 20.

[36] *Guidelines for Voluntary Mediation*, at 6.

the needs and expectations of the parties and to train accordingly.[37]

Because of the specific challenges raised by court-connected ADR providers, the *Guidelines for Court-Connected Programs* contain many provisions relating to the courts' responsibility for training: "Courts should specify the content of the training curriculum, the methods of training used, and qualifications of trainers."[38] "Courts should require 'satisfactory completion' of the requisite hours of training in the dispute resolution process."[39] "Courts should determine whether specific substantive knowledge should be required of the practitioner in certain types of disputes."[40] The standards also stress the importance of specific training in dispute resolution – even for those who have other expertise.[41] An unresolved issue relating to the training requirement is how to assess whether the neutral has actually learned the required material. While some programs incorporate a written exam into the training, there generally is little confidence that a written exam can test a practitioner's competence.[42]

---

[37] "Programs should identify the extent to which the parties' needs and reasonable expectation in a particular practice context require specialized substantive knowledge and select and/or train practitioners accordingly." "Programs should set forth and make available to the public and practitioners the skills, knowledge and other attributes necessary for competent practice in that program. These elements should:

    a. be tailored to the context, process, culture and jurisdiction;
    b. be directly related to the values and goals of the program;
    c. be developed with input from all stakeholders;
    d. set forth the tasks involved in the practice and the type and
    extent of substantive knowledge required; and
    e. articulate fair procedures for selection, screening, assessment, retraining and dismissal
    of practitioners in the program."
Commission on Qualifications II, at 20.

[38] *Guidelines for Court-Connected Programs*, Recommendation 3.1.

[39] *Guidelines for Court-Connected Programs*, Recommendation 3.3.

[40] *Guidelines for Court-Connected Programs*, Recommendation 2.6.

[41] *Guidelines for Court-Connected Programs*, Recommendation 3.5: "Courts should not accept prior professional experience as a substitute for training in dispute resolution." *Guidelines for Court-Connected Programs*, Recommendation 3.6: "Courts should not accept prior training in a dispute resolution process as adequate to meet the court's training requirement unless the court determines that the prior training is substantially equivalent to that which is required by the court for the same process." *Guidelines for Court-Connected Programs*, Recommendation 2.4: "Courts should not rely solely on academic degrees or professional licenses in a specific discipline to determine the competency of practitioners."

[42] *Guidelines for Court-Connected Programs*, Recommendation 2.5: "Courts should not rely solely

Some attention has also been given to the premise that competence is an on-going requirement,[43] and one method of assuring such competence is through the imposition of continuing education requirements.[44]

Mentorship/Apprenticeship

Early on, there has been recognition that training alone may not be a complete indicator of competence.[45] The *National Standards* posited that skills might be acquired through training and/or experience.[46] The *Guidelines for Court-Connected Programs* report *encourages* practitioners to participate in experiential learning settings, and suggests that "experiential learning should be *required* for all mediators"[47] [emphasis added]. Experiential learning can take the form of required observations of mediation and/or mediation of cases under observation and supervision.[48] The debate continues about whether such a requirement should include an assessment of how the trainee does in his or her mentorship or whether it should be used exclusively to provide the trainee with experience.

---

on performance on written tests to determine the competency of practitioners."

[43] *Guidelines for Court-Connected Programs*, Recommendation 2.8: "Courts should periodically re-evaluate the competency of dispute resolution practitioners."

[44] *Guidelines for Court-Connected Programs*, Recommendation 2.10: "Courts should ensure that practitioners participate in continuing education to maintain currency in their field of practice." See also "Courts should continue to monitor the performance of mediators to whom they refer cases and ensure that their performance is of consistently high quality." *National Standards for Court-Connected Mediation Programs*, SJI 1991, Standard 6.5, [hereinafter *National Standards*] and "The ADR Provider Organization's responsibilities under this Principle are continuing ones, which require the ADR Provider Organization to take all reasonable steps to monitor and evaluate the performance of its affiliated neutrals." *CPR-Georgetown Principles*, I. c.

[45] *See Selection, Training and Qualification of Neutrals: A Working Paper*, National Symposium on Court-Connected Dispute Resolution Research: A Report on Current Research Findings - Implications for Courts and Future Research Needs, State Justice Institute (1994), at 155 - 171.

[46] *National Standards* 6.1.

[47] *Guidelines for Court-Connected Programs* 3.4.

[48] *See, e.g.,* Florida Rules for Certified and Court-Appointed Mediators, Rule 10.100 which requires individuals wishing to be certified by the Florida Supreme Court to observe a number of mediations conducted by a certified mediator and to conduct a number of mediations under observation and supervision.

Settlement Rates

Settlement rates can provide useful information to a provider organization, but should not be the sole criterion to determine mediator competence.[49] It may be appropriate for a provider organization to investigate both unusually low and unusually high settlement rates. While low rates *may* indicate inferior skills, extremely high settlement rates *may* indicate a coercive practice.[50] For arbitrators, it probably is appropriate for a provider organization to monitor requests for trial de novo (in court-ordered arbitration context).

Sliding Scale of Responsibility Based on Level of Control

As discussed in the introduction, the phrase provider organization encompasses a wide range of providers. At one extreme are direct service providers who offer dispute resolution services for profit, and at the other extreme are courts that maintain a list or roster of independent service providers or agencies that provide employees with access to staff neutrals. Intuitively, it seems right that there would be different provider responsibility expectations based on the extent to which the provider maintains control over the individual practitioner and the degree of choice the parties have over the selection of the neutral. Predictably, the standards consistently provide that the greater the involvement of the parties in selection of the process and the neutral, the less responsibility the provider organization has for ensuring competence.[51] However, for party control to have any meaning, the parties must be knowledgeable and informed. Therefore, some standards call for provider organizations to take responsibility for education of the parties.[52]

The *Commission on Qualifications II* found that programs have higher responsibility to ensure practitioner competence when either of the following two

---

[49] *National Standards* 11.4: "Settlement rates should not be the sole criterion for mediation program funding, mediator advancement, or program evaluation." *See also Guidelines for Court-Connected Programs* 2.9: "Courts should not use settlement rates as the sole factor to determine whether dispute resolution practitioners are retained."

[50] *Guidelines for Court-Connected Programs* at 15.

[51] *Guidelines for Court-Connected Programs* 1.2: "The scope of the court's responsibility for ensuring the competence of practitioners increases as the extent to which parties may choose a practitioner decreases." *CPR-Georgetown Principles* I.a.: "The ADR Provider Organization's responsibilities under Principle I and I.a decrease as the ADR parties' knowing involvement in screening and selecting the particular neutral increases."

[52] "Programs should seek to maximize party choice in the process whenever possible and have a responsibility to educate parties to enable informed use of dispute resolution." *Commission on Qualifications II* at 20.

conditions are met:

> a. The use of dispute resolution is mandated and the practitioner is
> assigned to the parties without their input; or
> b. The outcome of the process is binding.[53]

By definition, the public justice system may have an even greater responsibility for the quality of dispute resolution that is provided by neutrals to whom it refers.[54] This responsibility arises because individuals, by filing a case with a court, have opted for a particular form of dispute resolution - a form of dispute resolution to which constitutional protections attach. An "alternative" form of dispute resolution (such as mediation or arbitration) that takes place at the direction or suggestion of the court may be rightly seen as having the approval of the court. That likelihood creates the necessity of a greater responsibility. The *SPIDR Law and Public Policy Report #2*, highlighted this responsibility: "The programs and rosters of neutrals to whom cases are referred, as well as the administration of such programs and rosters, should be beyond reproach and subject to public scrutiny. This includes the criteria and processes that pertain to inclusion and expulsion from the rosters, demographic and geographic diversity, ongoing oversight and evaluation of the neutrals' performance, and the provision of skill-enhancing training to roster members."[55] The later *Guidelines for Court-Connected Programs* included discussions of "equal opportunity," "use of rotation lists," and the importance of deferring to party choice.[56] An even greater responsibility likely will attach if the

---

[53] *Commission on Qualifications II* at 20.

[54] *SPIDR Law and Public Policy Committee Report #2*, Recommendation #5:

> The public justice system should take responsibility for the quality of the dispute resolution provided by the neutrals to whom it refers cases. The less choice given to parties as to whether to participate and as to selection of the neutral, the greater the public justice system's responsibility for assuring quality of the process.

See also, SPIDR Law and Public Policy Committee Report #2, Recommendation #4:

> When the public justice system refers a case to private dispute resolution, it should maximize party choice of neutral, particularly whenever the neutral will receive a fee for service as a result of the public referral. This choice will be a check against the perception or practice of favoritism and should be lifted only in exceptional cases. Further, qualifications for the pool of neutrals to which parties are referred should be based on the type of experience and training likely to be related to quality of practice, thus encouraging a large and diverse pool.

[55] *SPIDR Law and Public Policy Committee Report #2* at 16.

neutrals are provided immunity from liability. [57]

Evaluations

Putting training and apprenticeship programs in place for initial qualification may not be sufficient. Some standards require that provider organizations make a commitment to collect information for evaluation purposes. For example, the *National Standards* state that "[p]rograms should be required to collect sufficient, accurate information to permit adequate monitoring on an ongoing basis and evaluation on a periodic basis."[58] Such information must be reported to the court only if the program is court-operated or accepts court referrals.[59] When the provider organization is "court-connected," there should be a clearly identified person or entity responsible for oversight and evaluation.[60] One way to accomplish the evaluation is by conducting periodic surveys of participants.[61] *The Guidelines for Voluntary Mediation Programs Instituted by Agencies Charged with Enforcing Workplace Rights* specifically reference the need to ensure that confidentiality rules do not adversely impact on the provider's ability to collect meaningful data for evaluation purposes.[62] The data collected should be reviewed periodically in order to implement

---

[56] *Guidelines for Court-Connected Programs* 1.5: "Courts should use procedures for making referrals that: (1) create equal opportunity for qualified practitioners to be eligible to receive referrals; (2) rotate referrals among qualified practitioners ...(4) refer parties to particular practitioners only in exceptional circumstances in which the special needs of the parties warrant such a referral...."

[57] Quality control by the public justice system should be more substantial when the neutrals receiving referrals from the public justice system are granted immunity from liability. *SPIDR Law and Public Policy Committee Report #2*, Recommendation #6.

[58] *National Standards* 16.2.

[59] *National Standards* 2.3: *if court operated or referred by the court*, "the program or individual mediator should have the responsibility to report information to the court in order to permit monitoring and evaluation." [emphasis added] *if not*, the provider should have no responsibility to report to the court.

[60] *Guidelines for Court-Connected Programs* Recommendation 4.1: "Court-connected programs should clearly identify the person or entity responsible for the oversight and evaluation of court-connected dispute resolution programs and practitioners."

[61] *Guidelines for Court-Connected Programs* Recommendation 4.3: "Courts should require that practitioners or programs conduct periodic surveys of participants in the dispute resolution processes..."

[62] "Confidentiality rules should not preclude responsible, statistical monitoring and evaluation that

necessary adjustments in policies and procedures.[63]

Advertising/Information about Services

Absolute Rule

One way to approach advertising and provision of information is to list the provider organization's obligations. For example, the *National Standards* state that it is the court's obligation to provide information on the goals and limitations of the jurisdiction's programs, the basis for selecting cases and the way the program operates.[64] In addition, the *National Standards* would require disclosure about possible mediators, the selection process for mediators, party choice, fees (if any) and information on process.[65] The *Guidelines for Voluntary Mediation* go a step further and suggest that "[a]gencies should provide disputants access to information and technical assistance so that disputants can understand the mediation process and their alternatives to settlement .... When disputants are unrepresented ... they may lack access to basic information about their statutory rights, agency procedures, and the mediation process itself. It is essential that an agency mediation program provide technical assistance to unrepresented disputants."[66]

Rule of Reason

The CPR Institute for Dispute Resolution approached the provider organization's responsibilities from the standpoint of a rule of reason rather than an absolute rule. The *CPR-Georgetown Principles* require provider organizations to "take all reasonable steps to provide clear, accurate and understandable information" regarding services, operations, and fees and make "reasonable disclosure consistent with the nature, structure and services of the organization and the knowledge base of

---

protects disputants' confidentiality." *The Guidelines for Voluntary Mediation Programs Instituted by Agencies Charged with Enforcing Workplace Rights,* at 5.

[63] *Guidelines for Court-Connected Programs* Recommendation 4.2: "Courts should periodically review the operation of court-connected dispute resolution services and make adjustments in their policies and procedures to ensure that established goals are being met."

[64] *National Standards* 3.2a.

[65] *National Standards* 3.2b.

[66] *The Guidelines for Voluntary Mediation Programs Instituted by Agencies Charged with Enforcing Workplace Rights,* at 4.

the individual user."[67]

Access to ADR Services

Access to ADR services includes concrete access issues, such as offering the service in a place where individuals of various physical abilities can participate, as well as the broader access issues of the cost of the service and the hours during which the services are offered. In general, the standards suggest aspirational goals of accessibility, but stop short of mandates in this regard.

Fees/Expenses

At a minimum, most provider organization standards state that fees to be paid by users of dispute resolution services should be disclosed.[68] This policy is consistent with individual neutral ethical standards that tend to require disclosure. Disclosure alone, however, does not necessarily guarantee access if the fees for the service put it out of the reach of those with limited incomes. The *CPR-Georgetown Principles* acknowledge the importance of this issue by devoting a distinct principle to access issues. Once again, they use a "reasonableness" standard in suggesting the provider's responsibilities. Specifically, "ADR Provider Organizations should take all reasonable steps, appropriate to their size, nature and resources, to provide access to their services at reasonable cost to low-income parties."[69] The extent of this duty seems to hinge on a variety of factors: public vs. private entities (public providers may have higher duty)[70] and size, nature and resources.[71]

---

[67] *CPR-Georgetown Principles* II.

[68] *See, e.g., CPR-Georgetown Principles* II.a.

[69] *CPR-Georgetown Principles* IV.

[70] *National Standards* 1.1 "Mediation services should be available on the same basis as are other services of the court." *See also The Guidelines for Voluntary Mediation Programs Instituted by Agencies Charged with Enforcing Workplace Rights at 3*: "The mediation program should be accessible to disputants of all economic levels. Agencies should guard against creating a two-tiered system in which mediation is available only to the more affluent. If costs are to be borne by the disputants rather than the agency, the mediation program should be designed to account for disparate abilities to pay" and at 5: "Fees for mediation programs should reasonable allow for participation by disputants of all income levels.... Agencies should either charge no fees or minimal fees for participation in mediation, or, alternatively, provide for a reduced fee, fee waiver, or subsidy for those unable to pay the full fee."

[71] *CPR-Georgetown Principles* IV.

Range of Services

While the *Guidelines for Court-Connected Programs* contain a standard addressing access to a range of services,[72] the *CPR-Georgetown Principles* have no counterpart. This difference appears to be another example of the higher duty imposed on the public justice system. Public policy supports a variety of dispute resolution processes in order to enhance the opportunity for parties to choose the process that best meets their needs.

Disability/Diversity

Given the strong mandates of the Americans with Disabilities Act,[73] public entities must be concerned about access issues as they relate to disabilities.[74] In 2000, a workgroup comprised of mediation practitioners, trainers and administrators released *ADA Mediation Guidelines,* which are "mediation practice guidelines unique to conflicts arising under the ADA."[75] The standards are divided into four sections: I. Program and Case Administration; II. Mediation Process; III. Mediator Training; and IV. Ethics. The *Guidelines* adopt a "broad definition" of disability to include "chronic conditions, episodic symptoms and temporary disabilities,"[76] and they clearly state the provider organization's responsibility:

> Mediation provider organizations should have in place policies and procedures concerning accessibility for persons with disabilities. Essential components include procedures for requesting a disability accommodation, for grieving the denial of accommodations, and a

---

[72] *The Guidelines for Voluntary Mediation Programs Instituted by Agencies Charged with Enforcing Workplace Rights*, Recommendation #2. See also *Guidelines for Court-Connected Programs* Recommendation 1.3: "Courts should... encourage the availability of an array of services to meet the differing needs of various types of parties..."

[73] Americans with Disabilities Act of 1990, Pub. L. No. 101-336.

[74] Title II applies to services conducted by court employees or volunteers on behalf of courts and Title III applies to services and programs by private entities that operate a place of "public accommodations" (e.g., open for business to the general public). *See* Debbie Howells & Richard Cox, *The Americans with Disabilities Act: What You Need to Know*, THE RESOLUTION REPORT, Volume 12, Number 3, for more specific suggestions on accommodations.

[75] *ADA Mediation Guidelines*, 11 World Arbitration & Mediation Report 195 (July 2000).

[76] *ADA Mediation Guidelines*, I.B.1

nondiscrimination policy that includes disability. The policies and procedures should be communicated to the parties, to mediation participants, to mediators and to staff and volunteers.[77]

In addition to disability issues, given the changing demographics of this country, language and cultural issues may also create access issues. The *National Standards* addressed this issue by calling for each court to "develop policies and procedures that take into consideration the language and cultural diversity of its community at all stages of development, operation and evaluation of court-connected mediation services and programs"[78] and by suggesting that "courts should ensure that information about the availability of mediation services is widely disseminated in the languages used by consumers of court services."[79] Interestingly, the *CPR-Georgetown Principles* do not contain any references to either of these access issues.

Location/Hours of Service

The hours of service and location of services can also limit access. For example, individuals who work hourly jobs may not be able to access dispute resolution services that are available only during normal business hours of 9 a.m. to 5 p.m. Many community dispute resolution providers stress the importance of locations inside communities rather than in courthouses. For some parties, a courthouse location may be intimidating, rendering the program inaccessible. The *National Standards* addressed this issue by stating, "In choosing the location and hours of operation of mediation services, courts should consider the effect on the ability of parties to use mediation effectively and the safety of mediators and parties."[80]

Timing

The timing of the provision of dispute resolution services is the final access issue provider organizations should consider. Specifically, "[t]he mediation program should not delay access to the adjudicatory process,"[81] and "the design and operation

---

[77] *ADA Mediation Guidelines*, I.B.2.

[78] *National Standards* 1.2. See also *Guidelines for Court-Connected Programs* 1.3: "Courts should ensure wide access to services...."

[79] *National Standards* 1.5.

[80] *National Standards* 1.7.

[81] *The Guidelines for Voluntary Mediation Programs Instituted by Agencies Charged with*

of the mediation program should not undermine statutory or constitutional workplace rights."[82]

Protections

Finally, a provider organization has to provide some method of protection for parties utilizing its services. The importance of addressing issues of misconduct or poor practice was summed up by Michael D. Young, co-chair of JAMS Committee on Professional Standards and Public Policy, in the following manner:

> An isolated mistake in judgment by one neutral not only can hurt that individual's practice, but also may tar the user's perceptions of the provider organization under whose auspices the neutral served. When a provider recognizes the potential damage caused by an individual's mistake or poor performance, it seeks to maintain structures that ensure its neutrals render high quality and ethical services.[83]

There is a range of activities the provider organization can undertake, from merely providing information and allowing the market to govern to establishing a grievance mechanism enforced by the provider organization. Once again, to determine the provider organization's responsibilities, the standards tend to consider the degree of choice the parties retain in selection of process and neutral. Protections fall into two broad category types: those that address issues after the fact (i.e., grievance mechanisms and civil liability approaches) and those that are proactive (i.e., assessments).

Grievance Mechanism

The standards adopted specifically for public entities such as the courts state that at a minimum parties referred by the court to a mediation program "should have access to a complaint mechanism to address any grievances about the process."[84] The *National Standards* also state that the "courts should adopt procedures for removing

---

Enforcing Workplace Rights, at 3.

[82] *Id.*

[83] Young, *supra* note 16.

[84] *National Standards* 2.6. See also *Guidelines for Court-Connected Programs* 4.4: "Courts should require practitioners to adhere to an ethics code and to be subject to a grievance process."

from their roster of mediators those mediators who do not meet their performance expectations and/or ensuring that they do not receive further court referrals."[85] The *CPR-Georgetown Principles* go a step further and specifically address the responsibility of the provider organization to "provide mechanisms for addressing grievances about the Organization, and its administration or the neutral services offered...."[86]

Civil Liability

In addition to the grievance mechanism, parties may pursue civil remedies. While none of the standards suggest that immunity is appropriate,[87] some of the court provider organizations have pursued adoption of statutory immunity for court-connected neutrals,[88] which would limit the use of such remedies. The arguments in favor of limiting civil remedies include the desire to promote service by neutrals -- particularly those providers that rely on volunteers -- and to discourage lawsuits. Some have argued that implementation of alternative processes was intended to address some of the issues related to an overburdened judicial system; therefore, creating new causes of action to handle neutral misconduct would be counterproductive and should be limited. To date, while there have been cases against individual neutrals, there has not been legal activity against provider organizations.

Assessments

An ADR provider organization should "take all reasonable steps to monitor

---

[85] *National Standards* 6.6.

[86] *CPR-Georgetown Principles* VI.

[87] *See, e.g., National Standards* 14.1: "Courts should not develop rules for mediators to whom they refer cases that are designed to protect these mediators from liability. Legislatures and courts should provide the same indemnity or insurance for those mediators who volunteer their services or are employed by the court that they provide for non-judicial court employees." *See also Guidelines for Court-Connected Programs* 4.5: "Courts should consider the potential civil liability of practitioners and providers in the design of dispute resolution programs. The issue of civil liability may be addressed through ethical standards, specialized training, malpractice insurance and development of qualified immunity for neutrals in court-connected programs."

[88] *See, e.g.,* FLA. STAT. ANN § 44.107, which provides that an arbitrator or mediator appointed pursuant to court order shall have "judicial immunity in the same manner and to the same extent as a judge."

and evaluate the performance of its affiliated neutrals."[89] There are a variety of ways that provider organizations can implement assessments in order to provide some protection to consumers of their services. Among them are "consumer input, review of complaints, self-assessment, trouble-shooting, regular audits, peer review and visiting committees from other programs."[90] The *Commission on Qualifications II Report* goes on to suggest that assessments "can and should take place at various points," and various methods of assessing should be utilized in "complementary combinations."[91] The report explains that reliance on a single method may provide information relating to one aspect of performance, but neglect others. Finally, if a provider organization engages in assessment, the clear dictates of confidentiality will require that data collected for assessment purposes be protected.[92]

Market Forces

The final mechanism that protects the consumer of dispute resolution services is the free market. In essence, this mechanism removes responsibility from the provider organization by holding the market accountable for sorting out which providers are worthy of future use and which are not.

Conclusion

A fair amount of work regarding provider organization responsibilities has been completed, culminating in the recent publication of the *Principles for ADR Provider Organizations,* as drafted by the CPR-Georgetown Commission on Ethics and Standards of Practice in ADR. With regard to most of the important issues, existing standards provide a general consensus and clear guidance. The major exception is in the area of repeat players and the impact this situation has on impartiality. One would hope that CPR will monitor how these *Principles* are accepted by provider organizations and how they operate in practice. Given the experience with individual practitioner ethics, one would expect that the final word

---

[89] *CPR-Georgetown Principles* I.c. *See also, The Guidelines for Voluntary Mediation Programs,* at 6: "Agencies utilizing mediation programs for resolution of employment disputes have the responsibility to monitor and evaluate them periodically."

[90] *Commission on Qualifications II* at 12.

[91] *Id.*

[92] *The Guidelines for Voluntary Mediation Programs,* at 6.

on this topic has not yet been spoken.

Chapter X

Ethical Issues Specific to Arbitration

By Richard Chernick and Kimberly Taylor

Introduction

Because of the strict limits on judicial review of arbitration awards, it is essential that the arbitration process be fair and the arbitrator impartial. It is also important that the parties have confidence in the integrity of the process. As explored below, statutes, case law and the rules of various provider institutions, ADR organizations and trade associations set forth important ethical obligations and standards for persons who act as arbitrators.

Courts generally have focused on the procedural fairness of the arbitration process rather than the legal correctness of the award.[1] A body of authority has developed governing the conduct of neutral arbitrators in domestic (non-international) arbitrations. Special rules apply to non-neutral (party appointed) arbitrators and to arbitrators who serve in international matters.

The United States Arbitration Act[2] (commonly referred to as the Federal Arbitration Act, or FAA), governs the arbitration process in matters involving "commerce."[3] It has no express rules regarding arbitrator ethics other than to require *vacatur* of awards where the award was procured by "corruption, fraud or undue means" or where there was "evident partiality" by the arbitrator.[4]

The Uniform Arbitration Act, which has been adopted in most of the states, without change or with minor variations, as their arbitration law, was recently revised. The Revised Uniform Arbitration Act ("RUAA") has several provisions that relate to the integrity of the arbitration process, including

---

[1] Richard Chernick, *What the Courts have done to Encourage Arbitration*, 2 DISPUTE RESOLUTION ALERT 1 (Oct. 2002).

[2] 9 U.S.C. § 1 *et seq.*

[3] 9 U.S.C. § 2; Allied-Bruce Terminix Companies, Inc. v. Dobson, 513 U.S. 265 (1995).

[4] 9 U.S.C. § 10.

provisions relating to disclosures by arbitrators, disqualification of arbitrators and *vacatur* of awards on account of arbitrator conduct.[5]

The best-established code of ethics which creates a standard of conduct for arbitrators is the *Code of Ethics for Arbitrators in Commercial Disputes (ABA/AAA Code of Ethics)*.[6] It is regularly cited by courts as a standard for arbitrator conduct and is widely respected. As a freestanding code of ethics, it does not have force of law, but it is authoritative nonetheless, particularly in arbitrations conducted by the American Arbitration Association (AAA) which participated in its development. The *ABA/AAA Code of Ethics* is presently undergoing revision. The revised code in draft form has been approved by the ABA Section of Dispute Resolution Council. It is titled *The Code of Ethics for Arbitrators in Domestic and International Disputes*. It is referred to herein as the *Revised Code of Ethics*.[7]

Institutional providers of arbitration, such as AAA and JAMS, have rules and procedures that regulate and assure the integrity of the arbitration process. In the case of the AAA, such rules and procedures supplement the ABA/AAA Code of Ethics.[8]

California has adopted ethical standards for neutral arbitrators. Beginning July 1, 2002, a *neutral* arbitrator must comply with ethics standards adopted by the California Judicial Council. The standards address, *inter alia*,

- disclosure of interests, relationships or affiliations that may constitute conflicts of interest, including prior service as an arbitrator or other ADR entity;
- disqualifications;
- acceptance of gifts; and
- establishment of future professional relationships.[9]

---

[5] REVISED UNIFORM ARBITRATION ACT (RUAA). We will refer exclusively to the RUAA because it is now in the process of being proposed for adoption in the majority of states. The RUAA may be accessed at www.nccusl.org.

[6] American Bar Association & American Arbitration Association, *Code of Ethics for Arbitrators in Commercial Disputes* (1977) (hereinafter *ABA/AAA Code of Ethics*). The *ABA/AAA Code of Ethics* is reproduced at Appendix C.

[7] *Draft Code of Ethics for Arbitrators in Domestic and International Disputes* (hereinafter Revised Code of Ethics). The draft *Revised Code of Ethics* is reproduced at Appendix D.

[8] *See Statement of Ethical Principles for the American Arbitration Association, An ADR Provider Organization* available at www.adr.org, and *JAMS Ethics Guidelines for Arbitrators*, available at www.jamsadr.org and reproduced as Appendix E.

[9] CAL CIV. PROC. CODE §§ 1281.85, 1281.9 (a)(2) (2002); *See also Ethics Standards for Neutral Arbitrators in Contractual Arbitrations*, Cal. Rules of Court, Appendix, Div. VI (effective July 1, 2002) (hereinafter *California Ethics Standards*).

Arbitrators who are also lawyers may be controlled to some extent in their neutral activities by rules of professional ethics. In particular, the American Bar Association established a Commission on the Evaluation of Rules of Professional Conduct (also known as "Ethics 2000"), to evaluate and recommend revisions to the *ABA Model Rules of Professional Conduct*. Among the issues the Commission addressed is the extent to which lawyers participating in ADR proceedings should be regulated.[10]

Issues for Neutral Arbitrators in Domestic Arbitrations

Upholding the Integrity and Fairness of the Process

More than 30 years ago, the United States Supreme Court recognized that arbitrators should be held to a high standard of impartiality, observing, "It is true that arbitrators cannot sever all their ties with the business world, since they are not expected to get all their income from their work deciding cases, but we should, if anything, be even more scrupulous to safeguard the impartiality of arbitrators than judges, since the former have completely free rein to decide the law as well as the facts and are not subject to appellate review. We can perceive no way in which the effectiveness of the arbitration process will be hampered by the simple requirement that arbitrators disclose to the parties any dealings that might create an impression of possible bias."[11]

That fundamental principle is no less important today. Canon I of the *ABA/AAA Code of Ethics* recognizes that for commercial arbitration to be effective the public must have confidence in the integrity and fairness of the process.

To that end, Canon I also provides that an arbitrator should not solicit appointment for himself or herself nor accept appointment unless the arbitrator believes he or she can be available to conduct the arbitration promptly. Upon accepting an appointment to a case, the arbitrator should avoid entering into business or personal relationships or interests which might affect impartiality. Arbitrators should act in a manner that is fair to all parties, unaffected by "outside pressure, by public clamor, by fear of criticism or by self-interest." An arbitrator should not exceed the authority conferred by the parties, and should

---

[10] The ABA Section of Dispute Resolution worked with the Ethics 2000 participants to try to address ethics issues relating to lawyers in ADR proceedings, whether they serve as neutral arbitrators or in a representative capacity. See Chapters III, IV, and VIII, for more discussion of Ethics 2000.

[11] Commonwealth Coatings Corp. v. Continental Cas. Co., 393 U.S. 145, 148-149 (1968).

make all reasonable efforts to prevent delay, harassment, abuse or disruption of the arbitration process.[12] The *Revised Code of Ethics* is similar.

Courts determine the existence and enforceability of agreements to arbitrate unless the parties' agreement unmistakably places that responsibility on the arbitrator.[13] Where the agreement of the parties is adhesive, part of the determination of enforceability of the clause is an examination of the fairness of the process imposed on the adhering party (usually an employee, patient or consumer). Agreements that are unconscionable are not enforceable unless the offending provision can be severed.[14]

An arbitrator has the duty in such circumstances to assure the fairness of the process and to decline to proceed if the parties are unwilling to accept adjustments that will make the process meet minimum standards.[15] This issue is addressed more fully below.

The *California Ethics Standards for Neutral Arbitrators in Contractual Arbitrations* (*California Ethics Standards*) prescribe a general duty of arbitrators to act in a manner that upholds the integrity and fairness of the arbitration process and to maintain impartiality toward all participants at all times.[16] Standard 6 suggests that arbitrators have a duty to refuse appointment if they are unable to be impartial.

Neutrality and the Appearance of Neutrality

An essential tenet of arbitration is that the decision-maker be unbiased. Assurance of neutrality is achieved by providing disclosure of any relationship or interest that might suggest its absence, and permitting parties to cause the disqualification of the arbitrator based on that disclosure.

Initial Disclosures

While arbitrating parties often choose arbitrators based on their prior professional or business associations or expertise in a particular field, the goal of party choice and the desirability of arbitrator expertise must be balanced against

---

[12] *See ABA/AAA Code of Ethics*, Canon II.

[13] First Options of Chicago, Inc. v. Kaplan, 514 U.S. 938, 942-945 (1995).

[14] *E.g.*, Cole v. Burns Intern. Sec. Services, 105 F.3d 1465 (D.C. Cir. 1997); Graham Oil Co. v. ARCO Products Co., 43 F.3d 1244 (9th Cir. 1994); Armendariz v. Foundation Health Psychcare Services, Inc., 24 Cal. 4th 83 (2000).

[15] *See, e.g., AAA National Rules for the Resolution of Employment Disputes*, pp. 4-5 (effective Jan. 1, 2001); *JAMS Employment Arbitration Rules and Procedures* (Revised April 2002); *JAMS Policy on Employment Arbitration Minimum Standards of Procedural Fairness* (Revised April 1, 2002); *JAMS Financial Services Arbitration Rules and Procedures* (Revised June 2002).

[16] *California Ethics Standards for Neutral Arbitrators*, Standard 5

the parties' right to know "any relationship that might reasonably affect [the arbitrator's] partiality."[17]

Thus, arbitrators must disclose to the parties, "any dealings that might create an impression of possible bias."[18] Disclosure of facts creating a reasonable impression of partiality is essential to enable the parties to choose their arbitrators intelligently.[19] This includes substantial business dealings during a pending proceeding or substantial prior or continuing business relationships.[20] Social acquaintances, membership in professional organizations or insubstantial business dealings do not necessarily create an impression of bias.[21] "Because courts have given arbitration such a presumption of validity once the proceeding has begun, it is essential that the process by which the arbitrator is selected be certain as to the impartiality of the arbitrator."[22]

An arbitrator has a duty to make reasonable inquiry[23] and to disclose known facts.[24] The *California Ethics Standards* require an arbitrator to inform him or herself of matters required to be disclosed.[25] According to comment to the the *California Ethics Standards,* it is good practice to ask each participant to make an effort to disclose any matters that may affect the arbitrator's ability to be impartial.

Because arbitrator disclosure is critically important to party choice and the appearance of fairness, and because the parties to an arbitration give up significant rights to trial and appeal, most statutes and rules governing arbitration contain disclosure requirements and provisions for disqualification of nominees based on their disclosures.

FAA

The appointment of arbitrators is regulated by 9 U.S.C. § 5. It requires contract provisions specifying the manner of appointment to control the process. If no method is provided in the contract, or the parties are otherwise unable to

---

[17] Burlington N. R.R. Co. v. TUCO, Inc., 960 S.W.2d 629, 637 (Tex. 1997).

[18] Commonwealth Coatings Corp., 393 U.S. at 148-149.

[19] See Schmitz v. Zilveti, 20 F.3d 1043, 1047 (9th Cir. 1994).

[20] Commonwealth Coatings Corp., 393 U.S. 145.

[21] *Id.*

[22] Drinane v. State Farm Mut. Auto Ins. Co., 606 N.E.2d 1181, 1183 (Ill. 1992).

[23] RUAA § 12 (a).

[24] *Id.*, Comment 3. *See also* RUAA § 1 (4).

[25] *California Ethics Standards*, Standard 7 (b), Standard 7 (e).

agree, the court may name the arbitrator. There is no express process for disclosure or disqualification in the FAA, but case law suggests that arbitrators have the obligation to make disclosures bearing upon their fitness to serve, and parties have the right to request disqualification based on those disclosures. Even in the absence of a specific statutory disclosure obligation, the court's power to vacate an award for "evident partiality" makes it clear that that impartiality is an essential attribute of the arbitration process.

Arbitrators must disclose to the parties, "any dealings that might create an impression of possible bias."[26] Disclosure of facts creating a reasonable impression of partiality is essential to enable the parties to choose their arbitrators intelligently.[27] For example, a significant business relationship with either party or its representative must be disclosed.[28]

RUAA

Section 11 (b) of the RUAA provides that a proposed arbitrator "who has a known, direct and material interest in the outcome of the arbitration proceeding or a known, existing and substantial relationship with a party may not serve as [a neutral] arbitrator." Section 12 of the RUAA provides that before accepting appointment, the arbitrator shall disclose to all parties to the pending arbitration proceeding and any other arbitrator, "any known facts that a reasonable person would consider likely to affect the impartiality of the arbitrator in the arbitration proceeding, including: (1) a financial or personal interest in the outcome of the arbitration proceeding; and (2) an existing or past relationship with any of the parties to the agreement to arbitrate or the arbitration proceeding, their counsel or representatives, a witness, or another arbitrator."

According to the comments to RUAA Section 12, the arbitrator is not required to disclose *de minimis* interests or relationships:

> For example, if an arbitrator owned a mutual fund which as part of a large portfolio of investments held some shares of stock in a corporation involved as a party in an arbitration, it might not be reasonable to expect the arbitrator to know of such investment and in any event the investment might be of such an insubstantial nature so as not to reasonably affect the impartiality of the arbitrator.[29]

---

[26] Commonwealth Coatings Corp. v. Continental Cas. Co., 393 U.S. 145 at 148-149.

[27] *See* Schmitz v. Zilveti, 20 F.3d 1043 at 1047; W. KNIGHT ET AL., CALIFORNIA PRACTICE GUIDE, ALTERNATIVE DISPUTE RESOLUTION, ¶ 7:14 (2001).

[28] Commonwealth Coatings Corp. v. Continental Cas. Co., 393 U.S. 145 at 149.

[29] RUAA, §12, Comment 2.

The standard is objective, requiring disclosure of facts a reasonable person would consider likely to affect the arbitrator's impartiality. [30]

ABA/AAA Code of Ethics and Institutional Arbitration Rules

The *ABA/AAA Code of Ethics Canon II* states that "arbitrators should disclose the existence of any interests or relationships which are likely to affect their impartiality or which might reasonably create the appearance of partiality or bias."[31] Any doubt as to whether or not disclosure is to be made should be resolved in favor of disclosure.[32] The *Revised Code of Ethics* is similar.

This standard has been formally adopted by at least one court as its ethical guideline.[33] Canon II reflects the principle that disclosure of interests or relationships that might affect the impartiality of the arbitrator is essential to the perception that the process is fair. At the same time, the drafters recognized that the burden of detailed disclosure should not become so great as to make it impractical for persons in the business world to be arbitrators. Nevertheless, disclosure of potential conflicts is essential to a well-informed choice of arbitrators.

The *AAA Commercial Arbitration Rules*, Rule R-19, requires proposed arbitrators to disclose to the AAA (which in turn provides that disclosure to the parties) "any circumstance likely to affect impartiality or independence, including any bias or financial or personal interest in the result of the arbitration or any past or present relationship with the parties or their representatives." Where local law provides for more extensive disclosure, such as California, the administrative practice of the AAA is to follow that local procedure.

The *JAMS Ethics Guidelines for Arbitrators* requires disclosure of "any actual or potential conflict of interest or relationship or other information, of which the Arbitrator is aware, that reasonably could lead a party to question the Arbitrator's impartiality." Examples of types of information that should be disclosed are listed.[34] Similar language is contained in the *National Association of Securities Dealers' Code of Arbitration Procedure*, Rule 10312 (requiring disclosure of "any circumstance which might preclude such arbitrator from

---

[30] *See* ANR Coal. Co. v. Cogentrix of North Carolina, Inc., 173 F. 3d 493 (4th Cir. 1999); Beebe Med. Center, Inc. v. Insight Health Servs. Corp., 751 A.2d 426 (Del. Ch. 1999).

[31] *ABA/AAA Code of Ethics*, Canon II.

[32] *Id.*

[33] Safeco Ins. Co. of America v. Stariha, 346 N.W.2d 663, 666 (Minn. App. 1984).

[34] *JAMS Ethics Guidelines for Arbitrators*, Canon V.A. *See also JAMS Comprehensive Arbitration Rules and Procedures*, Rule 15 (h).

rendering an objective and impartial determination," and identifying specific information to be disclosed). Courts often cite such disclosure provisions.[35]

California

California adopted the first and most extensive state law on disclosure and disqualification of arbitrators in 1994. It has been revised several times to specify what must be disclosed, and California has the most developed jurisprudence on this subject of any state. It is for these reasons that we address California separately in these discussions.

California Code of Civil Procedure § 1281.9 (a) prescribes that in any arbitration pursuant to an arbitration agreement, a proposed neutral arbitrator shall disclose to all parties, in writing, within 10 calendar days of service of notice of the proposed nomination or appointment, the following information for the past five years:

1.   All matters that would cause a person aware of the facts to reasonably entertain a doubt that the proposed arbitrator would be able to be impartial, including the existence of any ground specified in California Code of Civil Procedure § 170.1[36] (standards for disqualification of a judge);

2.   Any matter required to be disclosed by ethics standards for neutral arbitrators, as adopted by the Judicial Council (*see* discussion below);

3.   Information concerning prior or pending arbitration proceedings in which the proposed neutral served or is serving as a party arbitrator for any party to the arbitration proceeding or for a lawyer for a party, or for which the proposed neutral arbitrator served or is serving as neutral arbitrator, and the results of each case arbitrated to conclusion, including:

- the date of the arbitration award
- identification of the prevailing party,
- names of the parties' attorneys, and
- the amount of monetary damages awarded, if any.

Standard 7 of the *California Ethics Standards*, entitled "Disclosure," identifies the matters that must be disclosed by a person nominated or appointed as an arbitrator. In summary, the specified areas of disclosure are the following:

---

[35] *See, e.g.*, William C. Vick Constr. Co. v. North Carolina Farm Bureau Fed., 472 S.E.2d 346, 348 (N. C. App. 1996) (citing *ABA/AAA Code of Ethics*); John E. Reid & Assocs v. Wickland-Zulawski & Assocs., 627 N.E.2d 348, 350-351 (Ill. App. 1994) (citing *ABA/AAA Code of Ethics*); Thomas James Associates, Inc. v. Owens, 1 S.W.3d 315, 317-318 (1999) (citing NASD).

[36] California Civil Procedure Code § 170.1 prescribes numerous grounds for disqualification of a judge, including (1) personal knowledge of disputed evidentiary facts, (2) prior service as a lawyer in the proceeding, (3) financial interest in the subject matter, (4) business, personal or family relationships with the parties or attorneys, (5) recusal would be in the interests of justice, (6) doubt (by judge or others) about the judge's ability to be impartial, or (7) physical impairment that disables the judge from perceiving the evidence or conducting the hearing.

1.	Any significant past, present or expected familial or personal relationship between the arbitrator or a member of the arbitrator's family and a party or lawyer in the arbitration;

2.	Any past, present or expected service as a dispute resolution neutral (arbitrator, referee or mediator) for a party or a lawyer for a party.

3.	Any past, present or expected attorney client relationship between the arbitrator and a party or a lawyer for a party.

4.	Any past, present or expected professional or financial relationship or affiliation between the arbitrator or a member of the arbitrator's family and a party or lawyer in the arbitration;

5.	Any significant relationship between the arbitrator or a member of his family and the dispute being arbitrated;

6.	The arbitrator's membership in any organization that practices invidious discrimination on the basis of race, sex, religion, national origin or sexual orientation;

7.	Any other matter that (a) might cause a person aware of the facts to doubt that the arbitrator would be able to be impartial, (b) leads the arbitrator to believe there is substantial doubt as to his or her ability to be impartial, or (c) otherwise leads the arbitrator to believe disqualification will further the interests of justice.[37]

"Family" usually means "immediate family" and includes spouse or domestic partner and minor children living in the arbitrator's household.[38] For some disclosures a broader definition of "extended family" is used. It includes all relatives to the third degree of relationship.[39] The arbitrator is deemed to have complied with the obligation to inform him or herself and to disclose such relationships if he or she seeks such information from the applicable relations and discloses all information in his or her possession.[40]

A neutral arbitrator may also be disqualified by any party on any ground specified in California Civil Procedure Code § 170.1 for disqualification of a judge. Therefore those standards operate as disclosure standards as well. Effective 2002, party-appointed (non-neutral) arbitrators *need not* make the disclosures.[41]

---

[37] There are special additional disclosures for consumer arbitrations regarding the provider's relationships with the parties and counsel. *See also* discussion on special concerns in matters in which arbitration is imposed on one party, *infra*.

[38] *California Ethics Standards,* Standard 2 (m).

[39] *Id.,* Standard 2 (n).

[40] *Id.,* Standard 7 (d)(1).

[41] CAL CIV. PROC. CODE § 1281.91(d). Many state courts require non-binding arbitration of disputes prior to trial. These processes are usually referred to as "judicial" or "court annexed arbitration." Often such processes have their own disclosure and disqualification standards. *See,*

It could be argued that a state-based disclosure provision such as this only applies to arbitrations not governed by the FAA because of the principle of preemption.[42] But it is likely a court would find such state-based rules to be pro-arbitration and not intended to defeat a party's right to its agreed contractual process.[43] On that basis, it is likely that these rules would be enforced in arbitrations governed by the FAA as well as by the California Arbitration Act.[44]

Continuing Duty to Disclose

Under some statutes, the disclosure requirement is expressly a continuing one and applies to relationships that arise or become evident during the course of the arbitration proceedings.

FAA

There is no provision in the FAA expressly requiring disclosures before or after appointment, but because a court may determine the existence of evident partiality on petition to vacate,[45] it would appear that a court may rely on relationships formed or conduct occurring after appointment.[46]

---

e.g., California Rules of Court, Rule 1606 (a), which imposes a duty on the arbitrator to determine whether any causes exists for her disqualification, based upon the grounds set forth in Code of Civil Procedure § 170.1. We do not address such proceedings in this chapter on contractual arbitration.

[42] *See* Doctor's Associates, Inc. v. Casarotto, 517 U.S. 681 (1996).

[43] *See* Commonwealth Coatings Corp. v. Continental Cas. Co., 393 U.S. 145 at 148-149.

[44] *See, e.g.,* Rosenthal v. Great Western Fin. Securities Corp., 14 Cal. 4th 394 (1996) (state summary procedure for compelling arbitration not anti-arbitration and hence enforceable notwithstanding jury trial right under the FAA). In some residential construction arbitrations, California arbitrators must make disclosures in the form of declarations. California Civil Procedure Code § 1281.95 provides that in binding arbitrations for any claim more than $3,000, pursuant to a contract for the construction or improvement or residential property consisting of one to four units, an arbitrator must make a written declaration signed under penalty of perjury disclosing: (1) Whether the arbitrator or his or her employer or arbitration service had or has a personal or professional affiliation with either party and; (2) Whether the arbitrator or his or her employer or arbitration service has been selected or designated as an arbitrator by either party in another transaction. If the arbitrator discloses an affiliation with either party, discloses that the arbitrator has been selected or designated as an arbitrator by either party in another arbitration, or fails to comply with this section, either party may disqualify the arbitrator from service. This is the only presently existing statutory disclosure obligation that requires information about the provider's relationships as distinguished from the neutral's relationships.

[45] 9 U.S.C. § 10.

[46] *Cf.* Erving v. Virginia Squires Basketball Club, 349 F. Supp. 716 (S.D.N.Y.), *aff'd.* 468 F.2d 1064 (2d Cir. 1972). *See also* IAN R. MACNEIL ET AL, FEDERAL ARBITRATION LAW § 28.2.3.6 (1995) (proposing a practice of disclosure and disqualification upon party objection as the most efficient and practical process choice rather than deferring the merits of these issues to a petition to vacate after the matter has been heard).

This suggests that it is the better practice to make disclosures of facts which first become known after appointment and prior to the issuance of the award, and relationships which are only formed after appointment (or to avoid creating such relationships).

Revised Uniform Arbitration Act

Section 12 (b) of the RUAA imposes a "continuing obligation to disclose to all parties to the agreement to arbitrate and arbitration proceeding and to any other arbitrators any facts that the arbitrator learns after accepting appointment which a reasonable person would consider likely to affect the impartiality of the arbitrator." The consequences of nondisclosure are the same for pre-appointment and post-appointment relationships and conduct.[47]

ABA/AAA Code of Ethics and Institutional Arbitration Rules

Canon II. C of the *ABA/AAA Code of Ethics* provides that the obligation to disclose interests or relationships is "a continuing duty which requires a person who accepts appointment as an arbitrator to disclose, at any stage of the arbitration, any such interests or relationships which may arise, or which are recalled or discovered."[48]

Similarly, Canon V.D. of the *JAMS Ethical Guidelines for Arbitrators provides*, "An Arbitrator's disclosure obligations continue throughout the course of the Arbitration and require the Arbitrator to disclose, at any stage of the Arbitration, any such interest or relationship that may arise, or that is recalled or discovered. Disclosure should be made to all parties."[49]

California

Neither the old nor the revised versions of California Code of Civil Procedure § 1281.9 explicitly makes the duty of disclosure a continuing one. Both versions of the statute require the proposed arbitrator to make the stated disclosures within 10 days of appointment, with no provision for later-discovered information. Effective January 1, 2002, a neutral arbitrator may be disqualified "upon the demand of any party" on the grounds enumerated in Code of Civil Procedure section 170.1 (relating to judicial disqualification) at any time "before the conclusion of the arbitration proceeding." Arguably, this creates a continuing duty to disclose the information set forth in California Civil Procedure Section 170.1. Section 170.3 sets forth the procedure for disqualification of a judge, "whenever a judge determines himself or herself to be disqualified," and Section

---

[47] RUAA § 12 (c), (d), (e).

[48] *See also ABA/AAA Code of Ethics,* Canon II.D.

[49] *See also JAMS Comprehensive Arbitration Rules and Procedures,* Rule 15 (h).

170.3 (b)(4) provides a procedure when the grounds for disqualification are learned after the judge has made rulings in the case.

The *California Ethics Standards* include a provision that would impose on the arbitrator a continuing obligation to inform him or herself of and disclose any matter required to be disclosed, from the notice of the arbitrator's proposed nomination or appointment until the conclusion of the arbitration. Standard 7(e). There is no continuing duty in consumer cases to make subsequent disclosures regarding provider relationships with parties or counsel.

Remedy for Failure to Disclose

FAA

Under federal law, "an arbitrator's decision may be set aside only for reasons stated in the Federal Arbitration Act, or for a small number of reasons created by the courts, including awards which violate public policy, awards based on a manifest disregard of the law, or where the arbitrators failed to conduct a fundamentally fair hearing."[50]

The Federal Arbitration Act provides that an award may be set aside if it "was procured by corruption, fraud, or undue means[,] . . . there was evident partiality or corruption in the arbitrators[,] . . . or for other misbehavior that prejudiced any party."[51] "Evident partiality" may be found when an arbitrator fails to disclose facts that might establish a bias.[52] This is true, even when no actual bias is present.[53] In *Commonwealth Coatings,* the court determined that the fact of the relationship or the interest in the subject matter of the arbitration, rather than the fact of non-disclosure, provides the basis for *vacatur.* But a leading treatise argues that under the FAA the non-disclosure of a relationship that might have given rise to the arbitrator's disqualification might implicate FAA § 10 (a) (4), vacatur on the ground that the arbitrator exceeded his power.[54]

---

[50] Denver & Rio Grande W. R.R. v. Union Pac. R.R., 119 F.3d 847, 849 (10th Cir. 1997). (collecting cases). *See* Stephen L. Hayford, *Law in Disarray: Judicial Standards for Vacatur of Commercial Arbitration Awards*, 30 GA. L. REV 731 (1996); Stephen L. Hayford, *A New Paradigm for Commercial Arbitrations: Rethinking the Relationship Between Reasoned Awards and the Judicial Standard for Vacatur,* 66 GEO. WASH. L. REV. 443 (1998).

[51] 9 U.S.C. § 10(a) (1-3).

[52] Schmitz v. Zilveti, 20 F.3d 1043 at 1046.

[53] *Id.* at pp. 1045-1049; Burlington N. R.R. Co. v. TUCO, Inc., 960 S.W.2d 629.

[54] *See* IAN R. MACNEIL ET AL, FEDERAL ARBITRATION LAW § 28.2.2 (1995).

Revised Uniform Arbitration Act

If the arbitrator fails to disclose a fact required to be disclosed, a court may, upon timely objection by a party, vacate an award.[55] However, "A party who does not object to the selection of the arbitrator or to any alleged bias on the part of the arbitrator at the time of the hearing waives the right to complain."[56]

California

"Generally, the merits of an arbitrated controversy are not subject to judicial review."[57] However, courts may vacate an arbitration award when a party's rights were substantially prejudiced by misconduct of the arbitrator, or in the proper circumstances, the arbitrator failed to disqualify him or herself. An award may also be vacated if the arbitrator was biased or prejudiced.[58]

> [W]here an ...arbitrator fails to disclose matters required to be disclosed by section 1281.9, subdivision (e), and a party later discovers disclosure should have been made, that failure to disclose constitutes one form of 'corruption' for purposes of section 1286.2, subdivision (b) and thus provides a ground for vacating an award. This is because the failure to disclose such matters, even if no actual bias is present, represents a kind of 'corruption' by creating the appearance that the . . . arbitrator is concealing something important and relevant to his or her impartial participation in the appraisal or arbitration process.[59]

Under the California Ethics Standards an arbitrator is disqualified if "at any time before the conclusion of the arbitration a party becomes aware that the arbitrator has made a material omission or material misrepresentation in his or her disclosure and [serves a timely notice of disqualification]."[60] Under Standard 8 (a)(1) an arbitrator is disqualified if he or she fails to make a timely disclosure and a party serves a timely notice of disqualification.

---

[55] RUAA, Section 12 (d).

[56] Bossley v. Mariner Fin. Group, Inc., 11 S.W.3d 349, 351 (Tex. App. 2000)). *See* RUAA § 12, Comment 4.

[57] Ceriale v. AMCO Ins. Co., 48 Cal. App. 4th 500, 504 (1996).

[58] CAL. CIV. PROC., Sections 1286.2 (c), (f); *see* CAL. CIV. PROC §§ 1281.9 (d), (e); CAL. CIV. PROC §170.1 (a); Cal. Code Jud. Ethics, Canon 3 (B)(5) and Canon 6 (D)(2)(a), (e), and (f).

[59] Michael v. Aetna Life & Cas. Ins. Co., 88 Cal. App. 4th 925, 937-938 (2001); *see also* Kaiser Foundation Hospitals, Inc. v. Superior Court, 19 Cal. App. 4th 513 (1993).

[60] *California Ethics Standards*, Standard 8 (a)(4).

Disqualification
Some statutes and rules oblige the proposed neutral to disqualify himself or herself upon request or demand of any party. Failure to do so may result in vacatur of the award.

FAA
There is no statutory procedure for disqualification, but case law suggests that parties have that right. Implicit in the concept of disclosure to the parties of "any dealings that might create an impression of possible bias"[61] is the right to ask an arbitrator with a relationship that meets the above standard to recuse him or herself.[62]

RUAA
If a fact is timely disclosed under § 12 (b), and a party timely objects to appointment or continued service based on the fact disclosed, the objection may be a ground for *vacatur* of the award.[63] Finally, a failure to disclose a known, direct, material interest in the outcome of the arbitration proceeding or a known, existing and substantial relationship with a party creates a presumption of evident partiality.[64]

ABA/AAA Code of Ethics and Institutional Rules
Canon II of the *ABA/AAA Code of Ethics* provides that an arbitrator must disclose any interest or relationship that might affect his or her impartiality or create an appearance of partiality or bias. Canon II (E) provides, "In the event that an arbitrator is requested by all parties to withdraw, the arbitrator should do so. In the event that an arbitrator is requested to withdraw by less than all of the parties because of alleged partiality or bias, the arbitrator should withdraw," unless the parties' agreement or the rules agreed to by the parties provide a method for resolving the question, in which case that procedure should be followed.[65] The arbitrator may elect not to withdraw if, after carefully considering the matter, the arbitrator "determines that the reason for the challenge is not substantial, and that he or she can nevertheless act and decide the case impartially and fairly, and that withdrawal would cause unfair delay or

---

[61] Commonwealth Coatings Corp. v. Continental Cas. Co., 393 U.S. 145 at 148-149)

[62] *See* IAN R. MACNEIL ET AL, FEDERAL ARBITRATION LAW § 28.2.3.6 (1995) (proposing a practice of disclosure and disqualification upon party objection as the most efficient and practical process choice.

[63] RUAA § 12 (c).

[64] RUAA § 12 (e).

[65] *See also ABA/AAA Code of Ethics,* Canon II.F.

expense to another party or would be contrary to the ends of justice."[66] The *Revised Code of Ethics* is similar.[67]

Institutional arbitration providers supervise the appointment and disclosure process in accordance with their rules and administrative procedures and practices. Where a disclosure results in a request to disqualify, the institution will determine the arbitrator's fitness to serve if the arbitrator does not voluntarily accept recusal.

The *AAA Commercial Arbitration Rules* provide for disqualification of proposed arbitrators in accordance with Rule R-19 (quoted above).[68] Disputes about disqualification are determined by the AAA as an administrative matter.

The *JAMS Ethics Guidelines for Arbitrators* provide that "An arbitrator should not proceed with the process unless all parties have acknowledged and waived any actual or potential conflict of interest. If the conflict of interest casts serious doubt on the integrity of the process, an arbitrator should withdraw, notwithstanding receipt of a full waiver."[69] JAMS resolves disputes as to arbitrator selection and removal as an administrative matter.[70]

Where the arbitration is non-administered, a court must determine an arbitrator's fitness to serve.[71] The FAA does not provide for judicial scrutiny of an arbitrator's qualifications in any proceeding other than an action to confirm or vacate an award.[72]

California

Failure to comply with the disclosure requirements of Code of Civil Procedure § 1281.9 will result in the arbitrator's disqualification, but the burden is on the parties to serve written notice of disqualification within 15 calendar days after the arbitrator's failure to comply.[73] Similarly, the arbitrator may be disqualified on the basis of the disclosure statement if any party serves notice of disqualification within 15 days after service of the statement.[74] The statutes

---

[66] *ABA/AAA Code of Ethics*, Canon II.F.

[67] *See Revised Code of Ethics*, Canon II.F.

[68] *AAA Commercial Arbitration Rules* Rule R-12.

[69] *JAMS Ethics Guidelines for Arbitrators*, Canon V.C.

[70] *See also JAMS Comprehensive Arbitration Rules and Procedures*, Rules 11 (d), 15 (i).

[71] 9 U.S.C., § 5. *See* RUAA at § 11(a).

[72] Marc Rich & Co., A.G. v. Transmarine Seaways Corp., 443 F. Supp. 386 (S.D.NY. 1978).

[73] CAL. CIV. PROC. CODE. § 1281.91(a).

[74] CAL. CIV. PROC. CODE § 1281.9(b)(1).

provide no requirement that disqualification be made in good faith or based upon good cause. There is apparently no limit on the number of neutrals who can be disqualified sequentially in this manner.[75]

Upon the demand of any party, an arbitrator must disqualify himself on any of the grounds specified in the California Code of Civil Procedure § 170.1 for disqualification of a judge.[76] Such disqualification is mandatory.

The California Code of Civil Procedure § 1281.6 permits a court to appoint the arbitrator where the parties' agreement has no method for appointment, or the agreed method has failed to result in an appointment. The statutory provisions for disclosure described above apply to such an appointment. A party may disqualify one court-appointed arbitrator without cause in any single arbitration, and upon a showing of cause, may challenge subsequent appointees.[77]

Under the *California Ethics Standards*, the arbitrator is disqualified if (a) he or she fails to make the required disclosure within the time required and a party timely serves a notice of disqualification, or (b) makes disclosure and based on that disclosure a party serves a timely notice of disqualification, or (c) makes a late disclosure and a party serves a timely notice of disqualification, or (d) a party becomes aware of an omission or material misrepresentation on the arbitrator's disclosure and timely serves a notice of disqualification.[78]

Acceptance of Gifts

According to the California Ethics Standards, arbitrators are prohibited from accepting gifts, bequests, favors or honoraria from parties or other persons having an interest in the arbitration. The arbitrator's family members are discouraged from accepting gifts, bequests, favors or honoraria from such persons. This obligation continues for two years from the conclusion of the arbitration.[79]

Acceptance of Subsequent Employment

The *California Ethics Standards* prohibit an arbitrator from accepting subsequent employment as a lawyer, expert witness or consultant from a party or a lawyer for a party in a pending arbitration.[80]

---

[75] W. KNIGHT ET AL., CALIFORNIA PRACTICE GUIDE, ALTERNATIVE DISPUTE RESOLUTION, (2001) pp. 7-20.

[76] CAL. CIV. PROC. CODE § 1281.9.

[77] CAL. CIV. PROC. CODE §1281.91.

[78] *California Ethics Standards*, Standard 8 (a)(1-4).

[79] *Id.* Standard 9. *See also JAMS Ethics Guidelines for Arbitrators* at Canon V.G.

[80] *California Ethics Standards,* Standard 10 (a).

An arbitrator may only entertain offers of subsequent employment in any other capacity (such as an arbitrator or mediator), if he or she discloses at the time of his or her appointment in a case that he or she intends to do so, but a party may disqualify the proposed arbitrator based on that disclosure.[81]

In consumer cases (defined in Standard 2 (d) and (e)), if the arbitrator has made the disclosure required by Standard 10 (b), when such an offer is made and disclosed to the parties in the first case, they have the right to consent or to refuse to consent thereto.[82]

Communicating with Parties

Canon III of the *ABA/AAA Code of Ethics* requires that "An arbitrator in communicating with the parties should avoid impropriety or the appearance of impropriety." If the parties' agreement or a provider's rules establishes the method of communication between the parties and the arbitrator, that method should be followed. The *Revised Code of Ethics* is similar.

The *AAA Commercial Arbitration Rules* provide that "There shall be no direct communication between the parties and a neutral arbitrator other than at a hearing, unless the parties and the arbitrator agree otherwise.[83] As with most institutional providers, AAA administrators act as intermediaries between the parties and the neutral arbitrators.

The *JAMS Comprehensive Arbitration Rules and Procedures* similarly provide that "No Party may have any *ex parte* communication with a neutral Arbitrator regarding any issue related to the Arbitration. Any necessary *ex parte* communication with JAMS, whether before, during or after the Arbitration Hearing, shall be conducted through the Case Manager. The Parties may agree to permit *ex parte* communication between a Party and a non-neutral Arbitrator."[84]

Parties sometimes agree to permit *ex parte* communications for purposes of scheduling or other administrative tasks. Such understandings ought to be documented in writing.[85] Where the arbitration is non-administered, it is more difficult to maintain strict rules against *ex parte* communications. It is not always possible to contact parties at the same time or for parties jointly to access the

---

[81] *Id.* Standards 10 (b), 10 (c).

[82] *Id.* Standard 10 (d). *See also JAMS Ethics Guidelines for Arbitrators,* Canon V.D (arbitrator should disclose any offer of subsequent employment and obtain a waiver of any conflict of interest).

[83] *AAA Commercial Arbitration Rules,* Rule R-20, as amended and effective on September 1, 2000.

[84] *JAMS Comprehensive Arbitration Rules and Procedures,* Rule 14. *See also* discussion at § B, *infra.*

[85] *See ABA/AAA Code of Ethics,* Canon III.B.1, 3.

arbitrator, particularly on matters of routine administration and scheduling. Nor is it always appropriate to contact the parties jointly, such as on matters of compensation. An understanding about these issues should be reached by the parties and arbitrator early in the process and documented in writing.

All institutional rules except from the no *ex parte* communication rule the situation where one party has defaulted or failed to appear after due notice and the hearing is conducted with only one side in attendance.[86]

Competence

Arbitrators, like judges, must instill confidence in the adjudicatory process. They do so by conducting proceedings fairly and evenhandedly and by performing their work diligently and with the highest level of competence. Canon IV of the ABA/AAA Code of Ethics recognizes that principle. "An arbitrator should perform duties diligently and conclude the case as promptly as the circumstances reasonably permit." The *Revised Code of Ethics* (Canon V) is similar. Canon IV of the revised code requires the arbitrator to make decisions "in a just, independent and deliberate manner." The arbitrator should not delegate his or her duty to others, although that standard should not prohibit an arbitrator from obtaining help from an associate or research assistant. The fact of such assistance and any compensation arrangements that affect the parties should be disclosed to them.[87]

Institutional providers may require arbitrators to agree to adhere to particular ethical standards. For example, The *JAMS Ethics Guidelines for Arbitrators*, Canon II, provides, "An Arbitrator should accept an appointment only if the Arbitrator meets the Parties' stated requirements in the agreement to arbitrate regarding professional qualifications. An Arbitrator should prepare before the Arbitration by reviewing any statements or documents submitted by the parties. An Arbitrator should refuse to serve or withdraw from the Arbitration if the Arbitrator becomes physically or mentally unable to meet the reasonable expectations of the Parties."

California

The *California Ethics Standards* establish a duty to refuse an appointment where the arbitrator is unable to be impartial.

Diligent and Fair Conduct of Proceedings

---

[86] *AAA Commercial Arbitration Rules*, Rule R-31, *JAMS Comprehensive Arbitration Rules and Procedures*, Rule 22(j), *JAMS Ethics Guidelines for Arbitrators*, Canon VI. *See also ABA Code of Ethics*, Canon III.B.2, *California Ethics Standards*, Standard 12.

[87] *See* discussion of just, independent and deliberate resolution of disputes submitted for decision, *infra*.

Canon IV of the ABA/AAA Code of Ethics obliges the arbitrator to conduct the proceedings fairly and diligently, treating all parties equally throughout the arbitration. The arbitrator should conclude the case as promptly as possible, while being patient and courteous to the parties, their lawyers and the witnesses. The arbitrator should also encourage similar conduct by the participants in the proceedings.[88]

The arbitrator should permit all parties the right to appear in person, and to be represented by counsel unless an agreement of the parties or the applicable rules provide otherwise. If notice of the arbitration hearing has been provided to all parties, and one party has failed to appear, the arbitrator may proceed with the hearing, but only upon satisfying himself or herself that notice has been given to the absent party.

The *ABA/AAA Code of Ethics,* Canon IV expressly permits an arbitrator to ask questions, call witnesses and request documents or other evidence when he or she determines that more information is required to decide the case.

An arbitrator may suggest to the parties that they discuss settlement of a case, but the arbitrator should not participate in the settlement discussions unless requested to do so by the parties. At the same time, an appointed arbitrator is free to act as a mediator if requested to do so by all parties or where authorized or required to do so by law. The arbitrator should not pressure any party to settle.[89]

The *JAMS Ethics Guidelines for Arbitrators,* Canon VI, is similar. It requires an arbitrator to "endeavor to provide an evenhanded and unbiased process and to treat all parties with respect at all stages of the proceedings." Canon VI advises the arbitrator to remain impartial, perform duties diligently, conclude the case as promptly as circumstances reasonable permit, and be courteous to the parties, lawyers and witnesses.

California

The *California Ethics Standards* address the conduct of the arbitration. Standard 11 requires the arbitrator, *inter alia,* to conduct the arbitration fairly, promptly and diligently, in a procedurally fair manner and in accordance with applicable law relating to the conduct of arbitration proceedings;[90] and to decide matters independently and uninfluenced by outside pressures or fear of criticism.[91]

---

[88] *ABA/AAA Code of Ethics,* Canon IV. *See also Revised Code of Ethics,* Canon IV.

[89] *ABA/AAA Code of Ethics* Canon IV.

[90] *California Ethics Standards*, Standard 11 (a).

[91] *Id.,* Standard 11 (b).

Just, Independent and Deliberate Resolution of Disputes Submitted for Decision

In addition to conducting the proceedings diligently and fairly, arbitrators instill confidence in the process when they resolve the disputes submitted to them in a just and independent manner. According to the *ABA/AAA Code of Ethics*, Canon V, "An arbitrator should, after careful deliberation, decide all issues submitted for determination. An arbitrator should decide no other issues." "The arbitrator should decide all matters justly, exercising independent judgment," unaffected by outside pressure and without delegating the duty to any other person.[92] Similarly, *JAMS Ethics Guidelines for Arbitrators,* Canon VIII expresses the tenet that "an arbitrator should make decisions in a just, independent and deliberate manner."

> An Arbitrator should, after careful deliberation and exercising independent judgment, promptly or otherwise within the time period agreed to by the parties, decide all issues submitted for determination and issue an award and/or decision. An arbitrator's decision should not be influenced by fear of criticism or by any interest in potential future case referrals by any of the parties or counsel, nor should an arbitrator issue an award that reflects a compromise position in order to achieve such acceptability. An arbitrator should not delegate the duty to decide to any other person.[93]

Maintenance of Confidentiality

One of the qualities of arbitration that attracts some parties is its non-public nature. Most provider rules and ethics guidelines provide that unless the parties otherwise agree or as may be required by applicable law, an arbitrator should keep confidential all matters relating to the proceedings and decision.[94] "Unless otherwise agreed by the parties, or required by applicable rules or law, an arbitrator should keep confidential all matters relating to the arbitration proceedings and decision."[95]

According to the ABA/AAA Code of Ethics, confidentiality also encompasses the obligation not to reveal the decision in advance of its issuance

---

[92] *Id. See ABA/AAA Code of Ethics* at Canon V (*accord*).

[93] *JAMS Ethics Guidelines for Arbitrators, Canon VIII.*

[94] *See, e.g., ABA/AAA Code of Ethics,* Canon VI.B.

[95] *ABA/AAA Code of Ethics,* Canon VI.B; *See also JAMS Ethics Guidelines for Arbitrators,* Canon IV (*accord*).

to the parties, not to inform anyone about the deliberations of the arbitrators and not to assist the parties in post award proceedings except as required or permitted by law.[96] The *Revised Code of Ethics* is similar.[97] The *JAMS Ethics Guidelines for Arbitrators* are similar as well.[98]

Arbitrators maintain the privacy of hearings and will routinely refuse to permit a non-party to observe or participate in the proceedings without the agreement of the parties.[99]

These ethical principles apply to arbitrators, not to the parties. It is a common misperception of arbitration confidentiality that the parties are somehow disabled from revealing facts about the process to third parties. Absent a protective order or separate confidentiality agreement, no institutional arbitration rules prohibit parties from revealing information about the process to third parties.

Arbitrators may not, except in limited circumstances, participate in post-award processes.[100] This obligation does not prevent submission to the parties of a draft or tentative award nor to an assistant or the provider organization.

Special Concerns in Matters in Which Arbitration is Imposed on One Party

Arbitration is increasingly being used as the exclusive or primary dispute resolution mode in a variety of business settings, including business/consumer transactions, health care, financial services industries, securities brokerage account relationships and employment relationships. Businesses hope by including mandatory arbitration clauses in their agreements that they will achieve effective, efficient and economical resolution of their disputes. Most, if not all, of these arbitration agreements are adhesive. They are included in standard form agreements that are by their nature non-negotiable.

Critics of arbitration assert that such arrangements intend to deny the involuntary contracting party statutory and due process rights and particularly the right to a trial by jury. There has been overreaching in some of these clauses,

---

[96] *ABA/AAA Code of Ethics,* Canon VI.C.

[97] *Revised Code of Ethics,* Canon VI.C.

[98] *JAMS Ethics Guidelines for Arbitrators,* Canon IV.

[99] *See AAA Commercial Arbitration Rules,* Rule R-25; *JAMS Comprehensive Arbitration Rules and Procedures,* Rule 26(c).

[100] *See* discussion at § A.12, *infra. See also California Ethics Standards,* Standard 13 (arbitrator must not use confidential information for personal gain and may not inform anyone of the award in advance of the time it is given to all parties).

including provisions that deny the adhering party the right to counsel, limit or bar discovery and limit or bar statutory remedies or punitive damages.[101]

Because an arbitration agreement was not negotiated or is contained in a contract of adhesion, however, does not mean that it is not enforceable.[102] While courts have generally left arbitrating parties to their own devices as a matter of substance, they have been careful to scrutinize the substantive and procedural fairness of private arbitration processes, particularly where the agreement to arbitrate is contained in a standard form agreement that is by its nature adhesive.

Courts determine the existence and enforceability of agreements to arbitrate. But parties frequently come to arbitration without any prior court scrutiny of the clause or the agreed arbitration process. If an issue of arbitrability or enforceability is raised, it must be determined by the arbitrator, subject to any later court review.

Where the agreement of the parties is adhesive, part of the determination of enforceability of the clause is an examination of the fairness of the process imposed on the adhering party (such as an employee or a patient or a consumer). Agreements that are unconscionable are not enforceable unless the offending part of the process can be severed.[103]

An arbitrator has the duty in such circumstances to assure the fairness of the process and to decline to proceed if the parties are unwilling to accept adjustments that will make the process meet minimum standards.[104]

California

Standard 7 (b)(12) of the *California Ethics Standards* imposes unique disclosure obligations on arbitrators in consumer cases (essentially imposed arbitration agreements involving the sale or lease of goods and services primarily for personal or family use and in most health care and non-collective bargaining employment agreements).[105]

Arbitrators are obligated to disclose extensive details about certain professional and financial relationships between the institutional provider and the

---

[101] *See, e.g.,* Armendariz v. Foundation Health Psychcare Services, Inc., 24 Cal. 4th 83; Stirlen v. Supercuts, Inc., 51 Cal. App. 4th 1519 (1997); Cole v. Burns Intern. Sec. Services, 105 F.3d 1465; Paladino v. Avnet Computer Tech. Inc., 134 F.3d 1054, 1059-1060 (11th Cir. 1998).

[102] *See* Armendariz v. Foundation Health Psychcare Services, Inc., 24 Cal. 4th 83; Cole v. Burns Intern. Sec. Services 105 F.3d 1465.

[103] *E.g.,* Cole v. Burns Intern. Sec. Services, 105 F.3d 1465; Armendariz v. Foundation Health Psychcare Services, Inc., 24 Cal. 4th 83.

[104] *See, e.g., AAA National Rules for the Resolution of Employment Disputes; JAMS Employment Arbitration Rules and Procedures; JAMS Policy on Employment Arbitration Minimum Standards of Procedural Fairness.*

[105] *See California Ethics Standards,* Standard 2 (d) and (e).

arbitrator and between the provider and the parties or their counsel (including all prior arbitrations and their results). These disclosures are phased in over time.[106] The arbitrator is not obligated to do more than to provide information known to him or her and to request the required information from the institution. The arbitrator is entitled to rely on information provided by the institution.[107]

Med-Arb, Arb-Med and Other Multiple Roles

Classic Med-Arb is a two-step process in which a neutral acts as mediator and attempts to facilitate a resolution of the dispute; if resolution is not achieved, the same neutral functions as arbitrator. Arbitration hearings may be conducted or the parties may simply ask the neutral to decide the case based on information received in the course of the mediation.

Mediators are usually expected to meet separately with the parties and to receive information that may not be shared with the other side. This access to confidential information and the ability to caucus separately with the parties are two important tools mediators use to facilitate resolution of disputes.

Arbitrators are expected not to receive ex parte communications and are expected to decide matters based on evidence presented in hearings which each side has the opportunity to challenge.

The Med-Arb process may cause parties to be reluctant to share adverse information with the mediator if that information might influence a later decision in the arbitration phase of the process. Parties may also be concerned that the ultimate decision might be reached based on evidence communicated to the neutral in a caucus and which therefore could not be challenged in the hearing. Determinations made by the neutral may thus not have the same degree of respect an arbitration award is usually accorded.

On the other hand, the process is efficient in that the presentation of information in the mediation phase need not be repeated in the arbitration phase of the process. Having a single neutral serve in both capacities avoids the necessity of educating two neutrals about the same dispute. The arbitrator has a keen sense of the parties' positions, gained through the joint and private sessions during the mediation. As a practical matter, the views of the mediator expressed during the course of the mediation phase should be persuasive in causing the parties to accept realistic evaluations of their positions. Because the parties understand that the mediator may ultimately decide the case, there is usually a greater incentive to settle at a mediation.[108]

---

[106] *California Ethics Standards,* Standard 7 (b) (12) (F).

[107] *California Ethics Standards,* Standard 7 (b)(12) (H).

[108] For a general discussion of this subject, *see* Barry C. Bartel, Comment, *Med-Arb as a Distinct Method of Dispute Resolution: History, Analysis and Potential,* 27 WILLAMETTE L. REV. 661 (1991).

Some neutrals are unwilling to serve in Med-Arb processes, either because they believe the process is inappropriate and they should not assist parties to engage in it, or because they believe they are personally unable to be effective in one or both phases of the process. A neutral should decline to serve if he or she has misgivings about the process or his or her effectiveness.[109]

Because of the differences in the roles of arbitrator and mediator, a Med-Arb should only be undertaken where the parties fully understand these issues and are willing to accept the risks. A stipulation or agreement between the parties should, at a minimum describe the possible difficulties with this mixed process, the inconsistencies in the roles of arbitrator and mediator, and the possible consequences to the parties. The stipulation should appoint the neutral to both roles, waive any right to disqualify the arbitrator based on his having functioned as mediator, and waive the right to seek to vacate or oppose confirmation of any award based on the arbitrator's dual role.[110]

These principles and concerns apply to any two-step resolution process in which the same neutral conducts both a non-binding step and a binding step.

The ADR process is inherently controlled by the parties. If one adopts the view that the parties should be permitted to craft their own process, there should be no prohibition against a neutral acting as mediator and arbitrator in the same case, notwithstanding the potential risks, so long as there is full understanding of those risks. The neutral should ensure that the parties have made an informed decision regarding their participation and the neutral's role.

Assisting the Parties with Process Choices

More so than any other adjudicatory procedure, the arbitration process is largely in the hands of the parties. Effective control over the process is achieved

---

[109] *See* American Arbitration Association, American Bar Association Section of Dispute Resolution, Society of Professionals in Dispute Resolution, MODEL STANDARDS OF CONDUCT FOR MEDIATORS (1994), Standard IV.

[110] Such a stipulation for a proceeding in California might include the following language: "(1) [NAME], who has been appointed as the arbitrator, may conduct a mediation in this matter. In this regard he may receive confidential communications from the parties *ex parte*. Some such information may not be admissible in the arbitration, if it goes forward. (2) The mediation shall be conducted in accordance with Cal. Evidence Code § 1115 *et seq*. (3) If the matter is not fully resolved, the mediator shall proceed to conduct an arbitration in this matter. (4) The fact that the arbitrator presided as mediator shall not provide any basis to seek the disqualification of him as arbitrator, whether pursuant to CCP § 1281.9 or otherwise, and the parties waive the right to do so. (5) The fact that the arbitrator presided as mediator shall not provide any basis for the award to be vacated or modified, and the parties agree not to seek to vacate or modify the award nor to oppose confirmation on such ground." *See generally*, COMMERCIAL ARBITRATION AT ITS BEST: SUCCESSFUL STRATEGIES FOR BUSINESS USERS § 1.9 (2) (Thomas J. Stipanowich & Peter H. Kaskell, Eds., 2001).

by thoughtful clause drafting and post-dispute negotiations and agreements which define the process.

While these matters are usually dealt with by counsel, the arbitrator, as the process expert, has a role to play in helping the parties to be aware of process choices and to make decisions about process that are reasonable for the nature of their dispute. This assistance may be offered at the preliminary hearing or at other points throughout the process. Arbitrators also have the power to impose some process choices on parties as part of the management of the arbitration.

This role is emphasized in AAA and JAMS rules for commercial arbitration and in the RUAA.[111] Proposed arbitrators are sometimes also approached by the parties for process advice prior to the commencement of the process. As long as the arbitrator conducts these discussions jointly with counsel and approaches the task of process design in a neutral fashion, such process advice and direction are within the arbitrator's proper role.

Participation in Post-award Proceedings

FAA

An arbitrator's testimony is neither required nor allowed to support, explain or attack an award.[112] This principle derives from the finality of an arbitration award and the doctrine of *functus officio*. Limited exceptions to this rule include testimony as to whether the award was intended to be final and issues as to alleged improper arbitrator conduct.[113] These rules support the notion that the arbitrator has an ethical duty not to inform anyone concerning their deliberations or to assist any party in post-arbitration proceedings except as may be required by law. [114]

California

An arbitrator's declaration or testimony is inadmissible to explain the reasons for the award or the merits of the controversy.[115] Exceptions to this

---

[111] See RUAA § 15 (a) (prehearing conferences) and Comment 2; *AAA Commercial Arbitration Rules, Rule R-10* (preliminary hearing); *JAMS Comprehensive Arbitration Rules and Procedures, Rule 16* (preliminary conference).

[112] *See generally* IAN R. MACNEIL ET AL, FEDERAL ARBITRATION LAW and cases therein cited.

[113] *Id.* § 38.5.3.

[114] *Id.*, §§ 32.6, 38.5.4. *See also* RUAA § 14 (d) (arbitrator incompetent to testify and may not be required to produce records as to any statement, conduct, decision or ruling occurring during arbitration proceeding).

[115] CAL. EVID. CODE § 703.5.

general rule are that an arbitrator may offer evidence on the issues of bias or disqualification or to support correction of the award in certain circumstances.[116]

Some institutional rules prohibit calling arbitrators or staff as witnesses.[117] *JAMS Ethics Guidelines for Arbitrators*, Canon V.F provides that an arbitrator should not participate in post-arbitration proceedings except where requested to make a correction or clarification of the award, as required by law, or where requested by all parties to participate in a subsequent dispute resolution procedure in the same case. The *ABA/AAA Code of Ethics* and the *Revised Code of Ethics* are similar.

Special Issues for Party-Appointed Arbitrators in Domestic Arbitrations

It is not uncommon for arbitration agreements to provide for party appointment of an arbitrator by each side and the selection of the third arbitrator jointly by the party appointed arbitrators or by an appointing authority. Unique questions are presented in situations where two of the arbitrators are party-appointed.

The *ABA/AAA Code of Ethics* deals with these questions in Canon VII. As the introductory note explains, a fundamental ground rule is that everyone involved in the case must know whether the party-appointed arbitrators are expected to be neutral or non-neutral. It is generally assumed they are non-neutral unless the parties agree otherwise in their arbitration clause, by applicable arbitration rules, by any governing law, or by a post-dispute stipulation.[118] Non-neutral, party-appointed arbitrators should observe all of the obligations imposed in the code, subject to the provisions set forth in Canon VII.

The *Revised Code of Ethics* refers to non-neutral party-appointed arbitrators as "partisan arbitrators." Canon IX of the *Revised Code of Ethics* addresses the extent to which party-appointed arbitrators must follow the processes of Canons I-VIII, but unlike the similarly structured Canon VII of the existing *ABA/AAA Code of Ethics*, Canon IX does not address the obligations of "partisan arbitrators." That subject is relegated to a supplement that delineates special obligations of party-appointed arbitrators who are deemed not to be neutral.

The placement of such matters is intended to separate non-neutral arbitrators from the "customary practice" of neutrality of party-appointed arbitrators.[119] That "customary practice" is accurate in international matters but is

---

[116] Century City Medical Plaza v. Sperling, Isaacs & Eisenberg, 86 Cal. App. 4th 865 (2001).

[117] *See, e.g., JAMS Comprehensive Arbitration Rules and Procedures*, Rule 30.

[118] The rules for arbitrators serving in international matters are quite different. *See* the section on special issues for arbitrators in international matters, *infra*.

[119] *Revised Code of Ethics*, Canon IX, Introductory Note.

not at all customary in domestic arbitrations. The drafters obviously intend to attempt to shift the prevailing view in the domestic arbitration community to match that on the international side. Time will tell whether this effort is successful. In the meantime, the structure of the *Revised Code of Ethics* will generate some confusion in domestic arbitrations.

Selection of Process

Parties may expressly choose this tripartite format or may reach the same result by selecting an institution that, by administrative practice, opts for three arbitrators unless the parties expressly provide to the contrary.[120]

In domestic arbitrations it is common for tripartite arbitration panels to be formed by the appointment of party arbitrators by each party and the selection of the presiding arbitrator jointly by the party arbitrators or the administering institution. The clause might read: "Each side shall select an arbitrator and they shall select the third arbitrator."

Although the clause rarely addresses the issue, it is usually assumed in domestic arbitrations that the party arbitrators will be non-neutral or at least predisposed to the position of the appointing party. Courts infer from such clauses that the absence of any restriction on who may be appointed permits the appointment of partisans.[121]

Neutrality

Non-neutral arbitrators are expected to comply with Canon I and uphold the integrity and fairness of the arbitration process. It is commonly accepted, however, that party-appointed arbitrators are not and cannot be neutral in the same sense an independent arbitrator or judge is.[122] Nor can they be neutral in the sense that the third arbitrator is.[123] Courts usually permit party-appointed

---

[120] *See, e.g., CPR Institute For Dispute Resolution Rules For Non-Administered Arbitration* (Revised and Effective September 15, 2000), Rule 5.1 (two party-appointed arbitrators and a presiding arbitrator unless the parties have agreed to the contrary); *UNCITRAL Arbitration Rules* (1976), Art. 5 (three arbitrators unless parties agree on one) and Art. 7 (parties appoint arbitrators and they appoint the third); *International Chamber of Commerce Rules of Arbitration* (in force as from January 1, 1998), Art. 8 (in tripartite arbitrations, parties each select one arbitrator; chairman is selected by the ICC Court unless agreement provides for arbitrators to make selection).

[121] Sunkist Soft Drinks, Inc. v. Sunkist Growers, Inc., 10 F.3d 753 (11th Cir. 1993) *cert. denied,* 513 U.S. 869 (1994). The same assumption is made by the *AAA Commercial Arbitration Rules,* Rule R-12 (b) and by the *ABA/AAA Code of Ethics, Canon VII* (Introductory Note). *But see* discussion of the *Revised Code of Ethics, supra.*

[122] Stef Shipping Corp. v. Norris Grain Co., 209 F. Supp. 249, 253-254 (S.D.N.Y. 1962).

[123] Astoria Medical Group v. Health Ins. Plan, 182 N.E.2d 85, 87 (N.Y. 1962).

arbitrators to have *ex parte* communications with parties, counsel and witnesses on matters of substance and permit conduct that clearly reveals a predisposition to the position of the party that appointed him or her.[124] By statute some party-appointed arbitrators in domestic arbitrations are required to be neutral.[125]

The *Revised Code of Ethics* provides that party-appointed arbitrators may have special skill or expertise in the subject matter of the proceeding and may be predisposed toward the position of the party which appointed them based on their special skill or expertise but should not have prejudged the issues in dispute.[126]

Disclosure

Disclosure by a party-appointed arbitrator is not required in AAA arbitrations;[127] however, the *ABA/AAA Code of Ethics* suggests that such disclosures ought to be made. Canon VII of the Code sets out specific standards for party arbitrators ("nonneutral arbitrators") and deals with such issues as *ex parte* contacts before and after appointment, disclosure of party arbitrators' interests and relationships, conduct of the hearing and the decision-making process. It is the responsibility of the neutral arbitrator to be sure that the parties have a common understanding of the roles of their respective appointed arbitrators, preferably early in the process and preferably documented in writing.

The *ABA/AAA Code of Ethics* requires nonneutral arbitrators to disclose their prior dealings with the other parties, but the disclosure "need not include as detailed information as is expected from persons appointed as neutral arbitrators."[128] The *Revised Code of Ethics* states that party-appointed arbitrators should disclose to the parties and the other arbitrators all interests and relationships which Canon II otherwise requires to be disclosed.[129] They are not required to withdraw if requested to do so by a party who did not appoint them.

RUAA

---

[124] *See, e.g.*, Employers Ins. of Wausau v. National Union Fire Ins.Co. of Pittsburgh, 933 F.2d 1481 (9th Cir. 1991) (court rejected a challenge to an award where a party-appointed arbitrator had performed consulting services with counsel on the issues in dispute and where *ex parte* communications had occurred throughout the matter by both party-appointed arbitrators.

[125] *See, e.g.*, Michael v. Aetna Life & Cas. Ins. Co., 88 Cal. App. 4th 925 at 937-938 (California Insurance Code provision for determination of amount of insured loss).

[126] *Revised Code of Ethics*, Canon IX.A.

[127] See *AAA Commercial Arbitration Rules*, Rule R-9(a).

[128] *ABA/AAA Code of Ethics*, Canon VII.B.

[129] *Revised Code of Ethics*, Canon IX.C.

The Revised Uniform Arbitration Act maintains the distinction between neutral and party-appointed arbitrators.[130] But disclosures are required of all arbitrators subject to the party's waiver of that obligation directly or as a result of the selection of rules of an administering body such as the AAA.

California

In California, disclosures are required only of a neutral arbitrator.[131] Prior to the enactment of these statutory disqualification standards in California, a court held that disclosures are only required of the neutral arbitrator because the party-appointed arbitrator was expected to be biased.[132] However, the conduct of a party-appointed arbitrator might nonetheless give rise to the *vacatur* of an award for corruption.[133]

Communication with Parties

The *ABA/AAA Code of Ethics* permits non-neutral arbitrators to consult with the parties which appointed them concerning the acceptability of persons under consideration for appointment as the third arbitrator and to consult concerning other aspects of the case provided they inform the other arbitrators and the other party they intend to do so.[134] Typically the parties will agree on the extent of *ex parte* communications and whether such communications will terminate at some point in the case (such as after the preliminary conference or prior to commencement of the evidentiary hearing).

The *Revised Code of Ethics* contains similar provisions in the Supplement at Paragraph D. It also prohibits any communications about deliberations and concerning any matter taken under consideration by the panel after the record is closed or the issue has been submitted for decision.

Special issues for Arbitrators in International Matters

Party-arbitrators

---

[130] *See* RUAA §23(a) (*vacatur*).

[131] CAL.CIV. PROC. CODE, §§ 1281.9 (a), (b), (c), and (d). *See* RUAA § 12, Comment 5.

[132] Tate v. Saratoga Savings & Loan Ass'n., 216 Cal. App. 3d. 843, 858 (1989).

[133] *Id.*

[134] *ABA/AAA Code of Ethics*, Canon VII.C.

As alluded to above, in international arbitrations party arbitrators are expected to be independent and not to engage in *ex parte* communications with their appointing party after their appointment.[135]

Failure to adhere to this practice may jeopardize enforcement of the award outside the United States. Because of the extremely broad definition of "international" arbitrations contained in California's International Arbitration Act,[136] this issue is of particular concern in California.

Revised Code of Ethics

The original *ABA/AAA Code of Ethics* received broad support in the United States among arbitrators, ADR provider organizations, and the courts. It had little influence outside the United States, however. The *Revised Code of Ethics* attempts to deal with this in a *Supplement to Code of Ethics for Arbitrators in Domestic and International Commercial Disputes*. The Supplement provides that in international matters, party arbitrators shall be and are neutral and independent.

International Bar Association Rules

The International Bar Association (IBA) has developed model rules that address, among other things, arbitrator ethics. The IBA requires international arbitrators to be impartial, independent (whether appointed by the parties or in some other fashion), competent, diligent and discreet. The 1987 IBA Guidelines deal with acceptance of appointment elements of bias, duties of disclosure, communication with parties, duties of diligence, involvement in settlement proposals, and confidentiality of deliberations.

Advertising and Promotion

The *Revised Code of Ethics* includes, at Canon VIII, guidelines for advertising or promotion of arbitral services. An arbitrator may disseminate advertisements that are discreet and professional, although it is inappropriate to solicit appointment in a particular case. "Advertising or promotion of an individual's general willingness or availability to serve as an arbitrator should be limited to a brief description of his or her professional credentials, experience, and relevant areas of expertise or activities, and such information as may be

---

[135] International Bar Association, *Rules of Ethics for International Arbitrators* (reflecting the continental view that every arbitrator, whatever the method of appointment, should be impartial and independent). See *ICC Rules of Arbitration*, Art. 7 (1) (every arbitrator shall be independent of the parties involved in the arbitration). *See also AAA International Arbitration Rules*, Art. 7.

[136] CAL. CIV. PROC. CODE § 1297.13.

required to facilitate contact and communication."[137] The advertising should not be inaccurate or likely to mislead, make comparison with other arbitrators, include statements about the quality of the arbitrator's work or success of his or her practice, or imply any willingness to accept an appointment without complying with the Code of Ethics.[138]

The *JAMS Ethics Guidelines for Arbitrators* provide, "An Arbitrator should avoid marketing that is misleading or that compromises impartiality. An Arbitrator should ensure that any advertising or other marketing to the public conducted on the Arbitrator's behalf is truthful."[139]

Similarly, Standard 15 of the *California Ethics Standards* provides, "(a) An arbitrator must be truthful and accurate in marketing his or her services and must not make any representation that directly or indirectly implies favoritism or a specific outcome. (b) An arbitrator must not solicit business from a participant in the arbitration while the arbitration is pending." This Standard omits the ABA/AAA Code's broader prohibition against solicitation.[140]

Compensation Issues

A potentially challenging issue for arbitrators is that of compensation. The *ABA/AAA Code of Ethics* treats the issue in Canon VI, which requires an arbitrator to be "faithful to the relationship of trust and confidentiality inherent" in the role. Specifically, subdivision D of Canon VI requires arbitrators to "scrupulously avoid bargaining with parties over the amount of payments or engaging in any communications concerning payments which would create an appearance of coercion or other impropriety." Further, unless the parties' agreement or applicable rules specify otherwise, the Code suggests that before accepting appointment, the arbitrator establish the basis of payment and inform all parties in writing. In cases conducted under the rules or administration of an institution, payments should be arranged by the institution to shield the arbitrator from discussing this issue with the parties. If the arbitration is not administered by an institution, all parties should be present during any discussion concerning fees.[141]

The *Revised Code of Ethics* is similar, but further cautions that, absent extraordinary circumstances, the arbitrator should not ask that his or her rate of compensation be increased during the pendency of the arbitration, and neither the

---

[137] *Revised Code of Ethics*, Canon VIII.

[138] *Id.*

[139] *JAMS Ethics Guidelines for Arbitrators*, Canon IX.

[140] *ABA/AAA Code of Ethics*, Canon I.B.

[141] *ABA/AAA Code of Ethics*, Canon VI.D.

payment of the arbitrator's fee nor the amount thereof should be contingent upon the outcome of the arbitration.[142] The admonitions apply to neutral and party-appointed arbitrators.

JAMS Ethics Guidelines for Arbitrators provide, "An Arbitrator may discuss issues relating to compensation with the Parties but should not engage in such discussions if they create an appearance of coercion or other impropriety and should not engage in *ex parte* communications regarding compensation."[143]

The *California Ethics Standards* state,

> (a) An arbitrator must not charge any fee for services or expenses that is in any way contingent on the result or outcome of the arbitration. (b) Before accepting appointment, an arbitrator, a dispute resolution provider organization, or another person or entity acting on the arbitrator's behalf must inform all parties in writing of the terms and conditions of the arbitrator's compensation. This information must include any basis to be used in determining fees and any special fees for cancellation, research and preparation time, or other purposes.[144]

Special Considerations for Institutional ADR Providers

Concerns exist about the partiality of arbitrators or institutional providers that have ongoing relationships with users, particularly employers, financial services providers or health care entities that impose arbitration on their constituents. Regulation of ADR provider organizations is being considered in a variety of contexts, most notably by the CPR-Georgetown Commission on Ethics and Standards of Practice in ADR. In May 2002, the Commission issued the *Principles for ADR Provider Organizations*.

The Commission was comprised of representatives from various ADR provider organizations, educational institutions, law firms and the judiciary. As stated in the preamble, "The Principles build upon the significant policy directives of the past decade which recognize the central role of the ADR provider organization in the delivery of fair, impartial and quality ADR services."

The nine Principles are aimed at addressing the Commission's desire to "establish standards of responsible practice…and to inform consumers, policy makers and the public generally;" to provide "meaningful disclosure of key information;" to convey "sufficient information about ADR Provider

---

[142] *Revised Code of Ethics,* Canon VII.

[143] *JAMS Ethics Guidelines for Arbitrators,* Canon IX.

[144] *California Ethics Standards*, Standard 14.

Organizations, their services and affiliated neutrals to make well-informed decisions about their dispute resolution options;" and to aid such organizations in meeting the expectations of its constituents "for fair, impartial and quality dispute resolution services and processes."[145]

The *CPR-Georgetown Principles for ADR Provider Organizations* include guidelines relating to quality and competence of service, information regarding services provided by and the operations of the provider, fairness and impartiality, access to services at a reasonable cost to low-income parties, disclosure of organizational conflicts of interest, complaint and grievance mechanisms, adherence to ethical guidelines, clear and accurate communications, and confidentiality.

Conclusion

As arbitration is used more widely in commercial and consumer settings, there will be increasing scrutiny on the fairness of the process. Courts have signaled that they regard their role more to assure procedural fairness than to police legal correctness; as a consequence unsuccessful litigants can be expected to focus their attention on the neutrality of the arbitrator (and the independence of the institutional provider) in order to develop grounds for vacatur. Arbitrators and providers have always regarded themselves as having a duty to assure fairness and neutrality, so the issue of arbitrator ethics will be a vital one in the developing arbitration marketplace.

---

[145] CPR-Georgetown Commission on Ethics and Standards of Practice in ADR, *Principles for ADR Provider Organizations* (May 2002). Preamble.

Chapter XI

Ethical Dilemmas Arising Out of Ombuds Practice

By Sharan Lee Levine, Philip J. Harter,
Paula A. Aylward and Judith S. Kaleta

Introduction

Government, academia and the private sector are answering demands for fairness and responsiveness by establishing ombuds.[1] Ombuds confidentially receive complaints or questions about alleged acts, omissions, improprieties and broader systemic problems within the ombuds' jurisdiction. They address, investigate or otherwise examine these issues independently and impartially. Ombuds may issue public reports with recommendations; they may work informally to resolve issues; and, when authorized, ombuds may advocate formally within the legal system.

Ombuds around the world have reduced litigation, improved morale and productivity, and satisfactorily resolved difficult and systemic problems. Ombuds have investigated and resolved concerns relating to procedure and process for employment options, illegal activity, workplace violence, deep-seated resentment associated with allegations of race discrimination, and matters relating to ethical and fair treatment.

The former Chief Parliamentary Ombudsman for Sweden noted that ombuds promote fairness in the entities in which they serve, describing ombuds as the "watchdog for legality and equity in administration."[2] An administrative law scholar and the author of the *Model Ombudsman Statute* wrote that the ombuds system is one of ethical self-governance that strives to freely hear complaints, give them deep consideration, and see that they are speedily

---

[1] "Ombudsman" is a Swedish word meaning "agent" or "representative." It, and the word "ombuds", are recognized internationally as gender-neutral terms, and the use of "ombuds" herein is intended to encompass all other forms of the word, such as "ombudsperson" or "ombudsman."

[2] Ulf Lundvik, *The Ombudsman as a Watchdog of Legality and Equity in the Administration,* OCCASIONAL PAPERS, December 1980, at 5.

reformed.[3] He further noted that ombuds assist individuals and organizations to attain what John Milton described as "the utmost bound of civil liberty."[4]

Another ombuds expert and author described the benefits of establishing organizational ombuds in words that may be appropriately applied to all types of ombuds:

> The question may well be raised whether the [adoption of ombuds offices within corporations] assures corporate morality and proper corporate conduct. While it may not prevent all future corporate disasters (the conduct of all individuals cannot be controlled), it should serve to prevent many and to avoid some of the most blatant problems, and, at a minimum, to limit and reduce potential disasters to relatively less significance. That, in itself, should be a sufficient justification.[5]

While the basic authorities of these persons called ombuds and the independence, impartiality and confidentiality with which they operate vary markedly, ombuds share essential characteristics. To be credible and effective, the office of the ombuds must be independent in structure, form and appearance. The ombuds' structural independence is the foundation upon which the ombuds' impartiality is built. The ombuds must conduct investigations and inquiries in an impartial manner, free from initial bias and conflicts of interest. Confidentiality is a widely accepted characteristic of ombuds, which helps ombuds perform the functions of the office.

The American Bar Association (ABA) has urged the establishment of ombuds offices. In 1969 the ABA adopted a resolution recommending that state and local governments consider establishing ombuds to inquire into administrative action and to make public criticism. The ABA adopted a resolution in 1971 recommending that the federal government experiment with establishing ombuds for limited phases of federal activity, in certain geographical areas or in specific agencies. The ABA recognized the contribution ombuds make in providing a means by which complaints are received, the underlying facts are developed through an informal inquiry or a more formal investigation, and those complaints found to have merit are suitably addressed in a means that fits the situation.

---

[3] WALTER GELLHORN, WHEN AMERICANS COMPLAIN 212 (1966) (paraphrasing John Milton).

[4] Id.

[5] Victor Futter, *An Answer to the Public Perception of Corporations: A Corporate Ombudsperson?*, 46 BUS. LAW. 29, 47 (1990).

Therefore, in August 2001, the ABA broadened its policies and adopted a resolution supporting the greater use of ombuds. This new policy was the culmination of years of collaboration and effort by and among ombuds, their attorneys, other ombuds experts, and ABA members. The policy addresses ombuds who are appointed within government, academia, and the private sector, and who respond to complaints from individuals within and outside the establishing entity. Furthermore, the ABA endorsed *Standards for the Establishment and Operation of Ombuds Offices (Ombuds Standards).*[6] The *Ombuds Standards* differentiate among different types of ombuds -- classical, organizational and advocate -- but the fundamental premise of the policy is that *all* ombuds must operate with certain basic authorities and essential characteristics. The three types of ombuds share the essential characteristics of independence, impartiality and confidentiality.

When established correctly, ombuds' offices serve as important and viable options to assist individuals who are or perceive themselves to be disenfranchised or ignored, passed over or harassed, neglected or abused. Furthermore, ombuds are often catalysts for positive change within an entity, thus expanding benefits beyond the individual who raises a concern to the ombuds.[7]

This chapter discusses the types and functions of ombuds, the ethical dilemmas that confront them, and the ways in which adherence to the *Ombuds Standards* in establishing and operating ombuds offices can effectively diminish, though not eliminate, ethical dilemmas that ombuds face.

History and Overview of the Standards for the Establishment and Operation of Ombuds Offices

Overuse of the terms "ombudsman," "ombuds" and "ombudsperson" was confusing to the public as well as to the entities establishing ombuds offices. In

---

[6] The ABA Administrative Law and Regulatory Practice Section, together with the Section of Dispute Resolution, joined to write the *Ombuds Standards*. Ultimately, they were also sponsored by the Section of Business Law, Labor and Employment Section, Section of State and Local Government Law, Government and Public Sector Lawyers, Senior Lawyers Division, National Conference of Administrative Law Judges, the Commission on Legal Problems of the Elderly, and the Standing Committee on Environmental Law. A copy of the *Ombuds Standards* is attached at Appendix I.

[7] The Report accompanying the ABA *Standards for the Establishment and Operation of Ombuds Offices* elaborates: "the Organizational Ombuds in one prominent company resolves several hundred workplace matters every year; that experience is echoed by other companies and increasingly by government agencies and academic institutions. Classical Ombuds have investigated and issued reports on important issues that need to be addressed by the body politic; a recent prominent example concerned prison conditions. Advocate Ombuds have been successful in protecting vulnerable populations, such as children and residents of nursing homes." The Report, at 3.

1997 the ABA Section of Administrative Law and Regulatory Practice sponsored a program concerning citizen interaction with the government and focused on ombuds at the federal, state, and local levels. Recognizing the various types of ombuds offices in and out of government and the proliferation of different processes by which the offices operate, the ABA Section of Administrative Law worked together with the ABA Section of Dispute Resolution to form a steering committee consisting of representatives of ombuds associations and other experts in the field.

The steering committee reviewed the ABA's 1969 resolution, which was limited to classical ombuds. The committee then set out to expand the policy to address ombuds who are appointed within government, academia and the private sector, and who respond to complaints from individuals both within and outside the entity. This process, the first time that all such groups had come together, was groundbreaking in its collaborative effort.

As the *Ombuds Standards* were developed, the importance of distinguishing among the different types of ombuds became apparent. The committee, therefore, clarified the means by which ombuds operate and defined ombuds' functions, to help prevent interference into those functions from the establishing entities, as well as to inform visitors to the office about the ombuds' role. The committee discussed concerns about protecting ombuds' communications, ensuring ombuds' independence while maintaining ombuds' accountability, and defining the parameters of ombuds' impartiality.[8] In its review, deliberations and drafting, the committee consulted with ombuds from federal, state and local agencies; academic institutions; companies; and non-profit organizations. The committee's review was also, in part, guided and informed by recent case law involving challenges to the ombuds' confidentiality and independence. As discussed below, case law determining common law privilege and interpreting statutes regarding confidentiality for ombuds has been infrequent, generally unpublished and inconsistent.

The committee's actions culminated in *Standards for the Establishment and Operation of Ombuds Offices*, which "provide advice and guidance on the structure and operation of ombuds offices so that ombuds may better fulfill their functions and so that individuals who avail themselves of their aid may do so with greater confidence in the integrity of the process."[9] Adherence to these

---

[8] The advocate ombuds' role has been described as a "hybrid, since it was designed to encompass both active advocacy and representation of residents' interests over those of other parties involved. . . in the classic model the ombudsman intervenes between the government and individual citizens. In the case of the Long-Term Care ombudsman program, however, intervention usually also includes a private third party – the nursing or board and care facility." From: *Real People Real Problems: An Evaluation of the Long-Term Care Ombudsman Programs of the Older Americans Act*, Division of Health Care Services, Institute of Medicine (1995) at 3.

[9] *Ombuds Standards*, Preamble.

Ombuds Standards helps protect ombuds from ethical dilemmas that arise out of their role and interdependent essential characteristics. However, the *Ombuds Standards* do not eliminate all potential dilemmas that are inherent in the ombuds' functions and essential characteristics.

Section A of the *Ombuds Standards* addresses the establishment and operations of an ombuds. It states that an entity establishing an ombuds should do so pursuant to a legislative enactment or a publicly available written policy (the charter). The charter should identify the ombuds' authority, functions and jurisdiction.

Section B of the *Ombuds Standards* articulates the essential qualifications of ombuds, who should "be of recognized judgment, objectivity and integrity." Furthermore, the establishing entity should provide ombuds with education relevant to their role and duties.

Section C identifies the ombuds' essential characteristics of independence, impartiality and confidentiality. Without them, an ombuds cannot discharge the duties of the office effectively.

Section D sets forth limitations on an ombuds' authority, to ensure independence, impartiality and confidentiality.

Section E of the *Ombuds Standards* notes the importance of establishing clear standards for removal of an ombuds. If removal becomes necessary, it must be only for good cause shown through the means of a fair procedure.

Section F raises the issue of whether a report made to an ombuds constitutes notice[10] to the entity. Because the law in this area continues to evolve, the *Ombuds Standards* do not address whether a communication to an ombuds will be deemed notice to anyone else including the entity in which the ombuds acts. Section F of the *Ombuds Standards* thus recognizes that important legal rights and liabilities may be affected.

Sections G, H and I define the three types of ombuds. Classical ombuds are defined in Section G. A classical ombuds receives complaints or inquiries from citizens about the functioning of the government, investigates the matter, and publishes a report making recommendations to resolve the issue. Organizational ombuds are described in Section H. An organizational ombuds strives to resolve the diverse issues that arise in the workplace. Finally, Section I defines an advocate ombuds as one who serves a designated vulnerable population and who, when justified by the facts of a particular case, becomes an advocate on behalf of an individual member of that group.

Ethical Dilemmas in Establishment, Authority and Accountability of Ombuds

---

[10] "Notice" refers to whether a person has legal cognizance of a matter. *See*, BLACKS LAW DICTIONARY 1087 (7th ed. 1999). This issue is discussed in greater detail *infra*.

The purpose of Sections A and D of the *Standards* is to urge the entity establishing an ombuds office to specify and define the ombuds' duties and any limitations on the ombuds' authority. When the entity properly establishes the ombuds' authority, and clearly sets forth the role and jurisdiction of the office, several potential dilemmas are avoided. Key to the ombuds' success is whether the ombuds' duties and responsibilities are well-defined, whether the ombuds instills confidence, maintains its boundaries and integrity, and is accountable to the people and institution in which the ombuds serves.

Ombuds encounter ethical problems if the charter is unclear about the kinds of complaints and questions the ombuds may receive. The charter should set forth precisely the kinds of matters that fall within the ombuds' jurisdiction. An ombuds whose charter is unclear may find itself working on matters that are more properly another's responsibility. This failure to provide specific guidelines could lead to the view that the ombuds is interfering with matters outside its jurisdiction and overstepping boundaries. For example, if an ombuds were asked to look into a substantive outcome already resolved by formal means by an agency, or an ombuds whose jurisdiction is limited to fielding employee grievances were asked to get involved in a substantive dispute, this would create ethical problems.

Section A, the establishment section, identifies a broad range of operations for all ombuds regardless of whether the ombuds is classical (receiving complaints from the general public), organizational (hearing complaints from employees in an organization), or advocate (representing the interest of a specific vulnerable population). For example, the *Ombuds Standards* suggest that an ombuds be authorized to receive complaints and questions about alleged acts, omissions, improprieties and systemic problems, to exercise discretion about whether to accept or decline such complaint or question, and to act on its own initiative, among other authorities. To help avoid confusion, a list of ombuds' functions, defining the methods by which the ombuds operates, are delineated in Section A (7) of the standards.

To further clarify the ombuds' role, the *Ombuds Standards* suggest that ombuds not be authorized to act on matters that could create a conflict of interest or be perceived to be the role of the legislature, of the executive or of management. For example, some may believe that the classical ombuds' investigative function is similar to that of an Inspector General and establish the ombuds position in the Office of an Inspector General. Locating an ombuds in that office, however, would raise questions about the control of resources and investigations and could create ethical dilemmas for the ombuds. Classical ombuds face conflicts if their functions include other formal roles. A classical ombuds should be authorized to conduct independent and impartial investigations, have subpoena power, issue reports, and advocate for change both within an entity and publicly.

Sections A and D of the *Ombuds Standards* likewise serve to ensure that an organizational ombuds' charter specifically outlines that the ombuds' role and function includes fielding questions and concerns from employees, though it may limit its authority to non-union employees. Those sections also ensure that an executive ombuds, appointed by the governor or agency head, might be granted authority to field questions and concerns about an agency action. However, the ombuds should be prohibited from acting as an appellate body because the ombuds could be viewed as substituting his/her judgment for that of the office which is under the ombuds' jurisdiction.

To avoid this problem, the *Ombuds Standards* recommend that the ombuds should not determine rights of individuals, nor make binding decisions relative to an individual or to a policy in the institution. Rather, the ombuds may make recommendations to the entity concerning an issue or policy. In addition, ombuds should not set aside law, policy or administrative decisions. Ombuds should not compel any action within the entity. The reason for these boundaries was well-expressed by the former Detroit City Ombudsman, Marie Farrell-Donaldson, in testimony offered before the Detroit City Charter Revision Commission on the issue of expanding the City ombuds' powers. She testified:

> . . . the ombudsman is in the position of reviewing policy. If we reach a point where we can recommend policy and enforce the implementation of that policy, two years from now, a citizen might come in and complain about that same policy.

A related concern in this regard is that if an ombuds can act as policy-maker based upon a confidential record, what happens to the processes and procedures in place to protect the due process rights of individuals?

The ombuds operates best by persuasion, which must be grounded in the ombuds' credibility. To enhance credibility, the ombuds should be well-qualified, as described in Section B of the standards. Essential to a well-defined function is a well-known and well-respected individual with well-defined duties and responsibilities in the role of ombuds. The ombuds' reasoned judgment is another critical factor limiting the possible ethical quandaries.

Consistent with this reasoned approach, Section E is written to protect both the ombuds and the entity creating the ombuds office. It acknowledges that an ombuds should be protected from removal for a well-documented report that was critical of an entity. This provision also allows an entity to ensure the accountability of an ombuds and further, to remove a rogue or nonfunctioning ombuds who fails to document findings, engages in misconduct, or exceeds the scope of the ombuds' authority.

Ethical Dilemmas and the Ombuds' Essential Characteristics of Independence, Impartiality and Confidentiality

Without sufficient independence, an ombuds office can be limited in the work it performs and its authority can be undercut. It can lose or fail to attain sufficient stature or respect within the entity. Without conducting inquiries and investigations in an impartial manner, an ombuds appears to be -- or is -- just another arm of the entity that created the office, and the office will not have the respect or trust of the community in which the ombuds works. An ombuds who fails to keep necessary information confidential will not be trusted sufficiently to be useful to the individual or entity.

Based on their essential characteristics, all ombuds -- classical, organizational, and advocate -- share similar ethical dilemmas. However, because of the difference in the way they function, ombuds also face different concerns.

Independence

The first essential characteristic of an ombuds is independence. To be credible and effective, ombuds must be independent in structure, function and appearance. An ombuds' independence is critical to and enables an ombuds' impartiality. Independence also helps to ensure confidentiality of an ombuds' communications.[11] The ombuds' independence can be enhanced by such simple functions as placing the office's physical location apart from the entity's human resources or management offices; by giving the ombuds a budget and authority to hire staff; by providing the ombuds separate phone, fax, computer and filing systems; by enabling the ombuds to enter into its own contracts with vendors and professionals.

Ombuds are effective and credible when they serve outside of line management or outside the executive branch over which they may have jurisdiction. Situated in this way, the ombuds is and appears to be truly independent. The following observation explains the importance of the ombuds' independence:

---

[11] In Garstang v. Superior Court of Los Angeles County, 39 Cal. App. 4th 526 (1995), the California Court of Appeals cited the independence and confidentiality of the ombuds' office as a basis to deny the plaintiff access to ombuds' communications. The court noted that parties participate in the ombuds' system at Caltech ". . .in the belief that the communications will not be disclosed. Caltech gives to all employees a strict pledge of confidentiality and assurance that they may rely on the confidentiality, independence and impartiality of the ombuds office." *Id*. at 534. The court further acknowledged that "the relationship between the ombuds office and Caltech's employees and management is worthy of societal support." *Id*. at 535. The court dismissed the plaintiff's claim that she did not know that ombuds' communications would be kept confidential, by noting that "the record reveals that every Caltech employee. . . was made aware of. . . Caltech's pledge of confidentiality, and that Caltech guaranteed the independence of the ombudsman office." It concluded that " . . . in the absence of evidence indicating that Caltech breached its confidentiality pledge and/or its guaranty that the ombudsman office would be independent, . . . the ombudsman's office is independent of all Caltech structures." *Id*. at 536.

> What gives an ombudsman's opinions the force they enjoy . . . is the ombudsman's detachment from 'politics.' An ombudsman, being mortal, may be mistaken; but whatever opinion he may express is universally accepted as having been shaped by his best judgment, uninfluenced by extraneous considerations.[12]

The *Ombuds Standards* address an ombuds' independence by encouraging entities to establish an ombuds as follows:

> The ombuds is and appears to be free from interference in the legitimate performance of duties and independent from control, limitation, or a penalty imposed for retaliatory purposes by an official of the appointing entity or by a person who may be the subject of a complaint or inquiry.

> In assessing whether an ombuds is independent in structure, function, and appearance, the following factors are important: whether anyone subject to the ombuds' jurisdiction or anyone directly responsible for a person under the ombuds' jurisdiction (a) can control or limit the ombuds' performance of assigned duties or (b) can, for retaliatory purposes, (1) eliminate the office, (2) remove the ombuds, or (3) reduce the budget or resources of the office.

An ombuds who is not independent will face ethical dilemmas. For example, an ombuds who is subject to the whims of management and fears job loss may hesitate to issue a public report on systemic problems within an entity or even a report intended for internal distribution, depending upon the volatility and sensitivity of the issue. Even if the ombuds' position is secure, because of the potential for funding cuts or other retaliatory action, an ombuds may hesitate to issue a report critical of an entity. For example, although a classical ombuds may be appointed by a legislature, the ombuds' budget may be controlled by an executive branch agency that is subject to the ombuds' jurisdiction. Alternatively, legislatively created ombuds may have their budgets cut by the legislature sitting in succession to the one that originally enabled the office. Organizational and advocate ombuds face similar issues.

Ethical dilemmas also arise when an entity interferes with an ombuds' independence by combining the ombuds' function with other, more formal, alternative dispute resolution functions. For example, an entity may locate an organizational ombuds in the human resources office and require the ombuds to serve as a fact finder on employee grievances. The ombuds' fact-finder report

---

[12] Gellhorn, When Americans Complain at 167.

would serve as the foundation for a potential disciplinary action. This commingling of functions undercuts an ombuds' independence and impartiality, and creates ethical dilemmas. What if the complainant is concerned about the actions of an employee in human resources or the fairness of a personnel policy and the ombuds' office is located with the Human Resources Department? In this case, the complainant may perceive a conflict of interest between the ombuds and the Human Resources department and, alternatively, the ombuds may be constrained from acting independently, as anticipated by the *Standards* paragraph C(1). When an ombuds is asked to perform management functions or to arbitrate company disputes, the ombuds is not, and does not appear to be, independent or impartial. This mixing of functions erodes the ombuds' ability to maintain confidentiality as well. Such intermingled functions could in and of themselves become a systemic problem.

Ombuds may have ethical dilemmas when faced with litigation, requests for confidential communications, access to documents in the entity over which the ombuds has jurisdiction, or other contentious legal issues. If the entity's legal counsel were also to provide legal counsel to the ombuds, there would be an inherent conflict of interest. Inevitably, the time will come when the actions recommended by the entity's counsel seek to protect the entity at the expense of someone else -- *viz*, an employee, a member of the public -- whom the ombuds is also charged to serve. To avoid this problem, the ombuds should have access to resources for independent legal advice and counsel. Independent legal counsel enables an ombuds to litigate to enforce the authority of its office.[13]

Impartiality

The second essential characteristic of an ombuds is impartiality in conducting inquiries and investigations. Impartiality fosters trust and confidence in the ombuds from all parties and enhances the ombuds' credibility. An ombuds who is perceived as an "employee advocate," a "voice of management," a "citizen's agent," or a "governmental representative" loses credibility and effectiveness. When seen as impartial, an ombuds is much more effective and generally achieves greater success.

With regard to an ombuds' impartiality, the *Ombuds Standards* urge the authorizing entity to establish the ombuds as follows:

---

[13] Paragraph A.8. of the *Ombuds Standards* provides that an ombuds has authority to "initiate litigation to enforce or protect the authority of the office as defined by the charter, as otherwise provided by these standards, or as required by law." *See also*, the United States Ombudsman Association's Model Act and the Older Americans Act, which requires each state agency to provide adequate legal counsel, without conflict of interest, to Long-Term Care ombuds. This Act also directs state agencies to ensure that these ombuds pursue administrative, legal, and other appropriate remedies on behalf of residents. 42 USC § 3058g(f)(1) and (2). The authority to file litigation is infrequently used.

The ombuds conducts inquiries and investigations in an impartial manner, free from initial bias and conflicts of interest. Impartiality does not preclude the ombuds from developing an interest in securing changes that are deemed necessary as a result of the process, nor from otherwise being an advocate on behalf of a designated constituency. The ombuds may become an advocate within the entity for change where the process demonstrates a need for it.

The ombuds' structural independence is the foundation upon which the ombuds' impartiality is built. Acting in an impartial manner requires that the ombuds be authorized to gather facts from relevant sources and apply relevant policies, guidelines and laws, to consider the rights and interests of all affected parties, and to identify appropriate actions to resolve the issue.[14] After the ombuds reaches a conclusion, the ombuds may become an advocate for change to implement that conclusion. For example, when an ombuds identifies a systemic problem, the ombuds may advocate for changes to correct the problem.[15] In this regard, the role of the ombuds is analogous to the role of a mediator in the sense that both serve as advocates for a fair and respectful process. The *Ombuds Standards* Section A(7)(d) identify that ombuds function by such means as facilitating, negotiating, and mediating.

On a human and personal level, it may be difficult for an ombuds to conduct inquiries and investigations in an impartial manner. Frequently an ombuds is selected from within an entity. Because of personal reputation and stature, a person already known to the entity could not afford to be derelict in the performance of duties.[16] But the ombuds may have friends who are subjects of complaints. A complainant may be someone with whom this ombuds had differences of opinions. Can this former entity "insider" be impartial in conducting an investigation of friends or enemies? All ombuds come to their positions possessing personal and professional background and histories, individual likes and dislikes, and life experiences.

> Inevitably, every ombudsperson confronts a situation that challenges his or her neutrality -- encountering a person who evokes strong like or dislike, receiving a complaint motivated by values that seem reprehensible, hearing a charge against a trusted and respected colleague, confronting an issue whose volatility or sensitivity might undermine organizational support for the

---

[14] *Ombuds Standards*, the Report, Section C(2) at 6.

[15] *Ombuds Standards,* Section C(2).

[16] Futter, *supra* note 5, at 39.

ombuds office.[17]

An ombuds' impartiality may also be affected by the ombuds' views of an entity's policies. Can an ombuds be professionally impartial when an ombuds personally disagrees with the entity's policies? Similarly, how do the factors of race, gender, sexual orientation, or age of the ombuds or any party affect the ombuds' view of the parties or problem?

One of the most effective principles for assuring neutrality and freedom from personal bias is for the ombuds primarily to assist others in problem-solving, and not to be the resolver. Thus, an ombuds should provide information and options to the complainant, and the ombuds should outline possible risks and benefits of each option. The ombuds would then let the complainant decide the best course of action and should not provide advice.[18]

To be impartial, an ombuds must not take sides during a conflict, must not have a personal stake in the outcome of a conflict, and must not have any conflicts of interest with those involved in the inquiry or investigation. Two organizational ombuds writing on the need for an organizational ombuds' neutrality offer the following advice:

> Ombudspeople must do all they can to ensure that they do not have, and do not appear to have, a conflict of interest between their position as ombuds and any other relationships with those in the institution, or with other affiliations in their lives.[19]

This admonition applies equally to classical and advocate ombuds.

Advocate ombuds must conduct investigations in an impartial manner, free from initial bias. Nevertheless, they may advocate for change if the investigation demonstrates a need for it. For example, Long-Term Care Ombuds are advocate ombuds who are established with the authority to receive complaints from residents of nursing homes and board-and-care facilities, and

---

[17] Howard Gadlin and Elizabeth Walsh Pino, *Neutrality: A Guide*, 13 NEGOTIATION J. 17, 18 (1997). Gadlin and Pino write about "neutrality" but their comments apply equally to "impartiality"; these terms are sometimes used interchangeably.

[18] As has been noted, "ombudspeople help by maintaining their neutrality, not by giving advice. When someone visits the ombuds office seeking advice on how to act so as to win a conflict or grievance, or how to protect himself or herself in a conflict or grievance, that person is asking the ombuds to serve as an ally. In such circumstances, giving advice is never neutral. . . An ombudsperson can help people by working with them to identify, construct, and evaluate options by helping them help themselves." *Id.* at 23.

[19] *Id.* at 24.

when necessary advocate for these constituents. In addition, Long-Term Care Ombuds are required to report to legislatures about trends and issues in long-term-care facilities. Therefore, the Long-Term Care Ombuds should begin the investigation in an impartial manner, taking the side of neither the nursing home resident nor the facility. If, however, the ombuds' investigation reveals institutional mismanagement or abuse of residents, the ombuds should become an advocate for the residents. This advocacy may include taking administrative, judicial or legislative action. This change in objectives and duties presents its own special challenges. Will it be difficult for the ombuds to shift from impartially conducting an investigation to advocating for change? More to the point, even if the ombuds subjectively believes they have shifted roles in an appropriate and ethical manner, will other stakeholders share the same perceptions?

A similar dilemma confronts a classical ombuds who is routinely called upon to investigate and criticize executive action. The duality of the ombuds' role may give the appearance of anti-government slant or bias. This can negatively affect the perception of the ombuds' impartiality, creating an ethical dilemma for the legislative ombuds.

An ombuds must be -- and must be perceived to be -- honest and fair in order to make the work of the office a success. The ombuds must have integrity to withstand pressures from management, friends and former entity colleagues. An ombuds must strive to keep biases out of any discussions with parties and out of any recommendation or report the ombuds may issue.

Confidentiality

The third essential characteristic of an ombuds is confidentiality. Individuals seek an ombuds' help because they wish to maintain privacy in the matters divulged. Some individuals fear retaliation, some fear increased harassment, and others fear embarrassment. For these reasons, they opt to use a confidential resource in lieu of other traditional complaint processes, such as grievance procedures or formal complaints or litigation.

Like a mediator, an ombuds serves as an alternative means of dispute resolution, a means by which issues may be raised, considered and resolved. The need for confidentiality in operating an ombuds' office may be compared to the need for confidentiality in mediation.

> One of the central functions of mediation is to encourage the parties to speak candidly about their interests, needs, fears, and desires. If a party has any concern over whether what it tells the mediator in confidence, or what it does in the negotiations, might be revealed to its detriment, any rational party would not be as forthcoming - it would want to protect against revealing too

much and hence maintain an adversarial position akin to litigation.[20]

If a complainant fears that the ombuds would disclose his identity or the matter discussed, an ombuds could not be an effective complaint handler. The *Ombuds Standards*, therefore, provide that the authorizing entity should establish an ombuds to operate confidentially:

> An ombuds does not disclose and is not required to disclose any information provided in confidence, except to address an imminent risk of serious harm. Records pertaining to a complaint, inquiry, or investigation are confidential and not subject to disclosure outside the ombuds' office. An ombuds does not reveal the identity of a complainant without that person's express consent. An ombuds may, however, at the ombuds' discretion disclose non-confidential information and may disclose confidential information so long as doing so does not reveal its source. An ombuds should discuss any exceptions to the ombuds' maintaining confidentiality with the source of the information.[21]

Confidentiality may be provided by law, written policy or agreement. The *Administrative Dispute Resolution Act* addresses confidentiality for ombuds serving within the federal government.[22] Some state ombuds have confidentiality provided for within the statutes that create their offices. These include ombuds offices established by Alaska,[23] Arizona,[24] Iowa,[25] Hawaii[26] and Nebraska,[27] and

---

[20] Philip J. Harter, *Neither Cop Nor Collection Agent: Encouraging Administrative Settlements by Ensuring Mediator Confidentiality*, 41 ADMIN L REV 315, 324 (1989).

[21] The *Ombuds Standards* note that a classical ombuds should not be required to discuss confidentiality with government officials and employees to the extent that an applicable statute makes clear that such an individual may not withhold information from the ombuds and that such a person has no reasonable expectation of confidentiality in information provided to the ombuds. See, *Ombuds Standards*, n. 3.

[22] 5 USC § 574. One of this chapter's authors, Philip J. Harter, helped draft the ADRA.

[23] ALASKA STAT. § 24.55.160(b). The Alaskan statute provides, "The ombudsman shall maintain confidentiality with respect to all matters and identities of the complainants or witnesses coming before the ombudsman. . ."

[24] ARIZ. REV. STAT. ANN. § 41-1378. The Arizona legislation provides, "If requested by the complainants or witnesses, the ombudsman-citizens aide shall maintain confidentiality with respect to those matters necessary to protect the identities of the complainants or witnesses. The ombudsman-citizens aide shall ensure that confidential records are not disclosed by either the ombudsman-citizens aide or staff to the ombudsman-citizens aide."

the Long-Term Care Ombuds established in the Older Americans Act.[28] Apart from these few statutes, however, there is no uniform protection.

The courts have not consistently recognized ombuds' confidentiality, though some courts have upheld an ombuds' privilege based on a common law theory[29] or on an implied-in-contract theory.[30] The first case in which a court recognized a privilege for an ombuds under federal law was *Shabazz v. Scurr*.[31] Courts have recognized a common law privilege under Federal Rule of Evidence 501 specifically for corporate ombuds.[32] Based on their recognition of the need

---

[25] IOWA CODE ANN. § 2C.8(b). The Iowa code provides that "the citizens' aide may maintain secrecy in respect to all matters including the identities of the complainants or witnesses coming before the citizens' aide. . ."

[26] HAW. REV. STAT. § 96-9(b). The Hawaii statute provides, "The ombudsman is required to maintain secrecy in respect to all matters and the identities of the complainants or witnesses coming before the ombudsman. . ."

[27] NEB. REV. STAT. ANN. § 81-8, 251. The law creating the Nebraska ombuds' office (called the "Public Counsel") states, "In discussing matters with which he or she has dealt, the Public Counsel need not identify those immediately concerned if to do so would cause needless hardship."

[28] 42 USC § 712(d).

[29] The common law privilege test requires a showing of four factors: (1) the communication must be one made in the belief that it will not be disclosed; (2) confidentiality must be essential to the maintenance of the relationship between the parties; (3) the relationship should be one that society considers worthy of being fostered; and (4) the injury to the relationship incurred by disclosure must be greater than the benefit gained in the correct disposal of litigation. This test was applied and found applicable to ombuds' communications in Kientzy v. McDonnell Douglas Corp., 133 F.R.D. 570 (E.D. Mo. 1991), McGuinness v. Barnes, 294 N.J. Super. 519; 683 A.2d 862 (1994) and Van Martin v. UTC, Docket No. 95-8389-CIV-UNGARO-BENAGES, (S.D. Fla. 1996) (per curiam).

[30] The implied-in-contract theory posits that when an individual decides to use the ombuds' resource, an agreement exists between the visitor and the ombuds that confidentiality will be maintained. The individual is advised about the confidential nature of the communications, and agrees that communications with the ombuds will remain confidential and that no one may waive this requirement except the ombuds. The implied-in-contract theory was recognized in Roy v. United Technologies, *Inc*, Case No: CIVIL H-89-680 (D. Conn 1990), in which the court held that the ombuds' communications met the common law test of privilege, and also found an independent basis for protection of these communications in an implied-contract theory. Though successful as between the ombuds and the complainant -- the "parties" to the implied-in-fact contract -- this theory may not be effective to protect discovery by persons who are not bound by the agreement.

[31] Shabazz v. Scurr, 662 F. Supp. 90 (S.D. Iowa 1987). In *Shabazz*, the US District Court was "...persuaded that the flow of information to the [ombuds'] office from citizens would be threatened if it became known that the statutory assurances of general confidentiality would not be respected in federal court. . ." The Court went on to note that ". . .anything which chills a citizen's willingness to come forward limits the [ombuds'] offices' effectiveness. . ." *Shabazz*, at 92.

for confidentiality for mediators and employee counselors, other courts appear likely to support the creation or recognition of an ombuds' privilege.[33] Some courts, however, have refused to recognize an ombuds' privilege.[34]

In response to the lack of clear direction from specific statutes or the courts, entities and ombuds have developed internal policies to attempt to ensure that an ombuds does not disclose and is not required to disclose information provided in confidence. Entities have ensured that the document establishing the ombuds office and also the entity's employee handbook, code of corporate conduct, management training data, and other materials distributed to employees, for example, explicitly note that ombuds' communications are confidential. Web sites and brochures describing the office and the services it performs should also include information about confidentiality.[35] The data-handling, the employee handbook, together with other recommended practices, are directed to helping establish a routine practice by the ombuds. These consistent practices will help protect ombuds' communications from discovery since such practices support the assertion of the implied contract theory, and the assertion of Federal Rule of Evidence 406,[36] or its analogous state evidentiary rule.

---

[32] In the following unpublished cases, an ombuds' privilege was also upheld: Roy v. United Technologies, Inc, Case No: CIVIL H-89-680; Kientzy v. McDonnell Douglas Corp., 133 F.R.D. 570; Jones v. McDonnell Douglas, Case No. 4:94-CV-355 (E.D. Mo. 1995); McMillan v. The Upjohn Company, Case No: 1:92:CV:826 (W.D. Mich, 3/8/95); Wagner v. The Upjohn Company, Case No. A91-2156CL (Mich. Cir. Ct., Kalamazoo Co., April 22, 1992). In addition, the California Court of Appeals, citing *Kientzy*, held that ombuds' communications are protected by the California Constitution in *Garstang*, 39 Cal. App. 4th 526, *supra* note 11.

[33] Foxgate Homeowners' Ass'n, Inc v. Bramalea California, Inc et al, 108 Cal. Rtr. d 642 (Cal. 2001), an example in the context of mediation. Oleszko v. State Compensation Insurance Fund, No 99-15207, DC No CV-95-00516-VRW, 2001, (9th Circuit) (communications with an Employee Assistance Program consultant were confidential and privileged from disclosure.) Kozlowski v. Upjohn, File No 94-5431-NZ (Mich. Cir. Ct. 1995) and NLRB v. Joseph Macaluso, 618 F.2d 51 (9th Cir 1980) (in the context of federal mediation).

[34] *See, e.g.,* Solorzano v. Shell Chemical Co, No. 99-2831, (E.D. La. 2000) and Carman v. McDonnell Douglas Corp, 114 F.3d 790 (8th Cir. 1997).

[35] Effectively then, separate from the "implied contract" that exists between ombuds and visitor is another: the contract between the entity and the ombuds. This ombuds-entity contract would be violated if the ombuds were required to disclose confidential communications. The entity establishing the ombuds office requires it to comply, and operate in accordance, with professional standards of ombuds' practice. The ombuds is expected to maintain confidentiality and impartiality. If the ombuds is required to disclose confidential communications, he is forced to breach the contract that is established with the entity, and with all visitors who have accessed the office in the past and who would access the office in the future.

[36] Federal Rule of Evidence 406 provides that "[e]vidence of the habit of a person or of the routine practice of an organization, whether corroborated or not and regardless of the presence of eyewitnesses, is relevant to prove that the conduct of the person or organization on a particular occasion was in conformity with the habit or routine practice."

To ensure visitor awareness, some ombuds advise every visitor to their offices about confidentiality. Unless clear statutory confidentiality exists, visitors are advised that if they accept the entity's offer to use the ombuds as a resource and accept the ombuds' offer to review the matter, then they agree to be bound by certain limitations. Visitors should not be permitted to abrogate the contract by attempting to waive confidentiality. Neither the entity nor the visitor may waive confidentiality with respect to communications to and from the ombuds; rather, the ombuds can prevent anyone from revealing that communication.[37]

As the process of developing the ABA *Ombuds Standards* and court decisions have revealed, uniformity and consistency in conducting ombuds' business and in maintaining confidentiality are essential to an effective ombuds' office. Because of the unsettled state of the law relating to confidentiality of communications or ombuds' privilege, many ombuds have understandably developed protocols in their own offices.

Some organizational ombuds have developed a statement of nondisclosure to advise the complainant of the terms of the relationship. Advocate ombuds may find it useful to develop a similar statement of nondisclosure that reminds individuals about nonconfidential and formal avenues available through which they may seek to resolve problems, report concerns, or institute a formal investigation. But a statement of nondisclosure may present an ethical dilemma for some classical ombuds. Some statutes provide that government officials and employees may not withhold information from ombuds. Thus, those officials and employees should have no reasonable expectation of confidentiality with respect to any information they provide an ombuds.

Therefore, the *Ombuds Standards* note that when the statute is clear, classical ombuds should not be required to discuss confidentiality. Will all employees be aware of the statutory distinctions? Will the concept of confidentiality be more confusing for employees in entities with organizational ombuds? While a government official or employee may be required by statute to provide information to a classical ombuds, disclosure may create an ethical dilemma for a classical ombuds if the ombuds believes that the employee may be subject to disciplinary action or unfair retaliation. Recognizing the potential confusion, a classical ombuds faces an ethical dilemma and may decide to advise officials and employees.

Absolute confidentiality would also present an ombuds with ethical dilemmas. Sometimes maintaining confidentiality would be inconsistent with competing societal interests. For example, an individual might tell an ombuds he intends harm to himself or others. Therefore, the *Ombuds Standards* and ombuds statutes and policies include an exception, to the otherwise required

---

[37] This privilege is consistent with that contained within the Uniform Mediation Act, Section 4(b).

confidentiality, to permit the ombuds to disclose confidential information to address an imminent risk of serious harm.

Some instances of imminent risk of serious harm, such as threatened physical harm to an individual, may be clear, but others may present the ombuds with a greater dilemma in deciding whether to disclose the confidential information. What should an ombuds do upon learning that the proposed location for a new playground was formerly a hazardous waste dumpsite? Or upon discovering ongoing embezzlement from the entity? Should the ombuds disclose to the entity's auditor what the ombuds has learned from a confidential source, or should the ombuds perhaps suggest that the auditor conduct an independent investigation? Even if an ombuds makes no finding and issues no report, an ombuds' referral to formal channels could link the ombuds to a formal proceeding. It may be difficult, although necessary, for an ombuds to act in a way that protects the identity of the source of the information.

Another ethical dilemma arises because confidentiality is not absolute. Does the ombuds have an obligation to inform the visitor that the ombuds would like to maintain confidentiality, even though the ombuds cannot ensure it? Surely in many circumstances, this would chill an individual's willingness to disclose a problem or candidly discuss issues.

Ethical dilemmas also arise when an ombuds' staff breaches confidentiality. Should the ombuds notify a complainant that a breach has occurred? Should the ombuds attempt to limit the further dissemination of confidential information? Should the ombuds try to retrieve documents that have been released? If the ombuds unsuccessfully asserts a privilege of confidentiality in a court proceeding, will the ombuds be deemed to have waived confidentiality in general, or will a waiver be found only with respect to that specific issue or complaint?[38]

Ombuds may face ethical dilemmas in everyday interactions. Consider: an officer of an organization asks the ombuds whether a particular person has complained or been complained about at any time. What response can the ombuds make, and continue to make, even when pressed hard by the officer? Perhaps the inquiry is phrased more generically: the officer asks whether a particular policy has ever been the subject of a complaint to the ombuds. The information-seeking goes both ways. Consider: A person lodges a complaint with the ombuds, having understood the importance of confidentiality to the ombuds' work. Nevertheless, this person later seeks to obtain all the records from the ombuds regarding similar complaints.

---

[38] *See*, McMillan v. The Upjohn Company, Case No: 1:92:CV:826, *supra* note 32, in which an ombuds provided a memorandum to the Upjohn Human Resources Department. While the Court found that the "cat was out of the bag" with respect to the memorandum, it limited disclosure to the one topic and granted a protective order to the remainder of the ombuds' communications.

Confidentiality protects the ombuds from responding to management and others about subjects the ombuds office investigates. The ombuds should not disclose names unless given express permission by the individuals to do so. Still, the ombuds may be responsive to management by carrying out inquiries and investigations in a responsible and professional manner, and by providing reports and making recommendations about systemic problems.

Ethical dilemmas may result when an ombuds begins to see a pattern or practice of questionable behavior within an organization. For example, an organizational ombuds may discover a pattern of discrimination. Should the ombuds continue to investigate? Or, recognizing an emerging pattern, does the ombuds at some point have a duty to ensure that the pattern -- and not just the particular instance -- is addressed by the entity?

Some offices do not retain records for this very reason. Some offices shred all records within a short time frame. Some offices refuse to respond to subpoenas, and others have asserted the privilege of confidentiality in the context of a court proceeding. Many offices put in place a nondisclosure policy with respect to office employees and visitors to the office.

An ombuds also faces an ethical dilemma when subpoenaed to provide records or to testify. For example, an organizational ombuds may be subpoenaed to testify about all complaints alleging discrimination that the ombuds has received. The issue usually arises when a complainant files a lawsuit against an entity. When an ombuds is confronted with a subpoena, the ombuds and its independent legal counsel must weigh the harm the disclosure may cause to the ombuds' essential characteristics. One organizational ombuds has described the potential harm as follows:

> If an Ombudsman appears as a witness in a specific case, in an apparently adversarial hearing, the image of the confidentiality of these practitioners will be damaged ... even in those cases where specific complainants to the Office have given permission for the Ombudsman to speak about them in a public hearing ....

> If an Ombudsman appears as a formal witness, the _image_ of confidentiality is damaged. Observers may or may not hear that permission was given by each party to the case, and may simply see that an Ombudsman will, after all, break confidentiality.

> If a workplace Ombudsman testifies in a way that appears to favor an employer against a worker or manager, it will appear ... that the Ombudsman is just a tool of management. If an Ombudsman testifies against the employer, it will sharply reduce the interest of employers to maintain ... this kind of in-house critic and change agent. And faced with this potential dilemma, practitioners themselves may lose their courage to be outspoken

in raising problems to management, and in support of those who blow the whistle.[39]

To avoid releasing confidential information in response to a subpoena, the ombuds and its legal counsel must educate the parties. It may be that plaintiff's counsel is unfamiliar with the ombuds' function, or fails to understand that the ombuds has not provided information to the defendant entity.

An ombuds may attempt to maintain confidentiality by shredding notes upon closing a file. Some data must be maintained to help the ombuds examine trends, systemic issues and problems, and areas of strength and weakness. But the data can potentially create a problem if certain terms are used, such as "sexual harassment," "race" or "age" discrimination, since these terms have particular legal meanings and implications. Identifying a matter in this way and listing it with others under the same category could produce the impression that a number of discrimination complaints have been raised with the ombuds.

The official act which establishes the ombuds office -- whether a legislative enactment or a publicly available written policy -- should authorize the ombuds to operate confidentially. Documents developed by the entity and information distributed by the ombuds should also include information about confidentiality. Finally, the ombuds should operate confidentially. Such consistent record-keeping and behavior will assist ombuds in asserting and protecting confidentiality in communications and documents, and may help diminish -- though not eliminate – the problems associated with subpoenas the ombuds faces.

Notice

Inextricably intertwined with the essential characteristics of ombuds is the question of notice. Ombuds meet with people who wish to discuss complaints and allegations of unfairness, maladministration and abuse of power. These persons fear retaliation or loss of privacy, among other negative repercussions. The ombuds' movement has grown, in part, in order to help people with sensitive questions and concerns to surface problems at a time, and in a manner that facilitates expeditious resolution. Importantly, this resolution ideally can be reached while avoiding personal identification. The ombuds serves as a buffer and intermediary.

The ombuds' barrier may be only semi-permeable. Some information generally must flow in both directions in order for the process and system to be effective. This can raise additional issues about the legal nature of the

---

[39] Mary Rowe, *Should an Ombudsman Testify*, THE OMBUDSMAN NEWS, Issue Seven, Winter 1989-90, emphasis added.

communications to the ombuds, and by the ombuds to the entity. If the ombuds is made aware of information, is that awareness sufficient to serve as notice to the entity in which the ombuds operates? Should it be? What impact does notice have on an ombuds' independence and the confidentiality of communication between an ombuds and a complainant? How does notice impact an individual's rights and remedies? Can an ombuds provide notice to an entity without revealing the identity of the complainant? Even a broadly-framed notice may ineluctably carry the potential of revealing the complainant's identity. These questions and issues illustrate the ethical dilemmas ombuds face as a result of their essential characteristics.

Some have proposed that an ombuds should be able to accept information on behalf of the complainant and then advise the organization, thereby putting the organization on notice of a particular issue. This would essentially make the ombuds an agent for the complainant. A related difficulty with this proposal is that for an ombuds to so act would be in derogation of the ombuds' role within the organization. Organizations provide other, formal resources to make reports to the organization and to provide it notice -- this is not the role of the ombuds. The ombuds should not be a repository of notice for the entity, and this position best protects and preserves the professional integrity and essential functions of the ombuds.

Whether a report or complaint made to an ombuds constitutes notice of a potential claim to the entity within which the ombuds works is a question that has been left unanswered by the *Ombuds Standards*. On the issue of notice, the *Ombuds Standards* state the following:

> These Standards . . . do not address the issue of whether a communication to the ombuds will be deemed notice to anyone, including any entity in or for which the ombuds acts. Important legal rights and liabilities may, however, be affected by the resolution of that issue.

In this section of the *Ombuds Standards*, the ABA recognizes that the law in this area is evolving. The courts have yet to provide clear guidance on the subject of when and if a complaint to an ombuds constitutes notice to the entity in which the ombuds works.[40] Yet the existence of the "Notice" Section within the *Ombuds Standards* signifies the importance of this issue in the operation of ombuds' offices.

The issue of notice is of particular importance to organizational ombuds and labor and employment legal counsel. Some employment lawyers are concerned that if an employee discusses a concern with an ombuds, the employee may lose a right of action. For example, what happens if an individual

---

[40] ABA *Standards for the Establishment and Operation of Ombuds Offices*, The Report, at 10.

confidentially raises an allegation of sexual harassment with an ombuds? The individual may have not yet filed a formal complaint, and has the individual failed to preserve a legal remedy? What if the individual believes that the report to the ombuds preserved the claim? There are no reported cases that answer these questions. We can only act on the fundamental principle that an ombuds' goal is to help, not harm. Therefore, entities that establish ombuds and ombuds themselves need to set policies to address these questions.

Entities that establish organizational ombuds and the ombuds themselves must articulate that an organizational ombuds is not a designated resource for employees' grievances. Complainants should be informed that the complaint to the ombuds is not notice to the entity and that failure to notify the entity may affect the individual's legal rights. The ombuds office is a voluntary and informal resource, in addition to -- and not instead of -- other grievance-handling systems. The employee may choose from a variety of other complaint-handling resources, including management, human resources and EEO officers. If a union member, the employee may have additional avenues for resolving complaints.

If an entity has no clear policy regarding notice, then in the event of litigation, the parties will be left to argue principles of the common law of agency. Although a properly established ombuds office will not meet any of the factual requisites of agency, it is the element of control -- or continuous subjection to the will of the principal -- which clearly exempts an ombuds from being an agent.

The closer on the independence spectrum that the ombuds is to management of an entity, the more likely the ombuds will be construed as an agent for notice to the entity. Thus, it is crucial that the ombuds be -- and be perceived to be -- separate from the rest of the entity. When an ombuds office has been properly established, with the requisite independence, confidentiality and impartiality, the office is not in the management hierarchy and the ombuds is not an agent for the entity.[41] This position should be made clear in the charter establishing the ombuds office, and in information describing the office.

Even were an ombuds deemed an "agent" of the entity, statements made to the ombuds would constitute notice to the entity <u>only if</u> (1) the ombuds were at a sufficiently high level in the company's management hierarchy to qualify as a proxy for the company; (2) the ombuds were charged with the duty to act on the knowledge and stop the harassment; or (3) the ombuds were charged with a duty to inform the company of the harassment.[42] Neither (1) nor (2) apply to ombuds,

---

[41] The existence of an agency relationship depends upon whether these requisites are met: (1) manifestations by the principal that the agent shall act for him; (2) agent's acceptance of the undertaking; and (3) understanding between the parties that the principal is to be in control of the undertaking. Restatement (Second) of Agency §1 cmt. b.

[42] *See, e.g.*, Meritor Sav Bank, FSB v. Vinson, 477 US 57, 65 (1986); Torres v. Pisano, 116 F. 3d 625 (2nd Cir. 1997). In *Torres,* the Court held that even though the complainant's supervisor <u>was</u>

since they are not in the management hierarchy, and are not charged with a duty to act to stop harassment. Factor (3) does not apply since ombuds are not charged with the duty to inform the company of harassment complaints. On the contrary, ombuds specifically inform employees and the company that all statements made to them will be held in confidence. Accordingly, communications made to an ombuds do not constitute notice to the entity.

Others have supported the position that disclosure to an ombuds should not be deemed to be notice to the entity. In identifying the benefits of keeping harassment complaints confidential, one litigation attorney whose practice includes employment law matters made the following observation:

> If communications with an ombudsman are privileged, shielded from discovery, and cannot be used to establish employer notice, an employer can assure its employees of strict confidentiality without fear that an employee's communication with the ombudsman will either trigger an employer duty to investigate and take action, or serve as a basis for imposing employee liability.[43]

The ombuds may find an unfair process and suggest to the entity that a formal investigation be conducted; however, ombuds do not conduct an investigation and recommend discipline or punishment or make other conclusions that could affect the employment or due process rights of an individual. To do so would potentially make the ombuds an agent of the entity.

In recognition of the concerns for individuals who seek an ombuds' assistance, for the entity in which the ombuds operates, and for the ombuds office itself, ombuds should establish a policy on notice. This policy should provide that as long as the ombuds functions in accordance with the *Ombuds Standards*, the ombuds should not be deemed an agent of any entity (other than the office of the ombuds), nor should any communication to the ombuds be imputed as notice to anyone, including the entity in which the ombuds acts.

Some may argue that there is an advantage in making the ombuds an agent for notice: an entity would be required to take corrective action. However, if an ombuds were to breach confidentiality and advise an entity about a confidential complaint, there would be no trust in the ombuds. The disadvantage

---

an agent of the entity, the entity had not received notice of the sexual harassment complaints since the complainant expressly asked the supervisor to keep the complaints confidential. The Court went further and stated that "the law will not presume in every case that harassed members of Title VII's protected classes do not know what is best for themselves and cannot make reasonable decisions to delay -- at least for a time -- pursuing harassment claims, perhaps for privacy or emotional reasons, until they are ready to do so." *Torres,* at 639.

[43] Mary Elizabeth McGarry, *Ombudsman Privilege: Keeping Harassment Complaints Confidential,* 214 N.Y.L.J 104 (1995).

outweighs the advantage because the entity would lose an independent, impartial and confidential complaint-handler.

Conclusion

Federal, state and local governments, academic institutions, corporations, and nonprofit organizations are establishing ombuds offices. The success of ombuds is attributable, and directly related to, how well-defined the ombuds offices are when they are authorized, and how the ombuds can operate in accordance with the *Ombuds Standards* and the essential characteristics. Although ombuds "may not prevent all future disasters. . . [they] should serve to prevent many and to avoid some of the most blatant problems, and, at a minimum, to limit and reduce potential disasters to relatively less significance. That, in itself, is sufficient justification."[44] These words may rightfully be applied to organizational, classical and advocate ombuds.

The ABA developed standards to provide guidance on the establishment and operation of ombuds offices. Adherence to the *Ombuds Standards* helps to protect ombuds from ethical dilemmas that arise out of their methods of operation, their functions and their interdependent essential characteristics. However, the *Ombuds Standards* do not eliminate all potential dilemmas that are inherent in the ombuds' essential characteristics. The truly successful ombuds, therefore, may be the one with the most accurate ethical compass.

---

[44] Futter, *supra* note 5, at 47.

Chapter XII

Ethics and Online Dispute Resolution

By Sandra A. Sellers and Gina Viola Brown

Introduction

The field of Online Dispute Resolution (ODR) is extremely new and is still developing rapidly. ODR promises to use the Internet and other emerging technologies to bring conflict resolution processes to parties for whom it is not practical to meet face-to-face, particularly in cross-border disputes. ODR processes overcome certain limitations of face-to-face traditional dispute resolution, but raise other new concerns not experienced in traditional processes, particularly with respect to building trust among the parties and establishing the integrity of the neutral. Parties participating in ODR processes do not sit at the same table or even in the same building. Rather, one party may be in Atlanta and another in Vancouver while the neutral is located in Tokyo. The parties and the neutral may be using an Internet-based dispute resolution service provided by an organization physically located in Amsterdam.

This chapter will discuss the ethical issues raised by ODR, focussing on the duties of the ODR provider (ODR Provider). For purposes of this chapter we define an ODR Provider as an entity or individual that provides dispute resolution services or processes in an online environment.[1] ODR Providers currently cover an extremely diverse range of processes, target markets and geographical regions.[2] No one ODR process fits all disputes, and organizations providing ODR services should be encouraged to continue to develop new models.

---

[1] For definitions of dispute resolution provider organizations, see Chapter IX or the *CPR-Georgetown Principles for ADR Provider Organizations* (May 2002) (hereinafter *CPR-Georgetown Principles*).

[2] For a list of ODR service businesses and organizations, *see* <http://www.ombuds.org/center/onlineadr.html >, a project of the University of Massachusetts Center for Information Technology and Dispute Resolution (visited April 23, 2002).

There are no published ethical guidelines for online neutrals or ODR Providers. To the extent that ODR is alternative dispute resolution (ADR), albeit in an online medium, ODR Providers and neutrals should observe existing ethical guidelines that apply to traditional ADR professionals, including the *Model Standards of Conduct for Mediators (Joint Standards)*, the *ABA/AAA Code of Ethics for Arbitrators in Commercial Disputes* and the CPR-Georgetown *Principles for ADR Provider Organizations (CPR-Georgetown Principles)*.[3] Online neutrals and provider organizations may also be bound by state ethical guidelines.[4]

However, the technology medium and the cross-border nature of most ODR disputes raise additional ethical issues and challenges for ODR Providers and online neutrals. This chapter will discuss efforts to create ethical standards for ODR, the unique issues raised by ODR, and recommended disclosures to address these issues. In discussing these ethical issues, the authors will refer to analogous offline ethical standards for guidance.

Efforts to Address Ethics and ODR

As soon as early ODR pioneers created web sites offering internet-based dispute resolution services, issues about ethics in ODR emerged.[5] ODR services handle disputes that arise from offline transactions as well as those disputes that arise between businesses conducting transactions online with other businesses (B2B) and between consumers and online merchants (B2C). Numerous governments, corporations, and other organizations have recommended the use of ODR to resolve online disputes and have also issued recommended guidelines for ODR.[6] The task of developing international ethical guidelines for these ODR processes is ongoing.

---

[3] For a discussion of the *Model Standards of Conduct for Mediators* (hereinafter *Joint Standards*) and the *Model Family Mediation Standards*, *see* Chapter V. For a discussion of ethics for provider organizations, *see* Chapter IX.

[4] However, it is difficult to ascertain which existing ethical guidelines may apply, particularly when the ODR Provider, the neutral and the disputants are located in different jurisdictions and are from different legal systems and cultures. For an analogous discussion, see Chapter V and Chapter VII on the unauthorized practice of law by mediators and arbitrators.

[5] Bruce L. Beal, *Online Mediation: Has Its Time Come?* 15 OHIO ST. J. ON DISP. RESOL. 735, 744 (2000). For a discussion of early ODR Provider sites, see Henry H. Perritt, Jr., *Dispute Resolution in Cyberspace: Demand for new Forms of ADR*, 15 OHIO ST. J. ON DISP. RESOL. 675 (2000).

[6] Organization for Economic Cooperation and Development, *Recommendations of the OECD Council Concerning Guidelines for Consumer Protection in the Context of Electronic Commerce* (visited April 23, 2002) <http://www.oecd.org/pdf/M00000000/M00000363.pdf>; Global Business Dialogue on Electronic Commerce (visited April 23, 2002) <http://consumerconfidence.gbde.org/adr_rec.html>; the Australian Best Practice Model for

In October 2000, the American Bar Association formed the Task Force on e-Commerce and Dispute Resolution (the Task Force).[7] The purpose of the Task Force was to propose protocols, guidelines and standards for parties to ODR and ODR Providers, focussing on multi-jurisdiction B2B and B2C transactions. The Task Force surveyed existing ODR Providers and e-commerce users, compiled existing guidelines and other recommendations by governmental and non-governmental organizations for online merchants concerning dispute resolution, and held public hearings. In each aspect of its work, the Task Force sought international input. The Task Force recognized concerns that disputants, particularly consumers in B2C transactions, need disclosure of information that will permit disputants to make informed choices about participating in ODR. The Task Force therefore determined to issue guidelines for recommended best practices for ODR Providers.[8] This chapter is based on the information gathered by the Task Force, the Task Force discussion, and the *Best Practices for Online Dispute Resolution Providers.*[9]

The Task Force concluded that ODR raises unique ethical issues and adds new dimensions to analogous offline issues. These issues include transparency of the ODR Provider organization and services, use of the technology itself, costs and funding of online services, impartiality and independence of the online neutral and ODR Provider, confidentiality in an online environment, quality assurance, and accountability.

Business (visited April 23, 2002) <http://www.ecommerce.treasury.gov.au>; American Bar Association Global Cyberspace Jurisdiction Project, London Meeting Draft, *Achieving Legal and Business Order in Cyberspace: A Report on Global Jurisdiction Issues Created by the Internet* (July, 2000) (visited April 23, 2002) <http://www.abanet.org/buslaw/cyber/initiatives/jurisdiction.html>.

[7] Information about the Task Force, as well as all documents compiled and produced by the Task Force, can be accessed at <http://www.law.washington.edu/ABA-eADR>.

[8] The Task Force's *Best Practices for Online Dispute Resolution Providers* have not been submitted to the ABA for formal approval. As a member of the Task Force and the ABA staff liaison to the Task Force respectively, Ms. Sellers and Ms. Brown have been involved in drafting the recommended best practices, and have drawn upon the basic principles set forth therein for their views in this Chapter. The views expressed in this Chapter are solely the views of the authors and are not the views of the ABA or the Task Force.

[9] The Task Force's *Best Practices for Online Dispute Resolution Providers* are intended to assist entities that provide ODR services, that is, resolution of disputes that occur online or disputes that lend themselves to being resolved online, and to consumers of those services. The term "online" describes the use of the Internet or related communications technologies such as email, videoconferencing, or interaction via a web site or chatroom. The Task Force recognized that it is wise not to be too constraining in an emerging, dynamic industry. Consequently, the recommended best practices do not place great emphasis upon form. Rather, the primary points are that the ODR Provider's service is clearly and comprehensively presented to the consumer in a manner that is consistent with the recommended best practices and in fact operates in the manner presented.

In this chapter the authors recommend ethical guidelines to address these issues. The unifying principle of these recommendations is disclosure. ODR professionals and provider organizations must be required to disclose information to permit disputants to determine which ODR process and provider organization is right for their dispute. Given the rapidly developing and international nature of the ODR industry, the authors have resisted recommending specific ethical requirements beyond disclosure. This chapter therefore places heavy emphasis upon the types of disclosures required to fulfill ethical obligations. There may come a time in the not very distant future when the ODR providers will look to designing a more specific set of guidelines as well as an enforcement mechanism for ODR.

Many of the ODR issues addressed below mirror ethical issues in ADR generally. Consequently, the following text may note an issue but refer to treatment elsewhere in this book rather than duplicate the discussion. This chapter, therefore, will focus on ethical issues that are peculiar to ODR or that at least may be impacted by the online environment.

Ethical Issues in ODR

What makes an ODR process different from an offline process? The definition of the process is the same, but the tools the parties and the neutral use to participate in the process are different. In traditional face-to-face ADR processes, the participants usually meet in person, at least for part of the process. This meeting permits the parties to utilize implicit observations, as well as explicit communications, to establish trust in each other and the process. In ODR, the participants rarely meet, and as a result the parties must rely solely on explicit information. The parties cannot judge the behavior or demeanor of the neutral or the other party and must rely upon external information.

Transparency of Organization and Services

On the Internet, not everything is what it seems. It is very easy to set up a web site and offer goods or services via the Internet, whether or not the site owner is legitimate. Visitors are dependent on the explicit information provided on the web site. Consequently, it is extremely important for an ODR Provider to inform users adequately about its organization's structure, the ODR process and the ODR neutrals so that disputants can make informed choices.[10] The *CPR-*

---

[10] This chapter assumes that disputants will have the choice to use ODR. It is not within the scope of this Chapter to address pre-dispute arbitration agreements. The international community is debating whether consumers in B2C disputes should be required to arbitrate, despite a pre-dispute agreement to arbitrate. For further discussion of pre-dispute arbitration contracts see Thomas J. Stipanowich, *Resolving Consumer Disputes, Due Process Protocol Protects Consumer Rights*, 53 DISP. RESOL. J 8, 12 (1999) and Jeremy Senderowicz, *Consumer Arbitration and Freedom of*

Georgetown Principles address disclosure of information about a provider's services and operations. Principle II states that ADR Provider Organizations should "take all reasonable steps" to provide information about the organization and its services.[11] ODR Providers should disclose even more specific information such as physical address and organizational structure. For offline organizations, we assume that this information is obvious or readily available; in the online world it may be either opaque or not available at all.

All information and disclosures should be accurately and completely stated, should be presented as clearly and simply as the substance permits, and should present the most important points in an appropriately conspicuous manner. All information and disclosures presented electronically should employ identifiable and accessible formats, should be printable, and should be downloadable electronically.

Recommended Disclosures

At a minimum, an ODR Provider should disclose the following specific information about its organization: a physical address, information about the organization's structure, a list of officers, and the jurisdiction of incorporation or organization.[12] In addition, the ODR Provider should explain its services and processes, including a description of the types of services and processes provided;[13] rules of procedure for all services and processes provided; nature of the outcome of each service and process and its legal consequences, whether binding or non-binding; and further possible avenues of action, including an appeal.[14]

It also is important at the outset for participants to know whether there are any requirements that must be met to participate in the service and process. For example, ODR Providers clearly should disclose whether there are any prerequisites for accessing the service (such as membership or residency in a

---

Contract: A Proposal to Facilitate Consumers' Informed Consent to Arbitration Clauses in Form Contracts, 32 COLUM. J.L. & SOC. PROBS. 275 (1999).

[11] *CPR-Georgetown Principles.*

[12] A Consumers International study of ADR Provider organizations concluded that most ODR Providers did not supply sufficient information about the organization's governing structure, CONSUMERS INTERNATIONAL, DISPUTES IN CYBERSPACE 2001:UPDATE OF ODR FOR CONSUMERS IN CROSS-BORDER DISPUTES at 10 (November 2001).

[13] See Marc Wilikens, et al., *Out of Court Dispute Settlement in Trans-Border Electronic Commerce* at 23, Joint Research Centre of the European Commission (visited on April 23, 2002) <http://dsa-isis.jrc.it/ADR/Reportv20apr.pdf>; Better Business Bureau, *BBBOnline Code of Online Business Practices* (visited April 23, 2000) <http://www.bbbonline.org/reliability/code/code.asp>.

[14] Global Business Dialogue on Electronic Commerce, *Consumer Confidence: Alternative Dispute Resolution*, September 14, 2001 (visited April 23, 2002) <http://consumerconfidence.gbde.org/adrtokyo2001.pdf>.

particular country or state) and whether the dispute must have a certain minimum value to be submitted to the ODR Provider for resolution. For B2C disputes, the provider should disclose whether the complainant must have submitted the matter to the merchant's customer complaints handling service prior to filing a complaint with the ODR Provider. Similarly, for B2B disputes, the ODR Provider should disclose whether the parties must have attempted direct negotiation prior to mediation, or whether the parties must have attempted mediation prior to arbitration, before initiating the ODR process.

Use of Technology and the Online Environment

ODR promises to use the Internet and other emerging technologies to bring conflict resolution processes to parties for whom it is not practical to meet face-to-face, particularly in cross-border disputes. By expanding the reach of traditional dispute resolution processes, these new technologies raise, to a certain extent, the public's expectations of dispute resolution providers. The technology brings dispute resolution to new forums. At the same time, providers of these services must be aware that for many users, the ODR process may be the disputant's only realistic option for resolution of the dispute.[15]

ODR Providers need to ensure that in adapting these processes to the new technology, the providers do not negatively impact the quality of the process. Standard VI of the *Model Standards of Conduct for Mediators* requires mediators to "conduct the mediation fairly, diligently, and in a manner consistent with the principle of self-determination by the parties."[16]

ODR Providers have an obligation to disclose information about the capabilities and limitations of their online systems, to provide a secure environment, to educate participants in how to use their online systems, and to ensure that the technology does not negatively impact the quality of the process.

Disclosures Regarding Online Systems

As noted earlier, ODR processes can overcome certain limitations of traditional face-to-face dispute resolution, particularly when disputants are in different and remote locations. ODR also can lessen the impact of stereotypes since participants cannot see each other's race, gender, age or physical disabilities. As new technologies are developed and incorporated into ODR systems, perhaps remote participants will enjoy many of the benefits of face-to-face interaction as well. However, these new technologies are expensive, and

---

[15] American Bar Association Global Cyberspace Jurisdiction Project, London Meeting Draft, *Achieving Legal and Business Order in Cyberspace: A Report on Global Jurisdiction Issues Created by the Internet* (July, 2000) (visited April 23, 2002) <http://www.abanet.org/buslaw/cyber/initiatives/jurisdiction.html>.

[16] *Joint Standards*, VI.

incorporating them into online systems is a matter of choice and marketing strategy for ODR Providers. Whatever the technology used, ODR Providers should disclose the online system's capabilities and limitations.

Recommended disclosures

ODR Providers should be required to disclose whether their systems accommodate the disputants' differences in language and culture. An ODR provider can anticipate that disputants from all over the world may access the site and should therefore provide information about the system's ability to provide services to disputants who speak different languages or come from different cultures.

The providers should also disclose whether the online environment incorporates audio and video streaming and other means to enhance the ODR process. The disputants should know whether the process will be handled by e-mail communication or whether additional communication tools are available. Providers also should disclose whether they have tools available for persons with low levels of literacy. If the system is solely text-based, low literacy disputants will have a difficult time using the system.

Providers should disclose whether their technology is accessible to persons with disabilities. The *ADA Mediation Guidelines* (*ADA Guidelines*) provide excellent guidance for ODR providers.[17] The *ADA Guidelines* recommend that providers formulate policies and procedures concerning access for disputants with disabilities.[18] The *ADA Guidelines* also recommend that providers establish a procedure for requesting an accommodation and for submitting a grievance if the request is denied.[19]

Education and Training in Use of Online Systems

Although some prior fledgling efforts existed, ODR became viable in 1999, and many organizations began providing ODR services in 1999-2000. Because many users are unfamiliar with dispute resolution and probably are even less familiar with ODR processes, ODR Providers have an obligation to inform their users about dispute resolution processes generally as well as how to use their ODR system.[20]

---

[17] *ADA Mediation Guidelines,* World Arbitration and Mediation Report, Volume 11, Number 7 (July 2000), pages 195-203.

[18] *Id.,* I.B.2.

[19] *Id.*

[20] Center for Dispute Settlement, *National Standards for Court-Connected Mediation Programs.* Standard 3.1 requires courts to inform their constituencies about mediation process and programs connected to the court. The commentary states that courts have the responsibility to provide

Different user constituencies have different educational needs. Neutrals skilled in traditional face-to-face ADR processes may need to be trained to use particular online technologies. Neutrals will need to adapt their communication and dispute resolution skills to overcome the peculiarities of the impersonal, abbreviated methods of online communication. Unfortunately, a skilled and experienced mediator will not automatically be an effective online mediator. An online mediator needs training and online experience in how to translate those skills to text-based communication.

Disputants may need basic information about different types of dispute resolution processes, including the costs and benefits of participating in dispute resolution and the possible effects the process may have on their legal recourse.[21] Disputants will also need assistance using the online system. ODR Providers should offer training or assistance to all participants. Market forces will influence the level of training given by the ODR Provider.

Recommended disclosures

Regardless of the type of training provided, the ODR Provider should disclose whether training or assistance will be given and sufficient details about the training to allow participants to make informed decisions about using that ODR service. In particular, ODR Providers should disclose the means used to educate potential participants in online procedures, including instructions, tutorials, help files, and the availability of support personnel. ODR Providers should also disclose whether they provide neutrals with training in the use of the ODR system and whether they provide training in adapting the neutrals' skills to the online environment.

Providing a Secure Environment

Beyond disclosure about the system's capabilities and limitations, online providers should employ electronic security mechanisms as part of their systems to preserve the confidentiality of the process and the privacy of participants, and to verify the identities of the parties using the system.[22] Because third parties may have more opportunities to access an ODR process than an offline process, online systems should provide security mechanisms and disclose the type of security utilized, including passwords, type of encryption (if any), secure server, and firewalls.

---

sufficient information about dispute resolution processes to parties and attorneys to allow them to make an informed choice.

[21] For instance, disputants may be contractually required to participate in a binding arbitration process.

[22] *See* Wilikens, et al., *supra* note 13, at 23.

Costs and Funding

Many commentators have discussed the costs of ODR services.[23] Consumer advocates argue that ODR should be offered free or at low cost to consumer participants seeking to resolve a dispute that arises from an online transaction.[24] Their rationale is that the consumer likely has little recourse to a court system either because of jurisdictional obstacles or because the amount of money in dispute is less than the costs of litigation. On the other hand, if the consumer does not bear the cost of the dispute resolution process, who will? As we will discuss later, if the online merchant bears the entire cost of the dispute, the merchant may be less willing to use a dispute resolution process, or there may be a perception that the merchant has special influence over the ODR provider.

The *CPR-Georgetown Principles* require ADR provider organizations to take reasonable steps to provide information about their fees[25] and to make their services available to low-income parties at a reasonable cost.[26] The *CPR-Georgetown Principles* are consistent with the *Model Standards of Conduct for Mediators*. The *Joint Standards* require a mediator to disclose fully and explain the basis for compensation. The *Joint Standards* also require mediators to charge reasonable fees that are "customary in the community."[27] The *ABA/AAA Code of Ethics for Arbitrators in Commercial Disputes* does not address fees and costs.[28]

The authors recommend that the costs of ODR processes should not be so high as to foreclose the opportunity to resolve a dispute, and the cost should be commensurate with the value of the dispute while taking into account the need to avoid frivolous claims. However, short of these aspirational goals, the authors recommend detailed disclosures about costs and funding.

Recommended disclosures

---

[23] *See* Perritt, *supra* note 5, at 698-699; CONSUMERS INTERNATIONAL, *supra* note 12; Wilikens, et al., *supra* note 13, at 23; U.S. Federal Trade Commission and Department of Commerce, *Summary of Public Workshop*, June 6-7, 2000 (visited April 23, 2002) <http://www.ftc.gov/bcp/altdisresolution/summary.htm>.

[24] CONSUMERS INTERNATIONAL, *supra* note 12, at 15.

[25] *CPR-Georgetown Principles*, Principle II.a.

[26] *Id.*, Principle IV.

[27] *Joint Standards*, VIII.

[28] *Code of Ethics for Arbitrators in Commercial Disputes* (1977). The 1977 Code is currently undergoing a revision process. *See* Chapter X for a detailed discussion of the 1977 Code and the revisions.

So that participants can make informed decisions about using that ODR service, the ODR Provider should disclose in advance the details of costs and funding, particularly any up-front costs for the process and the portion of cost each party will bear. In B2C disputes, if there is no cost to the consumer, or if the costs are subsidized, the source of the funding should be disclosed. In B2B disputes, if the costs will not be borne equally by the parties, the distribution should be explained.

Impartiality and Independence

The *Model Standards of Conduct for Mediators* state that "mediator impartiality is central to the mediation."[29] The *ABA/AAA Code of Ethics for Arbitrators in Commercial Disputes* also addresses arbitrator impartiality by requiring the arbitrator to "disclose any interest or relationship likely to affect impartiality or which might create an appearance of impartiality or bias."[30] ADR provider organizations also have a duty to ensure that the processes and services they provide are impartial. Principle III of the *CPR-Georgetown Principles* states that "the ADR Provider Organization has an obligation to ensure that ADR processes provided under its auspices are fundamentally fair and conducted in an impartial manner."[31]

Many existing ODR programs, particularly those involving B2C disputes, are dependent upon businesses to bear, or subsidize, the cost of the dispute resolution process. Some merchants refer all consumer disputes to a particular ODR Provider. This relationship may appear to give the merchant an unfair advantage because it is a repeat user of the ODR Provider's services whereas the consumer is likely a one-time user. One study has found that "repeat players" in dispute resolution processes fare better than one-time users.[32] At the same time, consumer advocates do not want the consumer to bear heavy, if any, costs. But someone has to bear the cost of developing ODR systems and the expenses of individual disputes. Because ODR Providers are not publicly funded like courts, it is unrealistic to expect ODR Providers to refuse relationships with merchants that can supply repeat business. An ODR Provider's independence may also be suspect if the provider refers customers to other services. For instance, an ODR Provider may refer users to a legal services organization if the users seek legal advice or assistance.

---

[29] *Joint Standards*, Standard II.

[30] *Code of Ethics for Arbitrators in Commercial Disputes*, Canon II.

[31] *CPR-Georgetown Principles*, Principle III.

[32] Lisa B. Bingham, *Employment Arbitration, The Repeat Player Effect*, EMPL. RIGHTS AND EMPLOYMENT POLICY J. 1(1) 189 (1997).

Short of complete independence from merchants or funders, how can the impartiality of ODR providers and the process be ensured? The focus should be placed on disclosing existing relationships between ODR Providers and businesses, and on ensuring impartiality of the neutrals. This approach is consistent with the *CPR-Georgetown Principles*.[33]

Recommended disclosures

An ODR Provider should disclose whether it has a relationship with other organizations, such as merchants and trade associations. It should also disclose the following: (1) whether it provides any referral compensation, including referral fees, rebates or commissions; (2) if such referral compensation is paid, to whom; and (3) the amount of the compensation or the basis for calculating the amount of the compensation. These disclosures should give consumers relevant information upon which to base their decision to participate in this provider's ODR process, or at least form the basis for further questions.

The ODR Provider's duty to ensure a fair and impartial process centers on the selection of the neutrals and impartiality of the neutrals. This duty is as important as appropriate disclosures. The provider should state clearly whether neutrals are required to certify that they have no conflicts of interest with respect to a particular dispute, and the provider should explain the process for disclosure of possible conflicts. If the neutrals are bound by a published set of ethical rules, the ODR Provider should identify those rules and post the full text of such rules or include a link to a page where the full text is posted.

Confidentiality, Privacy and Information Security

Confidentiality is regarded as an essential component of dispute resolution processes, particularly mediation and arbitration. The *Joint Standards*, the *ABA/AAA Code of Ethics for Commercial Arbitrators* and the *CPR-Georgetown Principles* all address issues of confidentiality.[34] Without guarantees of confidentiality, disputants may be unwilling to participate in these "alternative" processes or may become circumspect about sharing information. ODR Providers as well as the neutrals will accumulate information about the disputants and possibly the dispute. Because this information is in electronic format, it can easily be hacked or transferred to others, raising additional obligations for the ODR Provider to protect the confidentiality of the disputants and the process.

---

[33] *CPR-Georgetown Principles*, Principle V.b; For a more extensive discussion, *see* Chapter VIII.

[34] *Joint Standards,* Standard V; *Code of Ethics for Arbitrators in Commercial Disputes*, Canon VI; *CPR-Georgetown Principles,* Principle IX.

Privacy

Many jurisdictions now have privacy and information security laws concerning the processing and movement of personal data. Further, there exist a number of privacy "seals" or "trustmarks," which signify that online entities displaying their marks conform to specific privacy protection protocols. Many people fear that the security of online systems is vulnerable to penetration by hackers. Potential ODR participants must be assured that the ODR Provider will use reasonable, available precautions to prevent theft of confidential information and personally identifying data.

Recommended disclosures

Generally, ODR Providers should inform disputants about which laws or seals/trustmarks are applicable to them or to which they voluntarily adhere. More specifically, ODR Providers should disclose (1) what their privacy policies are; (2) how customer information may be used by the ODR Provider, including whether such information may be released, and if so, the circumstances under which that information may be released; (3) whether any ODR proceedings being conducted by the neutrals are monitored by the ODR Provider, and if so, under what circumstances; (4) whether the ODR Provider reviews customer information as part of a quality control process, and if so, who conducts the review; and (5) whether the ODR Provider's web site uses technological means to identify the participant and track the participant's online behavior.[35] If such means are used, the ODR Provider also should disclose whether it provides an opt-out opportunity and other relevant practices.

ODR Providers should disclose their record retention and disposition policies, particularly retention of information about individual participants, as well as records related to specific proceedings. They should disclose the forms of security used for all online processes, particularly protections against theft or disclosure of information provided by participants and information or documents related to specific proceedings. They should identify the security mechanisms used to safeguard information (e.g., data transmission protection protocols, firewalls, anti-virus software, and so forth).

Confidentiality of Specific Proceedings

Beyond privacy considerations, ODR Providers, like other ADR providers,[36] should disclose the scope of confidentiality accorded to the ODR

---

[35] Common technological devices used to identify users include session cookies, persistent cookies, web-bugs, and clear gifs. The European Commission DG Information Society, the Joint Research Centre report explains why cookies and other devices used to verify the identity of the parties involved are essential to the ODR process. *See* Wilikens, et al., *supra* note 13, at 23.

[36] *See* Chapter V, Section C.2.

processes and the legal basis for protection from disclosure. This disclosure should include whether mediated settlement agreements and arbitration decisions will be confidential or whether they will be available to the public.

The confidentiality of mediation proceedings is largely dependent upon the statutes and rules in the applicable jurisdiction. The difficulty for ODR Providers is determining which jurisdiction is applicable when the parties are spread across the globe. For states that have adopted the *Uniform Mediation Act* (*UMA*), ODR Providers should describe the broad scope of the *UMA* confidentiality protections.[37]

Many organizations have advocated publication of ODR arbitration decisions, mediation case statistics, or their aggregated data as a means of ensuring transparency in B2C disputes.[38] Others believe that data collected about dispute resolution processes will diminish the confidentiality traditionally ascribed to ADR proceedings and impede the development of the ODR field.

The *National Standards for Court-Connected Mediation Programs* recommend that court ADR programs should balance the need for confidentiality with the need for monitoring and evaluating dispute resolution programs.[39] The *Model Standards of Conduct for Mediators* contain a similar provision in the commentary to the confidentiality standard.[40] The *CPR-Georgetown Principles* require the provider organization to "take all reasonable steps to monitor and evaluate the performance of its affiliated neutrals.[41] The *CPR-Georgetown Principles* do not require the provider to monitor the program as a whole. Recognizing that program evaluation information can be misleading, the *CPR-Georgetown Principles* do require providers that publish statistics about settlement rates and similar measures to disclose the information in a "clear, accurate, and understandable manner," including how the rate is calculated.[42]

Recommended disclosures

At a minimum, ODR Providers should state whether arbitration decisions will be published, and if data concerning ODR proceedings are being aggregated, whether that data will be made available or published in aggregated form,

---

[37] UNIF. MEDIATION ACT (2001).

[38] Arbitration decisions and aggregate data are published for domain name disputes arbitrated online under the Internet Corporation for Assigned Names and Numbers (ICANN)'s Uniform Domain Name Dispute Resolution Policy (UDRP). *See* <http://www.icann.org/udrp>.

[39] *National Standards for Court-Connected Mediation Programs*, 9.5, 16.0.

[40] *Joint Standards*, V.

[41] *CPR-Georgetown Principles*, Principle I.c.

[42] *Id.*, Principle VIII.

including whether any personal identifying information in the proceeding data is removed prior to publication.

Qualifications and Selection of Neutrals

The ADR community continues to discuss whether there should be minimum standards of training, education and experience to ensure quality and competency of neutrals.[43] The *Model Standards of Conduct for Mediators* state that a mediator should have sufficient qualifications to meet the reasonable expectations of the parties.[44] In addition to the neutrals' duty of competence, there is general agreement that an ODR Provider has a duty to ensure the quality and competency of its neutrals and to disclose the steps taken to fulfill that duty.[45] The *CPR-Georgetown Principles* recommend that providers take all reasonable steps to ensure that their neutrals are qualified and competent.[46]

Qualifications

This chapter does not attempt to determine whether minimum standards should be met to act as an ODR neutral, what such minimums should be, or what standards an ODR Provider should establish. However, online disputants cannot judge neutrals assigned to ODR cases by their demeanor, their behavior, or even their office environment, but instead must rely on the information provided to them about the neutral. Therefore, we recommend that ODR Providers disclose detailed information about their qualifications requirements and the qualifications of each neutral.

Recommended disclosures

An ODR Provider should identify the minimum qualifications required for inclusion on its panel of neutrals, such as education or experience, profession, prior ADR experience and the like. For individual neutrals, the ODR Provider should disclose their qualifications, including ADR training, degrees or certificates, level of experience, and areas of expertise. As stated previously, the ODR Provider should disclose whether it provides additional training for neutrals, and if so, the type of training provided, particularly with respect to use of the online medium (and how it differs from traditional face-to-face ADR) and the technology used by that ODR Provider.

---

[43] *See* Chapter IX, Section II.B.

[44] *Joint Standards,* IV.

[45] Peter Maida, *Rosters and Mediator Quality: What Questions Should We Ask?* 8 DISP. RES. MAG. 17 (Fall 2001).

[46] *CPR-Georgetown Principles*, Principle I.

Selection

The selection of the neutral assigned to handle the case may have a significant impact on the resolution of the dispute and the disputants' perceptions of the process. The CPR *Principles* require disclosure about the selection process but do not require a particular type of selection process. The *National Standards for Court Connected Mediation Programs* recommend a mediator selection process that maximizes party choice.[47] However, the *National Standards* recognize a number of circumstances in which party choice may not be appropriate.[48]

The *ABA/AAA Code of Ethics for Arbitrators of Commercial Disputes* does not prohibit or require a particular arbitrator selection process, but according to the *Code*, it is "inconsistent with the integrity of the arbitration process for persons to solicit appointment for themselves."[49]

Recommended disclosures

We recommend a standard consistent with the *CPR-Georgetown Principles*. An ODR Provider should explain the criteria for selecting members of the panel of neutrals eligible to handle disputes. Similarly, the provider should explain the process for selecting the neutral assigned to handle a particular dispute, for example, by random assignment, party selection, or relevant education or experience.

Accountability for ODR Providers and Neutrals

Like traditional face-to-face ADR providers and neutrals, ODR Providers and neutrals should be accountable if they do not adhere to their ethical obligations. Because the ODR Provider, neutral and disputants may be located in different jurisdictions, it is especially important for the ODR Provider to disclose the guidelines and processes to which it adheres.

Recommended disclosures for neutrals

ODR Providers should disclose what steps they take to require neutrals to fulfill their responsibilities promptly, maintain communication with the parties, and comply with the stated ethical guidelines. They should describe what process they provide to allow participants to file complaints about a neutral. They

---

[47] *National Standards for Court-Connected Mediation Programs,* 7.0.

[48] *Id.*

[49] *Code of Ethics for Arbitrators in Commercial Disputes,* Canon I (1977).

should state whether they provide an appeals process for arbitration decisions rendered by the neutrals, and they should explain the basis for such appeals.

Recommended disclosures for ODR providers

ODR Providers should disclose whether they adhere to any published guidelines, such as those of a seal or trustmark program. If so, they should provide the full text of (or link to) any such guidelines or seal/trustmark requirements. They should disclose whether they provide a process for participants to file complaints concerning the ODR services rendered, both with the ODR Provider itself, and with any relevant external organizations (such as seal/trustmark providers). They should disclose the jurisdiction where complaints against the ODR Provider can be filed, and any relevant jurisdictional limitations.[50]

Conclusion

Many of the issues raised in this chapter are addressed in existing ADR ethical standards or are being debated in the general ADR community. However, ODR ethics must be considered separately due to the unique online environment, the cross-border nature of many online conflicts, and the need to allow this emerging field to reach its potential without premature restrictions. At this juncture, ODR Providers can meet most of their ethical obligations by full disclosure of information that will allow ODR participants to make informed choices. The international community is encouraged to collaborate in developing ODR ethical standards that may evolve as the field matures.

Conclusion

By John Feerick

The field of alternative dispute resolution is not new. Actually, it is quite ancient, with many examples of the use of ADR in ancient Greece and Rome. As early as 421 B.C., leaders of Greek city-states sought resolution of their conflicts through arbitration. Ancient Phoenician and Greek traders as well as medieval merchants of the Italian peninsula resorted to arbitration as a viable method of dispute resolution at the commercial level.

Mention of the benefits of ADR can be found in the writings of philosophers and in major religious texts. The Talmudic scriptures of the first and second centuries similarly addressed the subject of ADR, stating in the Sanhedrin, "What is that kind of justice within which peace abides? We must say, arbitration."

Louis IX was renowned as the "Arbiter of Europe," and in colonial America George Washington was sought out as an arbitrator of disputes. In 1850 Abraham Lincoln declared in a law lecture: "Discourage litigation. Persuade your negotiators to cooperate when they can. Point out to them how the nominal winner is often a real loser in fees, expenses and waste of time." More recently, former United States Senator George Mitchell gave eloquent expression to the possibilities of mediation in achieving a historic peace agreement in Northern Ireland.

In the past 75 years in the United States, statutes have been enacted to facilitate the use of ADR, and courts have followed suit in enforcing agreements that provide for ADR. In addition, court programs have developed to offer disputants a menu of options to resolve their controversies. In response, ADR provider organizations have appeared, lawyers and non-lawyers have assumed roles as neutrals, and programs, courses and writings on the subject of ADR have escalated.

As public justice systems give way, so to speak, to systems of private dispute resolution, it is imperative that such systems meet high standards of fairness so as to promote their use and vindicate the confidence of those who submit their disputes to the privacy of ADR. This book comes, therefore, at an important time in the history of the ADR movement, and also at a time when every area of human activity is being looked at from an ethical perspective. It reflects the dynamic forces surrounding in particular the fields of arbitration and mediation. It analyzes the special relationships that exist between clients and their lawyers. It examines the complementary roles played by ADR neutrals and members of the organized bar, as well as the tension that sometimes exists between them in terms of their respective obligations. Additionally, the book explores the special role played by lawyer-neutrals who engage primarily in mediation and arbitration, while it also examines the distinctive roles of non-lawyers taking part in the process.

Central to the operation of any fair and efficient system of dispute resolution, of course, is a system of ethical rules. Ethical norms not only protect the rights of the parties, but they serve as guidelines to those who participate in mediation and arbitration. They also help instill integrity and confidence in the process.

This book takes a critical look at ethics in ADR practice and explores a number of guidelines in the field. Among the sources discussed are the *Federal Arbitration Act* governing arbitration in matters involving interstate commerce; the *Uniform Arbitration Act*, which addresses a number of subjects including issues relating to integrity in the arbitration process, and the *Code of Ethics for Arbitrators in Commercial Disputes,* which was drafted by the American Bar Association and the American Arbitration Association. Also examined are JAMS' *Ethical Guidelines for Arbitrators* and various state laws, such as those of California, that assist and regulate the actions of arbitrators and mediators.

Foremost among the many responsibilities addressed is the need for neutrals to be impartial and to scrupulously avoid conflicts of interest. The book covers these significant areas as well as the duties of arbitrators and mediators to disclose any facts bearing on the issue of impartiality. It notes, for example, that while the *Federal Arbitration Act* and the ABA *Code of Ethics for Arbitrators in Commercial Disputes* require a continuing duty to disclose, the *California Code of Civil Procedure* is silent on the matter. It also surveys other important differences occurring among these guidelines. Another important challenge to the integrity of the ADR process arises, for example, from the intersection of mediation and arbitration with the legal system, which can create situations involving the unauthorized practice of law. The book involves these overlapping boundaries between arbitration, mediation and legal practice, as well as the ethical pitfalls and challenges that they pose to ADR disputants and practitioners. Other subjects treated include the practice of law from the perspective of both consumers and lawyers, the debate over multi-disciplinary practice, attorneys in non-adversarial roles, and situations in which out-of-state attorneys serve as arbitrators.

The topic of mediator ethics is thoroughly treated through an overview of various standards of conduct developed by professional organizations, ADR practitioners, state and federal courts, and bar associations. The standards receiving most attention include a mediator's impartiality, competence, capacity to mediate, and conflicts of interest. Also discussed are various aspects of the mediation process including party self-determination, confidentiality and fairness, and the different guidelines promulgated by a number of national organizations. Also addressed, in a separate chapter, are questions such as enforcement of ethical guidelines, methods for monitoring individual mediators, and means of educating both new and experienced mediators as to their ethical responsibilities.

Of particular interest to the reader is a comparison of the *Standards of Conduct for Mediators* (by the AAA, ABA, and the Society of Professionals in Dispute Resolution) and the *Model Standards of Practice for Family and Divorce Mediation* (by the Association of Family and Conciliation Courts, the ABA, and the National Council of Dispute Resolution Organizations). This comparison demonstrates the importance of creating guidelines for specific types of mediation involving special issues or sensitivity -- such as those involving domestic relations.

Rules of ethics for lawyers engaged in mediation are similarly scrutinized. Using the ABA's *Model Rules*, one chapter provocatively argues that, at all times, "lawyers' duties are to their clients -- not the process." It notes that mediation and "zealous advocacy" are compatible, but maintains that the ethical lawyer cannot always follow all of the mediation guidelines, such as accepting a duty to the process quite apart from what is in the best interests of the client. Thus, it sets the stage for a classic debate between those seeking to harmonize law and mediation and those who say they cannot be completely melded together.

Recognizing the changing landscape of litigation caused by the growth of ADR, one chapter examines the role of the trial lawyer in advising clients "in the civil dispute resolution business." This chapter considers topics such as the need to overcome the natural inclination of the client to see the attorney as a "litigation warrior" and the perception that "initiating settlement discussions with the opposition is [a] sign of weakness." It also addresses ethical standards and their implications for ADR, including a section on settlement negotiations and settlement process decisions.

Another interesting and timely chapter is devoted to the rapidly emerging field of Online Dispute Resolution. Among the subjects discussed are the unique challenges created by the online format, including "building trust among the parties and establishing the integrity of the neutral ..., disclos[ing] information about the capabilities and limitations of online systems," the specialized training necessary for all participants, "electronic security mechanisms [that] preserve security," and costs and funding of such systems.

As this book reveals, ADR has stood the test of time and has proven itself as an important partner of the judicial system in helping bring order and resolution to individuals and organizations involved in difficult circumstances affecting their well being. It necessarily follows that, given the significant roles they play, mediators, arbitrators and lawyers must fashion the best possible guidelines and promote the highest ethical standards to ensure the integrity of what they do and the interests of those they serve. These collective essays provide an important step toward achieving that goal.

Appendix A

MODEL STANDARDS OF CONDUCT FOR MEDIATORS

Introductory Note

The initiative for these standards came from three professional groups: the American Arbitration Association, the American Bar Association (Section of Dispute Resolution)[1], and the Society of Professionals in Dispute Resolution.

The purpose of this initiative was to develop a set of standards to serve as a general framework for the practice of mediation. The effort is a step in the development of the field and a tool to assist practitioners in it – a beginning, not an end. The standards are intended to apply to all types of mediation. It is recognized, however, that in some cases the application of these standards may be affected by laws or contractual agreements.

Preface

The Model Standards of Conduct for Mediators are intended to perform three major functions: to serve as a guide for the conduct of mediators; to inform the mediating parties; and to promote public confidence in mediation as a process for resolving disputes. The standards draw on existing codes of conduct for mediators and take into account issues and problems that have surfaced in mediation practice.

They are offered in the hope that they will serve an educational function and provide assistance to individuals, organizations, and institutions involved in mediation.

Mediation is a process in which an impartial third party – a mediator – facilitates the resolution of a dispute by promoting voluntary agreement (or "self-determination") by the parties to the dispute. A mediator facilitates communications, promotes understanding, focuses the parties on their interests, and seeks creative problem solving to enable the parties to reach their own agreement. These standards give meaning to this definition of mediation.

I.   **Self-Determination: A Mediator Shall Recognize that Mediation is Based on the Principle of Self-Determination by the Parties.**

Self-determination is the fundamental principle of mediation. It requires that the mediation process rely upon the ability of the parties to reach a voluntary, uncoerced agreement. Any party may withdraw from mediation at any time.

---

[1] The views set out in this publication have not been considered by the American Bar Association House of Delegates and do not constitute the policy of the American Bar Association.

COMMENTS:

- The mediator may provide information about the process, raise issues, and help parties explore options. The primary role of the mediator is to facilitate a voluntary resolution of a dispute. Parties shall be given the opportunity to consider all proposed options.
- A mediator cannot personally ensure that each party has made a fully informed choice to reach a particular agreement, but it is a good practice for the mediator to make the parties aware of the importance of consulting other professionals, where appropriate, to help them make informed decisions.

II.   **Impartiality: A Mediator Shall Conduct the Mediation in an Impartial Manner.**

The concept of mediator impartiality is central to the mediation process. A mediator shall mediate only those matters in which she or he can remain impartial and evenhanded. If at any time the mediator is unable to conduct the process in an impartial manner, the mediator is obligated to withdraw.

COMMENTS:

- A mediator shall avoid conduct that gives the appearance of partiality toward one of the parties. The quality of the mediation process is enhanced when the parties have confidence in the impartiality of the mediator.
- When mediators are appointed by a court or institution, the appointing agency shall make reasonable efforts to ensure that mediators serve impartially.
- A mediator should guard against partiality or prejudice based on the parties' personal characteristics, background or performance at the mediation.

III.   **Conflicts of Interest: A Mediator Shall Disclose all Actual and Potential Conflicts of Interest Reasonably Known to the Mediator. After Disclosure, the Mediator Shall Decline to Mediate Unless all Parties Choose to Retain the Mediator. The Need to Protect Against Conflicts of Interest Also Governs Conduct that Occurs During and After the Mediation.**

A conflict of interest is a dealing or relationship that might create an impression of possible bias. The basic approach to questions of conflict of interest is consistent with the concept of self-determination. The mediator has a responsibility to disclose all actual and potential conflicts that are reasonably known to the mediator and could reasonably be seen as raising a question about impartiality. If all parties agree to mediate after being informed of conflicts, the mediator may proceed with the mediation. If however, the conflict of interest casts serious doubt on the integrity of the process, the mediator shall decline to proceed.

A mediator must avoid the appearance of conflict of interest both during and after the mediation. Without the consent of all parties a mediator shall not subsequently establish a professional relationship with one of the parties in a related matter, or in an unrelated matter under circumstances which would raise legitimate questions about the integrity of the mediation process.

COMMENTS:

- A mediator shall avoid conflicts of interest in recommending the services of other professionals. A mediator may make reference to professional referral services or associations which maintain rosters of qualified professionals.
- Potential conflicts of interest may arise between the administrators of mediation programs and mediators and there may be strong pressures on the mediator to settle a particular case or cases. The mediator's commitment must be to the parties and the process. Pressures from outside of the mediation process should never influence the mediator to coerce parties to settle.

IV.   **Competence: A Mediator Shall Mediate only When the Mediator Has the Necessary Qualifications to Satisfy the Reasonable Expectations of the Parties.**

Any person may be selected as a mediator, provided that the parties are satisfied with the mediator qualifications. Training and experience in mediation, however, are often necessary for effective mediation. A person who offers herself or himself as available to serve as a mediator gives parties and the public the expectation that she or he has the competency to mediate effectively. In court-connected or other forms of mandated mediation, it is essential that mediators assigned to the parties have the requisite training and experience.

COMMENTS:

- Mediators should have available for the parties information relevant to training, education and experience.
- The requirements for appearing on a list of mediators must be made public and available to interested persons.
- When mediators are appointed by a court or institution, the appointing agency shall make reasonable efforts to ensure that each mediator is qualified for the particular mediation.

V.   **Confidentiality: A Mediator Shall Maintain the Reasonable Expectations of the Parties with Regard to Confidentiality.**

The reasonable expectations of the parties with regard to confidentiality shall be met by the mediator. The parties' expectations of confidentiality depend on the circumstances of the mediation and any agreements they may make. The mediator shall not disclose any matter that a party expects to be confidential unless given permission by all parties or unless required by law or other public policy.

COMMENTS:

- The parties may make their own rules with respect to confidentiality, or the accepted practice of an individual mediator or institution may dictate a particular set of expectations. Since the parties' expectations regarding confidentiality are important, the mediator should discuss these expectations with the parties.
- If the mediator holds private sessions with a party, the nature of these sessions with regard to confidentiality should be discussed prior to undertaking such sessions.
- In order to protect the integrity of the mediation, a mediator should avoid communicating information about how the parties acted in the mediation process, the merits of the case, or settlement offers. The mediator may report, if required, whether parties appeared at a scheduled mediation.
- Where the parties have agreed that all or a portion of the information disclosed during a mediation is confidential, the parties' agreement should be respected by the mediator.
- Confidentiality should not be construed to limit or prohibit the effective monitoring, research, or evaluation, of mediation programs by responsible persons. Under appropriate circumstances, researchers may be permitted to obtain access to statistical data and, with the permission of the parties, to individual case files, observations of live mediations, and interviews with participants.

VI. Quality of the Process: A Mediator Shall Conduct the Mediation Fairly, Diligently, and in a Manner Consistent with the Principle of Self-Determination by the Parties.

A mediator shall work to ensure a quality process and to encourage mutual respect among the parties. A quality process requires a commitment by the mediator to diligence and procedural fairness. There should be adequate opportunity for each party in the mediation to participate in the discussions. The parties decide when and under what conditions they will reach an agreement or terminate a mediation.

COMMENTS:

- A mediator may agree to mediate only when he or she is prepared to commit the attention essential to an effective mediation.
- Mediators should only accept cases when they can satisfy the reasonable expectations of the parties concerning the timing of the process. A mediator should not allow a mediation to be unduly delayed by the parties or their representatives.

- The presence or absence of persons at a mediation depends on the agreement of the parties and mediator. The parties and mediator may agree that others may be excluded from particular sessions or from the entire mediation process.
- The primary purpose of a mediator is to facilitate the parties' voluntary agreement. This role differs substantially from other professional client relationships. Mixing the role of a mediator and the role of a professional advising a client is problematic, and mediators must strive to distinguish between the roles. A mediator should therefore refrain from providing professional advice. Where appropriate, a mediator should recommend that parties seek outside professional advice, or consider resolving their dispute through arbitration, counseling, neutral evaluation, or other processes. A mediator who undertakes, at the request of the parties, an additional dispute resolution role in the same matter assumes increased responsibilities and obligations that may be governed by the standards of other professions.
- A mediator shall withdraw from a mediation when incapable of serving or when unable to remain impartial.
- A mediator shall withdraw from the mediation or postpone a session if the mediation is being used to further illegal conduct or if a party is unable to participate due to drug, alcohol, or other physical or mental incapacity.
- Mediators should not permit their behavior in the mediation process to be guided by a desire for a high settlement rate.

VII.   **Advertising and Solicitation: A Mediator Shall Be Truthful in Advertising and Solicitation for Mediation.**

Advertising or any other communication with the public concerning services offered or regarding the education, training, and expertise of the mediator shall be truthful. Mediators shall refrain from promises and guarantees of results.

COMMENTS:

- It is imperative that communication with the public educate and instill confidence in the process.
- In an advertisement or other communication to the public, a mediator may make reference to meeting state, national, or private organization qualifications only if the entity referred to has a procedure for qualifying mediators and the mediator has been duly granted the requisite status.

VIII.   **Fees: A Mediator Shall Fully Disclose and Explain the Basis of Compensation, Fees, and Charges to the Parties.**

The parties should be provided sufficient information about fees at the outset of a mediation to determine if they wish to retain the services of a mediator. If a mediator charges fees, the fees shall be reasonable, considering, among other things, the mediation service, the type and complexity of the matter, the expertise of the mediator, the time required, and the rates customary in the community. The better practice in reaching an understanding about fees is to set down the arrangements in a written agreement.

COMMENTS:

- A mediator who withdraws from a mediation should return any unearned fee to the parties.
- A mediator should not enter into a fee agreement which is contingent upon the result of the mediation or amount of the settlement.
- Co-mediators who share a fee should hold to standards of reasonableness in determining the allocation of fees.
- A mediator should not accept a fee for referral of a matter to another mediator or to any other person.

IX. **Obligations to the Mediation Process: Mediators have a duty to improve the practice of mediation.**

COMMENTS:

- Mediators are regarded as knowledgeable in the process of mediation. They have an obligation to use their knowledge to help educate the public about mediation; to make mediation accessible to those who would like to use it; to correct abuses; and to improve their professional skills and abilities.

Appendix B

MODEL STANDARDS OF PRACTICE
FOR FAMILY AND DIVORCE MEDIATION

Developed by
The Symposium on Standards of Practice
February, 2001

Overview and Definitions

Family and divorce mediation ("family mediation" or "mediation") is a process in which a mediator, an impartial third party, facilitates the resolution of family disputes by promoting the participants' voluntary agreement. The family mediator assists communication, encourages understanding and focuses the participants on their individual and common interests. The family mediator works with the participants to explore options, make decisions and reach their own agreements.

Family mediation is not a substitute for the need for family members to obtain independent legal advice or counseling or therapy. Nor is it appropriate for all families. However, experience has established that family mediation is a valuable option for many families because it can:

- increase the self-determination of participants and their ability to communicate;
- promote the best interests of children; and
- reduce the economic and emotional costs associated with the resolution of family disputes.

Effective mediation requires that the family mediator be qualified by training, experience and temperament; that the mediator be impartial; that the participants reach their decisions voluntarily; that their decisions be based on sufficient factual data; that the mediator be aware of the impact of culture and diversity; and that the best interests of children be taken into account. Further, the mediator should also be prepared to identify families whose history includes domestic abuse or child abuse.

These *Model Standards of Practice for Family and Divorce Mediation ("Model Standards")* aim to perform three major functions:

1. to serve as a guide for the conduct of family mediators;
2. to inform the mediating participants of what they can expect; and
3. to promote public confidence in mediation as a process for resolving family disputes.

The *Model Standards* are aspirational in character. They describe good practices for family mediators. They are not intended to create legal rules or standards of liability.

The *Model Standards* include different levels of guidance:

- Use of the term "may" in a *Standard* is the lowest strength of guidance and indicates a practice that the family mediator should consider adopting but which can be deviated from in the exercise of good professional judgment.
- Most of the *Standards* employ the term "should" which indicates that the practice described in the *Standard* is highly desirable and should be departed from only with very strong reason.
- The rarer use of the term "shall" in a *Standard* is a higher level of guidance to the family mediator, indicating that the mediator should not have discretion to depart from the practice described.

Standard I

A family mediator shall recognize that mediation is based on the principle of self-determination by the participants.

A. Self-determination is the fundamental principle of family mediation. The mediation process relies upon the ability of participants to make their own voluntary and informed decisions.
B. The primary role of a family mediator is to assist the participants to gain a better understanding of their own needs and interests and the needs and interests of others and to facilitate agreement among the participants.
C. A family mediator should inform the participants that they may seek information and advice from a variety of sources during the mediation process.
D. A family mediator shall inform the participants that they may withdraw from family mediation at any time and are not required to reach an agreement in mediation.
E. The family mediator's commitment shall be to the participants and the process. Pressure from outside of the mediation process shall never influence the mediator to coerce participants to settle.

Standard II

A family mediator shall be qualified by education and training to undertake the mediation.

A. To perform the family mediator's role, a mediator should:
   1. have knowledge of family law;
   2. have knowledge of an training in the impact of family conflict on parents, children and other participants, including knowledge of child development, domestic abuse and child abuse and neglect;
   3. have education and training specific to the process of mediation;
   4. be able to recognize the impact of culture and diversity;

B. Family mediators should provide information to the participants about the mediator's relevant training, education and expertise.

Standard III

A family mediator shall facilitate the participants' understanding of what mediation is and assess their capacity to mediate before the participants reach an agreement to mediate.

A. Before family mediation begins a mediator should provide the participants with an overview of the process and its purposes, including:
   1. informing the participants that reaching an agreement in family mediation is consensual in nature, that a mediator is an impartial facilitator, and that a mediator may not impose or force any settlement on the parties;
   2. distinguishing family mediation from other processes designed to address family issues and disputes;
   3. informing the participants that any agreements reached will be reviewed by the court when court approval is required;
   4. informing the participants that they may obtain independent advice from attorneys, counsel, advocates, accountants, therapists or other professionals during the mediation process;
   5. advising the participants, in appropriate cases, that they can seek the advice of religious figures, elders or other significant persons in their community whose opinions they value;
   6. discussing, if applicable, the issue of separate sessions with the participants, a description of the circumstances in which the mediator may meet alone with any of the participants, or with any third party and the conditions of confidentiality concerning these separate sessions;
   7. informing the participants that the presence or absence of other persons at a mediation, including attorneys, counselors or advocates, depends on the agreement of the participants and the mediator, unless a statute or regulation otherwise requires or the mediator believes that the presence of another person is required or may be beneficial because of a history or threat of violence or other serious coercive activity by a participant;
   8. describing the obligations of the mediator to maintain the confidentiality of the mediation process and its results as well as any exceptions to confidentiality;
   9. advising the participants of the circumstances under which the mediator may suspend or terminate the mediation process and that a participant has a right to suspend or terminate mediation at any time.
B. The participants should sign a written agreement to mediate their dispute and the terms and conditions thereof within a reasonable time after first consulting the family mediator.
C. The family mediator should be alert to the capacity and willingness of the participants to mediate before proceeding with the mediation and throughout the process. A mediator should not agree to conduct the mediation if the mediator reasonably believes one or more of the participants is unable or unwilling to

participate.

D. Family mediators should not accept a dispute for mediation if they cannot satisfy the expectations of the participants concerning the timing of the process.

Standard IV

A family mediator shall conduct the mediation process in an impartial manner. A family mediator shall disclose all actual and potential grounds of bias and conflicts of interest reasonably known to the mediator. The participants shall be free to retain the mediator by an informed, written waiver of the conflict of interest. However, if a bias or conflict of interest clearly impairs a mediator's impartiality, the mediator shall withdraw regardless of the express agreement of the participants.

A. Impartiality means freedom from favoritism or bias in word, action or appearance, and includes a commitment to assist all participants as opposed to any one individual.

B. Conflict of interest means any relationship between the mediator, any participant or the subject matter of the dispute, that compromises or appears to compromise the mediator's impartiality.

C. A family mediator should not accept a dispute for mediation if the family mediator cannot be impartial.

D. A family mediator should identify and disclose potential grounds of bias or conflict of interest upon which a mediator's impartiality might reasonably be questioned. Such disclosure should be made prior to the start of a mediation and in time to allow the participants to select an alternate mediator.

E. A family mediator should resolve all doubts in favor of disclosure. All disclosures should be made as soon as practical after the mediator becomes aware of the bias or potential conflict of interest. The duty to disclose is a continuing duty.

F. A family mediator should guard against bias or partiality based on the participants' personal characteristics, background or performance at the mediation.

G. A family mediator should avoid conflicts of interest in recommending the services of other professionals.

H. A family mediator shall not use information about participants obtained in a mediation for personal gain or advantage.

I. A family mediator should withdraw pursuant to *Standard IX* if the mediator believes the mediator's impartiality has been compromised or a conflict of interest has been identified and has not been waived by the participants.

Standard V

A family mediator shall fully disclose and explain the basis of any compensation, fees and charges to the participants.

A. The participants should be provided with sufficient information about fees at the outset of mediation to determine if they wish to retain the services of the mediator.

B. The participants' written agreement to mediate their dispute should include a description of their fee arrangement with the mediator.

C. A mediator should not enter into a fee agreement that is contingent upon the results of the mediation or the amount of the settlement.
D. A mediator should not accept a fee for referral of a matter to another mediator or to any other person.
E. Upon termination of mediation a mediator should return any unearned fee to the participants.

Standard VI

A family mediator shall structure the mediation process so that the participants make decisions based on sufficient information and knowledge.

A. The mediator should facilitate full and accurate disclosure and the acquisition and development of information during mediation so that the participants can make informed decisions. This may be accomplished by encouraging participants to consult appropriate experts.
B. Consistent with standards of impartiality and preserving participant self-determination, a mediator may provide the participants with information that the mediator is qualified by training or experience to provide. The mediator shall not provide therapy or legal advice.
C. The mediator should recommend that the participants obtain independent legal representation before concluding an agreement.
D. If the participants so desire, the mediator should allow attorneys, counsel or advocates for the participants to be present at the mediation sessions.
E. With the agreement of the participants, the mediator may document the participants' resolution of their dispute. The mediator should inform the participants that any agreement should be reviewed by an independent attorney before it is signed.

Standard VII

A family mediator shall maintain the confidentiality of all information acquired in the mediation process, unless the mediator is permitted or required to reveal the information by law or agreement of the participants.

A. The mediator should discuss the participants' expectations of confidentiality with them prior to undertaking the mediation. The written agreement to mediate should include provisions concerning confidentiality.
B. Prior to undertaking the mediation the mediator should inform the participants of the limitations of confidentiality such as statutory, judicially or ethically mandated reporting.
C. As permitted by law, the mediator shall disclose a participant's threat of suicide or violence against any person to the threatened person and the appropriate authorities if the mediator believes such threat is likely to be acted upon.
D. If the mediator holds private sessions with a participant, the obligations of confidentiality concerning those sessions should be discussed and agreed upon prior to the sessions.
E. If subpoenaed or otherwise noticed to testify or to produce documents the mediator

should inform the participants immediately. The mediator should not testify or provide documents in response to a subpoena without an order of the court if the mediator reasonably believes doing so would violate an obligation of confidentiality to the participants.

Standard VIII

A family mediator shall assist participants in determining how to promote the best interests of children.

A. The mediator should encourage the participants to explore the range of options available for separation or post divorce parenting arrangements and their respective costs and benefits. Referral to a specialist in child development may be appropriate for these purposes. The topics for discussion may include, among others:
  1. information about community resources and programs that can help the participants and their children cope with the consequences of family reorganization and family violence;
  2. problems that continuing conflict creates for children's development and what steps might be taken to ameliorate the effects of conflict on the children;
  3. development of a parenting plan that covers the children's physical residence and decision-making responsibilities for the children, with appropriate levels of detail as agreed to by the participants;
  4. the possible need to revise parenting plans as the developmental needs of the children evolve over time; and
  5. encouragement to the participants to develop appropriate dispute resolution mechanisms to facilitate future revisions of the parenting plan.
B. The mediator should be sensitive to the impact of culture and religion on parenting philosophy and other decisions.
C. The mediator shall inform any court-appointed representative for the children of the mediation. If a representative for the children participates, the mediator should, at the outset, discuss the effect of that participation on the mediation process and the confidentiality of the mediation with the participants. Whether the representative of the children participates or not, the mediator shall provide the representative with the resulting agreements insofar as they relate to the children.
D. Except in extraordinary circumstances, the children should not participate in the mediation process without the consent of both parents and the children's court-appointed representative.
E. Prior to including the children in the mediation process, the mediator should consult with the parents and the children's court-appointed representative about whether the children should participate in the mediation process and the form of that participation.
F. The mediator should inform all concerned about the available options for the children's participation (which may include personal participation, an interview with a mental health professional, the mediator interviewing the child and reporting to the parents, or a videotaped statement by the child) and discuss the costs and benefits of each with the participants.

Standard IX

A family mediator shall recognize a family situation involving child abuse or neglect and take appropriate steps to shape the mediation process accordingly.

A. As used in these Standards, child abuse or neglect is defined by applicable state law.

B. A mediator shall not undertake a mediation in which the family situation has been assessed to involve child abuse or neglect without appropriate and adequate training.

C. If the mediator has reasonable grounds to believe that a child of the participants is abused or neglected within the meaning of the jurisdiction's child abuse and neglect laws, the mediator shall comply with applicable child protection laws.

   1. The mediator should encourage the participants to explore appropriate services for the family.

   2. The mediator should consider the appropriateness of suspending or terminating the mediation process in light of the allegations.

Standard X

A family mediator shall recognize a family situation involving domestic abuse and take appropriate steps to shape the mediation process accordingly.

A. As used in these Standards, domestic abuse includes domestic violence as defined by applicable state law and issues of control and intimidation.

B. A mediator shall not undertake a mediation in which the family situation has been assessed to involve domestic abuse without appropriate and adequate training.

C. Some cases are not suitable for mediation because of safety, control or intimidation issues. A mediator should make a reasonable effort to screen for the existence of domestic abuse prior to entering into an agreement to mediate. The mediator should continue to assess for domestic abuse throughout the mediation process.

D. If domestic abuse appears to be present the mediator shall consider taking measures to insure the safety of participants and the mediator including, among others:

   1. establishing appropriate security arrangements;

   2. holding separate sessions with the participants even without the agreement of all participants;

   3. allowing a friend, representative, advocate, counsel or attorney to attend the mediation sessions;

   4. encouraging the participants to be represented by an attorney, counsel or an advocate throughout the mediation process;

   5. referring the participants to appropriate community resources;

   6. suspending or terminating the mediation sessions, with appropriate steps to protect the safety of the participants.

E. The mediator should facilitate the participants' formulation of parenting plans that protect the physical safety and psychological well-being of themselves and their children.

Standard XI

A family mediator shall suspend or terminate the mediation process when the mediator reasonably believes that a participant is unable to effectively participate or for other compelling reason.

A. Circumstances under which a mediator should consider suspending or terminating the mediation, may include, among others:
    1. the safety of a participant or well-being of a child is threatened;
    2. a participant has or is threatening to abduct a child;
    3. a participant is unable to participate due to the influence of drugs, alcohol, or physical or mental condition;
    4. the participants are about to enter into an agreement that the mediator reasonably believes to be unconscionable;
    5. a participant is using the mediation to further illegal conduct;
    6. a participant is using the mediation process to gain an unfair advantage;
    7. if the mediator believes the mediator's impartiality has been compromised in accordance with *Standard IV*.
B. If the mediator does suspend or terminate the mediation, the mediator should take all reasonable steps to minimize prejudice or inconvenience to the participants which may result.

Standard XII

A family mediator shall be truthful in the advertisement and solicitation for mediation.

A. Mediators should refrain from promises and guarantees of results. A mediator should not advertise statistical settlement data or settlement rates.
B. Mediators should accurately represent their qualifications. In an advertisement or other communication, a mediator may make reference to meeting state, national, or private organizational qualifications only if the entity referred to has a procedure for qualifying mediators and the mediator has been duly granted the requisite status.

Standard XIII

A family mediator shall acquire and maintain professional competence in mediation.

A. Mediators should continuously improve their professional skills and abilities by, among other activities, participating in relevant continuing education programs and should regularly engage in self-assessment.
B. Mediators should participate in programs of peer consultation and should help train and mentor the work of less experienced mediators.
C. Mediators should continuously strive to understand the impact of culture and diversity on the mediator's practice.

Special Policy Considerations for
State Regulation of Family Mediators and Court Affiliated Programs

The *Model Standards* recognize the *National Standards for Court Connected Dispute Resolution Programs* (1992). There are also state and local regulations governing such programs and family mediators. The following principles of organization and practice, however, are especially important for regulation of mediators and court-connected family mediation programs. They are worthy of separate mention.

A. Individual states or local courts should set standards and qualifications for family mediators including procedures for evaluations and handling grievances against mediators. In developing these standards and qualifications, regulators should consult with appropriate professional groups, including professional associations of family mediators.

B. When family mediators are appointed by a court or other institution, the appointing agency should make reasonable efforts to insure that each mediator is qualified for the appointment. If a list of family mediators qualified for court appointment exists, the requirements for being included on the list should be made public and available to all interested persons.

C. Confidentiality should not be construed to limit or prohibit the effective monitoring, research or evaluation of mediation programs by responsible individuals or academic institutions provided that no identifying information about any person involved in the mediation is disclosed without their prior written consent. Under appropriate circumstances, researchers may be permitted to obtain access to statistical data and, with the permission of the participants, to individual case files, observations of live mediations, and interviews with participants.

REPORT

The *Model Standards of Practice for Family and Divorce Mediation* (*"Model Standards"*) are the family mediation community's definition of the role of mediation in the dispute resolution system in the twenty-first century. The *Model Standards* are the product of an effort by prominent mediation-interested organizations and individuals to create a unified set of standards that will replace existing ones. They draw on existing codes of conduct for mediators and take into account issues and problems that have been identified in divorce and family mediation practice.

Between 1982 and 1984 the Association of Family & Conciliation Courts [AFCC] convened three national symposia on divorce mediation standards. Over forty individuals from thirty organizations attended to explore issues of certification, licensure and standards of practice. Drafts were distributed to over one hundred thirty individuals and organizations for comment and review. The result of the efforts was the 1984 *Model Standards of Practice for Family and Divorce Mediation* (*"1984 Model Standards"*) which have served as a resource document for state and national mediation organizations.

In tandem with the process convened by AFCC, the American Bar Association's Family Law Section drafted *Standards of Practice for Lawyer Mediators in*

Family Law Disputes, which were approved by the ABA House of Delegates in 1984 (*1984 ABA Standards*). The *1984 ABA Standards* were primarily developed for lawyers who wished to be mediators, a role at that time some thought inconsistent with governing standards of professional responsibility for lawyers. The *1984 ABA Standards* helped define how lawyers could serve as family mediators and still stay within the ethical guidelines of the profession. Several members of the Committee who worked on the *1984 Model Standards* participated in the drafting of the *1984 ABA Standards*. As a result the *1984 ABA Standards* were basically compatible with the *1984 Model Standards*.

Following promulgation of the 1984 *Model Standards* and *1984 ABA Standards* interest in mediation in all fields, and family mediation in particular, burgeoned. Interested organizations promulgated their own standards of practice. The Academy of Family Mediators, for example, promulgated its own standards of conduct based on the *1984 Model Standards*. Several states and courts have also set standards.

Other efforts were made by concerned organizations to establish standards of practice for mediation generally. For example, a joint Task Force of the American Arbitration Association, American Bar Association and the Society of Professionals in Dispute Resolution (SPIDR) published *Model Standards of Conduct for Mediators* in 1995.

In 1996, the ABA Family Law Section came to the conclusion that interest in and knowledge about family mediation had expanded dramatically since the *1984 ABA Standards* were promulgated and a fresh look at that effort was required. First, the *1984 ABA Standards* did not address many critical issues in mediation practice that have been identified since they were initially promulgated. They did not deal with domestic violence and child abuse. The *1984 ABA Standards* also did not address the mediator's role in helping parents define the best interests of their children in their post-divorce parenting arrangements. They made no mention of the need for special expertise and training in mediation or family violence.

Second, the *1984 ABA Standards* were inconsistent with other guidelines for the conduct of mediation subsequently promulgated. The Section believed that uniformity of mediation standards among interested groups is highly desirable to provide clear guidance for family mediators and for the public. Uniformity and clarity could not be provided within the framework of the *1984 ABA Standards*. The ABA Committee therefore decided to replace the *1984 ABA Standards* with a new document.

A committee, including representatives from AFCC, Academy of Family Mediators [AFM] and SPIDR, therefore, created a new draft of standards of practice for family mediation specially applicable to lawyers who sought to involve themselves in that process. Prof. Andrew I. Schepard of Hofstra University School of Law served as the committee's reporter. The Committee set several goals for the revised standards. First, the ABA Committee sought to insure that its revised standards were state of the art, addressing important developments in family mediation practice since the adoption of the *1984 ABA Standards* and *1984 Model Standards*. Second, the Committee sought to insure that its recommended standards were consistent, as far as is possible, with other standards of practice for divorce and family mediation.

To meet these goals, the Committee examined all available standards of practice, conducted research, and consulted with a number of experts on family and divorce mediation. It particularly focused on consultations with experts in domestic violence and child abuse about the appropriate role for mediation when family situations involved violence or the allegations thereof.

The Council of the ABA's Family Law Section concluded that other interested mediation organizations should be included in the process of drafting revised standards of practice for family mediation. Other mediation organizations also recognized that their current standards of practice for family mediation also needed review in light of developments in mediation practice since they were promulgated. These organizations included the National Council of Dispute Resolution Organizations (an umbrella organization which includes the Academy of Family Mediators, the ABA Section of Dispute Resolution, AFCC, Conflict Resolution Education Network, the National Association for Community Mediation, the National Conference on Peacemaking and Conflict Resolution, and the Society of Professionals in Dispute Resolution. In addition, the ABA Commission on Domestic Violence participated as an expert consultant.

The *Model Standards* that follow are thus the result of extensive and thoughtful deliberation by the family mediation community with wide input from a variety of voices.

Linda D. Elrod, Chair
Section of Family Law

February, 2001

Appendix C

The Code of Ethics for Arbitrators in Commercial Disputes (1977)

The Code of Ethics for Arbitrators in Commercial Disputes was prepared in 1977 by a joint committee consisting of a special committee of the American Arbitration Association and a special committee of the American Bar Association. It has been approved and recommended by both organizations.

Preamble
The use of commercial arbitration to resolve a wide variety of disputes has grown extensively and forms a significant part of the system of justice on which our society relies for fair determination of legal rights. Persons who act as commercial arbitrators therefore undertake serious responsibilities to the public as well as to the parties. Those responsibilities include important ethical obligations.

Few cases of unethical behavior by commercial arbitrators have arisen. Nevertheless, the American Bar Association and the American Arbitration Association believe that it is in the public interest to set forth generally accepted standards of ethical conduct for guidance of arbitrators and parties in commercial disputes. By establishing this code, the sponsors hope to contribute to the maintenance of high standards and continued confidence in the process of arbitration.

There are many different types of commercial arbitration. Some cases are conducted under arbitration rules established by various organizations and trade associations, while others are conducted without such rules. Although most cases are arbitrated pursuant to voluntary agreement of the parties, certain types of dispute are submitted to arbitration by reason of particular laws. This code is intended to apply to all such proceedings in which disputes or claims are submitted for decision to one or more arbitrators appointed in a manner provided by an agreement of the parties, by applicable arbitration rules, or by law. In all such cases, the persons who have the power to decide should observe fundamental standards of ethical conduct. In this code all such persons are called "arbitrators" although, in some types of case, they might be called "umpires" or have some other title.

Various aspects of the conduct of arbitrators, including some matters covered by this code, may be governed by agreements of the parties, by arbitration rules to which the parties have agreed, or by applicable law. This code does not take the place of or supersede such agreements, rules, or laws and does not establish new or additional grounds for judicial review of arbitration awards. While this code is intended to provide ethical guidelines in many types of arbitration, it does not form a part of the arbitration rules of the American Arbitration Association or of any other organization, nor is it intended to apply to mediation or conciliation. Labor arbitration is governed by the Code of Professional Responsibility for Arbitrators of Labor-Management Disputes, not by this code.

Arbitrators, like judges, have the power to decide cases. However, unlike full-time judges, arbitrators are usually engaged in other occupations before, during, and after the time that they serve as arbitrators. Often, arbitrators are purposely chosen from the same trade or industry as the parties in order to bring special knowledge to the task of deciding. This code recognizes these fundamental differences between arbitrators and judges.

In some types of arbitration, there are three or more arbitrators. In such cases, it is sometimes the practice for each party, acting alone, to appoint one arbitrator and for the other arbitrators to be designated by those two, by the parties, or by an independent institution or individual. The sponsors of this code believe that it is preferable for parties to agree that all arbitrators should comply with the same ethical standards. However, it is recognized that there is a long-established practice in some types of arbitration for the arbitrators who are appointed by one party, acting alone, to be governed by special ethical considerations. Those special considerations are set forth in the last section of the code, headed "Ethical Considerations Relating to Arbitrators Appointed by One Party."

Although this code is sponsored by the American Arbitration Association and the American Bar Association, its use is not limited to arbitrations administered by the AAA or to cases in which the arbitrators are lawyers. Rather, it is presented as a public service to provide guidance in all types of commercial arbitration.

CANON I. AN ARBITRATOR SHOULD UPHOLD THE INTEGRITY AND FAIRNESS OF THE ARBITRATION PROCESS.

A. Fair and just processes for resolving disputes are indispensable in our society. Commercial arbitration is an important method for deciding many types of disputes. In order for commercial arbitration to be effective, there must be broad public confidence in the integrity and fairness of the process. Therefore, an arbitrator has a responsibility not only to the parties but also to the process of arbitration itself, and must observe high standards of conduct so that the integrity and fairness of the process will be preserved. Accordingly, an arbitrator should recognize a responsibility to the public, to the parties whose rights will be decided, and to all other participants in the proceeding. The provisions of this code should be construed and applied to further these objectives.

B. It is inconsistent with the integrity of the arbitration process for persons to solicit appointment for themselves. However, a person may indicate a general willingness to serve as an arbitrator.

C. Persons should accept appointment as arbitrators only if they believe that they can be available to conduct the arbitration promptly.

D. After accepting appointment and while serving as an arbitrator, a person should avoid entering into any financial, business, professional, family or social relationship, or acquiring any financial or personal interest, which is likely to affect impartiality or which might reasonably create the appearance of partiality or bias. For a reasonable period of time after the decision of a case, persons who have served as arbitrators should avoid entering into any such relationship, or acquiring any such interest, in circumstances which might reasonably create the appearance that they had been influenced in the arbitration by the anticipation or expectation of the relationship or interest.

E. Arbitrators should conduct themselves in a way that is fair to all parties and should not be swayed by outside pressure, by public clamor, by fear of criticism or by self-interest.
F. When an arbitrator's authority is derived from an agreement of the parties, the arbitrator should neither exceed that authority nor do less than is required to exercise that authority completely. Where the agreement of the parties sets forth procedures to be followed in conducting the arbitration or refers to rules to be followed, it is the obligation of the arbitrator to comply with such procedures or rules.

G. An arbitrator should make all reasonable efforts to prevent delaying tactics, harassment of parties or other participants, or other abuse or disruption of the arbitration process.

H. The ethical obligations of an arbitrator begin upon acceptance of the appointment and continue throughout all stages of the proceeding. In addition, wherever specifically set forth in this code, certain ethical obligations begin as soon as a person is requested to serve as an arbitrator and certain ethical obligations continue even after the decision in the case has been given to the parties.

CANON II AN ARBITRATOR SHOULD DISCLOSE ANY INTEREST OR RELATIONSHIP LIKELY TO AFFECT IMPARTIALITY OR WHICH MIGHT CREATE AN APPEARANCE OF PARTIALITY OR BIAS.

Introductory Note
This code reflects the prevailing principle that arbitrators should disclose the existence of interests or relationships that are likely to affect their impartiality or that might reasonably create an appearance that they are biased against one party or favorable to another. These provisions of the code are intended to be applied realistically so that the burden of detailed disclosure does not become so great that it is impractical for persons in the business world to be arbitrators, thereby depriving parties of the services of those who might be best informed and qualified to decide particular types of case.

This code does not limit the freedom of parties to agree on whomever they choose as an arbitrator. When parties, with knowledge of a person's interests and relationships, nevertheless desire that individual to serve as an arbitrator, that person may properly serve.

Disclosure
A. Persons who are requested to serve as arbitrators should, before accepting, disclose
   1. any direct or indirect financial or personal interest in the outcome of the arbitration;

2. any existing or past financial, business, professional, family or social relationships which are likely to affect impartiality or which might reasonably create an appearance of partiality or bias. Persons requested to serve as arbitrators should disclose any such relationships which they personally have with any party or its lawyer, or with any individual whom they have been told will be a witness. They should also disclose any such relationships involving members of their families or their current employers, partners or business associates.

B. Persons who are requested to accept appointment as arbitrators should make a reasonable effort to inform themselves of any interests or relationships described in the preceding paragraph A.

C. The obligation to disclose interests or relationships described in the preceding paragraph A is a continuing duty which requires a person who accepts appointment as an arbitrator to disclose, at any stage of the arbitration, any such interests or relationships which may arise, or which are recalled or discovered.

D. Disclosure should be made to all parties unless other procedures for disclosure are provided in the rules or practices of an institution which is administering the arbitration. Where more than one arbitrator has been appointed, each should inform the others of the interests and relationships which have been disclosed.

E. In the event that an arbitrator is requested by all parties to withdraw, the arbitrator should do so. In the event that an arbitrator is requested to withdraw by less than all of the parties because of alleged partiality or bias, the arbitrator should withdraw unless either of the following circumstances exists.

1. If an agreement of the parties, or arbitration rules agreed to by the parties, establishes procedures for determining challenges to arbitrators, then those procedures should be followed; or,
2. if the arbitrator, after carefully considering the matter, determines that the reason for the challenge is not substantial, and that he or she can nevertheless act and decide the case impartially and fairly, and that withdrawal would cause unfair delay or expense to another party or would be contrary to the ends of justice.

CANON III AN ARBITRATOR IN COMMUNICATING WITH THE PARTIES SHOULD AVOID IMPROPRIETY OR THE APPEARANCE OF IMPROPRIETY.

A. If an agreement of the parties or applicable arbitration rules referred to in that agreement, establishes the manner or content of communications between the arbitrator and the parties, the arbitrator should follow those procedures notwithstanding any contrary provision of the following paragraphs B and C.

B. Unless otherwise provided in applicable arbitration rules or in an agreement of the parties, arbitrators should not discuss a case with any party in the absence of each other party, except in any of the following circumstances.

1. Discussions may be had with a party concerning such matters as setting the time and place of hearings or making other arrangements for the conduct of the proceedings. However, the arbitrator should promptly inform each other party of the discussion and should not make any final determination concerning the matter discussed before giving each absent party an opportunity to express its views.
2. If a party fails to be present at a hearing after having been given due notice, the arbitrator may discuss the case with any party who is present.
3. If all parties request or consent to it, such discussion may take place.

C. Unless otherwise provided in applicable arbitration rules or in an agreement of the parties, whenever an arbitrator communicates in writing with one party, the arbitrator should at the same time send a copy of the communication to each other party. Whenever the arbitrator receives any written communication concerning the case from one party which has not already been sent to each other party, the arbitrator should do so.

CANON IV. AN ARBITRATOR SHOULD CONDUCT THE PROCEEDINGS FAIRLY AND DILIGENTLY.

A. An arbitrator should conduct the proceedings in an evenhanded manner and treat all parties with equality and fairness at all stages of the proceedings.

B. An arbitrator should perform duties diligently and conclude the case as promptly as the circumstances reasonably permit.

C. An arbitrator should be patient and courteous to the parties, to their lawyers and to the witnesses and should encourage similar conduct by all participants in the proceedings.

D. Unless otherwise agreed by the parties or provided in arbitration rules agreed to by the parties, an arbitrator should accord to all parties the right to appear in person and to be heard after due notice of the time and place of hearing.

E. An arbitrator should not deny any party the opportunity to be represented by counsel.

F. If a party fails to appear after due notice, an arbitrator should proceed with the arbitration when authorized to do so by the agreement of the parties, the rules agreed to by the parties or by law. However, an arbitrator should do so only after receiving assurance that notice has been given to the absent party.

G. When an arbitrator determines that more information than has been presented by the parties is required to decide the case, it is not improper for the arbitrator to ask questions, call witnesses, and request documents or other evidence.

H. It is not improper for an arbitrator to suggest to the parties that they discuss the possibility of settlement of the case. However, an arbitrator should not be present or otherwise participate in the settlement discussions unless requested to do so by all parties. An arbitrator should not exert pressure on any party to settle.

I. Nothing in this code is intended to prevent a person from acting as a mediator or conciliator of a dispute in which he or she has been appointed as arbitrator, if requested to do so by all parties or where authorized or required to do so by applicable laws or rules.

J. When there is more than one arbitrator, the arbitrators should afford each other the full opportunity to participate in all aspects of the proceedings.

CANON V. AN ARBITRATOR SHOULD MAKE DECISIONS IN A JUST, INDEPENDENT AND DELIBERATE MANNER.

A. An arbitrator should, after careful deliberation, decide all issues submitted for determination. An arbitrator should decide no other issues.

B. An arbitrator should decide all matters justly, exercising independent judgment, and should not permit outside pressure to affect the decision.

C. An arbitrator should not delegate the duty to decide to any other person.

D. In the event that all parties agree upon a settlement of issues in dispute and request an arbitrator to embody that agreement in an award, an arbitrator may do so, but is not required to do so unless satisfied with the propriety of the terms of settlement. Whenever an arbitrator embodies a settlement by the parties in an award, the arbitrator should state in the award that it is based on an agreement of the parties.

CANON VI. AN ARBITRATOR SHOULD BE FAITHFUL TO THE RELATIONSHIP OF TRUST AND CONFIDENTIALITY INHERENT IN THAT OFFICE.

A. An arbitrator is in a relationship of trust to the parties and should not, at any time, use confidential information acquired during the arbitration proceeding to gain personal advantage or advantage for others, or to affect adversely the interest of another.

B. Unless otherwise agreed by the parties, or required by applicable rules or law, an arbitrator should keep confidential all matters relating to the arbitration proceedings and decision.

C. It is not proper at any time for an arbitrator to inform anyone of the decision in advance of the time it is given to all parties. In a case in which there is more than one arbitrator, it is not proper at any time for an arbitrator to inform anyone concerning the deliberations of the arbitrators. After an arbitration award has been made, it is not proper for an arbitrator to assist in post-arbitral proceedings, except as is required by law.

D. In many types of arbitration it is customary practice for the arbitrators to serve without pay. However, in some types of cases it is customary for arbitrators to receive compensation for their services and reimbursement for their expenses. In cases in which any such payments are to be made, all persons who are requested to serve, or who are serving as arbitrators, should be governed by the same high standards of integrity and fairness as apply to their other activities in the case. Accordingly, such persons should scrupulously avoid bargaining with parties over the amount of payments or engaging in any communications concerning payments which would create an appearance of coercion or other impropriety. In the absence of governing provisions in the agreement of the parties or in rules agreed to by the parties or in applicable law, certain practices relating to payments are generally recognized as being preferable in order to preserve the integrity and fairness of the arbitration process. These practices include the following.

1. It is preferable that before the arbitrator finally accepts appointment the basis of payment be established and that all parties be informed thereof in writing.

2. In cases conducted under the rules or administration of an institution that is available to assist in making arrangements for payments, the payments should be arranged by the institution to avoid the necessity for communication by the arbitrators directly with the parties concerning the subject.

3. In cases where no institution is available to assist in making arrangement for payments, it is preferable that any discussions with arbitrators concerning payments should take place in the presence of all parties.

CANON VII. ETHICAL CONSIDERATIONS RELATING TO ARBITRATORS APPOINTED BY ONE PARTY

Introductory Note

In some types of arbitration in which there are three arbitrators, it is customary for each party, acting alone, to appoint one arbitrator. The third arbitrator is then appointed by agreement either of the parties or of the two arbitrators, or, failing such agreement, by an independent institution or individual. In some of these types of arbitration, all three arbitrators are customarily considered to be neutral and are expected to observe the same standards of ethical conduct. However, there are also many types of tripartite arbitration in which it has been the practice that the two arbitrators appointed by the parties are not considered to be neutral and are expected to observe many but not all of the same ethical standards as the neutral third arbitrator. For the purposes of this code, an arbitrator appointed by one party who is not expected to observe all of the same standards as the third arbitrator is called a "nonneutral arbitrator." This Canon VII describes the ethical obligations that nonneutral party-appointed arbitrators should observe and those that are not applicable to them.

In all arbitrations in which there are two or more party-appointed arbitrators, it is important for everyone concerned to know from the start whether the party-appointed arbitrators are expected to be neutrals or nonneutrals. In such arbitrations, the two party-appointed arbitrators should be considered nonneutrals unless both parties inform the arbitrators that all three arbitrators are to be neutral or unless the contract, the applicable arbitration rules, or any governing law requires that all three arbitrators be neutral.

It should be noted that, in cases conducted outside the United States, the applicable law might require that all arbitrators be neutral. Accordingly, in such cases, the governing law should be considered before applying any of the following provisions relating to nonneutral party-appointed arbitrators.

A. *Obligations under Canon I*
Nonneutral party-appointed arbitrators should observe all of the obligations of Canon I to uphold the integrity and fairness of the arbitration process, subject only to the following provisions.

1. Nonneutral arbitrators may be predisposed toward the party who appointed them but in all other respects are obligated to act in good faith and with integrity and fairness. For example, nonneutral arbitrators should not engage in delaying tactics or harassment of any party or witness and should not knowingly make untrue or misleading statements to the other arbitrators.
2. The provisions of Canon I.D relating to relationships and interests are not applicable to nonneutral arbitrators.

B. *Obligations under Canon II*
Nonneutral party-appointed arbitrators should disclose to all parties, and to the other arbitrators, all interests and relationships which Canon II requires be disclosed. Disclosure as required by Canon II is for the benefit not only of the party who appointed the nonneutral arbitrator, but also for the benefit of the other parties and arbitrators so that they may know of any bias which may exist or appear to exist. However, this obligation is subject to the following provisions.

1. Disclosure by nonneutral arbitrators should be sufficient to describe the general nature and scope of any interest or relationship, but need not include as detailed information as is expected from persons appointed as neutral arbitrators.
2. Nonneutral arbitrators are not obliged to withdraw if requested to do so by the party who did not appoint them, notwithstanding the provisions of Canon II.E.

C. *Obligations under Canon III*
Nonneutral party-appointed arbitrators should observe all of the obligations of Canon III concerning communications with the parties, subject only to the following provisions.

1. In an arbitration in which the two party-appointed arbitrators are expected to appoint the third arbitrator, nonneutral arbitrators may consult with the party who appointed them concerning the acceptability of persons under consideration for appointment as the third arbitrator.
2. Nonneutral arbitrators may communicate with the party who appointed them concerning any other aspect of the case, provided they first inform the other arbitrators and the parties that they intend to do so. If such communication occurred prior to the time the person was appointed as arbitrator, or prior to the first hearing or other meeting of the parties with the arbitrators, the nonneutral arbitrator should, at the first hearing or meeting, disclose the fact that such communication has taken place. In complying with the provisions of this paragraph, it is sufficient that there be disclosure of the fact that such communication has occurred without disclosing the content of the communication. It is also sufficient to disclose at any time the intention to

follow the procedure of having such communications in the future and there is no requirement thereafter that there be disclosure before each separate occasion on which such a communication occurs.

3. When nonneutral arbitrators communicate in writing with the party who appointed them concerning any matter as to which communication is permitted under this code, they are not required to send copies of any such written communication to any other party or arbitrator.

D. *Obligations under Canon IV*

Nonneutral party-appointed arbitrators should observe all of the obligations of Canon IV to conduct the proceedings fairly and diligently.

E. *Obligations under Canon V*

Nonneutral party-appointed arbitrators should observe all of the obligations of Canon V concerning making decisions, subject only to the following provision.

1. Nonneutral arbitrators are permitted to be predisposed toward deciding in favor of the party who appointed them.

F. *Obligations under Canon VI*

Nonneutral party-appointed arbitrators should observe all of the obligations of Canon VI to be faithful to the relationship of trust inherent in the office of arbitrator, subject only to the following provision.

1. Nonneutral arbitrators are not subject to the provisions of Canon VI.D with respect to any payments by the party who appointed them.

Annotations

1. In applying the provisions of this code relating to disclosure, it might be helpful to recall the words of the concurring opinion, in a case decided by the U.S. Supreme Court, that arbitrators "should err on the side of disclosure" because "it is better that the relationship be disclosed at the outset when the parties are free to reject the arbitrator or accept him with knowledge of the relationship." At the same time, it must be recognized that "an arbitrator's business relationships may be diverse indeed, involving more or less remote commercial connections with great numbers of people." Accordingly, an arbitrator "cannot be expected to provide the parties with his complete and unexpurgated business biography," nor is an arbitrator called on to disclose interests or relationships that are merely "trivial" (a concurring opinion in *Commonwealth Coatings Corp. v. Continental Casualty Co.*, 393 US 145, 151#152, 1968).

Appendix D

REVISED CODE OF ETHICS FOR ARBITRATORS IN COMMERCIAL DISPUTES (2002) (DRAFT)

<u>WORKING DRAFT</u>

**THE CODE OF ETHICS FOR ARBITRATORS
IN DOMESTIC AND INTERNATIONAL COMMERCIAL DISPUTES**

SUPPLEMENT TO CODE OF ETHICS

**STATEMENT OF SPECIAL OBLIGATIONS OF PARTY-APPOINTED
ARBITRATORS WHO ARE NOT DEEMED NEUTRAL**

(Revised 2002)

This is a working draft. Its contents have not been approved or adopted by the American Bar Association, its Task Force on the Code of Ethics, any of the ABA Sections or Divisions represented on the Task Force, or any entity that sponsored or adopted the 1977 Code of Ethics for Arbitrators in Commercial Disputes.

<u>Introduction to 2002 Revision</u>

The original Code of Ethics for Arbitrators in Commercial Disputes was prepared in 1977 by a joint committee consisting of a special committee of the American Arbitration Association and a special committee of the American Bar Association.[1]

This 2002 Revision of the Code was prepared by a working group convened by the American Bar Association including representatives of its Sections of Dispute Resolution, Business Law, International Law and Practice, Litigation, and Torts and Insurance Practice and the Senior Lawyers Division and representatives of the American Arbitration Association and CPR Institute for Dispute Resolution.

The original 1977 Code was widely accepted by arbitrators throughout the United State of America and was cited favorably in a number of reported decisions of

---

[1]   <u>Editorial Note</u>. This paragraph and the following four paragraphs could be included in a booklet that would contain the Code. The final two paragraphs are for current information and should not be inserted in any booklet containing the Code following its approval by the sponsoring organizations.

United States courts. It was not widely used or referred to in arbitrations in countries other than the United States, or in international arbitrations.

The sponsors of the 2002 Revision recognized that since 1977 significant changes have taken place affecting the commercial transactions which form the subject matter of many commercial arbitrations, and affecting the arbitrations themselves. Arbitrations taking place within the United States, or in countries other than the United States, or international commerce, are increasingly affected by multi-national ownerships of or investments in the parties, or arise from international or multi-national transactions, or may require receipt of evidence from or pre- or post- hearing proceedings in multiple nations. To the extent that the original 1977 Code focused on standards and practices employed primarily within the United States, the sponsors felt that it provided inadequate guidance to arbitrators serving in matters requiring consideration of the standards and practices of nations other than the United States or of the international community.

The sponsors believe that with only one significant exception the ethical standards recognized by aribtrators and arbitral tribunals in the United States, in most other nations, and in the international community, although often articulated in different terms, are substantially the same. These essentially uniform standards are set out in the body of the 2002 Revised Code, consisting of Canons I through IX and the appended commentary.

There is a common type of arbitration in which each party or side appoints an arbitrator, and the party-appointed arbitrator or some third entity or institution appoints a third arbitrator. In most nations and in international arbitrations, all arbitrators, however appointed, are expected to be neutral, independent and free from bias. This expectation exists even as to the arbitrators appointed by the parties. This expectation also exists as to many but not all arbitrations within the United States. However, in a substantial number of arbitrations within the United States the expectation of the parties is that their party-appointed arbitrators may be inclined toward the positions of the parties that appointed them and in some instances may serve to an extent as advocates on their behalf. This role is in some instances recognized by the agreement of the parties or by the rules which they have adopted by their agreement, but more frequently finds no expression other than in the custom and practice of the particular line of commerce or in the submission of the dispute to arbitration.

In its Canon IX, the 2002 Code provides guidance for party-appointed arbitrators who serve as neutrals. In a Supplement which accompanies the Code guidance is provided for those arbitrators who may be expected to serve in other than a neutral capacity. The Supplement imposes obligations upon such arbitrators to ascertain or confirm and to disclose their status, to consult with their appointing parties with respect to potential consequences of their service other than in neutral capacities, and in any case of doubt to maintain neutral status unless and until a determination is made by the parties, the arbitral tribunal or the panel that they may do otherwise.

The sponsors seek approval and recommendation by the participating organizations and other organizations that provide, coordinate or administer the services of arbitrators. By adopting this Code those organizations will provide ethical guidance for their arbitration panel members. The sponsors deem it important that ethical standards be developed for such organizations as well but did not take any action on this subject pending the development of standards undertaken by the Working Group for ADR Provider Organizations convened by the CPR-Georgetown Commission on Ethics and Standards in ADR.

The views expressed herein have not yet been approved by the American Bar Association, CPR Institute or the College of Commercial Arbitrators and should not be construed as representing the policy of any of these institutions pending such approval.

The Code of Ethics for Arbitrators in Domestic and International Commercial Disputes

(2002 Revision)

PREAMBLE

The use of commercial arbitration to resolve a wide variety of disputes forms a significant part of the system of justice on which our society relies for fair determination of legal rights. Persons who act as commercial arbitrators therefore undertake serious responsibilities to the public as well as to the parties. Those responsibilities include important ethical obligations.

Few cases of unethical behavior by commercial arbitrators have arisen. Nevertheless, the American Bar Association, the CPR Institute for Dispute Resolution and the College of Commercial Arbitrators believe that it is in the public interest to set forth generally accepted standards of ethical conduct for guidance of arbitrators and parties in commercial disputes. By establishing this Code, the sponsors hope to contribute to the maintenance of high standards and continued confidence in the process of arbitration.

There are many different types of commercial arbitration. Some cases are conducted under arbitration rules established by various organizations and trade associations, while others are conducted without such rules. Although most cases are arbitrated pursuant to voluntary agreement of the parties, certain types of disputes are submitted to arbitration by reason of particular laws. This Code is intended to apply to all such proceedings in which disputes or claims are submitted for decision to one or more arbitrators appointed in a manner provided by agreement of the parties, by applicable arbitration rules, or by law. In all such cases, the persons who have the power to decide should observe fundamental standards of ethical conduct. In this Code all such persons are called "arbitrators" although, in some types of cases, they might be called "umpires," "referees," "neutrals," or have some other title.

Various aspects of the conduct of arbitrators, including some matters covered by this Code, may be governed by agreements of the parties, by arbitration rules to which the parties have agreed, or by applicable law. This Code does not take the place of or supersede such agreements, rules, or laws and does not establish new or additional grounds for judicial review of arbitration awards.

This Code is intended to provide ethical guidelines to all individuals serving as arbitrators in commercial disputes. In those instances where it has been approved and recommended by organizations that provide, coordinate or administer services of arbitrators it is intended to provide ethical standards for the members of their respective panels of commercial arbitrators. However it does not form a part of the arbitration rules of any such organization, nor is it intended to apply to persons engaged in such ADR processes as mediation, conciliation, court-annexed arbitration, mini-trial or early neutral evaluation. Labor arbitration in the United States is governed by the Code of Professional Responsibility for Arbitrators of Labor-Management Disputes sponsored by the National Academy of Arbitrators, not by this Code. While institutions that provide, coordinate or administer the services of arbitrators are not governed by this Code, it is expected that they will take into account the guidelines in this Code in the performance of their administrative functions.

Arbitrators, like judges, have the power to decide cases. However, unlike full-time judges, arbitrators are usually engaged in other occupations before, during, and after the time that they serve as arbitrators. Often, arbitrators are purposely chosen from the same trade or industry as the parties in order to bring special knowledge to the task of deciding. This Code recognizes these fundamental differences between arbitrators and judges.

The Code refers to the parties to arbitration and to their representatives collectively as "parties." The Code in some provisions refers to multi-arbitral panels as "the arbitrator."

The word "neutral," as used throughout the Code and in the Supplement, is intended to encompass not only the concept of neutrality but also the related concept of independence from any of the parties, their representatives and other arbitrators on the panel, the concept of freedom from bias respecting the parties and the issues in the arbitration, and even-handedness in conducting the arbitration.

In some types of arbitration there are three or more arbitrators. In some such cases it is the practice for each party, acting alone, to appoint one arbitrator and for the third arbitrator to be designated by these two, or by the parties, or by an independent institution or individual. The sponsors of this Code believe that it is preferable for parties to agree that all arbitrators – including any party-appointed arbitrators - should be neutral, independent and free from bias, and to comply with the same ethical standards once they have been appointed. This may be essential in arbitrations where the parties, the dispute, on the enforcement of any potential award may have international aspects because international customs, some rules, and the laws of some countries require that all arbitrators, including those appointed unilaterally by parties, shall observe the same ethical standards. However, parties in some domestic arbitrations in the United States have preferred and may continue to prefer that party-appointed arbitrators be non-neutral and governed by special ethical considerations. These special considerations do not appear in the Code itself but rather in a Supplement that follows the Code, entitled "Special Obligations Under Specific Canons of Party-Appointed Arbitrators Who Are Not Deemed Neutral."

Although this Code is sponsored by the American Bar Association, the CPR Institute for Dispute Resolution, the College of Commercial Arbitrators and other institutions, its use is not limited to arbitrations administered by such institutions or to cases in which the arbitrators are lawyers. Rather, it is presented as a public service to provide guidance in all types of commercial arbitration.

CANON I.   THE ARBITRATOR SHOULD UPHOLD THE INTEGRITY AND FAIRNESS OF THE ARBITRATION PROCESS.

A.   Fair and just processes for resolving disputes are indispensable in our society. Commercial arbitration is an important method for deciding many types of disputes. In order for commercial arbitration to be effective, there must be broad public confidence in the integrity and fairness of the process. Therefore, an arbitrator has a responsibility not only to the parties but also to the process of arbitration itself, and must observe high standards of conduct so that the integrity and fairness of the process will be preserved. Accordingly, the arbitrator should recognize a responsibility to the public, to the parties whose rights will be decided, and to all other participants in the proceeding. The provisions of this Code should be construed and applied to further these objectives.

B.   One should accept appointment as a neutral arbitrator only if fully satisfied (1) that he or she can serve without bias; (2) that he or she can serve independently from the parties, potential witnesses and the other arbitrators; (3) that he or she is competent to serve; and (4) that he or she can be available to commence the arbitration in accordance with the requirements of the case and thereafter to give to it the time and attention to its completion that the parties are reasonably entitled to expect.

C.   After accepting appointment and while serving as arbitrator a person should avoid entering into any financial, business, professional or personal relationship, or acquiring any financial or personal interest, which is likely to affect impartiality or which might reasonably create the appearance of partiality or bias. For a reasonable period of time after the decision of a case, persons who have served as arbitrators should avoid entering into any such relationship, or acquiring any such interest, in circumstances which might reasonably create the appearance that they had been influenced in the arbitration by the anticipation or expectation of the relationship or interest.

D.   Arbitrators should conduct themselves in a way that is fair to all parties and should not be swayed by outside pressure, by public clamor, by fear of criticism or by self-interest. They should avoid conduct and statements that give the appearance of partiality toward any party. They should guard against partiality or prejudice based on any party's personal characteristics, background or performance at the arbitration.

E.   An arbitrator's authority is derived from the agreement of the parties. The arbitrator should neither exceed that authority nor do less than is required to exercise that authority completely. Where the agreement of the parties sets forth procedures to be followed in conducting the arbitration or refers to rules to be followed, it is the obligation of the arbitrator to comply with such procedures or rules. The arbitrator has no ethical obligation to comply with any such procedures or rules that are unlawful, unconscionable, or inconsistent with this Code.

F.   The arbitrator should make all reasonable efforts to assure the prompt, economical and fair resolution of the matters submitted for decision. The arbitrator should endeavor to prevent delaying tactics, harassment of parties or other participants, or other abuse or disruption of the arbitration process.

G.   The ethical obligations of an arbitrator begin when first approached for appointment and continue throughout all stages of the proceeding. In addition, as set forth in this Code, certain ethical obligations continue even after the decision in the case has been given to the parties.

Comment to Canon I

One is not impartial and should not serve as a neutral arbitrator when he or she favors one of the parties or is prejudiced in relation to the subject matter of or issues involved in the dispute. A prospective arbitrator does not become partial or prejudiced by having acquired knowledge of the parties or of the applicable law or of the customs and practices of the business involved. A potential arbitrator is partial or prejudiced if, for example, prior to appointment he or she for any reason has formed an opinion as to the appropriate outcome of the case or any material issue involved in the case.

Existence of any of the matters or circumstances described in subparagraph C of Canon I does not render it unethical for one to serve as a neutral arbitrator where the parties have consented to the arbitrator's appointment or continued service following full disclosure of the relevant facts in accordance with Canon II. The matters set forth in subparagraphs B and D of Canon I reflect the arbitrator's obligation to the public and to the process, and therefore reflect circumstances where it is inappropriate for a neutral arbitrator to serve as such even though the parties have voiced no objection to the appointment or continued service following full disclosure.

During an arbitration, the arbitrator may be expected to engage in discourse with the parties or their counsel, to draw out arguments or contentions, to comment on the law or the evidence, to make interim rulings, and otherwise to control or direct the arbitration. These activities are integral parts of an active adjudicative process. Subparagraph D of Canon I is not intended to preclude or limit either full discussion of the issues during the course of the arbitration or the arbitrator's management of the proceeding.

This Canon requires an arbitrator to be diligent as to all aspects of the arbitration and to make a reasonable effort to render an enforceable award.

If an arbitrator is a member of a law firm or a business organization, the arbitrator should endeavor to assure that the firm or organization does not, without the consent of the parties, enter into or structure relationships which may affect the arbitrator's neutrality or create a reasonable appearance of partiality, bias or post-award remuneration.

CANON II.   **AN ARBITRATOR SHOULD DISCLOSE ANY INTEREST OR RELATIONSHIP LIKELY TO AFFECT IMPARTIALITY OR INDEPENDENCE OR WHICH MIGHT CREATE AN APPEARANCE OF PARTIALITY OR OTHER BIAS.**

    A.   Persons who are requested to serve as arbitrators should, before accepting, disclose:

    (1)   any known direct or indirect financial or personal interest in the outcome of the arbitration;

    (2)   any known existing or past financial, business, professional or personal relationships which are likely to affect impartiality or which the arbitrator believes may reasonably create an appearance of partiality or of lack of independence or bias in the eyes of any of the parties. Prospective arbitrators should disclose any such relationships which they personally have with any party or its lawyer, with any arbitrator, or with any individual whom they have been told will be a witness. They should also disclose any such relationships involving their immediate family or household members or their current employers, partners or professional or business associates that can be ascertained by reasonable efforts;

    (3)   the nature and extent of any prior knowledge he or she may have of the dispute; and

    (4)   any other matters, relationships or interests which they are obligated to disclose by the agreement of the parties, the rules or practices of the institution which is administering the arbitration, or applicable law regulating arbitrator disclosure.

B. Any doubt as to whether or not disclosure is to be made should be resolved in favor of disclosure.

C. Persons who are requested to accept appointment as arbitrators should make a reasonable effort to inform themselves of any interests or relationships described in subparagraph A.

D. The obligation to disclose the interests or relationships described in subparagraph A is a continuing duty which requires a person who accepts appointment as an arbitrator to disclose forthwith, at any stage of the arbitration, any such interests or relationships which may arise, or which are recalled or discovered.

E. Disclosure should be made to all parties unless other procedures for disclosure are provided in the agreement of the parties, the rules or practices of any institution which is administering the arbitration, or by law. Where more than one arbitrator has been appointed, each should inform the others of all matters disclosed.

F. In the event that a neutral arbitrator is requested by all parties to withdraw, the arbitrator should do so. In the event that a neutral arbitrator is requested to withdraw by less than all of the parties because of alleged partiality or bias, the arbitrator should withdraw unless either of the following circumstances exists:

(1) If an agreement of the parties, arbitration rules agreed to by the parties, or applicable law establishes procedures for determining challenges to arbitrators, then those procedures should be followed;

(2) If, in the absence of applicable procedures, the arbitrator after carefully considering the matter determines that the reason for the challenge is not substantial and that he or she can nevertheless act and decide the case impartially and fairly, and that withdrawal would cause unfair delay or expense to another party or would be contrary to the ends of justice.

G. An arbitrator appointed by a party need not withdraw at the request of a party that did not appoint the arbitrator.

H. In the event that compliance by a prospective arbitrator or arbitrator with any provision of this Code would require disclosure of any confidential or privileged information, he or she should either (i) secure the consent to the disclosure of the person who furnished the information or the holder of the privilege, or (ii) withdraw.

Comment to Canon II

This Canon reflects the prevailing principle that arbitrators should disclose the existence of interests, relationships or circumstances that are likely to affect their impartiality or independence or that might reasonably create an appearance in the eyes of the parties that they are biased against one party or favorable to another. These provisions of this Canon are intended to be applied realistically so that the burden of detailed disclosure does not become so great that it is impractical for persons in the business or legal worlds to be arbitrators, thereby depriving parties of the services of those who might be best informed and qualified to decide particular types of cases. However, Canon II provides that doubt as to whether or not disclosure is to be made should be resolved in favor of disclosure.[2]

Except as provided in the Comment to Canon I, Canon II does not limit the freedom of parties to agree on whomever they choose as an arbitrator. When parties, with knowledge of a person's interests and relationships, nevertheless desire that individual to serve as an arbitrator, that person may properly serve.

Comment to Subparagraph C.

The scope of a reasonable effort to become informed depends upon the circumstances. A single standard cannot be established for all situations. As a general proposition an inquiry by a principal or member of a firm or principal of a business organization should encompass the current or recent business or professional relationships of the other members of the firm or principals of the organization. However, it is sufficient for a member of a very large firm or principal of a large business organization to make such inquiries as would disclose relationships of the firm or organization which are likely to affect the arbitrators' partiality or which might create a reasonable appearance of partiality, lack of independence or bias on the part of the arbitrator.

Comment to Subparagraph F.

Since arbitration generally exists by virtue of agreement between or among the parties to submit their disputes to a non-judicial forum, it is appropriate that a neutral arbitrator withdraw upon the request of all parties. If the arbitrator has disclosed to the parties in advance that a fee will be charged if time has been set

---

[2]In applying the provisions of this Code relating to disclosure, it might be helpful to recall the words of the concurring opinion, in a case decided by the US Supreme Court, that arbitrators "should err on the side of disclosure" because "it is better that the relationship be disclosed at the outset when the parties are free to reject the arbitrator or accept him with knowledge of the relationship." At the same time, it must be recognized that "an arbitrator's business relationships may be diverse indeed, involving more or less remote commercial connections with great numbers of people." Accordingly, an arbitrator "cannot be expected to provide the parties with his complete and unexpurgated business biography," nor is an arbitrator called on to disclose interests or relationships that are merely "trivial" (a concurring opinion in *Commonwealth Coatings Corp. v. Continental Casualty Co.*, 393 US 145, 151-152 (1968).

aside for the arbitration and cannot be filled, in accordance with Canon VII a cancellation or termination charge is not improper.

In applying the provisions of Subparagraph F in the circumstance where less than all of the parties have requested that the arbitrator withdraw, it is appropriate to consider the timeliness of the request. Where the arbitrator has had minimal involvement in the case it may be preferable that the arbitrator withdraw. If the matter has proceeded to the point where substantial time and effort have been devoted to forming the arbitral tribunal and conducting the proceedings, and withdrawal will result in duplication of effort, significant expense, and significant delay in resolving the matter, the prejudice to the non-objecting party must be weighed against the credibility and seriousness of the basis for the request.

Although the Canons generally are for the guidance of arbitrators, not parties, the role of the parties should be noted. If a party is aware of material interests or relationships that the arbitrator has not disclosed or has overlooked, these should be made known promptly to the other parties or arbitrators or to the arbitral tribunal if one exists. In considering a request for withdrawal the arbitrator or tribunal may properly consider whether the requesting party was aware of the claimed relationship or interest at the time the arbitrator was appointed or delayed unduly in presenting its request after acquiring such knowledge.

Comment to Subparagraph G.
Although a neutral arbitrator who was appointed by a single party need not withdraw at the request of the non-appointing party, the arbitrator should nevertheless consider whether he or she can hear and decide the case with the impartiality contemplated by Subparagraph B of Canon I. If the arbitrator determines that he or she lacks such impartiality it is preferable that the arbitrator decline the appointment or withdraw.

CANON III.   AN ARBITRATOR IN COMMUNICATING WITH THE PARTIES SHOULD AVOID IMPROPRIETY OR THE APPEARANCE OF IMPROPRIETY.

A.   If an agreement of the parties or applicable arbitration rules establishes the manner or content of communications between the arbitrator and the parties, the arbitrator should follow those procedures notwithstanding any contrary provision of the following subparagraphs B and C.

B.   Unless otherwise provided in applicable arbitration rules or in an agreement of the parties, arbitrators should not discuss a case with any party in the absence of any other party, except in any of the following circumstances:

(1)   When the appointment of a prospective arbitrator is being considered, the prospective arbitrator (a) may ask about the

identities of parties, counsel or witnesses and the general nature of the case; and (b) may respond to inquiries from a party or its counsel designed to determine only his or her suitability and availability for the appointment. In any such dialogue the prospective arbitrator may receive information disclosing the general nature of the dispute, but should not permit the parties or their representatives the opportunity to discuss the details or merits of the case.

(2)   In an arbitration in which the two party-appointed arbitrators are expected to appoint the third arbitrator, each party-appointed arbitrator may consult with the party who appointed the arbitrator concerning the choice of the third arbitrator.

(3)   In an arbitration involving party-appointed arbitrators, each party-appointed arbitrator may consult with the party who appointed the arbitrator concerning arrangements for any compensation to be paid to the party-appointed arbitrator. Submission of routine requests for payment of compensation and expenses in accordance with such arrangements and communications pertaining solely to such requests for payment are not prohibited.

(4)   In an arbitration involving party-appointed arbitrators, each party-appointed arbitrator may consult with the party who appointed the arbitrator concerning the status of the arbitrator, as contemplated by Paragraph A of the Supplement which accompanies this Code.

(5)   Discussions may be had with a party concerning such matters as setting the time and place of hearings or making other arrangements for the conduct of the proceedings. However, the arbitrator should promptly inform any other party of the discussion and should not make any final determination concerning the matter discussed before giving any absent party an opportunity to express the party's views.

(6)   If a party fails to be present at a hearing after having been given due notice, the arbitrator may discuss the case with any party who is present.

(7)   If all parties request or expressly consent to it, such discussion may take place.

C.   Unless otherwise provided in applicable arbitration rules or in an agreement of the parties, whenever an arbitrator communicates in writing with one party, the arbitrator should at the same time send a copy of the communication to every other party, and, whenever the arbitrator receives any written communication concerning the case from one party which has not already been sent to every other party, the arbitrator should send or cause it to be sent to the other parties.

CANON IV.   AN ARBITRATOR SHOULD CONDUCT THE PROCEEDINGS FAIRLY AND DILIGENTLY.

A.   The arbitrator should conduct the proceedings in an evenhanded manner and treat all parties with equality and fairness at all stages of the proceeding.

B.   The arbitrator should perform duties diligently and conclude the case as promptly as the circumstances reasonably permit.

C.   The arbitrator should be patient and courteous to the parties, to their representatives and to the witnesses and should encourage similar conduct by all participants in the proceedings.

D.   Unless otherwise agreed by the parties or provided in applicable arbitration rules, the arbitrator should afford to all parties the right to appear in person and to be heard and due notice of the time and place of any hearing or pre-hearing conference. The arbitrator should allow each party fair opportunity to present its evidence and arguments. The arbitrator may preclude evidence which is irrelevant or cumulative or is otherwise protected from submission in the proceeding.

E.   The arbitrator should not deny any party the opportunity to be represented by counsel or by any other person chosen by the party to assist it.

F.   If a party fails to appear after due notice, the arbitrator should proceed with the arbitration when authorized to do so by the agreement of the parties, the applicable rules or by law. However, the arbitrator should do so only after receiving assurance that appropriate notice has been given to the absent party.

G.   When the arbitrator determines that more information than has been presented by the parties is required to decide the case, it is not improper for the arbitrator to ask questions, call witnesses, and request documents or other evidence, including expert testimony.

H.   It is not improper for an arbitrator to suggest to the parties that they discuss the possibility of settlement of the case or the use of mediation, conciliation or other dispute resolution processes. However, an arbitrator should not be present or otherwise participate in the settlement discussions or such other processes unless requested to do so by all parties. An arbitrator should not exert pressure on any party to settle or to utilize other dispute resolution processes.

I.   Nothing in this Code is intended to prevent a person from acting as a mediator or conciliator of a dispute in which he or she has been appointed as arbitrator, if requested to do so by all parties or where authorized or required to do so by applicable laws or rules.

J.   When there is more than one arbitrator, the arbitrators should afford each other the full opportunity to participate in all aspects of the proceedings.

Comment to Canon IV

Subparagraph J of Canon IV is not intended to preclude one arbitrator from acting in limited circumstances (*i.e.*, ruling on discovery issues) where authorized by the agreement of the parties or applicable rules or law. Nor does it preclude a majority of the arbitrators from proceeding with any aspect of the arbitration if an arbitrator is unable or unwilling to participate and such action is authorized by the agreement of the parties or applicable rules or law.

CANON V.   AN ARBITRATOR SHOULD MAKE DECISIONS IN A JUST, INDEPENDENT AND DELIBERATE MANNER.

A.   The arbitrator should, after careful deliberation, decide all issues submitted for determination. The arbitrator should decide no other issues.

B.   The arbitrator should decide all matters justly, exercising independent judgment, and should not permit outside pressure to affect the decision.

C.   The arbitrator should not delegate the duty to decide to any other person.

D.   In the event that all parties agree upon a settlement of issues in dispute and request the arbitrator to embody that agreement in an award, the arbitrator may do so, but is not required to do so unless satisfied with the propriety of the terms of settlement. Whenever the arbitrator embodies a settlement by the parties in an award, the arbitrator should state in the award that it is based on an agreement of the parties.

Comment to Canon V, Subparagraph C

Subparagraph C does not preclude an arbitrator from obtaining help from an associate or from a research assistant or other persons in connection with reaching his or her decision, so long as the arbitrator informs the parties of the use of such assistants or other persons and they agree to be bound by the provisions of subparagraphs A, B and C of Canon VI.

CANON VI.   AN ARBITRATOR SHOULD BE FAITHFUL TO THE RELATIONSHIP OF TRUST AND CONFIDENTIALITY INHERENT IN THAT OFFICE.

A.   An arbitrator is in a relationship of trust to the parties and should not, at any time, use or disclose confidential information acquired during the arbitration proceedings to gain personal advantage or advantage for others, or to affect adversely the interest of another.

B.   Unless otherwise agreed by the parties or required by applicable rules or law, the arbitrator should keep confidential all matters relating to the arbitration proceedings and decision.

C.   It is not proper at any time for an arbitrator to inform anyone of the final decision or of any interim decision in advance of the time it is given to all parties, with the exception of an organization which is administering the arbitration, under applicable rules or procedures. In a case in which there is more than one arbitrator, it is not proper at any time for an arbitrator to inform anyone about the substance of the deliberations of the arbitrators. After an arbitration award has been made, it is not proper for an arbitrator to assist in proceedings to enforce or challenge the award, except as is required by applicable rules or law or by the terms of the award, or if the parties agree that the arbitrator may do so.

D.   Except where otherwise agreed by the parties or required by applicable rules or law, when the award has been made the arbitrator may offer to return materials submitted by a party to that party or its representative. If the offer is not accepted, following due notice, the arbitrator may retain any of such materials or dispose of any of them in any manner reasonably calculated to prevent their use or disclosure.

E.   Unless the parties so request, an arbitrator should not appoint himself or herself to a separate office related to the subject matter of the dispute, such as receiver or trustee, nor should a panel of arbitrators appoint one of their number to such office.

CANON VII.   AN ARBITRATOR SHOULD BE GOVERNED BY STANDARDS OF INTEGRITY AND FAIRNESS WHEN MAKING ARRANGEMENTS FOR COMPENSATION AND REIMBURSEMENT OF EXPENSES.

A.   If persons who are requested to serve as arbitrators anticipate compensation for their services or reimbursement for their expenses, in making arrangements for such payments they are governed by the same high standards of integrity and fairness as apply to their other activities in the case. Accordingly, such persons should avoid any communications concerning the amount of or matters pertaining to such payments which would create an appearance of coercion or other impropriety.

B.   In the absence of governing provisions in the agreement of the parties or in applicable rules or law, certain practices relating to payments are generally recognized as being preferable in order to preserve the integrity and fairness of the arbitration process. These practices include the following.

(1)   Before the arbitrator finally accepts appointment, the terms and conditions of payment, including any cancellation fees and compensation for study and preparation time, should be established and all parties informed thereof in writing.

(2)   In cases conducted under the rules or administration of an institution that is available to assist in making arrangements for payments, the payments should be arranged by the institution to avoid the necessity for communication by the arbitrators directly with the parties concerning the subject.

(3)   In cases where no institution has been engaged by the parties to administer the arbitration, any communication with arbitrators concerning payments should take place in writing or in the presence of all parties.

C.   Absent extraordinary circumstances, the arbitrator should not ask that his or her rate of compensation be increased during the pendency of the arbitration.

D.   Neither the payment of an arbitrator's fee nor the amount thereof should be contingent upon the outcome of the arbitration.

CANON VIII.   AN ARBITRATOR MAY ENGAGE IN ADVERTISING OR PROMOTION OF ARBITRAL SERVICES IN A DISCREET AND PROFESSIONAL MANNER.

A.   Advertising or promotion of an individual's general willingness or availability to serve as an arbitrator should be limited to a brief description of his or her professional credentials, experience, and relevant areas of expertise or activities, and such information as may be required to facilitate contact and communication. Such advertising or promotion must not (a) be inaccurate or likely to mislead; (b) make comparison with other arbitrators or members of other professions; (c) include statements about the quality of the arbitrator's work or the success of the arbitrator's practice; or (d) imply any willingness to accept an appointment otherwise than in accordance with this Code. This Canon does not preclude an arbitrator, from printing, publishing or disseminating advertisements conforming to the foregoing standards in any electronic or print medium, from making personal presentations to prospective users of arbitral services conforming to such standards, or from responding to inquiries concerning the arbitrator's availability, qualifications, experience or fee arrangements.

B.   Although one may indicate a general willingness to serve as an arbitrator, it is inappropriate to solicit appointment as an arbitrator in a particular case.

CANON IX.   ARBITRATORS APPOINTED BY ONE PARTY SHOULD COMPLY WITH THE PROVISIONS OF THIS CODE UNLESS OTHERWISE REQUIRED BY THE AGREEMENT OF THE PARTIES OR APPLICABLE LAW OR ARBITRAL RULES, AND EXCEPT AS PROVIDED IN THIS CANON IX.

Introductory Note.

In some types of arbitration in which there are three arbitrators it is customary for each party, acting alone, to appoint one arbitrator. The third arbitrator is then appointed by agreement either of the parties or of the two arbitrators, or, failing such agreement, by an independent institution or individual. In arbitrations to which this Code applies, including those where arbitrators are appointed by the parties in this manner, all three arbitrators are customarily considered and are expected to be neutral and, except as provided on this Canon IX, the party-appointed arbitrators are expected to observe the same standards as the third arbitrator.

There are some types of tripartite arbitration in which it is expected by all parties that the two arbitrators appointed by the parties will not be considered or expected to be neutral. One who is asked or appointed to serve as a party-appointed arbitrator in an arbitration of this type should determine and disclose his or her status in accordance with the procedures described in the Supplement which accompanies this Code, entitled "Special Obligations of Party-Appointed Arbitrators Who Are Not Deemed Neutral". The Supplement also describes the ethical obligations of party-appointed arbitrators in these types of arbitrations.

A.   Obligations Under Canon I

Neutral party-appointed arbitrators should observe all of the obligations of Canon I to uphold the integrity and fairness of the arbitration process. They may have special experience or expertise in the areas of business, commerce or technology which are involved in the arbitration. A neutral party-appointed arbitrator does not contravene Paragraph B of Canon I if, by virtue of such experience or expertise, he or she has views on certain general issues or approaches likely to arise in the arbitration, but a neutral party-appointed arbitrator may not have prejudged any of the specific factual or legal determinations to be addressed on the arbitration.

B.   Obligations under Canon II

(1)   Neutral party-appointed arbitrators should disclose to all parties and to the other arbitrators all interests and relationships which Canon II requires to be disclosed.

Disclosure as required by Canon II is for the benefit not only of the party who appointed the arbitrator, but also for the benefit of the other parties and arbitrators so that they may know of any bias which may exist or appear to exist.

(2)   Neutral party-appointed arbitrators are not obliged to withdraw if requested to do so by a party who did not appoint them, as provided in subparagraph G of Canon II.

C.   Obligations under Canon III

Neutral party-appointed arbitrators may consult with the parties that appointed them as provided in subparagraph B of Canon III, but not concerning any other matters.

D.   Obligations under Canons IV, V and VI

Neutral party-appointed arbitrators should observe all of the obligations of Canons IV, V and VI.

E.   Obligations under Canon VII

Neutral party-appointed arbitrators should observe all of the obligations of Canon VII excepting only those provided for in subparagraph B of Canon VII.

F.   Obligations under Canon VIII

Neutral party-appointed arbitrators should observe all of the obligations of Canon VIII.

<u>SUPPLEMENT TO CODE OF ETHICS FOR ARBITRATORS IN</u>

<u>DOMESTIC AND INTERNATIONAL COMMERCIAL DISPUTES</u>

<u>Special Obligations of Party-Appointed Arbitrators</u>
<u>Who Are Not Deemed Neutral</u>

<u>Introductory Note</u>

There are some types of tripartite arbitrations in which it is anticipated by all parties that the two arbitrators appointed by the parties will not be considered to be neutral, but rather are expected to be supportive of the positions of the parties that appointed them. Such arbitrators are referred to in this Supplement as "partisan arbitrators."

Partisan arbitrators are expected to observe many – but not all – of the same ethical standards as arbitrators who are deemed neutral. This Supplement describes the ethical obligations that partisan arbitrators should observe and those that are not applicable to them. A partisan arbitrator is expected to observe all of the ethical obligations prescribed by the Code with the exceptions set forth in this Supplement. Partisan arbitrators are thus expected to adhere to the standards applicable to arbitrators who are neutral except as specifically excused. They too bear responsibility for the integrity and fairness of the process.

A.   Clarification of Status of Arbitrators

Except where it is clear from the outset, based upon the agreement of the parties, the rules of any tribunal administering the arbitration or applicable law, that all of the arbitrators are expected to be neutral, the party-appointed arbitrators have an ethical obligation to determine whether or not they are anticipated by the parties that appointed them to be neutral or to be partisan, and to provide a timely report of their determination to the parties and arbitrators. In so doing, party-appointed arbitrators should take into account that applicable rules or law may require that all arbitrators, including arbitrators appointed by one party, shall be neutral, and failing that awards may not be enforceable. Where party-appointed arbitrators have reasonable cause to believe that this might be the case, they should consult with and so inform the parties that appointed them, and should not act as partisans until the parties have been afforded the opportunity to consider and to make informed decisions with respect to their status. If they are unable to determine their anticipated status from any of the foregoing sources and no decision in that regard has been made by the arbitral panel or any tribunal administering the arbitration, they should continue to observe all of the obligations of neutral arbitrators.

B.   Obligations Under Canon I

Partisan arbitrators should observe all of the obligations of Canon I to uphold the integrity and fairness of the arbitration process, subject only to the following provisions:

(1) Partisan arbitrators may be predisposed toward the party who appointed them but in all other respects are obligated to act in good faith and with integrity and fairness. For example, partisan arbitrators should not engage in delaying tactics or harassment of any party or witness and should not knowingly make untrue or misleading statements to the other arbitrators.

(2) The provisions of subparagraphs B(1), B(2), C and D of Canon I, insofar as they relate to partiality or bias, relationships and interests, are not applicable to partisan arbitrators.

C. Obligations Under Canon II

(1) Partisan arbitrators should disclose to all parties and to the other arbitrators all interests and relationships which Canon II requires to be disclosed. Disclosure as required by Canon II is for the benefit not only of the party who appointed the arbitrator, but also for the benefit of the other parties and arbitrators so that they may know of any bias which may exist or appear to exist.

(2) Partisan arbitrators are not obliged to withdraw if requested to do so by the party who did not appoint them, as provided in subparagraph G of Canon II.

D. Obligations Under Canon III

Partisan arbitrators should observe all of the obligations of Canon III concerning communications with the parties, subject only to the following provisions:

(1) Partisan arbitrators may consult with the parties who appointed them as provided in subparagraph B of Canon III.

(2) Partisan arbitrators shall at the earliest practicable time disclose to the other arbitrators and to the parties whether or not they intend to communicate with the parties that appointed them concerning the case during the course of the arbitration. If they have disclosed their intention to engage in such communications, they may thereafter communicate with the

parties that appointed them concerning any other aspect of the case, except as provided in subparagraph (3). If such communication occurred prior to the time the person was appointed as arbitrator, or prior to the first hearing or other meeting of the parties with the arbitrators, the partisan arbitrator should, at or before the first hearing or meeting, disclose the fact that such communication has taken place. In complying with the provisions of this subparagraph, it is sufficient that there be disclosure of the fact that such communication has occurred without disclosing the content of the communication. A single timely disclosure of the partisan arbitrator's intention to participate in such communications in the future is sufficient, and there is no requirement thereafter that there be disclosure before or after each separate occasion on which such a communication occurs.

(3)   Partisan arbitrators may not at any time during the arbitration (i) disclose any deliberations by the arbitrators on any matter or issue submitted to them for decision or (ii) communicate with the parties that appointed them concerning the subject of any matter or issue taken under consideration by the panel after the record is closed or such matter or issue has been submitted for decision or (iii) disclose any final decision or interim decision in advance of the time that it is disclosed to all parties.

(4)   Unless otherwise agreed by the arbitrators and the parties, a partisan arbitrator may not communicate orally with the neutral arbitrator concerning the subject matter of the arbitration in the absence of the other partisan arbitrator. If a partisan arbitrator communicates in writing with the neutral arbitrator, he or she shall simultaneously provide a copy of the written communication to the other partisan arbitrator.

(5)   When partisan arbitrators communicate orally with the parties that appointed them concerning any matter as to which communication is permitted under the Code or Supplement, they are not obligated to disclose the contents of such oral communications to any other party or arbitrator.

(6)   When partisan arbitrators communicate in writing with the party who appointed them concerning any matter as to which communication is permitted under the Code or Supplement, they are not required to send copies of any such written communication to any other party or arbitrator.

(7)   Partisan arbitrators should comply with any agreement by the parties or order by the arbitral tribunal respecting unilateral communications with any party or anyone acting on behalf of a party.

E.   Obligations Under Canon IV

Partisan arbitrators should observe all of the obligations of Canon IV to conduct the proceedings fairly and diligently.

F.   Obligations Under Canon V

Partisan arbitrators should observe all of the obligations of Canon V concerning making decisions except that they are permitted to be predisposed toward deciding in favor of the party who appointed them.

G.   Obligations Under Canon VI

Partisan arbitrators should observe all of the obligations of Canon VI to be faithful to the relationship of trust inherent in the office of arbitrator.

H.   Obligations Under Canon VII

Partisan arbitrators should observe all of the obligations of Canon VII excepting only those provided for in subparagraph A of Canon VII.

I.   Obligations Under Canon VIII

Partisan arbitrators should observe all of the obligations of Canon VIII concerning advertising and promotion of arbitral services.

J.   Obligations Under Canon IX

The provisions of Canon IX are inapplicable to partisan arbitrators except as the obligations contained therein are also set forth as to partisan arbitrators in this Supplement.

Comment

In seeking to ascertain the agreement of the parties respecting the status of their party-appointed arbitrators, the initial inquiry should address any relevant express terms of their written or oral agreements. However, it may be necessary to inquire into agreements or understandings that have not been expressly set forth, but which may be implied from an established course of dealings of the parties or well-recognized custom and usage in their trade or profession.

Appendix E

JAMS
ETHICS GUIDELINES FOR ARBITRATORS

PREAMBLE

The purpose of these Ethics Guidelines is to provide basic guidance to JAMS arbitrators regarding ethical issues that may arise during or related to the arbitration process. Arbitration is an adjudicative dispute resolution procedure in which a neutral decision maker issues an award. Parties are often represented by counsel who argue the case before a single arbitrator or a panel of three arbitrators, who adjudicate, or judge, the matter based on the evidence presented.

Arbitration -- either entered into voluntarily after a dispute has occurred, or as agreed to in a pre-dispute contract clause -- is generally "binding." By entering into the arbitration process, the parties have agreed to accept an arbitrator's decision as final. There *are* instances when an arbitrator's decision may be modified or vacated, but they are extremely rare. The parties in an arbitration trade the right to appeal for a speedier, less expensive, private process in which it is certain there will be a resolution.

Other sets of ethics guidelines for arbitrators exist, such as those issued by the National Academy of Arbitrators and the American Arbitration Association. An arbitrator may wish to review these for informational purposes. Copies of each, as well as other reference materials, are kept in each JAMS/Endispute office.

These Guidelines are national in scope and are necessarily general. They are not intended to supplant applicable state or local laws or rules. An arbitrator should be aware of applicable state statutes or court rules, such as laws concerning disclosure, discovery procedures and privilege, that may apply to the arbitrations they are conducting. In the event that these Guidelines are inconsistent with such statutes or rules, an arbitrator should comply with applicable law.

In addition, most states have promulgated codes of ethics for judges and other public judicial officers. In some instances, these codes apply to certain activities of private judges, such as court-ordered arbitrations. Arbitrators should comply with codes that are specifically applicable to them or to their activities. Where the codes do not specifically apply, an arbitrator may choose to comply voluntarily with the requirements of such codes.

The ethical obligations of an arbitrator begin as soon as the arbitrator becomes aware of potential selection by the parties and continue even after the decision in the case has been rendered. These Guidelines apply to an arbitrator appointed either by one party or by a combination of parties. These Guidelines do not establish new or additional grounds for judicial review of arbitration awards. These Guidelines do not form a part of the arbitration rules of JAMS/Endispute.

JAMS/Endispute strongly encourages its arbitrators to confront directly ethical issues that may arise in their cases as soon as an issue becomes apparent, and to seek advice on how to resolve such issues from the Regional or local Director of Professional Services for their office or from a member of the Ethics Subcommitttee of the JAMS/Endispute Executive Committee.

I. AN ARBITRATOR SHOULD UPHOLD THE DIGNITY AND INTEGRITY OF THE OFFICE AND OF THE ARBITRATION PROCESS.

An arbitrator has a responsibility to the parties, to other participants in the proceeding, and to the profession. An arbitrator should seek to discern and refuse to lend approval or consent to any attempt by a party or its representative to use arbitration for a purpose other than the fair and efficient resolution of a dispute.

II. AN ARBITRATOR SHOULD BE COMPETENT TO ARBITRATE THE PARTICULAR MATTER.

An arbitrator should accept an appointment only if the arbitrator meets the parties' requirements regarding knowledge of relevant procedural and substantive issues. An arbitrator should prepare before the arbitration by reviewing any statements or documents submitted by the parties. An arbitrator should refuse to serve or withdraw from the arbitration if the arbitrator becomes physically or mentally unable to meet the reasonable expectations of the parties.

III. AN ARBITRATOR SHOULD INFORM ALL PARTIES OF THE ROLE OF THE ARBITRATOR AND THE RULES OF THE ARBITRATION PROCESS.

An arbitrator should ensure that all parties understand the arbitration process, the arbitrator's role in that process, and the relationship of the parties to the arbitrator.

In the event that, prior to or during the arbitration, all parties request an arbitrator to be present in discussions of settlement or of the possibility of combining arbitration with another dispute resolution process, the arbitrator should explain how the arbitrator's role and relationship to the parties may be altered, including the impact such a shift may have on the willingness of the parties to disclose certain information to the arbitrator serving in the settlement-related role. Nothing in these Guidelines is intended, however, to prevent an arbitrator from acting as a neutral in another dispute resolution process in the same case, if requested to do so by all parties. The parties should, however, be given the opportunity to select another neutral to conduct any such process.

IV. AN ARBITRATOR SHOULD MAINTAIN CONFIDENTIALITY APPROPRIATE TO THE PROCESS.

Unless otherwise agreed by the parties, or required by applicable rules or law, an arbitrator should keep confidential all matters relating to the arbitration proceedings and decision.

An arbitrator should not discuss a case with persons not involved directly in the arbitration unless advance approval or consent of all parties is obtained or where the identity of the parties and details of the case are sufficiently obscured to eliminate any realistic probability of identification. A commonly recognized exception is discussion of a problem in a case with an arbitrator not involved in the case. Any such discussion does not relieve the arbitrator who is acting in the case from sole responsibility for the decision and the discussion must be considered confidential.

An arbitrator may discuss a case with another member of the arbitration panel hearing that case, whether or not all panel members are present.

An arbitrator should not use confidential information acquired during the arbitration proceeding to gain personal advantage or advantage for others, or to affect adversely the interest of another. An arbitrator should not inform anyone of the decision in advance of giving it to all parties. Where there is more than one arbitrator, an arbitrator should not disclose to anyone the deliberations of the arbitrators.

An arbitrator should not participate in postarbitral proceedings, except (1) if requested to make a correction or clarification to an award, (2) if required by law or (3) if requested by all parties to participate in a subsequent dispute resolution procedure in the same case.

V. AN ARBITRATOR SHOULD ENSURE THAT THE ARBITRATOR HAS NO KNOWN CONFLICT OF INTEREST REGARDING THE CASE, AND SHOULD ENDEAVOR TO AVOID ANY PERCEPTION OF A CONFLICT OF INTEREST.

An arbitrator should disclose, or cause to be disclosed, as far in advance of the arbitration as practicable, any actual or potential conflict of interest or relationship or other information, of which the arbitrator is aware, that reasonably could lead a party to question the arbitrator's impartiality. Examples of the types of information that should be disclosed include pre-existing personal knowledge of the dispute; current or past business, managerial, consultive, familial or personal relationships with a party, its representative or a witness, including membership on a board of directors or service as a representative or advocate for a party; and current direct or indirect financial interest in the dispute, a party, its representative or a witness. Such financial interests include stock, bond or equity ownership (other than mutual fund shares or appropriate trust arrangements). An arbitrator should disclose any such relationship or interest involving members of the arbitrator's family, current employees, or partners of the arbitrator. In addition, an arbitrator should advise the parties of the extent of prior service as a neutral in matters involving a party, insurer, or counsel in the current arbitration. An arbitrator should make a reasonable effort to inform himself or herself of any of the above interests or relationships.

An arbitrator may establish social or professional relationships with lawyers and members of other professions. There should be no attempt to be secretive about such relationships but disclosure is not necessary unless some feature of a particular relationship might reasonably appear to impair impartiality.

An arbitrator should not proceed with the process unless all parties have acknowledged and waived any actual or potential conflict of interest. If the conflict of interest casts serious doubt on the integrity of the process, an arbitrator should withdraw, notwithstanding receipt of a full waiver.

An arbitrator's disclosure obligations continue throughout the course of the arbitration and require the arbitrator to disclose, at any stage of the arbitration, any such interest or relationship that may arise, or that is recalled or discovered. Disclosure should be made to all parties. Where more than one arbitrator is appointed, each should inform the others of the interests and relationships that have been disclosed.

An arbitrator should avoid conflicts of interest in recommending the services of other professionals. If an arbitrator is unable to make a personal recommendation without creating a potential or actual conflict of interest, the arbitrator should so advise the parties and refer them to a professional service or provider or association.

During the pendency of an arbitration, an arbitrator should decline to undertake any additional arbitration or dispute resolution work involving a party, insurer or counsel to the pending arbitration, unless the arbitrator believes it can be undertaken without an actual or apparent conflict of interest. In circumstances where the arbitrator believes it is appropriate to accept an additional engagement as a mediator or arbitrator involving a party, insurer or counsel to a party to the pending arbitration, the arbitrator should accept such work only after a written waiver of conflict has been obtained from the other parties to the pending arbitration.

After an award or decision is rendered in an arbitration, an arbitrator should refrain from any conduct involving a party, insurer or counsel to a party to the arbitration that would cast reasonable doubt on the integrity of the arbitration process, absent disclosure to and consent by all the parties to the arbitration. This does not preclude an arbitrator from serving as an arbitrator or in another neutral capacity with a party, insurer or counsel involved in the prior arbitration, provided that appropriate disclosures are made about the prior arbitration to the parties to the new matter.

An arbitrator should not accept a gift or item of value from a party, insurer or counsel to a pending arbitration. Unless a period of time has elapsed sufficient to negate any appearance of a conflict of interest, an arbitrator should not accept a gift or item of value from a party to a completed arbitration, except that this provision does not preclude an arbitrator from engaging in normal, social interaction with a party, insurer or counsel to an arbitration once the arbitration is completed.

Where relevant state or local rule or statute is more specific than these Guidelines as to arbitrator disclosure, it should be followed.

VI. AN ARBITRATOR SHOULD ENDEAVOR TO PROVIDE AN EVENHANDED AND UNBIASED PROCESS, AND TREAT ALL PARTIES WITH RESPECT AT ALL STAGES OF THE PROCEEDINGS.

An arbitrator should remain impartial throughout the course of the arbitration. This obligation applies to arbitrators appointed by fewer than all of the parties as well as arbitrators appointed by all of the parties. Impartiality means freedom from favoritism either by word or action. The arbitrator should be aware of and avoid the potential for bias based on the parties' backgrounds, personal attributes, conduct during the arbitration, or based on the arbitrator's pre-existing knowledge of or opinion about the merits of the dispute being arbitrated. An arbitrator should not permit any social or professional relationship with a party, insurer or counsel to a party to an arbitration to affect his or her decision-making. If an arbitrator becomes incapable of maintaining impartiality, the arbitrator should withdraw.

An arbitrator should perform duties diligently and conclude the case as promptly as the circumstances reasonably permit. An arbitrator should be courteous to the parties, to their representatives and to the witnesses, and should encourage similar conduct by all participants in the proceedings. An arbitrator should make all reasonable efforts to prevent the parties, their representatives, or other participants from engaging in delaying tactics, harassment of parties or other participants, or other abuse or disruption of the arbitration process.

Unless otherwise provided in an agreement of the parties, (1) an arbitrator should not discuss a case with any party in the absence of every other party, except that if a party fails to appear at a hearing after having been given due notice, the arbitrator may discuss the case with any party who is present; and (2) whenever an arbitrator communicates in writing with one party, the arbitrator should, at the same time, send a copy of the communication to every other party. Whenever an arbitrator receives a written communication concerning the case from one party that has not already been sent to each party, the arbitrator should do so. The obligations of this paragraph apply to arbitrators appointed by fewer than all of the parties as well as arbitrators appointed by all of the parties.

When there is more than one arbitrator, the arbitrators should afford each other full opportunity to participate in all aspects of the arbitration proceedings.

VII. AN ARBITRATOR SHOULD WITHDRAW UNDER CERTAIN CIRCUMSTANCES

An arbitrator should withdraw from the process if the arbitration is being used to further criminal conduct, or for any of the reasons set forth above -- insufficient knowledge of relevant procedural or substantive issues, a conflict of interest that has not or cannot be waived, the arbitrator's inability to maintain impartiality, or the arbitrator's physical or mental disability. In addition, an arbitrator should be aware of the potential need to withdraw from the case if procedural or substantive unfairness appears to have irrevocably undermined the integrity of the arbitration process.

VIII. AN ARBITRATOR SHOULD MAKE DECISIONS IN A JUST, INDEPENDENT AND DELIBERATE MANNER.

An arbitrator should, after careful deliberation and exercising independent judgment, promptly or otherwise within the time period agreed to by the parties, decide all issues submitted for determination and issue an award and/or decision. An arbitrator's decision should not be influenced by fear of criticism or by any interest in potential future case referrals by any of the parties or counsel, nor should an arbitrator issue an award that reflects a compromise position in order to achieve such acceptability. An arbitrator should not delegate the duty to decide to any other person.

If all parties agree upon a settlement of issues in dispute and request an arbitrator to embody that agreement in an award, the arbitrator should do so, unless the arbitrator believes the terms of the agreement are illegal, or unless the arbitrator believes the terms undermine the integrity of the arbitration process. If an arbitrator is concerned about the possible consequences of a proposed agreement, the arbitrator should inform the parties of that concern. In such circumstances, an arbitrator may request additional specific information, seek to educate the parties, refer one or more parties for specialized advice, or withdraw from the case.

IX. AN ARBITRATOR SHOULD UPHOLD THE DIGNITY AND INTEGRITY OF THE ARBITRATION PROCESS IN MATTERS RELATING TO MARKETING AND COMPENSATION.

An arbitrator should avoid marketing that is misleading or that compromises impartiality. An arbitrator should ensure that any advertising or other marketing to the public conducted on the arbitrator's behalf is truthful.

An arbitrator may discuss his or her compensation with the parties, but should not engage in such discussions if they create an appearance of coercion or other impropriety and should not engage in *ex parte* communications regarding compensation.

Appendix F

The Ten Commandments of Appropriate Dispute Resolution:

A Proposal

Originally Published in Carrie Menkel-Meadow, *Ethics and Professionalism:
Non-Adversarial Lawyering*, 27 Fla. St. L. Rev. 153, 167 (1999)

(Developed in conjunction with work for the ABA Dispute Resolution Section,
Ethics Subcommittee and the ABA-CPR Joint Initiative Committee on Ethics in ADR)

1. Lawyers should have an obligation to consider and inform the client about the possible methods of resolving a dispute, planning a transaction, or participating in legislative, administrative or other processes that might best address the client's needs. Lawyers should educate themselves and their clients about all available options for handling the client's matter.

2. Lawyers should promptly communicate all proposals to resolve disputes by any process suggested by other parties, clients or decision-makers.

3. Lawyers should consider and promptly communicate all substantive proposals for dispute resolution or transactional agreements to their clients, including both legally based remedies and resolutions and those that address other needs or interests. Lawyers should assist clients to consider non-legal concerns, including social, ethical, economic, psychological and moral implications of any possible solutions or proposals.

4. Lawyers should not misrepresent to or conceal from another person, a relevant fact or legal principle (including opposing counsel, parties, judicial officers, third party neutrals or other individuals who might rely on such statements).

5. Lawyers should not intentionally or recklessly deceive another person or refuse to answer material and relevant questions in representing clients (unless doing so would violate appropriate client confidentiality rules).

6. Lawyers, as representatives, should not agree to a resolution of a problem or participation in a transaction that they have reason to know will cause substantial injustice to the other party. In essence, a lawyer should do no harm.

7. A lawyer serving as third party neutral should decline to approve or otherwise sanction an agreement achieved by parties which the third party neutral has reason to know would effect an injustice on a party (or third party).

8. Lawyers serving as third party neutrals, such as arbitrators and mediators, should disclose all reasons the parties might consider relevant in determining if the neutral has any bias, prejudice or basis for not acting fairly and without improper interest in a matter.

9. Lawyers serving as client representatives or as third party neutrals should fully explain to their clients and parties any and all processes and procedures that will be used to facilitate solutions, make claims, or plan transactions so parties may understand and participate in the decision about what procedures to use.

10. Lawyers should treat all parties to a legal matter as they would wish to be treated themselves and should consider the effects of what they accomplish on behalf of their clients. In essence, lawyers should respect a lawyers' golden rule.

Appendix G

CPR-Georgetown Principles for ADR Provider Organizations

CPR-Georgetown Commission on Ethics and Standards of Practice in ADR
May 1, 2002

Principles for ADR Provider Organizations[1]

The CPR-Georgetown Commission on Ethics and Standards of Practice in ADR developed the following Principles for ADR Provider Organizations to provide guidance to entities that provide ADR services, consumers of their services, the public, and policy makers. The Commission is a joint initiative of the CPR Institute for Dispute Resolution and Georgetown University Law Center, with support from the William and Flora Hewlett Foundation. The Commission, which is chaired by Professor Carrie Menkel-Meadow of the Georgetown University Law Center, has also developed the CPR-Georgetown Proposed Model Rule of Professional Conduct for the Lawyer as Third Party Neutral (Final, 2002), and provided guidance to the ABA Ethics 2000 Commission in its reexamination of the Model Rules of Professional Conduct on ADR ethics issues.[2]

The Principles for ADR Provider Organizations were prepared under the auspices of the CPR-Georgetown Commission on Ethics and Standards of Practice in ADR, sponsored by CPR Institute for Dispute Resolution and Georgetown University Law Center, with support from the William and Flora Hewlett Foundation. CPR-Georgetown Commission members are noted on the final page of this document.

The Principles were drafted by a Commission committee co-chaired by Margaret L. Shaw and former staff director Elizabeth Plapinger, who also served as reporter. The Drafting Committee also included: Prof. Marjorie Corman Aaron, Howard S. Bellman, Christopher Honeyman, Prof. Carrie Menkel-Meadow, William K. Slate II *(see note 5 infra)*, Thomas J. Stipanowich, Hon. John L. Wagner, and Michael D. Young. Eric Van Loon and Vivian Shelansky also provided invaluable assistance in the drafting effort.

A second committee of the Commission, chaired by Charles Pou, developed the definition of ADR Provider Organization used in these Principles, as well as a taxonomy of ADR Provider Organizations which helped guide this effort. *See Taxonomy of ADR Provider Organizations*, Appendix A.

The final version of the Ethics 2000 proposal specifically addresses the lawyer's expanded role as ADR neutral and problem solver for the first time. It does so in four ways. *First*, the Ethics 2000 proposal recognizes the lawyer's neutral, nonrepresentational roles in the proposed Preamble to the Model Rules of Professional Conduct. *See* Ethics 2000 Proposal at Preamble para. [3] ("In addition to these representational functions, a lawyer may serve as a third-party neutral, a nonrepresentational role helping the parties to resolve a dispute or other matter. Some of these rules apply directly to lawyers who are or have served as third-party neutrals.") *Second*, the proposal indicates that a lawyer may have a duty to advise a client of ADR options. The proposed language to Comment 5 of Rule 2.1 states: "...when a matter is likely to involve litigation, it may be necessary under Rule 1.4 to inform the client of forms of dispute resolution that might constitute alternatives to litigation." *Third*, the Ethics 2000 proposal defines the various third-party roles a lawyer may play, including that of an arbitrator or mediator. *See* Proposed Rule 2.4. ("A lawyer serves as a third-party neutral when the lawyer assists two or more persons who are not clients of the lawyer to reach a resolution of a dispute or other matter that has arisen between them.") *Fourth*, the proposal addresses the unique conflicts of interest issues raised when lawyers and law firms provide both representational and neutral services. *See* Proposed Rule 1.12 (conflicts of interest proposal including screening procedures for former judges, arbitrators, mediators or other third-party neutrals. For a complete version of the Ethics 2000 report and status, *see http://www.abanet.org/cpr/ethics2k.html*.

The Principles for ADR Provider Organizations were developed by a committee of the CPR-Georgetown Commission, co-chaired by Commission member Margaret L. Shaw and former Commission staff director Elizabeth Plapinger, who also served as reporter.[3] The Principles were released for public comment from June 1, 2000 through October 15, 2001.[4] The final version reflects many of the substantive recommendations the Commission received during the comment period.[5]

---

[3] Ms. Plapinger is currently a CPR Fellow and Senior Consultant to the CPR Public Policy Projects, and a lecturer in law at Columbia Law School where she teaches ADR policy and process.

[4] The CPR-Georgetown Principles for ADR Provider Organizations have been the subject of several articles and public discussions during the comment period. *See, e.g., Special Feature: The CPR-Georgetown Ethical Principles for ADR Providers,* Disp. Resol. Mag. (ABA Dispute Resolution Section, Spring 2001), including Margaret Shaw and Elizabeth Plapinger, *The CPR-Georgetown Ethical Principles for Providers Set the Bar* at 14; Michael D. Young, *Pro: Principles Mitigate Potential Dangers of Mandatory Arbitration* at 18; Cliff Palesfsky, *Con: Proposed CPR Provider Ethics Rules Don't Go Far Enough* at 18. *See also* Carrie Menkel-Meadow, *Ethics in ADR: The Many "Cs" of Professional Responsibility and Dispute Resolution,* 28 Fordham Urban Law J., 979, 987-990 (April 2001); Reynolds Holding, *Private Justice: Can Public Count on Fair Arbitration,* The San Francisco Chronicle Francisco Chronicle, at A15 (October 8, 2001).

During the comment period, the CPR-Georgetown Provider Principles have also been used as guidelines for consideration of measurement of quality standards of dispute resolution programs in a variety of settings. For example, at the 2000 Annual Meeting of State Programs of Dispute Resolution sponsored by the Policy Consensus Institute in New Mexico, it was noted that a number of states have used the Principles for framing discussions and establishing standards and other evaluative criteria for assessing the quality of dispute resolution development. Additionally, it was suggested that the Provider Principles should serve broadly as templates for development and evaluation of state-sponsored dispute resolution programs. Internationally, during the comment period, the Provider Principles were translated into Italian and Spanish to provide guidance to relevant groups in Italy and South America.

[5] Drafting committee member and President of the American Arbitration Association William K. Slate II has declined to fully endorse the CPR-Georgetown Principles for ADR Provider Organizations, stating that he does not believe the Principles are fully applicable to the American Arbitration Association (AAA) because of its "unique size and complexity." While "endors[ing] the basic premises of the Principles which encourage transparency and disclosure" Mr. Slate explained his position in a letter of February 4, 2002 to Thomas J. Stipanowich, President of the CPR Institute for Dispute Resolution and also a drafting committee member. In the correspondence, which is on file at CPR, Mr. Slate stated, "I believe the ¡CPR-Georgetown] Principles will prove to be invaluable and [provide] appropriate guidelines for small provider organizations and for providers who serve in dual roles, by assisting in drafting agreements and then serving as neutrals. Although the AAA does not fall into either of these categories, the AAA endorses the basis premises of the Principles which encourage transparency and disclosure. As a result of my work with CPR on these Principles, the AAA has already developed an organizational ethical statement which has been posted for the past few months on the AAA website that we believe recognizes the unique size and complexity of the AAA in the ADR marketplace, while acknowledging and respecting the basic concerns that guided the CPR Principles." Mr. Slate also thanked the CPR-Georgetown Commission, and its sponsoring institutions, for providing "a true service to the advancement and credibility of alternative dispute resolution by recognizing the serious issues of ADR providers with actual or apparent conflicts of interest and convening a group to address these issues. I was pleased to be a part of this group and appreciate the consideration given to my opinions and perspective." Letter of 2/4/02 from William K. Slate to Thomas J. Stipanowich, on file at CPR.

Preamble

As the use of ADR expands into almost every sphere of activity,[6] the public and private organizations that provide ADR services are coming under greater scrutiny in the marketplace, in the courts, and among regulators, commentators and policy makers.[7] The growth and increasing importance of ADR Provider Organizations, coupled with the absence of broadly-recognized standards to guide responsible practice, propel this effort by the CPR-Georgetown Commission to develop the following Principles for ADR Provider Organizations.[8]

The Principles build upon the significant policy directives of the past decade which recognize the central role of the ADR provider organization in the delivery of fair, impartial and quality ADR services.[9] Several core ideas guide the Commission's effort, namely that:

- It is timely and important to establish standards of responsible practice in this rapidly growing field to provide guidance to ADR Provider Organizations and to inform consumers, policy makers and the public generally.

- The most effective architecture for maximizing the fairness, impartiality and quality of dispute resolution services is the meaningful *disclosure* of key information.

- Consumers of dispute resolution services are entitled to sufficient information about ADR Provider Organizations, their services and affiliated neutrals to make well-informed decisions about their dispute resolution options.

---

[6] Today, ADR processes or techniques are used in almost every kind of legal and nonlegal dispute and in all almost all sectors, including family, school, commercial, employment, environmental, banking, product liability, construction, farmer-lender, professional malpractice, etc. In the past decade, ADR has become a familiar part of federal and state courts, administrative practice, and regulatory and public policy development. The development of ADR systems for public and private institutions, as well as the use of ADR to arrange transactions are also well established. *See generally* Stephen D. Goldberg, Frank E.A. Sander, & Nancy H. Rogers, Dispute Resolution: Negotiation, Mediation and Other Process (Aspen Law and Business, 3rd ed., 1999).

[7] To date, much of the policy and case law development has focused on the fairness and integrity of ADR processes and forums that provide arbitration pursuant to contract in the areas of consumer services, health care and employment. *See, e.g., Circuit City Stores, Inc. v. Saint Clair Adams,* 279 F.3d 889 (9th Cir. 2002) (employment); *Cole v. Burns Int'l Security Services,* 105 F.3d 1465 (D.C. Cir. 1997) (employment); *Armendariz v. Foundation Health Psychcare Services, Inc.,* 24 Cal. 4th 83, 6 P.3d 669, 99 Cal. Rptr. 2d 745 (2000) (employment); *Engalla v. Kaiser Permanente Medical Group, Inc.,* 15 Cal. 4th 951, 938 P.2d 903, 64 Cal. Rptr.2d 843 (1997) (health care); *Ting v. AT&T,* 182 F. Supp.2d 902 (N.D. Cal. 2002) (consumer). *See also Green Tree Financial Corp.-Alabama v. Randolph,* 531 U.S. 79, 121 S. Ct. 513 (2000) (Truth in Lending Act claim).

Recent policy directives have recognized the central role of the ADR provider organization in the delivery of fair, impartial and quality ADR services. *See, e.g., Task Force on Alternative Dispute Resolution in Employment, A Due Process Protocol for Mediation and Arbitration of Statutory Disputes Arising out of the Employment Relationship* (1995)(hereafter cited as Employment Due Process Protocol); Society of Professionals in Dispute Resolution (SPIDR) Commission on Qualifications, *Ensuring Competence and Quality in Dispute Resolution Practice* (Draft Report 1994)(hereafter cited as SPIDR Report on Qualifications); American Arbitration Association, *Consumer Due Process Protocol: A Due Process Protocol for Mediation and Arbitration of Consumer Disputes* (May 1998)(hereinafter cited as Consumer Due Process Protocol); American Arbitration Association, American Bar Association, and American Medical Association, *Health Care Due Process Protocol: A Due Process Protocol for Mediation and Arbitration of Health Care Disputes* (June 1998)(hereafter cited as Health Care Due Process Protocol); Center for Dispute Settlement and Institute of Judicial Administration, *National Standards for Court-Connected Mediation* (1992); and JAMS Minimum Standards of Fairness for Employment Arbitrations (1995, 1998).

Commentators also have begun to consider the role of ADR provider organizations in the delivery of private justice and the procedural fairness of ADR forums. *See generally Carrie Menkel-Meadow, Do the 'Haves' Come Out Ahead in Alternative Judicial Systems?: Repeat Players in ADR,* 15 Ohio J. Dispute Res. 19 (Fall 1999); Lisa Bingham, *Focus on Arbitration After Gilmer: Employment Arbitration, The Repeat Player Effect,* 1 Employee Rights and Employment Policy J. 189 (1997); Thomas J. Stipanowich, *Behind the Neutral: A Look at Provider Issues,* Currents 1 (AAA, December 1998)("All providers, whether for-profit or non-profit, facilitate and implement ADR in one or more forms and for good or ill, they all compete in the marketplace without significant outside regulation."); David S. Schwartz, *Enforcing Small Print to Protect Big Business: Employee and Consumer Rights Claims in an Age of Compelled Arbitration,* 1997 Wis. L. Rev. 33.

[8] In publishing these standards, the drafters also note the increasing recognition of entity or organizational ethical responsibility or liability. *See generally* Ted Schneyer, *Professional Discipline for Law Firms?,* 77 Cornell L. Rev. 1 (Nov. 1992); New York Bar Disciplinary Rules governing law firm conduct, adopted May 1996.

[9] *See supra* 7.

- ADR Provider Organizations should foster and meet the expectations of consumers, policy makers and the public generally for fair, impartial and quality dispute resolution services and processes.

In addition to establishing a benchmark for responsible practice, the CPR-Georgetown Commission hopes that the Principles will enhance understanding of the ADR field's special responsibilities, as justice providers, to provide fair, impartial and quality process. This document hopes also to contribute to the ADR field's commitment to self-regulation and high standards of practice.

Scope of Principles

The following Principles were developed to offer a framework for responsible practice by entities that provide ADR services. In framing the nine Principles that comprise this document, the drafters tried to balance the need for clear and high standards of practice against the risks of over-regulating a new, diverse and dynamic field.

The Principles are drafted to apply to the full variety of public, private and hybrid ADR provider organizations in our increasingly intertwined private and public systems of justice.[10] A single set of standards was preferred because the Principles address core duties of responsible practice that apply to most organizations in most settings. The single set of Principles may also help alert the many kinds of entities providing ADR services of their essential, common responsibilities. Additional sector-specific obligations will likely continue to develop for particular kinds of ADR provider organizations, depending on their sector, nature of services and operations, and representations to the public. The proposed Principles were developed to guide responsible practice and, like ethical rules, are not intended to create grounds for liability.

Definition

The proposed Principles are intended to apply to entities and individuals which fall within the following definition:

> **An ADR Provider Organization includes any entity or individual which holds itself out as managing or administering dispute resolution or conflict management services.**

---

[10] For an overview of the array of organizations that offer dispute resolution services, *see Taxonomy of ADR Provider Organizations, infra* at Appendix A ("'ADR provider organizations' come in a wide variety of forms. These range from solo arbitrators and very small mediation firms to nationwide entities providing the gamut of neutral and management services. They also vary from new programs with short, informal referral lists to established public and private sector institutions that annually furnish thousands of disputants with panels of neutrals. These providers can differ considerably in their structures; in the kinds of neutrals they refer, parties they serve and cases they assist with; in their relationships with the neutrals they refer and with one or more of the parties using their services; in their approaches to listing, referring, and managing neutrals, and in their resources and management philosophies."). *See also* Thomas J. Stipanowich, *Behind the Neutrals: A Look at Provider Issues,* Currents 1 (AAA, December 1998) (Noting that "[t]he contemporary landscape of ADR ranges from complex, multi-faceted organizations of national and international scope to ad hoc arrangements among individuals" and includes "more specialized services marketing particular procedures, groups that have evolved to serve the special needs of a community, industry, or business sector; and mom-and-pop mediation services.")

The Taxonomy of ADR Provider Organizations, included as Appendix A, analyzes these diverse organizations along three major continua: the organization's structure, the organization's services and relationships with neutrals, and the organization's relationships with users or consumers.

Comment

This definition of an ADR Provider Organization includes entities or individuals that manage or administer ADR services, *i.e.,* entities or individuals who serve as ADR "middlemen."[11] The definition intends to cover all private and public entities, including courts and public agencies, that provide conflict management services, including roster creation, referral to neutrals, administration and management of processes, and similar activities. It is not intended to govern the individuals who provide direct services as neutrals;[12] rather this definition addresses the entities (either organizations or individuals) that administer or manage dispute resolution services.

The definition excludes persons or organizations who do not hold themselves out as offering conflict management services, although their services may incidentally serve to reduce conflict. These may include persons or organizations whose primary activities involve representing parties in disputes, providing counseling, therapy or similar assistance, or offering other services that may incidentally serve to reduce conflict. Importantly, however, if a law firm, accounting or management firm, or psychological services organization holds itself out as offering conflict management services as defined herein, it would be considered an ADR Provider Organization and fall within the ambit of these Principles.

---

[11] *See also* Consumer Due Process Protocol, *supra* note 7 ("An Independent ADR Institution is an organization that provides independent and impartial administration of ADR Programs for Consumers and Providers, including, but not limited to, development and administration of ADR policies and procedures and the training and appointment of Neutrals.")

[12] There are a number of ethics codes for ADR neutrals promulgated by national ADR professional organizations (*e.g.,* the ABA/AAA Code of Ethics for Arbitrators in Commercial Disputes (1977, under revision); the CPR-Georgetown Commission's Proposed Model Rule of Professional Conduct for the Lawyer as Third Party Neutral (Final, 2002); and the transdisciplinary ABA/AAA/SPIDR Model Standards of Conduct for Mediators (1995)), by state-wide regulatory or judicial bodies (*e.g.,* Florida Rules for Certified and Court- Appointed Mediators (Amended Feb. 3, 2000); Minnesota Rule 114; Virginia Code of Professional Conduct), as well as by individual court or community ADR programs (*e.g.,* D. Utah Code of Conduct for Court-Appointed Mediators and Arbitrators) and individual ADR provider organizations (*e.g.,* JAMS Ethics Guidelines for Mediators and Arbitrators).

Principles for ADR Provider Organizations

I. Quality and Competence of Services

The ADR Provider Organization should take all reasonable steps to maximize the quality and competence of its services, absent a clear and prominent disclaimer to the contrary.

  a. Absent a clear and prominent disclaimer to the contrary, the ADR Provider Organization should take all reasonable steps to maximize the likelihood that (i) the neutrals who provide services under its auspices are qualified and competent to conduct the processes and handle the kind of cases which the Organization will generally refer to them; and (ii) the neutral to whom a case is referred is competent to handle the specific matter referred.

  b. The ADR Provider Organization's responsibilities under Principles I and I.a decrease as the ADR parties' knowing involvement in screening and selecting the particular neutral increases.

  c. The ADR Provider Organization's responsibilities under this Principle are continuing ones, which requires the ADR Provider Organization to take all reasonable steps to monitor and evaluate the performance of its affiliated neutrals.

Comment

[1] With the growth of voluntary and mandatory ADR use in all kinds of private and public disputes, the Drafting Committee believes it is essential to hold the ADR Provider Organizations, which manage these forums and processes, to the highest standards of quality and competence. This Principle thus establishes that ADR Provider Organizations are responsible, absent specific disclaimer, for taking all reasonable steps to maximize the quality and competence of the services they offer.

   The Principle holds ADR Provider Organizations responsible for the quality and competence of the services they render, but articulates a rule of reason in determining the precise contours of that responsibility for each Organization. The nature of this obligation will vary with the circumstances and representations of the organization. The Drafting Committee adopts this approach over a more prescriptive rule because of the vastly different organizations that currently provide ADR management services.[13]

   Understanding that ADR Provider Organizations come in a variety of forms and hold themselves out as offering different levels of quality assurance, this Principle permits the Organization to limit its quality and competence obligation by a clear and prominent communication to that effect to the parties and the public. Specifically, the Principle provides that the ADR Provider Organization can diminish these obligations by a clear and prominent representation that the Organization intends a minimal or no warranty of quality or competence. Such a disclaimer may be appropriate, for example, where a bar association assembles a roster of available neutrals as a public service, but establishes only minimal criteria for inclusion and engages in no screening or assessment of the listed neutrals.

[2] Maximum quality and competence in the provision of neutral services has two main components under this Principle. The Organization is required to take all reasonable steps to maximize the likelihood that neutrals affiliated with the organization are qualified and competent (1) to conduct the

---

[13] *See supra* note 10 for a discussion of the varied landscape of ADR provider organizations; *see also Taxonomy of ADR Provider Organizations, infra* at Appendix A; Stipanowich, *supra* note 7, at 14 ("The provider's 'administrative' role varies greatly; in NASD arbitrations, case managers routinely sit in on hearings; at the AAA, case managers facilitate many aspects of the ADR process, while the CPR Institute for Dispute Resolution offers 'non-administered' procedures with minimal involvement by its employees.")

processes and handle the kind of cases which the organization will generally refer to them;[14] and (2) to handle the specific matter referred.[15]

[3] This Principle advisedly uses the related concepts of both qualification and competency. In the multidisciplinary field of conflict resolution, where neutrals come from a variety of professions of origin, there is no bright line between the concept of qualifications and competence. Unlike single disciplinary fields, where there are specific entry qualifications and examinations that certify that a practitioner is generally qualified to work in the field, no such universal entry standard exists in the conflict resolution field. Accordingly, the Principle uses the twin concepts of qualification and competency, as they are generally understood in the field today, as including a combination of process training and experience, and substantive education and experience.[16]

[4] Principle I.b reflects, and is consistent with ADR standards honoring party autonomy and knowing choice.[17] It provides that when knowledgeable parties have meaningful choice in the identification and selection of individual neutrals, the duty for assuring the quality or competence of the neutral chosen transfers in part from the administering Organization to the parties themselves. Where party choice is limited by contract, statute or court rules, the ADR Provider Organization retains responsibility for maximizing the likelihood of individual neutral competence and quality.

[5] Under Principle I.c, the ADR Provider Organization has a continuing duty to take all reasonable steps to oversee, monitor and evaluate the quality and competence of affiliated neutrals.[18] Determination of the specific monitoring and evaluation measures needed to fulfill this obligation will turn on the circumstances of each ADR Provider Organization. Currently, a spectrum of organizational oversight practice exists from extensive to modest monitoring of neutral performance. Some oversight measures used by Organizations include user evaluations, feedback forms, debriefings, follow-up calls, and periodic performance reviews.[19]

---

[14] As the dispute resolution field grows and becomes more specialized, ADR provider organizations are developing specialized panels or groups to handle disputes in particular subject areas, such as insurance or employment conflicts, or specific kind of processes, such as multiparty mediation. This Principle provides that neutrals be competent and qualified in their areas of general substantive and process expertise, as well being competent and qualified to serve in the specific matter referred. It does not suggest that all neutrals affiliated with an organization must be competent and qualified in all substantive areas and processes covered by the ADR provider organization.

[15] While there continues to be limited understanding about the mix and types of training, personal attributes and experience that predict effective performance, there is a growing willingness in the field to contemplate some objective criteria for judging competence. *See* Howard S. Bellman, *Some Reflections on the Practice of Mediation*, Negotiation J. 205 (July 1998). The current best practices standard for promoting competence relies on "some combination of training, experience, skills-based education, apprenticeships, internships, mentoring and supervised experience" and that "the appropriate combinations must be linked to the practice context." SPIDR Report on Qualifications, *supra* note 7, at 11-12. *See also* Margaret Shaw, *Selection, Training, and Qualifications of Neutrals*, National Symposium on Court-Connected Dispute Resolution Research (1994); Christopher Honeyman, *The Test Design Project: Performance-Based Assessment: A Methodology for Use in Selecting, Training, and Evaluating Mediators* (NIDR, 1995); Consumer Due Process Protocol, *supra* note 7, ("Elements of effective quality control include the establishment of standards for neutrals, the development of a training program, and a program of ongoing performance evaluation and feedback.")

[16] *See, e.g.*, SPIDR Report on Qualifications, *supra* note 7 and note 15 generally. For an example of how these combined concepts are used in the development of a roster of neutrals, see the roster entry criteria established by the U.S. Institute for Environmental Conflict Resolution for environmental mediators, at www.ecr.gov/r_entry.htm.

[17] *See, e.g.*, SPIDR Law and Public Policy Committee, *Mandated Participation and Settlement Coercion: Dispute Resolution as it Relates to the Courts* (1991).

[18] *See, e.g.*, National Standards for Court-Connected Mediation Programs, Standard 16, Evaluation ("Courts should ensure that the mediation programs to which they refer cases are monitored adequately on an ongoing basis, and evaluated on a periodic basis and that sufficient resources are earmarked for these purposes.")

[19] *See* SPIDR Report on Qualifications, *supra* note 7, at 12 (ADR Provider Organization should "be assessed on a regular basis," through such means as "consumer input, review of complaints, self-assessment, trouble-shooting, regular audits, peer review and visiting committees from other programs.")

II. Information Regarding Services and Operations

ADR Provider Organizations should take all reasonable steps to provide clear, accurate and understandable information about the following aspects of their services and operations:

a. The nature of the ADR Provider Organization's services, operations, and fees;

b. The relevant economic, legal, professional or other relationships between the ADR Provider Organization and its affiliated neutrals;

c. The ADR Provider Organization's policies relating to confidentiality, organizational and individual conflicts of interests, and ethical standards for neutrals and the Organization;

d. Training and qualifications requirements for neutrals affiliated with the Organization, as well as other selection criteria for affiliation; and

e. The method by which neutrals are selected for service.

Comment

[1] Reasonable and meaningful disclosure of key information about the ADR Provider Organization is the cornerstone of this document. In conformity with established ADR standards,[20] this Principle underscores the importance of clear, accurate and understandable information to informed decision-making by consumers of dispute resolution services and the public generally.

[2] This Principle, like this document generally, applies the rule of reason to the extent and form of the required disclosure. While some may prefer an absolute rule, the drafters believe that requiring reasonable disclosure consistent with the nature, structure and services of the organization and the knowledge base of the individual user, is more appropriate in this evolving field. Currently, ADR Provider Organizations come in a wide variety of organizational forms, provide a variety of services, and operate in an array of disparate settings.[21] These entities can differ considerably in their services, policies, relationships with the affiliated neutrals, affiliation criteria, markets, and their approaches to listing and referring cases to affiliated neutrals. A principle establishing an affirmative obligation to provide key information should recognize these differences, as well as differences in effective means of disclosure.[22]

[3] This Principle calls for reasonable disclosure of information about relevant financial relationships between the affiliated neutrals and the ADR Provider Organization. Information about specific compensation arrangements is not contemplated under this section. Rather, general statements of the existence or absence of consequential financial links, either direct or indirect, between the affiliated neutral and the ADR Provider Organization that may have an impact on the conduct of the Organization or the neutral, or may be reasonably perceived as having such an effect, are expected.[23]

[20] *See, e.g.*, SPIDR Report on Qualifications, *supra* note 7, at 6 ("It is the responsibility of . . . programs offering dispute resolution services to define clearly the services they provide . . . and provide information about the program and neutrals to the parties."); National Standards for Court-Connected Mediation, *supra* note 7, Standards 3.1-3.2.

[21] *See Taxonomy of ADR Provider Organizations, infra* at Appendix A; *see also supra* note 10 and accompanying text.

[22] We recognize that the kinds of disclosures advocated by this Principle will be different, for example, for a large international organization, like the American Arbitration Association, and a small mediation firm.

[23] In some organizations, there is no financial relationship with affiliated neutrals other than their inclusion on a roster. In other entities, affiliated neutrals are owners, employees, contributors, franchisees, independent contractors or stand in other consequential economic relationship to the ADR organization. *See Taxonomy of ADR Provider Organizations, infra* at Appendix A.

III. Fairness and Impartiality

The ADR Provider Organization has an obligation to ensure that ADR processes provided under its auspices are fundamentally fair and conducted in an impartial manner.

Comment

ADR parties and the public are entitled to fair processes and impartial forums. As justice providers, ADR Provider Organizations have an obligation to take all reasonable steps to ensure the impartiality and fundamental process fairness of their services. This mandate may have particular importance when the ADR Provider Organization undertakes to administer an in-house dispute resolution program, another organization's process or policy, or processes designed or requested by one party to a dispute. Recent ADR policy directives and case law provide the field, courts and regulators with important baselines of fundamental fairness and impartiality.[24] To date, key indicia of fair and impartial processes and forums include: competent, qualified, and impartial neutrals; rosters of neutrals that are representative of the community of users; joint party selection of neutrals; adequate representation; access to information; reasonable cost allocation; reasonable time limits; and fair hearing procedures.[25] Building on these standards, this Principle establishes an across-the-board obligation on the part of the ADR Provider Organization to ensure the impartiality and fundamental process fairness of its services.

IV. Accessibility of Services

ADR Provider Organizations should take all reasonable steps, appropriate to their size, nature and resources, to provide access to their services at reasonable cost to low-income parties.

Comment

As the profession and business of dispute resolution grows, ADR Provider Organizations have a responsibility to provide services to low-income parties at reasonable or no costs. This access-to-services obligation can be satisfied in various ways, depending on the circumstances of the ADR Provider Organization. For example, the Provider Organization can offer *pro bono* neutral services or sliding scale fees. The entity could also require its affiliated neutrals to participate as neutrals in dispute resolution programs offered by the courts, government, nonprofit groups or other institutions at below market rates or as volunteers.

V. Disclosure of Organizational Conflicts of Interest

a. The ADR Provider Organization should disclose the existence of any interests or relationships which are reasonably likely to affect the impartiality or independence of the Organization or which might reasonably create the appearance that the Organization is biased against a party or favorable to another, including (i) any financial or other interest by the Organization in the outcome; (ii) any significant financial, business, organizational, professional or other relationship that the Organization has with any of the parties or their counsel, including a contractual stream of referrals, a *de facto* stream of referrals, or a funding relationship between a party and the organization; or (iii) any other significant source of bias or prejudice concerning the Organization which is reasonably likely to affect impartiality or might reasonably create an appearance of partiality or bias.

---

[24] *See supra* note 7.

[25] *See, e.g.*, Employment Due Process Protocol, *supra* note 7; Consumer Due Process Protocol, *supra* note 7; and the Health Care Due Process Protocol, *supra* note 7. *See also Cole v. Burns Int'l Security Services*, 105 F.3d 1465 (D.C. Cir. 1997); *Engalla v. Kaiser Permanente Medical Group*, 15 Cal. 4th 951, 938 P. 2d 903, 64 Cal. Rptr. 2d 843 (1997).

b. The ADR Provider Organization shall decline to provide its services unless all parties choose to retain the Organization, following the required disclosures, except in circumstances where contract or applicable law requires otherwise.

Comment

Reflecting the field's longstanding reliance on reasonable disclosure to address the existence of interests or relationships which may effect fairness and impartiality,[26] this Principle imposes an independent duty of disclosure on the Organization to provide information about significant organizational relationships with a party or other participant to an ADR process. As with these Principles generally, the rule of reason is intended to apply to this provision.[27]

At issue is the potential for actual or perceived conflicts of interest involving ADR participants (such as, businesses, public institutions, and law firms) that have continuing professional, business or other relationships with the ADR Provider Organization. For example, an ADR Provider Organization may be under contract to an institutional party to provide a volume of ADR services; or a law firm may regularly choose a particular ADR Provider Organization to resolve disputes repeatedly, or represent a client or clients that does so; or a public institution may send most or all its employment disputes to a particular ADR Provider Organization by contract or *de facto* business relationship. Under this Principle, disclosure of such relationships between the Organization and repeat player parties or other repeat players to the other parties to the dispute would be required.

This Principle reflects the evolving concept of "organizational conflict and relationship."[28] Since ADR Provider Organizations perform functions which may have a direct or indirect impact on the dispute resolution process (in the creation of lists of neutrals for selection, scheduling or other administrative functions), concerns about organizational impartiality have begun to be raised by courts, policy makers and commentators.[29] While the drafters understand that this disclosure obligation may impose some additional costs, particularly for large ADR Provider Organizations, we believe that disclosure of organizational relationships and interests is critical to preserving user and public confidence in the independence and impartiality of ADR Provider Organizations and services.

---

[26] See *ABA/AAA Code of Ethics for Arbitrators in Commercial Disputes* (1977, under revision); *Commonwealth Coatings Corp. v. Continental Co.*, 393 U.S. 145, 151-52 (1968)(concurring opinion); Christopher Honeyman, *Patterns of Bias in Mediation*, J. of Dispute Resolution 141 (1985); CPR-Georgetown Commission on Ethics and Standards in ADR, *Proposed Model Rule of Professional Conduct for the Lawyer as Third Party Neutral* (Final, 2002).

[27] As with Principle II, we recognize that the extent and form of disclosures advocated by this Principle will be different depending on the nature of the ADR Provider Organization and is subject to the rule of reason. See generally Principle II, Comment [2].

[28] For an analysis of recent case law and repeat player issues in ADR, *see generally* Carrie Menkel-Meadow, *Do the 'Haves' Come Out Ahead in Alternative Judicial Systems?: Repeat Players in ADR*, 15 Ohio J. Dispute Res. 19 (Fall 1999); Lisa Bingham, *Focus on Arbitration After Gilmer: Employment Arbitration, The Repeat Player Effect*, 1 Employee Rights and Employment Policy J. 189 (1997); Thomas J. Stipanowich, *Behind the Neutral: A Look at Provider Issues*, Currents 1, 15 (AAA, December 1988)("providers should recognize that an ongoing, close connection between a provider and regular user may be a source of concern to the incidental user who is drawn into an ADR process by a pre-dispute ADR clause in a contract of the other party's devising.") *See also* JAMS Conflicts Policy, addressing both organizational conflicts and individual conflicts.

[29] See, e.g., Consumer Due Process Protocol, *supra* note 7, at 18 ("The consensus of the Advisory Committee was that the reality and perception of impartiality and fairness was as essential in the case of Independent ADR Institutions as it was in the case of individual Neutrals. . . . In the long term, ... the independence of administering institutions may be the greatest challenge of Consumer ADR.") In *Engalla v. Kaiser Permanente Medical Group, Inc.*, 15 Cal. 4th 951, 938 P 2d 903, 64 Cal. Rptr. 2d 843 (1997), the California Supreme Court strongly criticized the fairness and enforceability of Kaiser Permanente's mandatory malpractice self-administered arbitration program, and remanded the case for further factual consideration of claims of fraud. For an analysis of *Engalla*, see Carrie Menkel-Meadow, *California Court Limits Mandatory Arbitration*, 15 Alternatives 109 (September, 1997). While the suit filed by the family of the deceased lung cancer patient has since settled, the *Engalla* case has led to a comprehensive assessment and restructuring of the Kaiser arbitration process. *See* The Blue Ribbon Advisory Panel on Kaiser Permanente Arbitration, The Kaiser Permanente Arbitration System: A Review and Recommendations for Improvement (January 5, 1998). Kaiser has since hired an independent ADR provider organization to administer its formerly in-house program. *See* Justin Kelly, *Case Study Shows Consumer Confidence in Kaiser Arbitration Program*, adrworld.com, April 22, 2002; Davan Maharaj, *Kaiser Hires Outside to Oversee Arbitrations*, Los Angeles Times, November 11, 1998, at C11.

VI. Complaint and Grievance Mechanisms

ADR Provider Organizations should provide mechanisms for addressing grievances about the Organization, and its administration or the neutral services offered, and should disclose the nature and availability of the mechanisms to the parties in a clear, accurate and understandable manner. Complaint and grievance mechanisms should also provide a fair and impartial process for the affected neutral or other individual against whom a grievance has been made.

Comment

This Principle requires ADR Provider Organizations to establish and provide information about mechanisms for addressing grievances or problems with the Organization or individual neutral. Organizations should develop policies and procedures appropriate to their circumstances to provide this complaint review function.[30] The organizational oversight provided through these mechanisms is concerned primarily with complaints about the conduct of the neutral, or deficiencies in process and procedures used. The complaint and grievance mechanisms are not intended to provide an appeals process about the results or outcome of the ADR proceeding.

VII. Ethical Guidelines

    a. ADR Provider Organizations should require affiliated neutrals to subscribe to a reputable internal or external ADR code of ethics, absent or in addition to a controlling statutory or professional code of ethics.

    b. ADR Provider Organizations should conduct themselves with integrity and evenhandedness in the management of their own disputes, finances, and other administrative matters.

Comment

[1] Absent a controlling statutory or professional code of ethics, this Principle directs the ADR Provider Organization to require its neutrals to adhere to a reputable code of conduct. The purpose of this Principle is to help ensure that neutrals affiliated with the ADR Provider Organization are familiar with and conduct themselves according to prevailing norms of ethical conduct in ADR. To this end, ADR Provider Organization should take reasonable steps on an ongoing basis to educate its neutrals about the controlling code and ethical issues in their practices. An ADR Provider Organization may elect to develop an internal code, which conforms to prevailing ethical norms, or to adopt one or more reputable external codes.[31]

---

[30] For example, an Organization may provide a complaint form, and/or designate an individual within the entity to receive and follow up on complaints. Another Organization may develop a more formal procedure for filing, investigating and resolving complaints. *See, e.g.,* JAMS, Internal Procedures for Review and Resolution of Complaints Against Panel Members, Including Alleged Ethics Violations. In some states, disciplinary bodies have been established to review the conduct of state-certified ADR neutrals. For example, the Florida Mediator Qualifications Board was established by the Florida Supreme Court to govern the discipline of state-certified mediators in Florida. In the federal courts, the Northern District of California recently modified its local rules to provide that any complaint alleging a violation of ADR rules should be presented in writing and under seal directly to the U.S. Magistrate Judge who oversees the ADR programs in that court. (Local rule, effective May 2000).

[31] For examples of codes of conduct developed by an ADR provider organization, *see* JAMS's Ethical Guidelines for Mediators, Ethical Guidelines for Arbitrators, and the JAMS Conflicts Policy addressing both organizational and individual conflicts issues. *See* Principle V, Disclosure of Organizational Conflicts of Interest, *supra.* In addition, JAMS designated a senior executive as the organization's arbiter of service complaints, and has developed procedures for handling ethics-based complaints against panelists. *See* JAMS, Internal Procedures for Review and Resolution of Complaints Against Panel Members, Including Alleged Ethics Violations. *See also* Principle VI, Complaint and Grievance Mechanisms, *supra.*

[2] As the numbers of ADR Provider Organizations increase, it is particularly important that Organizations attend to issues of their own managerial, administrative and financial integrity. To this end, ADR Provider Organizations should consider adopting ethical guidelines for employees or other individuals associated with the Organizations who provide ADR management or administrative services, addressing such issues as impartiality and fair treatment in ADR administration, privacy and confidentiality, and limitations on gifts and financial interests or relationships.[32]

VIII. False or Misleading Communications

An ADR Provider Organization should not knowingly make false or misleading communications about its services. If settlement rates or other measures of reporting are communicated, information should be disclosed in a clear, accurate and understandable manner about how the rate is measured or calculated.

Comment

As providers of neutral dispute resolution services, ADR Provider Organizations should be vigilant in avoiding false or misleading statements about their services, processes or outcomes. With ADR Provider Organizations assuming greater prominence in the delivery of ADR, it is important that organizations take care not to foster unrealistic public expectations about their services, processes or results.

The reporting of settlement rates and other measures of reporting by ADR Provider Organizations and individual neutrals raises concern. Settlement rates can be calculated in various ways and reflect various factors (including the number of cases, the difficulty of cases, the time frame for inclusion, and the definition of settlement). This Principle calls for disclosure of how the settlement rates and other key reporting measures (such as "number of cases") are determined when ADR Provider Organizations use these measures to market their services.

IX. Confidentiality

An ADR Provider Organization should take all reasonable steps to protect the level of confidentiality agreed to by the parties, established by the organization or neutral, or set by applicable law or contract.

a. ADR Provider Organizations should establish and disclose their policies relating to the confidentiality of their services and the processes offered consistent with the laws of the jurisdiction.

b. ADR Provider Organizations should ensure that their policies regarding confidentiality are communicated to the neutrals associated with the Organization.

c. ADR Provider Organizations should ensure that their policies regarding confidentiality are communicated to the ADR participants.

---

[32] The American Arbitration Association recently adopted a Code of Ethics for Employees which addresses the ethical responsibilities of AAA employees in administering cases and other responsibilities. In the area of impartiality, for example, the Code provides, "[t]he appointment of neutrals to cases shall be based solely on the best interests of the parties." In the areas of Financial Transactions, the Code provides, *inter alia,* "[e]mployees shall avoid any financial or proprietary interest in contracts which the employee negotiates, prepares, authorizes or approves for the Association and shall not contract with family members." Additionally, the Code prohibits gifts to employees, stating: "Employees shall also observe the gift policy of the Association which prohibits the acceptance of gifts from neutrals, parties, advocates, vendors, or from firms providing services, regardless of the nature of the case or value of the intended gift." *Code of Ethics for Employees of the American Arbitration Association* (1998).

Comment

This Principle establishes the protection of confidentiality as a core obligation of the ADR Provider Organization. Given the varied sources of confidentiality protections, unsettled case law, and diverse regulatory efforts,[33] this Principle imposes a general obligation on the part of the ADR Provider Organization to establish, disclose and uphold governing confidentiality rules, whether set by party agreement, contract, policy or law. This Principle also makes it a core organizational obligation to communicate the Organization's confidentiality policies to neutrals and parties.[34]

---

[33] *See, e.g.,* Kathleen M. Scanlon, *Primer on Recent Developments in Mediation,* ADR Counsel In Box, No. 6, Alternatives (February 2001 and October 2001 Update)(overview of current ADR confidentiality policy, practice, case law and uncertainties)(October 2001 Update at www.cpradr.org, Members Only section); *Special Issue: Confidentiality in Mediation,* Disp. Resol. Mag., (Winter 1998) (for a review of policy issues and uncertainties, regulatory reforms, and case law); Christopher Honeyman, *Confidential. More or Less: The Reality, and Importance, of Confidentiality is Often Oversold by Mediators and the Profession.* Disp. Resol. Mag. 12, (Winter 1998); Proposed Model Rule 4.5.2 of the CPR-Georgetown Commission on Ethics and Standards in ADR's Proposed Model Rule of Professional Conduct for the Lawyer as Third Party Neutral (Final, 2002); Uniform Mediation Act & Reporter's Notes (jointly drafted by National Conference of Commissioners on Uniform State Law and ABA Section of Dispute Resolution) (adopted and recommended for enactment in all states by NCCUSL at 2001 Annual Meeting on August 10-17. 2001; adopted by ABA House of Delegates in February 2002).

[34] For an example of a public ADR Provider Organization's statement of confidentiality policy and rules, *see* U.S. Institute for Environmental Conflict Resolution, Confidentiality Policy and Draft Rule (1999).

Appendix A: Taxonomy of ADR Provider Organizations [35]

I. Definition of "ADR Provider Organization"

See Definition and Comment in the Principles for ADR Provider Organizations, *supra* at 5-6.

II. Taxonomy of ADR Provider Organizations

ADR Provider Organizations come in a wide variety of forms. These range from solo arbitrators and very small mediation firms to nationwide entities providing the gamut of neutral and management services. They also vary from new programs with short, informal referral lists to established public and private sector institutions that annually furnish thousands of disputants with panels of neutrals. These providers can differ considerably in their structures; in the kinds of neutrals they refer, parties they serve, and cases they assist with; in their relationships with the neutrals they refer and with one or more of the parties using their services; in their approaches to listing, referring, and managing neutrals; and in their resources and management philosophies.

To help organize our understanding of this diverse and dynamic field, we believe it is useful to categorize ADR Provider Organizations according to (i) their organizational structures, (ii) the nature of their services and relationships with neutrals, and (iii) the nature of their relationships with users or consumers. The following discussion looks closely at each of these three main categories and tries to identify the major distinguishing factors in each area. We hope this discussion helps to provide a framework for understanding and guiding the diverse entities which manage or administer dispute resolution and conflict management services.

A. ORGANIZATIONAL STRUCTURES

Nine distinguishing factors related to the organizational structure of ADR Provider Organizations were identified:

- Overall Organizational Status
- Overall Organizational Structure
- How Neutrals Are Listed
- How Neutrals Are Referred
- Organization's Role in Quality Control
- Organization's Stake in Dispute or Substantive Outcome
- Organization's Size
- Organization's Resources
- Organization's Operational Transparency

---

[35] CPR-Georgetown Commission member Charles Pou headed the Commission's effort to develop a taxonomy of ADR Provider Organizations, *see Principles for ADR Provider Organizations, supra* at note 1 (hereinafter referred to as ADR Provider Principles). The Commission's goal in developing the taxonomy was to describe, group and provide a framework for analysis of the many different kinds of entities that fall within the rubric of ADR Provider Organization. Mr. Pou is the primary author of the taxonomy. Commission members Bryant Garth and Michael Lewis also contributed to its development. The Taxonomy committee also played the lead role in formulating the definition of ADR Provider Organization included in the ADR Provider Principles.

1. Organizational Status:
Court • Public regulatory agency • Public dispute resolution provider agency • Other public entity (State dispute resolution agency, University, Administrative support agency, Office of Administrative Law Judges, Shared neutrals program) • Quasi-public (*e.g.,* community dispute resolution programs) • Private not-for-profit • Self-regulatory entity • Private industry programs for intra-industry disputes, franchisee disputes, consumers, employees, clients • Private for-profit

A variety of different kinds of organizations currently provide dispute resolution services. In recent years, many public entities have been established, or extended their activities, to serve as ADR Provider Organizations. These include court-annexed systems individually or centrally managed by a judge or an administrator, programs run in-house by government agencies with regulatory duties, programs in government agencies that employ staff neutrals, shared neutrals programs, expedited government contracting vehicles, and activities at government, academic, or other public entities interested in conflict management. On the private side, Provider Organizations include private sector non-profit entities and for-profit entities. Some private groups also serve as contractors to assist public agencies or others wishing to employ ADR more effectively.

2. Organizational Structure:
Corporation • Limited liability company • Partnership • Franchise • Law firm • Membership organization • Other entities

A variety of structures are used to arrange the business or other dealings of private provider organizations, including corporations, limited liability companies, partnerships, franchises, law firms, and membership organizations.

3. How Neutrals Are Listed:
Pure clearinghouse • Selective listing (objective) • Selective listing (subjective)

The ADR Provider Organization may list all neutrals who provide required data and serve simply as a clearinghouse. Alternatively, it may employ objective criteria and list all who are found to comply; or it may selectively limit listed neutrals in explicitly or implicitly subjective ways.

4. How Neutrals Are Referred:
Nonselective • Random panel selection • Subjective panel selection • Party-identified panels • Assignor of neutral • Mixture

The Organization may refer all of its listed neutrals to users requesting a panel of neutrals, or all who meet users' stated criteria, or a randomly selected subset of responsive neutrals; alternately, it may subjectively select a panel, or a single neutral, from among those that it (or the parties) deems appropriate for a given case. Some organizations employ a mix of these referral or selection techniques.

5. Organization's Role in Quality Control:
Certification of listed neutrals • Qualifications and selection process • Conflicts check • Performance evaluation • Discipline • Training • No role

Some management entities certify or otherwise indicate that the neutrals to whom they refer cases or employ are qualified, or even superior. Others offer no warranties of qualifications beyond the general accuracy of the information they supply about potential neutrals. Whatever warranties or disclaimers are made, a variety of informal and formal approaches to quality control are used. These generally include one or more of the following: requiring affiliated neutrals to receive approved training courses; requiring neutrals to show that they have certain kinds of experience, training, or references; providing ongoing in-service or other training and education to affiliated neutrals; offering informal, case-specific advice to neutrals; evaluating performance based on observation by the ADR Provider Organization's personnel or users' questionnaire responses; offering processes for receiving complaints, assessments, or other feedback from users; removing listed neutrals who, over time, are not selected by parties; and disciplining or removing neutrals who fail to meet ethical or other standards.

6. Organization's Stake in Dispute or Substantive Outcome:
None • Full party to dispute • Good will, future business • Membership organization • Non-profit mission • Administrative charge for matchmaking • Portion of neutral's fee • Other

Most ADR provider entities are explicitly independent and have no stake in the dispute. A few may be parties to cases for which they provide referrals, as in ADR programs that are managed internally by the private or public organization involved in the dispute (*e.g.*, an internally-managed corporate, university or governmental dispute resolution). Other ADR Provider Organizations may have some attenuated or perceived interest (programs using collateral duty or shared neutrals from the same, or another, agency). Some managing organizations provide ADR services as a public service, pursuant to a statutory mandate, as a means of improving or supplementing other services or activities, or as a way to fulfill other non-profit missions. Others provide services primarily in return for fees. Several other benefits may accrue to an ADR Provider Organization: service to members, good will that may influence other activities, or access to additional cases or clients.

7. Organization's Size:
Individual part-time solo • Individual full-time solo • Small entity • Large entity • Regional organization • National organization • International organization

ADR Provider Organizations may include a single individual for whom mediation, arbitration, or management or administrative services are a sideline, a full-time practitioner, a small specialized entity with several neutrals, a large entity that offers a diverse array of services and neutrals in several parts of the U.S., or a national or international organization with hundreds or thousands of available neutrals.

8. Organization's Resources:
Substantial paid staff and related resources devoted to program • Limited volunteer staff and few other resources

Staff and other resources available for operating a program vary dramatically and can have an impact on the nature and quality of services. A few providers devote no full-or part-time staff to their activities; they may, for example, use volunteers, simply provide a list of neutrals without more, or respond to requests on a "catch-as-catch can" basis. At the other extreme, some have substantial full-time staffs devoted to one or more provider roles (*e.g.*, setting standards for listing neutrals, admitting listed neutrals, furnishing panels, advising parties, assessing or disciplining listed neutrals).

9. Organization's Operational Transparency:
Opaque • Open decision making • Rules of procedure defining required competencies, disclosing standards and/or methods for selecting neutrals in individual cases

Some ADR Provider Organizations operate as black boxes, with little or no provision for oversight or openness; others are relatively more open and explicit about the processes by which neutrals are selected, assigned, and monitored; a few seek explicitly to assure openness and regularity via rules, standards, or methodologies.

B. ORGANIZATION'S SERVICES AND RELATIONSHIPS WITH NEUTRALS

Five key attributes of ADR Provider Organizations were identified in this area:

- Nature of Organization's Services
- Nature of Cases
- Nature of Process Assistance Furnished by Neutral
- Relation of Listed Neutrals to ADR Provider Organization
- Status of Neutral

1. Nature of Organization's Services:

Neutral who assists disputants • Clearinghouse list of available neutrals • Management service • Full service administration • Assignor of neutrals • Advisor • System design • Other consultant • Mixture

Some ADR Provider Organizations offer only certain limited kinds of neutral services; others offer a menu of ADR options, which may include training and consulting. A few operate purely as clearinghouses that do little beyond offering a list of neutrals for users to review, perhaps accompanied by a short brochure or generalized advice. Some court programs, for instance, simply maintain a binder containing resumes sent in by local neutrals. Many ADR Provider Organizations, however, offer a range of administrative, management, and consulting services, including helping parties select or design appropriate processes, finding suitable neutrals, and managing the case during the ADR process. Some Provider Organizations offer set management choices, while others offer parties tailored management (from full-service to self-administration) depending on the users' request. A few offer all of these neutral and management services, sometimes in settings where the Organization both manages a roster and provides neutrals' services for the same client.

2. Nature of Cases:

Number of parties (multiparty or two-party) • Complexity • Length • Subject matter (environmental/ policy • civil enforcement • mass tort, insurance, product liability, or similar litigation • commercial/business conflicts • small claims litigation • workplace/employment • family • consumer • labor-management • neighborhood • other)

ADR Provider Organizations assist parties in cases that vary in size, complexity, length, and number of parties, as well as in their subject matter. A few Provider Organizations offer services for cases involving a wide array of settings or subjects. Other Provider Organizations tend to specialize by subject matter. For instance, some Organizations deal mainly with environmental matters; others tend to focus primarily on a broad range of business, commercial, employment and public disputes. Most public Provider Organizations—for example, entities managing court-annexed ADR programs, state-wide court management organizations, and user-specific entities (like the FDIC's roster of neutrals for litigation stemming from bank closings)—deal mostly, or exclusively, with the kinds of cases they were established to support, though this may encompass a broad array of subject areas.

3. Nature of Process Assistance Furnished by Neutral:

System design • Other consulting • Training • Facilitation • Mediation • Case evaluation • Binding arbitration • Private judging • Specialized expertise in specific subject area • Hybrid ADR Processes • Mixture

The ADR Provider Organization may refer listed neutrals who offer a range of ADR processes and related services. The neutral's roles may also range from a brief consultations to extended conflict resolution interventions. Training and design consulting assignments may also include short or longer tenures.

4. Relation of Listed Neutrals to Organization:
Independent • Contractors • Franchisee • Staff • Other

Some management organizations have few, or no, dealings with neutrals beyond listing them. Other organizations work primarily, or exclusively, with neutrals who are contractors, subcontractors, employees, members or franchisees. Several provider organizations require most of their listed neutrals to pay a fee.

5. Status of Neutral:
Private full-time professional neutral • Private part-time • Public collateral duty • Public full-time • Judicial officer • Lawyer • Other professionals

An ADR Provider Organization may offer services from private full-time or part-time dispute resolution practitioners, public full-time practitioners, private individuals who serve occasionally as neutrals, public employees who offer neutral services on a collateral duty basis, or judicial officers whose activities as neutrals may be related to official duties. Apart from their employment status, neutrals referred by a Provider Organization may also come from a variety of professional or other backgrounds (*e.g.,* lawyer, judge, engineer, environmental scientist, social worker, therapist, among others).

C. ORGANIZATION'S RELATIONSHIPS WITH USERS OR CONSUMERS
Two key factors were identified in this area:
- Characteristics of Parties or Representatives
- Organization's Prior Relationship with a User or Representative

1. Characteristics of Parties or Representatives:
Unsophisticated/vulnerable/pro se/novice parties or representatives • Experienced/ fully represented parties or representatives • Individual v. Organization • Individual v. Individual • Other

ADR Provider Organizations deal with a variety of users. Organizations handling neighborhood, consumer, or family cases may often deal with cases involving exclusively first-time participants or similarly unsophisticated users. In many court programs and other settings, the Provider Organization may deal with some parties who are novices on one side and well-represented organizations, or ones that have great experience with ADR processes, on the other. These and other Provider Organizations—particularly in large commercial or labor disputes—deal largely with sophisticated repeat players (as parties and/or representatives) on one or all sides.

2. Organization's Prior Relationship with a User or Representative:
None • Repeat contractor • Long-term contractor • Financial dealings • Other (*e.g.,* board member)

An ADR Provider Organization may have had no dealings with any party or representative; may have worked one or more times with a party or with both parties, or their representatives; or may have a long-term service contract or other relationship with one party or law firm. A Provider Organization may also have certain types of prior, ongoing, or intermittent professional relations with parties or representatives, such as providing training, consulting, or systems design services. In some instances, a Provider Organization may have financial, business, professional or personal dealings with a party or representative.

CPR-GEORGETOWN COMMISSION ON ETHICS AND STANDARDS OF PRACTICE IN ADR*

Chair
Prof. Carrie Menkel-Meadow
Georgetown University
Law Center
Washington, DC

Prof. Marjorie Corman Aaron
University of Cincinnati
College of Law
Cincinnati, OH

Hon. Arlin M. Adams
Schnader, Harrison,
Segal & Lewis
Philadelphia, PA

Howard J. Aibel
LeBoeuf, Lamb,
Greene & MacRae
New York, NY

Tom Arnold
Arnold, White & Durkee
Houston, TX

Jonathan D. Asher
Legal Aid Society of
Metropolitan Denver
Denver, CO

Hon. Nancy F. Atlas
U.S. District Court
Houston, TX

Richard W. Austin
Pretzel & Stouffer
Chicago, IL

Margery F. Baker
Resolution Resources Inc.
Potomac, MD

Fred Baron
Baron & Budd
Dallas, TX

Howard S. Bellman
Madison, WI

John Bickerman
Bickerman Dispute
Resolution Group
Washington, DC

Sheila L. Birnbaum
Skadden, Arps, Slate,
Meagher & Flom
New York, NY

Hon. Wayne D. Brazil
U.S. District Court
Oakland, CA

William H. Champlin III
Tyler Cooper & Alcorn
Hartford, CT

Richard Chernick
Los Angeles, CA

Hon. Kenneth Conboy
Latham & Watkins
New York, NY

Frederick K. Conover II
The Faegre Group
Denver, CO

Hon. Mario M. Cuomo
Willkie Farr & Gallagher
New York, NY

John J. Curtin, Jr.
Bingham, Dana & Gould
Boston, MA

Dean John D. Feerick
Fordham University Law School
New York, NY

Lawrence J. Fox
Drinker, Biddle & Reath
Philadelphia, PA

Howard Gadlin
National Institute of Health
Bethesda, MD

Bryant Garth
American Bar Foundation
Chicago, IL

Shelby R. Grubbs
Miller & Martin
Chattanooga, TN

Prof. Geoffrey C. Hazard, Jr.
University of Pennsylvania
Philadelphia, PA

H. Roderic Heard
Wildman Harrold
Chicago, IL

James F. Henry
CPR Institute for
Dispute Resolution
New York, NY

Christopher Honeyman
Madison, WI

J. Michael Keating, Jr.
Chris Little & Associates
Providence, RI

Judith Korchin
Holland & Knight
Miami, FL

Duane W. Krohnke
Faegre & Benson
Minneapolis, MN

Hon. Frederick B. Lacey
LeBoeuf, Lamb,
Greene & MacRae
Newark, NJ

Prof. Homer LaRue
Howard University
School of Law
Washington, DC

Michael K. Lewis
ADR Associates, L.L.C.

Deborah Masucci
JAMS
New York, NY

Prof. Harry N. Mazadoorian
Quinnipiac Law School
Hamden, CT

* Affiliations and titles as of May 1, 2002

Prof. Barbara McAdoo
DRI Visiting Scholar
Hamline University
School of Law
Dispute Resolution Institute
St. Paul, MN

Bruce Meyerson
Steptoe & Johnson
Phoenix, AZ

Hon. Milton Mollen
Graubard Mollen Horowitz
Pomeranz & Shapiro
New York, NY

Jean S. Moore
Hogan & Hartson
Washington, DC

Robert C. Mussehl
Mussehl & Rosenberg
Seattle, WA

John E. Nolan, Jr.
Steptoe & Johnson
Washington, DC

Melinda Ostermeyer
Washington, DC

Wayne N. Outten
Lankenau Kovner & Kurtz
New York, NY

Charles Pou
Mediation Consortium
Washington, DC

Sharon Press
Supreme Court of Florida
Tallahassee, FL

Charles B. Renfrew
Law Offices of
Charles B. Renfrew
San Francisco, CA

Dean Nancy Rogers
Ohio State University
Columbus, OH

Prof. Frank E. A. Sander
Harvard Law School
Cambridge, MA

Robert N. Sayler
Covington & Burling
Washington, DC

Hon. William W. Schwarzer
U.S. District Court
San Francisco, CA

Kathleen Severens
U.S. Department of Justice
Washington, DC

Margaret L. Shaw
Co-Chair, Committee on ADR
Provider Organizations
ADR Associates, L.L.C.
New York, NY

Hon. Jerome B. Simandle
U.S. District Court
Camden, NJ

William K. Slate
American Arbitration
Association
New York, NY

Stephanie Smith
Hewlett Foundation
Menlo Park, CA

Larry S. Stewart
Stewart Tilghman
Fox & Bianchi
Miami, FL

Thomas J. Stipanowich
CPR Institute for
Dispute Resolution
New York, NY

Harry P. Trueheart III
Nixon, Hargrave,
Devans & Doyle
Rochester, NY

Hon. John J. Upchurch
CCB Mediation, Inc.
Daytona Beach, FL

Alvora Varin-Hommen
U.S. Arb. & Mediation Service
Bensalem, PA

Hon. John L. Wagner
Irell & Manella
Newport Beach, CA

Hon. William H. Webster
Milbank, Tweed,
Hadley & McCloy
Washington, DC

John W. Weiser
Bechtel Group, Inc.
San Francisco, CA

Michael D. Young
JAMS
New York, NY

CPR Staff

Elizabeth Plapinger
Co-Chair and Reporter,
Committee on ADR
Provider Organizations
CPR Institute for
Dispute Resolution
New York, NY

Kathleen Scanlon
Senior Vice President and
Director of Public
Policy Projects
CPR Institute for
Dispute Resolution
New York, NY

* Affiliations and titles as of May 1, 2002

Appendix H

National Standards for Court-Connected Mediation Programs

Center for Dispute Settlement – The Institute of Judicial Administration
1666 Connecticut Avenue, NW, Suite 501, Washington, DC 20009
202/265-9572

SJI

This document was developed under a grant from the State Justice Institute.
Points of view expressed herein are those of the authors and do not necessarily
represent the official position or policies of the State Justice Institute.

INTRODUCTION

These Standards for court-connected mediation programs have been developed to guide and inform courts interested in initiating, expanding or improving mediation programs to which they refer cases.

Courts across the country are seeking ways to provide a better quality of justice for various kinds of litigation, improve citizens' access to justice, save court and litigant costs, and reduce delays in the disposition of cases. As the use of new forms of dispute resolution as an alternative to litigation has become a more widely accepted and understood phenomenon, the number of court-connected dispute resolution programs has proliferated. In particular, courts are referring parties increasingly to mediation in civil, domestic relations and minor criminal cases. Because mediation usually requires less time and fewer resources than trials and produces earlier settlements, significant savings often can be realized in time and costs for both courts and litigants. The direct involvement of the parties in the process of reaching resolution also can provide a greater level of satisfaction, permit outcomes that may be better suited to the parties' needs and, in some cases, produce greater likelihood of compliance with agreements than traditional adjudicative processes.

Yet the greater the documentation of growing numbers of court-connected mediation programs, the clearer it becomes that there are wide variations in their design and implementation, and that there are few generally accepted methods of assessing their quality. The dearth of generally accepted principles to guide courts in designing, implementing and improving such programs risks not only the waste of scarce resources on programs that may be only marginally successful, but also confusion and dissatisfaction on the part of individual users as well as the public at large, who could come to view these programs as a form of second-class justice. Generally accepted standards promoting quality should assist the effectiveness of programming efforts, as well as their acceptance by users, including those whose only contact with the public justice system may be their participation in court-connected mediation programs.

Funded by the State Justice Institute, the Standards that follow were developed as a joint project of the Center for Dispute Settlement in Washington, D.C., and the Institute of Judicial Administration in New York City, with the active involvement of an 18-member Advisory Board comprised of experienced and respected individuals from throughout the country. A list of Advisory Board members and project staff follows this introduction. Points of view expressed in the Standards are those of the Advisory Board members and project staff, and do not necessarily represent the official position or policies of the State Justice Institute.

The Advisory Board includes judges, state and local court administrators, mediators and mediation program administrators, attorneys for both lower and higher income individuals and corporations, academics, evaluators, and officers of professional court and mediation organizations. The Standards that have resulted from the deliberations of this diverse Board as well as from input during a public comment period reflect consensus among people of very different perspectives and points of view.

Mediation is a term that has been used to describe a range of practices designed to help parties in conflict. Likewise, various kinds of relationships have been established between mediators and mediation programs and the courts. The terms "mediation" and "court-connected," as used in these Standards, are defined at the outset of this document (see Definitions at iv.)

The Standards recognize that mediation is used in many different types of cases, from minor criminal disputes, small claims disputes and domestic relations cases to complex civil matters. The Standards are intended to apply to court-connected mediation programs that handle all such cases, although some of the Standards will apply with more force in some types of programs than in others. The Standards are not intended, however, to apply to judicially-hosted settlement conferences. While judges often encourage parties to settle cases using some of the techniques used by mediators, judges are subject to their own codes of ethics, and their handling of the cases before them is within the exercise of their individual discretion. Nor are the Standards intended to apply across the board to programs at the appellate level. While many of the Standards may be applicable to programs handling cases on appeal, they have been developed with trial courts in mind.

The goal of the Standards is to inspire court-connected mediation programs of high quality. The Standards are intended to be used by courts as guidelines to achieving that end. They are not intended to be adopted in legislation or court rule, to create new duties and responsibilities that give rise to liability, or to function as rules that inhibit creativity and innovation. The Standards recognize that court-connected mediation programs need to be designed and implemented in ways that take account of local needs and circumstances. In some jurisdictions, for example, guidelines for "courts" will need to be read as applying to court administrators; in others, depending upon the size and structure of the court system, they will need to be read as applying to judges. Finally, the Standards should not discourage courts from adopting programs because current shortages of resources preclude adherence to all of their provisions. The Standards do not distinguish between required and recommended provisions. At the same time, they reflect the best thinking currently about what constitutes quality in court-connected mediation programming efforts.

The Standards are organized sequentially in the order in which issues might be expected to arise during a program's operation. Thus, they begin with provisions related to access, and end with program evaluation. There are a number of areas where, because of the interrelatedness of the topics, a certain degree of duplication occurs. Given the importance of each of the topics addressed, consolidation was rejected in favor of publishing a set of Standards, any one of which could stand on its own.

Overall, it is hoped that general acceptance and widespread implementation of these Standards will enhance confidence in and satisfaction with our public justice system. At a minimum, their publication should promote thoughtful dialogue about the critical issues they address.

DEFINITIONS

Mediation
Mediation is a term that has been used to describe a range of practices designed to help parties in conflict. In these Standards, the term is used to describe **a process in which an impartial person helps those parties to communicate and to make voluntary, informed choices in an effort to resolve their dispute**.

Court-Connected
These Standards are intended to apply to all programs that are court-connected, defined as **any program or service, including a service provided by an individual, to which a court refers cases on a voluntary or mandatory basis, including any program or service operated by the court**. The distinction sometimes is made between "court annexed" and "court-referred" mediation. Use of the term court-connected in these Standards is intended to apply equally to both.

NATIONAL STANDARDS
FOR COURT-CONNECTED MEDIATION PROGRAMS

1.0 ACCESS TO MEDIATION

1.1 Mediation services should be available on the same basis as are other services of the court.

COMMENTARY: Access to court-connected mediation services should be provided as broadly as possible. Specifically, courts should not make mediation available based on whether the parties are able to pay, whether they are represented, whether they have a particular physical disability or might have difficulty speaking or understanding English. Judges and court managers have already created mechanisms for providing in-court assistance for parties and witnesses falling into these categories. Offering or encouraging mediation through the court demands the same type of creativity to provide for open access to court-connected services. See Standard 13.0 on Funding. Mediation services should be located in a physical setting conducive to mediation and consistent with the requirements of the Americans with Disabilities Act and local statutes regarding disability.

1.2 Each court should develop policies and procedures that take into consideration the language and cultural diversity of its community at all stages of development, operation and evaluation of court-connected mediation services and programs.

COMMENTARY: Precisely how this principle would be implemented by a specific court must be determined by the circumstances in which judges and court administrators find themselves. At a minimum, however, judges or court administrators seeking to create a new mediation service or modify existing programs should seek ways to involve the client community in the task.

Some non-native speakers of English may wish to use the services of the court even though they are not legal immigrants. The court must think through carefully what its posture will be towards such litigants, and whether anything disclosed in mediation sessions is to be released to immigration authorities. Clearly, a policy of reporting would discourage mediation. If such a policy is adopted, the court should disclose that fact before permitting any mediations to go forward.

1.3   To ensure that parties have equal access to mediation, non-judicial screeners should have clearly stated written policies, procedures and criteria to guide their discretion in referring cases to mediation.

COMMENTARY: To ensure full access to mediation, all barriers created by gatekeepers need to be lowered. Many mediation programs do not rely on judges to make case-by-case determinations of the appropriateness of mediation. If court officials other than judges make decisions regarding referring cases to mediation, uniform policies, procedures and criteria minimize the risk that individual court officers will refer certain categories of cases to mediation more than others.

1.4   Courts should take steps to ensure that pro se litigants make informed choices about mediation.

COMMENTARY: When parties to mediation have neither legal representation nor access to legal information, they are often vulnerable to pressure to settle and to accept unfair results. When parties are unrepresented, courts should make special efforts to alert them to settlement alternatives (possibly through pre-mediation education). Similarly, courts should be sensitive to practices that make the uninformed perceive that they must settle. For example, courts could provide written information to parties containing answers to frequently asked questions (regarding statutory rights, for example). Alternative Disp. Resol. Comm., American Civ. Liberties Union, Draft Statement of Mediation Principles and Commentary 3 (1991).

Lawyers, or the availability of adequate legal information, may also act as a crucial check against uninformed, pressured settlements. See Standard 10.0 on Role of Lawyers in Mediation. This concern is especially important when the party is unsophisticated about legal processes and might easily be intimidated or manipulated. Generally, it is recognized that the mediator cannot provide the same protections provided by an individual's personal advocate. Some legal authority permits limited advice and drafting by the mediator, and at times, even requires the mediator to recommend obtaining outside legal advice. Some of these authorities also have drawn distinctions between "representation" and "protection of basic interests." See Vermont Bar Ass'n Prof. Responsibility Comm., Op. N. 80-12 (1980).

Courts should avoid two common responses to the problems presented by pro se litigants. Courts may tend to bar pro se disputants from any mediation. This provides the most complete assurance to courts that the customary courtroom protections afforded vulnerable litigants will not be lost in mediation, but it clearly defeats the goal of equal access to mediation. Further, pro se litigants are often the individuals who could most benefit from the lower cost and lack of procedural complexity of mediation. Exclusion of pro se litigants from mediation also may disadvantage those who may be able to represent themselves in the more flexible and informal mediation setting, as well as those who might otherwise benefit from other possible advantages of mediation such as higher quality solutions that meet their underlying needs.

Similarly, judges and administrators, working in an overburdened court system, may tend to make decisions regarding the referral of cases to mediation for entire classes or types of cases rather than on an individual basis. Neither option provides unrepresented parties with the degree of information or choice that is desirable.

1.5   Courts should ensure that information about the availability of mediation services is widely disseminated in the languages used by the consumers of court services.

COMMENTARY: A major barrier to the use of mediation is the lack of knowledge of availability and understanding of the process by individual litigants and their attorneys. Although lawyers' knowledge of mediation has increased dramatically in the past ten years, lack of familiarity remains. The public at large knows much less. See Standard 3.0 on Information for Judges, Court Personnel and Users.

Effective dissemination of material announcing availability of mediation services -- and what might be expected to result from use of the process -- requires materials in the languages of the court's consumers.

1.6   (a)   Courts should provide orientation and training for attorneys, court personnel and others regarding the availability and use of mediation services.

(b)   Prior to and at the filing of a case, courts should provide to the parties and their attorneys information regarding the availability of mediation.

COMMENTARY: Court personnel often are the gatekeepers for court services, especially for the poor and disadvantaged. Court clerks, and other court personnel likely to be in the position of answering questions regarding the court's services, need to understand the mediation process so that they can explain it to the public. Furthermore, although the past ten years have seen a vast increase in lawyers' knowledge about mediation, that knowledge is not evenly distributed. If lawyers are to be truly useful in helping their clients consider whether mediation might be the correct choice in a given litigation, they must become much more knowledgeable about the process. A successful mediation program needs to include educating members of the bar. See Standard 3.0 on Information for Judges, Court Personnel and Users.

Courts should aim to remove as many barriers as possible to the use of mediation. Informing litigants, as well as their counsel, upon filing about the availability of mediation ensures the best chance that a serious discussion about the viability of its use in a particular case can take place. The Supreme Court of Missouri, in Rule 17 (November 30, 1989), established that parties in most newly filed actions must receive written notice describing the availability and purpose of ADR options. In Jackson County, the Circuit court implementing rule (Local Rule 25.1) specifies that the parties must receive such notice from the Court if a pro se litigant, or from the party's attorney if represented. The attorney, in turn, must certify to the court that such notice was given to the client.

**1.7   In choosing the location and hours of operation of mediation
services, courts should consider the effect on the ability of
parties to use mediation effectively, and the safety of mediators
and parties.**

COMMENTARY: In contrast to litigation, mediation relies heavily on the
direct participation of the parties to a dispute. For mediation to be most effective, courts
should consider ways to encourage the participation of the parties.

The location at which mediation services are provided will have an impact on
participation by the parties in some disputes. Courts should consider the feasibility of
offering services in multiple locations. Mediation conducted in a number of decentralized
locations is more likely to attract disputants than a system designed to conduct all
mediations in a central facility. While the creation of a decentralized model for the
provision of mediation services may have relatively high start-up costs, the larger number
of cases a decentralized model will attract may off-set those costs over time.

Similarly, the hours of operation of mediation services will have an impact on
participation by some parties, who may need to attend during non-working hours. At the
same time, the safety of mediators and parties should be considered when scheduling the
time and place of mediations.

2.0   COURTS' RESPONSIBILITY FOR MEDIATION

**2.1   The degree of a court's responsibility for mediators or mediation
programs depends on whether a mediator or program is employed or
operated by the court, receives referrals from the court, or is chosen by
the parties themselves.**

> **a.   The court is fully responsible for mediators it employs and
> programs it operates.**
> **b.   The court has the same responsibility for monitoring the quality
> of mediators and/or mediation programs outside the court to
> which it refers cases as it has for its own programs.**
> **c.   The court has no responsibility for the quality or operation of
> outside programs chosen by the parties without guidance from
> the court.**

COMMENTARY: The Standards take the position that the method of referral,
rather than the sponsorship of the mediation program, should govern the court's
responsibility to monitor a program. The court should be responsible for monitoring both
its own selection of cases for mediation and the operation of all of the mediation
programs to which it refers cases.

This standard makes the court responsible for the quality of services provided
by all court-connected mediation programs. Although the court naturally has no direct
responsibility for the operation or administration of outside programs or mediators to

which it refers cases, it is responsible for monitoring the quality of the those individuals or programs that receive its imprimatur. This is so regardless of whether the court's referrals occur through the suggestion of a particular mediator or program by a judge or by court staff or through maintenance of a list of mediators that is provided to parties.

This approach is based on the same rationale as that taken by the Conference of State Court Administrators (COSCA) Committee on Alternative Dispute Resolution:

> The more closely connected to the court an alternative dispute resolution program is, the higher the degree of control the court should exercise.

COSCA Committee on ADR, "Report to the Membership," 3 (12/11/90 draft) (hereafter "COSCA Report").

COSCA offers the following discussion of its principle:

> If judges and court administrators institute a court-annexed program, they have responsibility for establishing program goals, structure, procedures, and the qualifications of those who serve as mediators, arbitrators and other types of neutrals. The court should regularly and rigorously monitor and evaluate the program's performance. Judges and court administrators should be prepared to modify any and all aspects of a program that fail to meet the court's goals.

> If judges and court administrators adopt a policy of referring a portion of the court's caseload to a dispute resolution program outside the court, they should establish mechanisms to review periodically the quality of the services provided by the program. The relationship of the court to the program should be maintained by an appointed liaison to ensure that communications with the program administrators are regular, clear and effective.

> The court has no direct responsibility to monitor or to evaluate private programs, but judges and court administrators should be knowledgeable about private programs in the community as well as the community needs that these programs address. The court should maintain some communication with private programs so that in

appropriate circumstances parties can be made
aware of the services of private programs and the
benefits they may offer.

Id. at 4.

**2.2   The court should specify its goals in establishing a mediation program or
in referring cases to mediation programs or services outside the court and
provide a means of evaluating whether or not these goals are being met.**

COMMENTARY: The court should ensure that program goals are clearly
articulated and related to its specific needs. Given the variety of possible goals of
referring cases to mediation, a court need not have a backlog of cases to institute a
mediation program or refer cases to outside mediators. Yet clarity of goals is important to
ensure that

--   A case or class of cases is referred to an appropriate
mediator or program.
--   The program is of high quality and suitable to the case or
class of cases referred.
--   The court has clear objectives by which to monitor and
evaluate the program's performance.

Among the possible goals are to:

--   provide a broader range of dispute resolution options
--   increase the involvement of parties in the process of
resolution of their disputes
--   provide a mechanism to deal with the real issues in dispute
--   facilitate the early resolution of disputes
--   decrease the cost to parties of resolving disputes
--   increase parties' satisfaction and compliance with the
results of dispute resolution
--   assist the parties in developing a wider range of outcomes
than are available through adjudication
--   provide access to a process that for many litigants is less
formal and intimidating than the traditional adjudicatory
process
--   increase the court's ability to resolve cases within given
resources.
--   increase the parties' ability to resolve their own disputes
without court intervention.

All too often courts implement programs based on models from other courts
without evaluating their own particular operating environments and needs. This situation
is likely to result not only in the court's failing to achieve the particular benefits it seeks

but also in litigants' confusion and dissatisfaction with the justice system as a whole. Even when a program is not initiated or operated by the court itself, the program's goals should be clear and relate directly to the rationale for a court's referring individual cases or categories of cases to it. Clarity of goals will facilitate effective monitoring and evaluation. (See Standard 16.0 on Evaluation.)

2.3 Program Management

a. **Information provided by the court to the mediator**
   (1) **When parties choose to go to mediation outside the court, the court should have no responsibility to provide any information to the mediator.**
   (2) **When a court makes a mandatory referral of parties to mediation, whether inside or outside the court, it should be responsible for providing the mediator or mediation program sufficient information to permit the mediator to deal with the case effectively.**

COMMENTARY: If the parties choose to use outside mediators, whether or not they are suggested by the court, the court should be able to rely on the parties to provide the mediator with whatever information is required. When the court requires the parties to participate in mediation, on the other hand, the Standards require the court to provide whatever information is needed. The precise information required will vary with the type of case and with whether the parties are represented. It includes such data as the case and parties' names; case type; dates of filing and referral to mediation; the amount of the claim and any counterclaim; any dispute motions, court orders and/or trial date; and the stage of discovery, where applicable.

b. **Information provided by the mediator or the parties to the court**

For purposes of quality control and the court's exercise of responsibilities to manage its caseload, providers of mediation services have the following responsibilities to provide information to the court:

   (1) **If the program is court-operated, or if the case is referred to an outside program or mediator by the court, the program or individual mediator should have the responsibility to report information to the court, in order to permit monitoring and evaluation.**
   (2) **If the mediator or program is chosen by the parties without guidance from the court, the provider should have no responsibility to report to the court.**

COMMENTARY: This standard makes the responsibility of the program to provide the court with certain data depend on the court's responsibility for monitoring its quality. Although a mediator or program chosen without guidance from the court has no responsibility to provide the court with data, the parties may be required to furnish the information in the case of mandatory mediation, or asked to furnish it in the case of voluntary mediation, to the extent that the information is necessary for the court to manage its docket. Such information may include case name and type, the date the case was referred, the name of the mediator or mediation program, the names of the parties or party representatives attending mediation, the outcome of the mediation, and, if the parties agree, any further court action required. Ordinarily, there is no need for the parties to furnish their agreements to the court.

2.4   Aggregate Information

Court-operated mediation programs and programs to which the court refers cases should be required to provide periodic information to the court. The information required should be related to:
a.   The court's objectives in establishing the program; and
b.   The court's responsibility for ensuring the quality of the services provided.

COMMENTARY: In addition to case-specific information, programs to which the court refers cases may be required to provide the court with aggregate information on a periodic basis, which will permit the court to monitor the quality of the services provided. The precise type of information required should depend in part on the program's goals. For example, information about parties' costs per case and time to resolution is important if the primary goal of the program is to save litigants time and money, whereas such information might not be important if the primary goal is to provide a more appropriate mechanism for resolution.
In general, however, the information should be adequate to permit:

--   effective case management by the court
--   monitoring of the quality of service provided (the percentage of cases reaching agreement, for example, and the average time between referral and agreement)
--   the nature of agreements, and information about the parties' satisfaction
--   evaluating whether the program is meeting its goals over time and the needs of litigants and the court

Periodic reports from programs, containing aggregate information about cases referred, is necessary to enable the court administration to determine whether the program is meeting its articulated goals as well as the needs of the court in referring individual cases or categories of cases to it. Such information should be evaluated regularly by the court administration to identify any deficiencies in the dispute resolution system.

2.5   The court should designate a particular individual to be responsible for supervision, monitoring and administration of court-connected mediation programs.

COMMENTARY: The presiding judge or the presiding judge's designee has the ultimate responsibility for the operation of court-connected mediation programs. For day-to-day administration, however, a member of the court staff, who should be a person in a senior management position, should be designated to operate court-based programs or to act as liaison with private, court-referred programs or mediators. This need not be a full-time position in a small jurisdiction.

The administrator should be knowledgeable about the goals, process and procedures of mediation, as well as about the court's process and procedures and its goals in referring individual cases or categories of cases to mediation. This individual should meet regularly with court administrators, groups of outside mediators who receive court referrals, and judges who refer cases to mediation, in order to ensure that the program is functioning effectively.

2.6   Complaint Mechanism

Parties referred by the court to a mediation program, whether or not it is operated by the court, should have access to a complaint mechanism to address any grievances about the process.

COMMENTARY: Increasing numbers of states have adopted official procedures allowing a party to register a grievance against a mediator or a mediation program and delineating an investigatory and disciplinary process. There seems to be widespread agreement that specific, written complaint mechanisms are needed, and several states have been developing proposals on this subject. Different models have been suggested, and questions have been posed concerning the level of formality needed, participation of parties and mediators complained about in the process, types of sanctions, and the procedures for appeal or review.

Any complaint mechanism should be based upon a clear code of ethical conduct by mediators. (See Standard 8.0 on Ethical Standards for Mediators.) The complaint process should screen complaints that do not allege ethical misconduct and refer these to program administrators in charge of supervising and reviewing mediators' skills or competence. (See Standard 16.0 on Evaluation.)

In Michigan, where the mediation of custody and visitation issues is offered on a voluntary basis by the court under state statute, the statute includes a grievance procedure.

> Parties may file a grievance in writing with the appropriate "Friend of the Court" office, the administrative bureau within the Office of Court

Administration responsible for implementing the statute. The office then investigates and decides the complaint. If the party is not satisfied with the decision, a further grievance in writing can be filed with the Chief Judge, who investigates and decides the matter. Each Friend of the Court office is required to maintain a record of each grievance received, together with its status. This information must be submitted to the State Office of Court Administration at least biannually. Public access to such reports is required.

Mich. Comp. Laws Ann. §552.526.

New Hampshire has also established a procedure to process complaints brought against marital mediators who are certified by the state. §328-C:7, Disciplinary Action. The State Board of Marital Mediation Certification (consisting of one Superior Court judge, one full-time marital master, one attorney, one mental health professional, and two members of the public) is required to hold a hearing in response to any complaint brought against a certified individual or program. The mediator or program is given an opportunity to respond in writing to the complaint, and to be present at the hearing. If the Board finds that there is a violation of a provision in the legislation dealing with marital mediation, it is authorized to: 1) issue a written warning; 2) suspend certification temporarily (and establish conditions for reinstatement); or 3) permanently suspend certification.

The Florida Statutes of Professional Conduct for Certified & Court Appointed Mediators provide detailed procedures for a Complaint Committee, to be composed of one judge or attorney and two court certified mediators. If the Complaint Committee finds probable cause to believe that alleged misconduct by a mediator would constitute a violation of the Standards, the Committee has discretion, before referring the matter to a hearing panel, to "meet with the complainant and the mediator in an effort to resolve the matter. This resolution may include sanctions if agreed to by the mediator." §2-5.0(H) 1991.

Although the Standards concluded that it would be inappropriate to require parties dissatisfied with mediation to mediate their complaints against the mediator, it considers it appropriate to offer parties the option of participating in mediation before launching a formal hearing against a mediator.

3.0   INFORMATION FOR JUDGES, COURT PERSONNEL AND USERS

3.1   Courts, in collaboration with the bar and professional organizations, are responsible for providing information to the public, the bar, judges and court personnel regarding the mediation process; the availability of programs; the differences between mediation, adjudication and other dispute resolution processes; the possibility of savings in cost and time; and the consequences of participation.

COMMENTARY: Establishing court mediation programs involves a significant investment in time and resources. The investment is justified if the programs are used by a significant number of people, who find that the programs meet their needs.

Experience with court mediation programs has shown that voluntary programs often are underutilized. In spite of the increasing number of ADR programs in courts and communities, mediation remains a largely unfamiliar process to judges, court administrators, citizens and attorneys. Judges, lawyers and clients tend to do things in the way to which they are accustomed and may resist new processes with which they are unfamiliar.

Judges and court administrators play a leadership role in the courts and their communities. Judges in some courts are responsible for deciding which cases go to mediation, explaining the process to disputants and helping to make program decisions regarding such issues as mandatory referral and choice of mediator. Their understanding and support of court mediation programs can make them powerful allies and help ensure a program's success.

The New Jersey Supreme Court Task Force on ADR addressed the need for judges and court personnel to have an understanding of the role of dispute resolution programs in the justice system. It recommended that judges and court personnel "be encouraged to develop and participate in educational and training programs," suggesting that they receive instruction about programs and how "to communicate information to disputants regarding the referral process and their rights." Supreme Ct. of the St. of N.J. Task Force on Disp. Resol., Final Report (1990), at 18, 20 (hereafter "N.J. Report").

Education of court administrators and judges should focus on the differences between mediation and adjudication, the participatory nature of mediation and the possibility of creative solutions that deal with future relationships. This information can help to ensure that they will be better advocates and wiser planners of mediation programs, better able to select cases appropriate for mediation and more expert at explaining mediation to parties and their attorneys.

Parties and attorneys may not choose mediation over adjudication because they are unfamiliar with the advantages of mediation, or because they do not know how to prepare for or participate in a mediation session. Mediators' experience is that, when attorneys understand mediation, they can facilitate the process and increase the likelihood of settlement. It follows that, with increased familiarity with mediation, more people will choose it in voluntary programs, more people will feel comfortable with it in mandatory programs, and more people will be better able to participate in both voluntary and mandatory programs.

Not only do courts have an interest in maximizing the use of mediation programs, but they also have a responsibility to ensure that parties and attorneys who have a choice between mediation and other alternative processes have enough information to enable them to make an informed choice. Although courts do not normally assume the responsibility of educating parties or attorneys, when they introduce new programs under their authority they should provide information about them.

Missouri Supreme Court Rule 17 and Jackson County Rule 25.1 require each court to provide notice of dispute resolution services to all parties to the action:

(a) In each civil action to which the early dispute resolution program applies, a notice of dispute resolution services shall be furnished to all parties to the action. The notice shall be provided to the party initiating the action at the time the action is filed. The opposing party shall receive the notice with the summons and petition. Other means of providing notice may be provided by local court rule.

(b) The notice shall advise parties of the availability and purposes of early dispute resolution services. The notice shall list individuals and organizations that provide such services. The notice may set out a brief description of the occupations and backgrounds of the individuals and organizations listed and fees that may be charged for their services.

Mo. Sup. Ct. R. 17.03.

The Judicial Council of California states that "each court should develop a pre-mediation education program based on current research and established court mediation practice." Judicial Council of Cal., Uniform Standards of Practice for Court-Connected Mediation of Child Custody and Visitation Disputes, §26(b) (1990). The council comments that "orientating parties prior to mediation may have several benefits . . . reducing their [parties'] fears; preparing the parties for sessions by giving them the opportunity to ask questions and raise concerns; helping to normalize the family crisis; and promoting an out of court settlement." Id.

In making its recommendations regarding mandated participation in court programs, the SPIDR Law and Public Policy Committee concluded: "Mandatory participation should only be used when a high quality program . . . . (iv) provides clarity about the precise procedures that are being required." The committee cautions, "It is important to inform parties about the dispute resolution procedures, especially if they are unrepresented." Society of Professionals in Dist. Resol., Mandated Participation and Settlement Coercion: Dispute Resolution as it Relates to the Courts (1991), at 3 (hereafter "SPIDR Report").

While the Standards endorse the principle that courts have the responsibility to educate and inform, they also support the role of the local bar and law schools in education. As courts take the primary initial responsibility to educate, they can encourage local bars and law schools to offer courses and CLE credits and encourage law schools to include mediation in particular and dispute resolution in general in the curricula.

3.2   Courts should provide the following information:

   a.   To judges, court personnel and the bar:

(1)	the goals and limitations of the jurisdiction's program(s)
(2)	the basis for selecting cases
(3)	the way in which the program operates
(4)	the information to be provided to lawyers and litigants in individual cases
(5)	the way in which the legal and mediation processes interact
(6)	the enforcement of agreements
(7)	applicable laws and rules concerning mediation

COMMENTARY: Recognizing the pressures and demands placed on judges' time, it may be necessary to provide flexible processes for informing them about court-connected mediation programs. The best introduction to mediation is to observe a live simulation. Where that is not possible, videotapes of mediations can be made available so that judges can view them as time permits. Written descriptions of process and programs should be prepared. Mediation program staff can meet individually with judges to provide further information. In Florida, for example, the court mediation office works closely with general civil division judges, holding periodic meetings to keep them informed of new developments or changes in program rules. In the United States District Court for the District of Columbia, program staff and consultants meet regularly with individual judges to discuss the program and the susceptibility to mediation of the judges' individual caseloads.

b.　　To users (parties and attorneys) in addition to the information in (a):

General information:
(1)	issues appropriate for mediation
(2)	the possible mediators and how they will be selected
(3)	party choice, if any, of mediators
(4)	any fees
(5)	program operation, including location, times of operation, intake procedures, contact person
(6)	the availability of special services for non-English speakers, and persons who have communication, mobility or other disabilities
(7)	the possibility of savings or additional expenditures of money or time

Information on process:
(1)	the purpose of mediation
(2)	confidentiality of process and records
(3)	role of the parties and/or attorneys in mediation
(4)	role of the mediator, including lack of authority to impose a solution

(5)	voluntary acceptance of any resolution or agreement
(6)	the advantages and disadvantages of participating in determining solutions
(7)	enforcement of agreements
(8)	availability of formal adjudication if a formal resolution or agreement is not achieved and implemented
(9)	the way in which the legal and mediation processes interact, including permissible communications between mediators and the court
(10)	the advantages and disadvantages of a lack of formal record.

COMMENTARY: At a minimum, courts should provide written information to explain the dispute resolution service to which parties are referred and instruct parties on how to use it. If a significant number of the population served is non-English speaking, the material should be available in other languages as well. (See Standard 1.0 on Access to Mediation.) Whether written information alone is sufficient may depend on the kind of disputes included, the sophistication of the parties, and whether or not parties are represented by attorneys.

The experience of dispute resolution professionals has been that, although it is helpful to talk and read about mediation, the process becomes most clear to people when they can see an actual or mock mediation. Program staff and funding constraints may make it impractical to consider regular demonstrations of mediations. It may be more feasible to have videotaped demonstrations and explanations available for viewing. The Judicial Council of California suggests "providing information in advance of mediation that may include individual presentation by the mediator, group instruction, video presentations, intake forms, and written materials." Uniform Standards of Practice, □26(b).

When parties are unrepresented and the court is concerned that a party will need extra information or assistance in making a choice, or the court has a special interest in encouraging the use of mediation, additional informational efforts may be required. The Judicial Council of California recommends that, in addition to premediation education, the mediator or court representative conduct an individualized orientation with the parties before beginning mediation. Uniform Standards of Practice, §26(b).

Courts also have the responsibility of providing information on mediation to the public at large. In order to encourage familiarity with and use of mediation, courts should inform the public about the mediation process, the availability of programs, the differences between mediation and adjudication, the possibility of savings in cost and time, and the advantages and disadvantages of participation in the determination of solutions.

Law enforcement agencies, social service agencies and schools can be approached to increase their understanding of available resources and to enable them to make appropriate referrals. For instance, the Superior Court Multi-Door Mediation Program in Washington, D.C., has made presentations including mediation demonstrations to parent-teacher groups, community groups and agencies such as the Office of Paternity and Child Support.

Another way to educate the community is by using advisory committees. When a court-connected mediation program is planned, an advisory committee on planning and implementation can be formed, which includes representatives of the local bar, judges, court, citizen groups, social service agencies and the schools. By participating on the committee, its members become informed and educated. These people then carry that information to their constituencies and provide information and education to the community at large.

3.3   The court should encourage attorneys to inform their clients of the availability of court connected mediation programs.

COMMENTARY: An issue in cases where parties are represented by counsel is whether it is sufficient for the court to provide information to counsel in the hope that it will be shared with the parties. Is there an infringement on the attorney/client relationship if the parties receive information on mediation programs from the court itself rather than from their attorneys? In New Jersey, the bar objected to the suggestion of mandatory attendance by parties at educational sessions as unnecessary and potentially costly for clients and raising the possibility of "interpos[ing] an intake specialist between the Bar and potential clients." The Task Force did recommend and the Supreme Court endorsed recommendations permitting mandatory referral to mediation for educational purposes. The Task Force also agreed that an "individual disputant's attorney has the primary role in explaining to the disputant the available CDR programs and processes." N.J. Report, at 18, 20.

Missouri Supreme Court Rule 17 and Jackson County Rule 25.1 have taken a different approach, setting strict requirements for attorneys to provide clients with "Notice of Dispute Resolution Services," as described under 3.1, supra.

Similarly, Colorado's Rules of Professional Conduct state that attorneys should advise their clients in all litigated cases of alternative forms of dispute resolution. (Colorado Rules of Professional Conduct, Rule 2.1 (January 1, 1993).)

4.0   SELECTION OF CASES AND TIMING OF REFERRAL

4.1   When courts must choose between cases or categories of cases for which mediation is offered because of a shortage of resources, such choices should be made on the basis of clearly articulated criteria. Such criteria might include the following:

    a.   There is a high probability that mediation will be successful in the particular case or category of case, in terms of both the number and quality of settlements.

    b.   Even if there is not a high probability that mediation will be successful in the particular case or category of cases, continuing litigation would harm non-parties, the dispute involves important continuing relationships, or the case, if not mediated, is likely to require continuing involvement by the court.

COMMENTARY: Available resources in the justice system are limited. Although ideally a full range of dispute resolution options should be made available to litigants in every case, the reality of limited funds and time to implement and monitor quality programs and services requires that choices be made between the kinds of options that can be provided and the types of cases in which those options will apply.

While the Standards do not recommend specific policies with respect to resource allocation, they do emphasize that choices should be made with thought and care, and guided by the premise of doing no harm. Examples of criteria that might be used by courts in allocating resources for court-connected mediation programs and services include a high probability of success measured both quantitatively and qualitatively, and potential negative impact on the parties, the court, or others if a case or type of case is litigated or mediated. Whatever the criteria for choice, such criteria should be clearly articulated by the court to enhance thoughtful decision-making as well as understanding and acceptance by court personnel, users and the public of the choices that are ultimately made.

4.2   **The following considerations may militate against the suitability of referring cases to mediation:**

    a.   **when there is a need for public sanctioning of conduct;**

    b.   **when repetitive violations of statutes or regulations need to be dealt with collectively and uniformly; and**

    c.   **when a party or parties are not able to negotiate effectively themselves or with assistance of counsel.**

COMMENTARY: Courts should consider carefully whether to exclude certain kinds of cases from mediation altogether, or to refer such cases to mediation only on a very selective, case-by-case basis.

For example, there is some conduct that the legislature has determined to be so intolerable to public health and welfare that criminal penalties should attach to its proven occurrence. While neighborhood justice centers typically mediate misdemeanor cases, and programs attached to prosecutors' offices mediate such cases as bad checks, serious criminal conduct may be inappropriate for mediation because of the potential for avoidance of sanctions the legislature has determined are important to deter future similar conduct and protect the public. Other conduct that is similarly intolerable to public health and welfare, although penalties attached to its proven occurrence are civil in nature, also may not be suitable for referral to mediation, such as the intentional dumping of toxic waste.

Likewise, there are some situations that need to be dealt with collectively and uniformly, such as a recurring pattern of consumer fraud. A manufacturer sued by numbers of customers for supplying defective products should not be allowed to continue such conduct by reaching individual private settlements. Such recurring practices may require court intervention to establish a clear rule for future conduct.

Finally, there are cases that courts should consider excluding from mediation because the parties are not able to negotiate effectively on their own behalf. One example is a case in which physical or psychological victimization has occurred that impairs the ability of one or both parties to protect their own interests during the process or to honor their agreements. It may be possible to introduce into the mediation process, on a case-by-case basis, a variety of special procedures to address this situation (see Standard 11.0 on Inappropriate Pressure to Settle). At a minimum courts should, in consultation with representatives of all of the interests involved, develop special protocols to govern referrals to mediation of these kinds of cases.

4.3   Courts should make available or encourage the availability of mediation to disputants before they file their cases in court as well as after judgment to address problems that otherwise might require relitigation.

COMMENTARY: Court-connected mediation programs and services generally are designed and implemented to provide alternatives to the litigation process. What often is forgotten is the goal of litigation prevention. Courts can play an important role in promoting the availability of mediation before disputes are filed in court as well as after cases have been settled or judgment has been rendered. Such promotion can take the forms of opening the caseloads of court-connected mediation programs and services to cases pre-filing and post-judgment, working directly with agencies and individuals in the community to encourage the provision of mediation, and advocating publicly through bar associations or otherwise for the increased availability of such services. To encourage pre-filing mediation, court statistical methods may have to be modified so that the court receives recognition for the services provided.

4.4   While the timing of a referral to mediation may vary depending upon the type of case involved and the needs of the particular case, referral should be made at the earliest possible time that the parties are able to make an informed choice about their participation in mediation.

COMMENTARY: There may be some types of cases where immediate referral to mediation is needed. Eviction cases are an example, as may be cases such as neighborhood disputes in which tensions are escalating.
In most other cases, the timing of a referral is variable. State statutes that address this issue differ. For example in the domestic relations area, child custody mediation in Alaska may be ordered within 30 days after a petition is filed (Alaska Stat. 25.2g.080 (1); California requires that such cases be ordered to mediation no later than 50 days after the filing of a petition (Cal. Civ. Code 4607a); in other states referrals can be made "at any time." Iowa Code Ann. 598.16, Kan. Sta. Ann. 23-602 (a); Me. Rev. Stat. Ann. tit. 19 636,637.
In other types of cases, the interests of court efficiency and speedy resolution of disputes appear to underlie references to timing. For example, New Hampshire Superior Court Rule 170 provides for mediation to be conducted no later than 210 days from the date the action was entered. Minnesota's Task Force on Alternative Dispute Resolution has recommended that in all civil cases parties should be required to meet within 45 days of the filing of a case to discuss management issues, including the selection of an ADR process and timing of its use, and communicate the results, in writing, to the court within another 15 days. Its reasoning is that "[e]arly case evaluation

and referral to an appropriate ADR process has proven to facilitate speedy resolution of disputes." Minnesota Supreme Court and State Bar Task Force on Alternative Dispute Resolution, Final Report, approved by Supreme Court June, 1990 (hereafter "Minn. Report").

There may be categories of cases, for example, small claims cases, where appropriate timing can be presumed by category of case. However, for many other cases, the timing of a referral should be determined on a case-by-case basis. In some kinds of cases early referral will be desirable before the parties' positions become hardened and substantial costs are incurred. In others, referral should be delayed to allow sufficient information to be gathered to ensure meaningful negotiations. In general a determination as to timing should take into account both the parties' capacity to mediate and the ripeness of the issues for mediation.

Courts should not lose sight of the fact that mediation itself is a case management tool that can be used to help parties determine and set a schedule for their discovery needs and thus create the conditions most conducive to assisted negotiations.

4.5   Courts should provide the opportunity on a continuing basis for both the parties and the court to determine the timing of a referral to mediation.

COMMENTARY: Assessment of the parties' capacity to mediate and the sufficiency of the information gathered through discovery should be conducted on a continuing basis. The danger is that a case assessed initially as not ready for mediation will be allowed to languish, with parties' positions allowed to harden and the opportunity for early resolution lost. Case tracking should be built into the court's case management system and provide for regular and periodic assessment of readiness for mediation.

4.6   If a referral to mediation is mandated, parties should have input on the question of when the case should be referred to mediation, but the court itself should determine timing.

Parties should have input in the question of when the case should be referred to mediation. As Minnesota's Task Force on Alternative Dispute Resolution has noted,

> Parties should have the opportunity to discuss among themselves . . . the timing of the ADR process. Such participation may lead to better cooperation in an ADR process, ultimately facilitating more efficient and less rancorous settlement of disputes.

Minn. Report, supra, at 14.

At the same time, the court should retain its ultimate responsibility for case management. If the final decision with respect to timing rests with the court, the possibility of delaying tactics on the part of one or both parties can be minimized.

4.7   Courts should establish presumptive deadlines for the mediation process, which may be extended by the court upon a showing by the parties that continuation of the process will assist in reaching resolution.

COMMENTARY: State statutes vary with respect to whether there is a limit on the length of time allowed for mediation, and how much time is allowed. For example, in Colorado custody/visitation mediation must be completed within 60 days. Colo. Rev. Stat. 14-10-129.5(1)(c). In Florida the outcome must be reported within 14 days after the referral. Fla. Stat. Ann. 39.429(3)(d). Other statutes are silent on the subject of time for mediation. (See e.g., Tex. Code Ann. 152.001 et seq.).

Since mediation is voluntary in the sense that parties are free to settle or not settle, its continuation could be assumed to reflect the parties' judgment that negotiations continue to be productive. At the same time, the courts have a clear interest in managing their cases and in preventing delay. Balancing these interests, the Standards recommend that courts establish presumptive deadlines for the process, deadlines integrated into existing case management procedures and time frames, and give the parties themselves, rather than the mediator, the opportunity to request an extension. The court should freely grant such requests if the parties can show that continuation will be helpful in reaching resolution. Since good mediation takes time, courts should not be unduly restrictive in establishing deadlines.

5.0   MANDATORY ATTENDANCE

5.1   Mandatory attendance at an initial mediation session may be appropriate, but only when a mandate is more likely to serve the interests of parties (including those not represented by counsel), the justice system and the public than would voluntary attendance. Courts should impose mandatory attendance only when:

a.   the cost of mediation is publicly funded, consistent with Standard 13.0 on Funding;

b.   there is no inappropriate pressure to settle, in the form of reports to the trier of fact or financial disincentives to trial; and

c.   mediators or mediation programs of high quality (i) are easily accessible; (ii) permit party participation; (iii) permit lawyer participation when the parties wish it; and (iv) provide clear and complete information about the precise process and procedures that are being required.

COMMENTARY: Many courts, by statute, court rule or rule of procedure, refer parties to mediation on a mandatory basis. In using the term "mandatory attendance" the intention of the Standards is to clarify that by referring parties to mediation on a mandatory basis a court should require only that they attend an initial mediation session, discuss the case, and be educated about the process in order to make an informed choice about their continued participation. See Standard 11.0 on Inappropriate Pressure to Settle.

There are both benefits and costs to mandated attendance. Among the benefits are that rates of voluntary usage of mediation are often low, even though parties reach agreement more often than not, regardless of whether their initial participation was voluntary or mandatory. The increased mediation caseloads resulting from mandated attendance allow more cost-effective administration of mediation programs and services. Settlements through mediation also free court resources for other cases. Finally, mandated attendance may increase future voluntary use by educating parties and their lawyers about the process.

On the other hand, mandatory referral risks forcing cases into a process that for one reason or another may be inappropriate. It may engender institutionalized programs that offer an inferior quality of justice, or, at a minimum, a costly and unnecessary hurdle for parties who prefer or are likely to resolve their cases through other means.

In weighing these costs and benefits, the Standards adopted SPIDR's recommendation that the appropriateness of mandatory referral depends on its application:

> Mandatory dispute resolution could either improve or impede the administration of justice. This uncertainty counsels for careful consideration before a compulsory program is instituted and careful monitoring as it is administered. At a minimum, participation should be compulsory only when the three conditions articulated in this Standard regarding funding, coercion to settle, and quality, are met.

SPIDR Report, at 16. (See also Standard 13.0 on Funding of Programs and Compensation of Mediators and Standard 11.0 on Inappropriate Pressure to Settle.)

In most courts mandatory attendance at a mediation session generally requires participation by parties (and often their insurers) with settlement authorization. The Standards endorse this practice. (See Standard 10.0 on The Role of Lawyers in Mediation.) The Standards recognize, however, that in cases involving large private entities or government agencies it may not be feasible to have all the parties whose assent is necessary to a final agreement present at the mediation. In such cases an alternative to physical presence may be availability by telephone.

5.2   Courts may use a variety of mechanisms to select cases for mandatory referral to mediation. Any mechanism chosen should provide for: individual assessment of each case to determine its appropriateness for mediation, which takes into account the parties' relative knowledge, experience and resources.

COMMENTARY: Various mechanisms have been used in different jurisdictions to select cases for mandatory referral to mediation, including (1) mandating referral to mediation by category of case with opt-out provisions (for example, more than half the states now mandate mediation of child custody cases); (2) mandating referral to some kind of ADR process by category of case, with a method for case-by-case screening to determine what particular process is appropriate (D.C. Super. Ct. Mandatory Arbitration R. I-IV; (3) mandating referral to mediation where one or both parties request it; (4) mandating referral to mediation by judicial determination on a case-by-case basis (Texas Civ. Prac. & Rem. Code Ann. §154.021 (West Supp. 1992); and (5) mandating the referral of a case to mediation by a special master in a case found to present "extraordinary circumstances" under Rule 53 of the Federal Rules of Civil Procedure.

Courts should balance the advantages and disadvantages of each approach. For example, the Minnesota Task Force on Alternative Dispute Resolution recommends that parties be required to select an ADR process, subject to court approval or court selection if the parties cannot agree:

> Such participation [by the parties in selection of a particular ADR process] may lead to better cooperation and a more positive attitude toward participation in an ADR process, ultimately facilitating more efficient and less rancorous settlement of disputes . . . . Referral of a case to an ADR process is dependent upon many factors, most of which are unique to the controversy being considered. For example, the relationships of the parties and the attitude of the parties toward ADR must be considered. Successful ADR depends on case-by-case selectivity. Across-the-board mandatory ADR will ultimately undercut its efficiency and acceptance. Judges should examine the factors in each case before determining that referral to an ADR process is appropriate.

Minn. Report, 14-15.

A recent evaluation of a pilot program in Hennepin County, Minnesota, found that the outcome of the case and the satisfaction of litigants both were highly dependent on the participants' initial reluctance or enthusiasm to engage in mediation. W. Kobbervig, Office of the St. Ct. Admin., Mediation of Civil Cases in Hennepin County: An Evaluation (1991).

On the other hand, leaving selection of a particular ADR process to the parties risks creating the opportunity for unnecessary procedural skirmishing. Case-by-case selection of cases for initial referral to mediation also may increase costs and delay for both the parties and the courts. Even without such efficiency considerations, such a mechanism may also result in underutilization of the process, particularly where judges and parties are not fully educated about the procedure and its benefits.

In the absence of research concerning the relative effects of courts' use of different mechanisms for selecting cases for mandatory mediation, the Standards do not recommend any one mechanism over another. Whichever mechanism is chosen, it is important for the court to ensure that each case mandated to participate is assessed individually, either before or during the initial session, to determine whether it is appropriate for mediation.

There are a number of considerations that may make individual cases inappropriate for mediation. Among them are physical or psychological victimization that has impaired the ability of a party to protect his/her own interests or honor his/her agreements; real inequality of knowledge or sophistication between the parties that cannot be balanced in the mediation; and significant resistance to settlement on the part of one or both parties. Proceeding with mediation under such circumstances is likely to be unproductive or harmful. Often these kinds of circumstances can be discovered only once the process has begun. Thus these Standards underscore the importance of viewing the first mediation session as an educational and screening process, with parties afforded the opportunity both then and later to opt out freely. Even if an individual case is determined to be appropriate for mediation and the parties choose to proceed, appropriateness should be assessed on a continuing basis to ensure that the process is terminated if circumstances come to light that warrant its discontinuation.

5.3 **Any system of mandatory referral to mediation should be evaluated on a periodic basis, through surveys of parties and through other mechanisms, in order to correct deficiencies in the particular implementation mechanism selected and to determine whether the mandate is more likely to serve the interests of parties, the justice system and the public than would voluntary referral.**

COMMENTARY: As SPIDR has stated:

> During the early period of a mandatory program, it is especially important that data be collected to determine whether it is meeting the goals set by planners. As part of this process, it is important to examine the effect of the program on such matters as the parties' costs, interest, and satisfaction as well as the effect on court resources. During early stages, data should be gathered to determine whether a substantial number of the participants believe that mandated participation has been so burdensome for them to pursue a trial or so injurious to other interests that, in their view, the costs of the mandate outweigh the benefits.

SPIDR Report, at 23.

Surveys of parties should be made part of the evaluation to ensure that it addresses qualitative as well as quantitative measures. (See also Standard 16.0 on Evaluation.) Evaluation data should be monitored carefully and used on an ongoing basis to correct any deficiencies identified in selection mechanisms.

6.0   QUALIFICATIONS OF MEDIATORS

6.1   **Courts have a continuing responsibility to ensure the quality of the mediators to whom they refer cases. Qualifications of mediators to whom the courts refer cases should be based on their skills. Different categories of cases may require different types and levels of skills. Skills can be acquired through training and/or experience. No particular academic degree should be considered a prerequisite for service as a mediator in cases referred by the court.**

COMMENTARY: In the most comprehensive effort to date to examine the subject of qualifications for mediators and arbitrators in both court-connected and independent programs and services, the Commission on Qualifications of the Society of Professionals in Dispute Resolution (SPIDR) states:

> The most commonly discussed purposes of setting criteria for individuals to practice as neutrals are: 1) to protect the consumer and 2) to protect the integrity of various dispute resolution processes. Concerns also have been raised, particularly about mandatory standards or certification, including 1) creating inappropriate barriers to entry into the field, 2) hampering the innovative quality of the profession, and 3) limiting the broad dissemination of peace-making skills in society.

Qualifying Neutrals: The Basic Principles (1989) (hereafter "SPIDR Commission").

Courts have a continuing responsibility to ensure the quality of the mediators to whom they refer cases. At the same time, courts should not set up barriers that inappropriately exclude competent mediators and should encourage diversity among service providers, including gender, racial and ethnic diversity.

Mediation requires a particular set of skills, knowledge and personal qualities. A variety of lists of mediator skills have been developed, such as those developed by the SPIDR Commission on Qualifications, the New Jersey Symposium on Critical Issues in Alternative Dispute Resolution, and individual mediation programs. The following list developed by SPIDR should be considered by courts and applied depending upon the type of case involved:

    a.   Skills necessary for competent performance as a neutral include:
        (1)   General
            (a)   Ability to listen actively;
            (b)   Ability to analyze problems, identify and separate the issues involved, and frame these issues for resolution or decision making;

	(c)	Ability to use clear, neutral language...;
	(d)	Sensitivity to strongly felt values of the disputants, including gender, ethnic, and cultural differences;
	(e)	Ability to deal with complex factual materials;
	(f)	Presence and persistence, i.e., an overt commitment to honesty, dignified behavior, respect for the parties, and an ability to create and maintain control of a diverse group of disputants;
	(g)	Ability to identify and to separate the neutral's personal values from issues under consideration; and
	(h)	Ability to understand power imbalances.
(2)	For mediation	
	(a)	Ability to understand the negotiating process and the role of advocacy;
	(b)	Ability to earn trust and maintain acceptability;
	(c)	Ability to convert parties' positions into needs and interests;
	(d)	Ability to screen out non-mediable issues;
	(e)	Ability to help parties to invent creative options;
	(f)	ability to help the parties identify principles and criteria that will guide their decision making;
	(g)	Ability to help parties assess their non-settlement alternatives;
	(h)	Ability to help parties make their own informed choices; and
	(i)	Ability to help parties assess whether their agreement can be implemented.

b. Knowledge of the particular dispute resolution process being used includes:

(1) Familiarity with existing standards of practice covering the dispute resolution process; and

(2) Familiarity with commonly encountered ethical dilemmas.

c. Knowledge of the range of available dispute resolution processes, so that, where appropriate, cases can be referred to a more suitable process;

d. Knowledge of the institutional context in which the dispute arose and will be settled;

e. In mediation, knowledge of the process that will be used to resolve the dispute if no agreement is reached, such as judicial or administrative adjudication or arbitration;

f. Where parties' legal rights and remedies are involved, awareness of the legal standards that would be applicable if the case were taken to a court or other legal forum; and

g. Adherence to ethical standards.

SPIDR Commission, *supra* at 20.

While many jurisdictions require their mediators to have a particular educational background or professional standing, no degree ensures competent performance. In fact, competence has been found in individuals with very different backgrounds and experiences, suggesting that performance may be attributable to personal characteristics rather than to education, profession, age or other criteria. While in some cases, such as complex civil cases, legal or other knowledge or experience related to the subject matter of the case may be appropriate, parties should be free in most circumstances to select a mediator of their choice. (*See* Standard 7.0 on Selection of Mediators).

Qualifications, rather, should be based on skills which may be acquired through training, experience, and skills-based education. These are the only criteria that have been correlated with successful mediation. *See, e.g.,* J. Pearson, N. Thoennes, and L. Vanderkoi, "Mediation of Child Custody Disputes," *Colorado Lawyer* Vol. 2, No. 2 (February, 1982) at 335. The amount of training and experience required for mediators handling divorce and child custody cases are typically higher, for example, than those for mediators handling cases in court-sponsored settlement weeks. A report to the National College of Juvenile and Family Law suggests that mediators in family and juvenile courts must have not only the necessary process skills but also an understanding of juvenile and family law and the concepts of child development. *Court Approved Alternative Dispute Resolution: A Better Way to Resolve Minor Delinquency, Status Office and Abuse/Neglect Cases,* Report by the Key Issues Curriculum Enhancement Project Faculty Consortium of the National College of Juvenile and Family Law 65-66 (1989).

The Standards make no recommendations with respect to the number of hours of training or experience that should be required. The amount of training and experience will vary depending upon the type of case being mediated.

6.2   Courts need not certify training programs but should ensure that the training received by the mediators to whom they refer cases includes role-playing with feedback.

COMMENTARY: While the Standards make no recommendations with respect to the numbers of hours of training that should be required, they do call for courts to ensure that the training received by the mediators to whom they refer cases includes role-playing with individualized feedback. While training, by itself, does not guarantee competence, experiential programs that allow participants to engage in simulations and receive individual observation and feedback are most likely to advance quality performance.

A number of jurisdictions require that mediators handling court-referred cases participate in a training program certified by the Court. (*See e.g.,* Florida Supreme Court Rules Governing Qualifications of Mediators and Arbitrators, September 23, 1988.) The Standards do not discourage, but do not require this practice.

6.3   Courts are responsible for determining that the mediators to whom they refer cases are qualified. The level of screening needed to determine

qualifications will vary depending upon the type of case involved.

COMMENTARY: Assuring that court-connected mediation programs and services are of high quality is of special concern when parties are mandated to participate. Even when courts refer parties to mediation on a voluntary basis, if the referral is specifically to court staff providing mediation services, to a particular program, or to a roster maintained by the court, such a referral carries the court's imprimatur. Thus the court should ensure that the mediators to whom such referrals are made, whether they are on the court's staff, employed by a program or on a roster, are qualified.

Courts presently have various methods to screen for qualifications. Some ask applicants to fill out questionnaires or submit curriculum vitae and paper-screen applicants. Others go one step further to conduct individual interviews. Sometimes courts rely on outside organization to certify mediators. Mentoring programs also can be required. See, e.g., Fla. R. Civ. Pro. 1.760. Performance-based testing has been advocated by several groups, including SPIDR's Commission on Qualifications, and has been used successfully by several court-connected mediation programs. (See, e.g., B. Honoroff, D. Matz and D. O'Connor, "Putting Mediation Skills to the Test," Negotiation Journal 37 (1990).

The level of screening needed will depend upon the type of case involved. For example, a higher level of screening will be required for domestic relations mediators than for those participating in court-sponsored settlement weeks.

6.4   Courts should orient qualified mediators to court procedures.

COMMENTARY: In addition to being trained in mediation skills and techniques, mediators to whom the court refers cases should be required to attend an orientation on court procedures. To be effective, mediators need to know the institutional context of the cases they are handling, including how the case was processed by the court before mediation, how it will be processed afterwards, and any time deadlines and reporting mechanisms that are in place. Mediators handling court-referred cases should also be informed routinely of any changes in court procedure. Dissemination of this information will ensure smooth functioning of court-connected mediation programs.

6.5   Courts should continue to monitor the performance of mediators to whom they refer cases and ensure that their performance is of consistently high quality.

COMMENTARY: It is not enough for courts to make an initial determination that the mediators to whom they refer cases are qualified. Monitoring their performance may be equal in importance to the initial selection process. It can ensure, for example, that programs once offering a collaborative problem-solving process do not degenerate into case status conferencing procedures. The quality of mediators' performance should be monitored by the courts on a continuing basis.

There are a number of mechanisms that have been used to monitor the quality of mediators' performance, and courts should consider using them in combination. Peer review and supervisor observation are valuable, as are client surveys, feedback from the judges who referred cases, and outcome data. The latter should be used with extreme caution, since success in helping parties reach agreement is not the only measure of mediators' competence.

Courts also should ensure that the mediators to whom they refer cases continue to improve their skills on an ongoing basis through additional training, study and practice. While continuing education by itself does not guarantee quality performance, it is a way in which mediators can maintain and enhance their skills and should be encouraged by the court. A number of jurisdictions require continuing education. See, e.g., Fla. Rules for Certified and Court-Appointed Mediators 10.010-10.290. Courts also should ensure that the mediators to whom they refer cases are updated continually on changes in court rules and procedures and on their ethical responsibilities.

6.6 Courts should adopt procedures for removing from their roster of mediators those mediators who do not meet their performance expectations and/or ensuring that they do not receive further court referrals.

COMMENTARY: Ongoing monitoring of mediator quality and removal of mediators who do not meet the court's performance expectations from the court's roster are the most critical components of any system that seeks to ensure mediator competence. Substandard mediator performance can be addressed in a variety of supportive ways. Courts can require that mediators who do not meet their performance expectations undergo additional training, supervision, and/or co-mediate with an experienced mediator for a designated period of time. Ultimately, however, courts also need to institute procedures to ensure that mediators who, even with additional help, are not performing at expected competence levels do not receive further referrals of cases from the court. Since the court cannot refer mediators to independent licensing or certification organizations, they should consider providing notice of removal and an opportunity to be heard. As an alternative to a formalized hearing process for removal, courts can review and reappoint panels of mediators or renew arrangements with mediation programs on an annual or other periodic basis.

7.0   SELECTION OF MEDIATORS

7.1 To enhance party satisfaction and investment in the process of mediation, courts should maximize parties' choice of mediator, unless there are reasons why party choice may not be appropriate. Such reasons might include:
    a.   there is significant inequality in the knowledge or experience of the parties.
    b.   the court has a particular public policy it is trying to achieve through mediation, which requires selection of a particular mediator or group of mediators.
    c.   party choice would cause significant and undesirable delay.

COMMENTARY: There are a number of mechanisms that have been used to select one or more mediators for a particular case:

1.   The parties agree on an individual and submit the name to the court. Their choice may be limited to a panel of mediators considered qualified by the court.

2.   The judge selects the mediator, subject to the parties' objections.

3.   The judge or court staff asks each party to submit a list of acceptable mediators. Court staff contact any individual who appears on both lists. If the lists do not contain a common name, the court gives the parties the opportunity to strike names for cause, then randomly chooses from those that remain.

4.   The judge or court staff provides the parties with a list of mediators. Each party may strike names for cause and the court then randomly chooses from those that remain.

5.   Court staff select the mediators, without input from the parties or the judge, based on the mediators' availability, rotation, or particular expertise.

Several policies favor maximizing the parties' role in selection of mediators. First, party choice may increase the parties' satisfaction with the process. Second, party choice may be the most effective way of ensuring the quality of mediators. Third, giving parties, as opposed to judges, the choice of mediators is a way of guarding against judicial favoritism in making referrals.

Several other policies argue against party choice. First, judges or program administrators may be better informed than the parties about mediators' qualifications. Second, it may be faster and more convenient for court personnel to choose the mediators. Third, if there is significant inequality in the knowledge or experience of the parties, the inequality may be exacerbated by leaving the selection of the mediator in the parties' hands. Fourth, court selection may give the process greater dignity and legitimacy, especially where the parties are unsophisticated or unrepresented and the mediator is a party's only contact with the court. Fifth, at least in cases of particular public significance, the court and public at large may have a stake in the choice of mediator.

Except in certain specified circumstances, the Standards endorse maximizing the parties' choice in order to enhance party satisfaction and investment in the process of mediation. Maximizing party choice includes allowing the parties to choose a mediator from among the court staff providing mediation services, among mediators available through a program to which the court refers cases, or among the names on a roster maintained by the court or to reject a mediator chosen by the court if the parties cannot agree. It also includes permitting parties to choose their own mediator as an alternative to mediators on the court's staff, in a program or on a roster.

While there may be risks to allowing parties to choose their own mediator as an alternative to a mediator who has been found qualified by the court, the advantages outweigh the disadvantages in most circumstances. Among the risks are the likelihood that indigent parties, and lower income parties for whom transaction costs already are high, will not have the same opportunity to select their own private mediator as higher income parties, resulting in the possibility of a two-tiered system of justice. In addition, if a significant number of higher-income parties opt out of the public system to employ private mediators, pressure on the public system to maintain a high level of quality could diminish and thus the quality of the public system might suffer.

On the other hand, allowing parties to choose their own alternative will lead to a more cooperative, positive attitude toward participation in mediation. When parties can choose mediators who they believe are best suited to handle their cases, particularly complex cases, they are likely to be more satisfied with the process. On balance, then, except in the following specific circumstances, the Standards favor permitting parties to choose their own mediator as an alternative to mediators on the court's staff, in a program, or on a roster.

The Standards recognize that there may be certain specific circumstances in which it is appropriate for courts to limit parties' choice of mediator. If parties have significantly unequal knowledge or experience, the court may need to step in to protect the disadvantages party by ensuring that choice is made from among mediators found to be qualified by the court.

Party choice also may need to be limited in situations where the court has a particular policy it is trying to achieve through mediation. For example, in domestic relations cases, the state has a significant interest in protecting the best interests of the child. In jurisdictions where thorough judicial review of mediated agreements cannot be ensured, the court may determine that parties should choose a mediator found to be qualified by the court. In addition, there may be cases or classes of cases in which the court is likely to have continuing involvement, such as suits against public institutions, and thus its concerns about the nature of the outcome of mediation would legitimize some limitation on party choice of a mediator.

Finally, the court may find that permitting parties to choose their own mediator would cause unacceptable delay in the proceedings, as in high volume, low stakes categories of cases, such as small claims, or in cases where the party-chosen mediator is unavailable for a period of time. Court assignment of a mediator, or assignment of mediator by the program to which the court refers cases, may serve court efficiency as well as party interests in small cases. Regardless of the type of case, the unavailability of a mediator chosen by the parties also may interfere with the court's needs to manage its docket. In this circumstance as well, limitation on party choice of mediator may be appropriate.

7.2 **When a court determines that it should refer the parties to a private mediator who will receive a fee, the court should permit the parties to choose from among a number of providers.**

COMMENTARY: Only under unusual circumstances should the courts require the use of a specific individual mediator when that mediator will receive a fee for services. Rule 53 of the Federal Rules of Civil Procedure and comparable state rules recognize that there are exceptional circumstances, particularly in complex cases, where either public policy or the needs of the court justify a judge's designating a particular individual to serve as special master and requiring that the master be paid by the parties. Even in these circumstances, however, many judges solicit the parties' views before making the appointment.

As the Society of Professionals in Dispute Resolution has stated:

> When the third party will receive a substantial fee,
> either from the court or from the parties who are

mandated to use the process, referral should not
be made to a particular individual except in
unusual circumstances. Instead, the parties
typically should be permitted to choose from a
panel of qualified persons and should be told the
qualifications of the panel members.

SPIDR Report, at 17.

Courts should avoid either the appearance or reality of "featherbedding" or
"cronyism." There is also a potential for perceived judicial abuse in that requiring the use
of a specific individual mediator may be seen as giving the judge control over the
mediator. Thus the Standards oppose this practice.

8.0   ETHICAL STANDARDS FOR MEDIATORS

**8.1   Courts should adopt a code of ethical standards for mediators, together
with procedures to handle violations of the code.**

**Any set of standards should include provisions that address the following
concerns:**
a.   Impartiality
b.   Conflict of Interest
c.   Advertising by Mediators
d.   Disclosure of Fees
e.   Confidentiality
f.   Role of Mediators in Settlement

COMMENTARY: In creating a code of ethics, courts should consider the dual
purposes of such a code: the promotion of honesty, integrity and impartiality in
mediation, and the effective operation of a mediation program. Confidentiality, for
instance, serves not only to protect the parties, but to build the parties' confidence in the
effectiveness of the system. A demonstration of bias by a mediator is not only unethical;
it can destroy the necessary foundation of good faith upon which mediation is built.

Each court should consider existing standards when drafting its code. Several
court mediation programs, the Association of Family and Conciliation Courts and the
American Bar Association's Family Law Section, have formulated standards of practice
for mediators. In addition, two national associations for professional mediators, the
Society for Professionals in Dispute Resolution ["SPIDR"] and the Academy of Family
Mediators ["AFM"], have developed standards or codes of ethics for their members. See
Program on Alter. Disp. Resol., Standards for Private and Public Mediators in the State of
Hawaii, (1986) ["Haw. Stds."]; Florida Standards of Professional Conduct for Certified
and Court-Appointed Mediators, (1991) ["Fla. Stds."]; Dispute Mediation Serv. of Dallas,
Inc., Code of Ethics for Staff and Mediators, (1986) ["Dal. Stds."]; Family Ct. Servs.,
Superior Ct. of Cal., Standards of Conduct Working Paper (1991) ["Cal. Stds."]; State
Bar of Texas Alternative Dispute Resolution Committee, Ethical Guidelines and

Standards of Practice for Impartial Third Parties in the State of Texas, Proposed, (1992) ["Texas Stds."]; SPIDR, Ethical Standards of Professional Responsibility (1991) ["SPIDR Stds."]; Academy of Fam. Mediators, Standards of Practice For Family and Divorce Mediation ["AFM Stds."]; Association of Fam. and Conciliation Cts., Model Standards of Practice for Family and Divorce Mediation, (1984) ["AFCC Stds."]; A.B.A., Standards of Practice for Lawyer Mediators in Family Disputes, (1984) ["ABA Stds."].

Most ethical standards for mediators are not described as "rules," but as "guides to reasonable behavior." See AFM Stds., Fla. Stds., Dal. Stds., Haw. Stds. These Standards take the position that this distinction is misplaced. Whether ethical standards are "rules" or "guides" is irrelevant if mediators who do not follow a standard are considered to have behaved unethically. If mediators' behavior differs from the standard, the implication is that it is "unreasonable," and "unreasonable" is equated with "unethical." T. Bishop, Standards for Family and Divorce Mediation, Disp. Resol. F., Dec. 1984, at 4. SPIDR responded to this distinction by setting a stricter standard of compliance with its ethical standards than "guides to reasonable behavior," stating that "adherence to these ethical standards by...SPIDR members and associates is basic to professional responsibility." SPIDR Stds. A better response may be to eliminate the distinction between "rules" and "guides" altogether.

The Advisory Board has reviewed a number of codes of ethics adopted by courts and associations throughout the country. Its recommendations on the subject may provide valuable guidance in designing ethical standards for mediation programs.

a.   **Impartiality**
        The mediator should maintain impartiality toward all parties.
        Impartiality means freedom from favoritism or bias either by
        appearance, word or by action, and a commitment to serve all
        parties as opposed to a single party.

Impartiality is at the heart of mediators' ethical responsibilities. SPIDR defines impartiality as freedom from favoritism or bias either by appearance, word or by action, and a commitment to serve all parties as opposed to a single party. SPIDR Stds.

The Hawaii, Florida, and AFCC Standards mirror this language. Hawaii and Florida define impartiality by adding freedom from bias in "appearance," in addition to "word" and "action." Haw. Stds., at §III(1); Fla. Stds., at §V(A); AFCC Stds., at 7-9. The Florida Standards require mediators to disclose "any circumstances bearing on possible bias, prejudice, or impartiality." Fla. Stds., at §V(A)(1).

Most standards contain language prohibiting the exchange of gifts or information that could bias mediators. For example, Florida forbids mediators from "accepting or giving a gift, request, favor, loan or any other item of value to or from a party, attorney, or any other person involved in any pending or scheduled mediation process." Fla. Stds., at §V(A)(3). This prohibition does not apply to mediators' fees, which are allowed and covered under a separate section. Id., at §VIII.

The broadly phrased "anything of value" could be construed to include any information which mediators could use for personal gain. The Dallas and Hawaii Standards address this possibility directly. The Dallas Standards state, "The mediator shall not collude with one party for personal or corporate gain." Dal. Stds., at §II(A)(5).

The Hawaii Standards expand upon this concept:

> Mediators shall not use information disclosed
> during the mediation process for private gain or
> advantage nor shall a mediator seek publicity
> from a mediation effort to enhance his or her
> position.

Haw. Stds., at §XI(2).

Mediators should not practice, condone, facilitate or collaborate with any form of discrimination on the basis of race, religion, national origin, marital status, political belief, mental or physical handicap, gender or sexual preference. Dal. Stds., at II.B. California adds that mediators should be aware of cultural differences and how they may affect parties' values and style of negotiating to avoid stereotypical attitudes toward parties in mediation. Cal. Stds., at 7.

Most standards recommend withdrawal by mediators who cannot maintain the requisite impartiality in a mediation.

b.   Conflict of Interest

The mediator should refrain from entering or continuing in any dispute if he or she perceives that participation as a mediator would be a clear conflict of interest. The mediator also should disclose any circumstances that may create or give the appearance of a conflict of interest and any circumstances that may raise a question as to the mediator's impartiality.

The duty to disclose is a continuing obligation throughout the process. In addition, if a mediator has represented either party in any capacity, the mediator should disclose that representation.

After the mediator discloses the prior representation, the parties may choose to continue with the mediator.

A mediator should disclose any known, significant current or past personal or professional relationship with any party or attorney involved in the mediation and the mediator and parties should discuss on a case-by-case basis whether to continue.

Conflicts of interest can arise due to both prior and future relationships between mediators and parties. These relationships may be professional or personal. Existing codes advocate three responses to conflicts of interest: abstention, withdrawal, and disclosure. The AFCC Standards is illustrative:

The mediator shall not proceed if previous legal or counseling services have been provided to one of the participants. If such services have been provided to both participants, mediation shall not proceed unless the prior relationship has been discussed, the role of the mediator made distinct from the earlier relationship and the participants have been given the opportunity to freely choose to proceed... The mediator should be aware that post-mediation professional or social relationships may compromise the mediator's continued availability as a neutral third party.

AFCC Stds., at II.B.1-2. See also SPIDR Stds., at §4.

The ABA Standards take a stronger position against attorneys acting as mediators for former clients:

The mediator shall not represent either party during or after the mediation process in any legal matters. In the event the mediator has represented one of the parties beforehand, the mediator shall not undertake the mediation.

ABA Stds., at III.A.

When disclosure is required, it is generally a continuing obligation:

A mediator must disclose any current or past representation or consulting relationship with any party or attorney involved in the mediation. Disclosure must also be made of any pertinent pecuniary interest. All such disclosures shall be made as soon as practical after the mediator becomes aware of the interest or the relationship.

Fla. Stds., at §V(B)(1). See also AFCC Stds., at II.3; SPIDR Stds., at §4 ("The duty to disclose is a continuing obligation throughout the process.")

The comment to the Florida Standards lists some subjects for disclosure, including membership on a board of directors, work as an advocate or representative, consulting for a fee, stock ownership (other than mutual fund or trust arrangements), previous business contact or other managerial, financial, or immediate family interest in a party. Comment to Fla. Stds. §V(B)(1). In addition to disclosure to the parties, the Florida Standards require disclosure to the court. Fla. Stds., at §V(B)(2).

Perceived conflicts sometimes warrant disclosure. Hawaii requires disclosure to the parties of any "prior relationships that might be perceived as a conflict of interest," and prohibits mediators from continuing the mediation

> unless (a) such prior relationships have been discussed; (b) the role of the mediator has been made distinct from earlier relationships; and (c) all of the parties freely choose to proceed.

Haw. Stds., at §III(2).

Both the Dallas and Florida Standards provide that a mediator should withdraw if he or she "believes or perceives that there is a clear conflict of interest...irrespective of the expressed desire of the parties." Fla. Stds., at §V(B)(3); Dal. Stds., at §II(9)(C).

c.   **Advertising by Mediators**
A mediator should not make exaggerated claims about the mediation process, its costs and benefits, its outcome or the mediator's qualifications.

No current ethical standards prohibit advertising by mediators. The SPIDR Standards suggests that advertising is not permissible "in some conflict resolution disciplines, such as labor arbitration" but does not indicate why advertising is acceptable for mediation and not labor arbitration. SPIDR Stds.

SPIDR, Florida, Hawaii, and the AFCC require that any statements about mediation services be honest and accurate. SPIDR Stds.; Fla. Stds., at §XI(B); Haw. Stds., at §X(3); AFCC Stds., IV 1984. For example, the Hawaii Standards state that "A mediator shall only make accurate statements about the mediation process, its costs and benefits, and the mediator's qualifications." Haw. Stds., at §X(3). Similarly, the SPIDR Standards require that "No claims of specific results or promises which imply favor of one side over another for the purpose of obtaining business should be made." SPIDR Stds., at §6. The Florida Standards caution against using the mediation process to incur future business. Fla. Stds., at §XI(A).

d.   **Disclosure of Fees**

Where costs and fees are funded by the parties, the mediator should enter into a written agreement with the parties that includes costs, fees, and time and manner of payment before beginning the mediation.

No commissions, rebates or other similar forms of remuneration should be given or received by a neutral for the referral of clients. Fees should not be based on the outcome of the dispute.

Ethical standards generally require disclosure of fees before services are rendered and prohibit fees based upon the outcome of the dispute.

SPIDR requires that mediators explain to the parties at the outset "the bases of compensation, fees, and charges, if any." SPIDR Stds. The Florida Standards require written disclosure of fees and costs, "including time and manner of payment," and Hawaii requires a written agreement with the parties before commencing the process. Fla. Stds., at §VII(A); Haw. Stds., at §IV(1).

SPIDR and Florida prohibit the acceptance of commissions or fees for the referral of mediation clients. SPIDR Stds.; Fla. Stds., at §VII(C). The SPIDR Standards state:

> No commissions, rebates, or other similar forms
> of remuneration should be given or received by a
> neutral for the referral of clients.

SPIDR Stds.

Hawaii and Florida prohibit basing fees on the outcome of the dispute. Haw. Stds., at §IV(2); Fla. Stds., at §VII(D).

e.   Confidentiality
In the absence of a statute to the contrary, the mediator should treat information revealed in a mediation as confidential, except for the following:
(1)   Information that is statutorily mandated to be reported.
(2)   Information that, in the judgment of the mediator, reveals a danger of serious physical harm either to a party or to a third person.
(3)   Information that the mediator informs the parties will not be protected.
The mediator should inform the parties at the initial meeting of any limitations on confidentiality.

Ethical standards require strict compliance with the promise of confidentiality as an integral element of the mediation process. According to SPIDR:

> Maintaining confidentiality is critical to the
> dispute resolution process. Confidentiality
> encourages candor, a full exploration of issues,
> and a neutral's acceptability. There may be some
> types of cases, however, in which confidentiality
> of the proceedings cannot necessarily be main-
> tained. Except in such instance, the neutral must
> resist all attempts to cause him or her to reveal
> any information outside the process. A
> commitment by the neutral to hold information in

confidence within the process also must be
honored.

SPIDR Stds., at §3.

There may be instances in which confidentiality is in conflict with other mediator
responsibilities. For example, mediators may learn of child abuse and be mandated by
statute to report it despite a general pledge of confidentiality. Similarly, lawyers who
mediate may feel obliged to report the unethical conduct of an attorney in the mediation
to a court or bar association.

In In Re: Waller, the District of Columbia Court of Appeals approved a
decision of the Board of Professional Responsibility, which held that the confidentiality
requirement of a trial court's civil mediation order was not intended to preclude a
disclosure by the mediator to the judge of a possible conflict of interest by one of the
attorneys. In Re: Waller, 573 A.2d 780 (D.C.App. 1990). The court may have been
swayed by the mediator's belief that his disclosure was consistent with the confidentiality
provision because "it was a matter that had nothing to do with the negotiations between
the parties but might affect the administration of justice in the Superior Court." Id., at
781.

The Dallas Standards include an exception to confidentiality when, in the
judgment of the mediator, there is a physical threat to a party or evidence of child abuse
(Dal. Stds., at §II(A)(7)-(8)), or there is evidence of unethical conduct by another
mediator. Id., at §IV.A.(1)-(2).

What is important is that the parties understand at the outset what is and is not
confidential. The AFCC Standards require mediators to explain to the parties all
exceptions to the promise of confidentiality:

> The mediator shall inform the parties at the initial
> meeting of limitations on confidentiality such as
> statutorily or judicially mandated reporting. The
> mediator shall inform the parties of circumstances
> under which mediators may be compelled to
> testify in court...The mediator shall discuss with
> the participants the potential consequences of
> their disclosure of facts to each other during the
> mediation process.

AFCC Stds., at IV.A.1-3.

Standards concerning confidentiality often include provisions protecting
records and other written information. As with verbal communications, parties can agree
to release written materials in certain circumstances. The Florida Standards provide:

> [Mediators] shall preserve and maintain the
> confidentiality of all mediation proceedings to the
> full extent required by law. [They] shall keep

confidential from opposing parties any
information obtained in individual caucuses
unless the party to the caucus permits disclosure.
[They] shall maintain confidentiality in the
storage and disposal of records and shall render
anonymous all identifying information when
materials are used for research, training or
statistical compilations.

Fla. Stds., at §VI(A)-(C).

Mediators should not be held to a standard that precludes participation in program evaluation and research. See Standard 9.0 on Confidentiality.

f.   Role of Mediators in Settlement
The mediator has the responsibility to see that the parties
consider the terms of the settlement and be sensitive to
inappropriate pressures to settle. In adhering to this standard,
the mediator may find it advisable to educate the parties or to
refer one or more parties for specialized advice.

By definition, mediation is a process in which decisions are made by the parties, not by mediators. Mediators, unlike the parties, have no stake in the outcome. However, they serve the parties and the process well when they educate the parties about the possible consequences of a proposed agreement, and are alert to whether continuation of the process would harm one or more of the participants. A history of violence between the parties, for example, raises the possibility of future problems if agreements require direct contact between the parties. Mediators cannot be expected to be able to foresee all possibilities of future problems, however. The primary responsibility is with the court at intake to ensure that appropriate cases go to mediation. In addition, courts have the responsibility to train mediators to be alert to possible dangers to the parties and to develop techniques for handling difficult cases. See Standard 11.0 on Inappropriate Pressure to Settle.

The primary responsibility for the resolution of a
dispute rests with the parties. The mediator's
obligation is to assist the disputants in reaching an
informed and voluntary settlement. At no time
and in no way shall a mediator coerce any party
into agreements or make substantive decisions for
any party. Mediators may make suggestions and
may draft proposals for the parties' consideration,
but all decisions are to be made voluntarily by the
parties themselves.

Haw. Stds., at §I(1).

A mediator shall inform the participants of their
right to withdraw from mediation at any time and
for any reason. If a mediator believes the
participants are unable to participate meaningfully
in the process or that a reasonable agreement is
unlikely, a mediator may suspend or terminate
mediation and encourage the parties to seek other
forms of assistance for the resolution of their
dispute. If participants reach a final impasse, a
mediator should not prolong unproductive
discussions that would result in emotional and or
monetary costs to the participants.

Id., at §X(2).

Both SPIDR and the ABA require mediators to terminate the mediation if they
believe that either continuation of the process or agreements proposed will be harmful to
the parties.

[Mediators] must be satisfied that agreements in
which [they have] participated will not impugn the
integrity of the process.

SPIDR Stds., at §6.

When the interests of parties not participating will be affected by the
mediation, some standards require mediators to consider those interests. This concern
applies especially to children in family and divorce mediations. Although some standards
make a general statement on this issue, Hawaii's standard includes a clause requiring the
mediator to withdraw if he or she believes those interests are not being served:

A mediator has a responsibility to promote
consideration of the interests of persons affected
by actual or potential agreements and not present
or represented at the bargaining table. Minimally,
a mediator has a duty to raise the possibility of
including additional representation in the
mediation. Where a mediator believes the best
interests of an absent party are not being served
and where the parties themselves refuse to
consider inclusive participation, a mediator is
encouraged to withdraw his or her services.

Haw. Stds., at §VI(2).

9.0   CONFIDENTIALITY

9.1   **Courts should have clear written policies relating to the confidentiality of both written and oral communications in mediation consistent with the laws of the jurisdiction. Among the issues such a policy should address specifically are:**
   a.   **the mediators and cases protected by confidentiality;**
   b.   **the extent of the protection;**
   c.   **who may assert or waive the protection; and**
   d.   **exceptions to the protection.**

COMMENTARY: The Standards do not prescribe any particular set of policies relating to confidentiality in mediation but rather call for courts to develop their own written policies. These policies should be clear and address four specific areas: 1) the mediators and types of cases protected; 2) the extent of the protection; 3) who may assert or waive the protection; and 4) exceptions to the protection.

Courts should consider the policy considerations which favor confidentiality in mediation. Some relate to evidentiary use, some to public disclosure, and some to both. The one most frequently cited is that confidentiality is required for the process to be effective. The assurance of confidentiality encourages parties to be candid and to participate fully in the process. A mediator's ability to draw out the parties' underlying interests and concerns may require discussion -- and sometimes admissions -- of facts that disputants would not otherwise concede. Further, because parties often speak in mediation without the expectation that they will later be bound in another forum by what they said, subsequent use of their communications also could be unfairly prejudicial, particularly when the parties' levels of sophistication are unequal. Confidentiality also helps ensure the mediator's continued neutrality, since a mediator's subsequent testimony at trial would inevitably favor one side or another and destroy his or her role as an "impartial broker." Finally, confidentiality in mediation may enhance the use of mediation and optimize the settlement potential of a case. Many parties are concerned about protecting private information, such as trademarks and trade secrets which are often difficult to protect in a court proceeding.

Confidentiality has both societal and evidentiary costs. When the government is a party to a dispute, confidentiality may frustrate accountability to the public and/or public access to the decision-making process. Confidentiality may also prejudice the interests of affected parties who are not represented at the bargaining table, for example the interests of homeowners in proximity to a toxic waste site.

Protecting information revealed in mediation may prejudice the interests of third parties in dispute with one or both of the mediating parties, whose communications could reveal a claim or defense available to the third party. It also may screen information about the commission of past or future crimes, such as the threat of violence during mediation by a defendant later accused of murder, or the incidence of child abuse which, if revealed, could warrant state intervention.

Finally, closed proceedings and outcomes eliminate one check on the integrity and appearance of fairness of the proceedings. This lack of openness may be of concern, particularly when mediation is mandated by the court.

In weighing the benefits of confidentiality protections against the potential costs of nondisclosure of information in order to determine their policies regarding confidentiality, courts should take care to preserve the integrity of the mediation process. At a minimum, policies regarding confidentiality in mediation should provide no less protection than policies regarding confidentiality in settlement conferences. It should be noted, however, that while court rules can protect confidentiality in many instances, they cannot create or modify the existing statutory law of privilege.

In developing their policies for confidentiality in mediation, courts may want to refer to settlement conference policies or to a model statute such as the one developed by the New Jersey Symposium on Critical Issues in Dispute Resolution to guide their deliberations. 1 Seton Hall Legis. J. 12, 72 (1988). Courts can also look to other current sources of protection of confidentiality in mediation, including Federal Rule of Evidence 408 and its state counterparts. Fed. R. Evid. 408. A number of states also have enacted statutes specifically protecting confidentiality in mediation. These statutes vary widely in terms of the nature and extent of the confidentiality protected. Some are very broad, and some cover only particular types of cases, programs or communications. See N. Rogers & C. McEwen, Mediation Law, Policy, Practice 95-146 (1989).

9.2   Courts should ensure that their policies relating to confidentiality in mediation are communicated to and understood by mediators to whom they refer cases.

COMMENTARY: It is important for mediators to whom the court refers cases to be knowledgeable about the law and the courts' policies relating to confidentiality in mediation. While the Standards require that such policies be in writing, written communication alone is likely to be insufficient. Mediators need to acquire the kind of full understanding that will enable them to convey the policies accurately to the parties and to act in accordance with them. Experience has shown, for example, that many mediators are unaware of the extent to which policies relating to confidentiality in mediation preclude the discussion of details of their cases with their colleagues.

Courts' policies relating to confidentiality in mediation should be covered thoroughly in training programs for mediators. In addition, courts have the responsibility to apprise mediators to whom they refer cases of any changes in their policies or in the way these policies can be applied.

9.3   Courts should develop clear written policies concerning the way in which confidentiality protections and limitations are communicated to parties they refer to mediation.

COMMENTARY: Parties in mediation need to understand clearly whether statements they may make in mediation or information they may disclose in connection with the mediation process will remain confidential and under what circumstances disclosure by the mediator or other parties may be permitted or required. Communicating this information accurately to parties can be extremely difficult, particularly given the complexity of confidentiality policies and the fact that they are subject to interpretive changes. Even if mediators themselves understand the complexities, they often are faced with the dilemma of overwhelming the parties in their explanation of legal niceties or misleading them in an effort to be succinct.

Given these dangers, courts should develop policies concerning the way in which confidentiality protections and limitations on the protections are communicated to parties they refer to mediation. Such policies should be clear and in writing to ensure that they are implemented appropriately.

9.4   Mediators should not make recommendations regarding the substance or recommended outcome of a case to the court.

COMMENTARY: Communications between courts and mediators relating to the substance or recommended outcome of cases destroy confidentiality and impugn the integrity of the process either by discouraging open communication or allowing mediators to use information revealed in confidence against a party's interest. See Standard 12.0 on Communications between Mediators and the Court.

9.5   Policies relating to confidentiality should not be construed to prohibit or limit effective monitoring, research or program evaluation.

COMMENTARY: Courts are responsible for ensuring the quality of the programs to which they refer cases, and they need adequate information to allow them to fulfill this responsibility. Policies on confidentiality should accommodate this need. See Standards 2.0 on Courts' Responsibility for Mediation Programs and 16.0 on Evaluation.

Effective research, monitoring or program evaluation may require not only collection of aggregate statistics, but also access to individual case files and/or observation of actual mediation sessions as well as interviews with parties, mediators and mediation program personnel. Courts must balance the need for this kind of data with the need to protect confidentiality.

There are a number of ways to effect such an accommodation. Data can be made available only to officially sanctioned research and evaluation efforts. The researchers and evaluators themselves can be bound by courts' confidentiality policies. Protocols can be developed to ensure, for example, that names are replaced by numbers and that specific identifying data are altered to protect individual parties. Procedures can be devised to provide that mediation sessions are observed only with the parties' permission.

Given the availability of such protocols and procedures and courts' need for data to fulfill its responsibility for ensuring quality, provision of information for the purposes of program monitoring, evaluation and research should not be construed as violating policies relating to confidentiality in mediation.

10.0   THE ROLE OF LAWYERS IN MEDIATION

10.1   Courts should encourage attorneys to advise their clients on the advantages, disadvantages, and strategies for using mediation.

COMMENTARY: Lawyers have several possible functions to perform in connection with their clients' participation in mediation:

1.   Before their clients decide whether to mediate, lawyers may give initial advice concerning whether it is in the clients' best interest to participate in mediation and what substantive rights will govern if the case goes to trial.

2.   Lawyers may attend mediation sessions and participate directly in mediation. Alternatively, they may participate indirectly by advising clients before, during, or after mediation sessions.

3.   Lawyers may review draft agreements reached in mediation or, alternatively, they may draft the agreements themselves.

4.   Following mediation, lawyers may complete the legal process, either by filing a consent decree or praecipe if agreement was reached, or by continuing the pre-trial process if issues remain to be resolved by the court.

5.   If necessary, lawyers may act to enforce any agreements reached in mediation.

The Standards deal explicitly with lawyers' roles in helping clients choose an appropriate process and in assisting their clients to participate in mediation.

Where participation in mediation is voluntary, courts should encourage lawyers to assist their clients in making an informed choice among the available processes. Although the information to be provided will vary with the circumstances, in most situations it will include consideration of the costs and potential benefits of mediation compared to alternative processes and of the substantive rules most likely to govern should the dispute be resolved by other means.

Even where participation in mediation is mandatory, legal advice prior to participation will be useful in explaining the process and considering how to exercise any options the parties may have. For example, even in a mandatory mediation scheme, the parties may be able to choose when to mediate, which mediator to use, and whether to conduct any discovery prior to mediation. Finally, regardless of whether they have any choices to make before entering mediation, all parties will benefit from discussing with their own attorneys the procedures governing mediation and the negotiating strategies they wish to use.

Some state statutes reflect a concern for disputants' who enter mediation without legal counsel, by requiring that they be informed of the risks of proceeding with mediation while unrepresented. For example, enforcement of a Minnesota civil mediation agreement is conditioned on its containing provisions that

> the parties were advised in writing that (a) the mediator has no duty to protect their interest or provide them with information about their legal rights; (b) signing a mediated settlement agreement may adversely affect their legal rights; and (c) they should consult an attorney before signing a mediated settlement agreement if they are uncertain of their rights.

Minn. Stat. Ann. §572.35(1). Similarly, parties in Kansas divorce mediation must be advised to obtain a lawyer before the process begins. Mediators are also required to advise the parties in writing to obtain legal help before drafting or reviewing agreements. Kan. Stat. Ann. §23-603(a)(5).

In the absence of state statutes, courts can adopt rules which encourage attorney participation. Colorado has adopted an ethical rule requiring that attorneys advise their clients of alternative forms of dispute resolution in any matter "involving or expected to involve litigation."

10.2   Parties, in consultation with their attorneys, should have the right to decide whether their attorneys should be present at mediation sessions.

COMMENTARY: Attorney attendance at mediation sessions has been the subject of considerable debate. The Minnesota Supreme Court and State Bar Association Task Force on Alternative Dispute Resolution recommends that attorneys be permitted to attend all alternative dispute resolution proceedings to "facilitate discussion with clients about their case." Minn. Report, at 16-17. In Alaska, a statute prohibits the exclusion of attorneys from divorce mediation sessions. Alaska Stat. §25.24.060(c). Two states take the opposite view, allowing mediators to exclude lawyers from proceedings at their discretion. The Florida rules of civil Procedure provide that mediators have discretion to direct counsel to be excluded unless a court orders otherwise. Fla. R. Civ. P. 1.720(d). Similarly, in California child custody and visitation mediation, mediators have "authority to exclude counsel from participation in the mediation proceedings where, in the discretion of the mediator, exclusion of counsel is deemed by the mediator to be appropriate or necessary." Cal. Civil Code §4607(d), 4351.5(e).

The Society of Professionals in Dispute Resolution opposes all efforts to exclude attorneys from mediation sessions where parties desire to have their lawyers present:

> Lawyers may act as a crucial check against
> uninformed and pressured settlements,
> particularly when they are knowledgeable about
> the dispute resolution process. It is the parties in
> consultation with their lawyers -- not public
> authorities -- who are in the best position to
> decide when the lawyers' presence is indicated.

SPIDR Report, at 20. The Standards have adopted this position.

Where one or more parties are unrepresented, mediators may reduce any actual or perceived imbalance that results by any one of the following means:

1. Advising unrepresented parties of their right to have an attorney present and of possible sources for obtaining legal representation.

2.   Maximizing the use of separate sessions, so that the unrepresented party will be less intimidated and so that the mediator may spend additional time with the unrepresented party, if necessary.

3.   As a last resort, the mediator may decide that the case is not appropriate for mediation.

10.3   **Courts and mediators should work with the bar to educate lawyers about:**
   a.   **the difference in the lawyer's role in mediation as compared with traditional representation; and**
   b.   **the advantages and disadvantages of active participation by the parties and lawyers in mediation sessions.**

<u>**COMMENTARY**</u>: The appropriate role for attorneys in mediation sessions varies with the type of case and the relative sophistication of the parties. Lawyers generally play a more active role in personal injury mediation than, for example, in divorce mediation, where it is common even for represented parties to attend sessions without their attorneys. In general, however, the attorney's role tends more to legal advice before and after the mediation session, to advice and coaching during mediation, and less to advocacy than the attorney's traditional role in trial-type proceedings.

Rogers and McEwen point out numerous benefits for parties when lawyers take an active role in mediating disputes. For instance, they state that allowing attorneys to participate may be the best means of ensuring an equitable settlement where a party does not possess the skills to negotiate or is overly emotional. N. Rogers and C. McEwen, <u>Mediation; Law, Policy, Practice</u> 22 (1989). Further, participation of lawyers in some cases can reduce the risk of harmful consequences if no settlement is reached by decreasing "the chances of harmful admissions and disclosure of matters of strategic importance by the client to the other party, which is of particular significance if no settlement results." <u>Id.</u> at 28-9. Rogers and McEwen also caution that the necessity of having attorneys present is at its greatest if the mediator reports the merits of the dispute to the trier of fact, "because mediation might become, in essence, a contested hearing at which each side tries to persuade the hearing officer." <u>Id.</u> at 29. <u>See</u> Standard 12.0 on Communications Between Mediators and the Court.

Having lawyers participate actively in mediation sessions, on the other hand, may have its drawbacks in reduced efficiency and, at times, in diminished participation by disputants in the process. In many cases, the best role for the lawyer may be a limited one, where the attorney educates the principals on the legal standards that courts might be expected to apply to their cases and advises them on negotiation strategies, while allowing the parties to negotiate on their own behalf. In other cases, especially where parties are unsophisticated, a more equal partnership between lawyer and client may be the most effective strategy.

The Standard takes the position that it is the parties, and not the mediators, who have the right to decide whether, and to what extent, their attorneys should participate in mediation sessions. The Standard adopts this position in order to maximize the parties' choice and protection, in full recognition of the fact that in some instances there will be a tension between attorneys' advocacy and problem-solving negotiation. Courts should not require the parties to play the dominant role in mediation if they do not choose to do so.

The greatest need in connection with this subject is the education of lawyers concerning their potential roles in mediation and the advantages and disadvantages of each of these possible roles in particular situations. For a discussion of the possible roles of clients in settlement conferences, <u>see</u> Leonard L. Riskin, <u>The Represented Client in a</u>

Settlement Conference: The Lessons of G. Heileman Brewing Co. v. Joseph Oat Corp., 69 Wash. U.L.Q. 1059 (1991); see also Standard 3.0 on Information for Judges, Court Personnel and Users. The attorney's role may be different in each context--before, during, and after the mediation session.

When a client decides to attend mediation sessions without an attorney but to have an attorney review the resulting agreement before it is signed, the attorney may apply different standards of review from those that would govern if the attorney were negotiating the agreement herself or himself. Some attorneys have considered whether the agreement is within an acceptable range of possible results, or "fair enough." See, e.g., D. Samuels and J. Shawn, The Role of the Lawyer Outside the Mediation Process, 2 Mediation Quarterly (1983).

11.0   INAPPROPRIATE PRESSURE TO SETTLE

11.1   Courts should institute appropriate provisions to permit parties to opt out of mediation. Courts also should consider modifying mediation procedures in certain types of cases to accommodate special needs, such as cases involving domestic violence. Special protocols should be developed to deal with domestic violence cases.

COMMENTARY: Fairness of the mediation process requires that both courts and mediators protect the parties' ability to make free and informed choices about whether or not to settle. There are different kinds of incentives and pressures on parties in mediation to settle, such as the cost and time of litigation, uncertainty of outcome at trial, the desire to avoid publicity and, often, the dynamics of the negotiation process itself. These kinds of incentives and pressures are to be distinguished from inappropriate practices and procedures which result in inappropriate pressure to settle.

Mandating referral to mediation often is appropriate. (See Standard 4.0 on Selection of Cases). However such a mandate inevitably places additional costs on parties such as the financial, time, travel or other costs associated with attending a mediation session. While these kinds of additional costs may be acceptable in most cases, particularly when mediation is likely to be helpful, there may be instances in which they result in inappropriate pressure to settle. It is for this reason that any mandatory referral system should include liberal opt-out provisions. Parties should also be permitted to reject a particular mediator assigned from among the court staff providing mediation services, from among mediators available through a program to which a court refers cases, or from among the names on a roster maintained by the court. (See Standard 7.0 on Selection of Mediators.)

Even requiring attendance at an initial mediation session risks creating inappropriate pressures to settle on some kinds of parties, such as those whose ability to protect their own interests has been impaired by psychological or physical victimization, or those who are substantially disadvantaged in relation to the other party in terms of knowledge, experience and/or resources. Depending upon available resources, courts should consider these kinds of cases carefully before referring them to mediation. (See Standard 4.0 on Selection of Cases).

Finally, courts should consider modifying the procedures of mediation when they make mandatory referrals in some kinds of cases, in order to minimize the potential for inappropriate pressure to occur. For example, one or both parties may be concerned that face-to-face meetings will create inappropriate pressures to settle. This may be a concern in cases where physical or psychological victimization has occurred or where other particular kinds of interpersonal dynamics exist between the parties caused by gender, culture or the parties' perceived relative status. When physical violence has occurred, parties always should be permitted to opt out of face-to-face meetings in mediation. In other circumstances, the issue should be considered by the court on a case-by-case basis and, at a minimum, discussed by the mediator with each of the parties at the outset of the initial mediation session. See also Standard 12.0 on Communications between Mediators and the Court.

11.2   Courts should provide parties who are required to participate in mediation with full and accurate information about the process to which they are being referred, including the fact that they are not required to make offers and concessions or to settle.

COMMENTARY: Inadequate information may lead parties to believe that they must settle in mediation. At a minimum, care should be taken to inform them at the outset that the mediator has no authority to impose a solution, and that no adverse consequences will be imposed as a result of their failure to settle. Informing parties that the mediator has no authority to impose a solution may be particularly important if a retired judge is serving as the mediator, because of the likelihood, given a retired judge's status, that parties may assume otherwise. When mediation involves unrepresented or unsophisticated parties, who may be more susceptible, courts should provide even fuller information. (See Standard 3.0 on Information for Judges, Court Personnel and Users).

Courts have the responsibility of ensuring that parties who are required to mediate are required only to attend an initial mediation session and to be educated about the process so they can make an informed choice about continued participation. (See Standard 4.0 on Selection of Cases.) While parties attending mediation may be required to bring with them the information they would need if they chose to continue participating, it should be made clear to them that they are not required to make offers or concessions or to settle their case in mediation. See Decker v. Lindsay, Texas Ct. App. 1st Dist., No. 01-91-01299-CV, Jan. 15, 1992.

In some jurisdictions, mandated referrals explicitly provide or are interpreted to provide that parties must participate in the process "in good faith." See Me. Rev. Stat. Ann. tit. 19, §§214, 752 (West Supp. 1991); and Wash. Rev. Code 59.20.080 (3) (1990). Although there is no doubt that successful mediation involves good faith, requirements to participate in good faith are vague, counterproductive, and cannot be enforced without the mediator's testimony. They may also pressure parties to make offers of settlement that might not be made in the absence of such provisions.

11.3   Courts should not systematically exclude anyone from the mediation process. Lawyers never should be excluded if the parties want them to be present.

COMMENTARY: Some parties, particularly those who are unsophisticated or lack negotiation experience, may want another person to be present during mediation. They may feel that the presence of another person will help protect their interests in mediation and prevent them from being coerced to settle in the process. For example, a tenant in dispute with a landlord who is perceived to be powerful may wish to have a neighbor present, or a woman who has been physically or psychologically victimized may wish to bring her own advocate. This other person may be a lawyer, but many times he or she is a lay person on whom a party relies for support.

Mediators should consider this issue carefully, particularly when the presence of another person is desired at the initial mediation session. It is important for parties in mediation to have the assurance that they will not be coerced to settle in the process. At the same time, the process may become unwieldy if additional people are permitted to be present, and the participation of others may itself become an issue between the parties.

Lawyers never should be excluded if the parties want them to be present. The parties and the mediator should make the decision about the presence of others on a case-by-case basis. (See Standard 10.0 on Role of Lawyers in Mediation.)

11.4   Settlement rates should not be the sole criterion for mediation program funding, mediator advancement, or program evaluation.

COMMENTARY: As court-connected mediation programs become institutionalized and an integral part of the public justice system, there is a danger that bureaucratic routinization may occur. Administrative rewards and incentives may come to focus on the numbers of settlements reached in mediation. The individual mediators themselves may begin to suffer from "burnout," focusing less on the particular issues and dynamics in each case than on whether the parties are able to reach agreement. All of these factors may result in undue pressure being placed on parties to settle so that the existence of programs and services can be justified.

Programs should adopt support systems for their mediators to minimize mediator "burnout" and guard against "selective facilitation," or the tendency of mediators to guide the parties inappropriately to a particular result. Ongoing training and peer review are important ways to ensure mediator quality. Such training and review should emphasize other aspects of the mediator's role besides promoting parties' agreement, such as communication skills and the ability to frame issues effectively. (See Standard 6.0 on Qualifications of Mediators.) Other ways can also be found to reward superior performance, such as giving mediators enhanced roles within the program itself, instituting special awards programs, or using them as trainers or mentors.

Likewise, program evaluation should not focus exclusively on the numbers of settlements reached in mediation (see Standard 16.0 on Evaluation), nor should program funding be entirely dependent upon this factor. Other goals articulated by the court in implementing the program should be taken into account. These may include increasing the involvement of parties in the process of resolving their disputes, increasing parties' satisfaction and compliance with the results of mediation, or assisting the parties to develop a wider range of outcomes than would be available through adjudication.

11.5 **There should be no adverse response by courts to nonsettlement by the parties in mediation.**

COMMENTARY: The failure of mediation to produce a settlement should not adversely affect the parties' treatment by the court. Such treatment may manifest itself in a number of ways. For example, courts may place a case that has not settled in mediation on a long trial list; they may draw inferences concerning the reasons a case did not settle that are adverse to one of the parties; they may solicit a recommendation from the mediator as to the best outcome for a case; or, they may require parties who have not settled in mediation to participate subsequently in a judicial settlement conference where they are pressured to come to agreement. Concern about the consequences of these kinds of practices may lead parties to settle in mediation involuntarily. Courts should take special care to avoid them.

12.0 **COMMUNICATIONS BETWEEN MEDIATORS AND THE COURT**

12.1 **During a mediation the judge or other trier of fact should be informed only of the following:**
   a. **the failure of a party to comply with the order to attend mediation;**
   b. **any request by the parties for additional time to complete the mediation;**
   c. **if all parties agree, any procedural action by the court that would facilitate the mediation; and**
   d. **the mediator's assessment that the case is inappropriate for mediation.**

COMMENTARY: The purpose of this standard is to insulate the mediator from the court during the mediation and, except for reports of violations of the court's orders (which preferably would be made to a judicial officer other than the trial judge), to keep from any judge who may be involved in a trial of the case if it does not settle, any information about the substance of the mediation. Thus the mediator's assessment of the inappropriateness of a particular case for mediation should be conveyed to the court without elaboration.

The policy rationales behind this concern were expressed by SPIDR:

> Settlement coercion tied to a neutral's evaluation
> has a significant negative impact on mediation.
> The coercion results in strategic argument by the
> parties, who accurately view the mediator as
> having an effect on an adjudicated outcome.
> Thus, the coercion destroys the environment of
> frank communication necessary for the

negotiation process. Further, the mediator's recommendation seems unlikely to provide the proper basis for judicial resolution . . . because mediators hold separate meetings with the parties and do not hear evidentiary presentations.

SPIDR Report, at 18.

The Missouri Supreme Court has a similar rule:

Except by agreement of the parties no lawyer or party shall communicate to the court, nor shall a court receive from any source, any information concerning: (1) a party's willingness or unwillingness to participate or to continue to participate in mediation; (2) why, or what caused the mediation to cease; (3) a party's willingness or unwillingness to be bound by the results of mediation; or (4) the results of mediation.

Mo. Sup. Ct. R. 17.06 (1989).

Thus the Standards reject the practice of a few courts where, in cases in which the parties do not reach agreement on child custody and visitation, the mediator (or "conciliation court counselor") is required to recommend to the judge which parent should be awarded custody. See McLaughlin v. Superior Court for San Mateo County, 140 Cal. App. 3d 473, 89 Cal. Rptr. 479 (1983) (either party may call as a witness or cross-examine a conciliation court counselor who renders a report to the judge).

The harm such practices can do to the mediation process outweighs any efficiencies that the court may achieve by using the mediator as part of its investigatory process:

This procedure [of mediators' recommendations to the trier of fact] is radically different from conventional mediation. It compromises the mediator's neutrality, discards any semblance of confidentiality, and confuses mediation with other procedures of a more investigatory nature.

L. Singer, Settling Disputes: Conflict Resolution in Business, Families, and the Legal System, 42-43 (1990).

In the opinion of J. Folberg and A. Taylor:

[A]llowing the mediator to make a recommendation and testify creates an untenable
Hobson's choice for divorcing parents: either

refrain from being candid in mediation
discussions or reveal relevant confidences
knowing that they can be used later against your
individual interests. This challenge has been
countered with the argument that parties to a
court-compelled mediation are unlikely to reveal
confidences that would threaten their desired
custody resolution, whether or not those
confidences would be revealed in court.

J. Folberg and A. Taylor, Mediation, 280 (1984).

A similar although less obvious problem exists where a statute or court rule
requires parties to make a "good faith" effort to mediate. See Me. Rev. Stat. Ann. tit. 4,
§581 (when "agreement through mediation is not reached on any issue, the court must
determine that the parties made a good faith effort to mediate the issue before proceeding
with a hearing"). See Standard 9.0 on Confidentiality.

Eric R. Max of the New Jersey Department of the Public Advocate, Office of
Dispute Settlement, points out that, although "in some cases it may be appropriate for a
judge to completely separate himself [sic] from the process, . . . in other cases he may
play a number of important roles during mediation. This includes supporting the process,
setting time deadlines and resolving discovery disputes . . . . Although he is not involved
in the substance of the mediation, a judge can greatly increase the effectiveness of the
process by working closely with the mediator." E. Max, Bench Manual for the
Appointment of a Mediator, 18 (1990).

In the interests of minimizing communications between the mediator and the
judge, however, all communications with the judge on procedural matters during the
mediation should be made by someone other than the mediator. Courts should develop an
administrative procedure or form for communication to enable conveying a mediator's
recommendation on procedural matters.

12.2 **When the mediation has been concluded, the court should be
informed of the following:**

    a.   **If the parties do not reach an agreement on
any matter, the mediator should report the
lack of an agreement to the court without
comment or recommendation.**

    b.   **If agreement is reached, any requirement that
its terms be reported to the court should be
consistent with the jurisdiction's policies
governing settlements in general.**

    c.   **With the consent of the parties, the mediators'
report also may identify any pending motions
or outstanding legal issues, discovery process,
or other action by any party which, if resolved
or completed, would facilitate the possibility of**

a settlement.

COMMENTARY: This standard is based on Rule 1.730 of the Florida Rules of Civil Procedure.

These Standards reject the approach of those who propose extensive communications between the mediator and the judge after a mediation in which settlement is not reached. Cf. E. Max, Bench Manual for the Appointment of a Mediator, 16 (1990). The Standards reject this approach.

Although communications between the mediator and any judge who may try the case should be discouraged, the Standards are not intended to preclude discussions with administrative staff responsible for the mediation program or reports to the court designed to permit monitoring of the quality of the mediation services being provided. (See Standards 16.0 on Evaluation and 2.0 on Courts' Responsibility for Mediation Programs.)

Mediation agreements should not be kept private per se, but should be treated as other court settlements. Parties may request that settlement terms be confidential as part of the mediated agreement. In those cases where the public interest demands, such as cases involving environmental or consumer protection issues, mediated agreements should not be held private.

12.3   **Whenever possible, all communications with the judge who will try the case should be made by the parties. Where the mediator must communicate with the trial judge, it is preferable for such communications to be made in writing or through administrative personnel.**

COMMENTARY: The purpose of this preference is to prevent any appearance of impropriety or threat to confidentiality. The rationale behind a preference for such communications to be made in writing or through administrative personnel is that it offers mediators the most complete protection from being questioned by judges about their mediations and, in turn, offers parties the most complete assurance of confidentiality and insulation of the eventual outcome of their case from influence by the mediators' observations. The Standards should not be read as endorsing the practice of some courts, however, which keeps the identity of the mediator from the judge or prohibits judges from knowing even that a case has been mediated. Such practices appear to go too far, by prohibiting mediators, where the parties agree, from communicating with judges or their law clerks concerning procedural matters, such as the need for discovery or extensions of time and failing to inform judges about the value of mediation in general and the performance of individual mediators in particular.

13.0   FUNDING OF PROGRAMS AND COMPENSATION OF MEDIATORS

13.1   Courts should make mediation available to parties regardless of the parties' ability to pay.
        a.   Where a court suggests (rather than orders) mediation, it should take steps to make mediation available to indigent litigants,

through state funding or through encouraging mediators who receive referrals from the court to provide a portion of their services on a free or reduced fee basis.

b.   **When parties are required to participate in mediation, the costs of mediation should be publicly funded unless in the view of the court the case is an exceptional one.**

COMMENTARY: Ideally mediation as a basic dispute resolution service should be funded by the public to the same extent as adjudication and other court services. See Standard 1.0 on Access.

The New Jersey Supreme Court's Task Force on Dispute Resolution recommends an annual legislative appropriation for alternative dispute resolution. Because "providing the best option for the resolution of each dispute is a public purpose of the Judiciary, [it] is, therefore, appropriately funded by that public." N.J. Report, at 25. The Minnesota Supreme Court and State Bar Association's Task Force on ADR, on the other hand, concludes that the fee in all ADR processes shall be set by the market-place . . . . The parties shall pay for the neutral. It is presumed that the parties shall split the costs of the ADR process on an equal basis." Minn. Report, at IV A (1)-(3).

The Standards take no position concerning the advisability of a court's charging fees to litigants for the use of other court services, such as transcripts or probation, or of increasing filing fees to pay for mediation or other services. They do state that court-connected mediation should be a part of the regular court budget and publicly funded to the same extent that adjudication and other court programs are funded.

Under present fiscal conditions this standard may have to be viewed as a goal rather than a minimal requirement. For example, some states rely on fees paid by the parties to fund mediation in whole or in part. If other court processes are offered free of charge, however, user fees for mediation programs could act as a disincentive to using mediation, regardless of the parties' ability to pay. SPIDR Report, at 16. The Society of Professionals in Dispute Resolution (SPIDR) has expressed a special concern about charging for mediation when it is offered as an alternative to the pursuit of a criminal complaint.

Harvard Law Professor Frank E. A. Sander, widely regarded as the originator of the multi-door courthouse concept, recently expressed concern about two funding alternatives developed by states and localities strapped for funds. One is overreliance on volunteers. While volunteers have a valuable role to play in many kinds of court-connected mediation programs, caution is needed:

> If ADR is to develop responsibly as a profession,
> its practitioners need to be reasonably
> compensated . . . . [I]f mediation is to be widely
> used in large-scale commercial and public policy
> disputes then we cannot look solely to volunteers.

F.E.A. Sander, Who Should Pay for Court-Connected ADR?, A.B.A. J., Feb. 1992, at 105. Professor Sander also addressed party payment of neutrals:

> The other solution adopted in some places (such
> as Florida and Texas) is to have the disputants pay
> the neutrals to whom the case has been referred.
> From the point of view of most commercial
> clients, this may not pose much of a problem . . . .
> But, [i]f the public justice system has an
> obligation to make available a range of dispute
> resolution options -- as I believe it does -- then we
> unfairly bias the choice by making court
> adjudication available free or for a modest filing
> fee, yet charging the parties for alternative
> processes that may be more appropriate in a
> particular case.

See also Minn. Report, at IV A (1)-(3) (concluding that the parties should pay equal amounts for mediation).

There are several options for providing publicly funded mediators. Courts may choose to provide trained staff mediators, whether from the ranks of professional mediators, former judges, magistrates, or court social workers, as one option. Alternatively, they may create a fund, either from legislative appropriations or from add-on filing fees, to compensate private mediators. The latter method has the advantage of maximizing the court's flexibility and the parties' ability to choose from among a number of qualified mediators.

The most short-sighted of the available options is the exclusive reliance on volunteers. Not only does it risk the demise of programs, or at the very least, a severe dilution of quality, after initial enthusiasm has waned and volunteer mediators want to be compensated; it also denigrates what should be a profession, with continuing commitment to improving skills, into a hobby. As Professor Sander puts it:

> What do we say to our talented young graduates
> who want to make a career of helping others
> resolve their disputes? That they should find
> some other work to support themselves and do
> dispute resolution in their spare time?

Id.

Where financing of ADR from general public funds is unavailable due to the current financial conditions of many of our court systems, Professor Sander advocates the use of add-on filing fees, as in California, as "a fairer form of assessment [than financing through volunteers or party fees] since the costs of improving the public dispute system are thus spread over all litigants, not simply imposed on the immediate disputants seeking to avail themselves of ADR procedures." Sander, supra, at 105.

Even under current fiscal constraints, a court should not require parties to participate in mediation unless public funds are available to compensate the mediators. This is the approach recommended by SPIDR. SPIDR Report, at 16. According to

Professor Sander, in addition to the arguments supporting the public funding of ADR procedures in general as part of the public justice system, "[w]here the referral to ADR is mandatory there is the added question whether it is fair or legal to compel users of the public justice system to use certain alternative processes and then to bill them for the cost." Sander, supra, at 105.

An exception to the requirement of public funding of mandatory mediation may be warranted in unusual cases, where state or local rules may authorize courts to appoint experienced special masters to manage and/or mediate in particularly large or complex cases and to order their costs to be borne by one or more of the parties. See Fed. R. Civ. P. 53; E. Max, Bench Manual for the Appointment of a Mediator 16 (1990).

Where the court suggests, rather than requires, mediation, it should take steps to ensure that mediation is available to low income parties. See Iowa Code Ann. §598.16 (costs "shall be paid in full or part by the parties...however, if the court determines that the parties will be unable to pay the costs without prejudicing their financial ability to provide themselves and any minor children with economic necessities, the costs may be paid in full or in part by the county"). An alternative approach is for each court to implement rules to provide for judicial review of the appropriateness of any fees charged to the parties for mediation services. If this review indicates that the fees are excessive or the parties do not have the financial ability to pay, a judge may reduce the fee or order other financial arrangements, including assignment of a mediator who has agreed to provide the services pro bono or for a reduced rate of compensation. Cf. Fla. Sup. Ct. Regs., Fla. Stat. Ann. §44.108 (West Supp. 1992). The Florida Standards of Professional Conduct for Court Appointed Mediators provide that, "[a]s a means of meeting the needs of the financially disadvantaged, a mediator should provide mediation services pro bono, or at a reduced rate of compensation whenever appropriate." Florida Standards of Professional Conduct for Court Appointed Mediators, §XIII(A) (1991).

13.2   In allocating public funds to mediation, a court may give priority for funding to certain types of cases, such as family and minor criminal matters.

COMMENTARY: Many courts already operate publicly funded mediation programs for some types of cases. Data from the National Center for State Courts' ADR Database illustrates the diversity of current funding sources for court-connected mediation programs. For example, most custody mediation programs use court-funded mediators (89 out of 110 programs), whereas almost 40 percent (21 out of 53) of tort programs rely on user fees to fund mediators.

PROGRAM SERVICES RENDERED							
BASIS	Cust./ Vis.	Con- tract	Tort	Small Claim	Land./ Tenant	Min. Crim.	Other
Free	89	43	44	33	31	15	28
Fixed Rate	13	16	17	2	3	1	10
Sliding Scale	4	1	1	0	0	0	2
Other	7	3	3	2	1	1	4

SOURCE OF FUNDS TO PAY NEUTRALS							
SOURCE	Cust./ Vis.	Con- tract	Tort	Small Claim	Land./ Tenant	Min. Crim.	Other
Court Budget	89	31	30	26	25	10	19
Non-Court Budget	11	2	2	0	2	2	6
Parties	10	19	21	0	3	0	12

The effect of the Standards would be that a court could operate either mandatory or voluntary programs in its priority areas, with public funding provided, and voluntary programs in other areas, with fees paid by the parties. Even in these lower priority, voluntary programs, provision should be made for serving indigent litigants.

13.3   **Where public funds are used, they may either: (a) support mediators employed by the court or (b) compensate private mediators. Where public funds are used to compensate private mediators, fee schedules should be set by the Court.**

COMMENTARY: In deciding whether to use public funds to support court-employed mediators or fees for private mediators, a court should consider the following:

- Does the size of its current or projected mediation caseload justify the hiring and training of full-time court personnel to mediate? Alternatively, should the court hire only one or more administrators to manage the use and compensation of private mediators?

- Which approach makes it more likely that the
  court can attract and retain qualified, experienced
  mediators?
- Which approach will produce a greater diversity
  of mediators in terms of race, sex, age, and
  experiences?
- Which approach will maximize the parties' choice
  among mediators?

The Standards conclude that the use of public funds to pay private mediators requires the uniformity, consistency, and predictability that can come only from having fee schedules set by a public body. The recommendation that fees or schedules be set by the court, or an administrative arm of the court, is based on a desire for a more flexible alternative to the setting of fees by the legislature.

13.4   **a.**   **Where courts offer publicly funded mediation services, courts should permit parties to substitute a private mediator of their own choosing except in those circumstances under which the court has decided that party choice is inappropriate.**

        b.   **Where parties elect to pay a private mediator, they should be permitted to agree with the mediator on the appropriate fee.**

COMMENTARY: This standard parallels Standard 7.0 on Selection of Mediators, which states that parties ordinarily should be given the widest possible latitude in selecting mediators, even beyond the mediators included on rosters of qualified mediators prepared by the court. The Standard on Selection also discuss the exceptional policy considerations that occasionally may override the general preference for party choice. The rationale behind these standards is to give the parties the widest possible latitude in selecting mediators, consistent with public policy.

Of the state statutes that establish the right of a private mediator to receive compensation, some, e.g., Haw. Rev. Stat. §672-3 (1985); Mont. Code Ann. §27-6-203 (1991), actually set the fee and specify who is responsible for payment. Other statutes delegate the task of setting and allocating fees to other bodies. Iowa Code Ann. §679.7 (West 1987) provides that the Training Coordination Council in the Department of Justice shall establish a sliding scale of fees to be charged based upon a party's ability to pay. Some statutes give the courts the explicit authority to order the parties in a particular dispute to bear the costs of engaging a mediator's services and to set a reasonable fee. E.g., Tex. Civ. Prac. & Rem. Code Ann. §154.054, (West Supp. 1992) (Compensation of Impartial Third Parties) ("The court may set a reasonable fee for the services of an impartial third party appointed..."). The Minnesota Supreme Court 's Task Force on ADR recommends that "[t]he fee in all ADR processes . . . be set by the marketplace." Minn. Report, at IV A(1)-(3).

When parties use their own funds to pay a private mediator on a voluntary basis, there appears to be no reason to override their own negotiations, based on market rates. In those states that require parties to pay for private mediators, on the other hand, it is appropriate for the court to set a range of fees.

14.0   LIABILITY OF MEDIATORS
Courts should not develop rules for mediators to whom they refer cases that are designed to protect those mediators from liability. Legislatures and courts should provide the same indemnity or insurance for those mediators who volunteer their services or are employed by the court that they provide for non-judicial court employees.

COMMENTARY: Immunity from liability is one means of encouraging the participation of individuals as mediators, especially where the risk of suit is not outweighed by the level of compensation for the mediators' services. As the Arizona Commission on the Courts put it, there is a need to "promote the use of mediation as an alternative form of dispute resolution and to encourage the participation of persons as professional or volunteer mediators," since mediators are "serving the courts and acting in the place of judges." Commission on the Courts, The Future of Arizona Courts 42 (1991). At the same time, these interests must be balanced against the concern for protecting litigants who may be harmed by incompetent service. As the Arizona Commission recognized, "the social value of a grant of immunity [must be measured] against the lost opportunity for recovery of claims." Id.

Several states have addressed the issue of mediators' liability by statute. See, e.g., Cal. Civ. Proc. Code §1297.432; Haw. Rev. Stat. §§672-679; Ill. Rev. Stat. ch. 111, para. 4804(B); Iowa Code §§13.14, 654A.15, 679.13; Me. Rev. Stat. Ann. tit. 4, §18(2-A); Miss. Code Ann. §69-2-49 (expired); Mont. Code Ann. §80-13-213; N.J. Rev. Stat. §§2A:23A-9(c), 34:13A-16(h); N.D. Cent. Code §6-09.10-04.1; Va. Code Ann. §8.01-581.23; Wash. Rev. Code §7.75.100; Wis. Stat. §93.50(2)(c). Statutes typically provide limited immunity for certain mediators, or absolute immunity for acts within the scope of their duties.

Statutes that provide limited immunity commonly protect mediators from civil liability for negligent acts or omissions. For instance, Colorado provides that mediators hired by the state's Office of Dispute Resolution are immune from liability unless they act "in bad faith, with malicious purpose or in a manner exhibiting willful and wanton disregard of human rights, safety, or property." Colo. Rev. Stat. §13-22-305(6). See also Okla. Stat. Ann. tit. 12, §1805(E) (To be liable, a mediator or agent must exhibit "gross negligence with malicious purpose or in a manner exhibiting willful disregard. . . ."); Wyo. Stat. §11-41-105(d) ("Mediators are immune from civil liability for any good faith act or omission within the scope of the performance . . . of their duties.")

Connecticut, under a general statutory provision of immunity, pays legal fees and costs for state employees acting within the scope of their employment, if the "act or omission is found not to have been wanton, reckless or malicious." All claims are reviewed by a panel before a mediator or expert appointed by the court is indemnified. Conn. Gen. Stat. §5.141d.

The Arizona Commission on the Courts recommended granting "qualified" immunity to mediators in court-annexed or government-sponsored programs. "Qualified immunity would apply to all acts or omissions of 'covered' mediators except those acts or omissions that could be characterized as exhibiting a reckless disregard of a substantial risk of significant injury to the rights of others, or intentional misconduct." Commission on the Courts, supra at 42. The Commission recommended certification and completion of an approved training program as a prerequisite to a grant of limited immunity.

Eight states provide absolute immunity from civil liability. Six states protect members of medical claim conciliation panels authorized to mediate malpractice claims, for acts within the scope of their duties. Haw. Rev. Stat§671-17; La. Rev. Stat. Ann. §1299.47(H); Mont. Code Ann. §27-6-106; Neb. Rev. Stat. §44-2844(3); Nev. Rev. Stat. §630.364; Utah Code Ann. §78-14-15. Minnesota provides absolute immunity to farm-lender mediators for acts within the scope of their duties. Minn. Stat. Ann. §583.26(7)(a). A Florida statute, recently amended, gives court-appointed mediators full judicial immunity "in the same manner and to the same extent as a judge." Fla. Stat. Ann. §44.107.

Other jurisdictions have taken a different approach. The New Jersey Supreme Court Task Force on Dispute Resolution, for example, considered mediators' liability in court-annexed programs but refrained from recommending immunity for mediators. N.J. Report, at 23-24. The Task Force concluded that it was premature to recommend immunity, given the likelihood that unforeseen circumstances might arise and given the risk of denying recovery for participants with valid claims of malpractice. However, because of the need to encourage the involvement of members of the public in providing dispute resolution services, the Task Force recommended that the state provide indemnification to any mediator found liable for malpractice, as well as underwrite the defense of any mediator sued as a result of participating in court-annexed programs.

The U.S. Justice Department has informed program administrators that it generally will defend court-connected volunteer mediators for the U.S. District Court and Court of Appeals for the District of Columbia if they are sued for malpractice. The District of Columbia Superior Court has purchased group insurance to cover all of its mediators, who are volunteers (although they may be paid modest stipends).

The Standards take the position that granting mediators immunity from liability inappropriately denies recourse to litigants injured by incompetent service, especially when litigants are required to pay for the service. Malpractice insurance is available in the private sector. It seems appropriate to expect mediators who are compensated for their services to purchase such insurance. In this context it should be noted that no court, to date, has upheld a finding of mediator liability.

Other methods than a grant of immunity are available to encourage the participation of volunteers and to protect court employees. Non-judicial court employees usually are protected from liability for negligent acts or omissions either through indemnification or insurance. The Standards recommend that whatever protections are in place for non-judicial court employees in any given jurisdiction be provided for mediators who serve as volunteers or are employed by the court and receive court referrals. This will allow courts to encourage the participation of individuals as mediators by those for whom the risk of suit otherwise would not be outweighed by the level of compensation for their services. At the same time, standards of liability for malpractice in mediation, as in any other profession, can continue to evolve and litigants who participate in court-connected mediation be protected from injury.

15.0   THE ENFORCEABILITY OF MEDIATED AGREEMENTS

15.1   Agreements that are reached through court-connected mediation should be enforceable to the same extent as agreements reached without a mediator.

Commentary: Basic contract principles dictate that an agreement among parties that contains all the elements of a contract should be enforceable when brought before a court. For matters already before the court, such an agreement may be presented to the court as a consent judgment, which is immediately enforceable through contempt or other post-judgment procedures. N. Rogers & C. McEwen, Mediation: Law, Policy, Practice 198 (1989).

Some states have codified these axioms. See Iowa Code Ann. §601A.15(9) (West 1988) (agreements reached in civil rights mediation must be issued as consent judgments which are enforceable by contempt); Ind. Code Ann. §22-9-1-6(n) (West 1991) (conciliated agreements in civil rights mediation are enforceable by a summary court procedure as consent judgments). More often, however, states require additional protections such as special language or court approval. See Colo. Rev. Stat. Ann. ꝺ13-22-308 (West Supp. 1991) (mediated agreements in court programs must be drafted as stipulations which are enforceable only after court review and approval); Mich. Comp. Laws. Ann. §552.513(2) (West 1988) (mediated agreements in domestic relations disputes must be drafted as a consent order and approved by court); N.D. Cent. Code §14-09.1-07 (1991) (domestic relations mediated settlements only binding after court approval); Cal. Bus. & Prof. Code §467.4 (West 1990) (mediated agreements under state-funded programs enforceable only if specified in writing); Mo. Sup. Ct. Rule 17.07 (mediated agreements enforceable only if not prohibited by law, the parties agree and settlement is adopted at conclusion of mediation); Minn. Stat. Ann. §572.35(1) (West 1988) (mediated agreements enforceable only if in writing stating that parties were given written notice that the mediator has no duty to protect their interests and that they should consult an attorney before signing if they are uncertain of the adverse effects that the agreement could have on their legal rights). These requirements are often based on the apprehension of legislatures that mediation is "second class justice" lacking in traditional court protections. These special protections are unnecessary in the context of court-connected mediation where other mechanisms safeguard the parties.

Firstly, contract law provides protection from various evils such as unconscionability, fraud, and mistake. Secondly, courts should institute monitoring and evaluation procedures to ensure that mediators are qualified and held accountable for their performance. See Standard 16.0 on Evaluation. Thirdly, legal advice should be available where it is needed. See Standard 11.0 on the Role of Lawyers in Mediation. Fourthly, courts can continue to utilize procedures traditionally applied in court-sponsored settlements. The only issue is whether an agreement reached through mediation (especially in cases where attorneys for the parties do not participate in the process) should be held to stricter or more lenient standards in order to be enforceable as a contract or judgment. If there is no reason to treat agreements that are mediated in court-connected programs any differently from other settlements, courts can follow whatever their usual practices are in connection with different types of agreements. Many courts, for example, review and modify agreements reached in class actions or in divorce actions involving children. In a few states, violating certain types of mediated agreements itself constitutes a violation of law. For instance, non-compliance with a settlement agreement in Minnesota environmental mediation is subject to a civil fine. Minn. Stat. Ann. §103F.421-5 (West Supp. 1991). Breaking a Georgia labor mediation agreement also constitutes a violation of the law. Ga. Code Ann. §45-19-32 (Michie 1990).

Although not required by the Standards, it is usually desirable to include in all agreements dispute resolution clauses that encourage or require the parties to return to mediation before they pursue other remedies for a claimed breach. Parties who do not wish to put their agreements in writing should be reminded that rules of the parties' agreement on confidentiality may preclude the mediator from testifying as a witness to the terms of an oral agreement. This limitation provides an additional reason to put settlements in writing.

The imposition of additional requirements on agreements reached through court-connected mediation is not only unnecessary, it is potentially harmful. By requiring more of agreements reached through court-connected mediation than of other settlements, these requirements could create the very second-class status that some policy makers fear.

16.0   EVALUATION

16.1   Courts should ensure that the mediation programs to which they refer cases are monitored adequately on an ongoing basis, and evaluated on a periodic basis and that sufficient resources are earmarked for these purposes.

COMMENTARY: Program monitoring is usually an internal function and involves ongoing assessment of how the program is operating and whether policies and procedures are being implemented as intended. Evaluation is often conducted by an external entity and involves periodic assessment to determine, from a policy perspective, whether the program is meeting the goals articulated for its implementation relative to other actual or potential programming efforts. For example, monitoring might answer the question "Are parties settling cases early in mediation?", while evaluation might determine whether parties are settling cases earlier in mediation than in litigation.

While monitoring and evaluation are undertaken for different purposes, both are essential to permit courts to fulfill their responsibility for ensuring the quality of the programs to which they refer cases. (See Standard 2.0 on Courts' Responsibility for Mediation Programs.)

The process of evaluation can have a number of goals: (1) to determine whether a program should be continued or discontinued; (2) to garner public or funding support for a program; (3) to assist in adjusting and improving a program; (4) to meet the requirements of a granting agency; and (5) to advance general knowledge about dispute resolution. See C. McEwen, Evaluating ADR Programs in Emerging Issues in State and Federal Courts (F. Sander ed., 1991). The goal of the evaluation prescribed in these Standards should be to ensure that the courts' mediation programs are meeting the specific goals articulated for their implementation and that they are being operated at levels of consistently high quality.

In this regard, disputants' perceptions of the legitimacy and fairness of the process are among the important elements of evaluation. Also among them are outcome measures, such as the extent to which mediated agreements maximize the parties' joint gains and/or endure over time. See, e.g., J. Pearson and N. Thoennes, Reflections on a Decade of Divorce Mediation Research, in The Mediation of Disputes: Empirical Studies in The Resolution of Conflicts (K. Kressel and D. Pruitt eds., 1987). Exclusive focus on efficiency measures, such as time and numbers of settlements, can have deleterious effects, such as increasing inappropriate pressures to settle in mediation and creating inferior forms of justice.

Evaluation should not be understood to involve the collection and analysis of quantitative data only. Qualitative data gathered through observations or open-ended interviews, for example, may provide special insights about the character and quality of mediation services.

Courts also should keep in mind that program evaluation can range from rigorous collection and analysis of a comprehensive empirical data base that may or may not compare "experimental" and control groups, and include rich observations and accounts of what mediators do, to periodic review of data collected on a regular, ongoing basis in individual case files. The level of evaluation conducted will depend upon program goals and resources and on the type of program being evaluated. For example, the newer and more experimental the program, the more rigorous should be the evaluation.

Courts also have choices with respect to who conducts the evaluation. Evaluation can be conducted in-house, by an outside entity such as a research firm or university, or by some combination of the two. There are advantages and disadvantages to each option. Outside evaluation preserves both the appearance and reality of objective assessment, but it may be more costly and likely to be limited to one particular stage of the program's operation. In-house evaluation may be less costly and provide ongoing feedback about the nature and effects of the program. There is a danger, however, that it will be used -- whether consciously or unconsciously -- by program personnel to justify continuation of the program. Outside evaluators may be retained simply to consult or carry out a segment of an in-house effort. However, their timetables and agendas may differ from those of program personnel. Courts should ensure that sufficient resources are earmarked for whichever option is selected.

Finally, courts should consider whether evaluation will be conducted on a program-by-program basis or coordinated throughout the jurisdiction. Program-by-program evaluation may be more costly, but it allows for program design variations to be taken into account when assessing the program's effects. At the same time, the effects of program design variations may make generalizations from research findings more difficult for system-wide program planners. It is for this reason that some states have recommended or implemented statewide evaluation programs:

> The (New Jersey) Task Force envisions a
> statewide evaluation program working closely
> with the vicinages to provide direction where

uniformity is required and technical assistance where it is needed. Prior to the implementation of new programs, the Statewide Committee on Dispute Resolution should determine categories of information to be required and should develop either uniform reporting forms or specific questions or data elements to be included in any such reporting forms. The Statewide Committee should, with the approval of the Supreme Court, seek appropriate resources to support such evaluation, including such options as monetary grants, establishing closer ties with local universities whose professors and graduate students may wish to participate in research efforts, and retaining paid consultants to help guide local and state evaluation efforts.

N.J. Report, at 37.

The degree to which coordinated assessment of court-connected mediation programs is needed may vary with the degree to which a jurisdiction is engaged in comprehensive statewide court-connected ADR program planning. As programs are initiated, however, consideration should be given to future system-wide data needs.

16.2   Programs should be required to collect sufficient, accurate information to permit adequate monitoring on an ongoing basis and evaluation on a periodic basis.

COMMENTARY: Monitoring and evaluation should be built into a program's routine functioning, with a carefully conceived information system which will provide accurate data on an ongoing basis. (See Standard 2.0 on Courts' Responsibility for Mediation Programs.) Policies relating to confidentiality should not be construed to prohibit or limit effective monitoring and evaluation. (See Standard 9.0 on Confidentiality).

The type of data collected should capture the timing and outcomes of key events, such as the date of referral, whether a mediation session was held, the date of the mediation session, whether agreement was reached, whether the agreement was a partial or complete resolution of the case, and the types of issues that were resolved (or unresolved). The program's information system should be designed to permit the monitoring of cases as well as the evaluation of mediation both in the short-run (e.g., the rate of settlement, the number of days from referral to resolution for both successfully and unsuccessfully mediated cases) and in the long run (e.g., the rate of compliance, the rate of relitigation). Programs also should be reminded that there are various sources of data for evaluation, including data that can be collected from the parties themselves (e.g., users' satisfaction with mediation, whether satisfaction varies by gender, area of law, or expectations). This data can be gathered through periodic surveys of participants, including the parties and their attorneys.

**16.3   Courts should ensure that program evaluation is widely
distributed and linked to decision-making about the program's
policies and procedures.**

COMMENTARY: Program evaluations should play a formative role in
program development. Courts need to ensure that the programs to which they refer cases
have "loopback" mechanisms in place which will translate research findings into program
improvements. Empirical evidence regarding the program's operation and consequences
should be used to identify deficiencies in the program's policies and procedures, to assess
those deficiencies and to find ways to correct them.

As programs become institutionalized, resistance to change may become
increasingly entrenched. As Craig McEwen has written:

> Do not assume ... that routine monitoring through
> collection and reporting of data about cases or
> case flow constitutes managerial evaluation.
> Evaluation is a state of mind after all. That state
> of mind includes a disposition to assess the worth
> of practices in the light of evidence and to make
> changes in response to that assessment.

McEwen, supra. In a similar vein the Conference of State Court Administrators cautions:

> Judicial planners should not become wedded to
> particular programs, structures or procedures, but
> rather should be willing to modify or to eliminate
> alternative programs if evaluation reveals the
> programs or procedures are not serving their
> defined purposes.

COSCA Report, at 3.

A continual process of evaluation, intervention on the basis of that evaluation,
and re-evaluation needs to be implemented. In some jurisdictions, such as New Jersey and
Florida, a statewide committee or the administrative office of the courts is designated to
ensure that program change based on evaluation occurs. In others, responsibility may rest
with the individual court.

Appendix I

AMERICAN BAR ASSOCIATION STANDARDS[1] FOR THE ESTABLISHMENT AND OPERATION OF OMBUDS OFFICES

PREAMBLE

Ombuds[2] receive complaints and questions from individuals concerning people within an entity or the functioning of an entity. They work for the resolution of particular issues and, where appropriate, make recommendations for the improvement of the general administration of the entities they serve. Ombuds protect: the legitimate interests and rights of individuals with respect to each other; individual rights against the excesses of public and private bureaucracies; and those who are affected by and those who work within these organizations.

Federal, state and local governments, academic institutions, for profit businesses, non-profit organizations, and sub-units of these entities have established ombuds offices, but with enormous variation in their duties and structures. Ombuds offices so established may be placed in several categories: A Classical Ombuds operates in the public sector addressing issues raised by the general public or internally, usually concerning the actions or policies of government entities or individuals. An Organizational Ombuds may be located in either the public or private sector and ordinarily addresses problems presented by members, employees, or contractors of an entity concerning its actions or policies. Both types may conduct inquiries or investigations and suggest modifications in policies or procedures. An Advocate Ombuds may be located in either the public or private sector and like the others evaluates claims objectively but is authorized or required to advocate on behalf of individuals or groups found to be aggrieved.

---

[1] These standards expand on a 1969 ABA resolution to address independence, impartiality, and confidentiality as essential characteristics of ombuds who serve internal constituents, ombuds in the private sector, and ombuds who also serve as advocates for designated populations.

[2] The term ombuds in this report is intended to encompass all other forms of the word, such as ombudsperson, ombuds officer, and ombudsman, a Swedish word meaning agent or representative. The use of ombuds here is not intended to discourage others from using other terms.

As a result of the various types of offices and the proliferation of different processes by which the offices operate, individuals who come to the ombuds office for assistance may not know what to expect, and the offices may be established in ways that compromise their effectiveness. These standards were developed to provide advice and guidance on the structure and operation of ombuds offices so that ombuds may better fulfill their functions and so that individuals who avail themselves of their aid may do so with greater confidence in the integrity of the process. Practical and political considerations may require variations from these Standards, but it is urged that such variations be eliminated over time.

The essential characteristics of an ombuds are:

- independence

- impartiality in conducting inquiries and investigations, and

- confidentiality.

ESTABLISHMENT AND OPERATIONS

A. An entity undertaking to establish an ombuds should do so pursuant to a legislative enactment or a publicly available written policy (the "charter") which clearly sets forth the role and jurisdiction of the ombuds and which authorizes the ombuds to:

(1) receive complaints and questions about alleged acts, omissions, improprieties, and systemic problems within the ombuds's jurisdiction as defined in the charter establishing the office

(2) exercise discretion to accept or decline to act on a complaint or question

(3) act on the ombuds's own initiative to address issues within the ombuds's prescribed jurisdiction

(4) operate by fair and timely procedures to aid in the just resolution of a complaint or problem

(5) gather relevant information

(6) resolve issues at the most appropriate level of the entity

(7) function by such means as:

(a) conducting an inquiry

(b)   investigating and reporting findings

(c)   developing, evaluating, and discussing options available to affected individuals

(d)   facilitating, negotiating, and mediating

(e)   making recommendations for the resolution of an individual complaint or a systemic problem to those persons who have the authority to act upon them

(f)   identifying complaint patterns and trends

(g)   educating

(h)   issuing periodic reports, and

(i)   advocating on behalf of affected individuals or groups when specifically authorized by the charter

(8)   initiate litigation to enforce or protect the authority of the office as defined by the charter, as otherwise provided by these standards, or as required by law.

QUALIFICATIONS

B.   An ombuds should be a person of recognized knowledge, judgment, objectivity, and integrity. The establishing entity should provide the ombuds with relevant education and the periodic updating of the ombuds's qualifications.

INDEPENDENCE, IMPARTIALITY, AND CONFIDENTIALITY

C.   To ensure the effective operation of an ombuds, an entity should authorize the ombuds to operate consistently with the following essential characteristics. Entities that have established ombuds offices that lack appropriate safeguards to maintain these characteristics should take prompt steps to remedy any such deficiency.

(1)   <u>Independence</u>. The ombuds is and appears to be free from interference in the legitimate performance of duties and independent from control, limitation, or a penalty imposed for retaliatory purposes by an official of the appointing entity or by a person who may be the subject of a complaint or inquiry.

In assessing whether an ombuds is independent in structure, function, and appearance, the following factors are important: whether anyone subject to the ombuds's jurisdiction or anyone directly responsible for a person under the ombuds's jurisdiction (a) can control or limit the ombuds's performance of assigned duties or (b) can, for retaliatory purposes, (1) eliminate the office, (2) remove the ombuds, or (3) reduce the budget or resources of the office.

(2) Impartiality in Conducting Inquiries and Investigations. The ombuds conducts inquiries and investigations in an impartial manner, free from initial bias and conflicts of interest. Impartiality does not preclude the ombuds from developing an interest in securing changes that are deemed necessary as a result of the process, nor from otherwise being an advocate on behalf of a designated constituency. The ombuds may become an advocate within the entity for change where the process demonstrates a need for it.

(3) Confidentiality. An ombuds does not disclose and is not required to disclose any information provided in confidence, except to address an imminent risk of serious harm. Records pertaining to a complaint, inquiry, or investigation are confidential and not subject to disclosure outside the ombuds's office. An ombuds does not reveal the identity of a complainant without that person's express consent. An ombuds may, however, at the ombuds's discretion disclose non-confidential information and may disclose confidential information so long as doing so does not reveal its source. An ombuds should discuss any exceptions to the ombuds's maintaining confidentiality with the source of the information.[3]

LIMITATIONS ON THE OMBUDS'S AUTHORITY

D. An ombuds should not, nor should an entity expect or authorize an ombuds to:

(1) make, change or set aside a law, policy, or administrative decision

(2) make binding decisions or determine rights

(3) directly compel an entity or any person to implement the ombuds's recommendations

---

[3] A classical ombuds should not be required to discuss confidentiality with government officials and employees when applying this paragraph to the extent that an applicable statute makes clear that such an individual may not withhold information from the ombuds and that such a person has no reasonable expectation of confidentiality with respect to anything that person provides to the ombuds.

(4)   conduct an investigation that substitutes for administrative or judicial proceedings

(5)   accept jurisdiction over an issue that is currently pending in a legal forum unless all parties and the presiding officer in that action explicitly consent

(6)   address any issue arising under a collective bargaining agreement or which falls within the purview of any existing federal, state, or local labor or employment law, rule, or regulation, unless the ombuds is authorized to do so by the collective bargaining agreement or unless the collective bargaining representative and the employing entity jointly agree to allow the ombuds to do so, or if there is no collective bargaining representative, the employer specifically authorizes the ombuds to do so, or

(7)   act in a manner inconsistent with the grant of and limitations on the jurisdiction of the office when discharging the duties of the office of ombuds.

REMOVAL FROM OFFICE

E.   The charter that establishes the office of the ombuds should also provide for the discipline or removal of the ombuds from office for good cause by means of a fair procedure.

NOTICE

F.   These standards do not address the issue whether a communication to the ombuds will be deemed notice to anyone else including any entity in or for which the ombuds acts. Important legal rights and liabilities may be affected by the notice issue.

CLASSICAL OMBUDS

G.   A classical ombuds is a public sector ombuds who receives complaints from the general public or internally and addresses actions and failures to act of a government agency, official, or public employee. In addition to and in clarification of the standards contained in Paragraphs A-F, a classical ombuds:

(1)   should be authorized to conduct independent and impartial investigations into matters within the prescribed jurisdiction of the office

(2)   should have the power to issue subpoenas for testimony and evidence with respect to investigating allegations within the jurisdiction of the office

(3)   should be authorized to issue public reports

(4)   should be authorized to advocate for change both within the entity and publicly

(5)   should, if the ombuds has general jurisdiction over two or more agencies, be established by legislation[4] and be viewed as a part of and report to the legislative branch of government.

ORGANIZATIONAL OMBUDS

H.   An organizational ombuds facilitates fair and equitable resolutions of concerns that arise within the entity. In addition to and in clarification of the standards contained in Paragraphs A-F, an organizational ombuds should:

(1) be authorized to undertake inquiries and function by informal processes as specified by the charter

(2) be authorized to conduct independent and impartial inquiries into matters within the prescribed jurisdiction of the office

(3) be authorized to issue reports

(4) be authorized to advocate for change within the entity.

ADVOCATE OMBUDS

I.   An advocate ombuds serves as an advocate on behalf of a population that is designated in the charter. In addition to and in clarification of the standards described in Paragraphs A-F, an advocate ombuds should:

(1)   have a basic understanding of the nature and role of advocacy

(2)   provide information, advice, and assistance to members of the constituency

(3)   evaluate the complainant's claim objectively and advocate for change relief when the facts support the claim

---

[4] The 1969 ABA Resolution, which remains ABA policy, provided that a classical ombuds should be "appoint[ed] by the legislative body or . . . by the executive with confirmation by the designated proportion of the legislative body, preferably more than a majority, such as two thirds."

(4)   be authorized to represent the interests of the designated population with respect to policies implemented or adopted by the establishing entity, government agencies, or other organizations as defined by the charter, and

(5)   be authorized to initiate action in an administrative, judicial, or legislative forum when the facts warrant.

Appendix J

ABA Section of Dispute Resolution Resolution on Mediation and the Unauthorized Practice of Law
(Adopted by the Section on February 2, 2002)

The ABA Section of Dispute Resolution has noted the wide range of views expressed by scholars, mediators, and regulators concerning the question of whether mediation constitutes the practice of law. The Section believes that both the public interest and the practice of mediation would benefit from greater clarity with respect to this issue in the statutes and regulations governing the unauthorized practice of law ("UPL"). The Section believes that such statutes and regulations should be interpreted and applied in such a manner as to permit all individuals, regardless of whether they are lawyers, to serve as mediators. The enforcement of such statutes and regulations should be informed by the following principles:

Mediation is not the practice of law. Mediation is a process in which an impartial individual assists the parties in reaching a voluntary settlement. Such assistance does not constitute the practice of law. The parties to the mediation are not represented by the mediator.

Mediators' discussion of legal issues. In disputes where the parties' legal rights or obligations are at issue, the mediator's discussions with the parties may involve legal issues. Such discussions do not create an attorney-client relationship, and do not constitute legal advice, whether or not the mediator is an attorney.

Drafting settlement agreements. When an agreement is reached in a mediation, the parties often request assistance from the mediator in memorializing their agreement. The preparation of a memorandum of understanding or settlement agreement by a mediator, incorporating the terms of settlement specified by the parties, does not constitute the practice of law. If the mediator drafts an agreement that goes beyond the terms specified by the parties, he or she may be engaged in the practice of law. However, in such a case, a mediator shall not be engaged in the practice of law if (a) all parties are represented by counsel and (b) the mediator discloses that any proposal that he or she makes with respect to the terms of settlement is informational as opposed to the practice of law, and that the parties should not view or rely upon such proposals as advice of counsel, but merely consider them in consultation with their own attorneys.

Mediators' responsibilities. Mediators have a responsibility to inform the parties in a mediation about the nature of the mediator's role in the process and the limits of that role. Mediators should inform the parties: (a) that the mediator's role is not to provide them with legal representation, but rather to assist them in reaching a voluntary agreement; (b) that a settlement agreement may affect the parties' legal rights; and (c) that each of the parties has the right to seek the advice of independent legal counsel throughout the mediation process and should seek such counsel before signing a settlement agreement.

Comments

1. *Mediation and the practice of law.* There is a growing consensus in the ethical opinions addressing this issue that mediation is not the practice of law. *See, e.g.,* Maine Bar Rule 3.4(h)(4) ("The role of mediator does not create a lawyer-client relationship with any of the parties and does not constitute representation of them."); Kentucky Bar Association Ethics Opinion 377 (1995) ("Mediation is not the practice of law."); Indiana Ethics Opinion 5 (1992) (same); Washington State Bar Association, Committee to Define the Practice of Law, Final Report (July 1999), adopted by Washington State Bar Association Board of Governors, September 1999 (same). *But see* New Jersey Supreme Court Advisory Committee on Professional Ethics, Opinion No. 676 (1994) (holding that when a lawyer serves as a third party neutral, he or she "is acting as a lawyer"). Essential to most of the common definitions of the practice of law is the existence of an attorney-client relationship. Because mediators do not establish an attorney-client relationship, they are not engaged in the practice of law when they provide mediation services. The Section recognizes that in some very extraordinary situations it might be possible for a mediator to inadvertently create an attorney-client relationship with a party in mediation. For example, if the parties were unrepresented, and the mediator did not clarify his/her role, it is conceivable, although extremely unlikely, that a party in mediation could mistakenly assume that the mediator's role was to advise and protect solely that party's interests. In mediations where the parties are represented by counsel or where the mediator properly explains (and preferably documents) his/her role, it would appear unlikely that either party in mediation could ever reasonably assume that the mediator was that person's attorney.

2. *Ethical rules governing mediators.* There is a growing body of ethical principles and standards governing the practice of mediation. Accordingly, even if a mediator's conduct is not inconsistent with state UPL statutes or regulations, there may be other sources of authority governing the mediator's conduct. *See, e.g.,* Mass. Uniform Rules on Dispute Resolution 9(c)(iv) ("A neutral may use his or her knowledge to inform the parties' deliberations, but shall not provide legal advice, counseling, or other professional services in connection with the dispute resolution process.").

3. *Ethical rules governing lawyers.* An important, but as yet unresolved question concerning the ethical rules applicable to lawyers is whether, and to what extent, the ABA Model Rules of Professional Conduct (or other rules governing the conduct of lawyers) apply to lawyers when they are serving as mediators and not engaged in the practice of law. If such rules were applied, in whole or in part, they would raise a host of imponderable issues for lawyer-mediators, including who is the client and how to discharge many of the traditional duties lawyers owe to clients. The ABA's Ethics 2000 Commission has made certain proposed revisions to the Model Rules that seemingly recognize this problem and attempt to resolve it by identifying a separate, neutral role for lawyers. The proposed new rule would state:

Lawyer Serving as Third-Party Neutral

(a) A lawyer serves as a third party-neutral when the lawyer assists two or more persons who are not clients of the lawyer to reach a resolution of disputes that have arisen between them. Service as a third-party neutral may include service as an arbitrator, mediator, or in such other capacity as will enable the lawyer to assist the parties to resolve their dispute.

(b) A lawyer serving as a third-party neutral shall inform unrepresented parties that the lawyer is not representing them. When the lawyer knows or reasonably should know that a party does not understand the lawyer's role in the matter, the lawyer shall explain the difference between the lawyer's role as a third-party neutral and the lawyer's role as one who represents a client.

Further, the Ethics 2000 Commission has recommended the following language be added to the Preamble of the Model Rules: "[3] In addition to these representational functions, a lawyer may serve as a third-party neutral, a nonrepresentational role helping the parties to resolve a dispute or other matter. Some of these Rules apply directly to lawyers who are or have served as third-party neutrals. See, e.g., Rules 1.12 and 2.4."

4. *UPL and multi-jurisdictional practice of lawyer-mediators.* Lawyer-mediators should be aware that, unless they are admitted to the bar in every state, they too are potentially affected by the issue of UPL and mediation. Many lawyer-mediators provide mediation services in more than one jurisdiction. If mediation is considered the practice of law, lawyer-mediators could be accused of violating UPL statutes when they serve in a jurisdiction in which they are not admitted to the bar. Although a lawyer may petition for temporary admission, requiring such admission substantially and unnecessarily burdens the practice of mediation outside of the mediator's local area.

This problem is compounded for lawyer-mediators who have ceased practicing law, serve only as a neutral, and later relocate to different states. These lawyer-mediators may face difficult bar admission issues, as a state may require a certain minimum years of active engagement in the practice of law to qualify for admission to the bar without examination. This problem arises because bar regulators' definitions of the active practice of law may not include the activities typical of mediation, whereas the regulators who enforce UPL statutes (typically the state Attorney General, local district attorneys, or a bar committee) may include such activities as the practice of law in their interpretation of UPL statutes. It would seem to be a perverse result if transplanted lawyers clearly engaged in the practice of law could do so without proving their command of their new jurisdiction's laws, while a mediator who has no intention of practicing law would be required to take the new jurisdiction's bar exam.

The ABA's Commission on Multijurisdictional Practice is currently considering proposals for modification of the Model Rules of Professional Conduct that would, if adopted by the ABA and enacted by the states, eliminate, or at least reduce, concerns about lawyer-mediators engaging in a multi-jurisdictional practice.

5. *Guidelines on legal advice.* The Virginia Guidelines on Mediation and the Unauthorized Practice of Law, drafted by the Department of Dispute Resolution Services of the Supreme Court of Virginia, and the North Carolina Guidelines for the Ethical

Practice of Mediation and to Prevent the Unauthorized Practice of Law, adopted by the North Carolina Bar in 1999, articulate a UPL standard for mediators that differs from the standard articulated in this Resolution. According to those Guidelines, a mediator may provide the parties with legal information but may not give legal advice. The Guidelines define legal advice as applying the law to the facts of the case in such a way as to (a) predict the outcome of the case or an issue in the case, or (b) recommend a course of action based on the mediator's analysis. The Section believes that adoption of the Virginia and North Carolina standards in other jurisdictions would be harmful to the growth and development of mediation.

It is important that mediators who are competent to engage in discussion about the strengths and weaknesses of a party's case be free to do so without running afoul of UPL statutes. Indeed, many parties, and their counsel, hire mediators precisely to obtain feedback about their case. Even though mediators who engage in these discussions do sometimes aid the parties by discussing possible outcomes of the dispute if a settlement is not reached and providing evaluative feedback about the parties' positions, this conduct is not the practice of law because the parties have no reasonable basis for believing that the mediator will provide advice solely on behalf of any individual party. This is the important distinction between the mediator's role and the role of an attorney. Parties expect their attorney to represent solely their interests and to provide advice and counsel only for them. On the other hand, a mediator is a neutral, with no duty of loyalty to the individual parties. (Thus, for example, when a judge conducts a settlement conference, acting in a manner analogous to that of a mediator and providing evaluation to the parties about their case, no one suggests that the judge is practicing law.)

6. *Discussion of legal issues.* This Resolution seeks to avoid the problem of a mediator determining, in the midst of a discussion of relevant legal issues, which particular phrasings would constitute legal advice and which would not. For example, during mediation of a medical malpractice case, if a mediator comments that "the video of the newborn (deceased shortly after birth) has considerable emotional impact and makes the newborn more real," is this legal advice or prediction or simply stating the obvious? In context, the mediator is implicitly or explicitly suggesting that it may affect a jury's damage award, and thus settlement value. S/he is raising, from the neutral's perspective, a point the parties (presumably the defendants) may have missed, which may distinguish this case from others (e.g., cases in which a baby died *in utero* or where there was no video of the newborn) in which lower settlement amounts were offered and accepted. Is the mediator absolved if s/he phrases the point as a "probing question"?

In their article, "A Well-Founded Fear of Prosecution: Mediation and the Unauthorized Practice of Law" (6 *Dispute Resolution Magazine* 20 (Winter 2000)), authors David A. Hoffman and Natasha A. Affolder illustrate this problem across a broader mediation context, setting out numerous alternative ways a mediator might phrase a point. They note that there would likely be very little professional consensus about which phrasings would constitute the practice of law and which would not. Even if mediators could agree as to where the line would be drawn among suggested phrasings, the intended meaning and impact of any particular statement might vary with the context and how the statement was delivered. Because mediation is almost always an informal and confidential process, it is virtually impossible – without an audio or video recording of a mediation – for regulators to police the nuances of the mediator's communications with the parties. Such recording would clearly be anathema to the mediation process.

7. _Settlement agreements_. The Virginia and North Carolina Guidelines' approach to the drafting of settlement agreements by a mediator is similar to the approach outlined in this Resolution. See "Guidelines on Mediation and the Unauthorized Practice of Law," Department of Dispute Resolution Services of the Supreme Court of Virginia, at 27-28 ("Mediators who prepare written agreements for disputing parties should strive to use the parties' own words whenever possible and in all cases should write agreements in a manner that comports with the wishes of the disputants. . . . Unless required by law, a mediator should not add provisions to an agreement beyond those specified by the disputants.") Ethics opinions in some states have approved the drafting of formal settlement agreements by mediators who are lawyers, even where the mediator incorporates language that goes beyond the words specified by the parties, provided that the mediator has encouraged the parties to seek independent legal advice. _See, e.g._, Massachusetts Bar Association Opinion 85-3 (attorney acting as mediator may draft a marital settlement agreement "but must advise the parties of the advantages of having independent legal counsel review any such agreement, and must obtain the informed consent of the parties to such joint representation").

8. _Resources_. A number of articles addressing the question of whether mediation is the practice of law have been published in recent years. In addition to the articles cited above, _see generally_, Symposium, "Is Mediation the Practice of Law?" _Forum_, Number 33 (NIDR, June 1997); Carrie Menkel-Meadow, "Is Mediation the Practice of Law?" _Alternatives_, May 1996, at 60; Bruce E. Meyerson, "Mediation Should Not Be Considered the Practice of Law," 18 _Alternatives_ 122-123 (CPR Institute for Dispute Resolution, June 1996); Andrew S. Morrison, "Is Divorce Mediation the Practice of Law? A Matter of Perspective," 75 _California Law Review_ 1093 (1987).

Appendix K

Florida Rules for Certified and Court-Appointed Mediators

PART I. MEDIATOR QUALIFICATIONS

Rule 10.100. General Qualifications

(a)   County Court Mediators. For certification a mediator of county court matters must be certified as a circuit court or family mediator or:

    (1)   complete a minimum of 20 hours in a training program certified by the supreme court;

    (2)   observe a minimum of 4 county court mediation conferences conducted by a court-certified mediator and conduct 4 county court mediation conferences under the supervision and observation of a court-certified mediator; and

    (3)   be of good moral character.

(b)   Family Mediators. For certification a mediator of family and dissolution of marriage issues must:

    (1)   complete a minimum of 40 hours in a family mediation training program certified by the supreme court;

    (2)   have a master's degree or doctorate in social work, mental health, or behavioral or social sciences; be a physician certified to practice adult or child psychiatry; or be an attorney or a certified public accountant licensed to practice in any United States jurisdiction; and have at least 4 years practical experience in one of the aforementioned fields or have 8 years family mediation experience with a minimum of 10 mediations per year;

    (3)   observe 2 family mediations conducted by a certified family mediator and conduct 2 family mediations under the supervision and observation of a certified family mediator; and

    (4)   be of good moral character.

(c)   Circuit Court Mediators. For certification a mediator of circuit court matters, other than family matters, must:

    (1)   complete a minimum of 40 hours in a circuit court mediation training program certified by the supreme court;

    (2)   be a member in good standing of The Florida Bar with at least 5 years of Florida practice and be an active member of The Florida Bar within 1 year of application for certification; or be a retired trial judge from any United States jurisdiction who was a member in good standing of the bar in the state in which the judge presided for at least 5 years immediately

preceding the year certification is sought;

(3) observe 2 circuit court mediations conducted by a certified circuit mediator and conduct 2 circuit mediations under the supervision and observation of a certified circuit court mediator; and

(4) be of good moral character.

(d) Dependency Mediators. For certification a mediator of dependency matters, as defined in Florida Rules for Juvenile Procedure 8.290(a) must:

(1) complete a supreme court certified dependency mediation training program as follows:

(A) 40 hours if the applicant is not a certified family mediator or is a certified family mediator who has not mediated at least 4 dependency cases; or

(B) 20 hours if the applicant is a certified family mediator who has mediated at least 4 dependency cases; and

(2) have a master's degree or doctorate in social work, mental health, behavioral sciences or social sciences; or be a physician licensed to practice adult or child psychiatry or pediatrics; or be an attorney licensed to practice in any United States jurisdiction; and

(3) have 4 years experience in family and/or dependency issues or be a licensed mental health professional with at least 4 years practical experience or be a supreme court certified family or circuit mediator with a minimum of 20 mediations; and

(4) observe 4 dependency mediations conducted by a certified dependency mediator and conduct 2 dependency mediations under the supervision and observation of a certified dependency mediator; and

(5) be of good moral character.

(e) Referral for Discipline. If the certification or licensure necessary for any person to be certified as a family or circuit mediator is suspended or revoked, or if the mediator holding such certification or licensure is in any other manner disciplined, such matter shall be referred to the Mediator Qualifications Board for appropriate action pursuant to rule 10.800.

(f) Special Conditions. Mediators who have been duly certified as circuit court or family mediators before July 1, 1990, shall be deemed qualified as circuit court or family mediators pursuant to these rules. Certified family mediators who have mediated a minimum of 4 dependency cases prior to July 1, 1997, shall be granted temporary certification and may continue to mediate dependency matters for no more than 1 year from the time that a training program pursuant to subdivision (d)(1)(B) is certified by the supreme court. Such mediators shall be deemed qualified to apply for certification as dependency mediators upon successful completion of the requirements of subdivision (d)(1)(B) and (d)(5) of this rule.

Rule 10.110. Good Moral Character

(a)   General Requirement. No person shall be certified by this Court as a mediator unless such person first produces satisfactory evidence of good moral character as required by rule 10.100.

(b)   Purpose. The primary purpose of the requirement of good moral character is to ensure protection of the participants in mediation and the public, as well as to safeguard the justice system. A mediator shall have, as a prerequisite to certification and as a requirement for continuing certification, the good moral character sufficient to meet all of the Mediator Standards of Professional Conduct set out in rules 10.200-10.690.

(c)   Initial Certification. The following shall apply in relation to determining the good moral character required for mediator certification:

   (1)   The applicant's good moral character may be subject to inquiry when the applicant's conduct is relevant to the qualifications of a mediator.
   (2)   A person who has been convicted of a felony shall not be eligible for certification until such person has received a restoration of civil rights.
   (3)   A person who is serving a sentence of felony probation shall not be eligible for certification until termination of the period of probation.
   (4)   In assessing whether the applicant's previous conduct demonstrates a present lack of good moral character the following factors shall be relevant:
      (A)   the extent to which the conduct would interfere with a mediator's duties and responsibilities;
      (B)   the area of mediation in which certification is sought;
      (C)   the factors underlying the conduct;
      (D)   the applicant's age at the time of the conduct;
      (E)   the recency of the conduct;
      (F)   the reliability of the information concerning the conduct;
      (G)   the seriousness of the conduct as it relates to mediator qualifications;
      (H)   the cumulative effect of the conduct or information;
      (I)   any evidence of rehabilitation;
      (J)   the applicant's candor during the application process; and
      (K)   disbarment or suspension from any profession.

PART II. STANDARDS OF PROFESSIONAL CONDUCT

Rule 10.200. Scope and Purpose

These Rules provide ethical standards of conduct for certified and court-appointed mediators. They are intended to both guide mediators in the performance of their services and instill public confidence in the mediation process. The public's use, understanding, and satisfaction with mediation can only be achieved if mediators embrace the highest ethical principles. Whether the parties involved in a mediation choose to resolve their dispute is secondary in importance to whether the mediator conducts the mediation in accordance with these ethical standards.

Committee Notes

2000 Revision. In early 1991, the Florida Supreme Court Standing Committee on Mediation and Arbitration Rules was commissioned by the Chief Justice to research, draft and present for adoption both a comprehensive set of ethical standards for Florida mediators and procedural rules for their enforcement. To accomplish this task, the Committee divided itself into two sub-committees and, over the remainder of the year, launched parallel programs to research and develop the requested ethical standards and grievance procedures.

The Subcommittee on Ethical Standards began its task by searching the nation for other states or private dispute resolution organizations who had completed any significant work in defining the ethical responsibilities of professional mediators. After searching for guidance outside the state, the subcommittee turned to Florida's own core group of certified mediators for more direct and firsthand data. Through a series of statewide public hearings and meetings, the subcommittee gathered current information on ethical concerns based upon the expanding experiences of practicing Florida certified mediators. In May of 1992, The "Florida Rules for Certified and Court Appointed Mediators" became effective.

In the years following the adoption of those ethical rules, the Committee observed their impact on the mediation profession. By 1998, several other states and dispute resolution organizations initiated research into ethical standards for mediation which also became instructive to the Committee. In addition, Florida's Mediator Qualifications Advisory Panel, created to field ethical questions from practicing mediators, gained a wealth of pragmatic experience in the application of ethical concepts to actual practice that became available to the Committee. Finally, The Florida Mediator Qualifications Board, the disciplinary body for mediators, developed specific data from actual grievances filed against mediators over the past several years, which also added to the available body of knowledge.

Using this new body of information and experience, the Committee undertook a year long study program to determine if Florida's ethical rules for mediators would benefit from review and revision.

Upon reviewing the 1992 ethical Rules, it immediately became apparent to the Committee that reorganization, renumbering, and more descriptive titles would make the Rules more useful. For that reason, the Rules were reorganized into four substantive groups which recognized a mediator's ethical responsibilities to the "parties," the "process," the "profession" and the "courts." The intent of the Committee here was to simply make the Rules easier to locate. There is no official significance in the order in which the Rules appear; any one area is equally important as all other areas. The Committee recognizes many rules overlap and define specific ethical responsibilities which impact more than one area. Clearly, a violation of a rule in one section may very well injure relationships protected in another section.

Titles to the Rules were changed to more accurately reflect their content. Additionally, redundancies were eliminated, phrasing tightened, and grammatical changes made to more clearly state their scope and purpose.

Finally, the Committee sought to apply what had been learned. The 2000 revisions are the result of that effort.

Rule 10.210. Mediation Defined

Mediation is a process whereby a neutral and impartial third person acts to encourage and facilitate the resolution of a dispute without prescribing what it should be. It is an informal and non-adversarial process intended to help disputing parties reach a mutually acceptable agreement.

Rule 10.220. Mediator's Role

The role of the mediator is to reduce obstacles to communication, assist in the identification of issues and exploration of alternatives, and otherwise facilitate voluntary agreements resolving the dispute. The ultimate decision-making authority, however, rests solely with the parties.

Rule 10.230. Mediation Concepts

Mediation is based on concepts of communication, negotiation, facilitation, and problem-solving that emphasize:
     (a)   self determination;
     (b)   the needs and interests of the parties;
     (c)   fairness;
     (d)   procedural flexibility;
     (e)   confidentiality; and
     (f)   full disclosure.

Rule 10.300. Mediator's Responsibility to the Parties

The purpose of mediation is to provide a forum for consensual dispute resolution by the parties. It is not an adjudicatory procedure. Accordingly, a mediator's responsibility to the parties includes honoring their right of self-determination; acting with impartiality; and avoiding coercion, improper influence, and conflicts of interest. A mediator is also responsible for maintaining an appropriate demeanor, preserving confidentiality, and promoting the awareness by the parties of the interests of non-participating persons. A mediator's business practices should reflect fairness, integrity and impartiality.

2000 Revision. Rules 10.300 - 10.380 include a collection of specific ethical concerns involving a mediator's responsibility to the parties to a dispute. Incorporated in this new section are the concepts formerly found in Rule 10.060 (Self Determination); Rule 10.070 (Impartiality/Conflict of Interest); Rule 10.080 (Confidentiality); Rule 10.090 (Professional Advice); and Rule 10.100 (Fees and Expenses). In addition, the Committee grouped under this heading ethical concerns dealing with the mediator's demeanor and courtesy, contractual relationships, and responsibility to non-participating persons.

Rule 10.310. Self-Determination

(a) Decision-making. Decisions made during a mediation are to be made by the parties. A mediator shall not make substantive decisions for any party. A mediator is responsible for assisting the parties in reaching informed and voluntary decisions while protecting their right of self-determination.

(b) Coercion Prohibited. A mediator shall not coerce or improperly influence any party to make a decision or unwillingly participate in a mediation.

(c) Misrepresentation Prohibited. A mediator shall not intentionally or knowingly misrepresent any material fact or circumstance in the course of conducting a mediation.

(d) Postponement or Cancellation. If, for any reason, a party is unable to freely exercise self-determination, a mediator shall cancel or postpone a mediation.

Committee Notes

2000 Revision. Mediation is a process to facilitate consensual agreement between parties in conflict and to assist them in voluntarily resolving their dispute. It is critical that the parties' right to self-determination (a free and informed choice to agree or not to agree) is preserved during all phases of mediation. A mediator must not substitute the judgment of the mediator for the judgment of the parties, coerce or compel a party to make a decision, knowingly allow a participant to make a decision based on misrepresented facts or circumstances, or in any other way impair or interfere with the parties' right of self-determination.

While mediation techniques and practice styles may vary from mediator to mediator and mediation to mediation, a line is crossed and ethical standards are violated when any conduct of the mediator serves to compromise the parties' basic right to agree or not to agree. Special care should be taken to preserve the party's right to self-determination if the mediator provides input to the mediation process. See Rule 10.370.

On occasion, a mediator may be requested by the parties to serve as a decisionmaker. If the mediator decides to serve in such a capacity, compliance with this request results in a change in the dispute resolution process impacting self-determination, impartiality, confidentiality, and other ethical standards. Before providing decision-making services, therefore, the mediator shall ensure that all parties understand and consent to those changes. See Rules 10.330 and 10.340.

Under subdivision (d), postponement or cancellation of a mediation is necessary if the mediator reasonably believes the threat of domestic violence, existence of substance abuse, physical threat or undue psychological dominance are present and existing factors which would impair any party's ability to freely and willingly enter into an informed agreement.

Rule 10.320. Nonparticipating Persons

A mediator shall promote awareness by the parties of the interests of persons affected by actual or potential agreements who are not represented at mediation.

Committee Notes

2000 Revision. Mediated agreements will often impact persons or entities not participating in the process. Examples include lienholders, governmental agencies, shareholders, and related commercial entities. In family and dependency mediations, the interests of children, grandparents or other related persons are also often affected. A mediator is responsible for making the parties aware of the potential interests of such non-participating persons.

In raising awareness of the interests of non-participating persons, however, the mediator should still respect the rights of the parties to make their own decisions. Further, raising awareness of possible interests of related entities should not involve advocacy or judgments as to the merits of those interests. In family mediations, for example, a mediator should make the parents aware of the children's interests without interfering with self-determination or advocating a particular position.

Rule 10.330. Impartiality

(a)   Generally. A mediator shall maintain impartiality throughout the mediation process. Impartiality means freedom from favoritism or bias in word, action, or appearance, and includes a commitment to assist all parties, as opposed to any one individual.

(b)   Withdrawal for Partiality. A mediator shall withdraw from mediation if the mediator is no longer impartial.

(c)   Gifts and Solicitation. A mediator shall neither give nor accept a gift, favor, loan, or other item of value in any mediation process. During the mediation process, a mediator shall not solicit or otherwise attempt to procure future professional services.

2000 Revision. A mediator has an affirmative obligation to maintain impartiality throughout the entire mediation process. The duty to maintain impartiality arises immediately upon learning of a potential engagement for providing mediation services. A mediator shall not accept or continue any engagement for mediation services in which the ability to maintain impartiality is reasonably impaired or compromised. As soon as practical, a mediator shall make reasonable inquiry as to the identity of the parties or other circumstances which could compromise the mediator's impartiality.

During the mediation, a mediator shall maintain impartiality even while raising questions regarding the reality, fairness, equity, durability and feasibility of proposed options for settlement. In the event circumstances arise during a mediation that would reasonably be construed to impair or compromise a mediator's impartiality, the mediator is obligated to withdraw.

Subdivision (c) does not preclude a mediator from giving or accepting de minimis gifts or incidental items provided to facilitate the mediation.

Rule 10.340. Conflicts of Interest

(a)   Generally. A mediator shall not mediate a matter that presents a clear or undisclosed conflict of interest. A conflict of interest arises when any relationship between the mediator and the mediation participants or the subject matter of the dispute compromises or appears to compromise the mediator's impartiality.

(b)   Burden of Disclosure. The burden of disclosure of any potential conflict of interest rests on the mediator. Disclosure shall be made as soon as practical after the mediator becomes aware of the interest or relationship giving rise to the potential conflict of interest.

(c)   Effect of Disclosure. After appropriate disclosure, the mediator may serve if all parties agree. However, if a conflict of interest clearly impairs a mediator's impartiality, the mediator shall withdraw regardless of the express agreement of the parties.

(d)   Conflict During Mediation. A mediator shall not create a conflict of interest during the mediation. During a mediation, a mediator shall not provide any services that are not directly related to the mediation process.

2000 Revision. Potential conflicts of interests which require disclosure include the fact of a mediator's membership on a related board of directors, full or part time service by the mediator as a representative, advocate, or consultant to a mediation participant, present stock or bond ownership by the mediator in a corporate mediation participant, or any other form of managerial, financial, or family interest by the mediator in any mediation participant involved in a mediation. A mediator who is a member of a law firm or other professional organization is obliged to disclose any past or present client relationship that firm or organization may have with any party involved in a mediation.

The duty to disclose thus includes information relating to a mediator's ongoing financial or professional relationship with any of the parties, counsel, or related entities. Disclosure is required with respect to any significant past, present, or promised future relationship with any party involved in a proposed mediation. While impartiality is not necessarily compromised, full disclosure and a reasonable opportunity for the parties to react are essential.

Disclosure of relationships or circumstances which would create the potential for a conflict of interest should be made at the earliest possible opportunity and under circumstances which will allow the parties to freely exercise their right of self-determination as to both the selection of the mediator and participation in the mediation process.

A conflict of interest which clearly impairs a mediator's impartiality is not resolved by mere disclosure to, or waiver by, the parties. Such conflicts occur when circumstances or relationships involving the mediator cannot be reasonably regarded as allowing the mediator to maintain impartiality.

To maintain an appropriate level of impartiality and to avoid creating conflicts of interest, a mediator's professional input to a mediation proceeding must be confined to the services necessary to provide the parties a process to reach a self-determined agreement. Under subdivision (d), a mediator is accordingly prohibited from utilizing a mediation to supply any other services which do not directly relate to the conduct of the mediation itself. By way of example, a mediator would therefore be prohibited from providing accounting, psychiatric or legal services, psychological or social counseling, therapy, or business consultations of any sort during the mediation process.

Mediators establish personal relationships with many representatives, attorneys, mediators, and other members of various professional associations. There should be no attempt to be secretive about such friendships or acquaintances, but disclosure is not necessary unless some feature of a particular relationship might reasonably appear to impair impartiality.

Rule 10.350. Demeanor

A mediator shall be patient, dignified, and courteous during the mediation process.

Rule 10.360. Confidentiality

(a)   Scope. A mediator shall maintain confidentiality of all information revealed during mediation except where disclosure is required by law.

(b)   Caucus. Information obtained during caucus may not be revealed by the mediator to any other mediation participant without the consent of the disclosing party.

(c)   Record Keeping. A mediator shall maintain confidentiality in the storage and disposal of records and shall not disclose any identifying information when materials are used for research, training, or statistical compilations.

Rule 10.370. Professional Advice or Opinions

(a)   Providing Information. Consistent with standards of impartiality and preserving party self-determination, a mediator may provide information that the mediator is qualified by training or experience to provide.

(b)   Independent Legal Advice. When a mediator believes a party does not understand or appreciate how an agreement may adversely affect legal rights or obligations, the mediator shall advise the party of the right to seek independent legal counsel.

(c)   Personal or Professional Opinion. A mediator shall not offer a personal or professional opinion intended to coerce the parties, decide the dispute, or direct a resolution of any issue. Consistent with standards of impartiality and preserving party self-determination however, a mediator may point out possible outcomes of the case and discuss the merits of a claim or defense. A mediator shall not offer a personal or professional opinion as to how the court in which the case has been filed will resolve the dispute.

Committee Notes

2000 Revision (previously Committee Note to 1992 adoption of former rule 10.090). Mediators who are attorneys should note Florida Bar Committee on Professional Ethics, formal opinion 86-8 at 1239, which states that the lawyer-mediator should "explain the risks of proceeding without independent counsel and advise the parties to consult counsel during the course of the mediation and before signing any settlement agreement that he might prepare for them."

2000 Revision. The primary role of the mediator is to facilitate a process which will provide the parties an opportunity to resolve all or part of a dispute by agreement if they choose to do so. A mediator may assist in that endeavor by providing relevant information or helping the parties obtain such information from other sources. A mediator may also raise issues and discuss strengths and weaknesses of positions underlying the dispute. Finally, a mediator may help the parties evaluate resolution options and draft settlement proposals. In providing these services however, it is imperative that the mediator maintain impartiality and avoid any activity which would have the effect of overriding the parties' rights of self-determination. While mediators may call upon their own qualifications and experience to supply information and options, the parties must be given the opportunity to freely decide upon any agreement. Mediators shall not utilize their opinions to decide any aspect of the dispute or to coerce the parties or their representatives to accept any resolution option.

While a mediator has no duty to specifically advise a party as to the legal ramifications or consequences of a proposed agreement, there is a duty for the mediator to advise the parties of the importance of understanding such matters and giving them the opportunity to seek such advice if they desire.

Rule 10.380. Fees and Expenses

(a)   Generally. A mediator holds a position of trust. Fees charged for mediation services shall be reasonable and consistent with the nature of the case.

(b)   Guiding Principles in Determining Fees. A mediator shall be guided by the following general principles in determining fees:
   (1)   Any charges for mediation services based on time shall not exceed actual time spent or allocated.
   (2)   Charges for costs shall be for those actually incurred.
   (3)   All fees and costs shall be appropriately divided between the parties.
   (4)   When time or expenses involve two or more mediations on the same day or trip, the time and expense charges shall be prorated appropriately.

(c)   Written Explanation of Fees. A mediator shall give the parties or their counsel a written explanation of any fees and costs prior to mediation. The explanation shall include:
   (1)   the basis for and amount of any charges for services to be rendered, including minimum fees and travel time;
   (2)   the amount charged for the postponement or cancellation of mediation sessions and the circumstances under which such charges will be assessed or waived;
   (3)   the basis and amount of charges for any other items; and
   (4)   the parties' pro rata share of mediation fees and costs if previously determined by the court or agreed to by the parties.

(d)   Maintenance of Records. A mediator shall maintain records necessary to support charges for services and expenses and upon request shall make an accounting to the parties, their counsel, or the court.

(e)   Remuneration for Referrals. No commissions, rebates, or similar remuneration shall be given or received by a mediator for a mediation referral.

(f) Contingency Fees Prohibited. A mediator shall not charge a contingent fee or base a fee on the outcome of the process.

Rule 10.400. Mediator's Responsibility to the Mediation Process

A mediator is responsible for safeguarding the mediation process. The benefits of the process are best achieved if the mediation is conducted in an informed, balanced and timely fashion. A mediator is responsible for confirming that mediation is an appropriate dispute resolution process under the circumstances of each case.

Committee Notes

2000 Revision. Rules 10.400 - 10.430 include a collection of specific ethical concerns involved in a mediator's responsibility to the mediation process. Incorporated in this new section are the concepts formerly found in rule 10.060 (Self-Determination), rule 10.090 (Professional Advice); and rule 10.110 (Concluding Mediation). In addition, the Committee grouped under this heading ethical concerns dealing with the mediator's duty to determine the existence of potential conflicts, a mandate for adequate time for mediation sessions, and the process for adjournment.

Rule 10.410. Balanced Process

A mediator shall conduct mediation sessions in an even-handed, balanced manner. A mediator shall promote mutual respect among the mediation participants throughout the mediation process and encourage the participants to conduct themselves in a collaborative, non-coercive, and non-adversarial manner.

Committee Notes

2000 Revision. A mediator should be aware that the presence or threat of domestic violence or abuse among the parties can endanger the parties, the mediator, and others. Domestic violence and abuse can undermine the exercise of self-determination and the ability to reach a voluntary and mutually acceptable agreement.

Rule 10.420. Conduct of Mediation

(a) Orientation Session. Upon commencement of the mediation session, a mediator shall describe the mediation process and the role of the mediator, and shall inform the mediation participants that:
(1) mediation is a consensual process;
(2) the mediator is an impartial facilitator without authority to impose a resolution or adjudicate any aspect of the dispute; and

(3) communications made during the process are confidential, except where disclosure is required by law.

(b)   Adjournment or Termination. A mediator shall:
(1) adjourn the mediation upon agreement of the parties;
(2) adjourn or terminate any mediation which, if continued, would result in unreasonable emotional or monetary costs to the parties;
(3) adjourn or terminate the mediation if the mediator believes the case is unsuitable for mediation or any party is unable or unwilling to participate meaningfully in the process;
(4) terminate a mediation entailing fraud, duress, the absence of bargaining ability, or unconscionability; and
(5) terminate any mediation if the physical safety of any person is endangered by the continuation of mediation.

(c)   Closure. The mediator shall cause the terms of any agreement reached to be memorialized appropriately and discuss with the parties and counsel the process for formalization and implementation of the agreement.

Committee Notes

2000 Revision. In defining the role of the mediator during the course of an opening session, a mediator should ensure that the participants fully understand the nature of the process and the limits on the mediator's authority. See rule 10.370(c). It is also appropriate for the mediator to inform the parties that mediators are ethically precluded from providing non-mediation services to any party. See rule 10.340(d).

Florida Rule of Civil Procedure 1.730(b), Florida Rule of Juvenile Procedure 8.290(o), and Florida Family Law Rule of Procedure 12.740(f) require that any mediated agreement be reduced to writing. Mediators have an obligation to ensure these rules are complied with, but are not required to write the agreement themselves.

Rule 10.430. Scheduling Mediation

A mediator shall schedule a mediation in a manner that provides adequate time for the parties to fully exercise their right of self-determination. A mediator shall perform mediation services in a timely fashion, avoiding delays whenever possible.

Rule 10.500. Mediator's Responsibility to the Courts

A mediator is accountable to the referring court with ultimate authority over the case. Any interaction discharging this responsibility, however, shall be conducted in a manner consistent with these ethical rules.

2000 Revision. Rules 10.500 - 10.540 include a collection of specific ethical concerns involved in a mediator's responsibility to the courts. Incorporated in this new section are the concepts formerly found in rule 10.040 (Responsibilities to Courts).

Rule 10.510. Information to the Court

A mediator shall be candid, accurate, and fully responsive to the court concerning the mediator's qualifications, availability, and other administrative matters.

Rule 10.520. Compliance with Authority

A mediator shall comply with all statutes, court rules, local court rules, and administrative orders relevant to the practice of mediation.

Rule 10.530. Improper Influence

A mediator shall refrain from any activity that has the appearance of improperly influencing a court to secure an appointment to a case.

Committee Notes

2000 Revision. Giving gifts to court personnel in exchange for case assignments is improper. De minimis gifts generally distributed as part of an overall business development plan are excepted. See also rule 10.330.

10.600. Mediator's Responsibility to the Mediation Profession

A mediator shall preserve the quality of the profession. A mediator is responsible for maintaining professional competence and forthright business practices, fostering good relationships, assisting new mediators, and generally supporting the advancement of mediation.

Committee Notes

2000 Revision. Rules 10.600 - 10.690 include a collection of specific ethical concerns involving a mediator's responsibility to the mediation profession. Incorporated in this new section are the concepts formerly found in rule 10.030 (General Standards and Qualifications), rule 10.120 (Training and Education), rule 10.130 (Advertising), rule 10.140 (Relationships with Other Professionals), and rule 10.150 (Advancement of Mediation).

Rule 10.610. Advertising

A mediator shall not engage in marketing practices which contain false or misleading information. A mediator shall ensure that any advertisements of the mediator's qualifications, services to be rendered, or the mediation process are accurate and honest. A mediator shall not make claims of achieving specific outcomes or promises implying favoritism for the purpose of obtaining business.

Rule 10.620. Integrity and Impartiality

A mediator shall not accept any engagement, provide any service, or perform any act that would compromise the mediator's integrity or impartiality.

Rule 10.630. Professional Competence

A mediator shall acquire and maintain professional competence in mediation. A mediator shall regularly participate in educational activities promoting professional growth.

Rule 10.640. Skill and Experience

A mediator shall decline an appointment, withdraw, or request appropriate assistance when the facts and circumstances of the case are beyond the mediator's skill or experience.

Rule 10.650. Concurrent Standards

Other ethical standards to which a mediator may be professionally bound are not abrogated by these rules. In the course of performing mediation services, however, these rules prevail over any conflicting ethical standards to which a mediator may otherwise be bound.

Rule 10.660. Relationships with Other Mediators

A mediator shall respect the professional relationships of another mediator.

Rule 10.670. Relationship with Other Professionals

A mediator shall respect the role of other professional disciplines in the mediation process and shall promote cooperation between mediators and other professionals.

Rule 10.680. Prohibited Agreements

With the exception of an agreement conferring benefits upon retirement, a mediator shall not restrict or limit another mediator's practice following termination of a professional relationship.

Committee Notes

2000 Revision. Rule 10.680 is intended to discourage covenants not to compete or other practice restrictions arising upon the termination of a relationship with another mediator or mediation firm. In situations where a retirement program is being contractually funded or supported by a surviving mediator or mediation firm, however, reasonable restraints on competition are acceptable.

Rule 10.690. Advancement of Mediation

(a)   Pro Bono Service. Mediators have a responsibility to provide competent services to persons seeking their assistance, including those unable to pay for services. A mediator should provide mediation services pro bono or at a reduced rate of compensation whenever appropriate.

(b)   New Mediator Training. An experienced mediator should cooperate in training new mediators, including serving as a mentor.

(c)   Support of Mediation. A mediator should support the advancement of mediation by encouraging and participating in research, evaluation, or other forms of professional development and public education.

PART III. DISCIPLINE

Rule 10.700. Scope and Purpose

These rules apply to all proceedings before all panels and committees of the mediator qualifications board involving the discipline or suspension of certified mediators or non-certified mediators appointed to mediate a case pursuant to court rules. The purpose of these rules of discipline is to provide a means for enforcing the Florida Rules for Certified and Court-Appointed Mediators.

Rule 10.710. Privilege to Mediate

Certification to mediate confers no vested right to the holder thereof, but is a conditional privilege that is revocable for cause.

Rule 10.720. Definitions

(a)   Board. The mediator qualifications board.

(b)   Center. The Florida Dispute Resolution Center of the Office of the State Courts Administrator.

(c)   Complaint. Formal submission of an alleged violation of the Rules for Certified and Court-Appointed Mediators, including allegations of a lack of good moral character. A complaint may originate from any person or from the Center.

(d)   Complaint Committee. Three members of the board from the division in which a complaint against a mediator originates.

(e)   Counsel. Counsel appointed by the center, at the direction of the complaint committee, responsible for presenting the complaint to the panel.

(f)   Division. One of 3 standing divisions of the mediator qualifications board, established on a regional basis.

(g)   Investigator. A certified mediator, or attorney, or other qualified individual appointed by the center at the direction of a complaint committee.

(h)   Mediator. A person certified by the Florida Supreme Court or an individual mediating pursuant to court order.

(i)   Panel. Five members of the board from the division in which a complaint against a mediator originates.

(j)   Qualifications Complaint Committee. Three members of the board selected for the purpose of considering referrals pursuant to rule 10.800.

Rule 10.730. Mediator Qualifications Board

(a)   Generally. The mediator qualifications board shall be composed of 3 standing divisions that shall be located in the following regions:
    (1)   One division in north Florida, encompassing the First, Second, Third, Fourth, Eighth, and Fourteenth judicial circuits;
    (2)   One division in central Florida, encompassing the Fifth, Sixth, Seventh, Ninth, Tenth, Twelfth, Thirteenth, and Eighteenth judicial circuits;
    (3)   One division in south Florida, encompassing the Eleventh, Fifteenth, Sixteenth, Seventeenth, Nineteenth, and Twentieth judicial circuits.

Other divisions may be formed by the supreme court based on need.

(b)   Composition of Divisions. Each division of the board shall be composed of:
    (1)   three circuit or county judges;
    (2)   three certified county mediators;
    (3)   three certified circuit mediators;
    (4)   three certified family mediators, at least 2 of whom shall be non-lawyers;
    (5)   not less than 1 nor more than 3 certified dependency mediators; and
    (6)   three attorneys licensed to practice law in Florida who have a substantial trial practice and are neither certified as mediators nor judicial officers during their terms of service on the board, at least 1 of whom shall have a substantial dissolution of marriage law practice.

(c)   Appointment; Terms. Eligible persons shall be appointed to the board by the chief justice of the Supreme Court of Florida for a period of 4 years. The terms of the board members shall be staggered.

(d)   Complaint Committee. Each complaint committee of the board shall be composed of 3 members. A complaint committee shall cease to exist after disposing of all assigned cases. Each complaint committee shall be composed of:

  (1)   one judge or attorney, who shall act as the chair of the committee;
  (2)   one mediator, who is certified in the area to which the complaint refers; and
  (3)   one other certified mediator.

(e)   Qualifications Complaint Committee. One member of each division shall serve as a member of the qualifications complaint committee for a period of 1 year. The qualifications complaint committee shall be composed of:
  (1)   one judge or attorney, who shall act as the chair of the committee; and
  (2)   two certified mediators.

(f)   Panels. Each panel of the board shall be composed of 5 members. A panel shall cease to exist after disposing of all assigned cases. Each panel shall be composed of:
  (1)   one circuit or county judge, who shall serve as the chair;
  (2)   three certified mediators, at least 1 of whom shall be certified in the area to which the complaint refers; and
  (3)   one attorney.

(g)   Panel Vice-Chair. Each panel once appointed shall elect a vice-chair. The vice-chair shall act as the chair of the panel in the absence of the chair.

Committee Notes

2000 Revision. In relation to (b)(5), the Committee believes that the Chief Justice should have discretion in the number of dependency mediators appointed to the Board depending on the number of certified dependency mediators available for appointment. It is the intention of the Committee that when dependency mediation reaches a comparable level of activity to the other three areas of certification, the full complement of three representatives per division should be realized.

Rule 10.740. Jurisdiction

(a)   Complaint Committee. Each complaint committee shall have such jurisdiction and powers as are necessary to conduct the proper and speedy investigation and disposition of any complaint. The judge or attorney presiding over the complaint committee shall have the power to compel the attendance of witnesses, to take or to cause to be taken the depositions of witnesses, and to order the production of records or other documentary evidence, and the power of contempt. The complaint committee shall perform its investigatory function and have concomitant power to resolve cases prior to panel referral.

(b)   Qualifications Complaint Committee. The qualifications complaint committee shall have jurisdiction over all matters referred pursuant to rule 10.800. The qualifications complaint committee shall have such jurisdiction and powers as are necessary to conduct the proper and speedy investigation and disposition of any good moral character complaint or other matter referred by the Center. The judge or attorney presiding over the qualifications complaint committee shall have the power to compel the attendance of witnesses, to take or to cause to be taken the depositions of witnesses, and to order the production of records or other documentary evidence, and the power of contempt. The qualifications complaint committee shall perform its investigatory function and have concomitant power to resolve cases prior to panel referral.

(c)   Panel. Each panel shall have such jurisdiction and powers as are necessary to conduct the proper and speedy adjudication and disposition of any proceeding. The judge presiding over each panel shall have the power to compel the attendance of witnesses, to take or to cause to be taken the depositions of witnesses, to order the production of records or other documentary evidence, and the power of contempt. The panel shall perform the adjudicatory function, but shall not have any investigatory functions.

(d)   Contempt. Should any witness fail, without justification, to respond to the lawful subpoena of the complaint committee, the qualifications complaint committee, or the panel or, having responded, fail or refuse to answer all inquiries or to turn over evidence that has been lawfully subpoenaed, or should any person be guilty of disorderly or contemptuous conduct before any proceeding of the complaint committee, the qualifications complaint committee, or the panel, a motion may be filed by the complaint committee, the qualifications complaint committee, or the panel before the circuit court of the county in which the contemptuous act was committed. The motion shall allege the specific failure on the part of the witness or the specific disorderly or contemptuous act of the person which forms the basis of the alleged contempt of the complaint committee, the qualifications complaint committee, or the panel. Such motion shall pray for the issuance of an order to show cause before the circuit court why the circuit court should not find the person in contempt of the complaint committee, the qualifications complaint committee, or the panel and the person should not be punished by the court therefor. The circuit court shall issue such orders and judgments therein as the court deems appropriate.

Rule 10.750. Staff

The center shall provide all staff support to the board necessary to fulfill its duties and responsibilities under these rules.

Rule 10.800. Good Moral Character; Professional Discipline

(a)   Good Moral Character.
    (1)   Prior to approving an applicant for certification or renewal as a mediator the Center shall review the application to determine whether the applicant appears to meet the standards for good moral character. If the Center's review of an application for certification or renewal raises any questions regarding the applicant's good moral character, the Center shall request the applicant to supply additional information as necessary. Upon completing this extended review, the Center shall forward the application and supporting material as a complaint to the qualifications complaint committee.

    (2)   If the Center becomes aware of any information concerning a certified mediator which could constitute credible evidence of a lack of good moral character, the Center shall refer such information as a complaint to the qualifications complaint committee.

    (3)   The qualifications complaint committee shall review all documentation relating to the good moral character of any applicant or certified mediator in a manner consistent, insofar as applicable, with rule 10.810. In relation to an applicant, the qualifications complaint committee shall either recommend approval or, if it finds there is probable cause to believe that the applicant lacks good moral character, it shall refer the matter to a hearing panel for further action. In relation to a certified mediator, the qualifications complaint committee shall dismiss or, if there is probable cause to believe that the mediator lacks good moral character, refer the matter to a hearing panel for further action.

    (4)   The panel shall take appropriate action on the issue of good moral character by dismissing the charges, denying the application in relation to an applicant, or imposing sanctions against a certified mediator pursuant to rule 10.830.

    (5)   All such hearings shall be held in a manner consistent, insofar as applicable, with rule 10.820.

(b)   Professional Discipline. Upon becoming aware that a certified mediator has been disciplined by a professional organization of which that mediator is a member, the Center shall refer the matter to the qualifications complaint committee.

Rule 10.810. Committee Process

(a)   Initiation of Complaint. Any individual wishing to make a complaint alleging that a mediator has violated one or more provisions of these rules shall do so in writing under oath. The complaint shall state with particularity the specific facts that form the basis of the complaint.

(b)   Filing. The complaint shall be filed with the center, or, in the alternative, the complaint may be filed in the office of the court administrator in the circuit in which the case originated or, if not case specific, in the circuit where the alleged misconduct occurred.

(c)   Referral. The complaint, if filed in the office of the court administrator, shall be referred to the center within 5 days of filing.

(d)   Assignment to Committee. Upon receipt of a complaint in proper form, the center shall assign the complaint to a complaint committee or the qualifications complaint committee within 10 days.

(e)   Facial Sufficiency Determination. The complaint committee or the qualifications complaint committee shall convene, either in person or by conference call, to determine whether the allegation(s), if true, would constitute a violation of these rules. If the committee finds a complaint against a certified mediator to be facially insufficient, the complaint shall be dismissed without prejudice and the complainant and the mediator shall be so notified. If the qualifications complaint committee finds a complaint against an applicant to be facially insufficient, the complaint shall be dismissed and the application approved if all other requirements are met. If the complaint is found to be facially sufficient, the committee shall prepare a list of any rule or rules which may have been violated and shall submit such to the center.

(f)   Service. The center shall send a copy of the list of rule violations prepared by the committee, a copy of the complaint, and a copy of these rules to the mediator or applicant in question. Service on the mediator or applicant shall be made by registered or certified mail addressed to the mediator or applicant at the mediator's or applicant's place of business or residence.

(g)   Response. Within 20 days of the receipt of the list of violations prepared by the committee and the complaint, the mediator or applicant shall send a written, sworn response to the center by registered or certified mail. If the mediator or applicant does not respond, the allegations shall be deemed admitted.

(h)   Preliminary Review. Upon review of the complaint and the mediator's or applicant's response, the committee may find that no violation has occurred and dismiss the complaint. The committee may also resolve the issue pursuant to subdivision (j) of this rule.

(i)   Appointment of Investigator. The committee, after review of the complaint and response, may direct the center to appoint an investigator to assist the committee in any of its functions. Such person shall investigate the complaint and advise the committee when it meets to determine the existence of probable cause. In the alternative to appointing an investigator, the committee or any member or members thereof may investigate the allegations, if so directed by the committee chair. Such investigation may include meeting with the mediator, the applicant and the complainant.

(j)   Committee Meeting with the Mediator or Applicant. Notwithstanding any other provision in this rule, at any time while the committee has jurisdiction, it may meet with the complainant and the mediator or applicant in an effort to resolve the matter. This resolution may include sanctions if agreed to by the mediator or applicant. If sanctions are accepted, all relevant documentation shall be forwarded to the center.

(k)   Review. If no other disposition has occurred, the committee shall review the complaint, the response, and any investigative report, including any underlying documentation, to determine whether there is probable cause to believe that the alleged misconduct occurred and would constitute a violation of the rules.

(l)   No Probable Cause. If the committee finds no probable cause, it shall dismiss the complaint and so advise the complainant and the mediator or applicant in writing.

(m)   Probable Cause Found. If probable cause exists, the committee may draft formal charges and forward such charges to the center for assignment to a panel. In the alternative, the committee may decide not to pursue the case by filing a short and plain statement of the reason(s) for non-referral and so advise the complainant and the mediator or applicant in writing.

(n)   Formal Charges and Counsel. If the committee refers a complaint to the center, the committee shall submit to the center formal charges which shall include a short and plain statement of the matters asserted in the complaint and references to the particular sections of the rules involved. After considering the circumstances of the complaint and the complexity of the issues to be heard, the committee may direct the center to appoint a member of The Florida Bar to investigate and prosecute the complaint. Such counsel may be the investigator appointed pursuant to this rule if such person is otherwise qualified.

(o)   Dismissal. Upon the filing of a stipulation of dismissal signed by the complainant and the mediator with the concurrence of the complaint committee, the action shall be dismissed. If an application is withdrawn by the applicant, the complaint shall be dismissed with or without prejudice depending on the circumstances.

Rule 10.820. Hearing Procedures

(a)   Assignment to Panel. Upon referral of a complaint and formal charges from a committee, the center shall assign the complaint and formal charges or other matter to a panel for hearing, with notice of assignment to the complainant and the mediator or applicant. No member of the committee shall serve as a member of the panel.

(b)   Hearing. The center shall schedule a hearing not more than 90 days nor less than 30 days from the date of notice of assignment of the matter to the panel.

(c)   Dismissal. Upon the filing of a stipulation of dismissal signed by the complainant and the mediator, and with the concurrence of the panel, a complaint shall be dismissed.

(d)   Procedures for Hearing. The procedures for hearing shall be as follows:

     (1)   No hearing shall be conducted without 5 panel members being present.

     (2)   The hearing may be conducted informally but with decorum.

     (3)   The rules of evidence applicable to trial of civil actions apply but are to be liberally construed.

     (4)   Upon a showing of good cause to the panel, testimony of any party or witness may be presented over the telephone.

(e)   Right to Defend. A mediator or applicant shall have the right to defend against all charges and shall have the right to be represented by an attorney, to examine and cross-examine witnesses, to compel the attendance of witnesses to testify, and to compel the production of documents and other evidentiary matter through the subpoena power of the panel.

(f)   Mediator or Applicant Discovery. The center shall, upon written demand of a mediator, applicant, or counsel of record, promptly furnish the following: the names and addresses of all witnesses whose testimony is expected to be offered at the hearing, together with copies of all written statements and transcripts of the testimony of such witnesses in the possession of the counsel or the center which are relevant to the subject matter of the hearing and which have not previously been furnished.

(g)   Panel Discovery. The mediator, applicant, or counsel of record shall, upon written demand of the counsel or the center, promptly furnish the following: the names and addresses of all witnesses whose testimony is expected to be offered at the hearing, together with copies of all written statements and transcripts of the testimony of such witnesses in the possession of the mediator, applicant, or counsel of record which are relevant to the subject matter of the hearing and which have not previously been furnished.

(h)   Failure to Appear. Absent a showing of good cause, if the complainant fails to appear at the hearing, the panel may dismiss a complaint for want of prosecution.

(i)   Mediator's or Applicant's Absence. If the mediator or applicant fails to appear, absent a showing of good cause, the hearing shall proceed.

(j)   Rehearing. If the matter is heard in the mediator's or applicant's absence, the mediator or applicant may petition for rehearing, for good cause, within 10 days of the date of the hearing.

(k)   Recording. Any party shall have the right, without any order or approval, to have all or any portion of the testimony in the proceedings reported and transcribed by a court reporter at the party's expense.

(l)   Dismissal. Upon dismissal, the panel shall promptly file a copy of the dismissal order with the center.

(m)   Sanctions. If, after the hearing, a majority of the panel finds that there is clear and convincing evidence to support a violation of the rules, the panel shall impose such sanctions included in rule 10.830 as it deems appropriate and report such action to the center.

(n)   Denial of Application for Certification. If, after a hearing, a majority of the panel finds by the preponderance of the evidence that an applicant should not be certified as a mediator, the panel shall deny the application and report such action to the center.

Rule 10.830. Sanctions

(a)   Generally. The panel may impose one or more of the following sanctions:
        (1)   Imposition of costs of the proceeding.
        (2)   Oral admonishment.
        (3)   Written reprimand.
        (4)   Additional training, which may include the observation of mediations.
        (5)   Restriction on types of cases which can be mediated in the future.
        (6)   Suspension for a period of up to 1 year.
        (7)   Decertification or, if the mediator is not certified, bar from service as a mediator under Florida Rules of Civil Procedure.
        (8)   Such other sanctions as are agreed to by the mediator and the panel.

(b)   Failure to Comply. If there is reason to believe that the mediator failed to timely comply with any imposed sanction, a hearing shall be held before a panel convened for that purpose within 60 days of the date when the center learned of the alleged failure to comply. A finding of the panel that there was a willful failure to substantially comply with any imposed sanction shall result in the decertification of the mediator.

(c)   Decertified Mediators. If a mediator has been decertified or barred from service pursuant to these rules, the mediator shall not thereafter be certified or assigned to mediate a case pursuant to court rule or be designated as mediator pursuant to court rule unless reinstated.

(d)   Decision to be Filed. Upon making a determination that discipline is appropriate, the panel shall promptly file with the center a copy of the decision including findings and conclusions certified by the chair of the panel. The center shall promptly mail to all parties notice of such filing, together with a copy of the decision.

(e)   Notice to Circuits. The center shall notify all circuits of any mediator who has been decertified or suspended unless otherwise ordered by the Supreme Court of Florida.

(f)   Publication. Upon the imposition of sanctions, the center shall publish the name of the mediator, a short summary of the rule or rules which were violated, the circumstances surrounding the violation, and any sanctions imposed.

(g)   Reinstatement. Except if inconsistent with rule 10.110, a mediator who has been suspended or decertified may be reinstated as a certified mediator. Except as otherwise provided in the decision of the panel, no application for reinstatement may be tendered within 2 years after the date of decertification. The reinstatement procedures shall be as follows:

    (1)   A petition for reinstatement, together with 3 copies, shall be made in writing, verified by the petitioner, and filed with the center.

    (2)   The petition for reinstatement shall contain:

        (A)   the name, age, residence, and address of the petitioner;

        (B)   the offense or misconduct upon which the suspension or decertification was based, together with the date of such suspension or decertification; and

        (C)   a concise statement of facts claimed to justify reinstatement as a certified mediator.

    (3)   The center shall refer the petition for reinstatement to a hearing panel in the appropriate division for review.

    (4)   The panel shall review the petition and, if the petitioner is found to be unfit to mediate, the petition shall be dismissed. If the petitioner is found fit to mediate, the panel shall notify the center and the center shall reinstate the petitioner as a certified mediator; provided, however, if the decertification has continued for more than 3 years, the reinstatement may be conditioned upon the completion of a certified training course as provided for in these rules. Successive petitions for reinstatement based upon the same grounds may be reviewed without a hearing.

Rule 10.840. Subpoenas

(a)   Issuance. Subpoenas for the attendance of witnesses and the production of documentary evidence for discovery and for the appearance of any person before a complaint committee, a panel, or any member thereof, may be issued by the chair of the complaint committee or panel or, if the chair of the panel is absent, by the vice-chair. Such subpoenas may be served in any manner provided by law for the service of witness subpoenas in a civil action.

(b)   Failure to Obey. Any person who, without adequate excuse, fails to obey a duly served subpoena may be cited for contempt of the committee or panel in accordance with rule 10.740.

Rule 10.850. Confidentiality

(a)   Generally. Until sanctions are imposed, whether by the panel or upon agreement of the mediator, all proceedings shall be confidential. After sanctions are imposed by a panel or an application is denied, all documentation including and subsequent to the filing of formal charges shall be public with the exception of those matters which are otherwise confidential pursuant to law or rule of the supreme court. If a consensual agreement is reached between a mediator and a complaint committee, only the basis of the complaint and the agreement shall be released to the public.

(b)   Witnesses. Each witness in every proceeding under these disciplinary rules shall be sworn to tell the truth and not disclose the existence of the proceeding, the subject matter thereof, or the identity of the mediator until the proceeding is no longer confidential under these disciplinary rules. Violation of this oath shall be considered an act of contempt of the complaint committee or the panel.

(c)   Papers to be Marked. All notices, papers, and pleadings mailed prior to formal charges being filed shall be enclosed in a cover marked "confidential."

(d)   Breach of Confidentiality. Violation of confidentiality by a member of the board shall subject the member to removal by the chief justice of the Supreme Court of Florida.

Committee Notes

1995 Revision. The Committee believed the rule regarding confidentiality should be amended in deference to the 1993 amendment to section 44.102, Florida Statutes, that engrafted an exception to the general confidentiality requirement for all mediation sessions for the purpose of investigating complaints filed against mediators. Section 44.102(4) specifically provides that "the disclosure of an otherwise privileged communication shall be used only for the internal use of the body conducting the investigation" and that "[Prior] to the release of any disciplinary files to the public, all references to otherwise privileged communications shall be deleted from the record."

These provisions created a substantial potential problem when read in conjunction with the previous rule on confidentiality, which made public all proceedings after formal charges were filed. In addition to the possibly substantial burden of redacting the files for public release, there was the potentially greater problem of conducting panel hearings in such a manner as to preclude the possibility that confidential communications would be revealed during testimony, specifically the possibility that any public observers would have to be removed prior to the elicitation of any such communication only to be allowed to return until the next potentially confidential revelation. The Committee believes that under the amended rule the integrity of the disciplinary system can be maintained by releasing the results of any disciplinary action together with a redacted transcript of panel proceedings, while still maintaining the integrity of the mediation process.

Rule 10.860. Interested Party

A mediator is disqualified from serving on a committee or panel proceeding involving the mediator's own discipline or decertification.

Rule 10.870. Disqualification of Members of a Panel or Committee

(a)   Procedure. In any case, any party may at any time before final disciplinary action show by a suggestion filed in the case that a member of the board before which the case is pending, or some person related to that member, is a party to the case or is interested in the result of the case or that the member is related to an attorney or counselor of record in the case or that the member is a material witness for or against one of the parties to the case.

(b)   Facts to be Alleged. A motion to disqualify shall allege the facts relied on to show the grounds for disqualification and shall be verified by the party.

(c)   Time for Motion. A motion to disqualify shall be made within a reasonable time after discovery of the facts constituting grounds for disqualification.

(d)   Action by Chair. The chair of the appropriate committee or panel shall determine only the legal sufficiency of the motion. The chair shall not pass on the truth of the facts alleged. If the motion is legally sufficient, the chair shall enter an order of disqualification and the disqualified committee or panel member shall proceed no further in the action. In the event that the chair is the challenged member, the vice-chair shall perform the acts required under this subdivision.

(e)   Recusals. Nothing in this rule limits a board member's authority to enter an order of recusal on the board member's own initiative.

(f)   Replacement. The center shall assign a board member to take the place of any disqualified or recused member.

(g)   Qualifications. Each assignee shall have the same qualifications as the disqualified or recused member.

Rule 10.880. Supreme Court Review

(a)   Right of Review. Any mediator or applicant found to have committed a violation of these rules or is otherwise sanctioned by a hearing panel shall have a right of review of the action taken by the panel. Review of this type shall be under the jurisdiction of the Supreme Court of Florida. Notice of review shall be filed with the clerk of the Supreme Court of Florida. A mediator shall have no right of review of any resolution reached pursuant to rule 10.810(j).

(b)   Rules of Procedure. The Florida Rules of Appellate Procedure shall be applicable to review by the Florida Supreme Court.

Rule 10.900. Mediator Ethics Advisory Committee

(a)   Scope and Purpose. The Mediator Ethics Advisory Committee shall provide written advisory opinions to mediators subject to these rules in response to ethical questions arising from the Standards of Professional Conduct. Such opinions shall be consistent with supreme court decisions on mediator discipline.

(b)   Appointment. The Mediator Ethics Advisory Committee shall be composed of 9 members, 3 from each geographic division served by the Mediator Qualifications Board. No member of the Mediator Qualifications Board shall serve on the committee.

(c)   Membership and Terms. The membership of the committee shall be composed of 1 county mediator, 1 family mediator, and 1 circuit mediator from each division and shall be appointed by the chief justice. At least one of the 9 members shall also be a certified dependency mediator. All appointments shall be for 4 years. No member shall serve more than 2 consecutive terms. The committee shall select 1 member as chair and 1 member as vice-chair.

(d)   Meetings. The committee shall meet in person or by telephone conference as necessary at the direction of the chair to consider requests for advisory opinions. A quorum shall consist of a majority of the members appointed to the committee. All requests for advisory opinions shall be in writing. The committee may vote by any means as directed by the chair.

(e)   Opinions. Upon due deliberation, and upon the concurrence of a majority of the committee, the committee shall render opinions. A majority of all members shall be required to concur in any advisory opinion issued by the committee. The opinions shall be signed by the chair, or vice-chair in the absence of the chair, filed with the Dispute Resolution Center, published in the Dispute Resolution Center newsletter, and be made available upon request.

(f)   Effect of Opinions. While reliance by a mediator on an opinion of the committee shall not constitute a defense in any disciplinary proceeding, it shall be evidence of good faith and may be considered by the board in relation to any determination of guilt or in mitigation of punishment.

(g)   Confidentiality. Prior to publication, all references to the requesting mediator or any other real person, firm, organization, or corporation shall be deleted from any request for an opinion, any document associated with the preparation of an opinion, and any opinion issued by the committee. This rule shall apply to all opinions, past and future.

(h)   Support. The Dispute Resolution Center shall provide all support necessary for the committee to fulfill its duties under these rules.

Committee Notes

2000 Revision.   The Mediator Ethics Advisory Committee was formerly the Mediator Qualifications Advisory Panel.

Appendix L

A Guide to Dispute Resolution Processes[1]

♦ **What Is Dispute Resolution?**

Dispute resolution is a term that refers to a number of processes that can be used to resolve a claim or dispute. Dispute resolution may also be referred to as alternative dispute resolution, appropriate dispute resolution, or ADR for short. Dispute resolution processes are alternatives to having a state or federal judge or jury decide the dispute in a trial. Dispute resolution processes can be used to resolve any type of dispute including family, neighborhood, employment, business, housing, personal injury, consumer, and environmental disputes.

♦ **Why Use Dispute Resolution?**

Dispute resolution processes have several advantages. For instance, many dispute resolution processes are cheaper and faster than the traditional legal process. Certain processes can provide the parties involved with greater participation in reaching a solution, as well as more control over the outcome of the dispute. In addition, dispute resolution processes are less formal and have more flexible rules than the trial court.

♦ **What Are the Different Types of Dispute Resolution Processes?**

Dispute resolution takes a number of different forms. Here are brief descriptions of the most common dispute resolution processes:

Arbitration

Arbitration is a private process where disputing parties agree that one or several individuals can make a decision about the dispute after receiving evidence and hearing arguments. Arbitration is different from mediation because the neutral arbitrator has the authority to make a decision about the dispute. The arbitration process is similar to a trial in that the parties make opening statements and present evidence to the arbitrator. Compared to traditional trials, arbitration can usually be completed more quickly and is less formal. For example, often the parties do not

---

[1] *The Guide to Dispute Resolution Processes* was made possible by the American Bar Association Section of Dispute Resolution with the support of the William and Flora Hewlett Foundation. The Guide is available free of charge as a service of the ABA Section of Dispute Resolution. Individuals and organizations are encouraged to make copies of this brochure and distribute as long as the copies are made available free of charge. Contact ABA Section of Dispute Resolution, 740 15th St. NW, Washington, DC 20005, (202) 662-1680, Fax (202) 662-1683, dispute@abanet.org.

have to follow state or federal rules of evidence and, in some cases, the arbitrator is not required to apply the governing law.

After the hearing, the arbitrator issues an award. Some awards simply announce the decision (a "bare bones" award), and others give reasons (a "reasoned" award). The arbitration process may be either binding or non-binding. When arbitration is binding, the decision is final, can be enforced by a court, and can only be appealed on very narrow grounds. When arbitration is non-binding, the arbitrator's award is advisory and can be final only if accepted by the parties.

Early Neutral Evaluation

Early neutral evaluation is a process that may take place soon after a case has been filed in court. The case is referred to an expert, usually an attorney, who is asked to provide a balanced and unbiased evaluation of the dispute. The parties either submit written comments or meet in person with the expert. The expert identifies each side's strengths and weaknesses and provides an evaluation of the likely outcome of a trial. This evaluation can assist the parties in assessing their case and may propel them towards a settlement.

Mediation

Mediation is a private process where a neutral third person called a mediator helps the parties discuss and try to resolve the dispute. The parties have the opportunity to describe the issues, discuss their interests, understandings, and feelings, provide each other with information and explore ideas for the resolution of the dispute. While courts can mandate that certain cases go to mediation, the process remains "voluntary" in that parties are not required to come to agreement. The mediator does not have the power to make a decision for the parties, but can help the parties find a resolution that is mutually acceptable. The only people who can resolve the dispute in mediation are the parties themselves.

There are a number of different ways that a mediation can proceed. Most mediations start with the parties together in a joint session. The mediator will describe how the process works, will explain the mediator's role and will help establish ground rules and an agenda for the session. Generally, parties then make opening statements. Some mediators conduct the entire process in a joint session. However, other mediators will move to separate sessions, shuttling back and forth between the parties. If the parties reach an agreement, the mediator can help reduce the agreement to a written contract, which may be enforceable in court.

Mini-Trial

A mini-trial is a private, consensual process where the attorneys for each party make a brief presentation of the case as if at a trial. The presentations are observed by a neutral advisor and by representatives (usually high-level business executives) from each side who have authority to settle the dispute. At the end of the presentations, the representatives attempt to settle the dispute. If the representatives fail to settle the dispute, the neutral advisor, at the request of the parties, may serve as a mediator or may issue a non-binding opinion as to the likely outcome in court.

Negotiation

Negotiation is a voluntary and usually informal process in which parties identify issues of concern, explore options for the resolution of the issues, and search for a mutually acceptable agreement to resolve the issues raised. The disputing parties may be represented by attorneys in negotiation. Negotiation is different from mediation in that there is no neutral individual to assist the parties negotiate.

Neutral Fact-Finding

Neutral fact-finding is a process where a neutral third party, selected either by the disputing parties or by the court, investigates an issue and reports or testifies in court. The neutral fact-finding process is particularly useful for resolving complex scientific and factual disputes.

Ombuds

An ombuds is a third party selected by an institution-for example, a university, hospital or governmental agency-to investigate complaints by employees, clients or constituents. The ombuds works within the institution to investigate the complaints independently and impartially. The process is voluntary, private and non-binding.

Private Judging

Private judging is a process where the disputing parties agree to retain a neutral person as a private judge. The private judge, who is often a former judge with expertise in the area of the dispute, hears the case and makes a decision in a manner similar to a judge. Depending on court rules, the decision of the private judge may be appealable in the public courts.

Settlement Conferences

A settlement conference is a meeting in which a judge or magistrate assigned to the case presides over the process. The purpose of the settlement conference is to try to settle a case before the hearing or trial. Settlement conferencing is similar to mediation in that a third party neutral assists the parties in exploring settlement options. Settlement conferences are different from mediation in that settlement conferences are usually shorter and typically have fewer roles for participation of the parties or for consideration of non-legal interests.

Summary Jury Trial

In summary jury trials, attorneys for each party make abbreviated case presentations to a mock six member jury (drawn from a pool of real jurors), the party representatives and a presiding judge or magistrate. The mock jury renders an advisory verdict. The verdict is frequently helpful in getting a settlement, particularly where one of the parties has an unrealistic assessment of their case.

♦ *If I Participate in Dispute Resolution, Can I Later File a Lawsuit?*

In most instances, dispute resolution processes do not preclude parties from later pursuing their case in court if they fail to reach a resolution. Parties can use dispute resolution before, or even after, they have filed a case in court. However, binding arbitration is final and prevents a party from bringing a court action.

♦ ***Do I Need an Attorney to Participate in Dispute Resolution?***
In many processes, you are not required to have an attorney to participate. In cases where the court or judge has referred the case to a dispute resolution process, attorneys often participate. The role of an attorney in a dispute resolution process varies depending upon the nature of the dispute and the type of dispute resolution process. In many dispute resolution processes, attorneys accompany their clients and participate either as counselors or as advocates.

For more information:

ABA Section of Dispute Resolution
http://www.abanet.org/dispute

American Arbitration Association
http://www.adr.org

Association of Family and Conciliation Courts
http://www.afccnet.org

Association for Conflict Resolution
http://www.acresolution.org

Center for Analysis of ADR Systems
http://www.caadrs.org

Conflict Resolution and Information Network
http://www.CRInfo.org

CPR Institute for Dispute Resolution
http://www.cpradr.org

JAMS
Mediation Information and Resource Center
http://www.mediate.com

National Arbitration Forum
www.arbitration-forum.com

National Association for Community Mediation
http://www.nafcm.org

Network of Communities for Peacemaking and Conflict Resolution
http://www.apeacemaker.net

Policy Consensus Initiative
http://www.policyconsensus.org

U.S. Department of Justice Office of Dispute Resolution
http://www.usdoj.gov/odr

Victim Offender Mediation Association
http://www.voma.org/

Appendix M

MODEL RULES FOR MEDIATION OF CLIENT-LAWYER DISPUTES

(Adopted by the American Bar Association
House of Delegates on August 4, 1998)

PREFACE

On February 4, 1992, the American Bar Association House of Delegates adopted the Report of the Commission on Evaluation of Disciplinary Enforcement (the "McKay Commission"). The Commission was created in February 1989 to conduct a nationwide evaluation of lawyer disciplinary enforcement and to provide a model for responsible regulation of the legal profession into the twenty-first century. Recommendation 3 of the McKay Commission Report called for jurisdictions to expand their systems of lawyer regulation by establishing mechanisms to resolve disputes between clients and lawyers and handle non-disciplinary complaints about lawyers. Mechanisms for fee arbitration, mediation, lawyer practice assistance and lawyer substance abuse counseling were recommended.

In 1996 the Joint Committee on Lawyer Regulation of the ABA Center for Professional Responsibility began drafting model rules for the mediation of complaints against lawyers which alleged lesser misconduct. The Committee reviewed mediation programs and rules from California, Colorado, Missouri, New York and Wisconsin. Additionally, the Committee studied the ABA *Model Rules for Fee Arbitration* that had been adopted in February 1995 by the America Bar Association House of Delegates. In 1997, the task of finalizing the mediation rules was passed to the ABA Standing Committee on Client Protection. In December 1997 the Committee circulated for comment a draft of the Model Rules to Association entities and judicial and legal organizations across the country. On August 4, 1998, at its Annual meeting in Toronto, the American Bar Association House of Delegates adopted the black-letter of the *Model Rules for Mediation of Client-Lawyer Disputes*.

The *Model Rules for Mediation of Client-Lawyer Disputes* are designed to assist jurisdictions interested in implementing a voluntary mediation program. The Model Rules will be subject to modification at the level of local implementation. The Comments do not add obligations to the Model Rules but provide guidance for conducting a mediation program in compliance with the Model Rules.

Mediation is a process by which those who have a dispute, misunderstanding or conflict come together and, with the assistance of a trained neutral mediator, resolve the issues and problems in a way that meets the needs and interests of both parties. Mediation can help to preserve the client-lawyer relationship. For both clients and lawyers, the mediation process is an alternative to litigation or other more formal and expensive dispute resolution mechanisms. The mediation process will benefit the public by directly addressing instances where a lawyer is alleged to have engaged in lesser misconduct but the misconduct does not warrant a formal disciplinary proceeding. The mediation process will also protect the public by removing matters involving lesser misconduct from the disciplinary system and thereby allowing disciplinary counsel to focus their efforts on more serious matters.

Rule 1. GENERAL PRINCIPLES AND JURISDICTION

A. **Definitions**.

(1) "Client" means a person or entity who directly or through an authorized representative consults or retains a lawyer in the lawyer's professional capacity.

(2) "Commission" means the Client-Lawyer Mediation Commission.

(3) "Lawyer" means any lawyer admitted to practice law in [name of jurisdiction], including any formerly admitted lawyer, any lawyer specially admitted by a court of this jurisdiction for a particular proceeding and any lawyer not admitted in this jurisdiction who practices law or renders or offers to render any legal services in this jurisdiction.

B. **Establishment; Purpose.** It is the policy of the [highest court of the jurisdiction] to encourage the informal resolution of disputes between lawyers who practice law in [name of jurisdiction] and their clients. To that end, the [highest court of the jurisdiction] hereby establishes through adoption of these rules, a program for mediation of client-lawyer disputes. The program includes mediations referred by [the lawyer disciplinary agency] and voluntary mediation requests made by the client or by the lawyer, if both the client and the lawyer agree to mediate.

C. **Jurisdiction.**

(1) Any lawyer is subject to these rules for mediation.
(2) The Commission has jurisdiction over disputes that involve lesser misconduct or no misconduct on the part of the lawyer and appear to be resolvable by mediation.
(3) The Commission has jurisdiction over disputes referred by [the lawyer disciplinary agency] and voluntary mediations in which a lawyer or client requests mediation and the other party agrees.

Comment

The mediation program described in these rules is part of this jurisdiction's comprehensive lawyer regulatory system. The comprehensive system includes: [a lawyer discipline and disability system, a client protection fund, mandatory arbitration of fee disputes, mediation, law office management assistance, and lawyer assistance programs].

Since mediation is a process that works by building consensus and agreement, the mediation process can preserve existing client-lawyer or other fiduciary relationships by allowing both sides to air their grievances and work together on a solution agreeable to all parties. When handled by a skilled mediator, the process can be simple and efficient, saving time and money for both parties. The lawyer's willingness to have a third party assist in resolving the dispute can demonstrate to the client that the lawyer's intention is to act in the client's best interest.

Mediation is not suitable when the dispute involves an allegation of lawyer misconduct, which, if true, would warrant a sanction restricting the lawyer's license to practice law. Mediation is appropriate when the dispute involves no allegation of lawyer misconduct or an allegation of lesser misconduct as defined in [jurisdiction's rules of disciplinary enforcement]. It is appropriate because there is little or no injury to a client, the public, the legal system, or the profession, and there is little likelihood of repetition by the lawyer.

Examples of disputes that might be referred to mediation include allegations of a lawyer's failure or refusal to return a client's file based on a fee dispute with the client, release a lien on a client's recovery in a case in which the lawyer has been succeeded by another lawyer, withdraw from representation upon being discharged by the client, conclude a legal representation by preparing an essential dispositive document, such as the findings of fact and conclusions of law in a divorce or the final account in an estate, return an unearned fee or a portion of the fee, comply with his or her agreement with a medical provider on the client's behalf or communicate concerning the status of a matter.

Other examples of situations in which the parties might agree to voluntary mediation could include allegations of a client's failure to pay or fulfill the contract, pay for costs (including future costs) or communicate with the lawyer.

The primary purpose of the program is to resolve complaints referred from the jurisdiction's lawyer disciplinary agency. Therefore, such referrals should be given priority over voluntary mediations.

Mediation can be used to complement fee arbitration proceedings. The Commission may accept jurisdiction in a dispute in which a fee arbitration proceeding is pending but has not yet begun. The intention is to solve the dispute in a less formal way, if possible, not to refer complainants back and forth between the two programs.

Rule 2. MEDIATION COMMISSION

A.   **Appointment of Commission.** The [highest court of the jurisdiction] shall appoint a Mediation Commission to administer the Mediation Program. The [highest court of the jurisdiction] shall designate one member to serve as Chair of the Commission.

B.   **Composition.** The Commission shall consist of [six] members, of whom at least one-third shall be nonlawyers. Members shall be appointed for terms of three years except where a vacancy has occurred in which event appointments shall be for the unexpired portion of the term being filled. Appointments shall be on a staggered basis so that the number of terms expiring shall be approximately the same each year. No members shall be appointed for more than two consecutive full terms, but members appointed for less than a full term (either originally or to fill a vacancy) may serve two full terms in addition to such part of a term.

C.   **Duties of the Commission.** The Commission shall have the following powers and duties to:

(1)   appoint and remove mediators and provide appropriate training;

(2)   interpret these rules;

(3)   establish written procedures not inconsistent with these rules;

(4)   issue an annual report and periodic policy recommendations, as needed, to the [state's highest court] regarding the program;

(5)   maintain all records of the Mediation Program;

(6)   determine challenges for cause where a mediator has not voluntarily acceded to a challenge;

(7)   educate the public and the bar about the Mediation Program;

(8)   perform all acts necessary for the effective operation of the program; and

(9)   establish fee schedules and oversee financial matters.

Comment

Overall authority to administer the Mediation Program is delegated by [the highest court of the jurisdiction] to the Commission. The court should ensure diversity in the membership of the Commission.

The Commission has authority to limit the types of matters accepted for mediation. Personal disputes and business matters where one of the parties is a lawyer but the allegations do not involve the practice of law are not appropriate for mediation under these rules. Mediation of disputes between lawyers is not precluded by these rules where the complaint otherwise meets the guidelines of matters that are appropriate for mediation.

The Commission has the authority to establish reasonable fees for the program and also to waive fees in cases of hardship. No fee should be charged a client if the charging of the fee would unduly restrict the client's access to the mediation process. Additionally, in mediations referred by [the lawyer disciplinary agency], the client should not be charged a fee for participating in the mediation.

With respect to the funding of the mediation program, it is envisioned that there will be minimal costs involved: lawyer and nonlawyer volunteers will be serving as mediators. The Commission may delegate the day-to-day administration of the Mediation Program to staff assigned to the lawyer disciplinary agency. However, a state or local bar association could administer this component of the lawyer regulation system.

Rule 3. MEDIATORS

A. **List of Approved Mediators.** The Commission shall maintain a list of approved mediators, both lawyers and nonlawyers, and shall adopt written standards for the appointment of the mediators. Mediators should represent all segments of the profession and the general population, including diversity on the basis of race, gender, and practice setting. Mediators shall be appointed for terms of [three] years and may be reappointed. The Commission may remove a mediator from the list of approved mediators for good cause, and may appoint a replacement member to serve the balance of the term of the removed member.

B. **Conflicts of Interest.** Within [20] days of the notification of appointment as a mediator, and prior to the initiation of the mediation, the mediator shall notify the Commission if he or she has previously acted as a mediator in the proceeding or in any other related proceeding or of any conflict of interest with a party to the mediation as defined in the [*Code of Judicial Conduct*] with respect to part-time judges. Upon notification of the conflict, the Commission shall appoint a replacement from the list of approved mediators.

C. **Challenges for Cause.** If either party has cause to object to participation by a mediator, a substitute shall be appointed by the Commission. A challenge for cause shall be filed within [15] days after service of the notice of appointment. A mediator shall accede to a reasonable challenge and the Commission shall appoint a replacement. If a mediator does not voluntarily accede, the Commission shall decide whether to appoint a replacement. The decision of the Commission on challenges shall be final.

D. **Duties.** The mediator shall have powers and duties to:
    (1) grant extensions of time as deemed appropriate;

(2)   reschedule or terminate the mediation if a party fails to appear; and

(3)   perform all acts necessary to conduct an effective mediation conference.

Comment

Written standards for the appointment of mediators should ensure appropriate training and experience for mediators as well as diversity in the background and experience of the mediators. Mediators should also be dispersed throughout the jurisdiction to increase access to the mediation process.

Mediators should be required to attend an appropriate training course, as determined by the Commission, which should include training in mediation theory, skills and the applicable provisions of the rules of professional conduct.

Mediators exercise a quasi-judicial role and should, therefore, be disqualified upon the same grounds and conditions applicable to part-time judges. The decisions of the mediators should be free from any appearance of outside influence.

Rule 4. THE PROCESS

A.   **Commencement of Mediation.**

(1)   **Referral from Lawyer Disciplinary Agency.** Within [15] calendar days after receipt by the Commission of a mediation referral from [the lawyer disciplinary agency], the Commission shall mail to both the lawyer and the complainant a copy of these rules and an agreement to mediate, together with a notice that shall include the name, address and telephone number of the mediation program and the date on which the referral for mediation was received. If the signed agreement to mediate is not returned to the Commission by both parties within [30] calendar days of mailing, the Commission shall close the file, notify the parties that it is closing the file because one or both parties failed to return the agreement, and inform the [lawyer disciplinary agency] of the identity of the party or parties who did not consent to mediation.

(2)   **Voluntary Mediation.** Within [15] calendar days after receipt by the Commission of the approved written application for voluntary mediation of a dispute and a signed agreement to mediate, the Commission shall notify the other party of the request and shall forward to that party an agreement to mediate, together with a copy of these Rules and a copy of the

written application. If the signed agreement is not returned to the program by the other party within [30] calendar days of mailing, the Commission shall close the file and notify the requestor that the other party did not consent to mediation.

B.   **Assignment of Mediators.** The Commission shall notify the parties of the assignment of a mediator within [15] calendar days after receipt of the fully executed agreement to mediate. The notice shall include the name, address and telephone number of the mediator assigned. The mediator shall be assigned at random from the available pool of qualified individuals. Upon withdrawal or removal of a mediator, the Commission shall notify the parties within [10] calendar days of the name, address and telephone number of a new mediator.

C.   **Mediation Hearing Date.** Within [15] calendar days after the date of mailing of the notice of the assignment of a mediator, the mediator shall arrange a mediation conference date which shall be scheduled to take place within [30] calendar days after the assignment notice mailing date, unless both parties to the mediation agree to a longer date. The mediator shall promptly notify the parties and the Commission of the place, date and time of the conference.

D.   **The Conference.**

(1)   Only the parties to the mediation, their lawyers, if any, and the mediator are required to be present during the mediation, but the mediator shall have authority to determine if others may be present at and participate in the mediation.

(2)   The mediator shall have the authority to meet separately with the parties.

(3)   If all parties and the mediator agree, the mediation may be conducted by telephone. In cases of hardship, the mediation may be conducted by telephone at the discretion of the mediator even if all parties do not agree.

(4)   If upon completion of the mediation, the parties have an agreement, the mediator shall reduce the agreement of the parties to writing. The parties shall sign as many originals as there are parties to the mediation. A copy of the signed agreement shall be made for the Commission's records. The mediator shall report to the Commission on the Mediation Summary Report form, which will indicate if the dispute was resolved, was not resolved, or did not proceed because a party did not appear (with an indication of which party did not

appear). Such agreement and/or report shall be submitted within [15] calendar days after the conclusion of the mediation.

(5) In the case of any mediation referred from the disciplinary agency, the following materials shall be transmitted to the [lawyer disciplinary agency] at the conclusion of the mediation:

a. A duplicate original of the signed mediation agreement described in Rule 4.D.4 above; and

b. the completed Mediation Summary Report form.

Comment

The overwhelming majority of complaints made against lawyers allege instances of lesser misconduct. Summary dismissal of these complaints is one of the chief sources of public dissatisfaction with the lawyer regulation system. These cases seldom justify the resources needed to conduct formal disciplinary proceedings and should be removed from the disciplinary system and handled administratively.

The mediation program established by these rules is designed to receive cases from a number of sources: the central intake office; the disciplinary agency; other agencies within the lawyer regulation system; the courts; or directly from the parties. Referrals from the disciplinary agency will usually be part of a diversion program or an agreement in lieu of discipline, in which a lawyer agrees to mediate a dispute with the understanding that the disciplinary matter will be dismissed upon successful completion of the mediation. Agreement of both the client and the lawyer is required for a matter to be referred to mediation from the disciplinary agency. Matters that come to the mediation program from the central intake office, other agencies, or directly from the parties are voluntary as described in these rules.

The mediator is authorized to determine the rules by which the mediation will proceed. The mediator should conduct the conference informally. At the outset, the mediator should make clear to the parties that the mediator is serving as a mediator and not a judge. The mediator's role is to facilitate communication and suggest ways of resolving the dispute; the mediator is not to impose a settlement on the parties. The mediator should make every effort to hear all the relevant facts, review all the relevant documents, become familiar with any controlling legal principles and seek to bring about an acceptable compromise between the parties. The mediator should make sure that any proposal offered for resolution of the matter is clearly understood by the parties and perceived to be fair.

Rule 5. CONFIDENTIALITY

A.   Except as provided in Rule 4.D.5 above, and Rule 5.B below, all communications, negotiations or settlement discussions by and between participants and/or mediators in the mediation shall remain confidential. All parties attending a mediation shall sign a written agreement that the proceeding will be confidential.

B.   Notwithstanding Rule 5.A above, lawyer mediators have a duty to, and nonlawyer mediators should, report conduct that would be reportable under the applicable rules of professional conduct or other applicable statutes or rules.

Comment

Confidentiality in a mediation hearing is of paramount importance. Nevertheless, the need to report lawyer misconduct takes precedence. Lawyer mediators have a duty to, and nonlawyer mediators should, report conduct that would be reportable under the jurisdiction's applicable rules or statutes. A lawyer having knowledge that another lawyer has committed a violation of the [rules of professional conduct] that raises a substantial question as to that lawyer's honesty, trustworthiness or fitness as a lawyer in other respects, must inform the appropriate professional authority. Nonlawyer mediators should refer to this standard in determining their responsibility to report lawyer misconduct. The fact that mediators have a duty to report lawyer misconduct should not have a chilling effect on those parties who are sincere in availing themselves of the benefits of mediation. All mediators may also be required by the laws in their jurisdiction to report to the appropriate agency evidence of other types of misconduct, i.e., child abuse or criminal conduct, that comes to light during a mediation.

Rule 6.   IMMUNITY

Communications to the Commission, mediators, or disciplinary counsel relating to lawyer misconduct or disability and testimony given in the proceedings shall be absolutely privileged, and no lawsuit predicated thereon may be instituted against any client or witness. Members of the Commission, mediators, disciplinary counsel, or any person acting on their behalf, and staff shall be immune from suit for any conduct in the course of their official duties.

Comment

The personnel involved in the mediation process are an integral part of the judicial process and are entitled to the same immunity, which is afforded prosecuting lawyers. Immunity protects the independent judgment of the mediation personnel and avoids diverting the attention of its personnel as well as its resources toward resisting collateral attack and harassment. A policy of conferring absolute immunity encourages those who have some doubt about a lawyer's conduct to submit the matter to the proper agency, where it may be examined and determined.

Appendix N

UNIFORM MEDIATION ACT

Drafted by the
NATIONAL CONFERENCE OF COMMISSIONERS
ON UNIFORM STATE LAWS

and by it

APPROVED AND RECOMMENDED FOR ENACTMENT
IN ALL THE STATES

at its

ANNUAL CONFERENCE
MEETING IN ITS ONE-HUNDRED-AND-TENTH YEAR
WHITE SULPHUR SPRINGS, WEST VIRGINIA
AUGUST 10–17, 2001

WITHOUT PREFATORY NOTE AND COMMENTS

Approved by the American Bar Association
Philadelphia, Pennsylvania, February 4, 2002

NATIONAL CONFERENCE OF COMMISSIONERS ON UNIFORM STATE LAWS DRAFTING COMMITTEE ON UNIFORM MEDIATION ACT:

MICHAEL B. GETTY, 1560 Sandburg Terrace, Suite 1104, Chicago, IL 60610, *Chair*
PHILLIP CARROLL, 120 E. Fourth Street, Little Rock, AR 72201
JOSE FELICIANO, 3200 National City Center, 1900 E. 9th Street, Cleveland, OH 44114-3485, *American Bar Association Member*
STANLEY M. FISHER, 1100 Huntington Building, 925 Euclid Avenue, Cleveland, OH 44115-1475, *Enactment Coordinator*
ROGER C. HENDERSON, University of Arizona, James E. Rogers College of Law, Mountain and Speedway Streets, Tucson, AZ 85721, *Committee on Style Liaison*
ELIZABETH KENT, P.O. Box 2560, Honolulu, HI, 96804
RICHARD C. REUBEN, University of Missouri-Columbia School of Law, Hulston Hall, Columbia, MO 65211, *Associate Reporter*
NANCY H. ROGERS, Ohio State University, Michael E. Moritz College of Law, 55 W. 12th Avenue, Columbus, OH 43210, *National Conference Reporter*
FRANK E.A. SANDER, Harvard University Law School, Cambridge, MA 02138, *American Bar Association Member*
BYRON D. SHER, State Capitol, Suite 2082, Sacramento, CA 95814
MARTHA LEE WALTERS, Suite 220, 975 Oak Street, Eugene, OR 97401
JOAN ZELDON, D.C. Superior Court, 500 Indiana Ave., Washington, DC 20001

EX OFFICIO

JOHN L. McCLAUGHERTY, P.O. Box 553, Charleston, WV 25322, *President*
LEON M. McCORKLE, JR., P.O. Box 387, Dublin, OH 43017-0387, *Division Chair*

AMERICAN BAR ASSOCIATION ADVISOR

ROBERTA COOPER RAMO, Sunwest Building, Suite 1000, 500 W. 4th Street, NW, Albuquerque, NM 87102

EXECUTIVE DIRECTOR

FRED H. MILLER, University of Oklahoma, College of Law, 300 Timberdell Road, Norman, OK 73019, *Executive Director*
WILLIAM J. PIERCE, 1505 Roxbury Road, Ann Arbor, MI 48104, *Executive Director Emeritus*

Copies of this Act may be obtained from:
NATIONAL CONFERENCE OF COMMISSIONERS
ON UNIFORM STATE LAWS
211 E. Ontario Street, Suite 1300
Chicago, Illinois 60611
312/915-0195
www.nccusl.org

ABA SECTION OF DISPUTE RESOLUTION
DRAFTING COMMITTEE ON UNIFORM MEDIATION ACT

THOMAS J. MOYER, *Co-Chair*, Supreme Court of Ohio, 30 E. Broad Street, Columbus, OH 43266

ROBERTA COOPER RAMO, *Co-Chair*, Modrall, Sperling, Roehl, Harris & Sisk, P.A., Sunwest Building, Suite 1000, Albuquerque, NM 87102

JAMES DIGGS, PPG Industries, 1 PPG Place, Pittsburgh, PA 15272

JOSE FELICIANO, Baker & Hostetler, 3200 National City Center, 1900 East 9th St., Cleveland, OH 44114

MICHAEL B. GETTY, 1560 Sandburg Terrace, Suite 1104, Chicago, IL 60610, *NCCUSL Representative*

EMILY STEWART HAYNES, Supreme Court of Ohio, 30 E. Broad Street, Columbus, OH 43266, *Reporting Coordinator*

RICHARD C. REUBEN, University of Missouri-Columbia School of Law, Hulston Hall, Columbia, MO 65211, *Reporter*

NANCY H. ROGERS, Ohio State University, College of Law and Office of Academic Affairs, 203 Bricker Hall, 190 N. Oval Mall, Columbus, OH 43210, *Coordinator, Faculty AdvisoryCommittee*

FRANK E.A. SANDER, Harvard Law School, Cambridge, MA 02138

JUDITH SAUL, Community Dispute Resolution Center, 120 W. State Street., Ithaca, NY 14850

ANNICE M. WAGNER, Court of Appeals of the District of Columbia, 500 Indiana Ave., NW, Washington, DC 20001

UNIFORM MEDIATION ACT

SECTION 1. TITLE. This [Act] may be cited as the Uniform Mediation Act.

SECTION 2. DEFINITIONS. In this [Act]:

(1) "Mediation" means a process in which a mediator facilitates communication and negotiation between parties to assist them in reaching a voluntary agreement regarding their dispute.

(2) "Mediation communication" means a statement, whether oral or in a record or verbal or nonverbal, that occurs during a mediation or is made for purposes of considering, conducting, participating in, initiating, continuing, or reconvening a mediation or retaining a mediator.

(3) "Mediator" means an individual who conducts a mediation.

(4) "Nonparty participant" means a person, other than a party or mediator, that participates in a mediation.

(5) "Mediation party" means a person that participates in a mediation and whose agreement is necessary to resolve the dispute.

(6) "Person" means an individual, corporation, business trust, estate, trust, partnership, limited liability company, association, joint venture, government; governmental subdivision, agency, or instrumentality; public corporation, or any other legal or commercial entity.

(7) "Proceeding" means:

(A) a judicial, administrative, arbitral, or other adjudicative process, including related pre-hearing and post-hearing motions, conferences, and discovery; or

(B) a legislative hearing or similar process.

(8) "Record" means information that is inscribed on a tangible medium or that is stored in an electronic or other medium and is retrievable in perceivable form.

(9) "Sign" means:

(A) to execute or adopt a tangible symbol with the present intent to authenticate a record; or

(B) to attach or logically associate an electronic symbol, sound, or process to or with a record with the present intent to authenticate a record.

SECTION 3. SCOPE.

(a) Except as otherwise provided in subsection (b) or (c), this [Act] applies to a mediation in which:

(1) the mediation parties are required to mediate by statute or court or administrative agency rule or referred to mediation by a court, administrative agency, or arbitrator;

(2) the mediation parties and the mediator agree to mediate in a record that demonstrates an expectation that mediation communications will be privileged against disclosure; or

(3) the mediation parties use as a mediator an individual who holds himself or herself out as a mediator or the mediation is provided by a person that holds itself out as providing mediation.

(b) The [Act] does not apply to a mediation:

        (1) relating to the establishment, negotiation, administration, or termination of a collective bargaining relationship;

        (2) relating to a dispute that is pending under or is part of the processes established by a collective bargaining agreement, except that the [Act] applies to a mediation arising out of a dispute that has been filed with an administrative agency or court;

        (3) conducted by a judge who might make a ruling on the case; or

        (4) conducted under the auspices of:

            (A) a primary or secondary school if all the parties are students or

            (B) a correctional institution for youths if all the parties are residents of that institution.

(c) If the parties agree in advance in a signed record, or a record of proceeding reflects agreement by the parties, that all or part of a mediation is not privileged, the privileges under Sections 4 through 6 do not apply to the mediation or part agreed upon. However, Sections 4 through 6 apply to a mediation communication made by a person that has not received actual notice of the agreement before the communication is made.

Legislative Note: To the extent that the Act applies to mediations conducted under the authority of a State's courts, State judiciaries should consider enacting conforming court rules.

SECTION 4. PRIVILEGE AGAINST DISCLOSURE; ADMISSIBILITY; DISCOVERY.

(a) Except as otherwise provided in Section 6, a mediation communication is privileged as provided in subsection (b) and is not subject to discovery or admissible in evidence in a proceeding unless waived or precluded as provided by Section 5.

(b) In a proceeding, the following privileges apply:

        (1) A mediation party may refuse to disclose, and may prevent any other person from disclosing, a mediation communication.

        (2) A mediator may refuse to disclose a mediation communication, and may prevent any other person from disclosing a mediation communication of the mediator.

        (3) A nonparty participant may refuse to disclose, and may prevent any other person from disclosing, a mediation communication of the nonparty participant.

(c) Evidence or information that is otherwise admissible or subject to discovery does not become inadmissible or protected from discovery solely by reason of its disclosure or use in a mediation.

Legislative Note: The Act does not supersede existing state statutes that make mediators incompetent to testify, or that provide for costs and attorney fees to mediators who are wrongfully subpoenaed. See, e.g., Cal. Evid. Code Section 703.5 (West 1994).

SECTION 5. WAIVER AND PRECLUSION OF PRIVILEGE.

(a) A privilege under Section 4 may be waived in a record or orally during a proceeding if it is expressly waived by all parties to the mediation and:

        (1) in the case of the privilege of a mediator, it is expressly waived by the mediator; and

(2) in the case of the privilege of a nonparty participant, it is expressly waived by the nonparty participant.

(b) A person that discloses or makes a representation about a mediation communication which prejudices another person in a proceeding is precluded from asserting a privilege under Section 4, but only to the extent necessary for the person prejudiced to respond to the representation or disclosure.

(c) A person that intentionally uses a mediation to plan, attempt to commit or commit a crime, or to conceal an ongoing crime or ongoing criminal activity is precluded from asserting a privilege under Section 4.

SECTION 6. EXCEPTIONS TO PRIVILEGE.

(a) There is no privilege under Section 4 for a mediation communication that is:

(1) in an agreement evidenced by a record signed by all parties to the agreement;

(2) available to the public under [insert statutory reference to open records act] or made during a session of a mediation which is open, or is required by law to be open, to the public;

(3) a threat or statement of a plan to inflict bodily injury or commit a crime of violence;

(4) intentionally used to plan a crime, attempt to commit or commit a crime, or to conceal an ongoing crime or ongoing criminal activity;

(5) sought or offered to prove or disprove a claim or complaint of professional misconduct or malpractice filed against a mediator;

(6) except as otherwise provided in subsection (c), sought or offered to prove or disprove a claim or complaint of professional misconduct or malpractice filed against a mediation party, nonparty participant, or representative of a party based on conduct occurring during a mediation; or

(7) sought or offered to prove or disprove abuse, neglect, abandonment, or exploitation in a proceeding in which a child or adult protective services agency is a party, unless the

[Alternative A: [State to insert, for example, child or adult protection] case is referred by a court to mediation and a public agency participates.]

[Alternative B: public agency participates in the [State to insert, for example, child or adult protection] mediation].

(b) There is no privilege under Section 4 if a court, administrative agency, or arbitrator finds, after a hearing in camera, that the party seeking discovery or the proponent of the evidence has shown that the evidence is not otherwise available, that there is a need for the evidence that substantially outweighs the interest in protecting confidentiality, and that the mediation communication is sought or offered in:

(1) a court proceeding involving a felony [or misdemeanor]; or

(2) except as otherwise provided in subsection (c), a proceeding to prove a claim to rescind or reform or a defense to avoid liability on a contract arising out of the mediation.

(c) A mediator may not be compelled to provide evidence of a mediation communication referred to in subsection (a)(6) or (b)(2).

(d) If a mediation communication is not privileged under subsection (a) or (b), only the portion of the communication necessary for the application of the exception from nondisclosure may be admitted. Admission of evidence under subsection (a) or (b) does not render the evidence, or any other mediation communication, discoverable or admissible for any other purpose.

Legislative Note: If the enacting state does not have an open records act, the following language in paragraph (2) of subsection (a) needs to be deleted: "available to the public under [insert statutory reference to open records act] or".

SECTION 7. PROHIBITED MEDIATOR REPORTS.

(a) Except as required in subsection (b), a mediator may not make a report, assessment, evaluation, recommendation, finding, or other communication regarding a mediation to a court, administrative agency, or other authority that may make a ruling on the dispute that is the subject of the mediation.

(b) A mediator may disclose:

(1) whether the mediation occurred or has terminated, whether a settlement was reached, and attendance;

(2) a mediation communication as permitted under Section 6; or

(3) a mediation communication evidencing abuse, neglect, abandonment, or exploitation of an individual to a public agency responsible for protecting individuals against such mistreatment.

(c) A communication made in violation of subsection (a) may not be considered by a court, administrative agency, or arbitrator.

SECTION 8. CONFIDENTIALITY. Unless subject to the [insert statutory references to open meetings act and open records act], mediation communications are confidential to the extent agreed by the parties or provided by other law or rule of this State.

SECTION 9. MEDIATOR'S DISCLOSURE OF CONFLICTS OF INTEREST; BACKGROUND.

(a) Before accepting a mediation, an individual who is requested to serve as a mediator shall:

(1) make an inquiry that is reasonable under the circumstances to determine whether there are any known facts that a reasonable individual would consider likely to affect the impartiality of the mediator, including a financial or personal interest in the outcome of the mediation and an existing or past relationship with a mediation party or foreseeable participant in the mediation; and

(2) disclose any such known fact to the mediation parties as soon as is practical before accepting a mediation.

(b) If a mediator learns any fact described in subsection (a)(1) after accepting a mediation, the mediator shall disclose it as soon as is practicable.

(c) At the request of a mediation party, an individual who is requested to serve as a mediator shall disclose the mediator's qualifications to mediate a dispute.

(d) A person that violates subsection [(a) or (b)][(a), (b), or (g)] is precluded by the violation from asserting a privilege under Section 4.

(e) Subsections (a), (b), [and] (c), [and] [(g)] do not apply to an individual acting as a judge.

(f) This [Act] does not require that a mediator have a special qualification by background or profession.

[(g) A mediator must be impartial, unless after disclosure of the facts required in subsections (a) and (b) to be disclosed, the parties agree otherwise.]

SECTION 10. PARTICIPATION IN MEDIATION. An attorney or other individual designated by a party may accompany the party to and participate in a mediation. A waiver of participation given before the mediation may be rescinded.

SECTION 11. RELATION TO ELECTRONIC SIGNATURES IN GLOBAL AND NATIONAL COMMERCE ACT. This [Act] modifies, limits, or supersedes the federal Electronic Signatures in Global and National Commerce Act, 15 U.S.C. Section 7001 et seq., but this [Act] does not modify, limit, or supersede Section 101(c) of that Act or authorize electronic delivery of any of the notices described in Section 103(b) of that Act.

SECTION 12. UNIFORMITY OF APPLICATION AND CONSTRUCTION. In applying and construing this [Act], consideration should be given to the need to promote uniformity of the law with respect to its subject matter among States that enact it.

SECTION 13. SEVERABILITY CLAUSE. If any provision of this [Act] or its application to any person or circumstance is held invalid, the invalidity does not affect other provisions or applications of this [Act] which can be given effect without the invalid provision or application, and to this end the provisions of this [Act] are severable.

SECTION 14. EFFECTIVE DATE. This [Act] takes effect ....

SECTION 15. REPEALS. The following acts and parts of acts are hereby repealed:
(1)
(2)
(3)

SECTION 16. APPLICATION TO EXISTING AGREEMENTS OR REFERRALS.

(a) This [Act] governs a mediation pursuant to a referral or an agreement to mediate made on or after [the effective date of this [Act]].

(b) On or after [a delayed date], this [Act] governs an agreement to mediate whenever made.

Appendix O

Model Rules of Professional Conduct 2002[1]

(Selected Rules)

RULE 1.2: SCOPE OF REPRESENTATION AND ALLOCATION OF AUTHORITY BETWEEN CLIENT AND LAWYER

(a)   Subject to paragraphs (c) and (d), a lawyer shall abide by a client's decisions concerning the objectives of representation and, as required by Rule 1.4, shall consult with the client as to the means by which they are to be pursued. A lawyer may take such action on behalf of the client as is impliedly authorized to carry out the representation. A lawyer shall abide by a client's decision whether to settle a matter. In a criminal case, the lawyer shall abide by the client's decision, after consultation with the lawyer, as to a plea to be entered, whether to waive jury trial and whether the client will testify.

(b)   A lawyer's representation of a client, including representation by appointment, does not constitute an endorsement of the client's political, economic, social or moral views or activities.

(c)   A lawyer may limit the scope of the representation if the limitation is reasonable under the circumstances and the client gives informed consent.

(d)   A lawyer shall not counsel a client to engage, or assist a client, in conduct that the lawyer knows is criminal or fraudulent, but a lawyer may discuss the legal consequences of any proposed course of conduct with a client and may counsel or assist a client to make a good faith effort to determine the validity, scope, meaning or application of the law.

Comment

Allocation of Authority between Client and Lawyer

[1]   Paragraph (a) confers upon the client the ultimate authority to determine the purposes to be served by legal representation, within the limits imposed by law and the lawyer's professional obligations. The decisions specified in paragraph (a), such as whether to settle a civil matter, must also be made by the client. See Rule

---

[1] © American Bar Association. Reprinted by permission of the American Bar Association. Copies of the *ABA Model Rules of Professional Conduct 2002* are available from Service Center, American Bar Association, 750 North Lake Shore Drive, Chicago, IL 60611-4497, 1-800-285-2221.

1.4(a)(1) for the lawyer's duty to communicate with the client about such decisions. With respect to the means by which the client's objectives are to be pursued, the lawyer shall consult with the client as required by Rule 1.4(a)(2) and may take such action as is impliedly authorized to carry out the representation.

[2]   On occasion, however, a lawyer and a client may disagree about the means to be used to accomplish the client's objectives. Clients normally defer to the special knowledge and skill of their lawyer with respect to the means to be used to accomplish their objectives, particularly with respect to technical, legal and tactical matters. Conversely, lawyers usually defer to the client regarding such questions as the expense to be incurred and concern for third persons who might be adversely affected. Because of the varied nature of the matters about which a lawyer and client might disagree and because the actions in question may implicate the interests of a tribunal or other persons, this Rule does not prescribe how such disagreements are to be resolved. Other law, however, may be applicable and should be consulted by the lawyer. The lawyer should also consult with the client and seek a mutually acceptable resolution of the disagreement. If such efforts are unavailing and the lawyer has a fundamental disagreement with the client, the lawyer may withdraw from the representation. See Rule 1.16(b)(4). Conversely, the client may resolve the disagreement by discharging the lawyer. See Rule 1.16(a)(3).

[3]   At the outset of a representation, the client may authorize the lawyer to take specific action on the client's behalf without further consultation. Absent a material change in circumstances and subject to Rule 1.4, a lawyer may rely on such an advance authorization. The client may, however, revoke such authority at any time.

[4]   In a case in which the client appears to be suffering diminished capacity, the lawyer's duty to abide by the client's decisions is to be guided by reference to Rule 1.14.

Independence from Client's Views or Activities

[5]   Legal representation should not be denied to people who are unable to afford legal services, or whose cause is controversial or the subject of popular disapproval. By the same token, representing a client does not constitute approval of the client's views or activities.

Agreements Limiting Scope of Representation

[6]   The scope of services to be provided by a lawyer may be limited by agreement with the client or by the terms under which the lawyer's services are made available to the client. When a lawyer has been retained by an insurer to represent an insured, for example, the representation may be limited to matters related to the insurance coverage. A limited representation may be appropriate because the client has limited objectives for the representation. In addition, the terms upon which representation is undertaken may exclude specific means that might otherwise be used to accomplish the

client's objectives. Such limitations may exclude actions that the client thinks are too costly or that the lawyer regards as repugnant or imprudent.

[7]   Although this Rule affords the lawyer and client substantial latitude to limit the representation, the limitation must be reasonable under the circumstances. If, for example, a client's objective is limited to securing general information about the law the client needs in order to handle a common and typically uncomplicated legal problem, the lawyer and client may agree that the lawyer's services will be limited to a brief telephone consultation. Such a limitation, however, would not be reasonable if the time allotted was not sufficient to yield advice upon which the client could rely. Although an agreement for a limited representation does not exempt a lawyer from the duty to provide competent representation, the limitation is a factor to be considered when determining the legal knowledge, skill, thoroughness and preparation reasonably necessary for the representation. See Rule 1.1.

[8]   All agreements concerning a lawyer's representation of a client must accord with the Rules of Professional Conduct and other law. See, e.g., Rules 1.1, 1.8 and 5.6.

Criminal, Fraudulent and Prohibited Transactions

[9]   Paragraph (d) prohibits a lawyer from knowingly counseling or assisting a client to commit a crime or fraud. This prohibition, however, does not preclude the lawyer from giving an honest opinion about the actual consequences that appear likely to result from a client's conduct. Nor does the fact that a client uses advice in a course of action that is criminal or fraudulent of itself make a lawyer a party to the course of action. There is a critical distinction between presenting an analysis of legal aspects of questionable conduct and recommending the means by which a crime or fraud might be committed with impunity.

[10]   When the client's course of action has already begun and is continuing, the lawyer's responsibility is especially delicate. The lawyer is required to avoid assisting the client, for example, by drafting or delivering documents that the lawyer knows are fraudulent or by suggesting how the wrongdoing might be concealed. A lawyer may not continue assisting a client in conduct that the lawyer originally supposed was legally proper but then discovers is criminal or fraudulent. The lawyer must, therefore, withdraw from the representation of the client in the matter. See Rule 1.16(a). In some cases, withdrawal alone might be insufficient. It may be necessary for the lawyer to give notice of the fact of withdrawal and to disaffirm any opinion, document, affirmation or the like. See Rule 4.1.

[11]   Where the client is a fiduciary, the lawyer may be charged with special obligations in dealings with a beneficiary.

[12]   Paragraph (d) applies whether or not the defrauded party is a party to the transaction. Hence, a lawyer must not participate in a transaction to effectuate criminal or fraudulent avoidance of tax liability. Paragraph (d) does not preclude

undertaking a criminal defense incident to a general retainer for legal services to a lawful enterprise. The last clause of paragraph (d) recognizes that determining the validity or interpretation of a statute or regulation may require a course of action involving disobedience of the statute or regulation or of the interpretation placed upon it by governmental authorities.

[13]   If a lawyer comes to know or reasonably should know that a client expects assistance not permitted by the Rules of Professional Conduct or other law or if the lawyer intends to act contrary to the client's instructions, the lawyer must consult with the client regarding the limitations on the lawyer's conduct. See Rule 1.4(a)(5).

RULE 1.4: COMMUNICATION

(a)   A lawyer shall:

(1)   promptly inform the client of any decision or circumstance with respect to which the client's informed consent, as defined in Rule 1.0(e), is required by these Rules;

(2)   reasonably consult with the client about the means by which the client's objectives are to be accomplished;

(3)   keep the client reasonably informed about the status of the matter;

(4)   promptly comply with reasonable requests for information; and

(5)   consult with the client about any relevant limitation on the lawyer's conduct when the lawyer knows that the client expects assistance not permitted by the Rules of Professional Conduct or other law.

(b)   A lawyer shall explain a matter to the extent reasonably necessary to permit the client to make informed decisions regarding the representation.

Comment

[1]   Reasonable communication between the lawyer and the client is necessary for the client effectively to participate in the representation.

Communicating with Client

[2]   If these Rules require that a particular decision about the representation be made by the client, paragraph (a)(1) requires that the lawyer promptly consult with and secure the client's consent prior to taking action unless prior discussions with the client have resolved what action the client wants the lawyer to take. For example, a

lawyer who receives from opposing counsel an offer of settlement in a civil controversy or a proffered plea bargain in a criminal case must promptly inform the client of its substance unless the client has previously indicated that the proposal will be acceptable or unacceptable or has authorized the lawyer to accept or to reject the offer. See Rule 1.2(a).

[3]   Paragraph (a)(2) requires the lawyer to reasonably consult with the client about the means to be used to accomplish the client's objectives. In some situations — depending on both the importance of the action under consideration and the feasibility of consulting with the client — this duty will require consultation prior to taking action. In other circumstances, such as during a trial when an immediate decision must be made, the exigency of the situation may require the lawyer to act without prior consultation. In such cases the lawyer must nonetheless act reasonably to inform the client of actions the lawyer has taken on the client's behalf. Additionally, paragraph (a)(3) requires that the lawyer keep the client reasonably informed about the status of the matter, such as significant developments affecting the timing or the substance of the representation.

[4]   A lawyer's regular communication with clients will minimize the occasions on which a client will need to request information concerning the representation. When a client makes a reasonable request for information, however, paragraph (a)(4) requires prompt compliance with the request, or if a prompt response is not feasible, that the lawyer, or a member of the lawyer's staff, acknowledge receipt of the request and advise the client when a response may be expected. Client telephone calls should be promptly returned or acknowledged.

Explaining Matters

[5]   The client should have sufficient information to participate intelligently in decisions concerning the objectives of the representation and the means by which they are to be pursued, to the extent the client is willing and able to do so. Adequacy of communication depends in part on the kind of advice or assistance that is involved. For example, when there is time to explain a proposal made in a negotiation, the lawyer should review all important provisions with the client before proceeding to an agreement. In litigation a lawyer should explain the general strategy and prospects of success and ordinarily should consult the client on tactics that are likely to result in significant expense or to injure or coerce others. On the other hand, a lawyer ordinarily will not be expected to describe trial or negotiation strategy in detail. The guiding principle is that the lawyer should fulfill reasonable client expectations for information consistent with the duty to act in the client's best interests, and the client's overall requirements as to the character of representation. In certain circumstances, such as when a lawyer asks a client to consent to a representation affected by a conflict of interest, the client must give informed consent, as defined in Rule 1.0(e).

[6]   Ordinarily, the information to be provided is that appropriate for a client who is a comprehending and responsible adult. However, fully informing the client according to this standard may be impracticable, for example, where the client is a child or suffers from diminished capacity. See Rule 1.14. When the client is an organization or

group, it is often impossible or inappropriate to inform every one of its members about its legal affairs; ordinarily, the lawyer should address communications to the appropriate officials of the organization. See Rule 1.13. Where many routine matters are involved, a system of limited or occasional reporting may be arranged with the client.

Withholding Information

[7]   In some circumstances, a lawyer may be justified in delaying transmission of information when the client would be likely to react imprudently to an immediate communication. Thus, a lawyer might withhold a psychiatric diagnosis of a client when the examining psychiatrist indicates that disclosure would harm the client. A lawyer may not withhold information to serve the lawyer's own interest or convenience or the interests or convenience of another person. Rules or court orders governing litigation may provide that information supplied to a lawyer may not be disclosed to the client. Rule 3.4(c) directs compliance with such rules or orders.

RULE 1.6: CONFIDENTIALITY OF INFORMATION

(a)   A lawyer shall not reveal information relating to the representation of a client unless the client gives informed consent, the disclosure is impliedly authorized in order to carry out the representation or the disclosure is permitted by paragraph (b).

(b)   A lawyer may reveal information relating to the representation of a client to the extent the lawyer reasonably believes necessary:

(1)   to prevent reasonably certain death or substantial bodily harm;

(2)   to secure legal advice about the lawyer's compliance with these Rules;

(3)   to establish a claim or defense on behalf of the lawyer in a controversy between the lawyer and the client, to establish a defense to a criminal charge or civil claim against the lawyer based upon conduct in which the client was involved, or to respond to allegations in any proceeding concerning the lawyer's representation of the client; or

(4)   to comply with other law or a court order.

Comment

[1]   This Rule governs the disclosure by a lawyer of information relating to the representation of a client during the lawyer's representation of the client. See Rule 1.18 for the lawyer's duties with respect to information provided to the lawyer by a prospective client, Rule 1.9(c)(2) for the lawyer's duty not to reveal information relating to the lawyer's prior representation of a former client and Rules 1.8(b) and 1.9(c)(1) for the lawyer's duties with respect to the use of such information to the disadvantage of clients and former clients.

[2]   A fundamental principle in the client-lawyer relationship is that, in the absence of the client's informed consent, the lawyer must not reveal information relating to the representation. See Rule 1.0(e) for the definition of informed consent. This contributes to the trust that is the hallmark of the client-lawyer relationship. The client is thereby encouraged to seek legal assistance and to communicate fully and frankly with the lawyer even as to embarrassing or legally damaging subject matter. The lawyer needs this information to represent the client effectively and, if necessary, to advise the client to refrain from wrongful conduct. Almost without exception, clients come to lawyers in order to determine their rights and what is, in the complex of laws and regulations, deemed to be legal and correct. Based upon experience, lawyers know that almost all clients follow the advice given, and the law is upheld.

[3]   The principle of client-lawyer confidentiality is given effect by related bodies of law: the attorney-client privilege, the work product doctrine and the rule of confidentiality established in professional ethics. The attorney-client privilege and work-product doctrine apply in judicial and other proceedings in which a lawyer may be called as a witness or otherwise required to produce evidence concerning a client. The rule of client-lawyer confidentiality applies in situations other than those where evidence is sought from the lawyer through compulsion of law. The confidentiality rule, for example, applies not only to matters communicated in confidence by the client but also to all information relating to the representation, whatever its source. A lawyer may not disclose such information except as authorized or required by the Rules of Professional Conduct or other law. See also Scope.

[4]   Paragraph (a) prohibits a lawyer from revealing information relating to the representation of a client. This prohibition also applies to disclosures by a lawyer that do not in themselves reveal protected information but could reasonably lead to the discovery of such information by a third person. A lawyer's use of a hypothetical to discuss issues relating to the representation is permissible so long as there is no reasonable likelihood that the listener will be able to ascertain the identity of the client or the situation involved.

Authorized Disclosure

[5]   Except to the extent that the client's instructions or special circumstances limit that authority, a lawyer is impliedly authorized to make disclosures about a client when appropriate in carrying out the representation. In some situations, for example, a lawyer may be impliedly authorized to admit a fact that cannot properly be disputed or to make a disclosure that facilitates a satisfactory conclusion to a matter. Lawyers in a firm may, in the course of the firm's practice, disclose to each other information relating to a client of the firm, unless the client has instructed that particular information be confined to specified lawyers.

Disclosure Adverse to Client

[6]   Although the public interest is usually best served by a strict rule requiring lawyers to preserve the confidentiality of information relating to the representation of their clients, the confidentiality rule is subject to limited exceptions. Paragraph (b)(1) recognizes the overriding value of life and physical integrity and permits disclosure reasonably necessary to prevent reasonably certain death or substantial bodily harm. Such harm is reasonably certain to occur if it will be suffered imminently or if there is a present and substantial threat that a person will suffer such harm at a later date if the lawyer fails to take action necessary to eliminate the threat. Thus, a lawyer who knows that a client has accidentally discharged toxic waste into a town's water supply may reveal this information to the authorities if there is a present and substantial risk that a person who drinks the water will contract a life-threatening or debilitating disease and the lawyer's disclosure is necessary to eliminate the threat or reduce the number of victims.

[7]   A lawyer's confidentiality obligations do not preclude a lawyer from securing confidential legal advice about the lawyer's personal responsibility to comply with these Rules. In most situations, disclosing information to secure such advice will be impliedly authorized for the lawyer to carry out the representation. Even when the disclosure is not impliedly authorized, paragraph (b)(2) permits such disclosure because of the importance of a lawyer's compliance with the Rules of Professional Conduct.

[8]   Where a legal claim or disciplinary charge alleges complicity of the lawyer in a client's conduct or other misconduct of the lawyer involving representation of the client, the lawyer may respond to the extent the lawyer reasonably believes necessary to establish a defense. The same is true with respect to a claim involving the conduct or representation of a former client. Such a charge can arise in a civil, criminal, disciplinary or other proceeding and can be based on a wrong allegedly committed by the lawyer against the client or on a wrong alleged by a third person, for example, a person claiming to have been defrauded by the lawyer and client acting together. The lawyer's right to respond arises when an assertion of such complicity has been made. Paragraph (b)(3) does not require the lawyer to await the commencement of an action or proceeding that charges such complicity, so that the defense may be established by responding directly to a third party who has made such an assertion. The right to defend also applies, of course, where a proceeding has been commenced.

[9]   A lawyer entitled to a fee is permitted by paragraph (b)(3) to prove the services rendered in an action to collect it. This aspect of the rule expresses the principle that the beneficiary of a fiduciary relationship may not exploit it to the detriment of the fiduciary.

[10]   Other law may require that a lawyer disclose information about a client. Whether such a law supersedes Rule 1.6 is a question of law beyond the scope of these Rules. When disclosure of information relating to the representation appears to be required by other law, the lawyer must discuss the matter with the client to the extent required by Rule 1.4. If, however, the other law supersedes this Rule and requires disclosure, paragraph (b)(4) permits the lawyer to make such disclosures as are necessary to comply with the law.

[11]   A lawyer may be ordered to reveal information relating to the representation of a client by a court or by another tribunal or governmental entity claiming authority pursuant to other law to compel the disclosure. Absent informed consent of the client to do otherwise, the lawyer should assert on behalf of the client all nonfrivolous claims that the order is not authorized by other law or that the information sought is protected against disclosure by the attorney-client privilege or other applicable law. In the event of an adverse ruling, the lawyer must consult with the client about the possibility of appeal to the extent required by Rule 1.4. Unless review is sought, however, paragraph (b)(4) permits the lawyer to comply with the court's order.

[12]   Paragraph (b) permits disclosure only to the extent the lawyer reasonably believes the disclosure is necessary to accomplish one of the purposes specified. Where practicable, the lawyer should first seek to persuade the client to take suitable action to obviate the need for disclosure. In any case, a disclosure adverse to the client's interest should be no greater than the lawyer reasonably believes necessary to accomplish the purpose. If the disclosure will be made in connection with a judicial proceeding, the disclosure should be made in a manner that limits access to the information to the tribunal or other persons having a need to know it and appropriate protective orders or other arrangements should be sought by the lawyer to the fullest extent practicable.

[13]   Paragraph (b) permits but does not require the disclosure of information relating to a client's representation to accomplish the purposes specified in paragraphs (b)(1) through (b)(4). In exercising the discretion conferred by this Rule, the lawyer may consider such factors as the nature of the lawyer's relationship with the client and with those who might be injured by the client, the lawyer's own involvement in the transaction and factors that may extenuate the conduct in question. A lawyer's decision not to disclose as permitted by paragraph (b) does not violate this Rule. Disclosure may be required, however, by other Rules. Some Rules require disclosure only if such disclosure would be permitted by paragraph (b). See Rules 1.2(d), 4.1(b), 8.1 and 8.3. Rule 3.3, on the other hand, requires disclosure in some circumstances regardless of whether such disclosure is permitted by this Rule. See Rule 3.3(c).

Withdrawal

[14]   If the lawyer's services will be used by the client in materially furthering a course of criminal or fraudulent conduct, the lawyer must withdraw, as stated in Rule 1.16(a)(1). After withdrawal the lawyer is required to refrain from making disclosure of the client's confidences, except as otherwise permitted by Rule 1.6. Neither this Rule nor Rule 1.8(b) nor Rule 1.16(d) prevents the lawyer from giving notice of the fact of withdrawal, and the lawyer may also withdraw or disaffirm any opinion, document, affirmation, or the like. Where the client is an organization, the lawyer may be in doubt whether contemplated conduct will actually be carried out by the organization. Where necessary to guide conduct in connection with this Rule, the lawyer may make inquiry within the organization as indicated in Rule 1.13(b).

Acting Competently to Preserve Confidentiality

[15]   A lawyer must act competently to safeguard information relating to the representation of a client against inadvertent or unauthorized disclosure by the lawyer or other persons who are participating in the representation of the client or who are subject to the lawyer's supervision. See Rules 1.1, 5.1 and 5.3.

[16]   When transmitting a communication that includes information relating to the representation of a client, the lawyer must take reasonable precautions to prevent the information from coming into the hands of unintended recipients. This duty, however, does not require that the lawyer use special security measures if the method of communication affords a reasonable expectation of privacy. Special circumstances, however, may warrant special precautions. Factors to be considered in determining the reasonableness of the lawyer's expectation of confidentiality include the sensitivity of the information and the extent to which the privacy of the communication is protected by law or by a confidentiality agreement. A client may require the lawyer to implement special security measures not required by this Rule or may give informed consent to the use of a means of communication that would otherwise be prohibited by this Rule.

Former Client

[17]   The duty of confidentiality continues after the client-lawyer relationship has terminated. See Rule 1.9(c)(2). See Rule 1.9(c)(1) for the prohibition against using such information to the disadvantage of the former client.

RULE 2.1: ADVISOR

In representing a client, a lawyer shall exercise independent professional judgment and render candid advice. In rendering advice, a lawyer may refer not only to law but to other considerations such as moral, economic, social and political factors, that may be relevant to the client's situation.

Comment

Scope of Advice

[1]   A client is entitled to straightforward advice expressing the lawyer's honest assessment. Legal advice often involves unpleasant facts and alternatives that a client may be disinclined to confront. In presenting advice, a lawyer endeavors to sustain the client's morale and may put advice in as acceptable a form as honesty permits. However, a lawyer should not be deterred from giving candid advice by the prospect that the advice will be unpalatable to the client.

[2]   Advice couched in narrow legal terms may be of little value to a client, especially where practical considerations, such as cost or effects on other people, are predominant. Purely technical legal advice, therefore, can sometimes be inadequate. It is

proper for a lawyer to refer to relevant moral and ethical considerations in giving advice. Although a lawyer is not a moral advisor as such, moral and ethical considerations impinge upon most legal questions and may decisively influence how the law will be applied.

[3] A client may expressly or impliedly ask the lawyer for purely technical advice. When such a request is made by a client experienced in legal matters, the lawyer may accept it at face value. When such a request is made by a client inexperienced in legal matters, however, the lawyer's responsibility as advisor may include indicating that more may be involved than strictly legal considerations.

[4] Matters that go beyond strictly legal questions may also be in the domain of another profession. Family matters can involve problems within the professional competence of psychiatry, clinical psychology or social work; business matters can involve problems within the competence of the accounting profession or of financial specialists. Where consultation with a professional in another field is itself something a competent lawyer would recommend, the lawyer should make such a recommendation. At the same time, a lawyer's advice at its best often consists of recommending a course of action in the face of conflicting recommendations of experts.

Offering Advice

[5] In general, a lawyer is not expected to give advice until asked by the client. However, when a lawyer knows that a client proposes a course of action that is likely to result in substantial adverse legal consequences to the client, the lawyer's duty to the client under Rule 1.4 may require that the lawyer offer advice if the client's course of action is related to the representation. Similarly, when a matter is likely to involve litigation, it may be necessary under Rule 1.4 to inform the client of forms of dispute resolution that might constitute reasonable alternatives to litigation. A lawyer ordinarily has no duty to initiate investigation of a client's affairs or to give advice that the client has indicated is unwanted, but a lawyer may initiate advice to a client when doing so appears to be in the client's interest.

RULE 3.3: CANDOR TOWARD THE TRIBUNAL

(a)   A lawyer shall not knowingly:

(1)   make a false statement of fact or law to a tribunal or fail to correct a false statement of material fact or law previously made to the tribunal by the lawyer;

(2)   fail to disclose to the tribunal legal authority in the controlling jurisdiction known to the lawyer to be directly adverse to the position of the client and not disclosed by opposing counsel; or

(3)   offer evidence that the lawyer knows to be false. If a lawyer, the lawyer's client, or a witness called by the lawyer, has offered material evidence and the lawyer comes to know of its falsity, the lawyer shall take reasonable remedial measures, including, if necessary, disclosure to the tribunal. A lawyer may refuse to offer evidence, other than the testimony of a defendant in a criminal matter, that the lawyer reasonably believes is false.

(b)   A lawyer who represents a client in an adjudicative proceeding and who knows that a person intends to engage, is engaging or has engaged in criminal or fraudulent conduct related to the proceeding shall take reasonable remedial measures, including, if necessary, disclosure to the tribunal.

(c)   The duties stated in paragraphs (a) and (b) continue to the conclusion of the proceeding, and apply even if compliance requires disclosure of information otherwise protected by Rule 1.6.

(d)   In an ex parte proceeding, a lawyer shall inform the tribunal of all material facts known to the lawyer that will enable the tribunal to make an informed decision, whether or not the facts are adverse.

Comment

[1]   This Rule governs the conduct of a lawyer who is representing a client in the proceedings of a tribunal. See Rule 1.0(m) for the definition of "tribunal." It also applies when the lawyer is representing a client in an ancillary proceeding conducted pursuant to the tribunal's adjudicative authority, such as a deposition. Thus, for example, paragraph (a)(3) requires a lawyer to take reasonable remedial measures if the lawyer comes to know that a client who is testifying in a deposition has offered evidence that is false.

[2]   This Rule sets forth the special duties of lawyers as officers of the court to avoid conduct that undermines the integrity of the adjudicative process. A lawyer acting as an advocate in an adjudicative proceeding has an obligation to present the client's case with persuasive force. Performance of that duty while maintaining confidences of the client, however, is qualified by the advocate's duty of candor to the tribunal. Consequently, although a lawyer in an adversary proceeding is not required to present an impartial exposition of the law or to vouch for the evidence submitted in a cause, the lawyer must not allow the tribunal to be misled by false statements of law or fact or evidence that the lawyer knows to be false.

Representations by a Lawyer

[3]   An advocate is responsible for pleadings and other documents prepared for litigation, but is usually not required to have personal knowledge of matters asserted therein, for litigation documents ordinarily present assertions by the client, or by someone on the client's behalf, and not assertions by the lawyer. Compare Rule 3.1. However, an assertion purporting to be on the lawyer's own knowledge, as in an affidavit by the

lawyer or in a statement in open court, may properly be made only when the lawyer knows the assertion is true or believes it to be true on the basis of a reasonably diligent inquiry. There are circumstances where failure to make a disclosure is the equivalent of an affirmative misrepresentation. The obligation prescribed in Rule 1.2(d) not to counsel a client to commit or assist the client in committing a fraud applies in litigation. Regarding compliance with Rule 1.2(d), see the Comment to that Rule. See also the Comment to Rule 8.4(b).

Legal Argument

[4]   Legal argument based on a knowingly false representation of law constitutes dishonesty toward the tribunal. A lawyer is not required to make a disinterested exposition of the law, but must recognize the existence of pertinent legal authorities. Furthermore, as stated in paragraph (a)(2), an advocate has a duty to disclose directly adverse authority in the controlling jurisdiction that has not been disclosed by the opposing party. The underlying concept is that legal argument is a discussion seeking to determine the legal premises properly applicable to the case.

Offering Evidence

[5]   Paragraph (a)(3) requires that the lawyer refuse to offer evidence that the lawyer knows to be false, regardless of the client's wishes. This duty is premised on the lawyer's obligation as an officer of the court to prevent the trier of fact from being misled by false evidence. A lawyer does not violate this Rule if the lawyer offers the evidence for the purpose of establishing its falsity.

[6]   If a lawyer knows that the client intends to testify falsely or wants the lawyer to introduce false evidence, the lawyer should seek to persuade the client that the evidence should not be offered. If the persuasion is ineffective and the lawyer continues to represent the client, the lawyer must refuse to offer the false evidence. If only a portion of a witness's testimony will be false, the lawyer may call the witness to testify but may not elicit or otherwise permit the witness to present the testimony that the lawyer knows is false.

[7]   The duties stated in paragraphs (a) and (b) apply to all lawyers, including defense counsel in criminal cases. In some jurisdictions, however, courts have required counsel to present the accused as a witness or to give a narrative statement if the accused so desires, even if counsel knows that the testimony or statement will be false. The obligation of the advocate under the Rules of Professional Conduct is subordinate to such requirements. See also Comment [9].

[8]   The prohibition against offering false evidence only applies if the lawyer knows that the evidence is false. A lawyer's reasonable belief that evidence is false does not preclude its presentation to the trier of fact. A lawyer's knowledge that evidence is false, however, can be inferred from the circumstances. See Rule 1.0(f). Thus, although a lawyer should resolve doubts about the veracity of testimony or other evidence in favor of the client, the lawyer cannot ignore an obvious falsehood.

[9]   Although paragraph (a)(3) only prohibits a lawyer from offering evidence the lawyer knows to be false, it permits the lawyer to refuse to offer testimony or other proof that the lawyer reasonably believes is false. Offering such proof may reflect adversely on the lawyer's ability to discriminate in the quality of evidence and thus impair the lawyer's effectiveness as an advocate. Because of the special protections historically provided criminal defendants, however, this Rule does not permit a lawyer to refuse to offer the testimony of such a client where the lawyer reasonably believes but does not know that the testimony will be false. Unless the lawyer knows the testimony will be false, the lawyer must honor the client's decision to testify. See also Comment [7].

Remedial Measures

[10]   Having offered material evidence in the belief that it was true, a lawyer may subsequently come to know that the evidence is false. Or, a lawyer may be surprised when the lawyer's client, or another witness called by the lawyer, offers testimony the lawyer knows to be false, either during the lawyer's direct examination or in response to cross-examination by the opposing lawyer. In such situations or if the lawyer knows of the falsity of testimony elicited from the client during a deposition, the lawyer must take reasonable remedial measures. In such situations, the advocate's proper course is to remonstrate with the client confidentially, advise the client of the lawyer's duty of candor to the tribunal and seek the client's cooperation with respect to the withdrawal or correction of the false statements or evidence. If that fails, the advocate must take further remedial action. If withdrawal from the representation is not permitted or will not undo the effect of the false evidence, the advocate must make such disclosure to the tribunal as is reasonably necessary to remedy the situation, even if doing so requires the lawyer to reveal information that otherwise would be protected by Rule 1.6. It is for the tribunal then to determine what should be done — making a statement about the matter to the trier of fact, ordering a mistrial or perhaps nothing.

[11]   The disclosure of a client's false testimony can result in grave consequences to the client, including not only a sense of betrayal but also loss of the case and perhaps a prosecution for perjury. But the alternative is that the lawyer cooperate in deceiving the court, thereby subverting the truth-finding process which the adversary system is designed to implement. See Rule 1.2(d). Furthermore, unless it is clearly understood that the lawyer will act upon the duty to disclose the existence of false evidence, the client can simply reject the lawyer's advice to reveal the false evidence and insist that the lawyer keep silent. Thus the client could in effect coerce the lawyer into being a party to fraud on the court.

Preserving Integrity of Adjudicative Process

[12]   Lawyers have a special obligation to protect a tribunal against criminal or fraudulent conduct that undermines the integrity of the adjudicative process, such as bribing, intimidating or otherwise unlawfully communicating with a witness, juror, court official or other participant in the proceeding, unlawfully destroying or concealing

documents or other evidence or failing to disclose information to the tribunal when required by law to do so. Thus, paragraph (b) requires a lawyer to take reasonable remedial measures, including disclosure if necessary, whenever the lawyer knows that a person, including the lawyer's client, intends to engage, is engaging or has engaged in criminal or fraudulent conduct related to the proceeding.

Duration of Obligation

[13]   A practical time limit on the obligation to rectify false evidence or false statements of law and fact has to be established. The conclusion of the proceeding is a reasonably definite point for the termination of the obligation. A proceeding has concluded within the meaning of this Rule when a final judgment in the proceeding has been affirmed on appeal or the time for review has passed.

Ex Parte Proceedings

[14]   Ordinarily, an advocate has the limited responsibility of presenting one side of the matters that a tribunal should consider in reaching a decision; the conflicting position is expected to be presented by the opposing party. However, in any ex parte proceeding, such as an application for a temporary restraining order, there is no balance of presentation by opposing advocates. The object of an ex parte proceeding is nevertheless to yield a substantially just result. The judge has an affirmative responsibility to accord the absent party just consideration. The lawyer for the represented party has the correlative duty to make disclosures of material facts known to the lawyer and that the lawyer reasonably believes are necessary to an informed decision.

Withdrawal

[15]   Normally, a lawyer's compliance with the duty of candor imposed by this Rule does not require that the lawyer withdraw from the representation of a client whose interests will be or have been adversely affected by the lawyer's disclosure. The lawyer may, however, be required by Rule 1.16(a) to seek permission of the tribunal to withdraw if the lawyer's compliance with this Rule's duty of candor results in such an extreme deterioration of the client-lawyer relationship that the lawyer can no longer competently represent the client. Also see Rule 1.16(b) for the circumstances in which a lawyer will be permitted to seek a tribunal's permission to withdraw. In connection with a request for permission to withdraw that is premised on a client's misconduct, a lawyer may reveal information relating to the representation only to the extent reasonably necessary to comply with this Rule or as otherwise permitted by Rule 1.6.

RULE 4.1: TRUTHFULNESS IN STATEMENTS TO OTHERS

In the course of representing a client a lawyer shall not knowingly:

(a)   make a false statement of material fact or law to a third person; or

(b)   fail to disclose a material fact when disclosure is necessary to avoid assisting a criminal or fraudulent act by a client, unless disclosure is prohibited by Rule 1.6.

Comment

Misrepresentation

[1]   A lawyer is required to be truthful when dealing with others on a client's behalf, but generally has no affirmative duty to inform an opposing party of relevant facts. A misrepresentation can occur if the lawyer incorporates or affirms a statement of another person that the lawyer knows is false. Misrepresentations can also occur by partially true but misleading statements or omissions that are the equivalent of affirmative false statements. For dishonest conduct that does not amount to a false statement or for misrepresentations by a lawyer other than in the course of representing a client, see Rule 8.4.

Statements of Fact

[2]   This Rule refers to statements of fact. Whether a particular statement should be regarded as one of fact can depend on the circumstances. Under generally accepted conventions in negotiation, certain types of statements ordinarily are not taken as statements of material fact. Estimates of price or value placed on the subject of a transaction and a party's intentions as to an acceptable settlement of a claim are ordinarily in this category, and so is the existence of an undisclosed principal except where nondisclosure of the principal would constitute fraud. Lawyers should be mindful of their obligations under applicable law to avoid criminal and tortious misrepresentation.

Crime or Fraud by Client

[3]   Under Rule 1.2(d), a lawyer is prohibited from counseling or assisting a client in conduct that the lawyer knows is criminal or fraudulent. Paragraph (b) states a specific application of the principle set forth in Rule 1.2(d) and addresses the situation where a client's crime or fraud takes the form of a lie or misrepresentation. Ordinarily, a lawyer can avoid assisting a client's crime or fraud by withdrawing from the representation. Sometimes it may be necessary for the lawyer to give notice of the fact of withdrawal and to disaffirm an opinion, document, affirmation or the like. In extreme cases, substantive law may require a lawyer to disclose information relating to the representation to avoid being deemed to have assisted the client's crime or fraud. If the lawyer can avoid assisting a client's crime or fraud only by disclosing this information, then under paragraph (b) the lawyer is required to do so, unless the disclosure is prohibited by Rule 1.6.

RULE 4.2: COMMUNICATION WITH PERSON REPRESENTED BY COUNSEL

In representing a client, a lawyer shall not communicate about the subject of the representation with a person the lawyer knows to be represented by another lawyer in the matter, unless the lawyer has the consent of the other lawyer or is authorized to do so by law or a court order.

Comment

[1]   This Rule contributes to the proper functioning of the legal system by protecting a person who has chosen to be represented by a lawyer in a matter against possible overreaching by other lawyers who are participating in the matter, interference by those lawyers with the client-lawyer relationship and the uncounselled disclosure of information relating to the representation.

[2]   This Rule applies to communications with any person who is represented by counsel concerning the matter to which the communication relates.

[3]   The Rule applies even though the represented person initiates or consents to the communication. A lawyer must immediately terminate communication with a person if, after commencing communication, the lawyer learns that the person is one with whom communication is not permitted by this Rule.

[4]   This Rule does not prohibit communication with a represented person, or an employee or agent of such a person, concerning matters outside the representation. For example, the existence of a controversy between a government agency and a private party, or between two organizations, does not prohibit a lawyer for either from communicating with nonlawyer representatives of the other regarding a separate matter. Nor does this Rule preclude communication with a represented person who is seeking advice from a lawyer who is not otherwise representing a client in the matter. A lawyer may not make a communication prohibited by this Rule through the acts of another. See Rule 8.4(a). Parties to a matter may communicate directly with each other, and a lawyer is not prohibited from advising a client concerning a communication that the client is legally entitled to make. Also, a lawyer having independent justification or legal authorization for communicating with a represented person is permitted to do so.

[5]   Communications authorized by law may include communications by a lawyer on behalf of a client who is exercising a constitutional or other legal right to communicate with the government. Communications authorized by law may also include investigative activities of lawyers representing governmental entities, directly or through investigative agents, prior to the commencement of criminal or civil enforcement proceedings. When communicating with the accused in a criminal matter, a government lawyer must comply with this Rule in addition to honoring the constitutional rights of the accused. The fact that a communication does not violate a state or federal constitutional right is insufficient to establish that the communication is permissible under this Rule.

[6]   A lawyer who is uncertain whether a communication with a represented person is permissible may seek a court order. A lawyer may also seek a court order in exceptional circumstances to authorize a communication that would otherwise be prohibited by this Rule, for example, where communication with a person represented by counsel is necessary to avoid reasonably certain injury.

[7]   In the case of a represented organization, this Rule prohibits communications with a constituent of the organization who supervises, directs or regularly consults with the organization's lawyer concerning the matter or has authority to obligate the organization with respect to the matter or whose act or omission in connection with the matter may be imputed to the organization for purposes of civil or criminal liability. Consent of the organization's lawyer is not required for communication with a former constituent. If a constituent of the organization is represented in the matter by his or her own counsel, the consent by that counsel to a communication will be sufficient for purposes of this Rule. Compare Rule 3.4(f). In communicating with a current or former constituent of an organization, a lawyer must not use methods of obtaining evidence that violate the legal rights of the organization. See Rule 4.4.

[8]   The prohibition on communications with a represented person only applies in circumstances where the lawyer knows that the person is in fact represented in the matter to be discussed. This means that the lawyer has actual knowledge of the fact of the representation; but such actual knowledge may be inferred from the circumstances. See Rule 1.0(f). Thus, the lawyer cannot evade the requirement of obtaining the consent of counsel by closing eyes to the obvious.

[9]   In the event the person with whom the lawyer communicates is not known to be represented by counsel in the matter, the lawyer's communications are subject to Rule 4.3.

RULE 4.4: RESPECT FOR RIGHTS OF THIRD PERSONS

(a)   In representing a client, a lawyer shall not use means that have no substantial purpose other than to embarrass, delay, or burden a third person, or use methods of obtaining evidence that violate the legal rights of such a person.

(b)   A lawyer who receives a document relating to the representation of the lawyer's client and knows or reasonably should know that the document was inadvertently sent shall promptly notify the sender.

Comment

[1]   Responsibility to a client requires a lawyer to subordinate the interests of others to those of the client, but that responsibility does not imply that a lawyer may disregard the rights of third persons. It is impractical to catalogue all such rights, but they include legal restrictions on methods of obtaining evidence from third persons and unwarranted intrusions into privileged relationships, such as the client-lawyer relationship.

[2]   Paragraph (b) recognizes that lawyers sometimes receive documents that were mistakenly sent or produced by opposing parties or their lawyers. If a lawyer knows or reasonably should know that such a document was sent inadvertently, then this Rule requires the lawyer to promptly notify the sender in order to permit that person to

take protective measures. Whether the lawyer is required to take additional steps, such as returning the original document, is a matter of law beyond the scope of these Rules, as is the question of whether the privileged status of a document has been waived. Similarly, this Rule does not address the legal duties of a lawyer who receives a document that the lawyer knows or reasonably should know may have been wrongfully obtained by the sending person. For purposes of this Rule, "document" includes e-mail or other electronic modes of transmission subject to being read or put into readable form.

[3]   Some lawyers may choose to return a document unread, for example, when the lawyer learns before receiving the document that it was inadvertently sent to the wrong address. Where a lawyer is not required by applicable law to do so, the decision to voluntarily return such a document is a matter of professional judgment ordinarily reserved to the lawyer. See Rules 1.2 and 1.4.

RULE 8.3: REPORTING PROFESSIONAL MISCONDUCT

(a)   A lawyer who knows that another lawyer has committed a violation of the Rules of Professional Conduct that raises a substantial question as to that lawyer's honesty, trustworthiness or fitness as a lawyer in other respects, shall inform the appropriate professional authority.

(b)   A lawyer who knows that a judge has committed a violation of applicable rules of judicial conduct that raises a substantial question as to the judge's fitness for office shall inform the appropriate authority.

(c)   This Rule does not require disclosure of information otherwise protected by Rule 1.6 or information gained by a lawyer or judge while participating in an approved lawyers assistance program.

Comment

[1]   Self-regulation of the legal profession requires that members of the profession initiate disciplinary investigation when they know of a violation of the Rules of Professional Conduct. Lawyers have a similar obligation with respect to judicial misconduct. An apparently isolated violation may indicate a pattern of misconduct that only a disciplinary investigation can uncover. Reporting a violation is especially important where the victim is unlikely to discover the offense.

[2]   A report about misconduct is not required where it would involve violation of Rule 1.6. However, a lawyer should encourage a client to consent to disclosure where prosecution would not substantially prejudice the client's interests.

[3]   If a lawyer were obliged to report every violation of the Rules, the failure to report any violation would itself be a professional offense. Such a requirement existed in many jurisdictions but proved to be unenforceable. This Rule limits the reporting obligation to those offenses that a self-regulating profession must vigorously endeavor to prevent. A measure of judgment is, therefore, required in complying with the

provisions of this Rule. The term "substantial" refers to the seriousness of the possible offense and not the quantum of evidence of which the lawyer is aware. A report should be made to the bar disciplinary agency unless some other agency, such as a peer review agency, is more appropriate in the circumstances. Similar considerations apply to the reporting of judicial misconduct.

[4] The duty to report professional misconduct does not apply to a lawyer retained to represent a lawyer whose professional conduct is in question. Such a situation is governed by the Rules applicable to the client-lawyer relationship.

[5] Information about a lawyer's or judge's misconduct or fitness may be received by a lawyer in the course of that lawyer's participation in an approved lawyers or judges assistance program. In that circumstance, providing for an exception to the reporting requirements of paragraphs (a) and (b) of this Rule encourages lawyers and judges to seek treatment through such a program. Conversely, without such an exception, lawyers and judges may hesitate to seek assistance from these programs, which may then result in additional harm to their professional careers and additional injury to the welfare of clients and the public. These Rules do not otherwise address the confidentiality of information received by a lawyer or judge participating in an approved lawyers assistance program; such an obligation, however, may be imposed by the rules of the program or other law.

RULE 8.4: MISCONDUCT

It is professional misconduct for a lawyer to:

(a)   violate or attempt to violate the Rules of Professional Conduct, knowingly assist or induce another to do so, or do so through the acts of another;

(b)   commit a criminal act that reflects adversely on the lawyer's honesty, trustworthiness or fitness as a lawyer in other respects;

(c)   engage in conduct involving dishonesty, fraud, deceit or misrepresentation;

(d)   engage in conduct that is prejudicial to the administration of justice;

(e)   state or imply an ability to influence improperly a government agency or official or to achieve results by means that violate the Rules of Professional Conduct or other law; or

(f)   knowingly assist a judge or judicial officer in conduct that is a violation of applicable rules of judicial conduct or other law.

Comment

[1]   Lawyers are subject to discipline when they violate or attempt to violate the Rules of Professional Conduct, knowingly assist or induce another to do so or do so through the acts of another, as when they request or instruct an agent to do so on the lawyer's behalf. Paragraph (a), however, does not prohibit a lawyer from advising a client concerning action the client is legally entitled to take.

[2]   Many kinds of illegal conduct reflect adversely on fitness to practice law, such as offenses involving fraud and the offense of willful failure to file an income tax return. However, some kinds of offenses carry no such implication. Traditionally, the distinction was drawn in terms of offenses involving "moral turpitude." That concept can be construed to include offenses concerning some matters of personal morality, such as adultery and comparable offenses, that have no specific connection to fitness for the practice of law. Although a lawyer is personally answerable to the entire criminal law, a lawyer should be professionally answerable only for offenses that indicate lack of those characteristics relevant to law practice. Offenses involving violence, dishonesty, breach of trust, or serious interference with the administration of justice are in that category. A pattern of repeated offenses, even ones of minor significance when considered separately, can indicate indifference to legal obligation.

[3]   A lawyer who, in the course of representing a client, knowingly manifests by words or conduct, bias or prejudice based upon race, sex, religion, national origin, disability, age, sexual orientation or socioeconomic status, violates paragraph (d) when such actions are prejudicial to the administration of justice. Legitimate advocacy respecting the foregoing factors does not violate paragraph (d). A trial judge's finding that peremptory challenges were exercised on a discriminatory basis does not alone establish a violation of this rule.

[4]   A lawyer may refuse to comply with an obligation imposed by law upon a good faith belief that no valid obligation exists. The provisions of Rule 1.2(d) concerning a good faith challenge to the validity, scope, meaning or application of the law apply to challenges of legal regulation of the practice of law.

[5]   Lawyers holding public office assume legal responsibilities going beyond those of other citizens. A lawyer's abuse of public office can suggest an inability to fulfill the professional role of lawyers. The same is true of abuse of positions of private trust such as trustee, executor, administrator, guardian, agent and officer, director or manager of a corporation or other organization.

Further Reading on Ethics in Dispute Resolution

Albin, C. *The Role of Fairness in Negotiation*, 9 NEG. J. 223 (1993).

Alfini, J. J. *E2K Leaves Mediation in an Ethics 'Black Hole'*, 7 DISP. RES. MAG. 3 (Spring 2001).

Alfini, J. J. *Settlement Ethics and Lawyering in ADR Proceedings: A Proposal to Revise 4.1*, 19 N. ILL. U. L. REV. 255 (1999).

APPLBAUM, A. I. ETHICS FOR ADVERSARIES: THE MORALITY OF ROLES IN PUBLIC AND PROFESSIONAL LIFE (1999).

Barton, B. H. *Why Do We Regulate Lawyers?: An Economic Analysis of the Justification for Entry and Conduct Regulation,* 33 ARIZ.ST L. J. 429 (Summer 2001).

Bingham, L. B. *Employment Arbitration, The Repeat Player Effect,* EMPLOYEE RIGHTS AND EMPLOY. POLICY J. 1(1) 189 (1997).

Blitman, B. A. *Mediator Ethics: Florida's Ethics Advisory Committee Breaks New Ground,* 7 DISP. RES. MAG. 10 (Spring 2001).

Breger, M. J. *Should An Attorney Be Required to Advise A Client of ADR Options?* 13 GEO. J. LEGAL ETHICS 427 (2000).

Brown, J. G., and Ayres, I. *Economic Rationales for Mediation*, 80 VA. L. REV.323 (1994).

Burns, R. P. *Some Ethical Issues Surrounding Mediation*, 70 FORDHAM L. REV. 691 (2001).

Burr, A. M. *Ethics in Negotiation: Does Getting to Yes Require Candor*, 56 DISP. RES. J. 8 (May-July, 2001).

Bush, R. A. B. *The Dilemmas of Mediation Practice: A Study of Ethical Dilemmas and Policy Implications*, 1994 J. DISP. RESOL.1 (1994).

CARBONNEAU, T. E. ALTERNATIVE DISPUTE RESOLUTION: MELTING LANCES AND DISMOUNTING THE STEEDS (1989).

Cohen, J. *Ethical Quandary: Advising the Client Who Wants to Apologize,* 5 DISP. RES. MAG. 19 (Spring 1999).

Condlin, R. *Cases On Both Sides: Patterns of Argument in Legal Dispute Resolution Bargaining,* 44 MD. L. REV. 65 (1985).

Consumers International, *Disputes in Cyberspace 2001:Update of ODR for Consumers in Cross-Border Disputes* (November 2001).

Craver, C. Negotiation Ethics: *How To Be Deceptive Without Being Dishonest/How To Be Assertive Without Being Offensive*, 38 S. TEX. L. REV. 713 (1997).

Daicoff, S. *Asking Leopards to Change Their Spots: Should Lawyers Change? A Critique of Solutions to Problems with Professionalism by Reference to Empirically-Derived Attorney Personality Attributes*, 11 GEO. J. LEGAL ETHICS 547 (1998).

Daly, M. C. *Choosing Wise Men Wisely: The Risks and Rewards of Purchasing Legal Services from Lawyers in a Multidisciplinary Practice,* 13 GEO. J. LEGAL ETHICS 217 (2000).

Dzienkowski, J. S., and Peroni, R. J. *Multidisciplinary Practice and the American Legal Profession: A Market Approach to Regulating the Delivery of Legal Services in the Twenty-First Century,* 69 FORDHAM L. REV.83 (October 2000).

Ensuring Competence and Quality in Dispute Resolution Practice: Report # 2 of the SPIDR Commission on Qualifications published by the Society of Professionals in Dispute Resolution (1995).

Feerick, J. D. *Standards of Conduct for Mediators*, 79 JUDICATURE 314 (1996).

Feldman, H. *Codes and Virtues: Can Good Lawyers be Good Ethical Deliberators?* 69 S. CAL L. REV. 885 (1996).

Fisher, R. *A Code of Negotiation Practices for Lawyers*, 1 NEGOTIATION J. 2 (1985).

FREUND, J. SMART NEGOTIATING: HOW TO MAKE GOOD DEALS IN THE REAL WORLD (1992).

Friedman, G. and Himmelstein, J. *Deal Killer or Deal Saver: The Consulting Lawyer's Dilemma,* 4 DISP. RES. MAG. 7 (Winter 1997).

FULLER, L. L. THE MORALITY OF LAW 193 (Rev. Ed. 1969).

Furlan, F. et al., *Ethical Guidelines for Attorney-Mediators: Are Attorneys Bound By Ethical Codes for Lawyers When Acting as Mediators?* 14 J. AM. ACAD. MATRIM. LAW 267 (1997).

Galanter, M. *Why The Haves Come Out Ahead: Speculations on the Limits of Legal Change,* 9 L. & SOCY REV. 95 (1974).

Garth, B. G. *Rethinking the Legal Profession's Approach to Collective Self-Improvement: Competence and the Consumer Perspective,* 1983 WIS. L. REV. 639 (May 1983/June 1983).

Garth, B. G. *Is Mediation the Practice of Law: The Wrong Question*, 33 NIDR FORUM 34 (June 1997).

Gerencser, A. E. *Alternative Dispute Resolution Has Morphed into Mediation: Standards of Conduct Must Be Changed,* 50 FLA. L. REV. 843 (1998).

Gillers, S. REGULATION OF LAWYERS: PROBLEMS OF LAW AND ETHICS, 5th ed., Aspen Law & Business (New York, 1998).

Gilson, R. J., and Mnookin, R. H. *Disputing Through Agents: Cooperation and Conflict Between Lawyers in Litigation,* 94 COLUM. L. REV. 509 (1994).

Golann, D. *Variations in Mediation: How - and Why - Legal Mediators Change Styles in the Course of a Case,* 2000 J. DISP. RESOL. 41.

Guernsey, T. F. *Truthfulness in Negotiation,* 17 U. RICH. L. REV. 99 (1982).

Gunning, I. R. *Diversity Issues in Mediation: Controlling Negative Cultural Myths,* 1995 J. DISP. RESOL. 55 (1995).

HAZARD, G. C. JR. ET AL., THE LAW AND ETHICS OF LAWYERING (3d ed. 1999).

Hazard, G. C. Jr. *The Lawyer' Obligation to be Trustworthy When Dealing With Opposing Parties,* 33 S.C. L. REV. 181 (1981).

Henikoff , J., and Moffitt , M. *Remodeling the Model Standards of Conduct for Mediators,* 2 HARV. NEGOT. L. REV. 87 (1997).

Hobbs, S. H. *Facilitative Ethics in Divorce Mediation: A Law and Process Approach,* 22 U. RICH. L. REV. 325 (1988).

Hoffman, D. A., and Affolder, N. A. *Mediation and UPL: Do Mediators have a Well-founded Fear of Prosecution?* 6 DISP. RES. MAG. 20 (Winter 2000).

Kaye, J. S. Lawyering for a New Age, 67 FORDHAM L. REV. 1 (1998).

Komoroske, F. *Should You Keep Settlements Secret?* TRIAL MAG. 55 (June 1999).

Kovach, K. K. *Good Faith in Mediation: Requested, Recommended or Required: A New Ethic,* 38 S. TEX. L. REV. 575 (1997).

Kovach, K. K. *Lawyer Ethics in Mediation: Time for a Requirement of Good Faith,* 4 DISP. RES. MAG. 9 (Winter 1997).

Kovach, K. K. *New Wine Requires New Wineskins: Transforming Lawyer Ethics for Effective Representation in A Non-adversarial Approach to Problem Solving: Mediation* 28 FORDHAM URB. L.J. 935 (2001).

Kovach, K. K., and Love, L. P. *'Evaluative' Mediation is an Oxymoron*, 14 ALTERNATIVES TO HIGH COST LITIG. 31 (1996).

Kronman, A. *Mistake, Disclosure, Information and the Law of Contracts*, 7 J. LEGAL STUDIES 1 (1978).

Kubiak, R. *Is ADR Practice by Non-Attorneys Authorized?* N. J. LAW J. (January 30, 1995).

Laflin, M. E. *Preserving the Integrity of Mediation through the Adoption of Ethical Rules for Lawyer Mediators,* 14 NOTRE DAME J. L. ETHICS AND PUB. POL'Y 479 (2000).

Lande, J. *How Will Lawyering and Mediation Practices Transform Each Other?* 24 FLA. ST. U. L. REV. 839 (1997).

Lansman, S. A. *A Brief Survey of the Development of the Adversary System* 44 OHIO ST. L. J. 713 (1983).

Lax, D., and Sebenius, J. *Three Ethical Issues in Negotiation,* 2 NEGOTIATION. J. 363 (1986).

Lempert, L. *In Settlement Talks, Does Telling the Truth Have Its Limits?,* 2 INSIDE LITIGATION 1 (1988) reprinted in LEGAL ETHICS 421-427 (Deborah L. Rhode & David Luban, eds., 2d ed. 1992).

Lerman, L. G. *Mediation of Wife Abuse Cases: The Adverse Impact of Informal Dispute Resolution on Women,* 7 HARV. WOMEN'S L. J. 57 (1984).

Levin , M. S. *The Propriety of Evaluative Mediation: Concerns About the Nature and Quality of an Evaluative Opinion,* 16 OHIO ST. J. DISP. RESOL. 267 (2001).

Loder, R. E. *Moral Truthseeking and the Virtuous Negotiator,* 8 GEO. J. LEGAL ETHICS 45 (1994).

Love, L. P. *Introduction, Symposium, Teaching a New Paradigm; Must Knights Shed Their Swords and Armor to Enter Certain ADR Arenas?* 1 CARDOZO ONLINE J. CONFLICT RESOL. (1999) at http://cardozo.yu.edu/cojcr/new-site/issues/vol1/vol1.htm.

Lowenthal, G. T. *The Bar's Failure to Require Truthful Bargaining By Lawyers,* 2 GEO. J. LEGAL ETHICS 411 (1988).

Luban, D. *Settlements and the Erosion of the Public Realm,* 83 GEO. L. J. 2619 (1995).

Shaw, M. *Mediator Qualifications: Report of a Symposium on Critical Issues in Alternative Dispute Resolution*, 12 SETON HALL LEGIS. J. 125 (1998).

McEwen, C. et al., *Bring in the Lawyers: Challenging the Dominant Approaches to Ensuring Fairness in Divorce Mediation*, 79 MINN. L. REV. 1317 (1995).

Menkel-Meadow, C. *Can They Do That? Legal Ethics in Popular Culture: Of Character and Acts*, 48 UCLA L. REV. 1305 (2001).

Menkel-Meadow, C. *Do the "Haves" Come Out Ahead in Alternative Judicial Systems?: Repeat Players in ADR*, 15 OHIO ST. J. DISP. RES. 19 (1999).

Menkel-Meadow, C. *Ethics and Professionalism in Non-Adversarial Lawyering*, 27 FLA. ST. U. L. REV. 153 (Fall 1999).

Menkel-Meadow, C. *Ethics and the Settlement of Mass Torts: When the Rules Meet the Road*, 80 CORNELL L. REV. 1159 (1995).

Menkel-Meadow, C. *Ethics in ADR Representation: A Road Map of Critical Issues*, 4 DISP. RES. MAG. 3 (Winter 1997).

Menkel-Meadow, C. *Ethics in ADR: The Many "Cs" of Professional Responsibility and Dispute Resolution*, 28 FORDHAM URB. L. J. 979 (2001).

Menkel-Meadow, C. *Ethics in Alternative Dispute Resolution: New Issues, No Answers from the Adversary Conception of Lawyers' Responsibilities*, 38 S. TEX. L. REV. 407 (1997)

Menkel-Meadow, C. *Is Mediation the Practice of Law?* 14 ALTERNATIVES TO HIGH COST LITIG. 57 (1996).

Menkel-Meadow, C. *Lying to Clients for Economic Gain or Paternalistic Judgment: A Proposal for a Golden Rule of Candor*, 138 U. PENN. L. REV. 761 (1990).

Menkel-Meadow, C. *Professional Responsibility for Third-Party Neutrals*, in DISP. RES. ALTERNATIVES (Practicing Law Institute, 1994).

Menkel-Meadow, C. *Public Access to Private Settlements: Conflicting Legal Policies*, 11 (6) ALTERNATIVES TO HIGH COST OF LITIG. 85 (June 1993).

Menkel-Meadow, C. *Pursuing Settlement in an Adversary Culture: A Tale of Innovation Co-opted or "The Law of ADR,"* 19 FLA. ST. U. L. REV. 1 (1991).

Menkel-Meadow, C. *The Art and Science of Problem Solving Negotiation*, TRIAL, 48 (June 1999).

Menkel-Meadow, C. *The Limits of Adversarial Ethics* in ETHICS IN PRACTICE (Deborah L. Rhode, ed. 2000).

Menkel-Meadow, C. *The Silences of the Restatement of the Law Governing Lawyers: Lawyering as Only Adversary Practice,* 10 GEO. J. LEGAL ETHICS 631 (1997).

Menkel-Meadow, C. *The Trouble with the Adversary System in a Post-Modern, Multi-Cultural World,* 38 WM. & MARY L. REV. 5 (1996).

Menkel-Meadow, C. *Toward Another View of Legal Negotiation: The Structure of Problem Solving,* 31 U.C.L.A. L. REV. 754 (1984).

Menkel-Meadow, C. *What's Gender Got to Do With It? The Morality and Politics of an Ethic of Care,* 22 NYU J. OF LAW AND SOCIAL CHANGE 265 (1996).

Menkel-Meadow, C. *Whose Dispute Is It Anyway? A Philosophical and Democratic Defense of Settlement (In Some Cases),* 83 GEO. L. J. 2663 (1995).

Meyerson, B. E. *Telling the Truth in Mediation: Mediator Owed a Duty of Candor,* 4 DISP. RES. MAG. 17 (Winter, 1997).

Meyerson, B. E. *Lawyers Who Mediate Are Not Practicing Law,* 14 ALTERNATIVES TO HIGH COST LITIG. 74 (1996).

MNOOKIN, R. H. ET AL., BEYOND WINNING: NEGOTIATING TO CREATE VALUE IN DEALS AND DISPUTES (2000).

Moberly, R. B. *Ethical Standards for Court-Appointed Mediators and Florida's Mandatory Mediation Experiment,* 21 FLA. ST. U. L. REV. 701 (1994).

Moberly, R. B. *Mediator Gag Rules: Is it Ethical for Mediators to Evaluate or Advise?* 38 S. TEX. L. REV. 669 (1997).

Moffitt, M. L. *Will this Case Settle? An Exploration of Mediators' Predictions,* 16 OHIO ST. J. ON DISP. RESOL. 39 (2000).

Morrison, A. *Defining the Unauthorized Practice of Law: Some New Ways of Looking at an Old Question,* 4 NOVA L. J. 363 (1980).

Nolan-Haley, J. *Court Mediation and the Search for Justice and Law,* 74 WASH. U. QUARTERLY 47 (1996).

Nolan-Haley, J. M. *Informed Consent in Mediation: A Guiding Principle for Truly Educated Decision Making,* 74 NOTRE DAME L. REV. 775 (1999).

Nolan-Haley, J. M. *Lawyers, Clients, and Mediation,* 73 NOTRE DAME L. REV 1369 (1998).

Norton, E. H. *Bargaining and the Ethic of Process,* 64 N.Y.U. L. REV. 493 (1989).

O'Brien, R. A. *Amending the Model Rules to Include the Role of Lawyer as Mediator: The Latest in the Debate,* 12 GEO. J. LEGAL ETHICS 107 (1998).

Palefsky, C. *Only a Start: Proposed ADR Provider Ethics Principles Don't Go Far Enough,* 7 DISP. RES. MAG. 3 (Spring 2001).

Pepper, S. *The Lawyer's Amoral Ethical Role: A Defense, A Problem and Some Possibilities,* 1986 AM. B. FOUND. RES. J. 613.

Pershbacher, R. R. *Regulating Lawyers' Negotiations,* 27 ARIZ. L. REV. 75 (1985).

Press, S. *Standards...and Results: Florida Provides Forum for Grievances Against Mediators,* 7 DISP. RES. MAG. 8 (Spring 2001).

Raiffa, H. *Post-Settlement Settlements,* 1 NEG. J. (1985).

RHODE, D. L. IN THE INTEREST OF JUSTICE: REFORMING THE LEGAL PROFESSION (2001).

Riskin, L. L. *Mediation and Lawyers,* 43 OHIO ST. L. J. 29 (1982).

Riskin, L. L. *Understanding Mediators' Orientations, Strategies, and Techniques: A Grid for the Perplexed,* 1 HARV. NEGOT. L. REV. 7 (1996).

Robert A. B. *The Dilemmas of Mediation Practice: A Study of Ethical Dilemmas and Policy Implications,* 1994 J. DISP. RESOL. 1 (1994).

ROBERT, A. B., AND FOLGER, J. P. THE PROMISE OF MEDIATION: RESPONDING TO CONFLICT THROUGH EMPOWERMENT AND RECOGNITION (1994).

Rose, C. M. R. *Trust in the Mirror of Betrayal,* 75 B.U. L. REV. 531 (1995).

Rubin, A. B. *A Causerie on Lawyers? Ethics in Negotiation,* 35 LA. L. REV. 577 (1975).

Rubin, M. H. *The Ethics of Negotiation: Are There Any?* 56 LA. L. REV. 447 (1995).

Rutherford, M. C. *Lawyers and Divorce Mediation: Designing the Role of "Outside Counsel,"* MEDIATION Q., June 1986.

Sabatino, J. M. *ADR as "Litigation Lite": Procedural and Evidentiary Norms Embedded within Alternative Dispute Resolution,* 47 EMORY L.J. 1289 (1998).

Schepard , A. *Preface to the Draft Model Standards,* 38 FAMILY AND CONCILATION COURT REVIEW 106 (2000).

SCHEPPELE, K. LEGAL SECRETS: EQUALITY AND EFFICIENCY IN THE COMMON LAW (1988).

Schwartz, M. L. *The Accountability and Professionalism of Lawyers,* 66 CAL. L. REV. 391 (1978).

Selection, Training and Qualification of Neutrals: A Working Paper, National Symposium on Court-Connected Dispute Resolution Research: A Report on Current Research Findings - Implications for Courts and Future Research Needs, State Justice Institute (1994).

Shaw M. L. and Plapinger, E. *Ethical Guidelines: ADR Provider Organizations Should Increase Transparency, Disclosure,* 7 DISP. RES. MAG. 14 (Spring 2001).

SHELL, G. R. BARGAINING FOR ADVANTAGE: NEGOTIATION STRATEGIES FOR REASONABLE PEOPLE (1999).

Shell, G. R. *When Is It Legal to Lie in Negotiations?* SLOAN MANANGMENT REVIEW 93 (Spring 1991).

Sherman, E. *Court-Mandated Alternative Dispute Resolution: What Form of Participation Should be Required?* 46 SMU L. REV. 2079 (1993).

Sherman, E. *'Good Faith' Participation in Mediation: Aspirational, not Mandatory,* 4 DISP. RES. MAG. 14 (Winter 1997).

Simon, W. H. *The Kaye Scholer Affair: The Lawyer's Duty of Candor and the Bar's Temptations of Evasion and Apology,* 23 LAW & SOC. INQUIRY 243 (1998).

Simon, W. H. *Homo Psychologicus: Notes on a New Legal Formalism,* 32 STAN. L. REV. 487 (1980).

Spiedel, R. *Has Pre-Dispute (Mandatory) Arbitration Outlived Its Welcome?,* 40 ARIZ. L. REV. 1069 (1998).

Stallworth, L. *Finding a Place for Non-Lawyer Representation in Mediation,* 4 DISP. RES. MAG. 19 (Winter 1997).

Stark , J. H. *The Ethics of Mediation Evaluation: Some Troublesome Questions and Tentative Proposals, from an Evaluative Lawyer Mediator,* 38 S. TEX. L. REV. 769 (1997).

Stempel, J. W. *Beyond Formalism and False Dichotomies: The Need for Institutionalizing a Flexible Concept of the Mediator's Role,* 24 FLA. ST. U. L. REV. 949 (1997).

Sternlight, J. R. *Lawyers' Representation of Clients in Mediation: Using Economics and Psychology to Structure Advocacy in a Nonadversarial Setting,* 14 OHIO ST. J. ON DISP. RESOL. 269 (1999).

Stipanowich, T. J. *Resolving Consumer Disputes, Due Process Protocol Protects Consumer Rights,* 53 DISP. RESOL. J 8 (1999).

Strudler, A. *On the Ethics of Deception in Negotiation,* 5 BUS. ETHICS Q. 805 (1995).

Symposium on Standards of Practice, *Model Standards of Practice for Family and Divorce Mediation,* 39 FAM. CT. REV. 121 (2001).

The Guidelines for Voluntary Mediation Programs Instituted by Agencies Charged with Enforcing Workplace Rights, ADR in the Workplace Initiative, Society of Professionals in Dispute Resolution (1998).

Walter, W. S. Jr. *Deceptive Negotiating and High Toned Morality,* 39 VAND. L. REV. 1387 (1986).

Wangerin, P. T. *The Political and Economic Roots of the ""Adversary System of Justice"" and "Alternative Dispute Resolution,"* 9 OHIO ST. J. DISP RESOL. 203 (1994).

Wasserstrom, R. *Roles and Morality* in THE GOOD LAWYER: LAWYERS' ROLES AND LAWYERS' ETHICS (David Luban, ed. 1983).

Watson, L. *Drafting Standards: Points of Reference for Triangulating Ethical Positions,* 7 DISP. RES. MAG. 13 (Spring 2001).

Webne-Behrman, H. M. *The Emergence of Ethical Codes and Standards of Practice in Mediation: The Current State of Affairs,* 1998 WIS. L. REV. 1289.

Welsh, N. A. *Making Deals in Court-Connected Mediation: What's Justice Got to Do With It?* 79 WASH. U. L.Q. 787 (2001).

Welsh, N. A. *The Thinning Vision of Self-Determination in Court-Connected Mediation: The Inevitable Price of Institutionalization?* 6 HARV. NEGOT. L. REV. 1 (2001).

Weston, M. A. *Checks on Participant Conduct in Compulsory ADR; Reconciling the Tension in the Need for Good-Faith Participation, Autonomy and Confidentiality,* 76 IND. L.J. 591 (2001).

Wetlaufer, G. B. *The Ethics of Lying in Negotiations,* 76 IOWA L. REV. 1219 (1990).

Yarn D. and Thorpe W. *Ethics 2000: The ABA Proposes New Ethics Rules for Lawyer-Neutrals and Attorneys in ADR,* 7 DISP. RES. MAG. 3 (Spring 2001).

Young, M. D. *The Right Balance,* 7 DISP. RES. MAG. 18 (Spring 2001).

Index

A

Absolute duty, 163
Acceptance of gifts, 180
Access, 89, 151, 157, 161, 171, 172, 173, 211, 243, 244
ADA Mediation Guidelines, 172, 173, 243
Administration of justice, 21
Administrative Dispute Resolution Act, 226
ADR in the Workplace Initiative, 158
Adversary ethics, 129
Adversary system, 57, 58, 61, 129, 151
Affirmative obligation to tell the truth, 148
Agreement to mediate, 21, 25, 27, 35, 81
Agreement to arbitrate, 182, 184, 189, 196, 200
Alfini, James J., 3, 65
American Arbitration Association Commercial Arbitration Rules, 185, 193, 195
American Bar Association Section of Administrative Law and Regulatory Practice, 216
American Bar Association House of Delegates, 136
American Bar Association Section of Dispute Resolution, 66, 94, 180, 216
American Law Institute, 141
Apprenticeship, 164, 166, 169
Arbitration,
   Commercial, 181, 203
   Mandatory, 159, 199
   Non-binding, 32
Arbitrator,
   Competence, 196
   Disqualification, 189
   Independent judgment, 198

Arb-med, 201
Aspirational, 67, 111, 125, 171, 245
Association for Conflict Resolution, 1, 34, 35, 156
Association of Family and Conciliation Courts, 66, 255
Attorney, trial counsel, 9, 10, 11, 16
Attorney-client privilege, 47
Aylward, Paula, 4, 213

B

Bargaining for Advantage Negotiation Strategies for Reasonable People, 141
Bernard, Phyllis, 1, 4, 89
Bok, Sissela, 127, 147
Brown, Gina Viola, 5, 237
Business to business transactions (B2B), 239, 242, 246
Business to consumer transactions (B2C), 239, 242, 246, 249

C

California Code of Civil Procedure, 186, 189, 194, 254
   § 1281.6, 194
   § 1281.9 (a), 186
   § 170.1, 186, 194
California Ethics Standards for Neutral Arbitrators in Contractual Arbitrations, 182, 183, 186, 190, 191, 194, 196, 197, 200, 209, 210
California Judicial Council, 180
Capacity to mediate, 65, 71-72, 85, 255
Case evaluation, 32
Center for Dispute Settlement, 157
Certification, *See* Credentialing
Chernick, Richard, 4, 179
Chief Parliamentary Ombudsman for Sweden, 213
Clinton, President Bill, 142

M

Mandated Participation and Settlement Coercion Dispute Resolution as it Relates to the Courts, 156
Materiality, 142
Med-arb, 201, 202
Mediated agreements, 79, 80
Mediation
  Advocacy, *See* Representation in mediation
  Confidentiality of mediation communications, 73, 74
  Nonparticipating parties, 78
Mediator
  Competence, 31, 70, 167
  Conflicts of interest, 68
  Impartiality, 68, 246
Menkel-Meadow, Carrie, 4, 119
Mentorship, 164, 166
Milton, John, 214
Misrepresentation, 120, 122, 132, 134, 135, 137, 138, 139, 140, 141, 144, 145, 191, 194
Mitchell, George, 253
Model Ombudsman Statute, 213
Model Rules of Professional Conduct, 1, 9, 20, 42, 53, 92, 93, 94, 127, 129, 131, 135, 137, 138, 181
Model Rule 1.2, 10, 12, 51, 54, 135, 136, 137
Model Rule 1.4, 10, 12, 13, 137
Model Rule 1.6, 46, 131
Model Rule 2.1, 10, 45, 46
Model Rule 3.2, 10
Model Rule 3.3, 49, 50, 129, 135, 142
Model Rule 4.1, 48, 50, 61, 128, 129, 131, 134, 135, 136, 142
Model Rule 4.2, 24, 47, 48, 61, 127
Model Rule 4.3, 61, 127
Model Rule 4.4, 51, 52, 138
Model Rule 5.6, 138
Model Rule 8.3, 138
Model Rule 8.4, 49, 61, 138

Moral-desert, 146

N

National Association of Securities Dealers' Code of Arbitration Procedure, 185
National Center for State Courts, 157
National Commissioners on Uniform State Laws, 141
National Council of Dispute Resolution Organizations, 66, 255
New Jersey Advisory Committee on Professional Ethics, 102
Norvell v. Credit Bureau, 98
Nyquist, Dean A., 106

O

Ombuds
  Confidentiality, 225-232
  Impartiality, 222-225
  Notice, 232-235
Ombuds Standards, See Standards for the Establishment and Operation of Ombuds Offices
Online dispute resolution
  Accountability, 251
  Confidentiality, 247-250
  Costs and funding, 245
  Education and training, 243-244
  Impartiality and independence, 246-247
  Qualifications, 250
  Secure environment, 244
  Technology, 242-243
  Transparency, 240-242
Online neutral, 238
Oversight, 113-114, 168

P

Palefsky, Cliff, 159
Peacemaker-lawyer, 23
Personal data, 248
Positional advocacy, 44
Positional negotiation, 32
Precedent, 45, 53

Precedential value, 153
Preparing the client for mediation, 14
Press, Sharon, 4, 155
Process fairness, 65, 75, 76, 77
Professional development, 65, 84
Professional misconduct, 49, 138
Promotion, 208
Property-entitlement, 130, 146
Provider organization, 1, 4, 19, 21,
    24, 30, 35, 114, 155-177, 199,
    208, 210, 237, 238, 239, 240, 241,
    245, 246, 249, 253
Public Justice System, 161

Q

Qualifications, 34-35, 70-71, 82, 83,
    157, 165, 193, 196, 217, 250
Qualifying Dispute Resolution
    Programs, 163

R

R.J. Edwards, Inc. v. Hert, 99
Raiffa, Howard, 149
Representation in mediation, 33, 41,
    44, 96
*Resolution on Mediation and the
    Unauthorized Practice of Law,*
    ABA Section of Dispute
    Resolution, 94-95
Restatements of Torts, 145
Revised Uniform Arbitration Act
    (RUAA), 179, 184, 189, 191, 192,
    203, 207
Roster, 28, 83, 158, 167, 168
Rule of Reason, 170

S

Sanhedrin, 253
Second Commission on
    Qualifications Report, 157
Selection (of the neutral), 21, 27, 30-
    34, 157, 167, 191, 204, 247, 250,
    251
Selection (of the process), 174, 205

Self-determination, 27-28, 65, 72,
    73-74, 76, 77, 89, 242, 254
Sellers, Sandra, 5, 237
Settlement discussions, 8, 9, 11, 12,
    13, 107, 141, 197
Settlement rates, 83, 164, 167, 249
Shabazz v. Scurr, 227
Shell, G. Richard, 141
Significant business relationship, 184
Society of Professionals in Dispute
    Resolution, 1, 27, 34, 156, 157
Spaulding v. Zimmerman, 140
*Standards for the Establishment and
    Operation of Ombuds Offices
    (Ombuds Standards)*, 215, 216,
    217, 218, 219, 221, 222, 223, 226,
    229, 233, 235, 236
Stare v. Tate, 144, 145
State Justice Institute, 157, 166
Suffolk County (New York) Bar
    Ethics Committee, 105

T

Talmudic scriptures, 253
Taylor, Kimberly, 4, 179
Technology, 57, 237, 238, 239, 242,
    243, 251
Training, 35, 70, 71, 76, 104, 112,
    116, 158, 164-166, 168, 169, 172,
    228, 243, 244, 250, 255
Transactional, 42, 120, 127, 130,
    131, 134, 138, 141, 146
Transformative, 31
Trump, Donald, 131
Truth-telling, 120, 123, 127, 142,
    150, 151

U

United States Arbitration Act, 179
Uniform Mediation Act (UMA), 1,
    249

V

Virginia Guidelines on Mediation and the Unauthorized Practice of Law, 80

Virzi v. Grand Trunk Warehouse & Cold Storage, 140

W

Washington, George, 253
Watergate, 127

Watson, Lawrence, 2, 7
Werle, Dr. Michael, 105
"Who blinks first," 8, 13, 23, 24

Y

Yarn, Douglas, 3, 19
Young, Michael D., 174

Z

Zealous Advocacy, 23, 40-41, 45, 125, 126, 127, 134, 255

About the Authors

ALFINI, JAMES J.

Professor Alfini teaches constitutional law, mediation theory and practice, legal ethics, and related courses. He served as dean of the Northern Illinois University College of Law for six years and previously was a member of the law faculty at Florida State University where he also served as Director of Education and Research of the Florida Dispute Resolution Center. While at Florida State, he served on the Florida Supreme Court Arbitration and Mediation Rules Committee. He received his undergraduate degree from Columbia University and his J.D. from Northwestern University. Professor Alfini has served as Chair of the American Bar Association Dispute Resolution Section and the Chair of the Association of American Law Schools Alternative Dispute Resolution Section. He has published numerous books and articles, including the co-edited *ADR Personalities and Practice Tips* published by the American Bar Association. He is also co-author of *Mediation Theory and Practice*, a law school textbook published by Lexis Law Publishing.

AYLWARD, PAULA A.

Paula A. Aylward has been an associate attorney with Levine & Levine since Spring 2000, where she has helped represent ombuds and co-authored a number of papers about ombuds issues. Ms. Aylward has been an attorney for over 11 years, and is licensed to practice law in Michigan, New York, Massachusetts and Texas. She worked as an Assistant District Attorney in Brooklyn and Queens, New York, for over five years. She was a featured speaker on the issue of Vulnerable Child Witnesses at a Queens County Bar Association event, and received the Young Israel of Queens Valley Community Service Award in 1996. Before becoming an attorney, Ms. Aylward worked at the Robert F. Kennedy Memorial Center for Human Rights, on Joseph P. Kennedy, Jr.'s first campaign for Congress, and at Citizens Energy Corporation, a non-profit energy company in Boston.

BERNARD, PHYLLIS

Phyllis Bernard is Professor of Law at the Oklahoma City University School of Law, where her teaching portfolio includes state and federal administrative, alternative dispute resolution, legal ethics, and state and local government law. She is the founding director of the OCU Center of Alternative Dispute Resolution, which has the mission of expanding the use of mediation, arbitration, negotiated settlement and non-litigious forms of dispute resolution through class instruction, scholarly research, and community outreach. Prof. Bernard heads the Early Settlement Central Mediation Program, the court annexed ADR programs for Oklahoma, Canadian and Cleveland counties operating under contract with the Oklahoma Supreme Court. Prof. Bernard holds a J.D. from the University of Pennsylvania Law School, master's in history from Columbia University Graduate School of Arts and Sciences, and a bachelor's in history (cum laude) form Bryn Mawr College. She is a member of the bars of the Court of Appeals for the District of Columbia, the United States District Court for the District of Columbia, the U.S. Court of Appeals for the D.C. Circuit, and the U.S. Supreme Court.

BROWN, GINA VIOLA

Gina Viola Brown is the Coordinator of ADR Research, Policy Analysis, and Law School Programs with the American Bar Association Section of Dispute Resolution in Washington, D.C. Ms. Brown has an undergraduate degree in political and social thought from the University of Virginia, a law degree from the Indiana University-Bloomington School of Law, and a master's of public affairs from the Indiana University School of Public and Environmental Affairs. Ms. Brown worked as an AmeriCorps attorney with the Housing Advocacy and Homelessness Prevention Project in Toledo, Ohio. She also worked as the Administrative Director with the Indiana Conflict Resolution Institute in Bloomington, Indiana.

CHERNICK, RICHARD

Richard Chernick is an arbitrator and mediator. He is Vice President and Managing Director of the JAMS Arbitration Practice. He has arbitrated and mediated commercial employment, entertainment, intellectual property, insurance, and real property cases and acted as a consultant on dispute resolution issues for business and lawyers on a full-time basis since 1994. Richard is a past president of the Los Angeles County Bar Association, the Legal Aid Foundation of Los Angeles, and past Chairman of the Board of Dispute Resolution Services, Inc., the dispute resolution program of the Los Angeles County Bar Association. Richard currently serves as Vice Chair of the Dispute Resolution Section of the American Bar Association. He is a member of the Blue Ribbon Panel of Experts advising the California Judicial Council on the development of neutral arbitrator ethics guidelines. He was the founding Chair of the ADR Committee of the State Bar of California. He served as ABA Advisor to NCCUSL's drafting committee revising the Uniform Arbitration Act. He is the co-author of the leading California practice guide on dispute resolution and of a practitioner's guide to international arbitration and mediation (to be published by Juris this year). He is member of the editorial boards of *World Arbitration & Mediation Report, Dispute Resolution Journal* (AAA) and *Dispute Resolution Magazine* of the ABA Section of Dispute Resolution.

FEERICK, JOHN D.

Dean John D. Feerick has served as Dean of Fordham University School of Law since 1982. He also holds the Leonard Manning Professorship at Fordham Law School. During his tenure as dean at Fordham Law School, he has served in a number of public positions: as a member of the New York State Law Revision Commission; as one of two representatives of New York City to the New York City Office of Collective Bargaining; as chairman of the New York State Commission on Government Integrity from 1987-1990; as a special New York State Attorney General from 1987-90; and as president of the Association of the Bar of the City of New York. He has been a mediator and arbitrator of many disputes, including labor disputes at the Jacob K. Javits Convention Center, the 1994 transit negotiations in New York, the NFL salary cap and recently in the NBA. He served as the first chair of the Ethics Committee of the Dispute Resolution Section of the American Bar Association, and previously chaired a joint committee of the American Bar Association, American Arbitration Association, and Spider that developed a set of ethical standards for mediators of disputes. He serves on a number of not-for-profit and public boards, and is a former chair of the Board of Directors of the American Arbitration Association. Dean Feerick is a graduate of Fordham College '58 and Fordham Law School '61, where he served as editor-in-chief of its Law Review. Dean Feerick is the author of several books, one of which was nominated for a Pulitzer Prize, and scores of articles.

FOX, LAWRENCE J.
Lawrence J. Fox is a partner (since 1976) and former Managing Partner in the Philadelphia firm of Drinker Biddle & Reath LLP, where he specializes in corporate and securities litigation and the counseling of lawyers and law firms. He received his LL.B. *cum laude* from the University of Pennsylvania School of Law in 1968, where he was Managing Editor of the *University of Pennsylvania Law Review*. He is currently an Adjunct Professor at the Penn Law School. He is a Fellow in the American College of Trial Lawyers, a Fellow in the American Bar Foundation and a member of the American Law Institute where he served as an adviser to the Restatement of the Law Governing Lawyers. He also has authored *Legal Tender: A Lawyer's Guide to Professional Dilemmas*, published in 1995 and numerous book chapters relating to internal investigations, sanctions, expert witnesses and other topics. Among Mr. Fox's many professional and community service activities, he is a member of the ABA Commission on the Evaluation of the Rules of Professional Conduct (Ethics 2000), Chair of the ABA Post-Conviction Death Penalty Representation Project (1996-present), Past Chair of the ABA Litigation Section and Past Chair of the ABA Standing Committee on Ethics and Professional Responsibility. He was sent by the United States State Department to Argentina (1997) and China (2002) as a Specialist and Speaker on the Role and Rights of Lawyers. He has made numerous television appearances on *Nightline*, *Cross-Fire*, the *Today Show*, *Talk Back Live*, *Burden of Proof*, *CNN* and *MSNBC* on topics ranging from the Clinton Impeachment to the Death Penalty.

GARTH, BRYANT
Bryant Garth was dean of Indiana University School of Law-Bloomington before joining the American Bar Foundation in 1990. He holds a J.D. from Stanford Law School and a Ph.D from the European University Institute in Florence. His research focuses on the legal profession, dispute processing, and the internationalization of legal practice. His book, with Yves Dezalay, entitled *Dealing in Justice: International Commercial Arbitration and the Construction of a Transnational Legal Order* was published in 1996 by the University of Chicago Press. They are continuing their collaboration in a project studying the role of internationalization in transforming the role of law in a variety of national settings, beginning in Latin America and continuing with a number of countries in Asia. He also is the co-editor, with Austin Sarat, of two recent volumes published by the Northwestern University Press in 1998: *Justice and Power in the Socio-Legal Studies and How Does Law Matter*. His professional activities include serving as a member of the Advisory Committee of the Open Society Institute's Law and Society Program, as a vice president of the International Association of Procedural Law, a member of the international advisory board of the Oxford Socio-Legal Studies series, and as a member of the Stanford Law School Board of Visitors. Five of his research projects have received grants from the National Science Foundation.

HARTER, PHILIP J.
Philip J. Harter is the Director of the Program on Consensus, Democracy and Governance at the Vermont Law School and Visiting Associate Professor of Law. Mr. Harter served as Chair of the Section of Administrative Law and Regulatory Practice of the American

Bar Association and was appointed by the President of the ABA as the Co-chair of its Task Force on Regulatory Reform in which capacity he represented the ABA in the regulatory reform debates before Congress. He was the official observer for the Section of Administrative Law and Regulatory Practice to the Uniform Mediation Act, the reporter for multi-section committee that developed Standards for Ombudsmen which were adopted by the ABA in August, 2001, and a member of the Section of Dispute Resolution. Mr. Harter has been a pioneer in both the theory and practice of the use of consensus and other forms of dispute resolution involving government agencies. In addition to serving as a mediator in many complex, controversial negotiations involving government policy, his research was the theoretical basis for negotiated rulemaking and has served as the foundation for the subsequent practice. His writing also formed much of the basis of the Administrative Dispute Resolution Act, including its confidentiality provisions. He was a principal draftsman of the Negotiated Rulemaking Act and the Administrative Dispute Resolution Act, both of which amended the seminal Administrative Procedure Act. The United States Court of Appeals for the District of Columbia Circuit appointed him as a mediator to assist the court in the resolution of its cases. Harter received the Federal Bar Association's prestigious Gellhorn Award for "improving the fairness and efficiency of the administrative process."

KALETA, JUDITH S.
Judith S. Kaleta is the Senior Counsel for Dispute Resolution and Dispute Resolution Specialist at the U.S. Department of Transportation. She leads the Department's efforts to increase the use of alternative dispute resolution by developing Departmental policy, designing and evaluating dispute resolution uses and programs, and identifying and eliminating barriers to ADR use. She a chairs the Department's Dispute Resolution Council and represents the Department on the Steering Committee of the Interagency ADR Working Group. Ms. Kaleta is also co-chair of the Ombudsman Committee of the American Bar Association's Dispute Resolution Section. She is a graduate of De Paul University and Loyola University of Chicago School of Law. Her chapter reflects her views and not those of the Department.

KOVACH, KIMBERLEE K.
Professor Kimberlee K. Kovach teaches in the Alternative Dispute Resolution area at the University of Texas School of Law, in Austin, Texas, where she also directs a Mediation Clinic. She is a Past Chair of the American Bar Association Section of Dispute Resolution, and currently on the Board of Directors of JUSTPEACE, a national conflict resolution project of the United Methodist Church. She has also chaired state and local bar association ADR Committees and Sections, as well as served on the local SPIDR Board of Directors. Kovach is the author of a textbook for law school use, *Mediation: Principles And Practice*, 2d Edition, published in March 2000. She has also written several articles on ADR topics, including *Good Faith in Mediation: A New Ethic*, at 38 South Tex. L. Rev. 575 (1997); a piece co-authored with Professor Lela P. Love, *Mapping Mediation: Risks of Riskin's Grid*, published at 3 Harv. Neg. L. Rev. 71 (1998); an article with Eric Galton, *Texas ADR: A Future so Bright We Gotta Wear Shades* at 31 St. Mary's L. J. 949 (2000); and *Life and Death Decision-Making in Neonatal Intensive Care Units: Can Mediation Help?* at 28 Cap. U. L. Rev. 251 (2000). Her most recent, *New Wine Requires New Wineskins: Transforming Lawyer Ethics for Effective*

Representation in a Non-adversarial Approach to Problem Solving - Mediation has just been published in the Fordham Urban Law Journal.

LEVINE, SHARAN LEE

Sharan Levine is a shareholder in the law firm of Levine & Levine in Kalamazoo, Michigan. Ms. Levine has been representing ombudsmen in government, academia and corporations since 1991. Ms. Levine is the chair of the Ombuds Committee of the Section of Administrative Law and Regulatory Practice, a member of the Ombuds Committee of the Section on Dispute Resolution and the Dispute Resolution Committee of the Business Law Section. She is an associate member of the Ombudsman Association, the United States Ombudsman Association and the International Ombudsman Institute. Ms. Levine attended Bennington College, received her B.A. from Florida Atlantic University and her J.D. from the Thomas M. Cooley Law School.

MENKEL-MEADOW, CARRIE

Carrie Menkel-Meadow is Professor of Law at Georgetown University Law Center and Visiting Professor at Harvard Law School. She has published extensively in the dispute resolution field, including the recent book, *Mediation: Theory, Practice and Policy* (Ashgate, 2001) and many articles on negotiation, mediation, ADR and ADR ethics. She currently chairs the CPR-Georgetown Commission on Ethics and Standards in ADR and serves on the Executive Committee of the American Bar Foundation. She has also published extensively on issues of feminist theory and gender and the law.

PRESS, SHARON

Sharon Press is Director of the Florida Supreme Court's Dispute Resolution Center, and an adjunct professor at Florida State University College of Law. Press mediates community and family disputes and regularly conducts mediation and arbitration training. She has conducted mediation and negotiation training in Argentina, Uruguay, and Haiti, worked with the Judiciary of the West Indies on developing court-connected ADR programs. Press received a J.D. from the George Washington University National Law Center, is admitted to practice in New York. She is a past president of the Society of Professionals in Dispute Resolution (SPIDR), serves on the Board of the Association for Conflict Resolution, and is an Honorary Fellow of the American College of Civil Trial Mediators.

SELLERS, SANDRA A.

Sandra A. Sellers is President of Technology Mediation Services, LLC, and a mediator with Bickerman Dispute Resolution Group. She mediates and arbitrates intellectual property, domain name, software, contract, employment, and other business disputes. With respect to online ADR, she is a founding member of Square Trade's B2B Panel, and also mediates online consumer disputes. She also arbitrates domain name disputes online with WIPO and CPR. She is a certified mediator and an attorney. Ms. Sellers is a member of the American Bar Association's E-Commerce and ADR Task Force, which is charged with drafting guidelines for e-commerce dispute resolution. Previously, Ms. Sellers was Vice President of Intellectual Property Education and Enforcement for the Software Publisher Assn., and a shareholder with Willian Brinks Hofer Gilson & Lione, where she specialized in intellectual property litigation. Ms. Sellers received her J.D. from George Washington University, and B.A. from Dickinson College.

TAYLOR, KIMBERLY
Kimberly Taylor joined JAMS in 1999. With a facilitative management style, she oversees the operations of JAMS offices in Southern California, negotiating agreements, and directing marketing, sales and other business affairs. She directs case management responsibilities in the region and oversees client outreach programs. An expert in the arbitration process, Ms. Taylor has developed training for staff and neutrals in arbitration, and conducts continuing education for staff and neutrals. Ms. Taylor assists clients on various arbitration issues, including recent developments in the law relating to employment and consumer financial services arbitrations. Ms. Taylor designed and implemented special procedures relating to Chapter 11 bankruptcy claims resolution and other large-scale dispute resolution matters. As a mediator, Ms. Taylor has successfully handled numerous cases involving discovery disputes, complex contract actions, multi-party commercial leases, appraisals for public agencies, and probate matters, including a complex multi-party, multi-million dollar trust. As a practicing attorney, Ms. Taylor handled a wide variety of cases, including business and commercial matters, insurance, employment, breach of contract, probate, family law, criminal and civil rights issues in a variety of settings, including law and motion jury and non-jury trials, and writs and appeals. Ms. Taylor teaches legal writing and frequently lectures on the subject of brief writing. Ms. Taylor acts as a resource on ADR and the law at JAMS, and is a frequent speaker and author of articles on ADR. Her articles have appeared in the *Los Angeles Daily Journal*, *California Lawyer* and other publications. Attended the Strauss Institute for Dispute Resolution, Pepperdine School of Law in negotiation, mediation advocacy and related topics. J.D., *cum laude*, Ventura/Santa Barbara College of Law, 1995.

WATSON, LAWRENCE M.
Following admission to the Florida Bar in 1969, Lawrence M. Watson joined the Carlton Fields law firm in Orlando. As an adjunct to his extensive trial practice, Mr. Watson developed substantial experience in alternative dispute resolution. He was in the first class of mediators certified by the Florida Supreme Court at the inception of Florida's statutory ADR program in 1988. Following his certification, Mr. Watson developed a substantial practice as a state and federal court mediator with a specialty in complex, multi-party claims. In 1997, Mr. Watson became a founding partner of Upchurch, Watson & White, a mediation and alternative dispute resolution firm with offices in Maitland and Daytona Beach, Florida. Upchurch, Watson & White now fields over 18 mediators and dispute resolution specialists who are actively serving the southeastern United States dispute resolution community. Mr. Watson is presently certified as a circuit court mediator in every circuit of Florida. He also serves as a mediator and a court-appointed arbitrator for the federal district courts of Florida and the American Arbitration Association. Mr. Watson is a Fellow in the American College of Civil Trial Mediators and is currently serving as President of that organization.

YARN, DOUG
Doug Yarn is Executive Director of the Consortium on Negotiation and Conflict Resolution (www.law.gsu.edu/CNCR), and Associate Professor of Law at Georgia State University College of Law where he teaches conflict resolution and ethics. An experienced litigator, mediator, facilitator, and arbitrator, Professor Yarn served as in-house attorney, mediator, and trainer for the American Arbitration Association from

1987-1994. He has trained mediators and arbitrators nationwide and designed conflict management systems for private and public entities, domestic and international. As a member of the Georgia Supreme Court's Commission on Dispute Resolution, he hears ethics cases and chairs the committee on evaluation. His publications include *The Dictionary of Conflict Resolution* (Jossey-Bass 1999), *Alternative Dispute Resolution: Practice and Procedure in Georgia* (2nd ed. Harrison 1997), *Alternative Dispute Resolution: Practice and Procedure in North Carolina* (Harrison 1998), and book chapters and articles. Professor Yarn's current research interests include the ethology and ethnology of conflict resolution, the evolution of conflict resolution processes, effect of peer groups on conflict handling among youth, effect of testosterone on lawyer preferences in handling conflict, and the social utility of dueling.